Public Finance

Irwin Publications in Economics

Harvey S. Rosen

Department of Economics
Princeton University

Public Finance

1985

Homewood, Illinois 60430

ISBN 0-256-02813-3

Library of Congress Catalog Card No. 84–80446

Printed in the United States of America

4 5 6 7 8 9 0 K 2 1 0 9 8 7 6

To My Parents

Preface

"It is a foolish thing to make a long prologue." (II Maccabees 2:32) I shall follow this Biblical advice, and be brief in describing the features of this book. The field of public finance has been changing rapidly in recent years. On the theoretical side, one of the main achievements has been to integrate the analysis of government spending and taxing more closely with basic economic theory. A prime example is the literature on optimal taxation, which has attempted to *derive* prescriptions for government fiscal behavior using standard economic tools, rather than to annunciate a set of ad hoc "principles" for tax design. On the empirical side, the most exciting development has been the widespread application of the tools of econometrics to understanding how tax and expenditure policies affect individual behavior, and how the government itself sets its policies.

The results of modern research have been slow in entering traditional texts. This book brings its readers up to many of the frontiers of current research. The approach to the material, while quite accessible to undergraduates, is basically the approach shared by most economists who are now active in the field.

The development of public finance has not proceeded free of controversy. In this book, disputes concerning both methodological issues and substantive problems are discussed at length. One reviewer of an early draft of the manuscript warned against displaying too much of the profession's dirty laundry in public. My feeling, however, is that "full disclosure" should apply not only in the market for securities, but in the market for ideas as well.

There is some tendency for economic analysis to lose touch with the reality it is supposed to describe. I have tried to avoid this tendency. The relevant institutional and legal setting is described in ample detail. Moreover, the links between economic analysis and current political issues are constantly emphasized.

Organization

Part One consists of two short chapters which provide a broad perspective on the role of government in the economy. Part Two discusses the methodological tools used in the study of Public Finance. These include the methods of empirical analysis (Chapter 3) and the fundamentals of theoretical welfare economics (Chapter 4). The remainder of the book follows the conventional tactic of analyzing government expenditure and revenue raising activities separately. Part Three (Chapters 5 through 10) deals with the expenditure side of the budget; various government programs are described and evaluated. Part Four (Chapters 11 through 13) provides a theoretical framework for discussing taxation. The major taxes are analyzed using this framework in Part Five (Chapters 14 through 18). Finally, Part Six considers public finance in a multijurisdictional setting; Chapter 19 deals with the special issues that arise under a federal system of government, Chapter 20 concerns international issues.

Some instructors may choose to do the tax side (Parts Four and Five) prior to the expenditure side (Part Three); the book is designed so that this can be easily done. In the same way, the chapters within Parts Three, Four, and Five can generally be taken up in any order desired without serious loss of continuity.

This book is designed for use in undergraduate programs, and graduate programs in public administration. It is assumed that readers are familiar with microeconomic theory at the level of the standard introductory course. Some use is made of indifference curve analysis, a topic that is not covered in all introductory courses. Indifference curves are carefully explained in the Appendix to the book. In addition, this Appendix provides a brief review of other topics in basic microeconomics: supply and demand, marginal analysis, and production possibilities curves. This review should be adequate to refresh the memories of readers who have been away from microeconomics for a while.

It is hoped that this book will whet readers' appetites to learn more about public finance. To this end, a large number of articles and books are cited within the chapters and at their ends. A typical citation consists of the author's name with the date of publication following in brackets. The full reference can then be found by consulting the consolidated bibliography that appears at the back of the book. These references vary considerably in technical difficulty; those who wish to pursue specialized topics further have to pick and choose.

Acknowledgments

It is a pleasure to acknowledge all the people who have helped in the preparation of this book. As a graduate student, I was fortunate to be taught by two of the world's outstanding figures in public finance, Martin Feldstein and Richard Musgrave. Feldstein and Musgrave differed considerably in their approaches to the subject, but they shared a fundamental outlook—public finance is not a mere academic exercise; its goal is to help us understand and perhaps improve real-world situations. The intellectual influence of both these men is evident throughout the text.

Several people have read various chapters and provided useful suggestions. Thanks are due to my colleagues at Princeton: Alan Blinder, David Bradford, Don Fullerton, Amy Gutmann, Edwin Mills, and Richard Quandt for their comments. Jonathan Eaton (University of Virginia), David Hartman (National Bureau of Economic Research), Robert Inman (University of Pennsylvania), Sharon Bernstein Megdal (University of Arizona), Wallace Oates (University of Maryland), and Amy Taylor (National Center for Health Services Research) made comments on and contributions to early drafts of the manuscript. Daniel Feenberg (National Bureau of Economic Research), Timothy J. Gronberg (Texas A&M University), Frederick W. Jones (University of Wisconsin-Parkside), Daphne A. Kenyon (Dartmouth College), Mark W. Plant (University of California at Los Angeles), Herbert E. Sim (University of Notre Dame), Harvey Watson (George Washington University), Jeffrey Wolcowitz (Harvard University), and George Zodrow (Rice University) reviewed either part or all of the manuscript. Their thoughtful comments and evaluations helped to bring the final form to this book. I am especially indebted to Richard Tresch (Boston College), who carefully read the entire manuscript, and to Douglas Holtz-Eakin, who did a tremendous job as a research assistant and as a critic. I also appreciate the typing assistance of Terry Butler, Constance Dixon, and Barbara Hickey.

Both my children were born while this book was in progress—Lynne in 1981, and Jonathan in 1983. Although I have not developed a complete theory of the impact of young children upon speed of textbook writing, there appear to be two effects, which (as usual) work in opposite directions: the "sleep-deprivation effect," which inhibits productivity, and the "future-college-tuition-payment effect," which serves as a great spur to work. As is often the case (see Chapter 3), it is hard to tell which effect dominates. On the off chance that future econometric research shows that the net effect is to increase productivity, I should give the kids my thanks.

Finally, I am grateful to my family lawyer for technical advice and encouragement.

Harvey S. Rosen

Contents

Public Finance

Part One

Introduction

People's views on how the government should conduct its financial operations are heavily influenced by their political philosophies. Some people care most about individual freedom, others care more about promoting the well-being of the community as a whole. Philosophical differences can and do lead to disagreements as to the appropriate scope for government economic activity.

However, forming intelligent opinions about governmental activity requires not only a political philosophy but also an understanding of what the government actually does. Where does the legal power to conduct economic policy reside? What does government spend money on, and how does it raise revenue?

Chapter 1 discusses how political views affect attitudes toward public finance, and Chapter 2 outlines the operation of the U.S. system of public finance. Together these two chapters provide a broad perspective which it will be useful to remember as various details are discussed in the rest of the book.

Public Finance and Attitudes toward Government

Sometimes it is said that man cannot be trusted with the government of himself. Can he, then, be trusted with the government of others? Or have we found angels in the forms of kings to govern him? Let history answer this question.

Thomas Jefferson

The year is 1030 B.C. For decades, the Israelite tribes have been living without a central government. The Bible records that the people have asked the prophet Samuel to "make us a king to judge us like all the nations" [I Samuel 8:5]. Samuel tries to discourage the Israelites by describing what life will be like under a monarchy:

> This will be the manner of the king that shall reign over you; he will take your sons, and appoint them unto him, for his chariots, and to be his horsemen; and they shall run before his chariots. . . . And he will take your daughters to be perfumers, and to be cooks, and to be bakers. And he will take your fields, and your vineyards, and your oliveyards, even the best of them, and give them to his servants. . . . He will take the tenth of your flocks; and ye shall be his servants. And ye shall cry out in that day because of your king whom ye shall have chosen. [I Samuel 9:11–18]

The Israelites are not deterred by this depressing scenario: "the people refused to hearken unto the voice of Samuel; and they said: 'Nay; but there shall be a king over us; that we also may be like all the nations; and that our king may judge us, and go out before us, and fight our battles' " [I Samuel 8:19–20].

This biblical episode illustrates an age-old ambivalence about government. Government is a necessity—"all the nations" have it, after all—but at the same time it has undesirable aspects. These mixed feelings toward government are inextricably wound up with its taxing and spending activities. The king will provide things that the people want (in this case, an army), but only at a cost. The resources for all government expenditures ultimately must come from the private sector. As Samuel so graphically explains, taxes can become burdensome.

Centuries have passed, mixed feelings about government remain, and much of the controversy still centers around its financial behavior. This book is about the taxing and spending activities of government, a subject usually called **public finance,** but sometimes referred to as **public sector economics** or simply **public economics.**

Our focus is on the microeconomic functions of government, the way government affects the allocation of existing resources and the distribution of income. Nowadays, the macroeconomic functions of government—the use of taxing, spending, and monetary policies to affect the overall level of unemployment and the price level—are usually taught in separate courses.

It is not always exactly clear whether certain subjects "belong" in public finance. Governmental regulatory policies have important effects upon resource allocation. Such policies have goals that sometimes can also be achieved by government spending or taxing measures. For example, if a goal of the government is to limit the size of corporations, one possible policy is to impose large taxes on big corporations. Another policy is to issue regulations making firms that exceed a particular size illegal. However, while corporate taxation is a subject of intense study in public finance, antitrust issues are generally treated only tangentially in public finance texts, and are covered instead in courses on industrial organizaton. Such a practice seems arbitrary, but it is necessary to limit the scope of the field. This book follows tradition by confining most attention to governmental spending and revenue-raising activities.

ALTERNATIVE VIEWS OF GOVERNMENT

Public finance economists analyze not only the effects of actual government taxing and spending activities, but what these activities ought to be. Views of how government should function in the economic sphere are influenced by general attitudes concerning the relationship between the individual and the state. Political philosophers have distinguished two major approaches.

Organic View

Society is conceived of as a natural organism. Each individual is a part of this organism, and the government can be thought of as its heart. The individual has significance only as part of the community, and the good of the individual is defined with respect to the good of the whole. Thus, the community is stressed above the individual. For example, in the *Republic* of Plato, an activity of a citizen is desirable only if it leads to a "just" society. Perhaps the most infamous instance of an organic conception of government is provided by Nazism: "National Socialism does not recognize a separate individual sphere which, apart from the community, is to be painstakingly protected from any interference by the State. . . . Every activity of daily life has meaning and value only as a service to the whole."[1]

The goals of the society are set by the state, which leads society towards their realization. Of course, there are considerable differences with respect to the choice of goals. Plato conceived of a state whose goal was the achievement of a golden age in which human activities would be guided by perfect rationality. On the other hand, Adolf Hitler [1971/ 1925, p. 393] viewed the state's purpose to be the achievement of racial purity: "The state is a means to an end. Its end lies in the preservation and advancement of a community of physically and psychically homogeneous creatures." According to Lenin [1968/1917, p. 198] the proletarian state has the purpose of *"leading the whole people* to socialism, . . . of being the teacher, the guide, the leader of all the working and exploited people."

Since societal goals can differ, a crucial question is how they are to be selected. Proponents of the organic view usually rely on some notion that certain goals are "natural" for the societal organism to pursue. Pursuit of sovereignty over some geographical area is an example of such a "natural" goal. (Think of the Nazi drive for domination over Europe.) However, despite the fact that philosophers have struggled for centuries to explain what *natural* means, the answer is far from clear.

Mechanistic View

In this view, government is not an organic part of society. Rather, it is a contrivance created by individuals to better achieve their individual goals. As the American statesman Henry Clay suggested in 1829, "Government is a trust, and the officers of the government are trustees; and both the trust and the trustees are created for the benefit of the people." Thus, the individual rather than the group is at center stage.

Accepting that government exists for the good of the people, we are still left with the problem of defining just what *good* is and how the government should act to promote it. There is virtually universal agreement that it is good for individuals when government protects them from violence. To do so government must have a monopoly on coercive

---

[1] Stuckart and Globke [1968, p. 330]. (Wilhelm Stuckart and Hans Globke were ranking members of the Nazi Ministry of the Interior.)

power. Otherwise, anarchy develops, and as the 17th century philosopher Thomas Hobbes [1963/1651, p. 143] noted, "the life of man [becomes] solitary, poor, nasty, brutish and short." Recent events in such countries as Lebanon and Northern Ireland, where private armies are common, confirm Hobbes's observation. Similarly, in *The Wealth of Nations*, Adam Smith argues that government should protect "the society from the violence and invasion of other independent societies," and protect "as far as possible every member of the society from the injustice or oppression of every other member of it" [1977/1776, Book V, pp. 182, 198].

The most limited government, then, is one whose sole function is to prevent its members from being subjected to physical coercion. Beyond that, Smith argued that government should have responsibility for "creating and maintaining certain public works and certain public institutions, which it can never be for the interest of any individual, or small number of individuals, to erect and maintain" [1977/1776, Book V, pp. 210–11]. Here one thinks of items such as roads, bridges, and sewers—the "infrastructure" required for society to function.[2]

At this point, opinions within the mechanistic tradition diverge. "Libertarians," who believe in a very limited government, argue that there is no further economic role for the government. In Smith's words, "Every man, as long as he does not violate the laws of justice, is left perfectly free to pursue his own interest his own way" [1977/1776, Book V, p. 180]. In contrast, those whom we might call "Social Democrats" believe that a substantial amount of government intervention is required for the good of individuals. These interventions can take such diverse forms as safety regulations for the workplace, laws banning racial and sexual discrimination in housing, or welfare payments to the poor. When Social Democrats are confronted with the objection that such interventions are likely to impinge upon individual freedom, they are apt to respond that "freedom" refers to more than the absence of physical coercion. An individual with a very low income may be "free" to spend that income as he or she pleases, but the scope of that freedom is quite limited indeed. Of course, between the Libertarian and Social Democratic positions there is a continuum of views with respect to the amount of government intervention that is appropriate.

VIEWPOINT OF THIS BOOK

The notion that the individual rather than the group is paramount is relatively new. Historian Lawrence Stone [1977, pp. 4–5] notes that prior to the modern period,

---

[2] Some argue that even these items should be provided by private entrepreneurs. Problems that might arise in doing so are discussed in Chapter 6.

It was generally agreed that the interests of the group, whether that of kin, the village, or later the state, took priority over the wishes of the individual and the achievement of his particular ends. 'Life, liberty and the pursuit of happiness' were personal ideals which the average, educated 16th-century man would certainly have rejected as the prime goals of a good society.

Since then, however, the mechanistic view of government has come to dominate Anglo-American political thought. This is not to say that its dominance is total. Whenever someone claims that something must be done in the "national interest," without reference to the welfare of some individual or group of individuals, he is implicitly taking an organic point of view. More generally, even in highly individualistic societies, people sometimes feel it necessary to act on behalf of, or even sacrifice their lives for, "the nation." As Arrow [1974, p. 15] observes, "the tension between society and the individual is inevitable. Their claims compete within the individual conscience as well as in the arena of social conflict."

Not surprisingly, Anglo-American economic thought has also developed along individualistic lines. The individual and his or her wants are the main focus in mainstream economics, a view that is reflected in this text. However, as stressed above, within the individualistic tradition, there is much controversy with respect to how active a role government should take. Thus, adopting a mechanistic point of view does not by itself provide us with an ideology which tells us whether any particular economic intervention should be undertaken.[3]

This point is important because economic policy is not based on economic analysis alone. The desirability of a given course of government action (or inaction) inevitably depends in part upon ethical and political judgments. As this country's ongoing public debate over what we have chosen to call public finance illustrates, reasonable people can disagree on these matters. We will attempt to reflect different points of view as fairly as possible.

SUMMARY

Public finance, also known as public sector economics or public economics, focuses on the taxing and spending activities of government and their influence on the allocation of resources and distribution of income.

---

[3] Note that this question really makes no sense in the context of an organic view of government, in which the government is above the people, and there is an assumption that it should guide every aspect in life.

Economists dealing with public finance both analyze actual policies and develop guidelines for government activities. In the latter role, economists are influenced by their attitudes toward the role of government in society.

In an organic view of society, individuals are valuable only in their contribution to the realization of social goals. These goals are determined by the government.

In a mechanistic view of society, government is a contrivance erected for the furtherance of individual goals. There is considerable disagreement over how the government should promote sometimes conflicting individual goals.

Individual decision making is the focus of much economics and is consistent with the mechanistic view of society adopted in this book. This does not eliminate much controversy over the appropriate role of the government in our economy.

DISCUSSION QUESTIONS

1. In *The End of Liberalism*, Theodore Lowi [1979, p. xii] offers the following "article" as part of a present-day constitution:

    Article VI: The public interest shall be defined by the satisfaction of the voters in their constituencies. The test of the public interest is reelection.

    What does this imply about the role of government in society? Do you agree or disagree? Why?

2. In his first state of the union address, President Ronald Reagan stated:

    The taxing power of government must be used to provide revenues for legitimate government purposes. It must not be used to regulate the economy or bring about social change.

    a. Is the statement more consistent with a "mechanistic" or "organic" view of government? Explain.
    b. Do you think that this goal for government is feasible? Why or why not?

SELECTED REFERENCES

Arrow, Kenneth J. *The Limits of Organization.* New York: W. W. Norton, 1974.

Lenin. "The Marxist Theory of the State and the Tasks of the Proletariat in the Revolution." In *Lenin on Politics and Revolution,* ed. James E. Connor. Indianapolis: Bobbs-Merrill, 1968, pp. 184–232.

Smith, Adam. *The Wealth of Nations.* London: J. M. Dent and Sons, Ltd., 1977. (Book V, Chapter I).

APPENDIX 1A
DOING RESEARCH IN PUBLIC FINANCE

Throughout the text, many books and articles are cited, both within and following the chapters. These references will be useful for those who want to delve into the various subjects in more detail. Students who are interested in writing term papers or theses on subjects in public finance should also consult the following journals which specialize in the field:

Journal of Public Economics
National Tax Journal
Public Finance
Public Finance Quarterly

The *Journal of Public Economics* is relatively technical compared to the others and will be of most use to those who have had a course in microeconomic theory at the intermediate level and have a working knowledge of calculus.

In addition, all the major general-interest economics journals frequently publish articles that deal with public finance issues. These include, but are not limited to

American Economic Review
Econometrica
Journal of Political Economy
Quarterly Journal of Economics
Review of Economics and Statistics

Articles on public finance in these and many other journals are indexed in the *Journal of Economic Literature.*

There are vast amounts of data available on government spending and taxing activity. The following useful sources of information are published by the U.S. Government Printing Office:

Statistical Abstract of the United States
Economic Report of the President
Budget of the United States
U.S. Census of Governments

All of the above are published annually, except for the *U.S. Census of Governments,* which appears every five years. *Facts and Figures on Government Finance,* published biannually by the Tax Foundation, is another compendium of data on government taxing and spending activities. For those who desire a long-run perspective, data going back to the 18th century are available in *Historical Statistics of the United States from Colonial Times to 1970* (U.S. Government Printing Office). Readers with a special interest in state and local public finance will want to read the reports issued by the U.S. Advisory Commission on Intergovernmental Relations.

In addition, students should consult the volumes included in the Brookings Institution's series on *Studies of Government Finance*. These books include careful and up-to-date discussions of important public finance issues using relatively nontechnical language. The American Enterprise Institute also provides useful tracts on current policy controversies. The working paper series of the National Bureau of Economic Research, available in many university libraries, is another good source of recent research on public finance. The technical difficulty of these papers is sometimes considerable, however.

CHAPTER 2

Government at a Glance

*I don't make jokes—I just watch government and
report the facts.*

Will Rogers

It is useful to have a broad description of the U.S. system of public
finance before delving into its details. We begin with a brief discussion
of the legal framework within which government conducts its economic
activities. Then we consider problems that arise in attempts to quantify
the role of government in the economy.

THE LEGAL FRAMEWORK[1]

The Founding Fathers' concerns about the role of government in the
economy are reflected in the Constitution. We will first discuss constitutional provisions relating to the spending and taxing activities of the
federal government and then turn to the legal status of states.

Federal Government

By virtue of Article 1, Section 8 of the Constitution, Congress is empowered "to pay the debts and provide for the Common Defense and
General Welfare of the United States." Over the years, the notion of
"general welfare" has been interpreted very broadly by Congress and
the courts, and at the present time this clause effectively puts no con-

---

[1] Much of this discussion is based upon Musgrave and Musgrave [1980, chap. 2], which
can be consulted for further details.

straints on government expenditure activity.[2] The Constitution puts no limits on the size of federal expenditure, either absolutely or relative to the size of the economy. Bills to appropriate expenditures (like practically all other laws) can originate in either house of Congress. An appropriations bill becomes law when it receives a majority vote in both houses and is signed by the president. If the president chooses to veto an expenditure bill, it can still be passed into law if it receives a two-thirds majority in each house.

How is Congress to raise the money to pay for these expenditures? Federal taxing powers are authorized in Article 1, Section 8: "The Congress shall have Power to lay and collect Taxes, Duties, Imports and Excises." Unlike expenditure bills, "All Bills for raising Revenue shall originate in the House of Representatives" (Article 1, Section 7). In light of the enormous dissatisfaction with British tax policy during the colonial period, it is no surprise that considerable care was taken to constrain governmental taxing power, as described in the following paragraphs.

1. "[A]ll Duties, Imports and Excises shall be uniform through the United States" (Article 1, Section 8). Congress cannot discriminate among states when it sets tax rates. If the federal government levies a tax on gasoline, the *rate* must be the same in every state. This does not, of course, imply that the per capita *amount* collected will be the same in each state. Presumably, states in which individuals drive more than average will have higher tax liabilities, other things being the same. Thus, it is still possible (and indeed, likely) that various taxes will make some states worse off than others.[3]

2. "[N]o direct Tax shall be laid, unless in Proportion to the Census or Enumeration herein before directed to be taken" (Section 9, Article 1). A direct tax is a tax levied upon a *person* as opposed to a *commodity*. Essentially, this provision says that if State A has twice the population of State B, then any direct tax levied by Congress must be such that it yields twice as much revenue from State A as from State B. In general, the only permissible direct tax is a *head tax*, under which every citizen has the same tax obligation.

In the late 19th century, attempts to introduce a federal tax on income were declared unconstitutional by the Supreme Court because income taxation leads to different tax burdens for different citizens. Given this decision, the only way to introduce an income tax was via a constitutional amendment. The 16th Amendment, ratified in 1913, declares that "Congress shall have power to levy and collect taxes on incomes, from whatever source derived, without appointment among the several

---

[2] Article 1 also mandates that certain specific expenditures be made. For example, Congress has to appropriate funds for an army and to maintain a court system.

[3] No tax law in history has even been struck down for violating this clause. However, a close call occurred in the early 1980s. Congress passed a tax on oil, which exempted oil from the North Slope of Alaska. A federal district court ruled that the tax was unconstitutional, but this decision was ultimately reversed by the Supreme Court.

states, and without regard to census or enumeration." Today, the individual income tax is one of the mainstays of the federal revenue system.

3. "No person shall be . . . deprived of life, liberty, or property, without due process of law; nor shall private property be taken for public use without just compensation" (Fifth Amendment). From the point of view of tax policy, this clause means that distinctions created by the tax law must be reasonable. However, it is not always simple to determine which distinctions are "reasonable" and doing so is an ongoing part of the legislative and judicial processes.

4. "No Tax or Duty shall be laid on Articles exported from any State" (Article 1, Section 9). This provision was included to assure the Southern states that their exports of cotton would not be jeopardized by the central government. It has not had much of an impact upon the development of the public finance system.

The federal government is not required to finance all of its expenditures by taxation. If expenditures exceed revenues, it is empowered "To borrow Money on the credit of the United States" (Article 1, Section 7). Recently, there has been some political support for a constitutional amendment to require a balanced federal budget, but so far the movement to adopt such an amendment has not succeeded.

State and Local Governments

According to the 10th Amendment, "The powers not delegated to the United States by the Constitution, nor prohibited by it to the States, are reserved to the States respectively, or to the people." Thus, explicit authorization for states to spend and tax is not required. However, the Constitution does put some limitations on states' economic activities. Article I, Section 10 states that "No State shall, without the Consent of the Congress, lay any Imports or Duties on Imports or Exports." Thus, international economic policy is in the hands of the federal government. In addition, various constitutional provisions have been interpreted as requiring that the states not (a) levy taxes arbitarily, (b) discriminate against outside residents, and (c) levy taxes on imports from other states.

States can impose spending and taxing restrictions on themselves in their own constitutions. State constitutions differ substantially with respect to the types of economic issues with which they deal. In recent years, one of the most interesting developments in public finance has been the movement of some states to amend their constitutions to limit the size of public sector spending.

From a legal point of view, the power of local governments to tax and spend is granted by the states. As a 19th century judge put it:

> Municipal corporations owe their origin to, and derive their powers and rights wholly from, the [state] legislature. It breathes into them the breath

of life, without which they cannot exist. As it creates, so it may destroy. If it may destroy, it may abridge and control. [*City of Clinton* v. *Cedar Rapids*, 1868]

It would be a mistake, however, to view localities as totally lacking in fiscal autonomy. Many towns and cities have substantial political power and do not respond passively to the wishes of state and federal governments. An interesting development in recent years has been the competition of states and cities for federal funds. The cities often are more successful in their lobbying activities than the states! [Perlez, 1983, p. B1.]

THE SIZE OF GOVERNMENT

What has been the result of these legal prescriptions for government taxing and spending activities? The first item that belongs in any such description is a measure of their magnitude. Just how big is government? The whole public debate concerning whether government is "too big" presupposes that there is some way of measuring it.

One measure often used by politicians and journalists is the number of workers in the public sector. However, inferences about the size of government drawn from the number of workers it employs can be misleading. Imagine a country where a few public servants operate an enormous computer that guides all economic decisions. In this country, the number of individuals in the government payroll certainly is an underestimate of the importance of government. Similarly, it would be easy to construct a scenario in which a large number of workers is associated with a relatively weak public sector. Although for many purposes it is useful to know the number of public-sector employees, it does not cast light on the central issue—the extent to which society's resources are subject to control of government.

A more sensible (and common) approach is to measure the size of government by the volume of its annual expenditures. These expenditures are basically of three types:

1. Purchases of goods and services. The government buys a wide variety of items, everything from missiles to services provided by forest rangers.
2. Transfers of income to people, businesses, or other governments. Here the government takes income from some individuals or organizations and transfers it to others. Examples are welfare programs like food stamps, and subsidies paid to farmers for production (or nonproduction) of certain commodities.
3. Interest payments. The government often borrows to finance its activities and, like any borrower, must pay interest for the privilege of doing so.

The federal government itemizes its expenditures in a document referred to as the **unified budget.**[4] In 1983, federal expenditures (excluding grants made to state and local governments) were $740.5 billion. When we add state and local government expenditures made that year, we arrive at a total of $1,224 billion [*Economic Report of the President, 1984,* pp. 308–9].[5] Figures on government expenditures are easily available and widely quoted. Typically when expenditures go up, people conclude that government has grown and vice versa.

Unfortunately, conventional budget expenditures can convey a misleading impression of the extent to which society's resources are under government control. There are at least two reasons for this, the exis-tance of off-budget items and "hidden" costs of government.

Off-Budget Items

Off-budget federal agencies are federally owned and controlled, but their fiscal activities are excluded by law from budget totals. These include entities such as the Rural Electrification and Revolving Telephone Fund (which makes loans to support the construction and operation of electric and telephone utilities in rural areas), and the better-known Tennessee Valley Authority, a regional supplier of electricity. The most important activity of off-budget agencies is making loans.[6] Our discussion will focus on the difficulties that off-budget credit activity creates for measuring the size of government.

Federal credit activities take the form of either direct loans or loan guarantees. **Direct loans** are made to individuals, businesses, nonprofit institutions, and local governments. Often the government lends at rates below the market rate of interest. The volume of direct federal loans has grown rapidly over time. In 1974, they totaled $4.1 billion; in 1981, the figure peaked at $26.1 billion; by 1983, it was down to $15.3 billion [Executive Office of the President, 1984, p. F-5]. **Loan guarantees** are promises to repay principal and interest in case a borrower defaults on a loan. The federal government guaranteed $10.3 billion worth of loans in 1974. The comparable figure in 1983 was $34.1 billion. To put these figures in perspective, in 1983 federal loans and loan guarantees amounted to roughly 10 percent of total funds raised in the credit market.[7]

---

[4] The publication of some kind of budget document is constitutionally required: "a regular Statement and Account of the Receipts and Expenditures of all public Money shall be published from time to time" (Article 1, Section 9).

[5] Federal grants to state and local governments were $85.7 billion in 1983.

[6] On-budget agencies also make loans, but the amount is relatively small. See Congressional Budget Office [1982d, p. 3].

[7] Computed from *Economic Report of the President* [1983, p. 237].

It should now be clear that even though they are omitted from the unified budget, government credit activities are important. If government expenditures fell slightly at the same time that credit activities rose substantially, one might erroneously conclude that the role of government in the economy was diminishing. In recognition of this fact, in the 1970s Congress mandated the creation of a **credit budget,** which estimates for each fiscal year the volume of new direct loans and loan guarantees made by the federal government.

However, it is not easy to interpret the economic significance of the credit budget. If the government taxes away $1 million from the private sector and spends the money on a tank, the cost to the private sector is $1 million.[8] If the government loans $1 million to a small business at a rate of interest below the market rate, then as long as the loan is repaid, apparently all that the private-sector loses is the difference between the subsidized interest rate and the market rate.

This line of reasoning suggests that government direct loans made **at** the market rate of interest have no net cost to the private sector. If the money is paid back, what's the difference? However, such reasoning fails to take into account the effect of government loan programs on the allocation of credit.

Assume for simplicity that there is a fixed amount of available credit during a given year. In competitive markets, the funds are allocated to projects on the basis of their expected rates of return. Lenders help to finance projects which are likely to be successful in the sense of making a lot of money. When the government steps in, funds are allocated to projects that otherwise might not have been able to gain financing. Our assumption that the amount of credit is fixed implies that some projects that otherwise would have been undertaken are *crowded out.*

Of course, it may be the case that the recipients of government loans are entirely worthy of support, even though they would not have been successful in borrowing on the private market. (Chapter 4 presents criteria for establishing which projects are "worthy.") The point is that the reallocation of credit induced by government loans has a cost in terms of the private investment projects that are crowded out. Therefore, an assessment of the economic significance of the credit budget requires knowing which private sector projects were sacrificed and what the returns on those projects would have been. Needless to say, this information is very hard to obtain.

To summarize: The federal government's off-budget credit activity is large in magnitude and scope. It is not included in the conventional

---

[8] Actually, the loss in welfare exceeds $1 million if the tax induces a less efficient pattern of economic activity. The notion of "efficiency" that is relevant here is described in Chapter 12.

budget, so the latter will tend to underestimate the extent to which government is affecting use of resources. However, it is difficult to quantify precisely the economic impact of government credit activities. Certainly, the ability to influence the allocation of capital enhances the power of the government.

Finally, we should note that some financial obligations incurred by the federal government appear in neither the unified budget nor the credit budget. Under the Social Security Program, for example, government commits itself to pay citizens pensions when they retire. In the private sector, when such obligations are made, it is considered prudent practice to establish a reserve fund sufficient to meet them. Additions to such reserves are considered a current expense. The federal government does not engage in this practice. If it did, the net obligation of the Social Security System for the future would have required setting aside about $300 billion during the fiscal year ending in 1981 [Friedman, 1981]. We see, then, that measures of the size of the official government budget depend upon somewhat arbitrary accounting decisions concerning which items are to be included.

"Hidden" Costs of Government

Some government activities can have substantial effects on resource allocation even if they involve little in the way of explicit outlays. For example, issuing regulations per se is not very expensive, but compliance with the rules can be very costly. Seat belt requirements raise the cost of cars. Various permit and inspection fees increase the price of housing. Some have argued that labor market regulations like the minimum wage create unemployment, and that regulation of the drug industry slows the pace of scientific development.[9]

It has been suggested that the costs imposed upon the economy by government regulations be published in an annual **regulatory budget.** In this way, an explicit accounting for the costs of regulation would be available for public scrutiny. Unfortunately, it is exceedingly difficult to compute the costs of regulation. For example, we can easily imagine even pharmaceutical experts disagreeing on what new cures *would* have been developed in the absence of drug regulation. Similarly, it is hard to estimate how much government mandated safety procedures in the workplace increase production costs. In view of such problems, it is unlikely that there will ever be an official regulatory budget.[10]

---

[9] See Weidenbaum [1978] for further discussion.

[10] It should be stressed that regulation is not necessarily a bad thing just because it creates costs. Like any other government activity, it can be evaluated only by assessing the benefits as well as the costs. (Problems in doing cost-benefit analysis are discussed in Chapter 9.)

Some Numbers

We reluctantly conclude that there is no feasible way to summarize in a single number the magnitude of government's impact on the economy. Having made this admission, we are still left with the practical problem of finding some reasonable indicator of government's size that can be used to estimate trends in the growth of government. Most economists are willing to accept conventionally defined government expenditure as a rough but useful measure. Like many other imperfect measures, it yields useful insights as long as its limitations are understood.

With all the appropriate caveats in mind, we present in Table 2.1 some data on expenditures made by all levels of U.S. government over

TABLE 2.1   State, Local, and Federal Government Expenditures (selected years)

	(1) Total Expenditures (billions)	(2) 1980 Dollars (billions)*	(3) 1980 Dollars per Capita	(4) Percent of GNP
1902	$ 1.6	$ 17.6	$ 222	7.7%
1938	17.7	107.9	830	20.9
1944	109.9	501.8	3,625	52.3
1950	70.3	233.6	1,539	24.7
1955	110.7	324.6	1,964	27.8
1960	151.3	389.9	2,158	30.0
1965	205.6	493.0	2,537	30.0
1970	333.0	655.5	3,199	34.0
1975	560.1	791.1	3,663	36.1
1980	958.7	958.7	4,210	36.5
1982	1,231.4	1,062.0	4,688	40.1

* Conversion to 1980 dollars was done using the GNP deflator, a price index produced by the government.

Source: For years prior to 1975, calculated from U.S. Bureau of the Census *Historical Statistics of the United States, Colonial Times to 1970* (Washington, D.C.: U.S. Government Printing Office, 1975), p. 1120. For 1975 and 1980, calculated from *Statistical Abstract of the United States: 1982–83*, 103d ed. (Washington, D.C.: U.S. Government Printing Office, 1982), p. 276. For 1982, from U.S. Bureau of the Census, *Governmental Finances in 1981–82* (Washington, D.C.: U.S. Government Printing Office, 1983), Table I, p. 15.

time. The first column indicates that annual expenditures have increased by a factor of about 741 since the turn of the century. This figure is a misleading indicator of the growth of government for several reasons:

1.   Over time because of inflation the dollar has decreased in value. In column 2, the expenditure figures are expressed in 1980 dollars. In

real terms, government expenditure in 1982 was about 60 times the
level in 1902.

2.   The population has also been growing over time. We expect that an
     increasing population by itself creates demands for a larger public
     sector. (For example, more roads and sewers are required to accom-
     modate more people.) Column 3 shows real government expendi-
     ture per capita. Now the increase from 1902 to 1982 is a factor of
     about 21.

3.   Finally, for some purposes it is useful to examine government ex-
     penditure compared to the size of the economy. If government dou-
     bles in size but at the same time the economy triples, then in a
     relative sense, government has shrunk. Column 4 shows govern-
     ment expenditure as a percentage of gross national product (GNP),
     the market value of goods and services produced by the economy
     during the year. In 1902, the figure was 7.7 percent, and in 1982, it
     was 40.1 percent.

In light of our previous discussion, the figures in Table 2.1 convey a
false sense of precision. Still, there is no doubt that in the long run the
economic role of government has grown enormously. With roughly two
fifths of GNP going through the public sector, government is an enormous economic force.[11]

To put the U.S. data in perspective, it helps to make some international comparisons. Table 2.2 shows figures on government expenditure
relative to gross domestic product for a number of developed coun-

TABLE 2.2   Government Outlays as a Percentage of Gross
            Domestic Product (selected countries, 1980)

Australia	30.4%
Canada	37.7
France	43.1
Germany	41.2
Japan	25.4
Sweden	57.2
United States	33.3
United Kingdom	42.2

Source: Computed from *National
Accounts of OECD Countries 1963–
1980*, volume II (Paris: OECD Department of Economics and Statistics,
1982), various pages.

---

[11] Interestingly, relative to the size of GNP, the rate of expenditure growth has slightly
tapered off in the last decade. But as growth slowed in this area, other dimensions of
government activity (such as off-budget lending) have been increasing. It is hard to say
what the effect is on balance.

tries.[12] The data indicate that the United States is not alone in having an important public sector. Indeed, compared to countries like Sweden and France, the U.S. public sector is relatively small.

EXPENDITURES

We now turn from the overall magnitude of government expenditures to their composition. It is impossible to reflect the enormous scope of government spending activity in a brief table. In the federal budget for fiscal year 1985, the list of programs and their descriptions required about 200 pages! The major categories of government expenditure and their growth over time are described in Table 2.3. The following aspects of the table are noteworthy.

TABLE 2.3   Expenditures by All Levels of Government ($ millions)

	1902	1938	1955	1970	1980	1982
National defense and international relations	$ 165	$ 1,041	$ 43,472	$ 84,300	$149,500	$ 204,275
Postal service	126	776	2,726	7,700	18,200	21,761
Education	258	2,653	12,710	55,800	143,800	166,057
Highways	175	2,150	6,520	16,700	33,700	35,121
Public welfare	41	1,233	3,210	17,500	64,800	78,821
Hospitals and health	63	678	3,428	13,600	43,300	52,766
Police, fire, and sanitation	141	835	3,194	10,300	34,100	40,321
Interest on general debt	97	1,513	5,684	18,400	76,000	121,786
Federal social security*	0	5	4,333	35,800	149,500	201,204
Other insurance trusts†	0	549	4,669	12,700	49,900	66,372
Miscellaneous‡	594	6,142	20,772	60,200	195,900	242,952
Total	$1,660	$17,675	$110,717	$333,000	$958,700	$1,231,436

* Officially known as OASDHI—old-age, survivors, disability, and health insurance.
† Includes, among other things, employee retirement and unemployment compensation.
‡ Includes natural resources, parks and recreation, housing and urban renewal, veterans services, financial administration, air and water transport, utilities, and state-run liquor stores.
Source: For years before 1970 U.S. Bureau of the Census, *Historical Statistics of the United States, Colonial Times to 1970* (Washington, D.C.: U.S. Government Printing Office, 1975), pp. 1120–21. For 1970 and 1980, idem, *Statistical Abstract of the United States* (Washington, D.C.: U.S. Government Printing Office, 1981), p. 276. For 1982, idem, *Governmental Finances in 1981–82* (Washington, D.C.: U.S. Government Printing Office, 1983), p. 15.

1.   National defense is and always has been an important component of government expenditure.[13] In 1982, the percentage of government expenditure devoted to defense (16.6 percent) was larger than it was at the turn of the century (9.9 percent), but quite a bit smaller than

---

[12] Gross domestic product differs from GNP in its treatment of production by foreign-owned companies. GNP includes U.S. production abroad and excludes the output of foreign-owned companies in the United States. GDP does the opposite, including the output produced domestically (although foreign owned) and excluding production abroad (even though it is U.S. owned).

[13] The bulk of expenditure on "national defense and international relations" is for military services.

in 1970 (25.3 percent). Of course, this observation by itself tells us little about whether "too much" or "too little" is spent on defense.

2.   The social security program has grown at an enormous rate. Essentially this program transfers income to individuals who are not working either because they are disabled or retired. Social security did not even exist 50 years ago; now it absorbs about as much of the budget as defense. A detailed analysis of the program is included in Chapter 8.

3.   Public welfare activities have also been increasing as a proportion of government spending. These include programs such as old-age assistance, Aid to Families with Dependent Children (AFDC), and the Medicaid program (which pays medical bills for the indigent).

4.   Payments of interest on debt are increasing in relative importance. This is because both interest rates and the size of the debt have been growing over time.

Note that the areas of greatest growth—social security, welfare, and interest payments—are relatively "uncontrollable" in the sense that they are determined by decisions made in previous years. Consider, for example, so-called **entitlement programs**—programs with cost determined not by fixed dollar amounts, but by the number of people who qualify. The laws governing social security, many public welfare programs, farm price supports, etc. include rules that determine who is entitled to benefits and how much recipients will receive. Expenditures on entitlement programs are therefore out of the hands of the current government, unless it changes the rules. Similarly, debt payments are determined by interest rates and previous deficits, again mostly out of the control of current decision makers. According to one estimate, about 75.3 percent of the federal budget in fiscal year 1982 was relatively uncontrollable. [*Facts and Figures on Government Finance,* 1983, p. 115]. In Chapter 10, we discuss whether government spending is "out of control" and if so, what can be done about it.

It is useful to break down total expenditures by the level of government making them. Of the $1,231.4 billion of direct expenditures made in 1982, the federal government accounted for about 57.7 percent, the states for 17.2 percent, and localities for 25.1 percent. State and local governments thus play a very important role in U.S. public finance. They account for the bulk of spending on items such as police and fire protection, education, and transportation. A substantial amount of public welfare expenditures are also made through the states. The complications that arise in coordinating the fiscal activities of different levels of government in a federal system are discussed in Chapter 19.

REVENUES

Tax Finance

The principal components of the U.S. tax system are noted in Table 2.4. Currently, personal income taxation is the single most important

TABLE 2.4 Revenue Collections, All Levels of Government ($ millions)

	1902	1938	1955	1970	1980	1982
Total revenues*	$1,694	$17,484	$106,404	$333,800	$932,200	$1,144,787
Personal income taxes	0	1,495	29,984	101,200	286,100	348,896
Corporate income taxes	0	1,498	18,604	36,600	77,900	64,240
Sales and gross receipts	515	3,815	17,221	48,600	112,000	139,311
Property taxes	706	4,440	10,735	34,100	68,500	81,918
Charges and miscellaneous	259	2,074	12,192	39,600	142,400	193,833
Utilities and liquor stores	62	877	3,688	8,600	25,600	33,611
OASDHI† (social security payroll tax)	0	387	5,087	38,500	139,400	181,598
Employee retirement	0	182	1,662	8,200	29,100	38,325
Unemployment compensation	0	731	1,345	3,200	13,700	17,103

* Individual items do not sum to totals because the totals include other items not shown separately.
† Old-age, survivors, disability and health insurance.
Sources: For years prior to 1960, U.S. Bureau of the Census, *Historical Statistics of the United States, Colonial Times to 1970* (Washington, D.C.: U.S. Government Printing Office, 1975), p. 1119. For 1970 and 1980, idem, *Statistical Abstract of the United States* (Washington, D.C.: U.S. Government Printing Office, 1981), p. 276. For 1982, idem, *Governmental Finances in 1981–82* (Washington, D.C.: U.S. Government Printing Office, 1983), p. 15.

source of revenue, accounting for about 30 percent of taxes raised by all levels of government. It may come as a surprise that the second single most important revenue source is neither sales, corporation, nor property taxation. Rather, number two is the tax levied on payrolls to finance social security payments. At the same time that social security expenditures have been increasing, so have the taxes raised to pay for them.

Property and sales taxes used to play a much greater role in the revenue structure than they do now. In 1902, property taxes accounted for 41 percent of all revenues raised, and sales taxes, 30 percent. By 1982, the comparable figures were 7 percent and 12 percent. It is also interesting to observe the relative rise and fall of corporation income taxes during this century. In 1902, taxes on corporate income did not exist. In 1955, they accounted for 17.5 percent of all revenue collected, but by 1982 this figure was down to 5.6 percent.

In 1982, the federal government collected about 60.1 percent of all tax revenues. The reader will recall that the proportion of direct expenditures made by the federal government was only 57.7 percent. Part of the discrepancy is accounted for by the fact that the federal government distributes grants to states and localities.

The federal government has not always been the biggest tax collector. In 1902, for example, only 37.4 percent of revenues were raised by the federal government; 51.3 percent were raised by localities, and the rest by the states.

Changes in the Real Value of Debt

In popular discussions, taxes are usually viewed as the only source of government revenue. However, when the government is a debtor and the price level changes, changes in the real value of the debt may be an important source of revenue. To see why, suppose that at the beginning of the year you owe a creditor $1,000, and the sum does not have to be repaid until the end of the year. Suppose further that over the course of the year, prices rise by 10 percent. Then the dollars which you use to repay your creditor are worth 10 percent less than those you borrowed from him. In effect, inflation has reduced the real value of your debt by $100 (10 percent of $1,000). Alternatively, your real income has increased by $100 as a consequence of inflation. Of course, at the same time, your creditor's real income has fallen by $100.[14]

At the end of fiscal year 1982, the federal government's outstanding debt was about $1,546.3 billion. During 1982, the rate of inflation was 6.0 percent [*Governmental Finance*, 1983b, p. 15]. Applying the same logic as above, inflation reduced the real value of the federal debt by $92.8 billion (= $1,546.3 × .06). In effect, this is as much a receipt for the government as any of the taxes listed in Table 2.4. However, the government's accounting procedures do not allow the inclusion of gains due to inflationary erosion of the debt on the revenue side of the account.

A Note on Deficit Finance

If expenditures exceed revenues, then by definition there is a deficit. The size of the federal government deficit, which was $110.6 billion in 1982 [Executive Office of the President, 1983, p. E-5], is a perennial source of acrimonious public debate. As noted above, recently there have even been serious attempts to amend the Constitution so as to make a balanced federal budget mandatory.[15]

We defer to a later chapter a discussion of the economic significance of government debt. Our concern here is with the problems involved in measuring its size. We have already shown that a good deal of arbitrariness is involved in measuring both expenditures and revenues. Therefore, it is inevitable that their difference, the deficit, is also an arbitrarily measured concept.

---

[14] If the inflation is anticipated by borrowers and lenders, one expects that the interest rate charged will be increased to take inflation into account. This phenomenon is discussed in Chapter 14.

[15] The constitutions of many states already require balanced budgets.

Consider the conventionally measured deficit of $110.6 billion for fiscal year 1982. If we treat as income in 1982 the implicit gains to the federal government due to inflationary erosion in the real value of the debt (shown above to be $92.8 billion), this deficit is reduced to a "mere" $17.8 billion (= $110.6 billion − $92.8 billion). Adding $17.3 billion of outlays by off-budget entities, the deficit is increased to $35.1 billion. If the increase in obligations of the social security system is taken into account, this deficit might increase by several more billions of dollars.

We could decrease the size of the deficit somewhat by including as income the implicit gains to the government from inflationary erosion of its contractual obligations (such as promises to pay its suppliers of goods and services), or increase the deficit by treating as an expenditure the decline in value of the government's capital assets as they age. (Think of bridges and roads deteriorating.) In addition, promises to pay future pension benefits to civil service and military employees might be taken into account.[16] The existence of the foregoing possible adjustments, as well as numerous others which can readily be imagined, underscores the arbitrariness of any number which purports to be "the" deficit. It therefore makes little sense to evaluate the economic operation of the public sector solely on the basis of the size of the deficit. What is more important is whether the levels of government services are optimal, particularly considering the costs of securing the resources required to provide these services.

A lively debate over the spending and financing activities of government is important in a democracy. The consequences of deficit versus other forms of finance are important and worthy of public consideration (see Chapter 11). Nevertheless, the tendency of both liberals and conservatives to evaluate the state of public finance solely on the basis of the deficit has tended to obscure and confuse the debate.

AGENDA FOR STUDY

This chapter has set forth a collection of basic "facts"—facts on governmental fiscal institutions, on the size and scope of government spending, and on the methods used by government to finance itself. Parts of the rest of this book are devoted to presenting more facts—filling in the rather sketchy picture of how our fiscal system operates. Just as important, we seek to explore the significance of these facts, to ask whether the status quo has led to desirable outcomes, and if not, how it can be improved.

---

[16] Leonard [1984] estimates that benefits promised to these groups exceed the currently and prospectively available assets by a trillion dollars.

SUMMARY

Legal constraints on federal and state government economic activity are embodied in the Constitution.

The federal government may effectively undertake any expenditures it wishes and may use debt and taxes to finance them. The federal government may not discriminate among states when choosing tax rates, and may not place a levy on state exports. The 16th Amendment empowers the federal government to levy a tax on personal income.

State governments are forbidden to levy tariffs on imports, discriminate against outside residents, or tax other states' products. Many states have adopted self-imposed requirements for a balanced budget.

All common measures of the size of government—employees, expenditures, revenues, etc.—involve some deficiency. In particular, these items miss the impact of off-budget activities and the costs of regulations. Nonetheless, there is strong evidence that the impact of the government sector on the allocation of national resources has increased over time.

The level of government expenditures has increased in both nominal and real absolute terms, in per capita terms, and as a percentage of gross national product.

The share of defense spending in federal expenditure has fallen in the long run, while social security, public welfare, and payments on outstanding debt have increased in importance. The combination of entitlement programs and interest payments has resulted in reduced yearly control over the level of expenditures.

Personal income and social security payroll taxes are currently the largest sources of government revenue. Since the turn of the century, property taxes have declined in importance, while corporate income taxes rose and then recently declined.

Measurement of the budget deficit requires making some rather arbitrary decisions concerning the definitions of "revenues" and "expenditures." As a result, deficit measures, while often a focal point in public discussion, are not a good way to summarize the state of public finance.

DISCUSSION QUESTIONS

1. In each of the following circumstances, decide whether the impact of government on the economy has increased or decreased and why. In each case, how does your answer compare to that given by standard measures of the size of government?

    a. Congress replaces federal student loan guarantees with outright, but smaller, direct grants to students.

    b. The ratio of government purchases of goods and services to gross national product falls.

    c. The federal budget is brought into balance by reducing grants-in-aid to state and local governments.

2. The federal government guarantees loans of $100 million to the Theta Beta Phi Sorority Sweatshirt Company. If the market interest rate is currently 10 percent, what is the cost of the program? Suppose that instead, the government makes a direct loan at a rate of 8 percent. What is the cost now?

3. Proponents of student loans argue that "the only objection is the reported default rate" [Drinan, 1983, p. E17]. Similarly, the vice chairman of the Chrysler company, which received millions of dollars of federal loan guarantees, stressed "we never really got a dime from the federal government. We only got guarantees [Chrysler's Stock Plea, 1983, p. D6]." Evaluate these claims.

SELECTED REFERENCES

Pechman, Joseph, A., ed. *Setting National Priorities—The 1984 Budget.* Washington, D.C.: Brookings Institution, 1983.

Facts and Figures on Government Finance—22nd Biennial Edition. Washington, D.C.: Tax Foundation, 1983.

Part Two

Tools of Public Finance

The dual tasks of an economist are to explain how the economy works—**positive economics**—and to determine whether or not it is producing good results—**normative economics.** In principle, positive analysis does not require value judgments, because its purpose is descriptive. Normative analysis, on the other hand, requires an ethical framework, because without one, it is impossible to say what is "good." Although it is sometimes difficult to keep the positive and the normative from getting entangled, most economists agree that the distinction is worthwhile. Discussions of how the world *is* should not be colored by a view of how it *ought* to be.

The next two chapters describe the tools used by public finance economists to analyze both normative and positive issues. To a large extent, they are the same as those used in other fields of applied economics. Despite the popularity of these tools, they are far from perfect. It is important to know their deficiencies as well as their strengths. Given their imperfections, why are the tools so widely used? A common response to this kind of query is the story about the compulsive gambler who plays roulette every night at the local casino, despite the fact that the wheel is fixed. When asked by a friend why he continues to play, the gambler replies, "It's the only game in town." Similarly, most[1] modern public finance economists are convinced that flawed as they may be, the standard tools of economics are the best available for studying the relationship between government and the economy.

---

[1] But not all! For example, a lively group of radical economists has rejected the standard tools. See Mermelstein [1973].

CHAPTER 3

Tools of Positive Analysis

It doesn't matter whether a cat is black or white so long as it catches mice.

Deng Ziaoping

A good subtitle for this chapter is "Why Is It So Hard to Tell what's Going On?" We constantly hear economists—and politicians—disagree vehemently about the likely consequences of various government actions. Consider the controversy over the likely effects of reduced income tax rates on the amount of labor that people will supply. Conservatives argue that lower tax rates will create incentives for people to work harder. Liberals are skeptical, arguing that no major changes can be expected. On each side there are economists to testify that their opinion is correct. Is it surprising that the cynical viewpoint expressed in the cartoon is so widespread?

An important reason for the lack of definitive answers is that economists are generally unable to perform carefully controlled experiments with the economy. To determine the effects of a fertilizer on cabbage growth, a botanist can treat one plot of ground with the fertilizer and compare the results with an otherwise identical unfertilized cabbage patch. The unfertilized patch serves as the "control group." Economists do not have such opportunities. Although the government can change the economic environment, there is no control group with which to make comparisons. Therefore, we never know for certain the extent to which changes in the economy are consequences of policy changes.

In the absence of controlled experiments, economists use other methods to analyze the impact of various government policies on economic behavior. Indeed, one of the most exciting developments in public fi-

*"That's the gist of what I want to say. Now get
me some statistics to base it on."*

•   •

nance in the last several decades has been the widespread use of modern statistical tools to study public policy issues.

Below, the debate over the effect of taxes on labor supply is used to provide an understanding of how empirical work is done in public finance. The general principles used are applicable to any number of problems.

THE ROLE OF THEORY

An assertion often heard in all kinds of arguments is that "The numbers speak for themselves." What do the numbers say about income tax rates and labor supply? The middle column of Table 3.1 gives information on how the proportion of the last dollar of earnings taken by the tax collector—the **marginal tax rate**—varied over the period 1942 to 1979. The next column shows how the average annual hours per worker has changed over time. The figures indicate that tax rates have increased, and the hours of work have decreased. The numbers appear to say that taxes have depressed labor supply.

TABLE 3.1   Income Tax Rates and Labor Supply

Year	Marginal Federal Income Tax Rate*	Annual Hours per Civilian Worker†
1942	10.7%	2,244
1944	19.4	2,065
1946	14.5	2,263
1948	12.1	1,925
1950	13.1	2,082
1952	18.1	2,024
1954	15.9	2,012
1956	16.7	2,034
1958	16.7	2,008
1960	17.2	2,014
1962	17.7	2,008
1964	15.6	2,012
1966	15.3	1,987
1968	17.3	1,970
1970	16.8	1,936
1972	16.4	1,953
1974	17.6	1,924
1976	18.5	1,915
1978	20.8	1,909
1979	19.0	1,905

* R. J. Barro and C. Sahasakul, *Measuring the Average Marginal Tax Rate for the Individual Income Tax*, National Bureau of Economic Research Working Paper No. 1060, 1983, pp. 19–20.

† Computed from U.S. Bureau of Economic Analysis, *The National Income and Product Accounts of the United States*, Washington, D.C.: U.S. Government Printing Office, various editions.

Is this inference correct? At the same time that tax rates were changing, so were numerous other factors that might influence labor supply. If *unearned income*—income from dividends, interest, etc.—were rising over the period, then people may have worked less because they were richer. Alternatively, changing attitudes—a decrease in the "Protestant ethic"—might have decreased labor supply. Neither of these effects, and you can certainly think of many more, is taken into account by the numbers given. Clearly, what we need to know is the *independent* effect of taxes on labor supply. This effect simply cannot be learned solely from examining the trends in the two variables over time. Here is a typical situation; when we turn to data for answers, *the numbers never speak for themselves.*

In a sense, this opens a Pandora's box. There are an unlimited number of variables that change over time. How do we know which ones have to be considered to find the tax effect? One major purpose of economic theory is to help isolate a small set of variables that are important in influencing behavior. The taxes and labor supply example illustrates how basic economic theory is useful in organizing thoughts.

The dominant theory of labor supply is that the work decision is based on the rational allocation of time.[1] Suppose that Mr. Rogers has only a certain number of hours in the day: How many hours should he devote to work in the market, and how many hours to leisure? Rogers derives satisfaction ("utility") from leisure, but to earn income he must work and thereby surrender leisure time. Rogers' problem is to find just the combination of income and leisure that maximizes his utility.

Suppose that Rogers' wage rate is $w per hour. The wage is the cost of Rogers' time. For every hour he spends at leisure, Mr. Rogers gives up $w in wages—time is literally money. However, a "rational" individual generally will *not* work every possible hour, even though leisure is costly. People spend time on leisure to the extent that it generates satisfaction that is valued in excess of its cost.

This model may seem absurdly simple. It does not account for the possibility that an individual's labor supply behavior may depend on the labor supply decisions of other family members. Neither does the model take into account whether the individual can work as many hours as desired. Indeed, the entire notion that people make their decisions by rationally considering costs and benefits may appear unrealistic.

However, the whole point of model building is to simplify as much as possible, so that a problem is reduced to its essentials. The literary critic Lytton Strachey said that "Omission is the beginning of all art" [Lipton, 1977, p. 93]. Omission is also the beginning of all good economic analysis. A model should not be judged on the basis of whether or not it is "true," but on whether the model is plausible and informative. Most of the work in modern economics is based on the assumption that maximization of utility is a good working hypothesis [see Becker, 1962]. It is this point of view that is taken throughout the book.

Imagine that Mr. Rogers has found his utility maximizing combination of income and leisure based on his wage rate of $w. Now the government imposes a tax on wage income of t percent. Then Rogers' after-tax or *net* wage is $(1 - t)w$. How will a "rational" individual react—work more, work less, or not change at all? In public debate, arguments for all three possibilities have been made with great assurance. In fact, however, the impact of earnings tax upon hours of work *cannot* be predicted on theoretical grounds.

To see this, first observe that the wage tax lowers the effective price of leisure. Prior to the tax, consumption of an hour of leisure cost Rogers $w. Under the earnings tax, because Rogers' net wage is lower, an hour of leisure costs him only $(1 - t)w$. Since leisure has become "cheaper,"

---

[1] The theory of labor supply is presented here verbally. A graphical exposition appears in Chapter 15.

there will be a tendency to consume more of it—to work less. This is called the *substitution effect.*

Another effect occurs simultaneously when the tax is imposed. Assume that Rogers will work a certain number of hours regardless of all feasible changes in the net wage. After the tax, Rogers receives only $(1 - t)w$ for each of these hours, while before it was $\$w$. In a real sense, Rogers has suffered a loss of income. To the extent that leisure is a *normal good*—consumption increases when income increases and vice versa—this income loss leads to less consumption of leisure. But less leisure means more work. Because the earnings tax has made Rogers poorer, it has induced him to work more. This is sometimes called the *income effect.*

Thus, the tax simultaneously produces two effects. It induces substitution toward the cheaper activity (leisure), and it reduces real income. Since the substitution effect and the income effect work in opposite directions, the impact of an earnings tax cannot be determined by theorizing alone. Consider the following two statements:

a. "With these high taxes, it's really not worth it for me to work as much as I used to."
b. "With these high taxes, I have to work more to maintain my standard of living."

For the person making statement (*a*) the substitution effect is dominating, while in statement (*b*) the income effect is dominating. Both statements can reflect perfectly rational behavior for the individuals involved.

The importance of the uncertainty caused by the conflict of income and substitution effects cannot be overemphasized. Only **empirical work**—analysis based on observation and experience as opposed to theory—can answer the question of how labor force behavior is affected by changes in the tax system. Even intense armchair speculation on this matter must be regarded with considerable skepticism.

Although we have developed the argument with a labor supply example, the lesson is more general; one major purpose of theory is to make us aware of the areas of our ignorance.

METHODS OF EMPIRICAL ANALYSIS

Theory helps to organize thoughts about how people react to changes in their economic environment. But it usually cannot tell what the magnitude of such responses will be. Indeed, in the labor supply case just discussed, theory alone cannot even predict the *direction* of the likely changes. Empirical work becomes necessary. There are three types of empirical strategies: personal interviews, experiments, and econometric estimation. With each technique, the connections to theory are vital.

Theory influences how the study is organized, what questions are asked, and how the results are interpreted.

Interviews

The most straightforward way to find out whether some government activity influences people's behavior is simply to ask them. In a crude way, this is the kind of empirical "analysis" done by reporters. ("Tell me, are you going to delay your retirement if the government lowers your social security benefit?") A number of quite sophisticated interview studies have been done to assess the effect of taxes on labor supply. A group of British lawyers and accountants were carefully questioned as to how they determined their hours of work, whether they were aware of the tax rates they faced, and if these tax rates created any incentives or disincentives to work. The responses suggested that relatively few people were affected by taxes [Break, 1957, p. 549]. A later survey of a group of affluent Americans told much the same story. "Only one-eighth . . . said that they have actually curtailed their work effort because of the progressive income tax. . . . Those facing the highest marginal tax rates reported work disincentives only a little more frequently than did those facing the lower rates" [Barlow, Brazer, & Morgan, 1966, p. 3].

Pitfalls of Interviews.   However, interpretation of these survey results must be done cautiously. After all, just because an individual cannot recite his or her tax rate does not mean that the individual is unaware of the discrepancy between before- and after-tax pay.

An old Chinese proverb counsels, "Listen to what a person says and then watch what he does." The fact that people *say* something about their behavior does not make it true. Some people are embarrassed to admit that financial considerations affect their labor supply decisions. ("I work for fulfillment.") Others complain about government just for the sheer fun of it, while in reality they are not influenced by taxes at all. If you want to find out what radio station a family listens to, what makes more sense: to ask them, or to see where the radio dial is set?

Experiments

At the outset, we stressed that the basic problem in doing empirical work in economics is the inability to do controlled experiments with the economy. However, the federal government has funded several major attempts to use experimental methodologies in the study of economic behavior. The idea underlying these social experiments is illustrated in the "Income Maintenance Experiment" that was conducted during the late 1960s.

The problem was to find out how the labor supply of the poor would change (if at all) when poor people were allowed to participate in certain kinds of income support programs.[2] By random selection, a sample of poor families was sorted into two groups. Families in the first group were allowed to participate in the income support program. The second group served as a control. At the end of several years, the labor supplies of the two groups were compared. Any differences in work effort, it was thought, could be attributed to the experimental treatment.

Pitfalls of Social Experiments.   Although such an experiment seems to be a promising way to learn about economic behavior, technical problems tend to diminish the usefulness of its results because classical methodology for experiments requires that samples be truly random. That is, the members of the sample must be representative of the population whose behavior is under consideration. In social experiments, it is virtually impossible to maintain a random sample, even if one is available initially. Some people leave the program to take new jobs. Others simply decide that they don't want to participate. Because such people *self*-select out of the sample, the characteristics of the group left are no longer "representative" of the population.

In addition, unlike plants or laboratory animals, human beings are conscious of the fact that they are participating in an experiment. This consciousness itself affects their behavior. A related point is that people within the group may react differently to a program when only a small number of participants is involved than they would when the program is universal.

One thing is certain. Social experiments are costly. An experiment conducted to learn how the housing decisions of the poor would be affected by rent subsidies cost $163.3 million.[3] Proponents of the experiments argue that the resulting knowledge is worth the cost, while detractors believe that the money would be better spent on other types of research.

Laboratory Experiments.   Certain kinds of economic behavior can also be studied in laboratory experiments, an approach often used by psychologists. An investigator recruits a group of people ("subjects") who perform various tasks. The investigator observes their behavior. To study labor supply, an investigator might begin by noting from the theory of labor supply that a key variable is the net wage rate. A possible

---

[2] Essentially, the programs provided poor families with a guaranteed annual payment, the amount of which depended upon their earnings in the labor market. See Pechman and Timpane [1975] and Chapter 15.

[3] In this Experimental Housing Allowance Program, $55.9 million went for payments to the members of the sample. The remainder was spent on administration and analysis of the data. See Ingram [1981].

experimental strategy would be to offer subjects different rewards for completing various jobs and record how the amount of effort varies with the reward.

Laboratory experiments are subject to some of the pitfalls of social experiments. The main problem is that the environment in which behavior is observed is artificial. Moreover, the characteristics of the subjects, who are often college undergraduates, are unlikely to be representative of the population as a whole. However, laboratory experiments are much cheaper than social experiments and provide more flexibility. Their popularity has been growing in recent years.[4]

Econometric Studies

Econometrics is the statistical analysis of economic data. It does not rely upon asking people for their opinions or subjecting them to experiments. Rather, the effects of various policies are inferred from the analysis of observed behavior. While economists are unable to control historical events, econometrics makes it possible to assess the importance of events that *did* occur.

In the simple labor supply model, it was suggested that annual hours of work (L) will depend upon the net wage rate (w_n). [By definition, $w_n = (1 - t)w$.] A bit of thought suggests that variables like nonlabor income (A),[5] age (X_1), and number of children (X_2) may also influence the hours of work decision. The econometrician chooses a particular algebraic form to summarize the relationship between hours of work and these explanatory variables. A particularly simple form is:

(3.1) $$L = \alpha_0 + \alpha_1 w_n + \alpha_2 A + \alpha_3 X_1 + \alpha_4 X_2 + \varepsilon$$

The α's are the **parameters** of the equation and ε is a **random error.** The parameters show how a change in a given right-hand side variable affects hours of work. If $\alpha_1 = 0$, the net wage has no impact on hours of work. If α_1 is greater than 0, increases in the net wage induce people to work more. The substitution effect dominates. If α_1 is less than 0, increases in the net wage induce people to work less. The income effect dominates.

The presence of the random error ε reflects the fact that there are influences on labor supply that are unobservable to the investigator. No matter how many variables are included in the study, there is always some behavior that cannot be explained by the model.

Clearly, if we knew the α's, all debate over effect of taxes on labor supply would be settled. The practical side of econometrics is to estimate the α's by application of various techniques. The most popular method

---

[4] V. L. Smith [1982] discusses the advantages of the experimental approach.

[5] The sum of dividends, interest, etc.

is called **multiple regression analysis.** The heat of the debate over labor supply indicates that this technique does not always lead to conclusive results. To understand why, we consider its application to the labor supply example.

For this purpose, ignore for the moment all variables in Equation (3.1) other than the net wage. Assume that hours of work decision can be written simply as

(3.2) $$L = \alpha_0 + \alpha_1 w_n + \varepsilon$$

Equation (3.2) is characterized as *linear* because if it is graphed with L and w_n on the axes, the result is a straight line.

Suppose now that information is obtained on hours of work and on after-tax wages for a sample of people. Plotting those observations gives a scatter of points like that in Figure 3.1A. Obviously, no single straight line can fit through all these points. The purpose of multiple regression analysis is to find the parameters of that line which fits "best".[6] Such a *regression line* is illustrated in Figure 3.1B. The regression line is a geometric representation of Equation (3.2), and its slope is an estimate of α_1.

After α_1 is estimated its "reliability" must be considered. Is it likely to be close to the "true" value of α_1? To see why this is an issue, suppose that our scatter of points looked like that in Figure 3.1C. The regression line is identical to that in Figure 3.1B, but the scatter of points is more diffuse. Even though the estimates of the α's are the same as those in Figure 3.1B, there will be less faith in their reliability. Econometricians calculate a measure called the *standard error* which indicates how much an estimated parameter can vary from the true value. When the standard error is small in relation to the size of the estimated parameter, the coefficient is said to be **statistically significant.**

This example assumed that there is only one explanatory variable, the net wage. Suppose that instead there were two variables in the equation: the net wage and nonlabor income. In analogy to fitting a *regression line* in a two-dimensional space, a regression *plane* can be fitted through a scatter of points in a three-dimensional space. For more than two variables, there is no convenient geometrical representation. Nevertheless, similar mathematical principles are applied to produce estimates of the parameters for any number of explanatory variables (provided that there are fewer variables than observations). The actual calculations are done with high-speed computers.

With estimates of the α's in hand, inferences can be made about the changes in L induced by changes in the net wage. Suppose that $\alpha_1 = 100$. Then if a tax increase lowered the wage by 50 cents, it can be predicted an individual would work 50 hours ($100 \times \$.50$) less per year.

---

[6] The best line is that which minimizes the sum of the squared vertical distances between the points on the line and the points in the scatter. See Gujarati [1978].

FIGURE 3.1   Multiple Regression Analysis

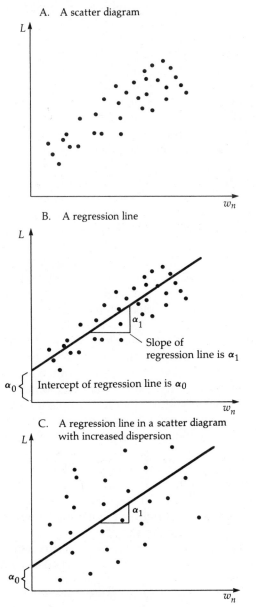

A.   A scatter diagram

B.   A regression line

Slope of
regression line is α_1

Intercept of regression line is α_0

C.   A regression line in a scatter diagram
with increased dispersion

Pitfalls of Econometric Analysis.   There are difficulties involved in doing econometrics which explain why different investigators may reach
contradictory conclusions.

For example, implicit in Equation (3.1) is the assumption that the
same equation can describe everyone's behavior. However, different
types of people may have different hours-of-work equations. The labor
supply of married women may react differently than that of married
men to change in the net wage. Similarly, the young and the old have
different behavioral patterns. Grouping together people with different
behavior results in misleading parameter estimates. Investigators generally do not know beforehand along what lines their samples should be
divided. Somewhat arbitrary decisions are required, and these may lead
investigators to different results.

A related problem is that the parameters may change over time. The
female labor supply equation for women using data from 1960 would
very likely show different results from an equation using 1985 data. In
part, this would be due to the impact of the women's movement upon
attitudes toward work, and hence, on the values of the α's. More generally, the reality that econometricians seek to understand is constantly
changing. Estimates obtained from various data sets may differ even if
the techniques used to obtain them are the same.

In addition, for an estimate of α_1 to be reliable, the regression equation must include all the relevant variables. Otherwise, some effects that
are actually due to an omitted variable may be attributed to the net
wage. Important variables are sometimes left out of an equation because
information on them is simply not available. For example, it is very
difficult to obtain reliable information on people's sources of nonlabor
income. Suppose that: (1) as nonlabor income increases (other things
being the same), people tend to work less; and (2) there is a tendency for
people with high wages also to have high nonlabor income. Then if nonlabor income is omitted from the equation, part of its effect on hours of
work will be attributed to the wage, and the estimate of α_1 will be lower
than its true value. In general, an estimate of α_1 will be biased unless all
the other variables that affect hours of work and that are also systematically related to the net wage are included.

A more severe version of this problem occurs when a potentially
important variable is inherently unmeasurable. Attitudes like "aggres-
siveness" may very well influence work decision, but there are no really
good ways for quantifying these attitudes.

Sometimes there are controversies over what variables should be included in a regression equation. Should an individual's educational level
be included? Some argue that education affects attitudes toward work
and therefore should be included as an explanatory variable. Others
believe that education only affects work decisions to the extent that it

changes the wage, and therefore should *not* be included. While economic theory helps give some structure to the search for explanatory variables, it is rarely definitive on this matter. Different investigators will make different judgments.

Also, to the extent that the variables are mismeasured, it is difficult to obtain reliable estimates of the behavior we seek to understand. Consider problems in measuring hours of work. Superficially, this seems like a straightforward issue—merely find out how much time elapses at the workplace. But a better measure would take into account coffee breaks and "goofing off" time. These are obviously more difficult to measure. Measuring the wage rate also presents substantial problems. Ideally, the computation should take into consideration not only what a worker receives in the paycheck at the end of the week, but also the value of fringe benefits—pension rights, insurance programs, access to a company car, etc.

Equation (3.1) assumes that all the explanatory variables affect hours of work in a linear fashion. This is a very convenient assumption, but certainly not the only possibility. An investigator might believe that hours of work depend on the net wage and the net wage squared—a quadratic relationship. It is therefore necessary to augment the equation with the variable w_n^2. Human behavior is sufficiently complex that any equation can only be an approximation of the truth. Unfortunately, economic theory gives little guidance with respect to what the correct functional form is, so investigators must choose specifications largely on the basis of intuition or convenience.

Finally, an important assumption is that variables on the right side of the equation affect the choice of the left-hand variable. If the reverse is true, serious problems arise. Suppose that α_1 of Equation (3.1) is found to be positive. One interpretation is that when the net wage increases, people choose to work more. Another plausible interpretation is that employers pay higher wages to people who work longer hours. Indeed, it might be the case that wage rates affect hours worked and *simultaneously* hours worked affect wages. If this is so, then the estimate of α_1 generated by multiple regression analysis does not measure just the effect of changes in the net wage on people's work decisions.

Several statistical techniques are available for dealing with the simultaneity problem. They tend to be complicated, and different techniques can lead to different answers. This is another source of discrepancies in the results of econometric studies.

CONCLUDING REMARKS

There are a number of tools available for those who seek to describe economic behavior. Theory plays a crucial role in helping to isolate a set of variables that might be important. Empirical work is then needed to see whether the theory is consistent with "real-world" phenomena. Currently the most widespread method of empirical work in economics is econometric analysis, because economists tend to be most comfortable with results based on data from real-world environments. However, honest econometricians may come to very different conclusions. The data they use are imperfect, and implementation requires that assumptions be made. Reasonable people can disagree on the proper interpretation of a particular set of "facts":

> Facts are simple
> and facts are straight
> Facts are lazy
> and facts are late
> Facts all come with points of view
> Facts won't do what I want them to.[7]

This does not mean that all hope of learning about the factors that influence economic behavior should be abandoned. The economist researching an empirical question will doubtless come across a number of studies, each making somewhat different assumptions, each emphasizing a somewhat different aspect of the problem, and each therefore arriving at a somewhat different conclusion. In many cases it is possible to reconcile the different studies and construct a coherent picture of the phenomenon under discussion. Feldstein has likened the economist who undertakes such a task to the maharajah in the children's fable about the five blind men who examined an elephant:

> The important lesson in that story is not the fact that each blind man came away with a partial and "incorrect" piece of evidence. The lesson is rather that an intelligent maharajah who studied the findings of these five men could probably piece together a good judgmental picture of an elephant, especially if he had previously seen some other four-footed animal. [1982b, p. 830]

On the numerous occasions throughout this book when we refer to the results of empirical studies, the caveats presented should be kept in mind. In cases where the profession has failed to achieve consensus, the opposing views will be discussed. But more generally, it is hoped that this introduction to empirical methodology will induce a healthy skepticism concerning claims about economic behavior that occur in public debate and begin with the magic words "studies have proved."

---

[7] From "Cross-Eyed and Painless" © 1980 Bleu Disque Music Co., Inc., Index Music, Inc., and E. G. Music, Ltd., by permission of David Byrne and Brian Eno.

SUMMARY

Because economists are unable to perform carefully controlled experiments with the economy, the effects of economic policy are often hard to determine.

Economic theory helps specify the factors that might affect a given kind of behavior. Generally, however, theory alone cannot say how important any particular factor is.

Empirical research attempts to measure both the direction and size of the effect of government policy changes on behavior. Common types of empirical studies are interview studies, social and laboratory experiments, and econometric analysis.

Interview studies consist of directly asking people how various policies affect their behavior. However, people may not actually react to policies in the way they say they do.

Social experiments subject one group of people to some policy and compare their behavior to another group that is not subject to the policy. These attempts are not entirely satisfactory because the experiment itself may affect people's behavior, because it is difficult to obtain a random sample, and because social experiments are quite costly.

Laboratory experiments are used to study some types of economic decisions, but in the artificial atmosphere subjects may not replicate real-world behavior.

Econometrics is the statistical analysis of economic data. In econometrics, the effects of various policies are inferred from the analysis of observed behavior.

Techniques such as multiple regression analysis are used to pick the "best" parameters for the model. It is the size and sign (positive or negative) of the estimated parameters that allow prediction of the effects of policy changes.

Econometrics is not without pitfalls. Misleading results will be obtained if data from greatly dissimilar groups are combined; if important variables are omitted; if the wrong mathematical form is adopted; if variables are incorrectly measured; or if the direction of causation is not only from the explanatory variables to the left-hand variable, but in the reverse direction, as well.

DISCUSSION QUESTIONS

1. Like economists, astronomers are generally unable to perform controlled experiments. Yet astronomy is considered more of an exact science than economics. Why?

2. A proposal is made to lower the rate of taxation on interest paid by savings accounts. You are asked to predict its impact.
   a. Are there any reasons to expect this proposal to increase savings? Lower savings?

  b. How would you construct a survey to investigate this issue?

  c. If you were to conduct an experiment to investigate the issue, would it be a social or laboratory experiment? Why? Describe your experiment.

  d. How would you conduct an econometric investigation? What data would you need? What algebraic function would you choose?

  e. In any of your studies did you consider variables other than tax rates? If so, why did you choose them?

SELECTED REFERENCES

Becker, Gary S. "Irrational Behavior and Economic Theory." *Journal of Political Economy* 70 (February 1962), pp. 1–13.

Gujarati, D. *Basic Econometrics.* New York: McGraw-Hill, 1978.

Pechman, Joseph A., and P. Michael Timpane, eds. *Work Incentives and Income Guarantees: The New Jersey Negative Income Tax Experiment.* Washington, D.C.: Brookings Institution, 1975.

Smith, Vernon L. "Microeconomic Systems as an Experimental Science." *American Economic Review* 72, no. 5 (December 1982), pp. 923–55.

CHAPTER 4

Tools of Normative Analysis

The object of government is the welfare of the people.
The material progress and prosperity of a nation
are desirable chiefly so far as they lead to the moral
and material welfare of all good citizens.

Theodore Roosevelt

As citizens we are called upon to react to and evaluate a constant flow of proposals concerning government's role in the economy. Should income taxes be raised? Is it a good idea to change the age at which social security payments begin? Should there be stricter controls on auto emissions? The list is virtually endless. Given the enormous diversity of the economic activities undertaken by government, some kind of *general* framework is needed to organize thoughts about the desirability of various government actions.

Without such a systematic framework, each government program would be evaluated on an ad hoc basis, and a coherent economic policy would be impossible to achieve. The framework used by most public finance specialists is **welfare economics,** the branch of economic theory concerned with the social desirability of alternative economic states. In this chapter we will sketch the fundamentals of welfare economics. The theory is used to distinguish those circumstances under which markets can be expected to perform well from those circumstances under which markets will fail to produce desirable results.

BASIC RESULTS OF WELFARE ECONOMICS[1]

Pure Exchange Economy

To examine welfare economics, we begin by considering a very simple economy: there are only two people who consume two commodities with fixed supply. The only economic problem here is to allocate amounts of the two goods between the two people. As simple as this model is, all the important results from the two good–two person case hold in economies with many people and commodities.[2] The two-by-two case is analyzed because of its simplicity.

The two people are Adam and Eve, and the two commodities are apples ("food") and fig leaves ("clothing"). An analytical device known as the **Edgeworth Box**[3] is used to depict the distribution of apples and fig leaves between Adam and Eve. In Figure 4.1, the length of the Edgeworth Box, *Os*, represents the total number of apples available in the economy; the height, *Or*, is the total number of fig leaves. The amounts of the good consumed by Adam are measured by distances from point

FIGURE 4.1   Edgeworth Box

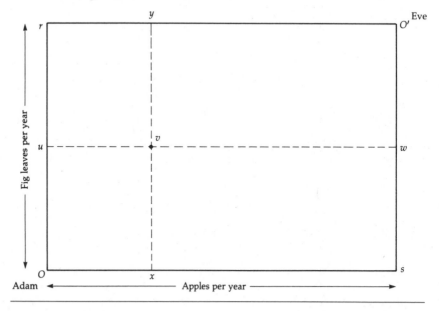

---

[1] Welfare economics relies heavily on certain basic economic tools, particularly indifference curves. For a review, see the appendix at the end of the book.

[2] See Chapter 11 of Henderson and Quandt [1980] where the results are derived using calculus.

[3] Named after the great 19th century economist F. Y. Edgeworth.

O; the quantities consumed by Eve are measured by distances from O'. For example, at point v, Adam consumes Ou fig leaves and Ox apples, while Eve consumes $O'y$ apples and $O'w$ fig leaves. Thus, any point within the Edgeworth Box represents some distribution of apples and fig leaves between Adam and Eve.

Now assume that Adam and Eve each have a set of conventionally shaped indifference curves which depict their preferences for apples and fig leaves. In Figure 4.2, both sets of indifference curves are super-

FIGURE 4.2   Indifference Curves in an Edgeworth Box

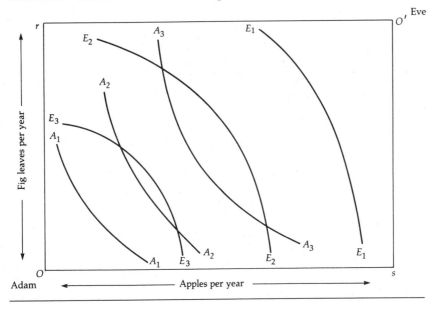

imposed onto the Edgeworth Box. Adam's are labeled with A's; Eve's are labeled with E's. The numbering of indifference curves corresponds to higher levels of happiness ("utility"). Adam is happier on indifference curve A_3 than on A_2 or A_1, and Eve is happier on indifference curve E_3 than on E_2 or E_1. In general, Eve's utility increases as her position moves toward the southwest, while Adam's utility increases as he moves toward the northeast.

Suppose that some arbitrary distribution of apples and fig leaves is selected—say point g in Figure 4.3. $A_g A_g$ is the indifference curve of Adam that runs through point g, and $E_g E_g$ is Eve's. Now pose the following question: Is it possible to reallocate apples and fig leaves between Adam and Eve in such a way that Adam is made better off, while Eve is made no worse off? A moment's thought suggests that there is such an allocation, at point h. Adam is better off at this point because indiffer-

FIGURE 4.3   Making Adam Better Off without Eve Being Worse Off

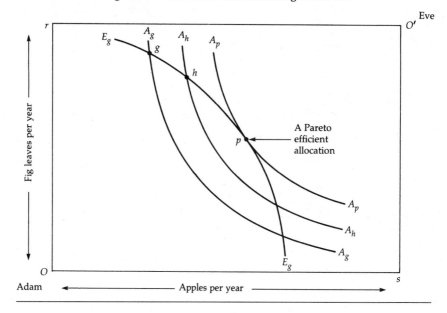

ence curve A_hA_h represents a higher utility level for him than A_gA_g. On the other hand, Eve is no worse off at h because she is on her original indifference curve, E_gE_g.

Can Adam's welfare be further increased without doing any harm to Eve? As long as it is possible to move Adam to indifference curves further to the northeast while still remaining on E_gE_g, it is possible. This process can be continued until Adam's indifference curve is just touching E_gE_g, which occurs at point p in Figure 4.3. The only way to put Adam on a higher indifference curve than A_pA_p would be to put Eve on a lower one. An allocation such as point p, at which the only way to make one person better off is to make another person worse off, is called **Pareto efficient.**[4] Pareto efficiency is often used as the standard for evaluating the desirability of an allocation of resources. If the allocation is not Pareto efficient, then it is "wasteful" in the sense that it is possible to make someone better off without hurting anybody else. When economists use the word *efficient,* they usually have the notion of Pareto efficiency in mind.

Point p is not the only Pareto efficient allocation which could have been reached by starting at point g. In Figure 4.4 we examine whether it is possible to make Eve better off without lowering the utility of Adam. Logic similar to that surrounding Figure 4.3 suggests moving Eve to

---

[4] Named after the 19th century economist Vilfredo Pareto.

FIGURE 4.4   Making Eve Better Off without Adam Being Worse Off

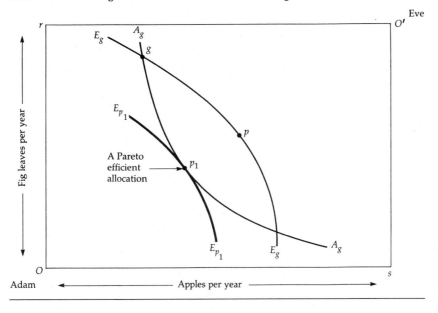

indifference curves further to the southwest, provided that the allocation remains on $A_g A_g$. In doing so, a point like p_1 is isolated. At p_1, the
only way to improve Eve's welfare is to move Adam to a lower indifference curve. Then, by definition, p_1 is a Pareto efficient allocation.

So far, we have been looking at moves that make one person better
off and leave the other at the same level of utility. In Figure 4.5 we
consider reallocations from point g that make Adam and Eve *both* better
off. At p_2, for example, Adam is better off than at point g ($A_{p_2}A_{p_2}$ is
further to the northeast than $A_g A_g$) and so is Eve ($E_{p_2}E_{p_2}$ is further to the
southwest than $E_g E_g$). Point p_2 is Pareto efficient, because at that point it
is impossible to make either individual better off without making the
other worse off. It should now be clear that starting at point g, a whole
set of Pareto efficient points can be found. They differ with respect to
how much each of the parties gains from the reallocation of resources.

Recall that the initial point g was selected arbitrarily. The exercise of
finding Pareto efficient allocations could be repeated with any starting
point. Had point k in Figure 4.6 been the original allocation, Pareto
efficient combinations of the commodities like p_3 and p_4 could have been
isolated. The key point is that there is a whole set of Pareto efficient
points in the Edgeworth Box. The locus of all the Pareto efficient points
is called the **contract curve,** and is denoted mm in Figure 4.7. Note that
for an allocation to be Pareto efficient (to be on mm), it must be a point at
which the indifference curves of Adam and Eve are "barely touching."

FIGURE 4.5   Making Both Adam and Eve Better Off

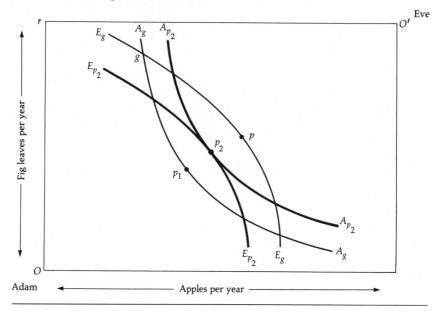

FIGURE 4.6   Starting from a Different Initial Point

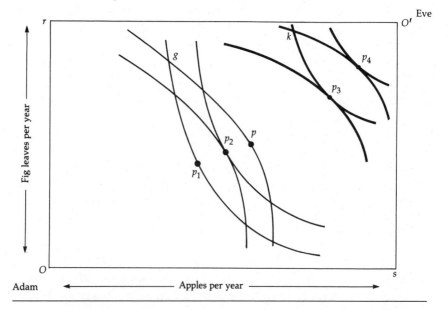

FIGURE 4.7   The Contract Curve

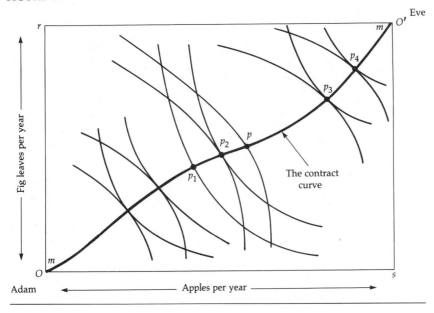

In mathematical terms, the indifference curves are tangent—the slopes of the indifference curves are equal.

In economic terms, the absolute value of the slope of the indifference curve indicates the rate at which the individual is willing to trade one good for an additional amount of another, called the marginal rate of substitution (MRS).[5] Hence, a Pareto efficient allocation of resources requires that marginal rates of substitution be equal for all consumers.[6] Algebraically, a necessary condition for Pareto efficiency is

(4.1) $$MRS_{af}^{Adam} = MRS_{af}^{Eve},$$

where MRS_{af}^{Adam} is Adam's marginal rate of substitution of apples for fig leaves, and MRS_{af}^{Eve} is defined similarly.

An Economy with Production

The analysis so far assumes that supplies of all the commodities are fixed. Consider what happens when productive inputs can shift between the production of apples and fig leaves, so that the quantities of

---

[5] The marginal rate of substitution is defined more carefully in the appendix at the end of the book.

[6] This assumes that a positive quantity of each commodity is consumed, an assumption that will be made throughout.

the two goods are alterable. Provided that the inputs are efficiently used, if more apples are produced, then fig leaf production must necessarily fall and vice versa. The **production possibilities curve** shows the maximum quantity of fig leaves that can be produced along with any given quantity of apples. A typical production possibilities curve is depicted as CC in Figure 4.8. As shown in Figure 4.8, one option available

FIGURE 4.8   Production Possibilities Curve

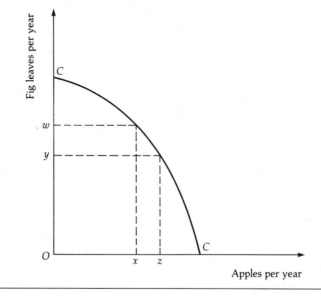

to the economy is to produce Ow fig leaves and Ox apples. The economy can increase apple production from Ox to Oz, distance xz. To do this, of course, inputs have to be removed from the production of fig leaves and devoted to apples. Fig leaf production must fall by distance wy if apple production is to increase by xz. The ratio of distance wy to distance xz is called the **marginal rate of transformation** of apples for fig leaves (MRT_{af}) because it shows the rate at which the economy can transform apples into fig leaves. Just as MRS_{af} measures the absolute value of the slope of an indifference curve, MRT_{af} measures the absolute value of the slope of the production possibilities curve.

When the production of apples and fig leaves is variable, the condition for Pareto efficiency in Equation (4.1) must be extended. The necessary condition for Pareto efficiency becomes

(4.2)
$$MRT_{af} = MRS_{af}^{\text{Adam}} = MRS_{af}^{\text{Eve}}$$

A simple arithmetic example demonstrates why the first equality in Equation (4.2) must hold. Suppose that at a given allocation Adam's

MRS_{af} is ⅓, and the MRT_{af} is ⅔. By the definition of MRT_{af}, at this allocation two additional fig leaves could be produced by giving up three apples. By the definition of MRS_{af}, if Adam lost three extra apples, he would require only *one* fig leaf to maintain his original utility level. Therefore, Adam could be made better off by giving up three apples and having them transformed into *two* fig leaves, and no one else would be made worse off in the process. Such a trade is *always* possible as long as the marginal rate of substitution does not equal the marginal rate of transformation. Only when the slopes of the curves for each are equal is it impossible to make someone better off without making anybody worse off. Hence, $MRT_{af} = MRS_{af}$ is a necessary condition for Pareto efficiency. The rate at which apples can be transformed into fig leaves (MRT_{af}) must equal the rate at which consumers are willing to trade apples for fig leaves (MRS_{af}).

The conditions for Pareto efficiency can be reinterpreted in terms of the notion of **marginal cost** (MC)—the incremental production cost of one more unit of output. It can be proved that the marginal rate of transformation along the production possibilities curve is the ratio of the marginal cost of apples (MC_a) to the marginal cost of fig leaves (MC_f), or $MRT_{af} = MC_a/MC_f$.[7] Substituting this relation into (4.2) gives us

(4.3)
$$\frac{MC_a}{MC_f} = MRS_{af}^{\text{Adam}} = MRS_{af}^{\text{Eve}}$$

as a necessary condition for Pareto efficiency.

The Fundamental Theorem of Welfare Economics

We have now described the necessary conditions for Pareto efficiency, but have given no indication as to whether or not a real-world economy will achieve this apparently desirable state. Will a market system naturally reach the contract curve? The Fundamental Theorem of Welfare Economics provides an answer: As long as producers and consumers act as perfect competitors, i.e., take prices as given, then under *certain conditions* a Pareto efficient allocation of resources will emerge. (These conditions are discussed below.) Thus, a competitive economy "automatically" allocates resources efficiently, without any need for centralized direction (shades of Adam Smith's "invisible hand"). In a way, the fundamental theorem merely formalizes an insight that social

---

[7] Intuitively, assume there is only one input, labor (L). Because the MRT_{af} is the absolute value of the slope of the production possibilities curve, by definition it is equal to $\Delta f/\Delta a$, where Δa is the change in the number of apples and Δf is the change in the number of fig leaves. Now, $\Delta f/\Delta a$ can be written as $(\Delta L/\Delta a)/(\Delta L/\Delta f)$. The numerator, $\Delta L/\Delta a$, shows the incremental amount of labor needed to produce an incremental amount of apples. Because labor is the only input, this is the marginal cost of apples. Similarly, $\Delta L/\Delta f$ can be interpreted as the marginal cost of fig leaves. Hence, $MRT_{af} = MC_a/MC_f$.

observers have long recognized: When it comes to providing goods and services, the free enterprise system has been amazingly productive.[8]

A rigorous proof of the fundamental theorem requires fairly sophisticated mathematics, but we can provide an intuitive justification. The essence of competition is that all people face the same prices—each consumer and producer is so small relative to the market that his actions alone cannot affect prices. In terms of our example, this means that Adam and Eve both pay the same prices for fig leaves (P_f) and apples (P_a). A basic result from the theory of rational choice[9] is that a necessary condition for Adam to maximize utility is

(4.4)
$$MRS_{af}^{\text{Adam}} = \frac{P_a}{P_f}$$

Similarly, Eve's utility maximizing bundle is characterized by

(4.5)
$$MRS_{af}^{\text{Eve}} = \frac{P_a}{P_f}$$

Equations (4.4) and (4.5) together imply that

$$MRS_{af}^{\text{Adam}} = MRS_{af}^{\text{Eve}}$$

This condition, however, is identical to Equation (4.1), one of the necessary conditions for Pareto efficiency.

Just as utility-maximizing consumers set the marginal rate of substitution equal to the price ratio, profit-maximizing producers set the marginal rate of transformation equal to the price ratio.[10] Taking this condition

(4.6)
$$MRT_{af} = \frac{P_a}{P_f}$$

together with (4.4) and (4.5) gives us (4.2), the necessary condition for Pareto efficiency. Hence, competition along with maximizing behavior on the part of all individuals leads to an efficient outcome.

We can take advantage of Equation (4.3) to write the conditions for Pareto efficiency in terms of marginal cost. Simply substitute (4.4) or (4.5) into (4.3) to find

(4.7)
$$\frac{P_a}{P_f} = \frac{MC_a}{MC_f}$$

To have a Pareto efficient allocation of resources it is necessary that prices be in the same ratios as marginal costs, and competition guaran-

---

[8] "The bourgeoisie, during its rule of scarce 100 years, has created more massive and more colossal productive forces than have all preceding generations together," according to Karl Marx and Friedrich Engels in *The Communist Manifesto*, Part I [Tucker, 1978, p. 477].

[9] This result is derived in the appendix to this book.

[10] See the book's appendix for a demonstration.

tees this condition will be met. The marginal cost of a commodity represents the additional cost to society of providing it. According to Equation (4.7), efficiency requires that the additional cost of each commodity be reflected in its price.

Choosing among Pareto Efficient Points: The Social Welfare Function

If properly functioning competitive markets allocate resources efficiently, what role does the government have to play in the economy? Only a very small government would appear to be appropriate. Its main function would be to establish a setting in which property rights are protected so that competition can work. Government provides law and order, a court system, and national defense. Anything more is superfluous. However, such reasoning is based on a superficial understanding of the fundamental theorem. Things are really much more complicated. For one thing, it has implicitly been assumed that efficiency is the only criterion for deciding whether or not a given allocation of resources is good. It is not obvious, however, that Pareto efficiency by itself is desirable.

To see why, consider Figure 4.9, which reproduces the contract curve mm derived in Figure 4.7. Compare the two allocations p_5 (at the lower left-hand corner of the box) and q (located near the center). Because p_5

FIGURE 4.9   Efficiency versus Equity

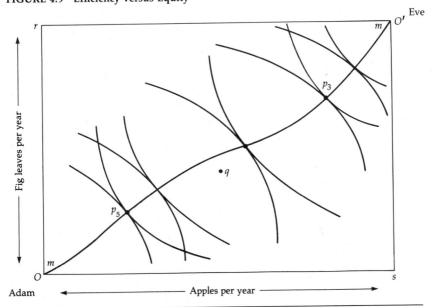

lies on the contract curve, by definition it is Pareto efficient. On the other hand, q is inefficient. Is allocation p_5 therefore better? That depends on what is meant by "better." To the extent that society prefers a relatively equal distribution of real income, q might be preferred to p_5, even though q is not Pareto efficient. On the other hand, society might not care about distribution at all, or perhaps care more about Eve than Adam. In this case, p_5 would be preferred to q.

The key point here is that the criterion of Pareto efficiency by itself is not enough to determine the desirability of alternative allocations of resources. Rather, explicit value judgments are required on the "fairness" of the distribution of utility. To formalize this notion, note that the contract curve implicitly defines a relationship between the maximum amount of utility that Adam can attain given a particular level of Eve's

FIGURE 4.10   Utility Possibilities Curve

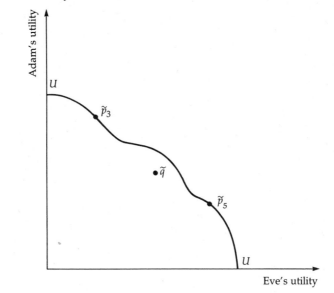

utility. In Figure 4.10, Eve's utility is plotted on the horizontal axis, and Adam's utility is recorded on the vertical axis. Curve UU is the **utility possibilities curve** dervied from the contract curve.[11] It shows the maximum amount of one person's utility given the utility attained by the

---

[11] The production possibilities curve in Figure 4.8 is drawn on the reasonable assumption that the absolute value of its slope continually increases as we move downward along it. The more apples that are produced, the more fig leaves must be given up to produce an apple. However, there is no reason to assume that this holds for the trade-off between individuals' utilities. This is why UU in Figure 4.10 is wavy rather than smooth.

other individual. Point $\tilde{p}_5$ corresponds to point p_5 on the contract curve in Figure 4.9. Here, Eve's utility is relatively high compared to Adam's. Point $\tilde{p}_3$ in Figure 4.10 corresponds to p_3 in Figure 4.9. Here, Adam's utility is relatively high, and Eve's relatively low. Point $\tilde{q}$ corresponds to point q in Figure 4.10. Because q is off the contract curve, $\tilde{q}$ must be inside the utility possibilities curve. This reflects the fact that at q, it is possible to increase one person's utility without decreasing the other's.

All points on or below the utility possibilities curve are attainable by society; all points above it are not attainable. By definition, all points on UU are Pareto efficient, but they represent very different distributions of real income between Adam and Eve. Which point is best? The conventional way to answer this question is to postulate a **social welfare function,** which embodies society's views on the relative deservedness of Adam and Eve. Imagine that just as an *individual*'s welfare depends upon the quantities of commodities he consumes, *society*'s welfare depends upon the utilities of each of its members. Algebraically, social welfare (W) is some function $F(\ )$ of each individual's utility:

(4.8) $$W = F(U^{\text{Adam}}, U^{\text{Eve}})$$

We assume that the value of social welfare increases as either U^{Adam} or U^{Eve} increases.[12] Society is better off when any of its members becomes better off. Note that we have said nothing about how "society" manifests these preferences. Under some conditions, members of society may not be able to agree on how to rank each other's utilities, and the social welfare function will not even exist. For the moment, we simply assume that it does exist.

Just as an individual's utility function for commodities leads to a set of indifference curves for those commodities, so does a social welfare function lead to a set of indifference curves between people's utilities.[13]

A typical set of social indifference curves is depicted in Figure 4.11. The downward slope of the curves indicates that if Eve's utility decreases, the only way to maintain a given level of social welfare is to increase Adam's utility, and vice versa. The level of social welfare increases as we move toward the northeast, reflecting the fact that increases in any individual's utility increase social welfare, other things being the same.

In Figure 4.12, the social indifference curves are superimposed upon the utility possibilities curve from Figure 4.10. Point i is not as desirable as point ii (point ii is on a higher social indifference curve than point i)

---

[12] Social welfare functions which depend only upon the utilities of individuals are sometimes referred to as "utilitarian" social welfare functions because of their association with the utilitarian social philosophers of the 19th century. Other social welfare functions are discussed in the next chapter.

[13] An important question discussed in Chapter 5 is whether it is valid to compare different individuals' utilities.

FIGURE 4.11   Social Indifference Curves

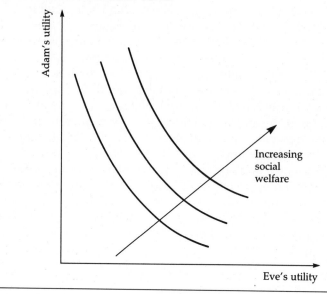

FIGURE 4.12   Maximizing Social Welfare

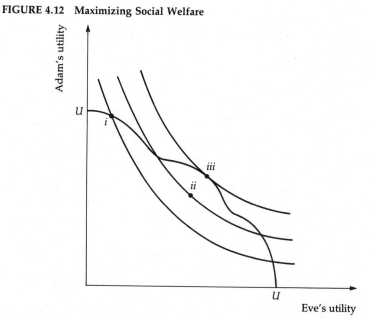

even though point *i* is Pareto efficient and point *ii* is not. Here, society's value judgments, embodied in the social welfare function, favor a more equal distribution of real income, inefficient though it may be. Of course, point *iii* is preferred to either of these. It is both efficient and "fair."

Now, the Fundamental Theorem of Welfare Economics indicates that a properly working competitive system will lead to some allocation on the utility possibilities curve. There is no reason, however, that it will be the particular point at which social welfare is at a maximum. We conclude that even if the economy generates a Pareto efficient allocation of resources, government intervention may be necessary to achieve a "fair" distribution of utility.

A second reason the fundamental theorem need not imply a minimal government has to do with the fact that the "certain conditions" required for its validity may not be satisfied by real-world markets. As we now show, an absence of these conditions may lead free markets to allocate resources inefficiently.

TYPES OF MARKET FAILURE

In the famous movie *Casablanca*, whenever something seems amiss, the police chief gives an order to "round up the usual suspects." Similarly, whenever markets appear to be failing to allocate resources efficiently, economists round up the same group of possible causes for the supposed failure. Monopoly, public goods, externalities, costly information, and nonexistence of markets are the "suspects" of market failure. Each may cause an economy with freely operating markets to generate an inefficient allocation of resources. Each type of market failure creates interesting and complicated questions concerning the appropriate governmental remedies discussed in subsequent chapters.

Monopoly

If some agents have market power, the ability to affect price, then the allocation of resources will generally be inefficient. An extreme form of such market power is **monopoly**—only one seller in the market for a given commodity. A monopolist can raise prices above marginal cost by supplying less output than a competitor would. Thus, Equation (4.7), one of the necessary conditions for Pareto efficiency, is violated. An insufficient quantity of resources is devoted to the monopolized good.

Public Goods

Price takers (those who cannot affect the market price) have no incentive to hide true preferences for a good. If bread costs 65 cents per loaf, and I would be willing to pay 68 cents, there is no reason for me to pretend that I do not want to buy it.

The essential characteristic of this example is that bread is consumed privately. When I eat a loaf of bread, no one else can possibly eat it simultaneously. This is sometimes referred to as *rivalness of consumption.* Moreover, producers of bread can easily exclude noncustomers from consuming bread. In contrast, a **public good** is characterized by the facts that consumption is not rival and excluding nonpayers is difficult. The classic example of a public good is a lighthouse. When the lighthouse turns on its beacon, it helps to guide all the ships in the vicinity. The fact that one person benefits from the lighthouse's services does not prevent anyone else from doing so simultaneously. Morever, in the absence of a technology to jam the signals, it is difficult to exclude nonpayers from taking advantage of them.

In using the lighthouse, people may have an incentive to hide their true preferences. Suppose that it would be worthwhile to me to have the lighthouse operate. I know, however, that once the beacon is lit, I can enjoy its services, whether I pay for them or not. Therefore, I may claim that the lighthouse means nothing to me, hoping that I can get a "free ride" after other people pay for it. Unfortunately, everyone has the same incentive, so the lighthouse may not get built at all, even though its construction could be very beneficial. The market mechanism may fail to force people to reveal their preferences for public goods, and possibly will result in insufficient resources being devoted to them.

Externalities

In the basic competitive model, people interact solely by trading with each other in the market. There are situations, however, in which economic agents affect each other in ways outside the market. Suppose that Eve sets up an apple press to manufacture cider, and the waste products associated with this process are dumped into a stream which flows into Adam's section of the Garden. As a consequence, Adam's drinking water is polluted and his utility declines.

The activity of one agent affecting the welfare of another in a way that is outside the market is termed an **externality.** In the presence of an externality, the market may fail to allocate resources efficiently. The problem is Eve's use of a scarce resource, water, in the production of cider. Despite the fact that water is scarce, if no one owns the stream, Eve does not have to pay for the water. Because the price of water (zero) does not reflect the fact that it is scarce, Eve "overuses" it.

All of this has a simple interpretation in the analytics of welfare economics. In the derivation of Equation (4.7), it was implicitly assumed that "marginal cost" meant marginal *social* cost—it took into account the incremental value of *all* of society's resources used in production. In the example above, however, Eve's marginal private cost is less than the marginal social cost because she does not have to pay for the water she uses. Hence, Equation (4.7) is not satisfied, and the allocation of resources is inefficient.[14]

Costly Information

The competitive model assumes that information on existing prices is somehow spread around at no cost, so that everyone can find the best price. In reality, this is not the case. "Shopping around" to find the lowest price requires time, which is a valuable commodity. Moreover, once information is obtained, it may be imperfect. (Is this car a lemon?) Thus, it is possible that individuals will not have the kind of information they need to make the right economic decisions, and inefficient patterns of resource allocation will emerge.

Nonexistence of Markets

The proof behind the fundamental theorem assumes that a market exists for each and every good.[15] It seems likely, however, that even if there were no public good or externality problem, markets for certain goods would fail to emerge. In a world of uncertainty, insurance is a "commodity" that is very important. Despite the existence of firms like Lloyd's of London, there are certain events for which insurance simply cannot be purchased on the private market. Suppose that you wanted to purchase unemployment insurance. The problem is that once you obtained such insurance you might take less care to keep your job than you would have originally. And since information on future employment prospects is costly, an insurance company could not tell whether or not you would be a good risk. Hence, no private firm goes into the business of providing unemployment insurance. A commodity that people would be willing to buy is not generally available on the private market, and resources may be inefficiently allocated.

OVERVIEW

The Fundamental Theorem of Welfare Economics states that a properly working competitive economy generates a Pareto efficient allocation of

---

[14] An externality can be positive—confer a benefit—as well as negative. Still, social and private marginal costs are unequal, and the allocation of resources is inefficient. In the case of the positive externality, not enough of the beneficial activity is pursued.

[15] In a formal sense, several of the previously listed illustrations of market failure are just different manifestations of the nonexistence of markets problem. For example, the public goods problem can be viewed as the failure of markets to emerge because it is too costly (or impossible) to gather information on people's true preferences.

resources without any government intervention. However, it is not obvious that an efficient allocation of resources is per se socially desirable; some argue that "fairness" must also be taken into account. In addition, in certain cases, the real-world economy is not "properly working." Hence, the market-determined allocation of resources is not likely even to be efficient, let alone equitable. There is then an opportunity for government to intervene in the economy to modify the distribution of income and enhance economic efficiency.

It must be emphasized that while distributional and market-failure problems provide opportunities for government intervention in the economy, they *do not require it*. The fact that the market-generated allocation of resources is imperfect does not mean that the government is actually capable of doing better. For example, in certain cases, the costs of setting up a government agency to deal with an externality could exceed the cost of the externality itself. Moreover, governments, like people, can make mistakes. Indeed, some argue that government is inherently incapable of acting efficiently, so that while in theory it can improve upon the status quo, in practice it never will. Thus, the fundamental theorem is only helpful in identifying situations in which intervention *may* lead to higher social welfare.

EVALUATION

Welfare economics provides the basis for most of the normative work in public finance. There are, however, some controversies surrounding the theory.

First of all, the underlying outlook is highly individualistic, with a focus on people's utilities and how to maximize them. This is brought out starkly in the formulation of the social welfare function, Equation (4.8). The basic point of view expressed in that equation is that a good society is one in which the members are happy. As suggested in Chapter 1, however, other societal goals are possible—to maximize the power of the state, to glorify God, etc. Welfare economics does not have much to say to people with such goals.

Because welfare economics puts people's preferences at center stage, it requires that these preferences be taken seriously. People know best what gives them satisfaction. If one believes that individuals' preferences are ill formed or corrupt, a theory that shows how to maximize their utility is essentially irrelevant. As Thomas O'Neill, Speaker of the House of Representatives, once suggested, "Often what the American people want is not good for them."

Musgrave [1959] developed the concept of **merit goods** to describe commodities that ought to be provided even if the members of society do not demand them. Government support of the fine arts is often justified on this basis. Operas and concerts should be provided publicly if individuals are unwilling to pay enough to meet their costs. But as Baumol and Baumol [1981] have noted,

> the term *merit good* merely becomes a formal designation for the un-
> adorned value judgment that the arts are good for society and therefore
> deserve financial support . . . [the] merit good approach is not really a
> justification for support—it merely invents a bit of terminology to desig-
> nate the desire to do so. [pp. 426–427]

Another possible problem with the welfare economics framework is its concern with *results*. Situations are evaluated in terms of the allocation of resources, and not of *how* the allocation was determined. Perhaps a society should be judged by the *processes* used to arrive at the allocation, not the actual results. Are people free to enter contracts? Are public processes democratic? If this view is taken, welfare economics lacks any normative significance.

On the other hand, the great advantage of welfare economics is that it provides a coherent framework for thinking about the appropriateness of various government interventions. The framework requires the formation of relevant questions whenever a government activity is proposed: Will it have desirable distributional consequences? Will it correct a market failure? Can it be done at a reasonable cost? If the answer to these questions is "no," the market should probably be left alone.

Of course, to answer these questions will often require substantial research, and in the case of the first question, value judgments as well. But just asking the right questions imposes a structure on the decision-making process. It forces the investigator to make ethical values explicit and it facilitates the detection of frivolous or self-serving programs.

SUMMARY

Welfare economics is the study of the desirability of alternative economic states.

A Pareto efficient allocation occurs when no person can be made better off without making another person worse off. A necessary condition for Pareto efficiency is that each person's marginal rate of substitution between two commodities equals the marginal rate of transformation. Pareto efficiency is the economist's benchmark of efficient performance for an economy.

Under certain conditions, competitive market mechanics will lead to Pareto efficient outcomes. This result, the Fundamental Theorem of Welfare Economics, relies on prices reflecting marginal social costs for each commodity.

Despite its appeal, Pareto efficiency has no obvious claim as an ethical norm. Society may prefer another, inefficient, allocation on the basis of equity, justice, or some other criterion. This provides one possible reason for government intervention in the economy.

A social welfare function summarizes society's preferences concerning the utility of each of its members. It may be used to find the allocation of resources that maximizes social welfare.

A second reason for government activity is "market failure," violations of the conditions required for the fundamental theorem to hold. Prominent among these are monopoly power, public goods, costly information, externalities, and nonexistent markets.

The fact that the market does not allocate resources perfectly does not necessarily mean that the government can do better. Each case must be evaluated on its own merits.

Welfare economics is based on an individualistic social philosophy. It does not pay much attention to the processes used to achieve results. Thus, although it provides a coherent and useful framework for analyzing policy, welfare economics is controversial.

DISCUSSION QUESTIONS

1. There is substantial government intervention in the U.S. economy. In each case can you rationalize the policy listed below using the considerations in this chapter? If not, why do they exist?
    a. Agricultural price supports (the government buys enough of a crop to ensure a minimum price).
    b. Maximum price laws for gasoline.
    c. Product safety standards.
    d. Zoning and land use laws.

2. In which of the following markets do you expect efficient outcomes? Why?
    a. Steel.
    b. Highway construction.
    c. Stock market.
    d. Retail food.

3. In 1982, several people died because of poisoned capsules of Tylenol pain reliever. Afterwards, strict government regulations were enacted to control the packaging of retail pharmaceuticals. Would private markets have reached the same result?

4. Laverne will trade two pizzas for one six-pack of beer and be equally happy. At the same time, Shirley will gladly exchange two of her six-packs for six pizzas. Is the allocation of beer and pizza Pareto efficient? Illustrate using an Edgeworth Box.

5. Imagine a simple economy with only two people, Augustus and Livia.
    a. Let the social welfare function be

$$W = U_L + U_A$$

where U_L and U_A are the utilities of Livia and Augustus, respectively. Graph the social indifference curves. How would you describe the relative importance assigned to their respective well-being?

b. Repeat **a** when

$$W = U_L + 2U_A$$

c. Assume that the utility possibility frontier is as given below:

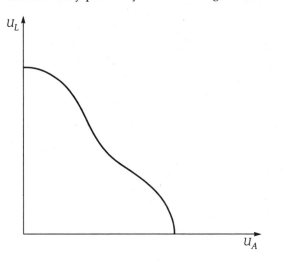

Graphically show how the optimal solution differs between the welfare functions given in parts **a** and **b**.

SELECTED REFERENCES

Bator, F. M. "The Simple Analytics of Welfare Maximization." *American Economic Review* 47 (March 1957), pp. 22–59.

Bator, F. M. "The Anatomy of Market Failure." *Quarterly Journal of Economics* 72 (August 1958) pp. 351–79.

Baumol, William J. *Economic Theory and Operations Analysis,* 4th ed. Englewood Cliffs, N.J.: Prentice-Hall, 1977, chapter 21.

Part Three

Analysis of Public Expenditure

Market outcomes need be neither efficient nor fair. This section examines how various kinds of "market failure" can be remedied by government intervention. Both the normative question of how the government ought to solve a particular problem and the positive question of how government actually changes the status quo are discussed.

The theory of welfare economics focused our attention on income distribution, public goods, externalities, and incomplete markets as possible sources of government intervention. These are taken up in Chapters 5 through 8.[1] Cost-benefit analysis, a practical set of rules for evaluating public expenditure decisions, is discussed in Chapter 9. Chapter 10 examines the important question of whether our political institutions are likely to produce economic policies that do in fact, increase the level of "social welfare."

---

[1] Public policy toward monopoly is discussed in Chapter 13.

CHAPTER 5

Income Distribution

And distribution was made unto every man according as he had need.

Acts 4:35.

"In general, the art of government consists in taking as much money as possible from one class of citizens to give to the other." While Voltaire's assertion is an overstatement, it is true that virtually every important political issue has implications for the distribution of income. Even when they are not explicit, questions of who will gain and who will lose lurk in the background of most public policy debates. This chapter first presents some alternative views of how the government should seek to alter the distribution of income, and then examines how government expenditures have in fact changed the income distribution.

At the outset, it should be noted that not everybody agrees that economists should consider distributional effects in their policy analyses. Notions concerning the "right" income distribution are value judgments and there is no "scientific" way to resolve differences on matters of ethics. Therefore, some argue that discussion of distributional issues is detrimental to objectivity in economics and that economists should restrict themselves to analyzing only the efficiency aspects of social issues.[1]

There are two problems with this view. The first it that, as emphasized in Chapter 4, the theory of welfare economics indicates efficiency by itself cannot be used to judge the desirability of a given state of affairs. Criteria other than efficiency must be brought to bear on ques-

---

[1] For additional arguments that economists should put distributional matters in the background, see Kristol [1980].

tions which involve comparing alternative allocations of resources. Of course, it can be asserted that only efficiency matters, but this in itself is a value judgment.

In addition, decision makers care about the distributional implications of policy. If economists ignore distribution, then policymakers will ignore economists. Policymakers may thus end up focusing only upon distributional issues and pay no attention at all to efficiency. The economist who systematically takes distribution into account can keep policymakers aware of both efficiency and distributional issues. In sum, although training in economics certainly does not confer a superior ability to make ethical judgments, economists *are* skilled at drawing out the implications of alternative sets of values and measuring the costs of achieving various ethical goals.

A related question is whether government ought to be involved in changing the income distribution. As noted in Chapter 1, some important traditions of political philosophy suggest that government should play no redistributive role. However, even the most minimal government conceivable influences income distribution. For example, when the government purchases materials for public goods, some firms receive contracts and others do not; presumably the owners of the firms receiving the contracts enjoy increases in their relative incomes. More generally, both the taxing and spending activities of government are bound to change the distribution of real income. Distributional issues are part and parcel of the government's functioning.

THE "OPTIMAL" INCOME DISTRIBUTION

Much of the widespread attention to governmental distribution policies is prompted by the simple observation that some people are rich and some are poor. The question of why there are large disparities in income has long occupied a central place in economics, and is far from definitively settled.[2] A person's place in the income distribution depends on items as diverse as inheritances from parents, physical strength, intelligence, effort, health, education, marriage decisions, and luck. Philosophical systems differ with respect to whether the government should try to modify the "natural" distribution of income, and if so, how. This section discusses some of the viewpoints that have received the most attention in economics.

Utilitarian Viewpoint

In welfare economics it is traditional that the welfare of society is defined by how well off its members are. Algebraically, if there are n

---

[2] For an excellent survey of alternative theories, see Atkinson [1975].

individuals in society and the ith individual's utility is U_i, then social welfare, W, is some function $F(\cdot)$ of individuals' utilities:[3]

(5.1) $W = F(U_1, U_2, \ldots, U_n).$

Equation (5.1) is sometimes referred to as a **utilitarian social welfare function** because of its association with the utilitarian social philosophers of the 19th century.[4] It is assumed that an increase in any of the U_is, other things being the same, increases W. A change which makes someone better off without making anyone worse off increases social welfare.

An important special case of Equation (5.1) is when social welfare is the sum of individual's utilities:

(5.2) $W = U_1 + U_2 + \cdots + U_n.$

This is referred to as an **additive social welfare function.**

A fundamental feature of utilitarian social welfare functions is their individualistic point of view. Unless an activity increases some person's utility, it cannot increase social welfare. Such an individualistic orientation takes individual's preferences seriously—if people like something, then by definition it is "good" for society. To the extent that people's preferences are viewed as corrupt or ill formed, the maximization of W is inappropriate as a social objective.

Suppose that the government's goal is to maximize the value of W given in Equation (5.2). Alone, this social welfare function has little implication for the appropriate governmental policy. If a few assumptions are made, however, quite strong results can be obtained. Assume that:

1. Individuals have identical utility functions which depend only upon their levels of income. These utility functions exhibit diminishing marginal utility of income—as an individual's income increases, he becomes better off, but at a decreasing rate.
2. The total amount of income available is fixed.

Under these assumptions and the additive social welfare function of Equation (5.2), the optimal income distribution is *complete equality*. To prove this, assume that the society consists of only two people, Peter and Paul. (It is easy to generalize the argument to cases where there is an arbitrary number of people.)

In Figure 5.1, the horizontal distance OO' measures the total amount of income available in society. Paul's income is measured by the distance

---

[3] This discussion ignores the problems that arise if the members of a society cannot agree upon a social welfare function. See Chapter 6.

[4] Actually, the utilitarians postulated that social welfare was the sum of utilities, Equation (5.2), but the label is now often used to describe the more general formulation of Equation (5.1).

FIGURE 5.1   A Model of the "Optimal" Distribution of Income

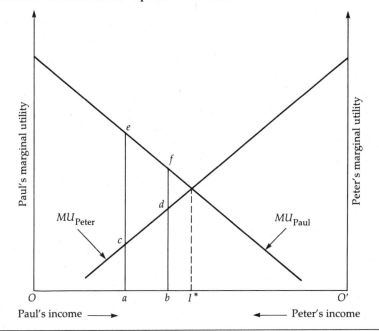

to the right of point O; Peter's income is measured by the distance to the left of point O'. Thus, any point along OO' represents some distribution of income between Paul and Peter. The problem is to find the "best" point.

Paul's marginal utility of income is measured by the vertical distance above point O. Following assumption 1, the schedule relating Paul's marginal utility of income to his level of income is downward sloping. It is labeled MU_{Paul} in Figure 5.1 Peter's marginal utility of income is the vertical distance above point O'. His marginal utility of income schedule is denoted MU_{Peter}. (Remember that movements to the left on the horizontal axis represent *increases* in Peter's income.) Because Peter and Paul have identical utility functions, MU_{Peter} is a mirror image of MU_{Paul}.

Assume that initially Paul's income is Oa and Peter's is $O'a$. Is social welfare as high as possible, or could the sum of utilities be increased if income were somehow redistributed between Paul and Peter? Suppose that ab dollars are taken from Peter and given to Paul. Obviously, this makes Peter worse off and Paul better off. However, the crucial question is what happens to the *sum* of their utilities. Because Peter is richer than Paul, Peter's loss in utility is smaller than Paul's gain, so that the sum of their utilities goes up. Geometrically, the area under each person's marginal utility of income schedule measures the change in his utility induced by the income change. Distributing *ab* dollars to Paul increases his utility by area *abfe*. Taking the *ab* dollars from Peter decreases his utility by area *abdc*. The sum of their utility therefore increases by *cefd*.

Similar reasoning suggests that as long as incomes are unequal, marginal utilities will be unequal, and the *sum* of utilities can be increased by distributing income to the poorer individual. Only at point *I**, where incomes and marginal utilities are equal, is social welfare maximized. Full income equality should be pursued.

The policy implications of this result are breathtaking, so the assumptions behind it require careful scrutiny.

Assumption 1.   The validity of assuming that individuals have identical utility functions is fundamentally impossible to determine. It simply cannot be known whether individuals derive the same amount of satisfaction from the consumption of goods, because satisfaction cannot be objectively measured.

Despite this, there are two possible defenses for the assumption.

First, although it cannot be *proved* that people derive the same utility from equal amounts of income, it is a reasonable guess. After all, if people generally do not vary wildly in their observable characteristics— weight, height, etc.—why should their utility functions differ?

Second, interpret the assumption not as a psychological statement, but as an *ethical* one. Specifically, in designing a redistributional policy, government ought to act *as if* all people have the same utility functions, whether they do or not.

Clearly, neither of these defenses will convince a skeptic, and the assumption remains troublesome.

A more technical, but equally important objection concerns the assumption of decreasing marginal utility of income. While it may be the case that the marginal utility of any given *good* decreases with its consumption, it is not clear that this is true for *income* as a whole. In terms of Figure 5.1, the results change drastically if the marginal utility of income schedules fail to slope down. Suppose that the marginal utility of income is constant at all levels of income. Then MU_{Peter} and MU_{Paul} are represented by an identical horizontal line. Whenever a dollar is taken from Peter, the loss in his utility is exactly equal to Paul's gain. Thus, the value of the sum of their utilities is *independent* of the income distribution. Government redistributive policy cannot change social welfare.

Assumption 2.   By this assumption, the total amount of income in the society, distance *OO'*, is totally fixed. The size of the pie does not change as the government redistributes its pieces. Suppose, however, that individuals' utilities depend not only on income, but on leisure as well. Each individual chooses how much leisure to surrender (how much to work) to maximize his utility. The taxes and subsidies enacted to redistribute income will generally change people's work decisions and diminish total real income.[5] Thus, a society whose goal is to maximize the sum of utilities faces an inescapable dilemma. On one hand, it prefers to equalize the distribution of income. However, in the process of doing so, it reduces the total amount of income available. The optimal income distribution must take into account the costs (in terms of lost real income) of achieving more equality. Some studies suggest that these costs may indeed be quite substantial. Browning and Johnson [1984] estimated that each dollar increase in the disposable incomes of the lowest 40 percent of the income distribution requires a reduction of more than *nine* dollars of the disposable incomes of the highest 60 percent. However, research on this topic is still at a formative stage.

Thus, even if we are willing to accept the assumption of identical utility functions, it cannot be concluded that the optimal distribution of income is complete equality. The answer depends upon the methods used to redistribute income and the effects that these have upon people's behavior.

The Maximin Criterion

According to the additive social welfare function of Equation (5.2), society is indifferent to the distribution of *utilities*.[6] If a unit of utility (or "util") is taken away from one individual and given to another, the sum of utilities is unchanged, and by definition, so is the level of social welfare. Other kinds of utilitarian social welfare functions do not carry this implication. Consider the social welfare function below:

(5.3) $$W = \delta_1 U_1 + \delta_2 U_2 + \cdots + \delta_n U_n$$

where the δ's are positive numbers. When the ith individual's utility increases by one unit, social welfare increases by δ_i units. The higher an individual's δ, the greater the weight that society attaches to a change in his or her utility. For this reason, the δ's are referred to as **social weights.** Suppose that a society attaches a great value to increasing the utilities of its poor. This society assigns high δ's to individuals with low utilities and vice versa. Thus, the strength of a society's preferences for equality can be measured by the relative magnitudes of the social weights for high- and low-utility individuals.

An extreme case is when weight is given *only* to the individual with the lowest utility. Everyone else has a δ of zero. Social welfare depends

---

[5] It is possible that taxes and subsidies will induce people to work more hours. However, even if their *money* incomes are higher, their real incomes (measured in terms of utility) are lower because the taxes and subsidies distort their behavior patterns. See Chapter 12.

[6] Equation (5.2) does *not* imply that society is indifferent to the distribution of *incomes*, as was proved in the preceding section.

only on the utility of the worst-off person, and society's goal is to maximize this person's utility. This social objective is often called the **maximin criterion** because the objective is to maximize the utility of the person with the minimum utility.[7] The maximin criterion implies that income distribution should be perfectly equal, *except* to the extent that departures from equality increase the welfare of the worst-off person. Consider a society with a rich person, Peter, who employs a poor person, Paul. The government levies a tax on Peter, and distributes the proceeds to Paul. However, when Peter is taxed, he cuts production and fires Paul. Moreover, the income that Paul receives from the government is less than his job-related income loss. In this hypothetical economy, satisfaction of the maximin criterion would still allow for income disparities.

The maximin criterion has received considerable attention, principally because of philosopher John Rawls' [1971] assertion that it has a special claim to ethical validity. Rawls' argument relies upon his notion of the **original position,** an imaginary situation in which people have no knowledge of what their place in society is to be. Because of this ignorance as to whether ultimately they will be rich or poor, Rawls believes that in the original position, people's opinions concerning distributional goals are impartial and fair. Rawls then argues that in the original position, people will adopt the maximin social welfare function because of the insurance it provides against disastrous outcomes. People are frightened that they may end up at the bottom of the income distribution, and therefore want the level at the bottom as high as possible.

Rawls' analysis has raised considerable controversy.[8] One important issue is whether decisions that people would make in the hypothetical original position have any superior claim to ethical validity. Why should the amoral and selfish views that individuals have in the original position be given special moral significance? Further, granted Rawls' view on the ethical validity of the original position, it is not obvious that rational self-interest would lead to the maximin criterion. Rawls' decision makers are so averse to risk that they are unwilling to take any chances whatsoever. However, people might be willing to accept a small probability of being very poor in return for a good chance of receiving a high income.

Finally, critics have noted that the maximin criterion has some peculiar implications. Feldstein [1976a, p. 84] considers the following scenario: "A new opportunity arises to raise the welfare of the least advantaged by a slight amount, but almost everyone else must be made substantially worse off, except for a few individuals who would become

---

[7] The maximin criterion can be regarded as a special case of Equation (5.1). The function $F(\cdot)$ takes the minimum of all the utilities.

[8] See Feldstein [1976a].

extremely wealthy." Because *all* that is relevant is the welfare of the worst-off person, the maximin criterion indicates that society should take advantage of this opportunity. Intuitively, however, such a course seems quite unappealing.

Pareto Efficient Income Redistribution

In our discussion of both utilitarian and maximin social welfare functions, we assumed that redistribution makes some people better off and others worse off. Redistribution was never Pareto efficient in the sense of allowing *all* individuals to be at least as well off as under the status quo. This is a consequence of the assumption that each individual's utility depends upon his income *only*. In contrast, imagine that high-income individuals are altruistic, so that their utilities depend not only on their own incomes, but those of the poor as well. Under such circumstances, redistribution can actually be Pareto efficient.

Assume that if (rich) Peter were to give his last dollar of income to (poor) Paul, then Peter's increase in satisfaction from doing a good deed would outweigh the loss of his own consumption. At the same time, assume that Paul's utility would increase if he received the dollar. Both individuals would be made better off by the transfer. Indeed, efficiency requires that income be redistributed until Peter's gain in utility from giving a dollar to Paul just equals the loss in Peter's utility caused by lower consumption.[9] Suppose that it is difficult for Peter to bring about the income transfer on his own, perhaps because he lacks enough information to know just who is really poor. Then if the government costlessly does the transfer for Peter, efficiency is enhanced.

In a formal sense, this is just an externality problem. Paul's behavior (his consumption) affects Peter's welfare in a way that is external to the market. As usual in such cases, it is possible that the government can increase efficiency.

Pushing this line of reasoning to its logical extreme, the income distribution can be regarded as a public good, because everyone's utility is affected by the degree of inequality.[10] Suppose that each person would feel better off if the income distribution were more equal. No individual acting alone, however, has enough income to change the income distribution—people have to act collectively. If the government uses its coercive power to force *everyone* who is wealthy to redistribute income to the poor, economic efficiency increases.

Although altruism doubtless plays an important part in human behavior,[11] it does *not* follow that altruistic motives explain the majority of

---

[9] See Hochman and Rodgers [1969].

[10] See Thurow [1971].

[11] See Becker [1976].

government income redistribution programs. The argument above *assumes* that in the absence of coercion, people will contribute less than an efficient amount to the poor. Some argue, however, that if people really want to give to the poor, they do so—witness the billions of dollars in charitable contributions made each year.

There are other reasons self-interest might favor income redistribution. For one there is always some chance that through circumstances beyond your control, you will become poor. An income distribution policy is a bit like insurance. When you are well off, you pay "premiums" in the form of tax payments to those who are currently poor. If bad times hit, the "policy" pays off, and you receive relief. The idea that government should provide a "safety net" is an old one. The 17th century political philosopher Thomas Hobbes [1963/1651, pp. 303–4] noted, "And whereas many men, by *accident* become unable to maintain themselves by their labour; they ought not to be left to the charity of private persons; but to be provided for, as far forth as the necessities of nature require, by the laws of the Commonwealth" [emphasis added].

In addition, some believe that income distribution programs help purchase social stability. If poor people become *too* poor, they may engage in antisocial activities such as crime and rioting. The link between social stability and changes in income distribution is not totally clear, however. It may be that some improvement in the well-being of the poor increase their aspirations and leads to demands for more radical change.

Nonindividualistic Views

The views of income distribution discussed so far have quite different implications, but they share a common outlook. In each, social welfare is some function of individuals' utilities, and the properties of the optimal income distribution are *derived* from the social welfare function. Some thinkers have approached the problem by specifying what the income distribution should look like independent of individuals' tastes. As Fair [1971, p. 552] notes, Plato argued that in a good society the ratio of the richest to the poorest person's income should be at the most four to one. Others have suggested that as a *first principle,* incomes should be distributed equally.[12]

In a less extreme proposal, Tobin [1970] suggested that only special commodities should be distributed equally, a position sometimes called **commodity egalitarianism.** In some cases, this view has considerable appeal. Most people believe that the right to vote should be distributed equally to all, as should the consumption of certain essential foodstuffs during times of war. Other types of commodity egalitarianism are more

---

[12] This view is considerably stronger than that of Rawls, who allows inequality as long as it raises the welfare of the worst-off individual.

controversial. Should all American children consume the same quality of primary school education, or should richer communities be allowed to purchase more? Should everyone receive the same type of health care? Clearly, limiting the range of the "special" commodities is a difficult problem.

Fair Processes

The positions discussed above take for granted that individuals' incomes are common property which can be redistributed as "society" sees fit. No attention is given to the fairness of either the processes by which the initial income distribution is determined or of the procedures used to redistribute it. In contrast, some argue that a just distribution of income is defined by the *process* that generated it. For example, it is a popular belief in the United States that if "equal opportunity" (somehow defined) were available to all, then the ensuing outcome would be fair, *regardless* of the particular income distribution it happened to entail.

The philosopher Robert Nozick [1974] has attacked the use of utilitarian principles to justify changes in the distribution of income. He argues that how "society" should redistribute its income is a meaningless question because "society" per se has no income to distribute. Only *people* receive income, and the sole possible justification for government redistributive activity is when the pattern of property holdings is somehow improper. Nozick's approach shifts emphasis from the search for a "good" social welfare function to a "good" set of rules to govern society's operation. The problem is how to evaluate social processes. It is hard to judge a process independent of the results generated. If a "good" set of rules consistently generates outcomes that are undesirable, how can the rules be considered "good"?

Social Mobility

Kristol [1980] argues that if there is sufficient social mobility, then the distribution of income is of no particular ethical interest. Suppose that those at the bottom of the income distribution (or their children) will occupy higher rungs on the economic ladder in future years. At the same time, some other people will move down, at least in relative terms. Then, even distributional statistics which remain relatively constant over time will conceal quite a bit of churning *within* the income distribution. Even if people at the bottom are quite poor, it may not be a major social problem if the people who are there change over time.

There have been several studies of income mobility. The U.S. Department of Health, Education and Welfare [1974] examined the American poverty population from 1967 to 1972. Only 20 to 30 percent of people who were classified as being poor in any one year were also poor for all six years. As Blinder [1980] notes, "While ghetto dwellers rarely trade places with Rockefellers, ours is not a stratified society" [p. 452]. On the other hand, there is probably not sufficient mobility to convince utilitarians and those of related philosophies that income inequality is unimportant.

Overview

We have surveyed a very wide range of opinions concerning fair income distribution. Their implications for government policy run the gamut from engineering complete equality to permitting the status quo. The scope of disagreement should not be surprising. Setting a distributional objective is no less than formalizing one's views of what a good society should look like, and this is an issue about which there will always be controversy. It should be stressed that these are normative rather than positive theories. Actual government redistributive policies *may* be guided by a number of these considerations, but it is not obvious that this is the case. As we shall see, it is difficult to find a coherent explanation of U.S. income distribution practices.

EXPENDITURE INCIDENCE: CONCEPTUAL PROBLEMS

We turn now from a discussion of how the government *ought* to redistribute income to how it actually does so. The way in which expenditure policy influences the distribution of real income is referred to as **expenditure incidence.** The government influences income distribution through its taxation as well as its expenditure policies. We will defer a discussion of the tax side to Chapter 11.

Expenditure incidence is difficult to determine for several reasons, which follow.

Problems in Income Measurement[13]

Discussing how government expenditure policy changes income distribution presupposes that we can measure income in the first place. In principle, a person's income during a given period is defined as the sum of the amount he or she consumes during that period and the amount he or she saves. In practice, it is difficult to obtain good measures of people's initial incomes for at least two reasons.

In the first place, some forms of income are hard to value. An important example is housework. Clearly, people who work within the home produce valuable services for themselves and their families, but it is not

---

[13] A more detailed discussion of these issues is included in Chapter 14.

clear how these services should be valued. Another example is the income provided by durable goods. A house provides its owner with a flow of housing services. The value of these services is the cost to the homeowner of renting a comparable dwelling. Again, however, it is often difficult to make such valuations. Moreover, it is not clear where to stop: should one impute income flows to stereo equipment, furniture, and food processors? Finally, some income is earned in the "underground economy" which includes illegal activities as well as legal transactions that are not reported to the government to evade taxation. Clearly, this is difficult to measure.

As well, the definition of income indicates that the concept makes sense only if it is measured over some period of time.[14] But it is not obvious what the time frame should be. A daily or weekly measure would be absurd, because even rich individuals could very well have zero incomes during some short periods of time. It makes much more sense to measure the flow of income over a year, as is customarily done. However, even annual measures may not reflect an individual's true economic position. After all, there can be unexpected fluctuations in income from year to year. From a theoretical point of view, lifetime income would be ideal, but the practical problems in estimating it are enormous.

Although distinguishing between different time periods may seem a mere academic quibble, it is really quite important. People tend to have low incomes when they are young, more when they are middle-aged, and less again when they are old and in retirement. Therefore, people who have *identical* lifetime incomes but are in different stages of the life cycle can show up in the annual data as having *unequal* incomes. Measures based on annual income will suggest more inequality than those constructed on the more appropriate lifetime basis.

Unit of Observation

Most people live with others, and at least to some extent make their economic decisions jointly. Should income distribution be measured over individuals or households? If there are economies achieved by living together, should they be taken into account in computing an individual's income? For example, are the members of a two-person household with total income of $30,000 as well off as a single individual with $15,000? Although two may not be able to live as cheaply as one, they may be able to live as cheaply as 1.5. If this is true, the members of the couple are better off in real terms. But finding just the right adjustment factor is not easy.

---

[14] In contrast, "wealth" measures the value of an individual's stock of assets at any point in time. Problems in measuring and taxing wealth are discussed in Chapter 18.

A related problem crops up when the structure of household formation changes over time. Consider what happens

> when higher living standards and/or more generous public transfer programs enable junior, or grandma and grandpa, to move into an apartment of their own. A new economic unit is formed, with a rather low income, thus bringing down the average level of income and raising its inequality. Both economic indicators will therefore signal a deterioration in welfare, though we may presume that these changes in living arrangements actually make the parties involved better off. [Blinder, 1980, p. 418]

Thus, especially when distributional comparisons are being made across time, changes in household composition must be taken into account.

Estimating Effects on Relative Prices

Suppose that the government decides to help the poor by subsidizing the consumption of low-income housing. How does this affect the distribution of income? A first guess would be that the people who get the subsidy gain and those who pay the taxes lose. If those who pay the taxes have higher incomes than the subsidy recipients, then the distribution of income tends to become more equal.

Unfortunately, this simple story is likely to be misleading. If the subsidy induces poor people to demand more housing, then the *pre*subsidy cost of housing may rise. Therefore, the subsidy recipients do not benefit to the full extent of the subsidy; the landlords reap part of the gain. However, on theoretical grounds alone it cannot be determined how much, if at all, housing prices are bid up. As shown in Chapter 11, this depends upon the shapes of the supply and demand curves for housing.

A housing subsidy program also affects the incomes of people who supply the inputs used in its construction. Thus, wages of workers in the building trades increase, as do prices of construction materials. If the owners of these factors of production tend to be middle and upper income, then there will be a tendency to make the distribution more unequal.

More generally, any government program sets off a chain of price changes which affects the incomes of people both in their roles as consumers of goods and as suppliers of inputs. A spending program that raises the relative price of a good you consume intensively makes you worse off, other things being the same. Similarly, a program that raises the relative price of a factor you supply makes you better off. The problem is that it is very hard to trace all the price changes generated by a particular policy. As a practical matter, economists are usually forced to assume that a given policy benefits the recipients only and that the effects of other price changes on income distribution are minor. In many cases, this is probably a good assumption.

Public Goods

Substantial government expenditure is for public goods—goods that may be consumed simultaneously by more than one person and for which it is difficult to exclude nonpayers. As noted in Chapter 4, the market does not force people to reveal how much they value public goods. But if we do not know how much each family values a public good, how can we determine its impact upon income distribution? The government spent $210 billion on defense in 1983. [*Economic Report of the President*, 1984, p. 305]. How much in dollar terms did this increase the real income of each family? Did each benefit by the same amount? If not, did the poor benefit less than the rich, or vice versa?

It is impossible to answer questions like these definitively. Unfortunately, alternative answers which are based on equally plausible assumptions can have very different implications. In a study using 1968 data, Musgrave, Case, and Leonard [1974] examined the distributional implications of expenditures on all pure public goods (such as defense) using three different assumptions: (*a*) a family's share of the benefit is in proportion to its total income; (*b*) its share is in proportion to the amount of taxes it pays; and (*c*) its share is proportional to the number of people in the family. Under assumption (*a*), public good expenditures increase the incomes of the poorest group[15] by 16.7 percent; under (*b*), by 13.2 percent; and under (*c*), by about 70 percent. The average percentage increase for *all* income groups was 16.7 percent. Thus, depending upon the assumptions, pure public goods expenditures have a very great redistributive impact, or none whatsoever.

Valuing In-Kind Transfers

In the early 1980s, headlines were made when the Agriculture Department offered 224 million pounds of surplus cheese, butter, and dried milk to poor Americans. The cheese program was a minor example of an **in-kind transfer**—a payment to individuals in terms of commodities or services as opposed to cash. We often think of in-kind transfers as being directed toward lower-income individuals: food stamps, Medicaid, and public housing come to mind. However, middle- and upper-income people are also the beneficiaries of in-kind transfers. A prominent example is education.[16]

Unlike pure public goods, in-kind transfers are not consumed by everyone. Nevertheless, it is difficult to estimate their value to beneficiaries. A convenient assumption is that a dollar spent by the government

---

[15] Less than $4,000 in 1968.

[16] Indeed, some middle- and upper-income people benefit from public assistance programs that are targeted for the poor. See Projector and Roen [1982, p. 48] for details.

on an in-kind transfer is equivalent to a dollar increase in the recipient's income. Unfortunately, there is no reason to believe that in-kind transfers are valued by beneficiaries on a dollar per dollar basis.

To see why, consider Jones, a typical welfare recipient who divides her monthly income of $300 between cheese and "all other goods." The market price of cheese is $2 per pound, and the units of "all other goods" are measured so that the price per unit is $1. In Figure 5.2, Jones's consumption of cheese is measured on the horizontal axis, and her consumption of all other goods on the vertical. Jones's budget constraint is line AB.[17] Assuming that Jones is interested in maximizing

FIGURE 5.2   An In-Kind Transfer Results in a Lower Utility Level than a Cash Transfer

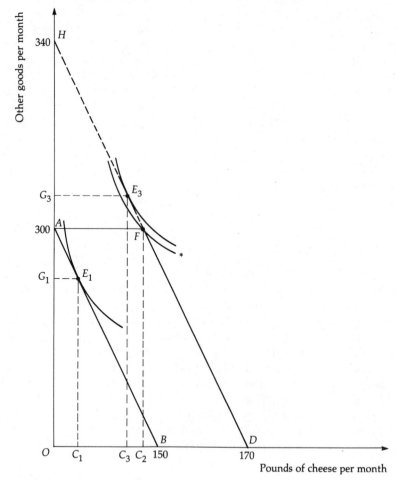

---

[17] For details on how to construct budget lines, see the Appendix at the end of the book.

utility, she consumes bundle E_1, which consists of OG_1 units of all other goods and OC_1 units of cheese.

Now suppose the government provides Jones with 20 pounds of cheese per month, which she is prohibited from reselling on the market. How does introduction of the cheese program change her situation? At any level of consumption of all other goods, Jones can now consume 20 more pounds of cheese than previously. Geometrically, her new budget constraint is found by moving 20 units to the right of each point on AB, yielding AFD. The highest indifference curve that can be reached subject to constraint AFD is marked with a (*) in Figure 5.2. It touches the constraint at its "corner"—at point F, where Jones's consumption of cheese is OC_2, and her consumption of all other goods is 300.

Compared to her original consumption bundle, Jones' consumption of both cheese *and* all other goods has gone up. Because the government provides her with free cheese, Jones can devote to all other goods money that otherwise would have been spent on cheese.

Now suppose that instead of giving Jones 20 pounds of cheese, the government gave her cash equal to its market value, $40 (=20 pounds $\times$ $2 per pound). An increase in income of $40 leads to a budget line that is exactly 40 units above AB at every point. This is represented in Figure 5.2 as line HD. Note that the cash transfer allows Jones to consume along segment HF. This opportunity was not available under the cheese program because Jones was not allowed to trade government cheese for any other goods.

Facing budget line HD, Jones maximizes utility at point E_3, where she consumes OG_3 of all other goods and OC_3 pounds of cheese. Comparing points E_3 and F we can conclude that: (1) under the cash transfer program, Jones consumes less cheese and more of all other goods than under the cheese giveaway program; and (2) $40 worth of cheese does *not* make Jones as well off as $40 of income. Because E_3 is on a higher indifference curve than point F, the cash transfer makes her *better* off. Intuitively, the problem with the cheese program is that it "forces" Jones to consume the full 20 pounds of cheese. She would prefer to sell some of the cheese and spend the proceeds on other goods.

Is an in-kind transfer always worse than the cash equivalent? Not necessarily. Figure 5.3 depicts the situation of Smith, whose income is identical to Jones's, and therefore faces exactly the same budget constraints (AB before the cheese program, and AFD afterwards). However, Smith has different tastes and thus a different set of indifference curves. Before the subsidy, he maximizes utility at point E_4, consuming OG_4 units of all other goods and OC_4 pounds of cheese. After the subsidy, he consumes OG_5 units of all other goods and OC_5 pounds of cheese. Smith would not be better off with a cash transfer because his most preferred point along HD is available under the cheese subsidy anyway. Because Smith is happy to consume *more* than 20 pounds of cheese, the restriction that he consume at least 20 pounds does him no harm.

FIGURE 5.3   An In-Kind Transfer Results in the Same Utility Level as a Cash Transfer

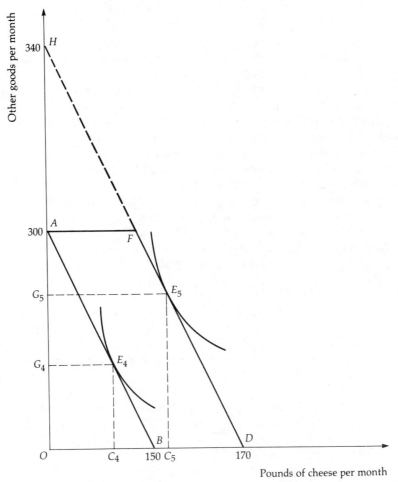

Thus, it cannot be known for certain whether an in-kind transfer will be valued less than a direct income transfer. Ultimately, the answer has to be found by empirical analysis. For example, several studies of the consumption patterns of the poor suggest that a dollar received in public housing is worth only about 80 cents received in cash [Weicher, 1979, p. 497].[18]

_____

[18] The structure of public housing programs differs somewhat from the cheese program analyzed above, because recipients have to pay some price for the housing. But the basic idea is the same. For further details, see Chapter 12.

In light of these observations, the obvious question is why the government bothers with in-kind transfers in the first place. We turn to this issue below, after we have discussed the actual structure of distributional policy in more detail.

Overview

In the theoretical models at the beginning of this chapter, it is clear who has what income and how government policy affects each person's income. In reality, none of this is obvious. Measures of income before intervention are calculated on an annual rather than a lifetime basis. Many important forms of income are ignored because they are too difficult to measure. Calculating the effect of government spending programs is no easier. These programs change relative prices and therefore real incomes in ways that are hard to discern. The transfers often take the form of public goods and in-kind payments upon which it is difficult to put a dollar value. Thus, any evidence on how government programs change the distribution of income should be interpreted with caution.

PROGRAMS FOR THE POOR

Before returning to the questions raised above, we will take a look at actual distribution policy. Most attention has focused on programs for the poor, and how these programs have affected the economic position of this segment. These issues are taken up in this section.

Federal Spending for Low-Income Individuals

Table 5.1 lists the federal government's outlays for programs that are designed, at least in part, to help the poor.[19] However, several points must be stressed before we examine the programs listed.

First, there is some arbitrariness in deciding whether certain programs are "for" the poor. Some programs that are not directed specifically at the poor do end up transferring considerable sums to them. Social security is usually considered an "insurance" program rather than a distributional program (see Chapter 8). Yet about 58 percent of the $138 billion in social security payments made in 1981 went to low-income households [Ladd and Doolittle, 1982, pp. 326–27]. Similarly, a substantial portion of unemployment insurance payments and veterans' pensions go to the poor.

At the same time, many of the benefits of some "low-income" programs go to middle- and upper-income people. All elderly people are eligible for medicare, not just the indigent aged. In 1981, only about 13

---

[19] The role of states and localities in distributional policy is discussed in Chapter 19.

TABLE 5.1   Some Federal Programs for Low-Income Individuals, 1982 ($ billions)

Cash transfers:
Aid to Families With Dependent Children (AFDC)	$ 8.0
Supplemental Security Income (SSI)	7.7

In-kind transfers:
Medicaid	$17.4
Medicare	44.8*
Food Stamps	11.0
Child Nutrition	4.0
Housing Assistance	7.9
Employment and Training	4.5
Social Services	6.7
Compensatory Education	4.0
Legal Aid	0.3†
Low-Income Energy Assistance	1.7

* Figure is for 1981. See U.S. Bureau of the Census, *Statistical Abstract of the United States: 1982–83* (Washington, D.C.: U.S. Government Printing Office, 1982), p. 104.

† Figure is for 1981. Source: Executive Office of the President, *Budget of the United States Government Fiscal Year 1982* (Washington, D.C.: U.S. Government Printing Office, 1982).

Source: Congressional Budget Office, *The Federal Government in a Federal System: Current Intergovernmental Programs and Options for Change* (Washington, D.C.: U.S. Government Printing Office, 1983), pp. 140–41, 152–53, 160–61, 172, 179, 185–86.

percent of medicare recipients were below the federal government's poverty line.[20]

In addition, a large number of families receive some sort of in-kind assistance from the federal government. According to the Census Bureau, in 1981 one sixth of all households received aid in the form of food stamps, medicaid, housing subsidies, or low-priced school lunches [U.S. Bureau of the Census, 1983a, p. 48]

Finally, not all people classified as poor receive benefits from federal programs. In 1981, 41.5 percent of all households below the government official poverty line received no benefits under any of the four programs mentioned in the previous paragraph.[21]

Given these caveats, the principal federal programs summarized in Table 5.1 are discussed below.

---

[20] Computed from U.S. Bureau of the Census [1983a, p. 91].

[21] [U.S. Bureau of the Census, 1983a, p. 48]. In 1981, the poverty line for a family of four was $9,287.

Aid to Families with Dependent Children (AFDC).[22]   In 1982, there were 10.4 million recipients. AFDC is a **means-tested program:** a family can qualify only if it can show that its financial resources are below a certain level. Benefit levels are set by the states, and they vary widely. In 1982, the maximum benefit level for a family of three was $96 in Mississippi and $513 in Connecticut. The amount of AFDC aid is reduced when other income becomes available to the family. The AFDC benefit is decreased by about 67 cents for each dollar of monthly earned income over $30.[23] The reduction of benefits when a recipient earns income is a general feature of all means-tested programs. Much concern has focused on whether this creates inappropriate work incentives for the poor. This important topic is discussed in Chapter 15.

Supplemental Security Income (SSI).   This is a federal welfare program which provides a minimum income guarantee for the aged. SSI, administered by the Social Security Administration, is means-tested. Benefits cannot be received unless income and assets are below a certain level. In December 1982, 3.9 million individuals received SSI aid. Federal SSI benefits are uniform, but individual states vary in the amount of supplemental benefits they provide. In December 1982, the average monthly benefit (combined state and federal) ranged from $146.03 (Arkansas) to $269.21 (California).[24]

Medicare and Medicaid.   Medicare pays for medical services rendered to people aged 65 or older. It is not means tested. In 1981, about 27.2 million people participated, about 4.4 million of whom were below the federal government poverty line.[25] Medicaid makes payments for medical expenses incurred by the indigent. To qualify, individuals must satisfy two criteria: (1) They must be aged, blind, disabled, or in certain types of families with dependent children; and (2) their income must be below a certain level. Each state sets its own income level, subject to some federal guidelines. In 1982, about 22 million people received Medicaid payments [Congressional Budget Office, 1983a].

Food Stamps and Child Nutrition.[26]   These are means-tested programs designed to eliminate hunger among the poor. A food stamp is a

---

[22] For further details, see Congressional Budget Office [1983a].

[23] By legislation passed in 1981, benefits are supposed to be reduced by $1 for each dollar earned. But due to the fact that working mothers are allowed to deduct certain expenses of working, the effective figure is more like 67 cents.

[24] See U.S. Department of Health and Human Services [1982, p. 243].

[25] See U.S. Bureau of the Census [1983a, p. 55].

[26] See U.S. Bureau of the Census [1983a, p. 20].

voucher issued by the government which can be used only for the purchase of food. Recipients purchase the stamps at a price below their face
value, with the difference being the subsidy. As of March 1982, 7.1
million households participated. These households had an average
gross monthly income of $657 for 2.9 persons and received an average of
$74 in food stamp subsidies. While the bulk of food stamp participants
made less than $625 monthly, 868,000 households with $1,250 or more
in gross monthly income also received subsidies.

Child nutrition programs are designed to benefit nursing mothers,
infants, children under five years old, and school children. The school
lunch program is the largest of these, with about 29 million children
affected as of March 1982 [U.S. Bureau of the Census, 1983a, p. 34].

Housing.   Housing programs provide the poor with direct assistance
with their rental payments and also subsidize the construction of low-
income housing operated by both private and public landlords. Unlike
the food stamp program, participation in housing programs is not con-
tingent on poverty alone, because there are many fewer subsidized
housing units available than there are eligible households. In 1982,
about 2.9 million households were assisted through the program, while
the number of households below the official government poverty line
was 11.7 million [U.S. Bureau of the Census, 1983a, p. 37].

Employment and Training.   Programs in these areas provide public-
sector jobs for those who are economically disadvantaged. The idea is to
provide training and work experience to those who cannot obtain it in
the private sector. In 1980, about 3.4 million people participated. There
are also some programs for dislocated workers—those who have lost
their jobs, for example, because of changes in the structure of trade.
However, these account for a relatively small proportion of the total.

Social Services.[27]   This includes child welfare, day care, rehabilitation
services, and numerous programs for children, youths, females, and
elderly persons. These programs are largely administered at the state
level. As of December 1980, there were about 7.9 million recipients.

Education.   Programs in this area provide funds to individual school
districts for compensatory education at the elementary and secondary
levels for disadvantaged students. About 5 million students were involved in 1981. There are also programs for the handicapped, for adults
returning to school, for bilingual students, etc. Not included in the table
is federal support of higher education. This mainly takes the form of

---

[27] See U.S. Department of Health and Human Services, *Social Services: Statistical Tables,
Summaries and Analyses* (Washington, D.C.: U.S. Government Printing Office, 1981).

student aid including some outright grants for students from low- and middle-income families, as well as loan subsidies and guarantees for those who borrow to meet their schooling costs.

Legal Aid (The Legal Services Corporation).   This entails legal services for the poor. In 1981, $328 million was spent, a rapid rise from the 1975 level of $71 million.[28]

Low-Income Energy Assistance Program.   This program provides funds to aid individuals with high fuel bills, energy-related emergencies, etc. In 1982, about 8 million assistance grants were made [Congressional Budget Office, 1983a, p. 184].

Evaluation of the "Poverty Budget": In-Kind Transfers Again

A striking feature of Table 5.1 is the importance of in-kind transfers. Yet, earlier it was suggested that welfare recipients might generally prefer cash to an in-kind transfer. Moreover, in-kind transfer programs often entail substantial administrative costs. In the case of the cheese program discussed above, costs were incurred for storage, transportation, and distribution of the cheese. (Indeed, the costs were so large that some communities chose not to participate.) Similarly, public housing programs require the services of bureaucrats to arrange contracts, set standards for the housing, and see that the standards are enforced. It would probably be cheaper just to send checks to the beneficiaries.

If in-kind transfers are less satisfactory than cash from the point of view of the recipients *and* entail more administrative costs, how can we account for their importance in the government's poverty budget? There are several possible explanations.

Paternalism.   The design of programs for the poor is influenced by paternalism. Donors may believe that the poor are not capable of making sensible spending decisions, so that the choices of commodities to be consumed must be made for them.

Commodity Egalitarianism.   Society cares not only about the distribution of income per se, but also about the distribution of certain "necessary" commodities—commodity egalitarianism. (See pp. 78–79.) For instance, in 1949 the U.S. Congress explicitly set as a national goal "a decent home and a suitable living environment for every American family" [Weicher, 1979, p. 470]. Note the distinction between this goal and

---

[28] See Executive Office of the President, Office of Management and Budget, *Budget of the United States Government Fiscal Year 1982* (Washington, D.C.: U.S. Government Printing Office, 1981).

"enough income so that every American family can live in a decent home, if it chooses." Legal services is an even clearer example of commodity egalitarianism—every citizen should have access to the judicial system.

Curb Welfare Fraud.   In-kind transfers may also help curb welfare fraud. The discussion so far has assumed that in means-tested programs there are no problems in identifying who is eligible and who is not. In reality, this is not the case, and people who do not qualify are sometimes able to obtain benefits. Nichols and Zeckhauser [1982] suggest that in-kind transfers may discourage ineligible persons from applying because some middle-class people may be quite willing to lie to receive cash, but less willing to commit fraud to obtain a commodity they do not really want. This is especially true if the commodity is difficult to resell, like an apartment in a public housing project. In the same way, creating "hassles" for welfare recipients (waiting in line, filling out a lot of forms) may discourage those who are not "truly needy" from applying. Thus, there is a trade-off. On one hand, a poor person would prefer $50 in cash to $50 worth of public housing. But if the in-kind program leads to less fraud, then more resources can be channeled to those who really need them. However, many would argue that the government has created far more than the "optimal" amount of administrative hurdles for welfare recipients. An example that received substantial public attention was a 1982 ruling by the Agriculture Department that children who received free school lunches had to obtain and submit the social security numbers of each adult who lived at home. This was felt by many to be an unfair burden upon the children.

Political Considerations.   In-kind transfers are attractive politically because they help not only the beneficiary, but also the producers of the favored commodity. A transfer program that increases the demand for housing benefits the building industry, which therefore becomes willing to lend its support to a political coalition in favor of the program. Similarly, the agricultural interests have always been avid supporters of food stamps. In the same way, the public employees who administer the various in-kind transfer programs can be expected to put their political support behind them. In 1977, when welfare reformers proposed that subsidized housing be phased out and replaced with cash grants, the Department of Housing and Urban Development registered vigorous opposition [Weicher, 1980, p. 51].

These explanations for in-kind transfers are not mutually exclusive, and they probably have all influenced policy design. Many economists, representing a broad range of political thought, believe that it would be preferable to replace in-kind transfers with direct cash grants.

Bottom Line: The Distribution of Income

With an understanding of the nature and magnitude of government distribution policies, we can now examine their impact. Table 5.2 shows the distribution of income in the United States for selected years since

TABLE 5.2   The Distribution of Money Income among Families for Selected
Years, 1947–1981

			Percentage Share			
Year	Lowest Fifth	Second Fifth	Middle Fifth	Fourth Fifth	Highest Fifth	Top 5 Percent
1947	5.0%	11.9%	17.0%	23.1%	43.0%	17.5%
1952	4.9	12.3	17.4	23.4	41.9	17.4
1957	5.1	12.7	18.1	23.8	40.4	15.6
1962	5.0	12.1	17.6	24.0	41.3	15.7
1967	5.5	12.4	17.9	23.9	40.4	15.2
1972	5.4	11.9	17.5	23.9	41.4	15.9
1977	5.2	11.6	17.5	24.2	41.5	15.7
1981	5.0	11.3	17.4	24.4	41.9	15.4

Source: U.S. Bureau of the Census, *Current Population Reports,* series P-60, no. 137 (Washington, D.C.: U.S. Government Printing Office, 1983), p. 47.

World War II.[29] These figures include cash transfers from the government, but exclude in-kind transfers. The table suggests that: *(a)* There is a lot of inequality. (The lowest 20 percent of the income distribution receives only about 5 percent of the income.) *(b)* The distribution has remained rather stable over time. The stability of the low income share seems curious in light of the increase in government transfer programs over time: in 1950, 8.8 percent of gross national product went to transfers; in 1978, the figure was 18.2 percent.[30] But perhaps it should not be so surprising. As suggested earlier, the composition of family units has been changing in a way that would tend to increase the number of "poor" families. And much of the aid has not gone to people at the very bottom of the income distribution anyway (see U.S. Bureau of the Census [1982, pp. 320–21]). Finally, the work incentives created by the programs may have induced beneficiaries to work less, so that even as their transfer income rose, their labor income fell (see Chapter 15).

What about the effect of in-kind transfers? According to the results surveyed by Blinder [1980], if it is assumed that each dollar of in-kind transfers is valued as a dollar by recipients, the share of income received

[29] Looking at the share of total income going to each section of the income distribution is just one of many ways of characterizing the amount of inequality. Blinder [1980] provides a discussion of several others.

[30] These computations are based upon Cohen [1980, p. 490].

by the lowest fifth increases by two percentage points. If in-kind transfers are valued at 70 percent of the dollar amount, they increase the share of the lowest fifth by about 1.5 percentage points. Thus, in-kind payments have somewhat reduced the amount of income inequality.[31]

CONCLUDING REMARKS

Whatever refinements are made in measuring income, there is no doubt that its distribution is unequal. Whether or not this is a "problem" depends upon your political and ethical views. However, in the United States there does appear to be a consensus that government intervention is called for to increase the material well-being of those at the bottom of the income distribution. How far to go is another question. In the framework of conventional welfare economics, the optimal amount of income redistribution depends upon the trade-off between the benefits from more equality and the efficiency costs generated by the tax-transfer system.

When we turn from the theory of income distribution to its actual practice, the most striking phenomenon is the prevalence of a wide variety of in-kind transfers. Economists' criticisms of these programs have concentrated on their lack of efficiency and on the fact that many poor people receive little or no aid. However, the academic discussion of the pros and cons of various systems barely hints at the emotions surrounding the debate over welfare. The current structure is often accused of degrading the poor. According to one welfare mother, "It's like I heard of girls that say they got a pimp. I mean, the pimp takes them and treats them like a queen for a little while and then starts stripping them of all their values, their moral character and then just degrades them to the lowest—that's welfare" [Schoen, 1983, p. 23].

Some would go further and suggest that *any* welfare system leads to spiritual problems:

> Welfare, like many other expressions of noble intentions, has a seed of corruption in it. You might, at first, accept charity because you really need it. But if you don't stop accepting it the very moment you can make a living on your own—even a modest living—then you lose your soul. [Kenan, 1982, p. A29]

But proponents of transfers to the poor are quick to point out that they are not the only beneficiaries of public "charity." A number of govern-

---

[31] The impact of cash transfers upon the income distribution has also been analyzed. Using a somewhat different sample from that in Table 5.2, Danziger and Plotnick [1977] estimate that in 1974, cash transfers increased the share of income going to the bottom quintile from 0.9 percent to 3.8 percent.

ment expenditure and tax programs benefit middle- and upper-income people. Spending by the National Science Foundation increases the incomes of scientists; support for college education increases the incomes of professors; and defense programs increase the incomes of munitions manufacturers. Indeed, sometimes programs that are ostensibly for other purposes are actually nothing more than income distribution programs favoring various groups. For example, most economists believe that farm price supports have a negligible efficiency purpose and are only a veiled way of transferring income to the politically powerful agricultural interests. (In fiscal year 1983, these programs cost $28 billion, about $3 billion more than all farm income [Robbins, 1983, p. 1]. Similarly, the location of certain U.S. military bases may serve only to raise incomes in key legislative districts.

However, "welfare to the rich" does not carry that label. Perhaps that is why no one worries about them losing *their* souls.

SUMMARY

Optimal Income Distribution

Economists analyze distributional issues not because they have the "right" answers, but rather to determine the consequences of alternative government policies on the distribution of income and to draw out the implications of various ethical goals.

The "optimal" distribution of income depends upon the particular social welfare function employed. There are a number of different opinions as to what form the social welfare function should take.

In the utilitarian approach, social welfare is a function of individual utilities:
If (1) social welfare is the sum of identical utility functions which depend only on income; (2) there is decreasing marginal utility of income; and (3) the total amount of income is fixed, then income should be equally distributed. These are quite strong assumptions, and weakening them gives radically different results.

The maximin criterion states that the best income distribution maximizes the utility of the member of society who has the lowest utility. Rawls has argued that the maximin criterion has a compelling ethical justification, but his argument has been criticized.

It is possible that income distribution is much like a public good—everyone derives utility from the fact that income is equitably distributed, but no single person may accomplish the needed redistribution. This raises the possibility of Pareto efficient redistribution in which no one is made worse as a result of the redistributive activity.

Other views of income distribution do not follow the utilitarian framework. Some believe that it is a first principle that income, or at least certain goods, be distributed equally. Others argue that the distribution of income is not a relevant question. As long as the distribution arises from a "fair" process, the actual income distribution is irrelevant. These views sidestep the problem of how to judge the "fairness" of a process without looking at the results.

Incidence of Government Expenditure

Income before transfers is hard to measure correctly. Some goods and services are not marketed, and the values of the services provided by durable goods are not observed. Moreover, it is not clear what time period—month, year, lifetime—or what unit of observation—individual, household, family—is appropriate.

A government program can change the entire set of relative prices in the economy, creating losses and gains for various individuals. It is difficult to trace out all of these price changes, so economists generally focus only on the prices in the markets directly affected.

Much government expenditure is for public goods. Since people do not reveal how they value public goods, it is difficult to determine how real incomes are affected.

Many government programs provide goods and services (in-kind transfers) instead of cash. Recipients are not legally allowed to sell the goods and services so received. If recipients would prefer to consume less, the value of the in-kind transfer is less than the market price, but exactly how much less is hard to determine.

In general, beneficiaries would prefer cash to in-kind transfers. However, the prevalence of in-kind transfer programs may be due to paternalism, commodity egalitarianism, administrative feasibility, or political attractiveness.

Statistics on U.S. income distribution have been remarkably stable since 1947. However, government in-kind transfer programs may serve to increase the income share of the lowest income quintile by as much as 2 percentage points.

DISCUSSION QUESTIONS

1. Are the concepts of "fairness" and "equality" in the distribution of income synonymous? To what extent is income inequality consistent with fairness? What are the implications of your answer for government expenditure policy?

2. Suppose that there are only two people, Simon and Charity, who must split a fixed income of $100. For Simon, the marginal utility of income is:

$$MU_s = 400 - 2I_s$$

while for Charity, marginal utility is:

$$MU_c = 400 - 6I_c + 2I_s$$

where I_c, I_s are the amounts of income to Charity and Simon, respectively.

a. What is the optimal distribution of income if the social welfare function is additive?

b. What is the optimal distribution if society values only the utility of Charity? What if the reverse is true? Comment on your answers.

c. Suppose instead that:

$$MU_c = 400 - 6I_c$$

Answer **(a)** and **(b)** for this case.

d. Finally, comment on how your answers change if the marginal utility of income for both Simon and Charity is constant:

$$MU_c = 400$$
$$MU_s = 400$$

3. Consider the following programs:
    a. Subsidized bus fares for the elderly.
    b. Purchase of helicopters for the Air Force.
    How might each program affect the distribution of income?

4. Evaluate: "To win the 'War on Poverty' does not require more government expenditures. What is needed is more sensible use of expenditures already being made." Base your answer not only on historical experience, but upon the relevant economic arguments as well.

SELECTED REFERENCES

Atkinson, A. B. *The Economics of Inequality.* Oxford: Oxford University Press, 1975.

Blinder, Alan S. "The Level and Distribution of Economic Well-Being." in *The American Economy in Transition,* ed. Martin Feldstein. Chicago: University of Chicago Press, 1980, pp. 415–79.

Hochman, H. M., and J. D. Rodgers. "Pareto Optimal Redistribution." *American Economic Review* 59 (1969), pp. 542–57.

Kristol, Irving. "Some Personal Reflections on Economic Well-Being and Income Distribution." In *The American Economy in Transition,* ed. Martin Feldstein. Chicago: University of Chicago Press, 1980, pp. 479–86.

CHAPTER 6

Public Goods

*There exists an intrinsic connection between the
common good on the one hand and the structure and
function of public authority on the other. The moral
order, which needs public authority in order to
promote the common good in human society, requires
also that the authority be effective in attaining that
end.*

Pope John XXIII

What goods and services should the public sector provide, and in what
amounts? As the annual debate over the government budget demonstrates, this question lies at the leart of some of the most important
controversies over public policy. In this chapter we will discuss the
conditions under which public provision of commodities is appropriate.[1]
Special attention is paid to understanding why markets may fail to provide particular goods at Pareto efficient levels.

Even if the marketplace does not provide certain goods efficiently,
other better mechanisms are not obvious. A common alternative method
of deciding resource allocation is the political process, and in this chapter we discuss some of the procedures used in public decision making.
This analysis sheds light not only on the relatively narrow issue of
economic efficiency, but also more generally on the ability of democracies to make sensible choices. We begin by examining the subject of so-
called public goods.

---

[1] Note that public *provision* does not necessarily imply public *production*. For example,
the federal government provides national defense using weapons produced in the private
sector.

PUBLIC GOODS DEFINED

A **public good** (sometimes called a **collective good**) has two characteristics: (1) Once it is provided, the additional resource cost of another person consuming the good is zero—consumption is *nonrival*. (2) To prevent anyone from consuming the good is either very expensive or impossible—consumption is *nonexcludable*. Consider the lighthouse example from Chapter 4. Once the beacon is lit, the resource cost of an additional ship using it for guidance is zero. Moreover, no particular vessel can be excluded from taking advantage of the signal.

There are several aspects of our definition of public good worth noting.

First, even though everyone consumes the same quantity of the good, there is *no* requirement that this consumption be valued equally by all. We expect that owners of ships with relatively valuable cargoes would place a higher value on being guided safely to shore than those with inexpensive cargoes, other things being the same. Indeed, people might differ over whether the value of certain public goods is positive or negative. When a new missile system is constructed, each person has no choice but to consume its services. For those who view the system as an enhancement to their safety, the value is positive. Others believe that additional missiles only provoke the Russians, and thus make life less safe. Presumably such individuals would value an additional missile negatively. They would be willing to pay not to have it around.

Second, classification as a public good is not an absolute. It depends upon market conditions and the state of technology. Suppose that a jamming device were invented which made it possible to prevent ships from obtaining the lighthouse signal unless they purchased a special receiver. In this case, part (2) of the definition of public good would no longer be satisfied. A scenic view can be considered a public good when there is a small number of people involved. But as the number of sightseers increases, the area may become congested. The same "quantity" of scenic view is being "consumed" by each person, but its quality can decrease with the number of people. Hence, the nonrivalness criterion of the definition is no longer satisfied.

In many cases, then, it is useful to think of "publicness" as a matter of degree. A "pure" public good satisfies the definition exactly. Consumption of an "impure" public good is to some extent rival or excludable. It is difficult to think of many examples of really pure public goods. However, just as analysis of pure competition yields important insights into the operation of actual markets, so the analysis of pure public goods help us to understand problems confronting public decision makers.

Closely related to this point is the fact that a good can satisfy one part of the definition of a public good and not the other. Consider the streets of a downtown urban area during rush hour. In most cases, nonexcludability holds, because it is infeasible to set up enough toll booths to monitor traffic. But consumption is certainly rival, as anyone who has ever been caught in a traffic jam can testify. On the other hand, many people can enjoy a huge seashore area without diminishing the pleasure of others. Despite the fact that individuals do not rival each other in consumption, exclusion is quite possible if there are only a small number of access roads.

Finally, a number of things that are not conventionally thought of as commodities have public good characteristics. An important example is honesty. If each citizen is honest in commercial transactions, then all of society benefits due to the reduction of the costs of doing business. Such cost reductions are characterized both by nonexcludability and nonrivalness. Similarly, some argue that a "fair" income distribution is a public good [see Thurow, 1971]. If income is distributed fairly, each person gains satisfaction from living in a good society, and no one can be excluded from having that satisfaction.

EFFICIENT PROVISION OF PUBLIC GOODS

Reinterpretation of the Private-Good Case

To derive the conditions for efficient provision of a public good, it is useful to begin by reexamining private goods from a slightly different point of view than that used in Chapter 4. Assume again a society populated by two people, Adam and Eve. There are two private goods, apples and fig leaves. In Figure 6.1A, the quantity of fig leaves (f) is measured on the horizontal axis, and the price per fig leaf (P_f) is on the vertical. Adam's demand curve for fig leaves is denoted by D_f^A. The

FIGURE 6.1   Horizontal Summation of Demand Curves

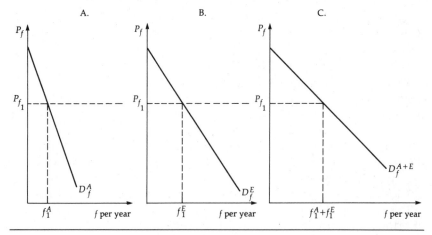

demand curve shows the quantity of fig leaves that Adam would be willing to consume at each price, other things being the same.[2] Similarly, D_f^E in Figure 6.1B is Eve's demand curve for fig leaves.

Suppose now that we want to derive the *market* demand curve for fig leaves. To do so, we simply add together the number of fig leaves each person demands at every price. In Figure 6.1A, at price P_{f_1} Adam demands f_1^A, the horizontal distance between D_f^A and the vertical axis. Figure 6.1B indicates that at the same price, Eve demands f_1^E. The total quantity demanded at price P_{f_1} is therefore $f_1^A + f_1^E$. The market demand curve for fig leaves is labeled in Figure 6.1C. As we have just shown, the point at which price is P_{f_1} and quantity demanded in $f_1^A + f_1^E$ lies on the market demand curve. Similarly, finding the market demand at any given price involves summing the horizontal distance between each of the private demand curves and the vertical axis at that price. This process is sometimes called **horizontal summation.**

Figures 6.2A and 6.2B reproduce the private demand curves depicted in Figures 6.1A and 6.1B. Figure 6.2C superimposes the market supply

FIGURE 6.2   Efficient Provision of a Private Good

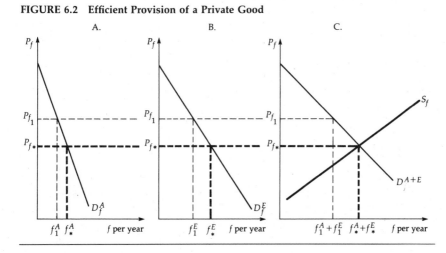

curve, labeled S_f, upon the market demand curve D_f^{A+E} from Figure 6.1C. Equilibrium in the market occurs at the price where the quantities demanded and supplied are equal. This occurs at price P_{f*} in Figure 6.2C.

At this price, Adam consumes quantity f_*^A and Eve consumes f_*^E. Note that there is no reason to expect f_*^A and f_*^E to be equal. Due to different tastes, incomes, and other characteristics, Adam and Eve demand different quantities of fig leaves.

---

[2] Demand curves are explained in the appendix to this book.

The equilibrium in Figure 6.2C has a significant property: the allocation of fig leaves is Pareto efficient. In consumer theory, a utility-maximizing individual sets the marginal rate of substitution of fig leaves for apples (MRS_{fa}) equal to the price of fig leaves (P_f) divided by the price of apples (P_a): $MRS_{fa} = P_f/P_a$.[3] Because only relative prices matter for rational choice, the price of apples can be arbitrarily set at any value. For convenience, set $P_a = \$1$. Thus, the condition for utility maximization reduces to $MRS_{fa} = P_f$. The price of fig leaves thus measures the rate at which an individual is willing to substitute fig leaves for apples. Now, Adam's demand curve for fig leaves (D_f^A) shows the maximum price per fig leaf that he would pay at each level of fig leaf consumption. Therefore, the demand curve also shows the MRS_{fa} at each level of fig leaf consumption. Similarly, D_f^E can be interpreted as Eve's MRS_{fa} schedule.

In the same way, the supply curve S_f in Figure 6.2C shows how the marginal rate of transformation of fig leaves for apples (MRT_{fa}) varies with fig leaf production.[4]

At the equilibrium in Figure 6.2C, Adam and Eve both set MRS_{fa} equal to P_{f*}, and the producer also sets MRT_{fa} equal to P_{f*}.[5] Hence, at equilibrium

(6.1) $$MRS_{fa}^{\text{Adam}} = MRS_{fa}^{\text{Eve}} = MRT_{fa}$$

Equation (6.1) is the necessary condition for Pareto efficiency derived in Chapter 4. As long as the market is competitive and functions properly, the Fundamental Theorem of Welfare Economics guarantees that this condition holds.

Public Good Case

Suppose that Adam and Eve both enjoy displays of fireworks. Eve's enjoyment of fireworks does not diminish Adam's and vice versa. If there is a fireworks display, it is impossible to exclude either individual from "consuming" it. Hence, a fireworks display is a public good.

The quantity of fireworks consumed is measured by the number of rockets (r) that are exploded. In Figure 6.3A, Adam's consumption of rockets is measured on the horizontal axis, and the price per rocket (P_r) is on the vertical. Adam's demand curve for rockets is D_r^A. Similarly,

---

[3] See the Appendix to the book for a proof.

[4] To demonstrate this, note that under competition, firms produce up to the point where price equals the marginal cost, the incremental cost of the last unit produced. Hence, the supply curve S_f shows the marginal cost of each level of fig leaf production. As noted in Chapter 4, $MRT_{fa} = MC_f/MC_a$. Because $P_a = \$1$ and price equals marginal cost, then $MC_a = \$1$, and $MRT_{fa} = MC_f$. We can therefore identify the marginal rate of transformation with marginal cost, and hence with the supply curve.

[5] A demonstration that profit-maximizing firms set the marginal rate of transformations equal to the price ratio is included in the appendix at the end of the book.

FIGURE 6.3   Vertical Summation of Demand Curves

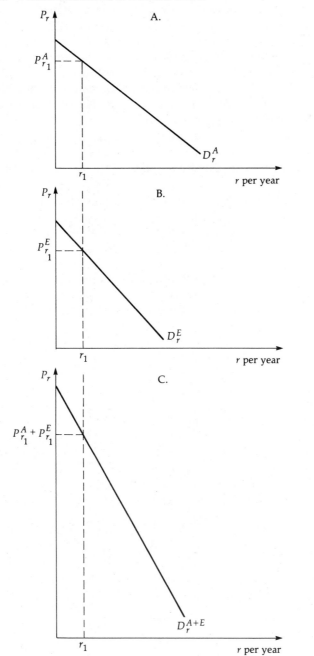

Eve's demand curve for rockets is D_r^E in Figure 6.3B. How do we derive the total demand for rockets? To find the market demand curve for fig leaves—a private good—we horizontally summed the individual demand curves. That procedure makes it possible for Adam and Eve to consume *different* quantities of fig leaves at the same price. For a private good, this is fine. However, the services produced by the rockets—a public good—*must* be consumed in *equal* amounts. If Adam consumes a 10-rocket fireworks display, then Eve must also consume a 10-rocket fireworks display. It literally makes no sense to try to sum the quantities of a public good that the individual would consume at a given price.

Instead, to find the total demand for rockets, we add the prices that each would be willing to pay for a given quantity. The demand curve in Figure 6.3A tells us that Adam is willing to pay $P_{r_1}^A$ per rocket when he consumes r_1 rockets. Eve is willing to pay $P_{r_1}^E$ when she consumes r_1 rockets. Their total willingness to pay for r_1 rockets is therefore $P_{r_1}^A + P_{r_1}^E$. The total demand curve for rockets, D_r^{A+E} is shown in Figure 6.3C. It indicates the total willingness to pay at each quantity of rockets. Therefore, the vertical distance between the point r_1 and the total demand curve is $P_{r_1}^A + P_{r_1}^E$. D_r^{A+E} is determined by repeating this procedure for each level of public-good production. For a public good then, the total demand curve is found by **vertical summation** of the individual demand curves.

Note the symmetry between private and public goods. With a private good, everyone has the same *MRS*, but people can consume different quantities. Therefore, demands are summed horizontally over the differing quantities. For public goods, everyone consumes the same quantity, but people can have different *MRS*s. Vertical summation is required to find the total demand curve.

The efficient quantity of rockets is found at the point where market demand equals market supply. In Figure 6.4C, the supply curve S_r is superimposed on the market demand curve D_r^{A+E}.[6] The intersection occurs at output r_* where the price is equal to $(P_{r_*}^A + P_{r_*}^E)$.

Once again prices can be interpreted in terms of marginal rates of substitution. Reasoning as before, P_r^A is Adam's marginal rate of substitution of rockets for apples (MRS_{ra}^{Adam}), and P_r^E is Eve's marginal rate of substitution (MRS_{ra}^{Eve}). Therefore, $P_r^A + P_r^E$ equals $MRS_{ra}^{Adam} + MRS_{ra}^{Eve}$. From the production point of view, price still represents the marginal rate of transformation, MRT_{ra}. Hence, the equilibrium in Figure 6.4C is characterized by the condition:

(6.2) $$MRS_{ra}^{Adam} + MRS_{ra}^{Eve} = MRT_{ra}.$$

---

[6] This analysis does not consider explicitly the production possibilities frontier which lies behind this supply curve. See Samuelson [1955].

FIGURE 6.4   Efficient Provision of a Public Good

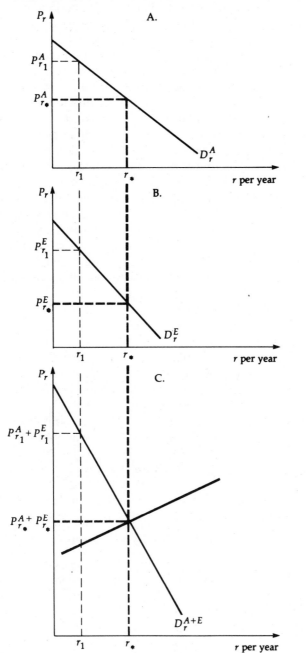

Contrast this with the conditions for efficient provision of a private good described in Equation (6.1). For a private good, efficiency requires that each individual have the same marginal rate of substitution, and that this equal the marginal rate of transformation. For a pure public good, the *sum* of the marginal rates of substitution must equal the marginal rate of transformation.[7] Because everybody must consume the same amount of the public good, its efficient provision requires that the *total* valuation they place on the last unit provided—the sum of the MRSs—equal the incremental cost to society of providing it—the MRT.

As stressed in Chapter 4, under a reasonably general set of conditions, one can expect a decentralized market system to provide goods efficiently. In the absence of "market imperfections," the efficient quantity of fig leaves ($f_*^A + f_*^E$) in Figure 6.2C will be generated. Will similar forces lead to output r_* in Figure 6.4? The answer turns on the extent to which Adam and Eve reveal their true preferences for fireworks. When a private good is exchanged in a competitive market, an individual has no incentive to lie about how much he values it. If Eve is willing to pay the going price for a fig leaf, then she has nothing to gain by failing to make the purchase. This kind of behavior is implicitly assumed in the usual stories of how the forces of supply and demand produce an equilibrium.

But in the case of the public good, there may be incentives for people to hide their true preferences. These arise because it is impossible to exclude anyone from consuming the good. Adam may falsely claim that fireworks mean nothing to him. If he can get Eve to foot the entire bill, he can still enjoy the show and yet have more money to spend on apples and fig leaves. This incentive to let other people pay while you enjoy the benefits is known as the **free rider problem.** Of course, Eve also would like to be a free rider. Where there are public goods, "any one person can hope to snatch some selfish benefit in a way not possible under the self-policing competitive pricing of private goods" [Samuelson, 1954, p. 389]. Hence, there is a good chance that the market will fall short of providing the efficient amount of the public good. No "automatic" tendency exists for markets to reach allocation r_* in Figure 6.4.

Is the Free Rider Problem Really a Problem?

Some suggest that the free rider problem necessarily leads to inefficient levels of public goods; therefore, government provision of public goods is *required* for economic efficiency. The argument is that the government can somehow find out everyone's true preferences, and then using its coercive power, force everybody to pay for public goods. If all

---

[7] This analysis assumes that the taxes required to finance the public good can be raised without distorting economic decisions in the private sector. When this is not the case, the condition for efficient provision changes. See Atkinson and Stern [1974]. The analysis also assumes that the good cannot be priced on the market. This issue is discussed below.

this is possible, then the government can avoid the free rider problem and ensure that public goods are provided at appropriate levels.

It must be emphasized that free ridership is not a *fact;* it is a *hypothesis* about how people behave. To be sure, one can find examples in which public goods are not provided because people fail to reveal their preferences. On the other hand, much evidence suggests that individuals can and do act collectively without government coercion: "Thousands of churches, music halls, libraries, scientific laboratories, art museums, theaters, and other such facilities have been financed by voluntary contributions to fund drives conducted by private societies" [V. L. Smith, 1980, p. 585].[8] One prominent economist has even argued, "I do not know of many historical records or other empirical evidence which show convincingly that the problem of correct revelation of preferences has been of any practical significance" [Johansen, 1977, p. 147].

These observations do not prove that free ridership is irrelevant. Although *some* goods that appear to have "public" characteristics (nonrivalness and nonexcludability) are privately provided, others that "ought" to be provided (on grounds of efficiency) may not be. Moreover, the quantity of those public goods that are privately provided may be insufficient. The key point is that the importance of the free rider problem is an empirical question whose answer should not be taken for granted.

Marwell and Ames [1981] conducted laboratory experiments to investigate the importance of free rider behavior. Subjects in the experiment were given a number of tokens which they invested in an "individual exchange" or in a "group exchange." Investments in the individual exchange earned a set amount, regardless of the behavior of other group members. The return was "excludable" in the sense that it neither affected nor was affected by the other members. On the other hand, "The group exchange . . . paid its cash earnings to *all* members of the group by a pretest formula, regardless of who invested. . . . [It] provided a joint, nonrival, nonexcludable, or *public* form of payoff" [p. 297]. The incentive to free ride was provided by the fact that the group exchange could offer a substantially larger return.

> Under these circumstances, all members of the group would be better off if all the group's resources were invested in the group exchange than if all were invested in the individual exchange. On the other hand, each individual would be best off if she/he invested in the individual exchange while everyone else invested in the group exchange. [p. 297]

What did the results show? On average, people voluntarily contributed 40 to 60 percent of their resources to the provision of the public

---

[8] There is even some evidence of successful private provision of that classic public good, the lighthouse [see Coase, 1974]. Groves and Ledyard [1977] describe some mechanisms which induce people to reveal their true preferences to a government agency.

good. Some free riding therefore was present in the sense that the subjects failed to contribute a substantial portion of their resources. On the other hand, the results flatly contradicted the notion that free riding will lead to zero or trivial amounts of a public good. People's notions of fairness and responsibility may work counter to the pursuit of narrow self-interest.

As was stressed in Chapter 3, caution must be exercised in interpreting the results of laboratory experiments. The setting is artificial and the sample of individuals being observed is restricted. The results do suggest, however, that more research on the relevance of the free rider problem is called for.

Private Substitutes for Public Goods

In some cases, the services provided by public goods can be obtained privately. The commodity "protection" can be obtained from a police force, which is a public good. Alternatively, to some extent protection can also be gained by purchasing strong locks, burglar alarms, and bodyguards, which are private goods. A large backyard can serve many of the functions of a public park. Even substitutes for services provided by public courts of law can be obtained privately. For example, because of the enormous costs of using the government's judicial system, companies sometimes bypass the courts and instead settle their disputes before mutually agreed-upon neutral advisers.[9]

In these cases, public and private provision can be thought of as two different technologies for producing the same (or similar) outputs. The problem is to find the efficient mix between public and private provision. There are advantages to each method. Under public provision, any fixed administrative costs of a given program can be spread over a large group of people. Instead of everyone having to spend time negotiating an arrangement for garbage collection, the negotiation is done by one office for everybody. On the other hand, costs of public provision may be higher than they would be in the private sector. Some argue that public sector managers, because they do not have to make profits, are less efficient than their private-sector counterparts.[10] The issue is complicated further if society has distributional goals. Public provision may be desirable if society believes a certain quantity of the commodity should be consumed uniformly. Public education is an example.

The extent to which services currently provided by the government should be "privatized" is an important political debate. Conservatives

---

[9] In 1981, the average litigation fee paid by very large companies was roughly $5.2 million [Lewin, 1982, p. D1].

[10] Anecdotal evidence abounds. For example, there was a public scandal in 1984 when it was learned that the Pentagon paid $1,118.26 for a plastic stool cap. For a systematic discussion of the evidence, see the studies cited in Inman [1979].

want more functions provided by the private sector, while liberals prefer government provision. Part of the controversy stems from fundamental differences regarding the extent to which government should intervene in the economy (see Chapter 1). Part is due to differences of opinion about the relative efficiencies of public versus private provision. Unfortunately, little empirical evidence is available on the latter topic.

SOCIAL CHOICE[11]

The extent to which various goods should be provided collectively is controversial. However, for at least some important public goods like national defense, it is hard to imagine a decentralized market system. A public decision has to be made. In democratic societies, various voting procedures are used to decide what quantities of public goods to provide. This section discusses and evaluates some of these procedures.

Unanimity Rules and the Lindahl Procedure

The irony of the free rider problem is that *everyone* could be better off if the public good were provided efficiently, but because people act in their narrow self-interest, not enough is provided. This suggests that in principle, if a vote were taken on whether to provide the good in an efficient quantity, consent would be unanimous as long as there was a suitable tax system to finance it. A procedure designed to elicit such unanimous agreement was proposed in the early 20th century by Erik Lindahl [1919/1958].

To understand Lindahl's procedure, assume again that there are two individuals, Adam and Eve, and one public good, rockets for fireworks (r). Suppose Adam is told that his share of the cost of rocket provision will be 30 percent. Then if the market price per rocket is P_r, Adam's price per rocket is $.30 \times P_r$. Given this price, the prices of other goods, his tastes, and his income, there is some quantity of rockets that Adam will want to consume. More generally, let S^A denote Adam's share of the cost of rocket provision. For any particular value of S^A, Adam demands some quantity of rockets. As his tax share increases and it becomes more expensive for him to obtain rockets, he demands a smaller quantity.

In Figure 6.5, the horizontal axis measures the quantity of rockets. Adam's tax share is measured by the vertical distance from point O. The curve D_r^A shows how the quantity of rockets demanded by Adam decreases as his tax share increases.

In the same way, define S^E as Eve's share of the cost of rocket provision. (By definition, $S^A + S^E = 1$.) When S^E goes up, the quantity de-

---

[11] This section relies heavily on the excellent survey by Mueller [1976], which should be consulted for further details.

FIGURE 6.5   Lindahl's Model

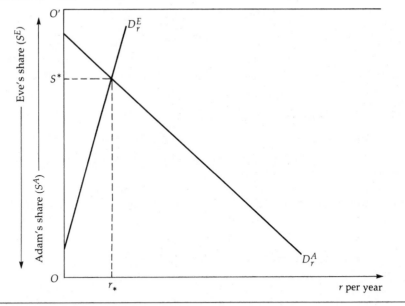

manded by Eve decreases. In Figure 6.5, Eve's tax share increases as we move down along the vertical axis from O'. (Thus, the distance OO' is 1.) Her demand schedule is denoted D_r^E. It slopes upward because upward movements along the vertical axis represent a *lower* price to her.

An obvious similarity exists between the role of tax shares in the Lindahl model and market prices in the usual theory of demand. But there is an important difference. Instead of each individual facing the same price, each faces a "personalized price" per unit of public good, which depends upon his or her tax share. The tax shares are referred to as **Lindahl prices.**

An equilibrium in the model is a set of Lindahl prices such that at those prices each person votes for the same quantity of the public good. In Figure 6.5, this occurs when Adam's tax share is OS^* and Eve's tax share is $O'S^*$. At these Lindahl prices, both parties agree that r_* rockets should be provided.

The Feasibility of Unanimity Rules. The Lindahl model shows the existence of tax shares and a level of public good provision that is agreeable to *all* members of society. The big question is how the economy reaches the equilibrium. Imagine that an auctioneer announces some initial set of tax shares. On the basis of their respective demand schedules, Adam and Eve vote for the number of rockets they want. If agreement is not unanimous, the auctioneer announces another set of tax shares. The process continues until Adam and Eve unanimously agree upon the quantity of rockets (r_* in Figure 6.5). The determination of the quantity of public goods, then, is done in a way quite similar to the market process. Like the outcome of a market process, it can be shown that the allocation is Pareto efficient.[12]

As a practical method for providing public goods, there are two main problems with Lindahl's procedure. First, it assumes that people vote sincerely. If Adam can guess the maximum amount that Eve would spend for rockets rather than do without them, he can try and force her to that allocation. Eve has the same incentives. Strategic behavior may prevent Adam and Eve from reaching the Lindahl equilibrium.

Second, it may take a lot of time to find the set of tax shares agreed upon by everyone. In this example, there are only two parties. In most important cases, many people are likely to be involved. To get everyone to agree is likely to involve very high decision-making costs. Indeed, although unanimity rules guarantee that no one will be "exploited," they often lead to situations in which *no* decisions are made. Historically, when organizations adopted a unanimity rule, it was often expressly because the participants wanted to make sure that no actions were taken![13]

Majority Voting Rules

Unanimity is clearly a difficult state to reach. As a result, voting systems not requiring unanimity may be desirable. With a **majority voting rule,** one more than half of the voters must favor a measure for it to be approved.

Although the mechanics of majority voting are familiar, it is useful to review them carefully. Consider a community with three voters, I, II, and III, who have to choose between three levels of missile provision, A, B, and C. Level A is "small," level B is "moderate," and level C is "large." The voters' preferences are depicted in Figure 6.6. Each column shows how the voter ranks the choices. For example, voter II most prefers level C, but given a choice between B and A, would prefer B.

Suppose that an election were held on whether to adopt A or B. Individual I would vote for A while II and III would vote for B. Hence, B would win by a vote of 2 to 1. Similarly, if an election were held between

---

[12] Intuitively, assume as above that $P_a = 1$. Then Eve sets $S^E P_r = MRS_{ra}^{Eve}$, and Adam sets $S^A P_r = MRS_{ra}^{Adam}$. Therefore $MRS_{ra}^{Eve} + MRS_{ra}^{Adam} = S^E P_r + S^A P_r = P_r(S^E + S^A) = P_r$. But P_r represents MRT_{ra}, so $MRS_{ra}^{Eve} + MRS_{ra}^{Adam} = MRT_{ra}$, which is the necessary condition for Pareto efficiency of Equation (6.2). For further details, see Mueller [1976].

[13] In 17th century Poland, the structure of government was essentially feudal. None of the nobles wanted to lose any power to the monarch. Hence, the monarch had to promise to take no actions unless he received the unanimous consent of the Polish parliament [see Massie, 1980, p. 228].

FIGURE 6.6   Voter Preferences that Lead to an Equilibrium

Choice \ Voter	I	II	III
First	A	C	B
Second	B	B	C
Third	C	A	A

B and C, B would win by a vote of 2 to 1. Level B wins any election against its opposition, and thus is the option selected by majority rule. Note that the selection of B is independent of the order in which the votes are taken.

·Do we always expect majority decision rules to yield such clear-cut results? Not necessarily. Suppose that the preferences for various levels of missile provision are as depicted in Figure 6.7. Again, imagine a series

FIGURE 6.7   Voter Preferences that Lead to Cycling

Choice \ Voter	I	II	III
First	A	C	B
Second	B	A	C
Third	C	B	A

of paired elections to determine the most preferred level. In an election between A and B, A would win by a vote of 2 to 1. If an election were held between B and C, B would win by a vote of 2 to 1. Finally, in an election between A and C, C would win by the same margin. This is a disconcerting result. The first election suggests that A is preferred to B; the second that B is preferred to C. Conventional notions of consistency suggest that A should therefore be preferred to C. But in the third election, just the opposite occurs. Although each individual voter's preferences are consistent, the community's are not. This phenomenon is referred to as the **voting paradox.**

Moreover, in the situation depicted in Figure 6.7, the ultimate outcome depends crucially on the order in which the votes are taken. If the first election is between propositions A and B and the winner (A) runs against C, then C is the ultimate choice. On the other hand, if the first election is B versus C, and the winner (B) runs against A, then A is chosen. Under such circumstances, the ability to control the order of voting—the agenda—confers great power. **Agenda manipulation** is the process of organizing the order of votes to assure a favorable outcome.

A related problem is that paired voting can go on forever without a decision being reached. After the election between A and B, A wins. If C challenges A, then C wins. If B then challenges C, B wins. The process can continue indefinitely, a phenomenon called **cycling.**

Clearly, the majority rule does not *have* to suffer from these problems. After all, the elections associated with Figure 6.6 went perfectly smoothly. What is the source of the difference? It turns on the structure of individual preferences for various levels of missile procurement. Consider again the people in Figure 6.7. Because voter I prefers A to B to C, it follows that A gives voter I more utility than B, and B more than C. The schedule denoted I in Figure 6.8 depicts this relationship. The schedules labeled II and III do the same for the other voters.

We define a **peak** in an individual's preferences as a point at which all the neighboring points are lower.[14] Voter I has a single peak at point A.

FIGURE 6.8   Graphing the Preferences from Figure 6.7

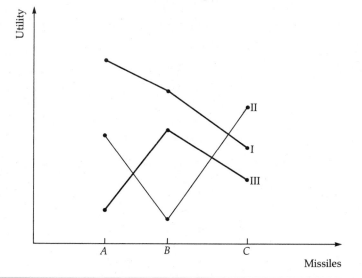

---

[14] For this analysis, the absolute amount of utility associated with each alternative is irrelevant. The vertical distances could change, but as long as the pattern of peaks stays unchanged, so does the outcome of the election.

Voter III has a single peak at point B. Voter II has two peaks, one at A and one at C. It turns out that II's preferences are the ones that lead to the voting paradox. If II had *any* set of single-peaked preferences, majority voting would lead to a consistent decision. This is why no voting paradox problems emerge from Figure 6.6. There, each voter has single peaked preferences. More generally, if all voters' preferences are single peaked, then the voting paradox will not occur.

Because multipeaked preferences can throw a wrench into majority voting, it is important to know whether they are likely to be important as a practical matter. Consider again voter II in Figure 6.7 whose preferences have two peaks. This voter prefers either very large or very small missile expenditures to a quantity in the middle. Although such preferences are not necessarily "irrational," they do seem a bit peculiar.[15] It is tempting to conclude, then, that multipeaked preferences are just a theoretical curiosity, and not of much practical importance.

When issues are not based upon a single dimension, however, multipeaked preferences are a serious possibility. Suppose that a community is trying to decide how to use a vacant building. Choice A is an abortion clinic, choice B is an adult book store, and choice C is a draft counseling center. Unlike the choice between different levels of missile expenditure, here the alternatives do not represent more or less of a single characteristic. It is easy to imagine multipeaked preferences emerging.

The Median Voter Rule.   Let us now return to the simple case in which all alternatives being considered represent smaller or greater amounts of a single characteristic. People rank each alternative on the basis of this single characteristic. An example is how much of some public good to acquire. Define the **median voter** as the voter whose preferences lie in the middle of the set of all voters' preferences; half the voters want more missiles than the median voter, and half want less. As long as all preferences are single peaked, the outcome of majority voting reflects the preferences of the median voter.[16] This is called the **median voter rule.**

To demonstrate the median voter rule, assume that there are five voters: Donald, Daisy, Huey, Dewey, and Louie. They are deciding how large a party to give together, and each of them has single-peaked preferences for party sizes. The most preferred level for each voter is noted in Figure 6.9. *Because preferences are single peaked,* the closer an expenditure level is to a given voter's peak, the more he or she prefers it. A movement from zero party expenditure to $5 would be preferred to no

---

[15] Perhaps voter II believes that moderate numbers of missiles will provide little if any real protection, so that unless expenditures are large, they might as well be close to nothing.

[16] See Black [1948]. When there is an even number of voters, there may be a tie between two median voters which must be broken arbitrarily.

FIGURE 6.9   Preferred Level of Party Expenditure

Voter	Expenditure
Donald	$ 5
Daisy	100
Huey	150
Dewey	160
Louie	700

money for parties by all voters. A movement from $5 to $100 would be approved by Daisy, Huey, Dewey, and Louie, and from $100 to $150 by Huey, Dewey, and Louie. Any expenditure in excess of $150, however, would be blocked by at least three voters: Donald, Daisy, and Huey. Hence, the majority votes for $150. But this is just the amount preferred by Huey, the median voter. The election results mirror the median voter's preferences.

To summarize: when all preferences are single peaked, majority voting yields a stable result. Moreover, the choice selected reflects the preferences of the median voter. However, when all voters' preferences are not single peaked, then a voting paradox may emerge.[17] Because multipeaked preferences may be important in many realistic situations, majority voting cannot be depended upon to yield consistent public choices.

Logrolling

Some argue that an important problem with simple majority voting is that it does not allow people to register how strongly they feel about the issues. Whether voter I just barely prefers A to B or has an enormous preference for A has no influence on the outcome. **Logrolling** systems allow people to trade votes and hence register how strongly they feel about various issues. Suppose that voters Smith and Jones prefer not to have more missiles, but this preference is not strongly felt. Brown, on the other hand, definitely wants more missiles. With a logrolling system, Brown may be able to convince Jones to vote for more missiles if Brown promises to vote for a new road to go by Jones' factory.

Vote trading is controversial. Its proponents argue that trading votes leads to efficient allocations of public goods, just as trading in commodities leads to efficient provision for private goods. Proponents also emphasize its potential for revealing the intensity of preferences and estab-

---

[17] The presence of one or more voters with multipeaked preferences does not *necessarily* lead to a voting paradox. It depends upon the number of voters and the structure of their preferences. See Question 3 at the end of this chapter.

lishing a stable equilibrium. Moreover, the compromises implicit in vote trading are necessary for a democratic system to function. As the English statesman Edmund Burke noted, "All government—indeed, every human benefit and enjoyment, every virtue and every prudent act—is founded on compromise and barter." (Married readers will believe this!)

Opponents of logrolling stress that it is likely to result in special-interest gains not sufficient to outweigh general losses. Large amounts of waste can be incurred. A famous example is the Clinch River Breeder Reactor, a nuclear power facility in Tennessee. For years, Congress voted to continue funding the $8.8 billion project, even though virtually all experts agreed that it was based on outmoded technology and was potentially dangerous. Why? One important reason was that Tennessee was the home state of Senate Majority Leader Howard Baker, whose vote would be important on a number of other Senators' key projects. Finally, in 1983, after spending more than $1.7 billion, Congress agreed to close what one newspaper called the "Clinch River Rathole."

Many other anecdotal reports of the effects of logrolling can be found. See the article below for a particularly outlandish episode.

It Began as a Rather Ordinary Piece of Legislation*

By DAVID SHRIBMAN

Special to The New York Times

WASHINGTON, Nov. 8—It began last spring as a rather ordinary piece of legislation: some emergency highway money for states suffering flood damage.

Then both the House and Senate took turns lathering on projects worth $140 million. By last week the bill had grown to double its original cost, given a plum to the nation's trucking industry, included funds for one of House Speaker Thomas P. O'Neill Jr.'s favored projects, and provided miscellaneous "goodies," as one legislator put it, for a number of powerful Republicans.

Even now, a week after it passed the House, on a voice vote before a near-empty chamber, the legislation, known as the Surface Transportation Technical Corrections Act of 1983, evokes whispers, muffled laughter, and even some embarrassment in the chambers, cloakrooms, and anterooms of the Capitol. The history of the bill seems to show, once again, that while most members of Congress are, in principle, opposed to pork-barrel legislation, many members are able to finesse principle and vote for it, for the greater good of the home district.

"It depends on what section of the country you come from," said one lawmaker, "whether you regard this as legislation at its best or legislation at its worst."

Senate Action Is Blocked

With Congress worried about its own security, troubled about Ameri-

* By David Shribman, *The New York Times,* November 9, 1983. Copyright © 1983 by The New York Times Company. Reprinted by permission.

cans in Lebanon and the Caribbean, and concerned about the lingering budget deficit, the highway legislation is not one of the most visible items on Capitol Hill. It is one of the scores of bills that slip down the Congressional slide, the hand of skillful legislators often moving quicker than the eyes staring down from from the gallery.

Final Senate action on the package is being blocked by Senator Bob Packwood, Republican of Oregon, who was angered by the concession to the trucking industry. The affair has split Congress by houses rather than by party, and members on both sides are not working to resolve the stalemate.

The stream of new projects that the House added began with approval for planning and design funds for a portion of Interstate 93 known to Bostonians as the Central Artery. The Congressional provision, worth as much as $100 million, would be a major step toward a plan to depress the highway, which now bisects Boston, and to revitalize a portion of the city. The project has long been regarded as a favorite of Mr. O'Neill, a Massachusetts Democrat.

"To get the Central Artery we had to deal with the Republicans on the Public Works Committee," said one legislator. "They wouldn't bite for the atery unless they got a little something, too."

Here is what the Republicans got:

¶Improvements on a portion of a road that connects an interstate highway near Dry Ridge, Kentucky, with another highway near Owenton, Kentucky. The project is in the district of Representative Gene Snyder, the ranking Republican on the Public Works Committee. The cost: $20.5 million.

¶Widening a road connecting a community college with a new shopping mall in the Fort Smith, Arkansas, area. The project is in the district of Representative John Paul Hammerschmidt, the second ranking Republican on the committee. The cost: $8.5 million.

¶Improvements on a stretch of highway in Altoona, Pennsylvania. The project is in the district of Representative Bud Shuster, the third ranking Republican on the committee. The cost: $8 million.

¶Highway work in Moorehead, Minnesota. The project is in the district of Representative Arlan Stangeland, the fourth ranking Republican on the committee. The cost: $3 million.

"Let's just say that this has something for everyone," said Representative Bob Edgar, Democrat of Pennsylvania. "I would hope that with the high deficits that members of Congress would be a little embarrassed about this."

This bill and its ornaments, inevitably described on Capitol Hill as a "Christmas tree," is the product of an unusual set of circumstances. The legislation, without any of the projects, was passed routinely late this spring. The Senate added a provision involving the use of domestic materials in federally funded highway and transit projects, made some technical transfers of funds for projects in Atlanta and Baltimore, and expected the differences to be resolved in the customary fashion, by a House-Senate conference committee.

But the Senate additions opened the legislative floodgates, and instead of agreeing to a conference committee, the House decided to add a few more items of its own, beginning with the Boston highway project that Speaker O'Neill had coveted.

"I didn't know the House could do that," said Senator Daniel Patrick Moynihan, Democrat of New York, "but I guess they can do anything."

The additions came as the House sought unanimous consent for the additions, a procedure that gives any lawmaker a chance to object and, therefore, an opportunity to win inclusion of legislation he favors. That is how Representative Geraldine Ferraro, Democrat of Queens, won approval of a provision to give states more power to limit two-tandem trucks on portions of interstate highways.

'There Was No Other Way'

"I said I'd object," she said. "That was the only way to get everyone to sign onto it. I didn't want to do it that way. You don't make friends doing that kind of thing, but for me there was no other way."

By the time the House was finished with the bill, it included a number of other highway projects and a two-year extension of antitrust immunity for certain rate-making practices used by trucking companies. "We went to our friends and asked for this," said

George G. Mead, vice president for government relations for the American Trucking Associations. "We used our juice. We rattled our sabre."

The trucking companies' victory distressed Senator Packwood, who, as chairman of the Senate Commerce Committee, had offered the companies a three-year extension but who said he wanted to remove all of the companies' antitrust immunity.

"They added a whole bunch of projects, but adding truck deregulation was the straw that broke the camel's back," said Senator Robert T. Stafford, the Vermont Republican who heads the Senate Environment and Public Works Committee.

"We worked very hard to keep our bill clean," said Senator Lloyd Bentsen, Democrat of Texas. "These additions are a serious mistake. There are always those who try to do this, and they won't get away with it this time."

A large number of other voting schemes have been proposed and analyzed.[18] Like simple majority voting and logrolling, none has entirely desirable properties. The next section explains why.

Arrow's Impossibility Theorem

Our focus so far has been on how society solves the problem of deciding what quantities of public goods to provide. A more general problem is to evaluate the desirability of the entire allocation of resources. Can a rule be determined that indicates whether one state of affairs is socially more desirable than another? In the language of welfare economics, such a rule to guide public choice is called a **social welfare function.** In Chapter 4 it was *assumed* that a social welfare function existed. No attention was paid to where it came from. Is it necessarily

---

[18] These include point voting (each person is given a fixed number of "points" which are cast for the different alternatives), plurality voting (the alternative with the most votes wins), Borda counts (each alternative is ranked by each voter, and the ranks are totaled to choose), Condorcet elections (the alternative that defeats the rest in paired elections wins), and exhaustive voting (the proposal favored *least* by the largest number of voters is repeatedly removed until only one remains). See Mueller [1976] for further details.

the case that a group of people will be able to arrive at a social welfare function?

The answer depends on the characteristics required. Intuitively, it seems desirable that the function be consistent and that it reflect the preferences of society's members. Arrow [1951] suggested that a social welfare function should satisfy the following criteria:

1. It must rank all possible outcomes, and the ranking mut be consistent; if A is preferred to B, and B is preferred to C, then A is preferred to C.
2. It must be responsive to individuals' preferences. Specifically, assume that for a given set of preferences, A is socially preferred to B. Then if individual preferences change so that some people raise A to a higher rank, and no one lowers it in rank, then A remains socially preferred to B. In a sense, this is an antidiscrimination clause. If society is undertaking a given activity and a subgroup in the population which had been against the activity suddenly decides to favor it, society cannot go back and stop the activity just to "get" the subgroup.
3. Social preferences must satisfy the Pareto condition. Suppose that A is an allocation so that no member of society has a lower utility than at B, and one or more members have higher levels of utility at A than at B. In such a situation, the social welfare function must prefer A to B.
4. Dictatorship is ruled out. Social preferences must not reflect the preferences of only a single individual.
5. Society's preferences between any two alternatives must not depend upon the existence of other alternatives. Suppose that when alternatives A, B, and C are available, society prefers A to B and B to C. If option C were not available, the societal decision rule must still prefer A to B. This assumption is called the independence of irrelevant alternatives.

Taken together, these criteria seem quite reasonable. Basically, they say that society's choice mechanism should be logical and respect the preferences of individuals. Unfortunately, the stunning conclusion of Arrow's analysis is that in general it is *impossible* to find a social welfare function that satisfies all these criteria.[19] A democratic society cannot be expected to be able to make consistent decisions.

This result, sometimes called Arrow's Impossibility Theorem, thus casts doubt on the very ability of democracies to function. Naturally, the theorem has generated a great deal of debate, much of which has fo-

---

[19] The proof involves fairly sophisticated mathematics. The procedure of proof is to show that if all five conditions are imposed, then phenomena like the voting paradox can arise.

cused on whether other sets of criteria might allow formation of a social welfare function. It turns out that if any of the five criteria other than the first is dropped, a social welfare function that satisfies the other four *can* be constructed. But whether or not it is permissible to drop any of the criteria depends upon one's views of their ethical validity.

It is important to note that Arrow's theorem does not state that it is *necessarily* impossible to find a consistent social welfare function, but only that whether society will be able to do so cannot be guaranteed. For certain patterns of individual preferences, no problems arise. An obvious example is when members of society have identical preferences. Some radical theorists have suggested that the real significance of Arrow's theorem is it shows the need for a virtual uniformity of tastes if a democracy is to function. They then argue that many capitalist institutions have the express purpose of molding people's tastes to make sure that uniformity emerges. An example used is mandatory public education.

Others have argued that Arrow's theorem does not really have much to say about the viability of democratic processes. Buchanan [1960] views the inconsistencies of majority voting as having beneficial aspects:

> Majority rule is acceptable in a free society precisely because it allows a sort of jockeying back and forth among alternatives, upon none of which relative unanimity can be obtained. . . . It serves to insure that competing alternatives may be experimentally and provisionally adopted, tested, and replaced by new compromise alternatives approved by a majority group of ever-changing composition. This is democratic choice process, whatever may be the consequences for welfare economics and social welfare functions. [p. 83]

Another important question raised by Arrow's theorem concerns use of a social welfare function in economic analysis. If it does not "exist," can economists use the social welfare function to rank alternative states? A number of economists have rejected the function's use. They argue that it is merely a way of introducing ethical views about the desirability of various economic states and not a representation of "society's" preferences. As such, a social welfare function does not isolate the correct allocation of resources. However, most economists believe that the function is an important tool. It may not provide "the" answer, but can be used to draw out the implications of alternative sets of value judgments. As long as this interpretation is kept in mind, the social welfare function often helps to provide valuable insights.

OVERVIEW

The subjects of public goods and social choice are closely linked simply because the nature of public goods often requires that they be provided collectively.

Analysis of these subjects leaves one feeling vaguely pessimistic. The line between public and private goods is often hard to draw. Even if a good is public, it is not clear whether government provision is appropriate. And if public provision turns out to be called for, Arrow's theorem leads to severe doubts about the possibility of making consistent collective decisions. In short, the existence of public goods may imply government intervention, but decisions on how to intervene are very difficult to make. Perhaps this should come as no real surprise. It simply reflects the difficulties that people have always had in trying to devise good systems for making collective judgments.

Although the discussion of public decision making in this chapter sheds light on some important questions, it is based on a very unrealistic view of government. In this view, government is essentially a big computer that elicits from citizens their preferences and uses this information to try to produce social decisions. The state has no interests of its own; it is neutral and benign.

In fact, of course, government is done by *people*—politicians, judges, bureaucrats, and others. To understand the realities of public choice, one must study the goals and behavior of the people who govern. The results of such an analysis have implications for the ability of government to deal with *all* types of market failure, not just the public goods problem. Hence, a systematic analysis of government behavior is deferred until the other types of market failure have been discussed, and appears in Chapter 10.

SUMMARY

Public goods are characterized by nonrivalness and nonexcludability in consumption. Thus, each person consumes the same amount, but not necessarily the preferred amount, of the public good.

Efficient provision of public goods requires that the *sum* of the individual *MRS*s equal the *MRT*, unlike private goods where *each MRS* equals the *MRT*.

Market mechanisms are unlikely to provide public goods efficiently because people have the incentive to free ride on others, misrepresenting their preferences to pay less than the value of the good.

Casual observation and laboratory studies indicate that people do not fully exploit free riding possibilities. Nonetheless, in certain cases, free riding is likely to be a significant problem.

Economists have studied several methods of providing public goods:
  Lindahl pricing results in a unanimous decision to provide an efficient quantity of public goods, but relies on honest revelation of preferences.
  Majority voting may lead to inconsistent decisions regarding public goods if some people's preferences are not single peaked.

Logrolling allows voters to express the intensity of their preferences by trading votes. However, agenda control still affects the provision of public goods, and minority gains may come at the expense of greater general losses.

Arrow's Impossibility Theorem explains why each provision mechanism has problems. It states that in general it is impossible to find a social welfare function which simultaneously satisfies a number of apparently reasonable criteria. The implication is that democracies are inherently prone to inconsistency regarding public goods and other decisions.

Even though it may be impossible for a society to decide upon a social welfare function, the concept is still useful for many purposes.

DISCUSSION QUESTIONS

1. Which of the following do you consider public goods? Private goods? Why?
   a. Wilderness areas.
   b. Roads.
   c. Crime protection.
   d. Television programs.
   e. Education.
   f. Movies.

2. Tarzan and Jane live alone in the jungle and have trained Cheetah both to patrol the perimeter of their clearing and harvest tropical fruits. Cheetah can collect three pounds of fruit an hour and currently spends 6 hours patrolling, 8 hours picking, and 10 hours sleeping.
   a. What are the public and private goods in this example?
   b. If Tarzan and Jane are each currently willing to give up one hour of patrol for two pounds of fruit, is the current allocation of Cheetah's time Pareto efficient? Should he patrol more or less?

3. Suppose that there are five people—1, 2, 3, 4, and 5—who rank projects A, B, C, and D as follows:

1	2	3	4	5
A	A	D	C	B
D	C	B	B	C
C	B	C	D	D
B	D	A	A	A

   a. Sketch the preferences, as in Figure 6.8.
   b. Will any project be chosen by a majority vote rule? If so, which one? If not, explain why. Whose preferences are "at fault"?

4. Consider three "social states" that differ only in terms of the existence of a single tax program:

    a. A new tax is levied which results in all employees of the U.S. auto industry being laid off permanently.

    b. Another tax level results in some layoffs, but continued production.

    c. No tax is levied.

    In each case, the tax is used to buy national forest land.

      i. How would you rank choices **a, b,** and **c**?

     ii. Suppose **a** is not an option. Would you choose **b** or **c**?

   iii. Does the "social welfare function" indicated by your answers to **(i)** and **(ii)** satisfy the independence of irrelevant alternatives?

5. Suppose that in a given referendum, the conditions required for the median voter rule are satisfied. Construct an example to demonstrate that the outcome can be inefficient, i.e., that Equation (6.2) is violated. (Hint: Write down marginal benefits and marginal costs for each voter, and remember that the marginal costs [tax burdens] can differ across voters.)

SELECTED REFERENCES

Buchanan, James M. "Social Choice, Democracy, and Free Markets." In *Fiscal Theory and Political Economy—Selected Essays,* ed. James M. Buchanan. Chapel Hill: University of North Carolina Press, 1960, pp. 75–89.

Coase, Ronald H. "The Lighthouse in Economics." *Journal of Law and Economics,* October 1974, pp. 357–76.

Marwell, Gerald and Ruth E. Ames. "Economists Free Ride, Does Anyone Else? Experiments on the Provision of Public Goods, IV." *Journal of Public Economics* 15, no. 3 (June 1981), pp. 295–310.

Mueller, Dennis C. "Public Choice: A Survey." *The Journal of Economic Literature* 14, no. 2 (June 1976), pp. 395–433.

Samuelson, Paul A. "Diagrammatic Exposition of a Theory of Public Expenditure." *Review of Economics and Statistics* 37 (1955), pp. 350–56.

CHAPTER 7

Externalities

*We have always known that heedless self-interest was
bad morals; we know now that it is bad economics.*
Franklin D. Roosevelt

A common observation is that the world is becoming an ever more
interdependent place. The notion of interdependence occupies a central
position in economics. After all, that is what markets are all about—
people interacting as they trade goods and services.

Simple supply and demand models make it clear that people's actions
have consequences for the welfare of others. Suppose large numbers of
suburbanites decide that they want to live in an urban setting. As they
move to the city, the price of urban land increases. Urban property
owners are better off, but the welfare of tenants already there is lowered. Merchants in the city benefit from increased demand for their
products, while their suburban counterparts are worse off. By the time
the economy settles into a new equilibrium, the distribution of real
income has changed substantially.

In this example, all the effects are transmitted *via changes in market
prices.* Suppose that prior to the change in tastes, the allocation of resources was Pareto efficient. The shifts in supply and demand curves
change relative prices, but the Fundamental Theorem of Welfare Economics guarantees that these will be brought into equality with the
relevant marginal rates of substitution. Thus, the fact that the behavior
of some people can affect the welfare of others does *not* necessarily cause
"market failure." As long as the effects are transmitted via prices, there
are no adverse consequences for economic efficiency.[1]

---

[1] Of course, the new pattern of prices may be more or less desirable from a distributional point of view, depending upon one's ethical judgments as embodied in the social
welfare function.

However, people also affect each other in direct ways external to the market, often as the unintended by-product of some activity. Suppose that Sluggo operates a factory that dumps its garbage into a river nobody owns. Bill makes his living by fishing from the river. Sluggo's activities make Bill worse off in a direct way that is not the result of price changes. An **externality** occurs when the activity of one agent affects the welfare of another in a way that is outside the market. Unlike effects that are transmitted through market prices, externalities adversely affect economic efficiency.

In this chapter we will analyze these inefficiencies and possible remedies for them. One of the most important applications of externality theory has been the debate over environmental quality, and much of the discussion focuses on this issue.

THE NATURE OF EXTERNALITIES

In the pollution example just given, clean water is an input to Sluggo's production process. Clean water gets "used up" just like all other inputs: land, labor, capital, and materials. Clean water is also a scarce resource with alternative uses, such as fishing by Bill and swimming. As such, efficiency requires that for the water he uses, Sluggo should pay a price which reflects the fact that water is a scarce resource valued for other activities. Instead, Sluggo pays a zero price and as a consequence, uses the water in inefficiently large quantities.

Posing the externality problem this way allows us to expose its source. Sluggo uses his other inputs efficiently because he must pay their owners prices that reflect their value for alternative uses.[2] Otherwise, the owners of the inputs simply sell them elsewhere. However, if no one owns the river, everyone can use it for free. An externality, then, is a consequence of the failure or inability to establish property rights. If someone owned the river, then a price would have to be paid for its use, and the externality would not materialize.

Suppose that Bill owned the stream. He could charge Sluggo a fee for polluting which reflected the damage done to his catch. Sluggo would take these charges into account when making his production decisions and no longer use the water inefficiently. On the other hand, if Sluggo owned the stream, he could make money by charging Bill for the privilege of fishing in it. The amount of money that Bill would be willing to pay Sluggo for the right to fish in the stream would depend upon the amount of pollution present. Hence, Sluggo would have an incentive not to pollute "too much." Otherwise, he could not make much money from Bill.

---

[2] The situation is no different if Sluggo owns some of the inputs himself. In that case, the price "paid" by Sluggo is the income forgone by not selling those inputs to other producers.

The point is that as long as *someone* owns a resource, its price reflects the value for alternative uses, and the resource is therefore used efficiently. In contrast, resources that are owned in common are abused because no one has an incentive to economize in their use.

To expand on the subject, note the following characteristics of externalities:

First, they can be produced by consumers as well as firms. Just think of the person who smokes a cigar in a crowded room, lowering the welfare of others by using up the common resource, fresh air.

Second, externalities can be positive or negative. If I spray my trees to kill gypsy moths, my neighbors benefit directly by my actions. If there is no way to get them to pay me for these benefits, I do not consider them when deciding how much to spray, but I do less spraying than is justified by the beneficial spillovers I create. In the case of a positive externality, then, an inefficiently *low* level of the activity is undertaken.

Finally, public goods can be viewed as a special kind of externality. Specifically, when an agent creates an externality with full effects felt by every person in the economy, the externality is a pure public good. At times, the boundary between public goods and externalities is a bit fuzzy. In the tree-spraying example above, for instance, the classification would depend on the distance at which the effects of the insecticide dissipated. If I kill the whole community's gypsy moths, then I have, in effect, created a pure public good. If only a few neighbors are affected, then it is an externality. Although externalities and public goods are quite similar from a formal point of view, in practice it is usually useful to distinguish between them.

GRAPHICAL ANALYSIS[3]

Figure 7.1 analyzes the Sluggo-Bill example described earlier. The horizontal axis measures the amount of output, Q, produced by Sluggo's factory, and the vertical axis measures dollars. The curve labeled MB indicates the marginal benefit to Sluggo of each level of output; it is assumed to decline as output increases. Think of MB as showing the incremental revenue that Sluggo receives from the sale of each unit of output. Also associated with each level of output is some marginal *private* cost, MPC. Marginal private costs reflect payments made by Sluggo to the factors of production, and are assumed here to increase with output. As a by-product of its activities, the factory produces pollution which makes Bill worse off. Assume that as the factory's output, Q, increases, so does the amount of pollution it creates. The marginal damage inflicted upon Bill by the pollution at each level of output is denoted

---

[3] It is assumed throughout this section that there are no other inefficiencies in the economy.

FIGURE 7.1   An Externality Problem

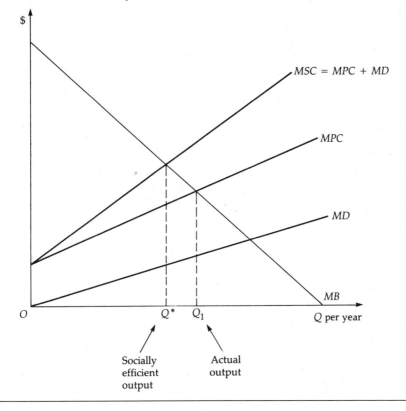

by *MD*. *MD* is drawn sloping upward, reflecting the assumption that as Bill is subjected to pollution, he becomes worse off at an increasing rate.

If Sluggo is interested in maximizing profits, how much output does he produce? Sluggo produces each unit of output for which the marginal benefit *to him* exceeds the marginal cost *to him*.[4] In terms of Figure 7.1, he produces all levels of output for which *MB* exceeds *MPC*, but does not produce where *MPC* exceeds *MB*. Thus, he produces up to the output at which *MPC* intersects *MB*, at output Q_1.

From the point of view of society, production should take place as long as the marginal benefit *to society* exceeds the marginal cost *to society*. The marginal cost to society has two components. First is the inputs purchased by Sluggo. Their value is reflected in *MPC*. Second is the marginal damage done to Bill as reflected in *MD*. Hence, marginal social cost is *MPC plus MD*. Graphically, the marginal social cost schedule is

---

[4] This reasoning is a typical example of marginal analysis in economics. See the appendix to the book for further explanation.

found by adding together the heights of *MPC* and *MD* at each level of output. It is depicted in Figure 7.1 as *MSC*. Note that by construction, the vertical distance between *MSC* and *MPC* is *MD*. (Because *MSC* = *MPC* + *MD*, it follows that *MSC* − *MPC* = *MD*.)

Efficiency from a social point of view requires production of only those units of output for which *MSC* exceeds *MB*. Thus, output should be produced just up to the point at which the schedules intersect, at Q^*.

Implications.   This analysis suggests several observations, as described below.

First, unlike the case in which externalities are absent, there is no reason to expect private markets to produce the socially efficient level of output. In particular, when a good is associated with a negative externality, "too much" of it is produced relative to the efficient output.[5]

Second, the model not only shows that efficiency would be enhanced by a move from Q_1 to Q^*, but also provides a way to measure the benefits from doing so. Figure 7.2 replicates from Figure 7.1 the marginal benefit (*MB*), marginal private cost (*MPC*), marginal damage (*MD*), and marginal social cost (*MSC*) schedules. When output is cut from Q_1 to Q^*, Sluggo loses profits. To calculate the precise size of his loss, recall that the *marginal* profit associated with any unit of output is the difference between marginal benefit and marginal private cost. If the marginal private cost of the eighth unit is $10 and its marginal benefit is $12, then the marginal profit is $2. Geometrically, the marginal profit on a given unit of output is the vertical distance between *MB* and *MPC*. If Sluggo is forced to cut back from Q_1 to Q^*, he therefore loses the difference between the *MB* and *MPC* curves for each unit of production between Q_1 and Q^*. In Figure 7.2, this is represented as area *dcg*.

At the same time, however, Bill becomes better off because the less Sluggo produces, the fewer the damages done to Bill's fishery. For each unit that Sluggo's output is reduced, Bill gains an amount equal to the marginal damage associated with the unit of output. In Figure 7.2, Bill's gain for each unit of output reduction is the vertical distance between *MD* and the horizontal axis. Therefore, Bill's gain when output is reduced from Q_1 to Q^* is the area under the marginal damage curve between Q^* and Q_1, *abfe*. Now note that *abfe* equals area *cdhg*. This is by construction—the vertical distance between *MSC* and *MPC* is *MD*, which is the same as the vertical distance between *MD* and the horizontal axis.

In sum, if output were reduced from Q_1 to Q^*, Sluggo would lose area

---

[5] Note that this model assumes the only way to reduce pollution is to reduce output. If antipollution technology is available, it may be possible to maintain output and still reduce pollution. However, the analysis is basically the same, since the adoption of the technology requires the use of resources.

FIGURE 7.2   Gains and Losses from Moving to an Efficient Level of Output

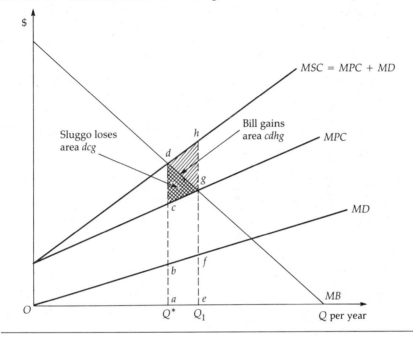

dcg and Bill would gain area *cdhg*. If from society's point of view, a dollar to Sluggo is equivalent to a dollar to Bill, then moving from Q_1 to Q^* yields a net gain to society equal to the difference between *cdhg* and *dcg*, which is *dhg*.

Third, the analysis implies that zero pollution is not socially desirable as a general rule. Finding the "right" amount of pollution requires trading off its benefits and costs, and this generally occurs at some positive level of pollution. Because virtually all productive activity involves some pollution, the requirement that pollution be set at zero would be equivalent to no production whatsoever, clearly an inefficient solution. If all this seems only like common sense, it is. But note that the U.S. Congress has set as a national goal that "the discharge of pollutants into the navigable waters be eliminated by 1985" [Baumol and Oates, 1979, p. 211]. The adoption of such infeasible objectives is not only silly, but, as shall be argued later, may actually hinder *any* movement away from points like Q_1.

Finally, to implement the framework of Figure 7.2, it is not enough to be able to draw some hypothetical marginal damage and benefit curves. Their actual shapes for any given pollutant must be determined, at least approximately. However, difficult practical questions arise when it comes to identifying and valuing the damage done by pollution.

What Activities Produce Pollutants?   The types and quantities of pollution associated with various production processes must be identified. Consider "acid rain," a phenomenon that has caused widespread concern. Scientists have shown that acid rain forms when sulfur oxides and nitrogen oxides emitted into the air react with water vapor to create acids. These acids fall to earth in rain and snow, increasing the general level of acidity with potentially harmful effects on plant and animal life.

However, it is not known just how much of acid rain is associated with productive activities and how much with natural activities such as plant decay and volcanic eruptions. Moreover, it is hard to determine what amounts of nitrogen and sulfur emissions generated in a given region eventually become acid rain. It depends in part on local weather conditions and in part on the extent to which other pollutants such as nonmethane hydrocarbons are present. Finally, some scientific studies have indicated there is no strong evidence that acidification has been getting worse over time [Funkhauser, 1983, p. A27].

Which Pollutants Do Harm?   The ability of health practitioners to conduct large-scale controlled experiments on the effects of pollution is severely limited. Hence, it is often difficult to pinpoint just what effect a given pollutant has. Recently, considerable alarm has been caused by the presence of the waste product dioxin in certain areas. Dioxin has been shown to be toxic to some animals. But it is unknown just what concentrations of the chemical are dangerous to humans or how long it takes for the bad effects to manifest themselves. Some scientists have argued that dioxin does not pose much of a problem, while others believe that it merits extreme concern [Boffey, 1983, p. 1]. This kind of uncertainty can obviously lead to serious problems in formulating environmental policy. Lave and Omenn [1981, p. 45] argue that some of the air pollutants which have been the focus of U.S. environmental policy are considerably less dangerous than other pollutants that are officially ignored.

What Is the Value of the Damage Done?   Even if the physical damage a pollutant creates is determined, the value of getting rid of it must be calculated. When economists think about measuring the "value" of something, typically they think in terms of people's willingness to pay for it. If you are willing to pay $162 for a bicycle, that is its "value" to you.

Unlike bicycles, there is no explicit market in which pollution is bought and sold. How then can people's marginal willingness to pay for pollution removal be measured? Some attempts have been made to infer it indirectly by studying housing prices. When people shop for houses, they consider both the quality of the house itself and the characteristics of the neighborhood, such as cleanliness of the streets and quality of schools. Suppose in addition that families care about the level of air pollution in the neighborhoods. Consider two identical houses situated in two identical neighborhoods, except that the first is in an unpolluted area, and the second is in a polluted area. We expect that the house in the unpolluted area has a higher price. This price differential measures people's willingness to pay for clean air.

These observations suggest a natural strategy for estimating people's willingness to pay for clean air. Examine houses that are identical in all respects except for the surrounding air quality and compare their prices. The apparent problem is to find such houses. Luckily, the necessity of doing so can be avoided if the statistical technique of multiple regression analysis is used (see Chapter 3). Harrison and Rubinfeld [1978] used data from 1970 to estimate a regression equation in which the left-hand variable is the value of owner-occupied homes in a given community.[6] The right-hand variables include the factors that should influence house value: number of rooms, age of house, crime rate in the town, etc. The right-hand side also includes a measure of air pollution, the concentration of nitrogen oxide measured in parts per hundred million.

If the equation is specified correctly, then the parameter multiplying the nitrogen oxide variable indicates the *independent* effect of the pollutants on house values, and hence, people's willingness to pay for their removal. Harrison and Rubinfeld's estimates [1978, p. 91] suggest that when the annual average concentration of nitrogen oxide is about five parts per hundred million, a middle-income family would be willing to pay almost $1,500 for a one part per hundred million improvement. (In their sample, the average value of a home was $22,532.)

As stressed in Chapter 3, the validity of econometric analysis depends in part upon the completeness with which the model is specified. If there are important determinants of housing prices omitted by Harrison and Rubinfeld, then their estimate of the pollution effect may be unreliable. More fundamentally, the use of a willingness-to-pay measure can be questioned. People may be ignorant about the effects of air pollution upon their health, and hence underestimate the value of reducing it. The econometric approach is promising, but it does not close the debate.

We conclude that implementing the framework of Figure 7.2 requires the skills of biologists, engineers, ecologists, and health practitioners, among others. A resolutely interdisciplinary approach to investigating the pollution problem is needed. Having said this, however, it must be emphasized that even with superb engineering and biological data, sensible decisions simply cannot be reached without applying the economist's tool of marginal analysis.

---

[6] Specifically, it is the logarithm of the median value of owner-occupied homes.

POSSIBLE REMEDIES: HOW DO WE GET FROM HERE TO THERE?

A number of alternative solutions for achieving the efficient level of output Q^* have been proposed, as follows.[7]

Taxes

Sluggo produces inefficiently because the prices he faces for inputs incorrectly signal social costs. Specifically, because his input prices are "too low," the price of his output is "too low." A natural solution, suggested by the British economist A.C. Pigou, is to levy a tax on the polluter that makes up for the fact that some of his inputs are priced too low. A **Pigouvian tax** is a tax levied upon each unit of a polluter's output in an amount just equal to the marginal damage it inflicts *at the efficient level of output.* Figure 7.3 reproduces the example of Figures 7.1 and 7.2. In this case, the marginal damage done at the efficient output Q^* is distance *cd.* This is the Pigouvian tax. (Remember that the vertical distance between *MSC* and *MPC* is *MD.*)

FIGURE 7.3   Analysis of a Pigouvian Tax

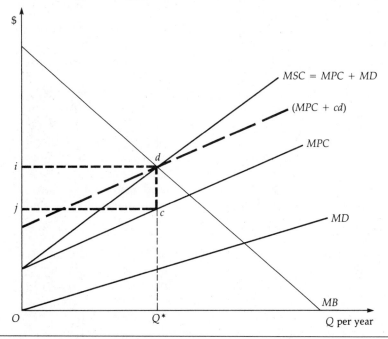

How does Sluggo react if a tax of *cd* dollars per unit of output is imposed? The tax raises Sluggo's effective marginal cost. For each unit he produces, Sluggo has to make payments both to the suppliers of his inputs (measured by *MPC*) *and* to the tax collector (measured by *cd*). Geometrically, Sluggo's new marginal cost schedule is found by adding *cd* to *MPC* at each level of output. This is done by shifting up *MPC* by a vertical distance equal to *cd*.

Profit maximization requires that Sluggo produce up to the output at which marginal benefit equals marginal cost. This now occurs at the intersection of *MB* and *MPC* + *cd* which is at the efficient output Q^*. In effect, the tax forces Sluggo to take into account the costs of the externality that he generates, and hence, induces him to produce efficiently. Note that the tax brings in revenue of *cd* dollars for each of the *id* units produced ($id = OQ^*$). Hence, tax revenue is $cd \times id$, which is equal to area of rectangle *ijcd* in Figure 7.3.[8] It would be tempting to use these revenues to compensate Bill, who still is being hurt by Sluggo's activities, although to a lesser extent than before the tax. However, caution must be exercised. If it becomes known that anyone who fishes along the river receives compensation for fishing there, then some people may choose to fish there who otherwise would not have done so. Then an inefficiently large amount of fishing would be done in the river. The key point is that compensation to the victim of the pollution is not necessary to achieve efficiency.

There are practical problems in implementing a Pigouvian tax scheme. In light of the above-mentioned difficulties in estimating the marginal damage function, it is bound to be hard to find the "correct" tax rate. Still, sensible compromises can be made. Suppose that a certain type of automobile produces noxious fumes. In theory, a tax based upon the number of miles driven will enhance efficiency. But a tax based on mileage might be so cumbersome to administer as to be infeasible. The government might instead consider levying a special sales tax upon the car, even though it is not ownership of the car per se that determines the size of the externality, but the amount it is driven. The sales tax would not lead to the most efficient possible result, but it still might lead to a substantial improvement over the status quo.

More generally, the tax approach assumes that it is known who is doing the polluting and in what quantities. In many cases, these questions are very hard to answer. Of course, the relevant issue is not whether Pigouvian taxes are a perfect method of dealing with externalities, but whether or not they are likely to be better than the other alternatives. In the few places where such taxes have been tried, such as the Ruhr River Basin in West Germany, they appear to have been rather successful [Baumol and Oates, 1979, Chapter 18].

---

[8] It is assumed that these tax revenues are spent by the government in such a way that none of the schedules in Figure 7.3 changes position.

Subsidies

The efficient level of production can be obtained by paying the polluter not to pollute. Although this notion may at first seem peculiar, it works in very much the same way as the tax scheme. This is because a subsidy for not polluting is simply another method of raising the polluter's effective cost of production.

Suppose that the government announces that it will pay Sluggo a subsidy of *cd* for each unit of output that he does *not* produce. What will Sluggo do? In Figure 7.4, Sluggo's marginal benefit at output level Q_1 is

FIGURE 7.4   Analysis of a Pigouvian Subsidy

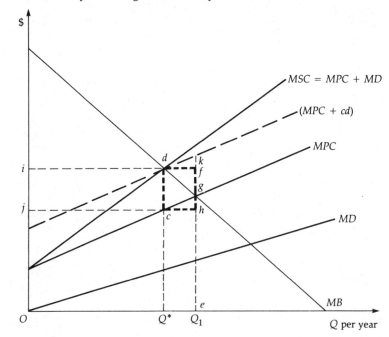

measured by the distance between *MB* and the horizontal axis, *ge*. The marginal cost of producing at Q_1 is the sum of the amount that Sluggo pays for his inputs (which we read off the *MPC* curve), *and* the subsidy of *cd* which he foregoes by producing. Once again, then, the perceived marginal cost schedule is *MPC* + *cd*. At output Q_1, this is distance *ek* (= *eg* + *gk*). But *ek* exceeds the marginal benefit, *ge*. As long as the marginal cost exceeds the marginal benefit, it does not make sense for Sluggo to produce the Q_1st unit of output. Instead, he should forego its production and accept the subsidy. The same line of reasoning indicates that Sluggo will choose not to produce any output in excess of Q^*. At all output levels to the right of Q^*, the sum of the marginal private cost and the subsidy exceeds the marginal benefit. On the other hand, at all points to the left of Q^*, it is worthwhile for Sluggo to produce even though he has to give up the subsidy. For these output levels, the total opportunity cost, $MPC + cd$, is less than the marginal benefit. Hence, the subsidy induces Sluggo to produce just to Q^*, the efficient output.

The distributional consequences of the tax and subsidy schemes differ dramatically. Instead of having to pay the tax of $idcj$, Sluggo receives a payment equal to the number of units of foregone production, ch, times the subsidy per unit, cd, which equals rectangle $dfhc$ in Figure 7.4. That an efficient solution can be associated with different income distributions is no surprise. It is analogous to the result from Chapter 4; there is an infinite number of efficient allocations in the Edgeworth Box, each of which is associated with its own distribution of real income.

In addition to the problems associated with the Pigouvian tax scheme, the subsidy program has a few of its own. To determine the size of the subsidy, the government must know Q_1, the output that Sluggo would have produced in the absence of any government intervention. Such information is *not* required for the tax scheme. This distinction is crucial because under the subsidy program, Sluggo has an incentive to exaggerate the size of his profit-maximizing output. The more production he can claim to be foregoing, the greater the payments to which he is entitled. Administration of a subsidy program would require measures to deal with this kind of problem.

Second, the analysis is short run in that it does not involve the possibility that the number of polluting firms will change. The subsidy leads to higher profits, so firms which would not have located along the river may be induced to do so by the lure of these profits. Hence, the subsidy may induce an inefficiently large amount of production along the river.

Third, the subsidy payments have to be raised by taxes levied somewhere in the economy. In general, taxation distorts people's incentives. And it is not obvious that these distortion effects would be less costly than the externality itself. (The efficiency costs of taxation are discussed in detail in Chapter 12.)

Finally, subsidies may be undesirable from a moral perspective. As Mishan [1971a, pp. 24–25] notes:

> It may be argued [that] the freedom to operate noisy vehicles, or pollutive plant, does incidentally damage the welfare of others, while the freedom desired by members of the public to live in clean and quite surroundings does not, of itself, reduce the welfare of others. If such arguments can be sustained, there is a case . . . for making polluters legally liable.

Auction Pollution Permits

Another method of achieving Q^* is to sell producers permits to pollute. The government announces that it will sell permits to dump into the river the amount of garbage associated with output Q^*. Firms bid for the right to own these permissions to pollute, and the permissions go to the firms with the highest bids. The fee charged is that which "clears the market"—the amount of pollution equals the level set by the government.

In the simple model, the pollution permit and the Pigouvian tax are identical. Both achieve the efficient level of pollution. Implementing both requires knowledge of who is polluting and in what quantities. Baumol and Oates [1979, p. 251] argue that pollution permits have some advantages over the tax scheme from a practical point of view. One of the most important is that the permit scheme reduces uncertainty about the ultimate level of pollution. If the government is *certain* about the shapes of the marginal private cost and marginal benefit schedules of Figure 7.3, then it can safely predict how a Pigouvian tax will affect behavior. But if there is misinformation about these schedules, it is hard to know for sure how much a particular tax will reduce pollution. If the authorities can make a reasonable guess about the appropriate level of pollution, there is more certainty that the policy will achieve it.

Moreover, when the economy is experiencing inflation, the market price of pollution rights would be expected to keep pace automatically, while changing the tax rate could require a lengthy administrative procedure. On the other hand, one possible problem with the auctioning scheme is that large firms might be able to buy up pollution licenses in excess of the firms' cost-minimizing requirements to deter other firms from entering the market. Whether such strategic behavior is likely to occur is hard to predict.

Establish Property Rights

If the root cause of an externality is the absence of property rights, then perhaps the most straightforward way to "cure" the problem is to put the resource in question into private hands. Suppose that property rights to the river are assigned to Sluggo. Assume further that it is costless for Bill and Sluggo to bargain with each other. Is it possible for the two parties to strike a bargain which will result in output being reduced from Q_1?

Sluggo would be willing to not produce a given unit of output as long as he received a payment which exceeded his net incremental gain from producing that unit ($MB - MPC$). On the other hand, Bill would be willing to pay Sluggo not to produce a given unit as long as the payment were less than the marginal damage done to him, MD. As long as the amount that Bill is willing to pay Sluggo exceeds the cost to Sluggo of not producing, then the opportunity for a bargain exists. Algebraically, the requirement is that $MD > (MB - MPC)$. Figure 7.5 (which reproduces the information from Figure 7.1) indicates that at output Q_1,

FIGURE 7.5   Coase Theorem

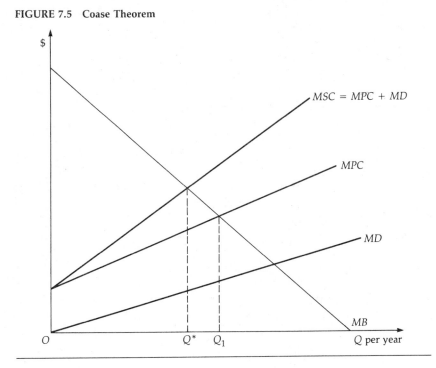

$MB - MPC$ is zero, while MD is positive. Hence, MD exceeds $MB - MPC$, and there is scope for a bargain.

Similar reasoning indicates that the payment Bill would be willing to make exceeds $MB - MPC$ at every output level to the right of Q^*. In contrast, to the left of Q^*, the amount of money that Sluggo would demand to reduce his output would exceed what Bill would be willing to pay. Hence, Bill pays Sluggo to reduce output just to Q^*, the efficient level. We cannot tell without more information exactly how much Bill will end up paying Sluggo. This depends upon the relative bargaining strengths of the two parties. Regardless of how the gains from the bargain are divided, however, production ends up at Q^*.

Now suppose that the shoe is put on the other foot, and Bill is assigned the property rights to the stream. The bargaining process now consists of Sluggo paying Bill for Bill's permission to pollute. Bill is willing to accept some pollution as long as the payment is greater than the marginal damage (MD) to his fishing enterprise. Sluggo finds it worthwhile to pay for the privilege of producing as long as the amount is less than the value of $MB - MPC$ for that unit of output. Reasoning similar to that above suggests that they have every incentive to reach an agreement whereby Bill sells Sluggo the right to produce at Q^*.

The conclusion is that the efficient solution will be achieved *independently* of who is assigned the property rights, as long as *someone* is assigned those rights. This result, known as the **Coase Theorem,** implies that once property rights are established, no government intervention is required to deal with externalities [Coase, 1960]. The Coase Theorem is especially attractive to those who are predisposed against government intervention in the economy. However, there are at least two reasons society cannot always depend upon the Coase Theorem to "solve" externality problems.

First, the theorem requires that the costs of bargaining do not deter the parties from finding their way to the efficient solution. However, externalities like air pollution involve literally millions of people (both polluters and pollutees). It is difficult to imagine them getting together for negotiations at a sufficiently low cost.[9]

Second, the theorem assumes that resource owners can identify the source of damages to their property and legally prevent the damages. Consider again the important case of air pollution. Even if property rights to air were established, it is not clear how owners would be able to identify which of thousands of potential polluters was responsible for dirtying their air space and for what proportion of the damage each was liable.

The Coase Theorem, then, is most relevant for cases in which there are a few parties involved and the sources of the externality are well defined.

Regulation

Under regulation, each polluter is told to reduce pollution by a certain amount or else face legal sanctions. In terms of the diagrammatic analysis, Sluggo would simply be ordered to reduce output to Q^*.

Regulation is likely to be inefficient when there is more than one firm. To see this, assume that there are two firms, X and Z, which generate the same externality. In Figure 7.6, output of firms X and Z is measured on the horizontal axis and dollars on the vertical. MB_X is the marginal benefit schedule for X and MB_Z the schedule for Z. For expositional ease only, X and Z are assumed to have identical MPC schedules and profit-maximizing outputs $X_1 = Z_1$.

Suppose it is known that the marginal damage at the efficient level of total output is d dollars. Then efficiency requires that each firm produce at the point of intersection of its marginal benefit curve with the sum of its marginal private cost curve and d. The efficient outputs are denoted

---

[9] Of course, as we have emphasized earlier, there is no guarantee that the transactions costs of implementing a government solution will be less.

FIGURE 7.6   Two Polluting Firms

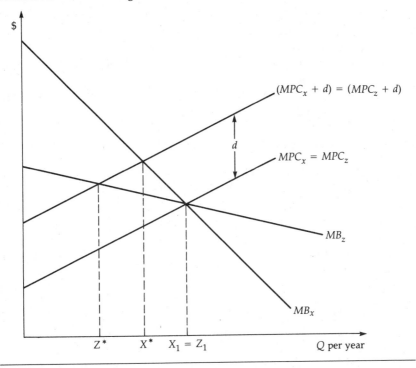

X^* and Z^* in Figure 7.6. The crucial thing to observe is that efficiency does *not* require the firms to reduce pollution equally. The efficient reduction in production of Z is much greater than the of X. Here this is due to different MB schedules, but in general, each firm's appropriate reduction in output depends upon the shapes of its marginal benefit *and* marginal private cost curves. Hence, a regulatory rule that mandates all firms to cut back by equal amounts (either in absolute or proportional terms) leads to some firms producing too much and others too little.

   Intuitively, this analysis simply illustrates that the costs and benefits of pollution reduction are likely to differ from case to case. A car that operates in a relatively uninhabited area creates less damage than one that operates in a heavily polluted area. What sense does it make for both cars to have exactly the same emissions standard? Under U.S. policy, all cars must meet standards that were set to improve the air quality in just a half dozen heavily polluted cities. Clearly the policy is inefficient. Of course, the regulatory body could assign each polluter its specially designed production quota. But in the presence of a large number of polluters, this is administratively infeasible.

Evaluation

Except in cases where the Coase Theorem is likely to be relevant, the presence of externalities requires some kind of intervention to achieve efficiency. Implementing any environmental policy entails a host of difficult technical issues. No policy is likely to do a perfect job. However, of the options available, most economists prefer Pigouvian taxes or the sale of pollution permits. Generally, these are more likely to achieve efficient outcomes than is either subsidies or direct regulation.

THE U.S. RESPONSE: THE CLEAN AIR ACT

How do real-world responses to externality problems compare to the solutions suggested by theory? The main federal law dealing with air pollution is the Clean Air Act of 1963 and subsequent amendments.[10] In the clean air amendments passed in 1970, Congress set national air quality standards that were to be met *independent of the costs of doing so*. An Environmental Protection Agency (EPA) was established to set the standards, and ensure that the states attained the standards by 1975. In short, the U.S. response has been regulation rather than market incentives.

Has the Clean Air Act accomplished its goals? By and large, the cleanup deadline has been ignored even by the Congress [Lave & Omenn, 1981, p. 9]. In 1982, EPA officials indicated that between 400 and 500 counties, in every state except North Dakota, were in violation of at least one standard [Shabecoff, 1982, p. 14E]. Effective control of air pollution has not occurred.

We have already shown why a regulatory approach like the Clean Air Act is likely to be inefficient. Why has it been so ineffectual as well? Baumol [1976] emphasizes how the efficacy of regulation depends upon the vigilance of the regulator, that is:

> the promptness with which orders are issued, the severity of their provisions, the strength of the regulator's resistance to demands for modifications, his effectiveness in detecting and documenting violations, his vigor and success in prosecuting them, and the severity of the penalties imposed by the judicial mechanism. [p. 445]

This is a tall order, especially considering the political pressures under which the regulator is likely to be acting. In contrast, Pigouvian taxes "depend not on the watchfulness of the regulator but on the reliable tenacity of the tax collector. They work by *inviting* the polluter to avoid his payments through the loophole deliberately left to him—the reduction of his emissions" [Baumol, 1976, p. 446].

---

[10] An excellent summary of the act's provisions is provided by Lave and Omenn [1981].

In addition, L. J. White [1976] has documented how the "or else" approach of regulation often backfires. The ultimate threat is to close down the polluting factory. In many cases, however, such closure would create major dislocations among workers and/or consumers and is therefore politically unthinkable. Hence, the regulator's threat is not credible, and pollution continues. A tax, in contrast, is not nearly so unwieldy a policy instrument.

White's analysis is consistent with a rather bizarre political situation that developed in late 1982. Environmentalists accused the head of the EPA under President Ronald Reagan, Ann Gorsuch, of trying to gut the Clean Air Act and thus expose the environment to damage. What action prompted these charges? All she did was announce her intention to stringently carry out the provisions of the act! Gorsuch threatened to impose the statutory sanctions for areas that did not meet air quality standards. The sanctions included withholding federal highway funds and federal grants [Mrs. Gorsuch, 1982]. Presumably, both Gorsuch and the environmentalists realized that actually enforcing the law would lead to a public outcry and perhaps an eventual change in the statute.

This is not to say that the direct regulation is never useful. When very toxic substances are involved, it might be the best solution. But in general, the regulatory approach is probably the source of much of the failure in environmental policy. Why then is it so popular? Perhaps legislators like the immediate sense of "doing something" that enacting regulations gives them, even though more passive measures like Pigouvian taxes would probably do the job better. A cynic would argue that the regulatory solution is the result of politicians' desire to have it both ways: Pass noble sounding legislation to please environmentalists, but make it unworkable to keep business happy.

IMPLICATIONS FOR INCOME DISTRIBUTION

Our main focus so far has been on the efficiency aspects of externalities. Welfare economics indicates that to maximize social welfare requires taking distributional as well as efficiency considerations into account. However, attempts to assess the distributional implications of environmental improvement raise a number of difficult questions.

Who Benefits from Pollution Reduction?   In our simple model, the distribution of benefits is a trivial issue because there is only one type of pollution and one pollution victim. In reality, there are many different types of individuals who suffer differently from various externalities. There is some evidence that poor neighborhoods tend to have more exposure to air pollution than those inhabited by high-income individuals [Baumol and Oates, 1979, p. 178]. If this is true, lowering the level of air pollution might make the distribution of real income more equal, other things being the same. On the other hand, the benefits of environmental programs which enhance the quality of recreational areas such as national parks probably benefit mainly high-income families, who tend to be their main users [Baumol and Oates, 1979, p. 180].

Even knowledge of who is suffering from a given externality does not tell us how much it is worth to them to have it removed. Accounting for willingness to pay can have a major impact on conclusions about the distribution of benefits. Suppose that a high-income family would be willing to pay more for a given improvement in air quality than a low-income family. Then even if a cleanup program reduces more of the *physical* amount of pollution for low-than high-income families, in *dollar* terms the program can end up favoring those with high incomes.

Who Bears the Costs of Pollution Reduction?   Suppose that large numbers of polluting firms are induced to reduce output by government policy. As these firms contract, the demand for the inputs they employ falls, which tends to make the owners of these inputs worse off.[11] Some of the polluters' former workers may suffer unemployment in the short run and be forced to work at lower wages in the long run. If these workers have low incomes, environmental cleanup makes the distribution of real income more unequal.

The extent to which the poor bear the costs of environmental protection is a source of bitter public controversy. A critic of environmentalism argued "Let's face it, a family in Harlem or the Texas barrio is a lot more concerned about jobs and cheap electricity than in visiting the beautiful wilderness. . . . Where's the sensitivity and concern to those people by all these organizations and groups litigating in the District of Columbia?"[12] Environmentalists have labeled such assertions as "job blackmail," and argue that there is no good evidence that the poor are really hurt.

Another consideration is that if polluting firms are forced to take into account marginal social costs, their products will tend to become more expensive. From an efficiency point of view, this is totally desirable, because otherwise prices give incorrect signals concerning full resource costs. Nevertheless, there will be a tendency for buyers of these commodities to be made worse off.[13] If the commodities so affected tend to be consumed primarily by high-income groups, then the distribution of real income will become more equal, other things being the same. Thus, to assess the distributional implications of reducing pollution, we also

---

[11] More specifically, under certain conditions, those inputs used relatively intensively in the production of the polluting good will suffer income losses. See Chapter 11.

[12] Dan M. Burt, quoted in "In Watt's Corner," *San Francisco Chronicle*, October 1, 1981, p. 18. For further argument along these lines, see Tucker [1982].

[13] One cannot know a priori how high consumer prices will rise. It depends upon the shapes of the supply and demand schedules. See Chapter 11.

need to know the pattern of demand for the goods produced by polluting companies.

It is obviously a formidable task to determine how the costs of pollution control have been distributed. In one careful study, Dorfman and Snow [1975] estimated that the higher a family's income, the *smaller* the proportion of its income reduced by antipollution measures. They estimated that in 1976, for a household in the lowest fifth of the income distribution, pollution controls cost between 2 and 2.5 percent of family income. For a household in the highest fifth of the income distribution, the figure was closer to 1.8 percent. If these results are correct, they pose a serious dilemma for those who favor *both* a more equal income distribution and a cleaner environment.

A CAUTIONARY NOTE ON POSITIVE EXTERNALITIES

Most of the focus in this chapter has been on negative externalities. We did observe, however, that spillover effects could just as well be positive. The formal analysis of this case is symmetrical. Suppose that when a scientist does research, the marginal private benefit *(MPB)* and marginal cost *(MC)* schedules are as depicted in Figure 7.7. The scientist chooses research output R_1, where $MC = MPB$. Assume further that the

FIGURE 7.7   A Positive Externality

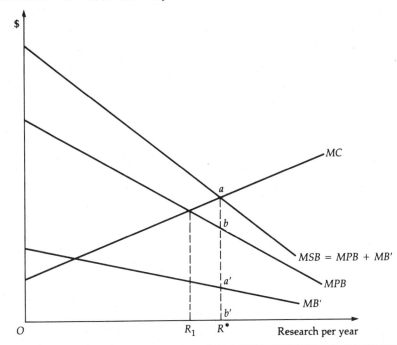

scientist's work enables industrial firms to produce their products more cheaply, but that the firms do not have to pay for using scientific results because these are part of "general knowledge."[14] In Figure 7.7, the marginal benefit to other firms of each quantity of research is denoted MB'. The marginal *social* benefit of research is the sum of MPB and MB', which is depicted as schedule MSB.

Efficiency requires the equality of marginal cost and marginal *social* benefit, which occurs at R^*. Hence, an insufficient quantity of research is done. Just as a negative externality can be corrected by a Pigouvian tax, a positive externality can be corrected by a Pigouvian subsidy. Specifically, if the scientist is given a subsidy equal to the marginal external benefit at the optimum—distance ab in Figure 7.7—the scientist will be induced to produce efficiently.[15] The lesson is clear: When an individual or firm produces positive externalities, the market will underprovide the activity or good, but an appropriate subsidy can remedy the situation.[16]

Implications

Many people who have never heard the term "positive externality" nevertheless have a good intuitive grasp of the concept and its policy implications. They understand that if they can convince the government their activities create beneficial spillovers, they may be able to dip into the treasury for a subsidy. When requests for such subsidies are considered, two factors should be kept in mind:

1. One way or another, the subsidy has to come from resources extracted from taxpayers. Hence, implicit in all subsidies is a redistribution of income from taxpayers as a whole to the particular recipients. Even if the efficiency consequences of the subsidy are desirable, the distributional implications may not be. This depends upon the value judgments embodied in the social welfare function.
2. When the presence of a beneficial externality is claimed, its precise nature must be determined. The fact that an activity is socially desirable per se does *not* mean that a subsidy is required for efficiency. A subsidy is appropriate only if the market does not allow those performing the activity to capture the full marginal return. For example, a brilliant surgeon who does much good for humanity creates no positive externality as long as the surgeon's salary reflects the incremental value of his or her services.

We illustrate these points with two examples.

---

[14] If the scientist produces an invention, then this type of situation can partially be avoided by patent laws. But in many cases, the results of "pure" research are not patentable, even though they may be used for commercial purposes.

[15] Note that by construction, $ab = a'b'$.

[16] All the difficulties concerning problems in measuring the quantity and value of the externality are still relevant.

Owner-Occupied Housing. Through a variety of provisions in the U.S. federal income tax code, owner-occupied housing receives a substantial subsidy. (These provisions are detailed in Chapter 15.) It is estimated that this subsidy was worth almost $32 billion to the 65 percent of American families who were homeowners in 1981. [Congressional Budget Office, 1981, p. 39]. How can this subsidy be justified? Arguments usually boil down to an assertion that home ownership creates positive externalities. Homeowners take good care of their property, keep it clean, etc., all of which makes the other people in their neighborhoods better off, hence, the externality. In addition, homeownership provides an individual with a stake in the nation. This tends to increase social stability, another desirable spillover effect.

It is indisputable that careful maintenance of property creates positive externalities. But is it home ownership as such that induces this desirable behavior? Aaron [1972] argues that the beneficial side effects associated with home ownership are probably a consequence of the fact that homeowners tend to have relatively high incomes. (In March 1983, the median income for renters was $14,199, and for homeowners $24,148 [U.S. Bureau of Census, 1983c, p. 19].) Neither is there any evidence that low ownership rates necessarily contribute to social instability. In Switzerland, which is not known for its revolutionary tendencies, only about 28 percent of the dwellings are owner occupied [Melton, 1979, p. 4].

Of course, even if the subsidy does not contribute to correcting an inefficiency, it might be justifiable on equity grounds. But as just noted, homeowners tend to have higher incomes than renters. Thus, only if the distributional objective is to increase income *inequality* does a subsidy for home ownership make sense from this point of view.

Higher Education. The federal government has been supporting higher education on a large scale since the mid-1960s.[17] In 1965, outlays for direct loans, grants, and work-study programs amounted to $250 million. This figure reached $6.3 billion by 1981. As of 1983, the most extensive program was the guaranteed student loan program which covered about 2.8 million undergraduates and 1.4 million graduate and professional students. Under this program, the federal government guarantees private lenders that it will repay loans on which students default and subsidizes the difference between the rates charged and the market rate of interest. The role of outright grants has decreased since the 1970s, although the amounts involved—$1.4 billion in 1983—are not trivial.

---

[17] For further details, see Executive Office of the President, Office of Management and Budget, *Budget of the United States Government for Fiscal Year 1983* (Washington, D.C.: U.S. Government Printing Office, 1982). There is also substantial support for higher education from the states.

One rationalization for subsidizing higher education is that it produces externalities. This argument is quite convincing for primary and secondary schooling. Such schooling not only increases an individual's earning capacity, it also contributes to the literate and well-informed populace that is generally agreed to be necessary for a smoothly functioning modern democracy.[18] Some argue that college education should be subsidized because it increases productivity. This may be true,[19] but *as long as the earnings of college graduates reflect their higher productivity, there is no externality.* In fact, the earnings of college graduates are substantially higher than their counterparts who have not attended college. Mincer [1974, p. 92] estimates that other things being the same, each year of schooling increases annual earnings between 5 and 11 percent. For the externality argument to be convincing, a case has to be made that the productivity gain *exceeds* this differential.

Even if such evidence were produced, it would not justify the form of current programs which subsidize all eligible students at the same rate. Are the external benefits of all kinds of college training equal? Do art history, accounting, and premedical courses all produce the same externalities? If not, efficiency requires that they be subsidized differentially.

It is observed that if the subsidies were cut, fewer people would attend college. This is probably true, but alone is no justification for the subsidy. If there were subsidies for young people who wanted to open auto repair shops and these were cut, then the number of auto repair shops would also decline. Why should a potential car mechanic be treated differently than a potential classicist?

Some argue that if government subsidies for college students were removed, students from poorer families would bear the brunt of the burden, because they find it especially difficult to obtain loans from the private sector. This argument has considerable merit. By their very nature, it is difficult to provide collateral for loans for "human capital" investments, so markets for these loans may not materialize. One possible remedy for this market failure is for the government to make loans available at the *going rate* of interest. Unless the existence of a positive externality can be established, there is no efficiency basis for subsidizing the interest rate.

The theory of welfare economics recognizes that it is possible to justify an inefficient program if it produces "desirable" effects on income distribution. Subsidies for college students represent a transfer from taxpayers as a whole to college goers. Since the lifetime incomes of college attendees are higher than those of the population as a whole,

---

[18] Bowen [1964] provides further details.

[19] There is some controversy with respect to whether the higher incomes associated with more education are actually due to enhanced productivity, or to the fact that college is a "screening device" that identifies for prospective employers those individuals with high ability. [See Aaron, 1978, Chapter 3.]

such a transfer is desirable if the goal is to increase the inequality of the income distribution.

When subsidies for college students came under attack in 1981, the president of the Association of Student Loan Funds argued that "The government is spending about $2 billion a year [under the guaranteed student loan program] to support $20 billion in credit to students. . . . That's an outstanding bargain for the government, the students and the institutions" ["Cuts in Federal Aid," 1981, p. 67]. To be sure, the subsidized loans are a great deal for students and colleges, both of whom have lobbied intensely for their maintenance. In the absence of persuasive evidence on externalities, however, the benefit to society as a whole is less clear.

ECONOMISTS AND EXTERNALITIES

The presence of externalities creates problems that are as complicated as they are important. It would not be surprising to find a great deal of disagreement among economists on how public policy should be designed. In the case of externalities, however, this is generally not true. To be sure, there has been some wrangling about the extent to which private individuals can be relied upon to bargain their way to efficient solutions without government intervention. In general, though, for cases in which externalities affect large numbers of people, economists agree that intervention is appropriate, and that it should take the form of market incentives to produce efficiently. As we have seen, this approach has been rejected in the United States, and progress in improving the environment has been less than satisfactory. It is depressing and ironical that in the area of environmental policy, "where economists speak almost with one voice and a high degree of confidence, their counsel rarely creates a ripple and has yet to produce a single case of significant influence on federal or local policy" [Baumol, 1976, p. 44].

SUMMARY

An externality occurs when the activity of one person affects another person outside of the market mechanism. Externalities may generally be traced to the absence of property rights.

Externalities cause market price to diverge from social costs and benefits. This generally brings about an inefficient allocation of resources.

A Pigouvian tax is a tax levied on the polluters' output in an amount equal to the marginal social damage at the efficient output. Such a tax gives the producer a private incentive to produce the efficient output.

A subsidy for output *not* produced can induce polluters to produce at the efficient level. However, subsidies can lead to too much production, are administratively difficult, and are regarded by some as ethically unappealing.

Pollution rights may be auctioned off to individual polluters. This fixes the total level of pollution, an advantage when administrators are uncertain how polluters will response to Pigouvian taxes.

The Coase Theorem indicates that private parties may bargain towards the efficient output *if* property rights are established. However, bargaining costs must be low and the source of the externality easily identified.

Regulation is likely to be inefficient because the social value of pollution reduction varies across firms, locations, and the populace. Nevertheless, this is the most widespread form of environmental policy—a source of dismay to economists. A prime example is the U.S. Clean Air Act and its amendments.

Each approach to the externality problem has different implications for the distribution of income. As always, the social welfare function may indicate that the most efficient solution is not the most desirable.

Positive externalities generally lead to underprovision of an activity. A subsidy can correct the problem, but care must be taken to avoid wasteful subsidies.

DISCUSSION QUESTIONS

1. Which of the following are examples of an externality?
   a. After a heavy snowfall, I shovel the sidewalk in front of my house.
   b. Mr. Hunt tries to "corner the silver market." Silver prices skyrocket, making other silver holders quite wealthy.
   c. The Rolling Stones play an outdoor concert at the local football stadium.

2. In Figure 7-A, the number of parties that Cassanova gives per month is measured on the horizontal axis, and dollars are measured on the vertical.

FIGURE 7-A   **Private Marginal Costs and Benefits**

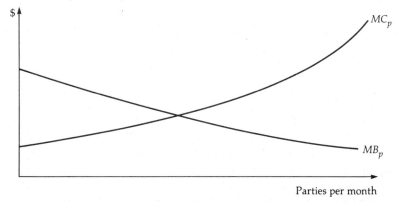

MC_p is the marginal cost of providing parties and MB_p is Cassanova's marginal benefit schedule from having parties.

a. Graphically, show how many parties Cassanova will host.

b. Suppose there is a fixed marginal benefit, b, per party to Cassanova's friends. Illustrate this on your graph.

c. What is the socially (no pun intended) optimal level of parties? How could the Social Committee induce Cassanova to throw this number?

d. On your graph, show the optimal subsidy per party and the total amount paid to Cassanova. Who gains and loses under this plan?

3. For each of the following situations, is the Coase Theorem applicable? Why or why not?

a. Two cottages share a small pond. One cottager fishes, while the other prefers to hold games of water polo.

b. The heat from a copper smelter interferes with the neighboring ice company, but aids an adjacent dry cleaner.

c. The pollution from a copper smelter drifts out over a surrounding residential area.

4. A stream runs directly from a power plant to a brewery. The power plant uses the water for cooling, but the dirt produced by the power plant interfers with the brewery. Together, the brewer and the power plant operators agree that the power plant will pay for the cost of cleaning the water before it gets to the brewery. However, in addition, the local government imposes a Pigouvian tax on water polluters which the power plant must pay.

a. Graph this situation showing the power plant's relevant benefit and cost schedules without the equipment, with the equipment, and with both the tax and the equipment.

b. What is the net result? Is it efficient?

SELECTED REFERENCES

Baumol, William J., and Wallace E. Oates. *Economics, Environmental Policy, and the Quality of Life.* Englewood Cliffs, N.J.: Prentice-Hall, 1979.

Coase, Ronald H. "The Problem of Social Cost." *Journal of Law and Economics,* October 1960, pp. 1–44.

Lave, Lester B., and Gilbert S. Omenn. *Clearing the Air: Reforming the Clean Air Act.* Washington, D.C.: Brookings Institution, 1981.

White, Lawrence J. "Effluent Charges as a Faster Means of Achieving Pollution Abatement." *Public Policy* 24, no. 1 (Winter 1976), pp. 111–25.

CHAPTER 8

Social Insurance

*It is easier for a mother to take care of 10 children
than for 10 children to take care of a mother.*
Yiddish Proverb

Life is full of uncertainties. Unexpected events like fires or illness can dramatically lower people's well-being. One way to gain some protection against such eventualities is to purchase insurance. In return for paying premiums to the insurance company, an individual is guaranteed compensation in the event of certain losses. A number of federal government programs also replace income losses that are consequences of events largely outside personal control. These programs, collectively referred to as **social insurance,** are listed in Table 8.1. As the table indicates, expenditures on social insurance are a large proportion of both federal government expenditures and gross national product.

Although the various programs serve quite different functions, several share these common characteristics: (1) participation is compulsory; (2) eligibility and benefit levels depend, in part, on past contributions made by the worker; (3) benefit payments begin with some identifiable occurrence such as unemployment, illness, or old age; and (4) the programs are *not* means tested—financial distress need not be established to receive benefits.

Each social insurance program has been intensively studied by economists.[1] It is impossible to do justice to each in a single chapter. Thus, most of our discussion is devoted to the largest social insurance program, Social Security. However, the techniques of the analysis are relevant for evaluating the other programs, as well.

---

[1] For a fine survey, see Danziger, Haveman, and Plotnick [1981].

TABLE 8.1   Major Social Insurance Programs (billions of 1980 dollars)

Program	Date Enacted	1965	1983
Social Security	1935	41.4	150.4
Unemployment Insurance	1935	6.3	27.8
Workers' Compensation	1908	4.5	25.8
Veterans' Disability Compensation	1917	5.6	7.8
Railroad Retirement	1937	2.5	2.9
Black Lung	1969	0	1.5
Medicare	1965	0	46.3
Total as percent of federal expenditure		17.8%	37.4%
Total as percent of GNP		3.2%	9.0%

Source: Figures for 1965 are computed by adjusting numbers from S. Danziger, R. Haveman, and R. Plotnick, "How Income Transfers Affect Work, Savings, and the Income Distribution," *Journal of Economic Literature* 19, no. 3 (September 1981), p. 977. Figures for 1983 are computed from Executive Office of the President, Office of Management and Budget, *The Budget of the United States Government, for Fiscal Year 1982* (Washington, D.C.: U.S. Government Printing Office, 1981).

WHY HAVE SOCIAL INSURANCE?

According to the Fundamental Theorem of Welfare Economics, private markets generally provide commodities in efficient quantities. What is special about the "commodity" insurance?

Adverse Selection

Some argue that private markets for certain kinds of insurance will fail to emerge [see Diamond, 1977]. Consider the problem of obtaining insurance against loss of income in case you become disabled due to illness or age. Private insurance companies do indeed sell policies which provide a fixed annual income in the event of disablement. However, such policies—called "annuities"—are normally sold only to fairly large *groups* of people. Employers with many workers can make collective purchases for their employees, as can unions for their members. Insurance companies usually do not sell these annuities to individuals or very small groups.

To see why, consider a company selling annuities to a large group in which some members are prone to heart disease and others are not. As long as the group is reasonably large, the insurance company can make a good guess as to how many heart attacks will occur, even though it does not know exactly who the victims will be. It can then use this information to set the premium for the policy.

The situation of an insurance company contemplating selling such a policy to an individual is quite different. We can expect an individual who knows he is especially likely to collect benefits to have an especially high demand for insurance, a phenomenon known as *adverse selection*. However, even if the insurance company requires a physical examination, chances are that the individual will know more about his health status than the company does. Due to adverse selection and the fact that the individual has better information about his health, the insurance company must charge a higher premium for individual coverage than for group coverage to break even. These higher premiums exacerbate the adverse selection problem. Only individuals who know that they are at great risk will pay the high prices. This in turn, requires a further increase in premiums, and the vicious cycle continues. Thus, many people who are not part of some large group find the cost of insurance so high that they choose not to insure. The market fails to provide an efficient amount of insurance. In essence, social insurance solves this problem by forcing everybody into one big group—the country.

Is adverse selection empirically important enough to justify the provision of social insurance? It depends upon the particular program being considered. On one hand, there are well-developed markets for health insurance, and policies can be obtained by most people either as part of a group or on an individual basis. In contrast, there is not much of a market for insurance against losses caused by unemployment brought about by the business cycle.

Even if the market does fail to provide certain kinds of insurance, this does not explain why social insurance is *compulsory*. Why not construct a system in which people are permitted to purchase insurance from the government on a voluntary basis? Individuals could buy all their insurance this way, or supplement part of it with private purchases, or choose to remain uninsured altogether.[2] We must therefore look to other considerations to explain the basic structure of U.S. social insurance programs.

Other Justifications

Paternalism.   The usual argument is that individuals are not farsighted enough to buy enough insurance for their own good and therefore the government must force them to. For example, it is popularly believed that in the absence of social security, most people would not accumulate enough assets to finance an adequate level of consumption during their retirement. This argument raises two issues. First, is it true that people really would fail to provide for themselves adequately without social security? To find out would require estimating how people would behave in the absence of the program. As noted below, this is very difficult to do. Second, even if it is true, it does not necessarily follow that the

---

[2] There would still be an adverse selection problem, but at least everyone would be able to obtain insurance if they so desired.

government should step in. Those with a highly individualistic philosophical framework believe that people should be left to make their own decisions, even if this occasionally results in mistakes.

A related consideration is that individuals who can opt out of a social insurance program may believe that if they put themselves in a sufficiently desperate situation, society will feel obliged to come to their aid. For example, society may feel it intolerable to have destitute elderly citizens around. Realizing this, some younger people may not bother to save for their old age, gambling that they will be "bailed out." Part of the justification for a compulsory system may be to eliminate such games.

Economize on Decision-Making Costs.   Insurance and annuity markets are complicated, and it is likely to involve quite a bit of time and effort for an individual to choose the right policy. If public decision makers can select an appropriate program for everybody, individuals do not have to waste resources on making their own decisions. A clear criticism here is that there is no reason to believe the government would necessarily choose the right kind of policy. After all, different people have different needs, so it might be better to let people shop around on their own.

Income Distribution.   We noted above that benefits from social insurance programs are determined *in part* by past contributions. In fact, for some of the programs, the link between benefits and earlier contributions is quite weak. Some people do better than they would have if they had purchased private insurance, and some do worse. To an extent, then, social insurance programs are also income distribution programs. This helps explain why the programs are compulsory. Otherwise, those who "lose" might opt out of them.

Regardless of the rationale, however, the United States *does* provide several forms of social insurance. In the next section we will explore the best known, Social Security.

THE STRUCTURE OF THE SOCIAL SECURITY SYSTEM[3]

Social Security—officially, Old Age, Survivors, Disability and Health Insurance (OASDHI)—is the largest single domestic spending program. It is expected that social security expenditures will soon exceed even those on defense. In brief, the system works as follows: During their working lives members of the system and their employers make contributions via

---

[3] Much of this section is based upon Munnell [1977] and Pellechio [1981].

a tax on payrolls.[4] Upon retirement, members are eligible for payments based in part upon their contributions. Social security also provides benefits for disabled workers and for dependents and survivors of disabled and retired workers. There is also a health insurance plan providing medical benefits for the aged sick—**Medicare.** In addition, the **Supplemental Security Income Program** provides special benefits for very poor elderly, blind, and/or disabled persons.

Basic Components

Pay-as-You-Go Financing.   Originally, the Social Security Program (begun in 1935) was broadly similar to a private insurance system. During their working lives, individuals deposited some portion of their salaries into a fund. Over time, the fund would accumulate interest, and upon retirement, the principal and accrued interest would be used to pay benefits. This plan was scrapped almost immediately. In 1939 the system was converted to a **pay-as-you-go** basis, meaning that the benefits paid to current retirees come from payments made by those who are presently working. Each generation of retirees is supported by payments made by the current generation of workers, *not* by drawing down an accumulated fund. An important reason for the switch to pay-as-you-go was the perception that the savings of many of the elderly had been wiped out by the Great Depression, and they deserved to be supported at a level higher than that possible with only a few years of contributions.[5]

Although there still is a **social security trust fund,** it now holds only enough money to finance about one year of benefit payments and serves simply as a contingency fund to smooth out payment flows. Pay-as-you-go financing has some profound implications which are discussed later in this chapter.

Explicit Transfers.   Another key change in the 1939 legislation was a broadening of the scope of the program. The 1935 act provided primarily for monthly retirement benefits for insured workers aged 65 and over. In 1939, monthly benefits for dependents and survivors of insured workers were introduced. Thus, social security not only provides insurance, but

---

[4] When the program was started in the 1930s, coverage was compulsory only for workers under 65 engaged in commerce or industry. Domestic workers, the self-employed, and some other groups were excluded. Over the years, coverage has expanded, and today, virtually every member of the population who works is covered either by social security or some other government retirement program.

[5] The early social security recipients received very high returns on their contributions. An extreme case is that of Ida Fuller, the first beneficiary, who paid about $22 in social security taxes. She lived until the age of 99, and collected about $20,000 in benefits. ["Your Stake in the Fight," September 1981, p. 504.]

it transfers income between individuals, as well. The transfer function has grown in importance over time, and culminated with the enactment of **Supplemental Security Income** (SSI) in 1972. SSI, although administered by the Social Security Administration, is not insurance by the conventional definition.[6] It is a welfare program which provides a federal minimum income guarantee for the aged. As in most welfare programs, to qualify for benefits, an individual must pass a means test— benefits cannot be received unless income and assets are below a certain level. In 1981, SSI benefits amounted to about $8.5 billion [Danziger, Haveman, & Plotnick, 1981, p. 977].

Benefit Structure.   The calculation of an individual's social security benefits depends in a complicated way upon his or her earnings history, age, and other personal circumstances. The first stage is to calculate the **average indexed monthly earnings** (AIME). This represents the individual's average wages in covered employment over the length of his or her working life.[7] Not all years of work are included. (For example, for a worker reaching 62 years of age in 1982, just the highest 26 years of indexed wages were included.) Only annual wages up to a given ceiling are included in the calculation. This ceiling is the same as the maximum amount of wages subject to the social security payroll tax (discussed in the section on financing below). In addition, if the individual elects to work after 62, then years of higher earnings after that age can be substituted for years of lower earnings before it.

The next step is to substitute the AIME into a benefit formula to find the individual's **primary insurance amount** (PIA), which is the basic benefit payable to a worker who retires at age 65 or who becomes disabled. The benefits formula is structured so that the PIA increases with the AIME but at a slower rate. For a person retiring in 1983, the PIA is 90 percent of the first $254 of AIME, plus 32 percent of AIME between $254 and $1,528, plus 15 percent of AIME above $1,528. Thus, for a worker with an AIME of $25, the PIA was $22.50, while for a worker with an AIME of $1,100, the PIA was $499.32. The maximum monthly benefit for an individual was $639.54; for a family, $1,151.96 [*Retirement and Survivor's Insurance*, 1983]. Note that workers with low AIMEs are entitled to benefits that are a higher proportion of their earnings than those with high AIMEs.

The amount of an individual's actual benefit depends not only on the PIA but also on two factors.

---

[6] There is a broader sense in which any transfer program can be considered insurance. See Chapter 5.

[7] Wages earned over different years are not directly comparable because of changes in the price level over time. To correct for this, wages are indexed by the percentage increase in all workers' wages.

The Age at which the Benefit Is Drawn.   Currently, a worker can retire as early as age 62, but if he or she does so, benefits are reduced by 5/9 percent for each month before the age of 65. If retirement is delayed past 65, benefits are increased by 1/12 percent for every month after 65 and before retirement, up to age 72. Legislation passed in 1983 increases by two months a year the retirement age for people reaching age 62 in the years 2000 to 2005. Under the new regime, retirement benefits will still be available at age 62, but there is a greater benefit reduction for electing to retire early.

The Recipient's Family Status.   When a fully insured single worker retires at 65, the actual monthly benefit is just equal to the primary insurance amount. A worker with a dependent wife, husband, or child, receives an additional 50 percent of the PIA.

Three additional rules have an important effect upon the benefit structure:

1. The amount that an individual can earn and still receive full benefits is strictly limited by the **earnings test.**[8] In 1982, the initial earnings level for retirees between the ages of 65 and 70 was $6,000 annually. For each dollar earned in excess of $6,000, 50 cents of benefits were withheld.
2. Historically, social security benefits have not been subject to the personal income tax. But beginning in 1984, up to one half of the benefits received by individuals whose incomes exceed certain base amounts were subject to tax. These base amounts are $25,000 for a single taxpayer, and $32,000 for married taxpayers.
3. Benefits are corrected for inflation. As already noted, in the computation of AIME, past earnings are adjusted by an index of wage growth. Moreover, once a person becomes eligible for a social security benefit, the purchasing power of the benefit is maintained through annual cost-of-living increases based on the minimum of (*a*) the increase in prices as measured by the consumer price index; and (*b*) the increase in wages as measured for purposes of defining the benefit base.[9]

Financing.   The payroll tax is a flat percentage of an employee's annual gross wages up to a certain amount. Half the tax is paid by employers and half by employees.[10] The legislative intention was apparently that the cost of the program be shared equally by workers and employees.

---

[8] The earnings test does not apply to capital and rental incomes or to other pensions.

[9] The minimum rule is in effect only when the ratio of the assets in the Social Security Trust Fund to estimated outgo falls below a certain percentage.

[10] An exception is the year 1984, when the employee rate was 6.7 percent, and the employer rate 7.0 percent.

However, it may be the case that employers can "shift" part or all of their share to employees in the form of a lower pretax wage. Whether such shifting occurs is a complicated question which is discussed in Chapter 11. For now, we merely note that it is highly unlikely that the true division of the costs of the program is really 50–50.

As benefits have grown over time, so have the payroll tax rates. The 1984 tax rate, 7 percent (on the employer and employee *each*), is seven times its original level. (See Table 8.2.) It is scheduled to rise to 7.05

TABLE 8.2   Social Security Tax Rates (selected years 1937–1983)

Year	Maximum Taxable Earnings (dollars)	Employer and Employee, each (percent)
1937	$ 3,000	1.000%
1950	3,000	1.500
1955	4,200	2.000
1960	4,800	3.000
1965	4,800	3.625
1970	7,800	4.800
1975	14,100	5.850
1981	29,700	6.650
1983	35,700	6.700
1984	37,800	7.000*

* 1984 was a one-time exception; the employer rate was 7 percent and the employee rate 6.7 percent.

Source: A. J. Pellechio and G. P. Goodfellow, "Individual Gains and Losses from Social Security before and after the 1983 Social Security Amendments," mimeo (Washington, D. C.: Department of Health and Human Services, 1983), p. 6, except for 1984 figure which is from Deborah Rankin, "The Give and Take of Social Security," *New York Times*, December 25, 1983, p. F7.

percent in 1985 and 7.65 percent in 1990 and thereafter. Legislation passed in 1977 mandated that maximum taxable earnings rise automatically with future increases in average wages.

Distributional Issues

Our description of social security indicates that it serves as much more than a corrective for the nonavailability of certain types of insurance. If providing insurance were the only objective, then each individual would receive approximately the same return on his or her contributions.[11] In fact, some people earn higher returns than others. Implicitly, the people who earn low returns are taxed to subsidize those who receive high returns.

---

[11] Specifically, each individual would receive an "actuarially fair return," meaning that on average, the benefits received would equal the premiums paid. The calculation must be made "on average" because total benefits depend upon the length of the individual's life, which cannot be known in advance with certainty.

Due to the complexity of the social security law, it is difficult to make many general statements concerning who gains and who loses. The most straightforward way to explore distributional issues is to actually compute the expected lifetime net benefits from social security for several representatives individuals and see which ones come out ahead. The first step in this computation is to estimate the expected lifetime value of the social security benefits to which the worker is entitled.[12] Although an individual is not guaranteed these benefits by contract and could theoretically be deprived of them by a legislative change, past experience and the current political environment suggest that these benefits will continue to be paid. The value of future social security payments is an important part of a family's assets and is often referred to as **social security wealth** [Feldstein, 1974a].

The second step in the net benefit calculation is to find the expected lifetime value of the costs of being in the system—the payroll taxes collected from the individual. Of course, both an individual's social security wealth and future payroll taxes depend upon wage growth over time. The calculations reported below, which are from Pellechio [1981], assume that real wages grow by 1 percent a year.[13]

Table 8.3 shows how social security affects men and women of different earnings levels and different ages. The computations are done for the year 1981, as the law stood in that year. Each cell of the table gives the following information: (1) annual retirement benefit; (2) social security wealth for people of different marital status (married individuals are assumed to have spouses with no earnings covered by social security); and (3) lifetime value of payroll taxes. The net benefit from the social security system can be calculated simply as (2) minus (3). (When the difference is negative, then the figure shows the individual's *loss* from the system.) Thus, a woman who was 40 years old in 1981 and had earnings of $20,000 can expect an annual retirement benefit of $6,867. If she is single, her social security wealth is $103,212, if married, $147,844. Her lifetime payroll taxes are $73,357. Thus, if she is single, her net benefit from the system is $29,855; if married to an uncovered husband, it is $74,487.

Table 8.3 illustrates several ways in which social security redistributes income.[14] First, single men with low earnings can expect small gains

---

[12] Because social security benefits received depend upon the length of life, the actual value is uncertain, and actuarial tables must be used to compute the value "on average," or the "expected" value. Because benefits and costs occur over time, lifetime magnitudes must be computed as "present values." Those unfamiliar with this concept should consult Chapter 9.

[13] By definition, this means that the rate of nominal wage growth minus the inflation rate is 1 percent.

[14] All of these results ignore possible effects that social security might have upon before-tax prices. See Chapter 11.

TABLE 8.3 Estimated Benefits and Costs of Social Security by Age, Income, Sex, and Marital Status (1981)

Earnings	Men (age)				Women (age)			
	30	40	50	60	30	40	50	60
$10,000								
Retirement Benefit	$ 4,412	$ 4,452	$ 4,492	$ 4,536	$ 4,412	$ 4,452	$ 4,492	$ 4,536
Social Security Wealth								
Single	43,557	44,157	46,191	52,411	66,998	66,916	68,129	72,197
Married	88,508	88,639	90,482	96,839	95,384	95,853	98,592	107,073
Lifetime Payroll Taxes	38,408	38,698	34,910	26,436	39,329	39,366	35,255	26,445
$20,000								
Retirement Benefit	6,916	6,867	6,693	6,674	6,916	6,867	6,693	6,674
Social Security Wealth								
Single	68,275	68,109	68,822	77,114	105,020	103,212	101,510	106,226
Married	138,737	136,718	134,814	142,482	149,514	147,844	146,897	157,539
Lifetime Payroll Taxes	76,451	72,020	61,292	44,016	78,294	73,357	61,983	44,035
$29,700								
Retirement Benefit	8,232	7,799	7,235	6,860	8,232	7,799	7,235	6,860
Social Security Wealth								
Single	81,266	77,356	74,390	79,266	125,002	117,224	109,722	109,190
Married	165,135	155,280	145,721	146,457	177,963	167,916	158,782	161,935
Lifetime Payroll Taxes	106,608	93,016	73,279	47,132	109,345	95,000	74,305	47,160

Source: A. J. Pellechio, "Individual Gains and Losses from Social Security: Calculations in 1981 According to Social Security Law and an Agenda for Reform," mimeo, (Rochester, N.Y.: University of Rochester, 1981).

from the social security system, while their counterparts with higher earnings can expect losses. Women of all ages gain from the system, but the gains are larger for those with lower earnings. For most age groups, social security transfers income from high-income to low-income individuals.

At all earnings levels, women gain more than men. This is a consequence of the well-known fact that females have longer life expectancies than males. The greater longevity of women increases their lifetime payroll tax payments only slightly, but has a large effect on their benefits.

Social security redistributes income from single individuals to those married with uncovered spouses. Consider a 40-year-old woman earning $20,000. According to the table, if she is single, her net benefit from social security is $29,855. If married, she receives an extra benefit for her husband equal to 50 percent of her own benefit. Moreover, if she dies, the husband is entitled to her full benefit as a surviving spouse. These extra benefits raise her social security wealth to $147,844. If the husband had no covered earnings, then this increase in social security wealth comes at no extra cost to the family.

In most cases, social security distributes income from two-earner to one-earner couples. Consider a family in which the wife has higher lifetime covered earnings than the husband. (The qualitative results are the same when the roles are reversed.) If the benefit the husband would receive on the basis of his earnings history turns out to be less than 50 percent of his wife's benefit, then the husband is entitled to *no more* than the 50 percent of his wife's benefit which he would have received even without working. If his benefit is more than 50 percent of hers, he gains only the difference between his benefit and 50 percent of hers. Thus, even though the spouse with lower earnings is subject to the payroll tax during his or her working life, he or she does not gain very much in terms of social security wealth.

Finally, social security currently redistributes income across generations. The amounts involved depend upon individual circumstances. Consider single males of different ages, all of whom earn $20,000 in 1981. The system deals the 30-year-old a lifetime loss of $8,176, while the 60-year-old comes out ahead by $33,098. Men with the same earnings but who are married to nonworking wives all gain from the system, but the size of the gain increases with age. Similarly, for both single women and women married to uncovered husbands, social security is a "better deal" for the old.

Much of this intergenerational redistribution was made possible by a unique set of historical circumstances. In the decades after social security was established, more and more occupations were brought into the system. At the same time, the size of the labor force was itself increasing, as were real wages. In such an environment, benefits for retirees could be increased without large payroll tax increases for current workers. It is unlikely that such forces will create similar windfalls for the current generation of workers when they retire. Indeed, as the cartoon suggests, there are widespread fears that the social security system will go bankrupt altogether.

Mike Peters. Reprinted with permission.

IT'S ANOTHER ONE OF YOUR CHECKS FROM THE SOCIAL SECURITY OFFICE...

Is Social Security Bankrupt?

In 1982, newspaper headlines blared that social security was bankrupt. The trust fund that paid benefits had run out of money, in part because of large benefit increases that had been voted in earlier years, and in part because payroll tax receipts were low due to the recession taking place that year. To deal with this problem on a short-term basis, Congress gave the Social Security Administration permission to borrow from funds set aside to cover Medicare benefits.

This short-term crisis focused attention on the long-run problems of the system. As emphasized above, the social security system endows each individual with a certain amount of wealth. It had been estimated that by the late 1970s the value of social security wealth exceeded $5.5 *trillion* (in 1981 dollars).[15] Although this sum is an *asset* as far as future recipients are concerned, it is of course a *liability* from the point of view of the social security system. However, as pointed out earlier, the sys-

---

[15] This amount is derived by taking Feldstein's [1982a, p. 641] figure and adjusting it for changes in the consumer price index.

tem has a relatively trivial amount of assets. Thus, judged by standards applicable to the private sector, the social security system is technically bankrupt.

However, this analogy is misleading, because it ignores the fact that the government can use its coercive powers to raise by taxation the money it needs to meet its obligations. The question then becomes whether taxes scheduled for collection under the current law will be sufficient to meet the scheduled benefits. Most studies suggest that the answer is no. As of 1981, Boskin, Arvin, and Cone [1981] estimated that the system had a long-term deficit of over $1,304.4 billion (in 1981 dollars).[16] The major reason for this deficit is the anticipated change in the age structure of the population. When the post–World War II baby boom generation retires (beginning in 2010), it is predicted that the ratio of retirees to workers will increase from slightly less than one in three to about one in two. In a pay-as-you-go system, a fall in the number of workers relative to retirees tends to create a deficit, other things being the same. The deficit can be removed only by raising taxes and/or reducing the ratio of benefits to before-tax wages.

In 1983, a number of changes were made in the system to reduce this deficit. These included subjecting some portion of benefits to personal taxation, moving up scheduled increases in the payroll tax rate, and introducing a less generous system for making cost-of-living adjustments. However, many observers believe that the system is still in need of a major overhaul. We defer a discussion of some suggested reforms to a later section of this chapter.

THE EFFECTS OF SOCIAL SECURITY ON ECONOMIC BEHAVIOR

In recent years, several investigators have argued that the social security system influences people's economic decisions in a way that is detrimental to the economy's efficient operation. Most of the discussion has focused on the impact of Social Security upon saving behavior and labor supply decisions.[17] As we shall see, all the difficulties in doing empirical work that were explained in Chapter 3 arise here with a vengeance. The impact of social security on behavior remains a controversial subject, so this section is best regarded as a report on "research in progress," rather than a compendium of definitive conclusions.

---

[16] Like all computations concerning the long-run financial status of social security, this estimate is sensitive to assumptions on future rates of wage growth, inflation, etc.

[17] These issues are discussed here because they are important and have been the subject of much research. Some fascinating questions which have not received as much attention surround the impact of social security on family structure. For example, how has decreased parental need for children's support in old age changed family relationships?

Savings Behavior

The starting point for most work on social security and savings is the life-cycle theory of savings, which suggests that individuals' consumption and savings decisions are based upon lifetime considerations. During their working lives, individuals save some portion of their incomes to accumulate wealth from which they can finance consumption during retirement.[18] Such funds can be invested until they are needed, thus increasing society's capital stock.

The introduction of a social security system can substantially alter the amount of lifetime savings. Such changes are the consequences of three effects.

First, workers realize that in exchange for their social security contributions, they will receive a guaranteed retirement income. If they view social security taxes as a means of "saving" for these future benefits, they will tend to save less on their own. But as emphasized above, with a pay-as-you-go system, the contributions are not actually saved—they are paid out immediately to the current beneficiaries. Thus, there is no public saving to correspond to the loss of private saving, which means a reduction in the amount of total capital accumulation. This phenomenon is referred to as the **wealth substitution effect.**

Second, social security may induce people to retire earlier than they would have, because to receive benefits, they have to reduce their participation in the labor force. However, if the length of retirement increases, the individual has more nonworking years during which consumption must be financed, but fewer working years to accumulate funds. This **retirement effect** tends to increase saving.

Finally, suppose that an important reason for saving is the bequest motive—people want to leave an inheritance for their children. Suppose further that people realize that the social security system tends to shift income from children (worker/taxpayers) to parents (retiree/benefit recipients). (Recall the discussion surrounding Table 8.3.) Then parents may save more to increase bequests to their children, and hence offset the distributional effect of social security. In essence, people increase their saving to undo the impact of social security on their children's incomes. This is referred to as the **bequest effect.**

Given that the three effects work in different directions, on the basis of theory alone it cannot be known how social security affects savings. Econometric analysis is necessary. The first step is to specify a mathematical relationship which shows how the amount of saving depends upon social security wealth and other variables that might plausibly have an effect. Alternatively, an investigator can just as well posit a

---

[18] Of course, savings are also accumulated for other reasons as well: to finance the purchase of durables, to use in case of a "rainy day," etc. For a more complete discussion of the life-cycle theory, see Feldstein [1974a].

relation which explains the amount of *consumption* as a function of the same variables, because by definition, saving and consumption are opposite sides of the same coin—anything that raises consumption by a dollar must lower saving by the same amount.

In a controversial study, Feldstein [1974a] assumed that consumption during a given year is a function of private wealth at the beginning of the year, disposable income during the year and during the previous year, corporate retained earnings, and social security wealth. Income and private wealth are included because they are measures of the individual's capacity to consume. The previous year's disposable income is included to allow for the possibility that people may take a while to adjust their savings habits to changes in their incomes—they react to last year's as well as this year's income. Retained earnings are corporation profits that are not distributed to shareholders. Although technically held by the corporations, these sums represent income to the stockholders and hence, should influence their level of saving.

Feldstein estimated the regression equation with annual U.S. data from 1929 to 1976, using statistical methods similar to those described in Chapter 3. For our purposes, the key question is the sign and magnitude of the parameter multiplying the social security wealth variable. Feldstein found a positive and statistically significant value of 0.018.[19] This positive sign suggests that increases in social security wealth increase consumption and hence, decrease saving. Thus, the wealth substitution effect dominates the retirement and bequest effects.

To assess the quantitative importance of the coefficient, consider the fact that in 1976, the value of Social Security Wealth (in 1976 dollars) was $3,238 billion. A coefficient of .018 implies that Social Security reduced personal saving in 1976 by $58 billion (= .018 × $3,238). In comparison, during 1976 private saving was $95 billion. The $58 billion is thus 38 percent of the potential private saving of $153 billion (the sum of $58 billion and $95 billion). Thus, if Feldstein's calculations are correct, the pay-as-you-go nature of the social security system has had a huge negative impact upon capital accumulation in the United States. Given the current concern that some of America's "productivity crisis" is due to insufficient capital, this is a serious matter indeed.[20]

Feldstein's study has spawned a considerable amount of controversy, much of which has centered on whether his equation contains all the explanatory variables that it should. Munnell [1977] has suggested that the rate of unemployment is an important determinant of the aggregate amount of saving, because during years of high unemployment, people

---

[19] This estimate is from a revision and update of the 1974 paper. See Feldstein [1982a].

[20] Interestingly, when social security was introduced during the 1930s, the perception that it decreased saving was regarded as a virtue. This was because of the belief that a major cause of the Great Depression was the failure of people to consume enough.

are likely to draw down their savings to maintain their standard of living. She argued further that Feldstein's failure to include the unemployment rate in the equation tends to make his coefficient on the social security wealth variable appear higher than it actually is. This is because through time, social security wealth and unemployment have tended to move in opposite directions. (During the decade of the 1930s, social security wealth was zero for most of the years, and the unemployment rate was very high. Later on, social security wealth increased while the unemployment rate came down.) Thus, part of the variation in saving that might be caused by fluctuations in unemployment is reflected in the coefficient of the social security wealth variable. When Munnell estimated an equation similar to Feldstein's, but includes the rate of unemployment, she found that social security wealth still reduces personal saving, but the magnitude is only about 10 percent of that found by Feldstein. Obviously, the implications for capital accumulation are much less portentous.

Other studies have used different data sets and methods of estimation. Leimer and Lesnoy [1982] found evidence that social security might even have *increased* saving. In their survey of the available evidence, Danziger, Haveman, and Plotnick [1981, p. 1006] concluded that social security has a negative effect on savings, but it is probably not very large.

Labor Supply Behavior

The social security system influences lifetime work effort in two different ways. For those over 62 years of age, the structure of benefits provides some incentives for partial or complete retirement. For most younger workers, the system changes the reward for additional work but with effects that are hard to predict. We discuss each of these in turn.

Retirement Decisions.   In 1929, 45 percent of the men over 65 were retired. By 1950, the retirement rate for this group was 75.5 percent, and by 1980, it was 88.2 percent. A number of factors have doubtless contributed to this phenomenon: rising incomes, changing life expectancies, differences in occupations, etc. Many investigators believe that social security has played a key role in this dramatic change in retirement patterns.

The retirement incentive is illustrated nicely by a numerical example in Feldstein [1976b]. By the late 1970s, a man who earned about the average wage throughout his life could retire at age 65 with benefits equal to approximately 46 percent of his preretirement gross earnings. If he had a nonworking wife, he would receive a dependent's benefit equal to one half of his own, making the total benefit 69 percent of former gross earnings. But as noted above, in the late 1970s, social security benefits were untaxed, while labor-market earnings were subject to income and payroll taxes. Suppose that the tax rate on additional income for our person was 15 percent, so that for every dollar earned, he could keep only 85 cents. Thus, the percent of *after*-tax earnings replaced by social security was 81 percent (=69/85). For such an individual, earning a dollar generated a gain of only 19 cents over what he would have gotten with no work at all. Hence, social security weakens the incentive to continue participation in the work force past the age of 65.

For workers who wish to participate in the labor market on a full-time basis, social security puts a high implicit tax on earnings via the earnings test. Those receiving social security are permitted to earn only a small amount of money in the market without having their benefits reduced. In 1982, retirees between the ages of 65 and 70 could earn no more than $6,000 without suffering a reduction of benefits. For each dollar earned above this amount, benefits are reduced by 50 cents—in effect, a 50 percent rate of taxation.[21]

A number of econometric studies have been done to assess the impact of social security upon retirement decisions. Many of them are consistent with the hypothesis that the system increases the likelihood of retirement and reduces the amount of labor supplied by those who continue to work. Danziger, Haveman, and Plotnick [1981, p. 966] argue that social security may have accounted for about half of the increase since 1950 in the retirement rate for older men. However, this estimate is much in doubt. One important reason for the uncertainty is the fact that many of the variables influencing labor supply decisions of the aged are difficult to measure and sometimes unavailable altogether. These include: health status, local labor market conditions, and the amount of wealth accumulated in private pensions. As better data become available, more reliable answers will be obtained.

Labor Supply of Younger Workers.[22]   From a theoretical point of view, the effect of social security upon the labor supply of younger workers is ambiguous. To see why, consider first a worker for whom the expected present value of social security benefits just equals the payroll taxes paid. In this case, social security contributions would not really be perceived as a "tax," but just a requirement to "save" in a particular way.[23] Hence, there would be no effect on labor supply at all.

---

[21] For recipients between the ages of 62 and 65 who lose some benefits because of the earnings test, there is an upward adjustment of benefits they can receive after age 65. In some cases, this adjustment is so large that it actually creates an incentive to work more. See Blinder, Gordon, and Wise [1980].

[22] The arguments in this section are based on Feldstein [1976b].

[23] This assumes that the implicit rate of return paid by social security is the same as is elsewhere available to the worker.

However, as shown above, social security does, in fact, tax some people and subsidize others. For many individuals who are subsidized, the more they contribute to the system, the greater the size of the subsidy. In effect, the social security system increases the reward for an additional hour of work. If work effort increases with the net wage, then the social security system increases labor supply for such workers. For workers who are taxed by the system, the result is just the opposite.

So far we have been ignoring the fact that the payroll tax is levied on earnings only up to the covered maximum. For those workers whose earnings are above this amount, the payroll tax has no impact upon the reward received for one more hour of work. However, for such people, the tax does have an "income effect"—it lowers income. If leisure is a normal good, less of it is consumed and labor supply is increased.

It is clear that the effects of social security on labor supply are complicated and can influence people quite differently depending upon their particular circumstances. There is currently no consensus on the answer.

Social Security and Behavior: Implications

Many economists believe that the social security system depresses both work effort and saving. However, the evidence is murky, and many others are unconvinced. It should be stressed that even if future research establishes more firmly that the system does distort economic decisions, this is not necessarily a bad thing. If society wants to achieve some level of income security for its members, then presumably it should be willing to pay for that security in terms of some loss of efficiency. On the other hand, efforts should be made to structure the system so that labor and savings incentives are adversely affected as little as possible.

SOCIAL SECURITY REFORM

Much of the recent public discussion of reform of social security has been prompted by the realization that due to changing demographic trends, it will be impossible to maintain current benefit levels unless revenues are increased. As noted above, several provisions to reduce benefits were enacted in 1983. Any additional benefit reductions are likely to meet with insurmountable political opposition unless they are also phased in very gradually so as to give all those affected the opportunity to change their plans appropriately.[24] There is a general consensus that society cannot renege on the promises it has made to the current generation of the elderly.

---

[24] See Congressional Budget Office [1982c] for a number of suggestions for reducing benefits.

Of course, the other way to eliminate the deficit is to increase revenues. Further major increases in the payroll tax appear politically infeasible, so the funds would have to come from general government revenues. In practice, this means financing social security from federal personal income tax collections. Those who regard the social security system mainly as a transfer program often favor this method of finance. Under the income tax, the average rate of taxation tends to increase with income.[25] Hence, those with high incomes bear a disproportionately high share of the burden, which is desirable if the goal is to equalize the distribution of income.[26]

However, for those who view social security primarily as an insurance program, the payroll tax is more appropriate because it maintains the link between contributions and benefits. Some proponents of social security favor payroll tax finance because it insulates the system from political pressures to emasculate it. The idea is that a link between taxes and benefits—no matter how tenuous—creates an obligation on the part of the government to maintain the system that promised the benefits. Franklin Roosevelt articulated this position with typical eloquence:

> Those taxes were never a problem of economics. They are politics all the way through. We put those payroll contributions there so as to give the contributors a legal, moral, and political right to collect their pensions. With these taxes in there, no damn politician can ever scrap my Social Security Program. ["Your Stake in the Fight," 1981, p. 504]

The reforms mentioned so far keep intact the basic structure of the social security system. Thinking about a major overhaul requires a careful statement of the goals of the program. As noted earlier, although social security is called "social insurance," apparently one of its important objectives is to redistribute income. Thus, there are really two distinct goals: to force individuals to insure themselves by reallocating income from their working years to their retirements, and to distribute income to those elderly citizens who would otherwise lack a "socially adequate" level of support. Many of the problems with social security stem from the fact that it attempts to meet both objectives through a single structure of benefits and taxes. Several economists have suggested that the system be restructured so as to meet the two objectives separately.[27]

Under this separation proposal, the compulsory saving aspect of social security would continue to be funded out of earmarked payroll taxes. Each individual would have the *same* rate of return on his or her contributions. This is in marked contrast to the current system, which

---

[25] The structure of the federal income tax is described in detail in Chapter 14 below.

[26] This statement assumes that those who pay the income tax are unable to shift its burden. That this might not be the case is shown in Chapter 11.

[27] See, for example, Munnell [1977], Boskin, Arvin, and Cone [1981], and Pellechio [1981].

gives different people very different rates of return. (Recall the discussion surrounding Table 8.3.)

Of course, for many people who had low earnings during their working lives, the return on their lifetime contributions might not provide a level of support considered adequate by society. Under the separation proposal, the retirement incomes of such people would be supplemented by direct transfers, the amounts of which would be based upon personal circumstances. Supplemental Security Income, which is funded out of general revenues, is a mechanism already in place for making such transfers. Presumably, it could be expanded to allow for as much redistribution to the elderly poor as society desired.

Pellechio [1981] has noted two implications of this proposal. First, family status would no longer have a major effect upon the value of a person's social security wealth. If a one-earner couple and a two-earner couple paid the same amount into the system, they would receive the same benefits. The problem of supporting nonworking spouses could be dealt with by crediting each spouse with half of the total taxes paid by the couple. In this way, even if a divorce occurred, each spouse would carry with him or her a given balance upon which retirement payments would be based.

Second, the earnings test would be eliminated. Because benefits would be the returns from what an individual had already paid into the system, there would be no reason for benefits to be limited by the amount of other income. Presumably, elimination of the earnings test would diminish some of the work disincentives discussed above. However, under the reform, all social security benefits would be subject to income tax—just like any form of ordinary income.

As Boskin, Arvin, and Cone [1981, p. 8] observed, general financing of the transfer part of social security would require it to compete openly with other government priorities. Policymakers and the public would have to determine explicitly the value of transfers to the elderly relative to other social objectives.

Social security is an emotional political issue, and any attempts to tinker with the system, let alone overhaul it, will be met with fierce resistance. The changes of 1983 came only after they were recommended by a bipartisan commission, and they probably would not have been implemented without the pressure of the short-term financial crisis. At this time, it is unlikely that any major changes will be made in the system.

UNEMPLOYMENT INSURANCE

Unemployment Insurance (UI) was established in 1935, the same year as social security. Like the social security system, it has grown in importance over time and has come under attack for creating adverse incentives.

The purpose of the program is to replace income lost due to unemployment. About 97 percent of all wage earners are covered, and in fiscal year 1981, about 4.1 million workers received UI benefits each week [M. M. Smith, 1981]. The number of weeks for which an individual can receive unemployment compensation is determined by a complicated formula which depends upon work history and the state in which the person works. In most states, the regular maximum length of time is 26 weeks. However, this period can be extended if the state unemployment rate exceeds certain levels.

In most states, the benefit formula is designed so that the **gross replacement rate**—the proportion of pretax earnings replaced by UI—is about 50 percent.[28] Consider Smith, who makes $300 a month before taxes. Given a 50 percent gross replacement rate, if Smith becomes unemployed, he receives a monthly benefit of $150. It would seem, then, that Smith loses half his income when he becomes unemployed. But this ignores the fact that Smith's earnings are subject to tax. Assume that Smith's income tax rate is 14 percent, and his payroll tax rate is 7 percent. Then if Smith works, his take-home pay is only $237. If Smith becomes unemployed, UI therefore replaces 63 percent (=$150/$237) of his net earnings; he loses only 37 percent of his previous take-home pay. In general, as long as UI benefits are not taxed, the proportion of net income replaced by UI—the **net replacement rate**—exceeds the gross replacement rate. The higher the tax rate on earnings, the more dramatic the disparity.[29]

The fact that net replacement rates can be quite high is important when considering the incentive effects of UI. Normally, when we think of insuring against an event, we imagine the event as being largely out of the individual's control.[30] One reason that UI is so controversial is that in many cases, an individual's employment status is quite under his or her control. A worker's behavior on the job can influence the probability that he or she will lose it. Similarly, an unemployed worker can control the intensity with which he or she seeks a new job. Considerable attention, both in academic and political discussions, has been focused on the question of whether UI actually *causes* some unemployment. The high net replacement rates of UI may make workers more likely to accept employment in industries where the probability of future layoffs is great. In addition, UI may induce the unemployed to spend more time looking for work than otherwise would have been the case.

This issue has been the subject of many econometric studies. Typically, investigators estimate regressions in which the variable on the left-hand side is the number of weeks unemployment insurance is received.

---

[28] However, there is a maximum benefit level that cannot be exceeded.

[29] For further examples, see Feldstein [1974b].

[30] But not totally! People can set fires to their homes to collect home insurance, or feign illness to get health benefits.

The explanatory variables include personal characteristics of the worker such as sex and marital status, as well as the UI weekly benefit amount. If UI encourages unemployment, the coefficient on the weekly benefit amount should be positive; higher benefits lead to a longer duration of unemployment. In a careful study, Classen [1979] found that a 10 percent increase in the weekly benefit amounts leads to a 6 to 10 percent increase in duration of unemployment, other things being the same.

The fact that UI extends the duration of unemployment is not necessarily undesirable. If workers take more time to search, they may find jobs that are more appropriate for their skills. Hence, the efficient allocation of resources is enhanced. More generally, if society believes it is worthwhile to maintain income levels for those who are involuntarily unemployed, then it may be willing to pay the price in terms of some increased voluntary unemployment.

Still, there is a sense that the program is not working as well as it might. One suggestion for revamping it would be to have recipients pay federal income taxes on all UI receipts.[31] Under the personal income tax, the higher your income, the larger the proportion of additional income you pay in tax. Thus, if UI benefits were taxed, then net replacement rates would be lowered disproportionately for those with substantial income from other sources such as spouse's earnings, interest, dividends, etc. With smaller benefits going to those with high incomes, more could be targeted for low-income people. At the same time, reducing the net replacement rates for those with high incomes would reduce their incentive to stay out of work. Solon [1982] estimated that among a sample of high-income UI claimants in 1979, the imposition of benefit taxation induced about a 10 percent reduction in the length of time they collected benefits.

CONCLUSIONS

A thought suggested by this chapter is that social insurance programs have had unintentional consequences. It is hard to imagine that the designers of the social security program really wanted to generate huge income redistributions based upon marital status. Similarly, no one wanted to design an unemployment insurance system that created unemployment. Feldstein [1976b] has suggested that the unintended creation of distributional anomalies and economic inefficiencies is also common to other forms of social insurance. For example, he argued that Medicare and Medicaid ignited an unintended explosion of health-care costs.

The extent to which social insurance actually is responsible for current economic problems is unknown. There does seem to be a wide-

---

[31] Currently, benefits are taxable on joint tax returns reporting $18,000 of adjusted gross income including benefits. For a single return, the figure is $12,000.

spread consensus, however, that U.S. social insurance policy fails to operate in a fair and efficient way. Part of this is due to the fact that our social insurance programs are largely an inheritance from the 1930s, when economic conditions were vastly different than they are today. Part is also due to the failure of policymakers to fully think through the implications of their programs and to precisely define their goals. Unfortunately, prospects for serious reform are remote because the current forms of social insurance have become almost sacrosanct. Nonetheless, it would make more sense to remain faithful to the objectives of the original programs rather than to their particular structures.

SUMMARY

Social insurance programs replace income lost due to different events. They share characteristics of private insurance, but participation is mandatory.

Public provision of social insurance may be justified on grounds of adverse selection, decision-making costs, income distribution, or simply paternalism.

Social security (OASDHI) is the largest social insurance program, indeed the largest domestic spending program. It provides retirement incomes, health insurance (Medicare), and minimum incomes for the aged (Supplemental Security Income—SSI).

Social security benefits are calculated in two steps. Average indexed monthly earnings (AIME) are derived from the worker's earnings history and determine the primary insurance amount (PIA). To compute actual benefits, the PIA is adjusted according to retirement age, family status, and other earnings.

Benefits are not paid out of a fund of previous contributions, but out of current payroll taxes. This pay-as-you-go financing explicitly transfers income from younger to older citizens. Moreover, SSI adds to the transfer aspect by including an income guarantee.

The social security structure has important distributional impacts, best examined by calculating the difference between lifetime benefits (social security wealth) and lifetime taxes. These calculations broadly indicate that social security redistributes incomes from high- to low-income individuals, from men to women, and from young to old. Married couples with one earner in the family tend to gain relative to either two-earner couples or individuals.

Economic theory indicates that social security may affect savings and labor supply. However, theory does not give clear implications, and empirical studies have been conducted to fill this gap.

Social security may reduce private savings—the *wealth substitution effect*—or increase savings—the *retirement* and *bequest* effects. Numerous studies have produced conflicting results. A general conclusion is that savings have been reduced, but the magnitude of this effect is not clear.

The percentage of retired older workers has increased dramatically since the introduction of social security and much evidence indicates that this is the result of disincentives in the system. In principle, social security may affect the labor supply of younger workers as well, but thus far there has not been much research on this subject.

There have been calls to reform social security, both to reduce its impact on saving and work incentives and to insure its solvency. Some of the changes enacted in 1983 were to partially tax the benefits of relatively high-income recipients and to gradually to raise the retirement age. These changes, although politically difficult to make, leave the basic structure unchanged. More fundamental reforms would separate the forced savings and transfer aspects of the program.

Unemployment Insurance (UI) replaces income lost due to unemployment. The key event—unemployment—is somewhat under the control of workers. Econometric evidence indicates that UI has increased the duration of unemployment.

DISCUSSION QUESTIONS

1. "Social security improves economic welfare. Because the system distributes current earnings of the young (which they would save anyway) to the old, the old are better off and the young unaffected." Discuss carefully.

2. Suppose that private savings accounts pay interest of 5 percent per year. A social security system is set up which also pays a return of 5 percent a year. Further, suppose that there are two types of people:
   a. Type I people may take out loans now by promising to repay the loans out of their social security benefits in the future.
   b. Type II people are refused these loans.
   What are the labor supply effects of the Social Security program for each type of person? Be sure to discuss both the amount of labor supplied when working and the timing of the retirement decision.

3. Suppose that participation in the current social security program were made optional. What do you expect would happen to aggregate private saving?

4. Some states pay unemployment insurance to those who quit their jobs as well as to those who are laid off. Does this improve or impair economic efficiency? Should these benefits be subject to the personal income tax?

SELECTED REFERENCES

Congressional Budget Office. *Financing Social Security: Issues and Options in the Long Run.* Washington, D.C.: U.S. Government Printing Office, November 1982.

Danziger, Sheldon; Robert Haveman; and Robert Plotnick. "How Income Transfers Affect Work, Savings, and the Income Distribution." *Journal of Economic Literature* 19, no. 3 (September 1981), pp. 975–1028.

Feldstein, Martin S. "Unemployment Compensation: Adverse Incentives and Distributional Anomalies." *National Tax Journal* 27 (June 1974), pp. 231–44.

Munnell, Alicia H. *The Future of Social Security.* Washington, D.C.: Brookings Institution, 1977.

(9.2) $PV = R_0 + \dfrac{(1 + g)R_1}{(1 + g)(1 + i)} + \dfrac{(1 + g)^2 R_2}{(1 + g)^2(1 + i)^2} + \cdots$

$+ \dfrac{(1 + g)^T R_T}{(1 + g)^T(1 + i)^T}$

A glance at Equation (9.2) indicates that it is equivalent to Equation (9.1) because all the terms involving $(1 + g)$ cancel out. The moral of the story is that the *same answer* is obtained whether real or nominal magnitudes are used. It is crucial, however, that dollar magnitudes and discount rates be measured consistently. If real values are used for the Rs, then the discount rate must also be measured in real terms—the market rate of interest *minus* the expected inflation rate. Alternatively, if the market rate of interest is used for discounting, then returns should be measured in nominal terms.

DECISION-MAKING CRITERIA: THE PRIVATE SECTOR

Suppose that a firm is considering two mutually exclusive projects, X and Y. The real benefits and costs of project X are B^X and C^X, respectively; and those for project Y are B^Y and C^Y. For both projects, the benefits and costs are realized immediately. The firm's decision maker must answer two questions. First, should either project be done at all: are the projects **admissible?** (The firm has the option of doing neither project.) Second, if both projects are admissible, which is **preferable?** Because both benefits and costs occur immediately, answering these questions is simple. Compute the net return to project X, $B^X - C^X$, and compare it to the net return to Y, $B^Y - C^Y$. A project is admissible only if its net return is positive, i.e., the benefits exceed the costs. If both projects are admissible, the firm should choose the project with the higher net return.

In reality, most projects involve a stream of real benefits and returns that occur over time rather than instantaneously. Suppose that the initial benefits and costs of project X are B_0^X and C_0^X, those at the end of the first year are B_1^X and C_1^X, and those at the end of the last year are B_T^X and C_T^X. We can characterize project X as a stream of net returns (some of which may be negative):

$$(B_0^X - C_0^X), (B_1^X - C_1^X), (B_2^X - C_2^X), \ldots , (B_T^X - C_T^X)$$

The present value of this income stream (PV^X) is

$$PV^X = B_0^X - C_0^X + \frac{B_1^X - C_1^X}{(1 + i)} + \frac{B_2^X - C_2^X}{(1 + i)^2} + \cdots + \frac{B_T^X - C_T^X}{(1 + i)^T}$$

where i represents the real rate of return that is generally available to the owners of the firm, the opportunity cost of their funds.

Similarly, suppose that project Y generates streams of costs and benefits B^Y and C^Y over a period of T' years. (There is no reason for T and T' to be the same.) Project Y's present value is:

$$PV^Y = B_0^Y - C_0^Y + \frac{B_1^Y - C_1^Y}{1 + i} + \frac{B_2^Y - C_2^Y}{(1 + i)^2} + \cdots + \frac{B_{T'}^Y - C_{T'}^Y}{(1 + i)^{T'}}$$

Since both projects are now evaluated in present value terms, we can use the same rules that were applied to the instantaneous project described above. The **present value criteria** for project evaluation are that: (1) a project is admissible only if its present value is positive; and (2) if two projects are mutually exclusive, then the preferred project is the one with the higher present value.

The discount rate plays a key role in the analysis. Different values of i can lead to very different conclusions concerning the admissibility and comparability of projects.

Consider the two projects shown in Table 9.2, a research and development program (R&D) and drilling a new oil well. Both require an

TABLE 9.2   Comparing the Present Values of Two Projects

	Annual Net Return	
Year	R&D	Oil Well
0	−$1,000	−$1,000
1	600	–0–
2	–0–	–0–
3	550	1,200

	PV	
$i =$	R&D	Oil Well
0	$ 150	$ 200
.01	128	165
.03	86	98
.05	46	37
.07	10	−21

initial outlay of $1,000. The R&D project produces a return of $600 at the end of the first year and $550 at the end of the third year. The well, on the other hand, has a single large payoff of $1,200 in three years.

As the calculations show, the discount rate chosen is of some importance. For low values of i, the oil well is preferred to R&D. However, higher discount rates weigh against the oil drilling project (where the returns are concentrated further into the future) and may even make the project inadmissible.

Thus, considerable care must be taken that the value of i used represents as closely as possible the firm's actual opportunity cost of funds. If the discount rate chosen is too high, it will tend to discriminate against projects with returns that come in the relatively distant future and vice versa.

Several criteria other than present value are often used for project evaluation. As we shall see, they can sometimes give misleading answers, and therefore, the present value criteria are preferable. However, these other methods are popular, so it is necessary to understand them, and to be aware of the problems their use entails.

Internal Rate of Return

A firm is considering the following project: It spends $1 million today on an advertising campaign and reaps a benefit of $1.04 million in increased profits a year from now. If you were asked to compute the advertising campaign's "rate of return," you would probably respond "4 percent." Implicitly, you calculated that figure by finding the value of ρ that solves the following equation:

$$-\$1,000,000 + \frac{\$1,040,000}{(1 + \rho)} = 0$$

We can generalize this procedure as follows: If a project yields a stream of benefits (B) and costs (C) over T periods, the **internal rate of return** (ρ) is defined as the ρ which solves the equation

(9.3) $B_0 - C_0 + \dfrac{B_1 - C_1}{1 + \rho} + \dfrac{B_2 - C_2}{(1 + \rho)^2} + \cdots + \dfrac{B_T - C_T}{(1 + \rho)^T} = 0$

The internal rate of return is that discount rate which would make the present value of the project just equal to zero.

An obvious admissibility criterion is to accept a project if ρ exceeds the firm's opportunity cost of funds, i. For example, if the project earns 4 percent while the firm can get 3 percent on other investments, then the project should be done. The corresponding comparability criterion is that if two mutually exclusive projects are both admissible, then the one with the higher value of ρ should be chosen.

However, project selection on the basis of the internal rate of return can lead to bad decisions. Consider project X which requires the expenditure of $100 today and yields $110 a year from now, so that its internal rate of return is 10 percent. Project Y requires $1,000 today, and yields $1,080 in a year, generating an internal rate of return of 8 percent. Assume that the firm can borrow and lend freely at a 6 percent rate of interest.

On the basis of internal rate of return, X is clearly preferred to Y. However, the firm makes only $4 profit on X ($10 minus $6 in interest costs), while it makes a $20 profit on Y ($80 minus $60 in interest costs). Contrary to the conclusion implied by the internal rate of return, the firm should prefer Y, the project with the higher profit. In short, when projects are of different sizes, the internal rate of return can give poor guidance. In contrast, the present value rule gives correct answers even when the projects differ in scale. The present value of X is $-100 + 110/1.06 = 3.77$, while that of Y is $-1{,}000 + 1080/1.06 = 18.87$. The present value criterion says that Y is preferable, as it should.

Sometimes it is impossible even to find a unique value of the internal rate of return. Consider the following three-period project:

Period	$B - C$
0	100
1	−260
2	165

Using Equation (9.3), we find this project's internal rate of return by solving:

$$100 - \frac{260}{1 + \rho} + \frac{165}{(1 + \rho)^2} = 0$$

This is a quadratic equation in ρ, and has *two* roots, $\rho = .1$ and $\rho = .5$.[4] The two values have quite different implications, and there is no obvious way to choose between them.

Benefit-Cost Ratio

Suppose that a project yields a stream of benefits $B_0, B_1, B_2, \ldots, B_T$, and a stream of costs $C_0, C_1, C_2, \ldots, C_T$. Then the present value of the benefits, B, is

$$B = B_0 + \frac{B_1}{1 + i} + \frac{B_2}{(1 + i)^2} + \cdots + \frac{B_T}{(1 + i)^T}$$

and the present value of the costs, C, is

$$C = C_0 + \frac{C_1}{1 + i} + \frac{C_2}{(1 + i)^2} + \cdots + \frac{C_T}{(1 + i)^T}$$

The **benefit-cost ratio** is defined as B/C.

---

[4] Multiplying the equation through by $(1 + \rho)^2$ yields $100(1 + \rho)^2 - 260(1 + \rho) + 165 = 0$ which is equivalent to $\rho^2 - 0.6\rho + 0.05 = 0$. Applying the quadratic formula, $\rho = (.6 \pm \sqrt{.36 - .2})/2 = (.6 \pm .4)/2 = .1$ or $.5$.

Admissibility requires that a project's benefit-cost ratio exceed one. Application of this rule always gives correct guidance. To see this, note simply that $B/C > 1$ implies that $B - C > 0$, which is equivalent to the present value criterion for admissibility.

As a basis for comparing admissible projects, however, the benefit-cost ratio is virtually useless. Consider a community that is considering two methods for disposing of toxic wastes. Method I is a toxic waste dump with $B = \$250$ million, $C = \$100$ million, and therefore a benefit-cost ratio of 2.5. Method II involves sending the wastes in a rocket to Saturn, which has $B = \$200$ million, $C = \$100$ million, and therefore a benefit-cost ratio of 2. The town fathers choose the dump because it has the higher value of B/C. Now suppose that in calculating the benefits and costs of the dump, the analysts inadvertently neglected to take into account crop damage of $40 million that would be caused by seepage. If the $40 million is viewed as a reduction in the dump's benefits, then its B/C becomes $\$210/\$100 = 2.1$, and the dump is still preferred to the rocket. However, the $40 million can just as well be viewed as an increase in costs, in which case $B/C = \$250/\$140 = 1.79$. Now the rocket looks better than the dump!

We have illustrated that there is an inherent ambiguity in computing benefit-cost ratios because benefits can always be counted as "negative costs" and vice versa. Thus, by judicious classification of benefits and costs, any admissible project's benefit-cost ratio can be made arbitrarily high. In contrast, a glance at Equation (9.1) indicates that such shenanigans have no effect whatsoever on the present value criterion because it is based upon the *difference* between benefits and costs rather than their *ratio*.

We conclude that the internal rate of return and the benefit-cost ratio can lead to incorrect inferences. The present value criterion is the most reliable guide.

THE PUBLIC SECTOR DISCOUNT RATE

Sensible decision making by the government also requires present value calculations. However, the way in which the public sector should compute costs, benefits, and discount rates differs from that used in the private sector. This section discusses problems in the selection of a public sector discount rate. In the next, we turn to problems in evaluating costs and benefits.

As suggested above, the discount rate chosen by private individuals should reflect the rate of return available on alternative investments. Although in practice it may be difficult to pinpoint this rate, from a conceptual point of view there is agreement that the opportunity cost of funds to the firm gives the correct value of i.[5]

There is less consensus on the conceptually appropriate discount rate for government projects. Several possibilities have been proposed, some of which are discussed below.[6]

Before-Tax Rate of Return in the Private Sector

Suppose that the last $1,000 of private investment in the economy yields an annual rate of return of 16 percent. If the government extracts $1,000 from the private sector for a project, and the $1,000 is entirely at the expense of private sector investment, then society loses the $160 that would have been generated by the private sector project. Thus, the opportunity cost of the government project is the 16 percent rate of return in the private sector. Because it measures the opportunity cost, the 16 percent should be used as the discount rate. Note that it is irrelevant whether or not this return is taxed. Whether it all stays with the investor or part goes to the government, the before-tax rate of return measures the value of output that the funds would have made available to society.

Weighted Average of Before- and After-Tax Returns

Contrary to the assumption made above, it is likely that some of the funds for the government project would come at the expense of consumption as well as investment. As just argued, for those funds coming out of investment, the before-tax rate of return is the opportunity cost and therefore the appropriate discount rate. But this is not the case for funds that come at the expense of consumption. Consider Nelson, who is deciding how much to consume and how much to save this year. For each dollar Nelson consumes this year, he gives up one dollar of consumption next year *plus* the rate of return he would have earned on the dollar saved. Hence, the opportunity cost to Nelson of a dollar of consumption now is measured by the rate of return he would have received if he had saved the dollar. Now suppose that the before-tax yield on a project available to Nelson is 16 percent, but he must pay 50 percent of the return to the government in the form of taxes. All that Nelson gives up when he consumes an additional dollar today is the *after*-tax rate of return of 8 percent. Because the after-tax rate of return measures what an *individual* loses when his or her consumption is reduced, it is the

---

[5] One reason for the practical difficulties is the fact that there are hundreds of different types of securities on the market, many of which offer different rates of return. Things are complicated further because returns on investments are subject to various taxes, which introduces a difference between the market rate of return and the owner's opportunity cost. See Chapter 14.

[6] See Tresch [1981, Chapter 24] for further discussion of the alternative views.

opportunity cost of dollars that comes at the expense of consumption. In short, dollars that come at the expense of consumption should be discounted by the after-tax rate of return.

Because funds for the public sector come at the expense of both private-sector consumption and investment, a natural solution is to use a weighted average of the before- and after-tax rates of return, with the weight on the before-tax rate equal to the proportion of funds that comes from investment, and that on the after-tax rate the proportion that comes from consumption. In the above example, if one quarter of the funds came at the expense of investment and three quarters at the expense of consumption, then the public-sector discount rate would be 10 percent ($\frac{1}{4} \times$ 16 percent $+ \frac{3}{4} \times$ 8 percent). Unfortunately, in practice it is hard to determine what the proportions of sacrificed consumption and investment actually are for a given government project. The funds are collected from a variety of taxes, each of which has a different effect upon consumption and investment. And even with information on the impact of each tax upon consumption and investment, it is difficult in practice to determine which tax is used to finance which project.

None of this is very important if the magnitudes of pre- and post-tax rates of return are fairly close. In fact, there are large differences. Feldstein [1977] has estimated that the before-tax rate of return in the post–World War II period was about 12 percent, and the after-tax rate only 5 percent. Therefore, the inability to reliably determine a set of weights lessens the usefulness of this approach as a practical guide to determining discount rates.

Social Discount Rate

A third view is that public expenditure evaluation should involve a **social rate of discount,** which measures the valuation that *society* places upon consumption that is sacrificed in the present.[7] But why should "society's" view of the opportunity cost of foregoing consumption differ from the opportunity cost revealed in market rates of return?

Several reasons have been suggested for believing that the social discount rate is lower.

Concern for Future Generations.   It is the duty of public-sector decision makers to care about the welfare not only of the current generation of citizens, but of future generations, as well. The private sector, on the other hand, is concerned only with its own welfare. Hence, from a social point of view, the private sector devotes too few resources to saving—it applies too high a discount rate to returns in the future.

---

[7] Complications arise in implementing this approach when public funds come at the expense of private investment. See Tresch [1981, pp. 500–505].

As Gramlich [1981, p. 97] notes, the idea of government as the guardian of the interests of future generations may be appealing, but it assumes a degree of omniscience and benevolence that is unrealistic. Moreover, even totally selfish individuals often find it in their personal interest to engage in projects that will benefit future generations. If future generations are expected to benefit from some project, then the anticipated profitability will be high, which will encourage investment today. Private firms plant trees today in return for profits on wood sales which may not be realized for many years.[8]

Paternalism. Even from the point of view of their own narrow self-interest, people may not be farsighted enough to adequately weigh benefits in the future; they therefore discount such benefits at too high a rate. Pigou [1932, Chapter 2] described this problem as a "defective telescopic faculty." The government should use the discount rate that individuals *would* use if they knew their own good. This is, of course, a paternalistic argument—government forces citizens to consume less in the present, and in return, they have more in the future, at which time they presumably thank the government for its foresight. Like all paternalistic arguments, this raises the fundamental philosophical question of when it is appropriate to impose public preferences.

Market Inefficiency. When a firm undertakes an investment, it generates knowledge and technological know-how that can benefit other firms. This process has been called **learning by doing** [Arrow, 1962]. In a sense, then, investment creates positive externalities, and by the usual kinds of arguments, investment is underprovided by private markets (see Chapter 7). By applying a discount rate lower than the market's, the government can correct this market inefficiency. The enormous practical problem here is measuring the actual size of the externality. Moreover, the theory of externalities suggests that a more appropriate remedy would be to determine the size of the marginal external benefit at the optimum, and grant a subsidy of that amount (see again Chapter 7).

It appears, then, that none of the arguments concerning the inadequacy of market rates provides much specific guidance with respect to the choice of a public-sector discount rate. Where does this leave us? It would be difficult to argue very strongly against any public rate of discount in a range between the before- and after-tax rates of return in the private sector. One practical procedure is to evaluate the present value

---

[8] Why should people invest in a project whose returns may not be realized until after they are dead? Investors can always sell the rights to future profits to members of the younger generation, and hence consume their share of the anticipated profits during their lifetimes.

of a project over a range of discount rates and see whether or not the present value stays positive for all reasonable values of i. If it does, the analyst can feel some confidence that the conclusion is not sensitive to the discount rate.

VALUING BENEFITS AND COSTS

A second consideration is valuing benefits and costs. From a private firm's point of view, estimating these factors is relatively straightforward. The benefits from a project are the revenues received, and the costs are the firm's payments for inputs. Both are measured by market prices. The evaluation problem is more complicated for the government because *social* benefits and costs may not be reflected in market prices. However, there are several potential ways to measure the benefits and costs of public sector projects.

Market Prices

As noted in Chapter 4, in a properly functioning competitive economy, the price of a good simultaneously reflects marginal social costs of its production and its marginal value to consumers. It would appear that if the government uses inputs and/or produces outputs that are traded in private markets, then market prices should be used for valuation.

The problem is that real-world markets have many imperfections—monopoly, externalities, uncertain information, etc. In such a world, prices do not necessarily reflect marginal social costs and benefits. As McKean [1977, p. 123] has suggested, "There are enough things wrong with observed market prices to make one's hair stand on end."

The relevant question, however, is not whether market prices are perfect, but whether they are likely to be superior to alternative measures of value. Such measures would either have to be made up or derived from highly complicated—and questionable—models of the economy. And, whatever their problems, market prices provide plenty of information at a low cost. Most economists believe that in the absence of any glaring imperfections, market prices should be used to compute public benefits and costs.

Adjusted Market Prices[9]

The prices of goods that are traded in imperfect markets generally do not reflect their marginal social cost. The **shadow price** of such a commodity is its underlying social marginal cost. Although market prices of goods in imperfect markets diverge from shadow prices, in some cases

---

[9] This section is based upon Layard [1977, pp. 18–22].

the market prices can be used to *estimate* the shadow prices. The relevant circumstances are discussed below.

Monopoly.   Suppose that a public project uses a monopolistically produced input. In contrast to perfect competition under which price is equal to marginal cost, a monopolist's price is above marginal cost (see Chapter 4). Should the government value the input at its market price (which measures its value to consumers) or at its marginal production cost (which measures the incremental value of the resources used in its production)?

The answer depends upon the impact of government purchase on the market. If production of the input is expected to increase by the exact amount used by the project, then the social opportunity cost is the value of the resources used in the extra production—the marginal production cost. On the other hand, if no more of the input will be produced, then the government's use comes at the expense of private consumers, whose value of the input is measured by the demand price. If some combination of the two responses is expected, then a weighted average of price and marginal cost is appropriate.[10]

Taxes.   If an input is subject to a sales tax, the price received by the producer of the input is less than the price paid by the purchaser. This is because some portion of the purchase price goes to the tax collector. When the government purchases an input that is subject to sales tax, should the producer's or purchaser's price be used in the cost calculations? The basic principle is the same as that for the monopoly case. If production is expected to expand, then the producer's supply price is appropriate. If production is expected to stay constant, the purchaser's price should be used. For a combination of responses, a weighted average is required.

Unemployment.   Like most microeconomic tools, cost-benefit analysis generally assumes that all resources are fully employed. Nevertheless, a project may involve hiring workers who are currently involuntarily unemployed. Because hiring an unemployed worker does not lower output elsewhere in the economy, the wage the worker is paid does not represent an opportunity cost. All that is foregone when the worker is hired is the leisure he or she was consuming, the value of which is presumably low if the unemployment is involuntary. There are two complications, however: (1) If the government is running its stabilization policy so as to maintain a constant rate of employment, then hiring an unemployed worker may mean reducing employment and output elsewhere in the economy. In this case, the social cost of the worker is

---

[10] Note the similarity to the discount rate problem above.

his or her wage. (2) Even if the worker is involuntarily unemployed when the project begins, it is not necessarily the case that he or she would have continued to be so during its entire duration. But forecasting an individual's future employment prospects is a difficult problem indeed. In light of the current lack of consensus on the causes and nature of unemployment, the pricing of unemployed resources remains a problem with no agreed-upon solution. In the absence of a major depression, valuation of unemployed labor at the going wage is probably a good approximation for practical purposes.

Consumers' Surplus

In many cases, private firms are small relative to the economy. Therefore, they do not have to be concerned that changes in the amount they produce will affect the market price of their product. In contrast, public-sector projects can be so large that they induce changes in market prices. For example, a government irrigation project could bring so much land into production that the market price of food falls. But if the market price changes, how should the additional amount of food be valued—at its original price, at its price after the project, or at some price in-between?

The situation is depicted in Figure 9.1. Pounds of food are measured on the horizontal axis, the price per pound is measured on the vertical,

FIGURE 9.1   Measuring the Change in Consumers' Surplus

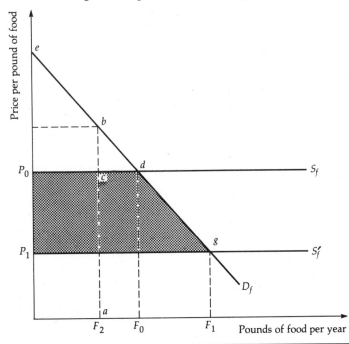

and D_f is the demand schedule for food. Prior to the irrigation project, the supply curve is labeled S_f, and market price and quantity are P_0 and F_0, respectively. (The supply curve is drawn horizontally for convenience. The main points would still hold even if it sloped upward.)

Suppose that after more land is brought into production by the irrigation project, the supply curve for food shifts to S_f'. At the new equilibrium, the price falls to P_1, and food consumption increases to F_1. How much better off are consumers? Another way of stating this question is, "How much would consumers be willing to pay for the privilege of consuming F_1 pounds of food at price P_1 rather than F_0 pounds at price P_0?"

To provide an answer, begin by recalling that the demand curve shows the *maximum* amount that individuals *would be willing* to pay for each pound of food they consume. Consider some arbitrary amount of food, F_2. The most people would be willing to pay for the F_{2th} pound of food is the vertical distance up to the demand curve, *ab* dollars. Before the irrigation project, consumers in fact had to pay only *ac* per pound. In a sense, then, on their purchase of the F_{2th} pound of food, consumers enjoyed a "surplus" of *bc* dollars. The amount by which the sum that individuals would have been *willing* to pay exceeds the sum they *actually* have to pay is called the **consumers' surplus.**

Of course, the same exercise could be repeated at any level of output, not just as F_2. When the price is P_0 for each level of consumption, the consumers' surplus at each output level equals the distance between the demand curve and the horizontal line at P_0. Summing the surpluses for each pound of food purchased, we find that the total consumers' surplus when the price is P_0 is the area P_0ed. More generally, consumers' surplus is measured by the area under the demand curve and above a horizontal line at the market price.

When the price of food falls to P_1 as a consequence of the irrigation project, consumers' surplus is still the area under the demand curve and above a horizontal line at the going price, but because the price is now P_1, the relevant area is P_1eg. Consumers' surplus has therefore increased by the difference between areas P_1eg and P_0ed—area P_1P_0dg. Thus, the area behind the demand curve between the two prices measures the value to consumers of being able to purchase food at the lower price.[11] Provided that the planner can estimate the shape of the demand curve, the benefit of the project can be measured.

---

[11] Consumers' surplus gives only an approximation to the true value of the change in consumer welfare. This is because the consumers' surplus measure ignores the fact that as price changes, so do people's real incomes, and this may change the value that they place on additions to their income (the *marginal utility of income*.) However, Willig [1976] has shown that consumers' surplus is likely to be a pretty good approximation in most cases, and it is used widely in applied work.

Inferences from Economic Behavior

We have so far been dealing with cases in which market data can serve as a starting point for analysis. Sometimes the good in question is not explicitly traded, so no market price exists. We discuss two examples of how people's willingness to pay for such commodities can be estimated.

The Value of Time.   Suppose that if the government builds a road it will save each traveler half an hour a day. While it is true that "time is money," to do benefit-cost analysis we need to know *how much* money. A common way to estimate the value of time is to take advantage of the theory of leisure/income choice. If people have control over the amount they work, they will work just until the point where the subjective value of leisure is equal to the income they gain from one more hour of work—the after-tax wage rate. Thus, the after-tax wage can be used to value the time that is saved.[12]

Although this is a useful approach, it has two major problems: (1) Some people cannot choose their hours of work. Involuntary unemployment represents an extreme but common case. (2) Not all uses of time away from the job are equivalent. For example, to avoid spending time on the road, a person who hated driving might be willing to pay at a rate exceeding his wage. On the other hand, a person who used the road for pleasure drives on weekends might not care very much about the opportunity cost of time, particularly if he or she could not work on weekends anyway.

Several attempts have been made to estimate the value of time by looking at people's choices between modes of transportation that involve different traveling times. Suppose that in a given community people can commute to work either by bus or by train. The train takes less time, but is more expensive. By seeing how much extra money people are willing to pay for the train, we can infer how much they are willing to pay to reduce their commuting time, and hence how they value that time. Of course, other characteristics of people, such as their income, affect their choice of travel mode. Statistical techniques similar to those described in Chapter 3 can be used to take these other variables into account. Several such studies done using British data [Layard, 1977, p. 24] found the effective cost of traveling time to be about one quarter the before-tax wage rate, or, assuming a 20 percent tax rate on earnings, about 30 percent of the after-tax wage rate.

The Value of Life.   A newspaper reporter once asked the head of the Federal Occupational Safety and Health Administration "how do you

---

[12] For further details, see Chapter 15.

place dollar values on human life or health?" [Shabecoff, 1981, p. E9]. It's a hard question. Our religious and cultural values suggest that life is priceless. When a child falls down a mineshaft, no one stops to compute the costs of rescuing her. Similarly, if a person were asked to value his own life, it would not be surprising if the response indicated that only the sky was the limit.

From the point of view of cost-benefit analysis, such a position presents obvious difficulties. If the value of life is infinite, then any project which leads even to a single life being saved has an infinitely high present value. This leaves no sensible way to determine the admissibility of projects. If *every* road in America were a divided four-lane highway, it is doubtless true that traffic fatalities would decrease. Would this be a good project?

Two methods for assigning finite values to human life have been considered by economists. The first requires measuring the individual's lost earnings; the second requires estimating the value the individual puts on changes in the probability of death.

Lost Earnings.   The value of life is the present value of the individual's net earnings over his lifetime.[13] If an individual dies as a consequence of a given project, then the cost to society is just the expected present value of the output he would have produced. This approach is often used in law courts to determine how much compensation the relatives of accident fatalities should receive. However, if this approach is taken literally, it means that society would suffer no loss if the aged infirm or severely handicapped were summarily executed. This implication is sufficiently bizarre that the method is rejected by many economists.

Probability of Death.   A second approach has as its starting point the notion that most projects do not actually affect with *certainty* a given individual's prospects for living. Rather, it is more typical for a change in the *probability* of a person's death to be involved.[14] For example, you do not know that cancer research will save *your* life. All that can be determined is that it may reduce the probability of your death. The reason this distinction is so important is that even if people view their lives as having infinite value, they very often accept increases in the probability of death for finite amounts of money. An individual driving a light car is subject to a greater probability of death in an auto accident than his counterpart in a heavy car, other things being the same. People are willing to accept the increased risk of death because of the money they can save by purchasing the lighter car.

Another way that people reveal their risk preferences is by their occu-

---

[13] See Klarman [1965] for an example using this approach.
[14] See Mishan [1971b] for further details.

pational choices. Some jobs involve a higher probability of death than others. Suppose we compare two workers who have identical job qualifications (education, experience, etc.), but one is in a riskier job than the other. The individual on the riskier job is expected to have a higher wage to compensate him for the higher probability of death. The difference between the two wages provides an estimate of the value that people place on a decreased probability of death. Using data from 1967, Thaler and Rosen [1976] estimated that for each .01 increase in the probability of death in an occupation, the yearly earnings in the occupation increased by about $2,000.[15] (In terms of 1983 dollars, the figure is about $6,000).

An appealing aspect of this approach is that it puts the analysis on the same willingness to pay basis that is so fruitful in other contexts. It remains highly controversial, however. Broome [1978] has argued that the probabilistic approach is irrelevant once it is conceded that *some* people's lives are *certainly* going to be at stake. The fact that we happen to be ignorant of just who will die is beside the point. If this position is taken, we are back where we started, with no way at all to value projects that involve human life.

This academic controversy has become a matter of public concern, because of various proposals to subject government safety regulations to cost-benefit analysis. In an attack on one proposal, the president of the Amalgamated Clothing and Textiles Workers Union said, "It seems incredible that in 1981 anyone could seriously suggest trading lives for dollars" [Finley, 1981, p. A23]. Unfortunately, in a world of scarce resources, we have no choice in the matter. The only question is whether or not sensible ways for valuing will be used.

Valuing Intangibles

Some benefits and costs seem impossible to value, no matter how ingenious the investigator. One of the benefits of the space program is increased national prestige. Creating national parks gives people the thrill of enjoying beautiful scenery. The mind boggles at putting a dollar value on these "commodities." Three points must be kept in mind when intangible items might be important.

First, intangibles can subvert the entire cost-benefit exercise. By claiming that they are large enough, *any* project can be made admissible.[16]

---

[15] The cost-benefit analyst should also consider the psychological cost of bereavement to families and friends, and the changes in financial status of relatives.

[16] In Israel, a careful cost-benefit analysis of a canal between the Mediterranean and Dead Seas indicated that it was not worthwhile. But it was suggested that building the canal was part of the fulfillment of the Zionist dream. Who can argue with visionaries? The canal was authorized.

Second, the tools of cost-benefit analysis can sometimes be used to force planners to reveal limits on how they value intangibles. Suppose that a space program's measurable costs and benefits are C and B, respectively, and its intangible benefits, such as national prestige, are an unknown amount X. Then if the measured costs are greater than measured benefits, X must exceed $(C - B)$ for the program to be admissible.[17] With this information, it may become clear that the intangible is not valuable enough to merit doing the project. If $(C - B)$ for the space program were $10 million per year, people might agree that its contribution to national prestige was worth it. But if the figure were $10 billion, a different conclusion might emerge.

Finally, even if it is impossible to measure certain benefits, there may be alternative methods of attaining them. If so, systematic study of the costs of the various alternatives should be done to find the cheapest way possible. This is sometimes called **cost-effectiveness analysis.** Thus, while it may be impossible to put a dollar value on "national security," it still may be feasible to subject the costs of alternative weapons systems to careful scrutiny.

SOME PITFALLS IN COST-BENEFIT ANALYSIS

In addition to the problems we have already discussed, Tresch [1981] has noted a number of common errors in cost-benefit analysis.

The Chain-Reaction Game

The idea here is to make a proposal look especially attractive by counting secondary profits arising from it as part of the benefits. If the government builds a road, the primary benefits are the reductions in transportation costs for individuals and firms. At the same time, though, profits of local restaurants, motels, and gas stations probably increase. This leads to increased profits in the local food, bed-linen, and gasoline-production industries. If enough of such secondary effects are added to the benefit side, then eventually a positive present value can be obtained for practically any project.

The major flaw with this procedure arises from the fact that the calculation should take into account the losses as well as the profits induced by the project. It is just as easy to find a list of secondary losses as gains. After the road is built, the profits of train operators will decrease as some of their customers turn to cars for transportation. Increased auto use may bid up the price of gasoline, which will decrease the welfare of

---

[17] A similar strategy can be applied to intangible costs.

many gasoline consumers. In short, if secondary benefits are counted, secondary losses must be also.

It is essentially impossible to trace through all the secondary benefits and losses of a project. The best strategy is probably to assume that such secondary gains and losses approximately offset each other, and focus attention on the difficult enough problems of assessing primary benefits and costs.

The Labor Game

In 1982, the Congress debated and eventually passed a multibillion-dollar bill to improve the quality of the nation's roads. Although some of the public debate concerned the benefits that would follow from improved highways, proponents of the bill emphasized the fact that the project would employ a lot of labor. Indeed, the measure was often referred to as a "highway repair and job-creation bill."

This is a typical example of the argument that a given project should be implemented because of all the employment that it will "create." Essentially, the wages of the workers employed are viewed as *benefits* of the project. This is absurd, because wages belong on the cost, not the benefit side of the calculation. Of course, as suggested above, it is true that if workers are involuntarily unemployed, their social cost is less than their wage. But even in an area with high unemployment, it is unlikely that all the labor used in the project would have been unemployed, or that all those who were unemployed would have remained so for a long time.

The Double-Counting Game

Suppose that the government is considering irrigating some land which currently cannot be cultivated. It counts as the project's benefits the sum of (1) the increase in value of the land, *and* (2) the present value of the stream of net income obtained from farming it. The problem here is that a farmer can *either* farm the land and take as gains the net income stream, *or* sell the land to someone else. Under competition, the sales price of the land just equals the present value of the net income from farming it. Because the farmer cannot do both simultaneously, counting both (1) and (2) represents a doubling of the true benefits.

This error may seem so silly that no one would ever commit it. However, Tresch [1981, p. 561] points out that at one time double counting was the official policy of the Bureau of Reclamation within the U.S. Department of the Interior. The Bureau's instructions for cost-benefit analysts indicated that the benefits of land irrigation be computed as the *sum* of the increase in land value and the present value of the net income from farming it.

DISTRIBUTIONAL CONSIDERATIONS

So far, we have not taken into account the distributional effects of public projects. In the private sector, normally no consideration is given to the question of who receives the benefits and bears the costs of a project. A dollar is a dollar, regardless of who is involved. Some economists have argued that the same view be taken in public-project analysis. If the present value of a project is positive, it should be undertaken regardless of who gains and loses. This is because as long as the present value is positive, the gainers *could* compensate the losers and still enjoy a net increase in utility. This notion, sometimes called the **Hicks-Kaldor criterion,** thus bases project selection on *potential* gains in social welfare.[18] The actual compensation does not have to take place.

Others believe that because the goal of government is to maximize social welfare (not profit), the distributional implications of a project should be taken into account. Moreover, because it is the *actual* pattern of benefits and costs that really matters, the Hicks-Kaldor criterion does not provide a satisfactory escape from grappling with distributional issues.

One way to avoid the distributional problem is to assume that the government can and will costlessly correct any undesirable distributional aspects of a project by making the appropriate transfers between gainers and losers.[19] The government works continually in the background to ensure that income stays optimally distributed,[20] so that the cost-benefit analyst need only be concerned with computing present values. Again, reality gets in the way. The government may have neither the power nor the ability to distribute income optimally.[21]

Suppose that cost-benefit analyst believes that some group in the population is especially deserving. This distributional preference can be taken into account by assuming that a dollar benefit to a member of this group is worth more than a dollar going to others in the population. This, of course, tends to bias the selection of projects in favor of those

---

[18] See Hicks [1940] and Kaldor [1939].

[19] "Costlessly" in this context means that the transfer system costs nothing to administer, and the transfers are done in such a way that they do not distort people's economic behavior. See Chapter 12.

[20] It may be useful at this point to recall the problems involved in defining an optimal income distribution. See Chapter 5.

[21] Moreover, as the government works "behind the scenes" to modify income distribution, relative prices will probably change. But as relative prices change, so do the benefit and cost calculations. Hence, efficiency and equity issues cannot be separated as neatly as suggested here.

which especially benefit the preferred group. Although much of the discussion of distributional considerations has focused on income as the basis for classifying people, presumably characteristics like race, ethnicity, and sex can be used, as well.

Suppose that the policymaker who actually has to make the decision supplies the cost-benefit analyst with the criteria for membership in the preferred group. The analyst still faces the question of precisely how to weight benefits to members of that group relative to the rest of society. It will matter a lot whether a dollar to a poor person is counted as twice a dollar to a rich person, or 50 times as much. As usual, the resolution of such issues depend upon value judgments. All the analyst can do is induce the policymaker to state explicitly his or her value judgments and understand their implications.

A potential hazard of introducing distributional considerations is that political concerns will come to dominate the entire cost-benefit exercise. Depending upon how weights are chosen, any project can generate a positive present value, regardless of how inefficient it is. In addition, incorporating distributional considerations substantially increases the information requirements of cost-benefit analysis. The analyst needs to estimate not only benefits and costs, but also how they are distributed across the population. As noted in Chapter 5, it is difficult indeed to assess the distributional implications of government fiscal activities.

UNCERTAINTY

So far we have been assuming that all benefits and costs are known with certainty. However, many important debates over project proposals center around the fact that their outcomes are not known for sure. How much will a job-training program increase the earnings of trainees? Is it likely that a nuclear reactor will blow up? If it does, what will be the damages?

Suppose that two projects are being considered. They have identical costs, and both affect only one citizen, Smith. Project X guarantees a benefit of $1,000 with certainty. Project Y creates a benefit of zero dollars with a probability of one in two, and a benefit of $2,000 with a probability of one in two. Which project does Smith prefer?

Note that on average, the benefit from Y is equal to that from X. This is because the expected benefit from Y is $\frac{1}{2} \times \$0 + \frac{1}{2} \times \$2,000 = \$1,000$. Nevertheless, if Smith is risk averse, she prefers X to Y. This is because project Y subjects Smith to risk, while X is a sure thing. In other words, if Smith is risk averse, she would be willing to trade project Y for a *certain* amount of money less than $1,000—she is willing to give up some income in return for gaining some security. The most obvious evidence that people are in fact willing to pay to avoid risk is the widespread holding of insurance policies of various kinds.

Therefore, when the benefits or costs of a project are risky, they must be converted into **certainty equivalents**—the amount of *certain* income that the individual would be willing to trade for the set of uncertain outcomes generated by the project. The computation of certainty equivalents requires information on both the distribution of returns from the project and how risk averse the people involved are. The method of calculation is described in the appendix to this chapter.

The calculation of certainty equivalents presupposes that the random distribution of costs and benefits is known in advance. In some cases, this is reasonable assumption. For example, in estimating the benefits from a dam, engineering and weather data could be used to estimate how it would reduce the probability of flood destruction. In many important cases, however, it is hard to assign probabilities to various outcomes. There is not enough experience with nuclear reactors to gauge the likelihood of various malfunctions. Similarly, how do you estimate the probability that a given weapons system will deter foreign aggression? As usual, the best the analyst can do is to make explicit his or her assumptions, and determine the extent to which substantive findings change when these assumptions are modified.

AN APPLICATION OF COST-BENEFIT ANALYSIS: RECREATIONAL USE OF THE WHITE CLOUD PEAKS[22]

The White Cloud Peaks lie about 30 miles north of Sun Valley, Idaho. This public area occupies about 20,000 acres, supports a large variety of wildlife, and with some development could provide excellent opportunities for hiking, camping, fishing, and hunting. The White Cloud Peaks also appear to have substantial deposits of the valuable metal, molybdenum, and the late 1960s, a company requested permission to mine these deposits. The land cannot be used for mining and for recreation simultaneously. Should the White Cloud Peaks be developed for recreational purposes? Should the area be mined instead? Or should it be left alone altogether?

Krutilla and Fisher [1975] (hereafter referred to simply as K & F) employed the tools of cost-benefit analysis to answer these questions. We discuss here only one component of K & F's study—an examination of whether the incremental costs of developing the White Cloud Peaks for recreational use would exceed the incremental benefits. The analysis well illustrates several of the issues raised in this chapter.

Estimating the costs and benefits of developing the White Cloud Peaks for "recreation" requires that just what *kind* of recreation by specified. Constructing roads for Jeeps has very different costs and benefits than extending hiking trails. K & F assumed that the land would be used

---

[22] This section is based on Krutilla and Fisher [1975, chap. 7].

in such a way that its basic ecology would be preserved. Specifically, they assumed that development would take the form of creating four additional trails, which would allow more access for visitors.

Earlier sections of this chapter indicated that cost-benefit analysis entails selecting a discount rate and specifying the costs and benefits for each year. These are now discussed in turn.

Discount Rate

As usual, there is no compelling theoretical reason to choose one particular discount rate, so K & F followed the sensible practice of selecting several and seeing whether the substantive results are sensitive to the differences. We report below their results for discount rates of 7 percent and 10 percent.

Costs

Creating additional trails requires immediate outlays for equipment and labor, estimated to be $23,000 in 1971. This figure is recorded in row

TABLE 9.3 Incremental Costs for Expanded Recreational Use of White Cloud Peaks

		Present Value	
Trail Extensions		*i = 7%*	*i = 10%*
(1) Initial outlays: $23,000		$ 23,000	$ 23,000
(2) Maintenance outlays per year: $12,092		170,981	119,835
(3) Total present value of trail extensions costs (sum of rows *(1)* and *(2)*)		193,981	142,835
Sanitary Facilities			
Outlays for equipment:			
(4) In year 1, nine toilets at a cost of $750 per toilet		$ 6,750	$ 6,750
(5) In year 30, nine toilets		887	387
(6) In year 60, nine toilets		114	20
(7) Maintenance and operation outlays per year: $100		1,414	990
(8) Total present value of sanitation costs (sum of rows *(4)*, *(5)*, *(6)*, and *(7)*)		$ 9,165	$ 8,147
(9) Present value of all costs (sum of rows *(3)* and *(8)*)		$203,146	$150,982

Source: Computations based on Krutilla and Fisher [1975, p. 163].

(1) of Table 9.3. Because these capital outlays are made immediately, their present value is also $23,000, regardless of the discount rate.

After the trails are put in, yearly expenditures must be made for their maintenance. The estimated annual cost is $12,092. Because these costs are incurred over time, however, they must be discounted. Row (2) of Table 9.3 shows the discounted present value of these maintenance expenditures over a 50-year period for both $i = 7$ percent and $i = 10$ percent. Note how the present value of maintenance is smaller with the higher discount rate.

The total cost of extending the trails is given in row (3). It is the present value of the capital and maintenance outlays.

If the goal is to expand recreational use *while maintaining the quality of the environment*, then appropriate sanitation facilities are required. K & F estimated that initially nine toilets, at a cost of $750 per toilet, are needed. The total expenditure, $6,750, is recorded in row (4). The toilets have to be replaced at 30-year intervals. Rows (5) and (6) show the present value of the same $6,750 toilet expenditure made 30 and 60 years in the future, respectively. In addition, the sanitation facilities have to be maintained at an annual cost of $100. The present value of this stream of expenditures at the two discount rates is recorded in row (7). Row (8) gives the sum of all the sanitation costs, and row (9) adds these to the costs of extending the trails. In terms of our earlier notation (p. 182), the future in row (9) represent C, the present value of the project's costs, at each discount rate.

Benefits

A key piece of information is required: how much would people be willing to pay for the privilege of using the new trails? On the basis of survey studies of other recreational areas, K & F estimated that in the initial year (1971), a typical user would be willing to pay $10 per day. They further estimated that the area would be used 4,600 recreation-days that year, making the first year's benefit $46,000.

The analysis required estimates of benefits in future years as well. K & F assumed that use of the area would grow initially by 10 percent per year, and that willingness to pay would increase by 4 percent per year.[23] Of course, an uninterrupted growth rate of 10 percent a year over a long period of time would result in the area being overrun by visitors. On the basis of discussions with district rangers and other experts, K & F postulated a maximum number of possible users consistent with maintaining environmental quality. After this figure is reached, the annual number of visits is not allowed to grow.

On the basis of K & F's willingness-to-pay calculations, the benefits flowing from the increased expenditures for recreational use are as

---

[23] As use increases, some congestion occurs, which tends to lower people's willingness to pay. (A visit to a crowded wilderness area isn't as pleasant as a visit to a quiet one.) K & F estimated the dampening effect of increased congestion costs and factored it into their willingness-to-pay calculations.

TABLE 9.4   Incremental Benefits for Expanded
              Recreational use of White Cloud
              Peaks

Present Value

$i = 7\%$	$i = 10\%$
$991,000	$390,000

Source: Krutilla and Fisher
[1975, p. 171].

shown in Table 9.4. In terms of our earlier notation, Table 9.4 gives the value of B, the present value of the benefits, for each discount rate.

Computation of the net present value of the project is now straight-forward. For each discount rate, take the benefit value from Table 9.4, and subtract from it the cost figure from row (9) of Table 9.3. This computation reveals that when $i = 7$ percent, benefits minus costs are $787,854, and when $i = 10$ percent, benefits minus costs are $239,018. Thus, for either choice of discount rate, $(B - C)$ exceeds zero, and by the present value criterion, the project is admissible. This does not complete the analysis, however, because we still have to find out whether the net present value exceeds that of the alternative project, molybdenum mining. However, discussion of that part of the study would take us too far afield. Interested readers should consult Krutilla and Fisher [1975] for further details.

Comments

This White Cloud Peaks analysis illustrates some important aspects of practical cost-benefit studies:

1. The analysis is often interdisciplinary because economists alone do not have the technical expertise to evaluate all costs and benefits. Thus, engineers were required to predict construction costs of the trails, wilderness-use experts to estimate the maximum number of campers the area can support, etc.
2. Evaluation of costs and benefits, especially those arising in the future, is likely to require some ad hoc assumptions. As shown above, it is difficult enough to estimate *current* willingness to pay for a commodity that is not priced on the market; projecting such figures decades into the future is even tougher. In most cases, all the analyst can do is assume that willingness to pay follows some pattern of growth, and see whether the substantive results change when alternative reasonable patterns are postulated. Moreover, in situations characterized by so much uncertainty, it may overburden the analysis to include distributional considerations. An investigator who can

barely predict the total number of users two decades in the future can hardly be expected to estimate the distribution of their incomes as well.

3. For all its limitations, cost-benefit analysis is a remarkably useful way of summarizing information. It also forces analysts to make explicit their assumptions so that the *reasons* for their ultimate recommendation are clear.

CONCLUDING REMARKS

Much effort has been devoted to refining the techniques of cost-benefit analysis. Have these methods been put to work by the government? Stipulations that certain kinds of federal projects be subjected to cost-benefit analysis began appearing in the late 1930s.[24] However, it was not until the mid-1960s that such analysis received major public interest. At that time, President Lyndon Johnson's Great Society (a catchall term for a number of social programs) was leading to a tremendous expansion in the scope and magnitude of government programs. With so many new projects being proposed, some kind of systematic evaluation procedure seemed needed.

Thus was born the *Planning Programming Budget System* (PPBS), which was adopted by the federal government in 1965. It mandated that each program's costs and benefits be computed, and that they be compared to the returns of relevant alternatives. Furthermore, common analytic techniques were to be used throughout the government, where possible.

However, PPBS does not appear to have induced major changes in the style of government project selection, and there are several probable reasons for its failure. This was partly due to the many practical difficulties in implementing cost-benefit analysis, particularly when there is no consensus as to what the government's objectives are. In addition, many bureaucrats lacked either the ability or the temperament to perform the analysis—particularly when it came to their own programs. And neither were politicians particularly eager to see their pet projects subjected to careful scrutiny.

Nevertheless, PPBS did introduce some tendency toward more systematic evaluation of government projects. Many government bureaucracies have created planning and analysis units and hired social scientists to staff them. The use of cost-benefit analysis received further encouragement when the Reagan administration announced that it would subject proposals for new regulations to cost-benefit analysis.

---

[24] Gramlich [1981, pp. 7–11] provides a concise and useful discussion of the history of cost-benefit analysis in the United States.

On the other hand, in certain vital areas not only has cost-benefit analysis failed to take hold, it has been expressly forbidden. For example, the Occupational Safety and Health Act of 1970 stated that the Secretary of Labor "shall set the standard which most adequately assures, *to the extent feasible* . . . that no employee will suffer material impairment of health or functional capacity" [italics added] ["A High Court Win for OSHA," 1981, p. 59]. In 1981, a Supreme Court majority interpreted this as meaning that the costs of achieving a given improvement in health are strictly irrelevant. Justice Brennan wrote, "Congress itself defined the basic relationship between costs and benefits by placing the 'benefit' of worker health above all other considerations save those making attainment of this 'benefit' unachievable" ["A High Court Win," 1981, p. 59].

However, as Justice Rehnquist pointed out, feasibility is really "no standard at all"—the only perfectly safe factory is an empty factory [MacAvoy, 1981, p. F3]. Although cost-benefit analysis is surely an imperfect tool, it is the only analytical framework available for making consistent decisions. Forbidding cost-benefit analysis amounts to outlawing sensible decision making.

SUMMARY

Cost-benefit analysis is the practical use of welfare economics to evaluate potential projects.

Cost-benefit analyses consider net benefits received over time. To make these comparable, the present value of all future net benefits is computed using either the nominal values and the nominal interest rate or real values for net benefits and the real interest rate.

Other methods—internal rate of return, benefit-cost ratio—can lead to incorrect decisions when the scales of projects differ or items are difficult to categorize as benefits or costs. The present value criterion is superior in this context.

Choosing the discount rate is critical in cost-benefit analyses. In public-sector analyses three measures have been proposed: the before-tax private rate of return, a weighted average of before- and after-tax private rates of return, and the social discount rate. Choosing among them depends upon the type of private activity displaced—investment or consumption—and the degree to which private markets are believed to reflect society's preferences.

In private decisions, benefits and costs are measured by market prices.
On the other hand, the benefits and costs of public projects may be measured in several ways:
Market prices serve well if there is no strong reason to believe that they depart from social marginal costs.

Shadow prices adjust market prices for deviations from social marginal costs due to monopoly power, taxes, unemployed resources, etc. In each case, the investigator must determine the value of resources in their alternative uses. This may be the market price, including the distortion if production is constant and consumption is displaced, or the cost of inputs if production increases and private consumption is unchanged.

If the resource, especially labor, is currently unemployed and will remain so for the duration of the project, the opportunity cost is small. However, forecasting employment is quite difficult.

Consumers' surplus measures the benefit to consumers of changes in market prices. If large government projects change equilibrium prices, analysts may measure consumers' surplus by estimating the shape of the demand curve.

For nonmarketed commodities, no prices are available. In some instances, the values of these commodities can be inferred by observing people's behavior. Two examples are computing the benefits of saving time and the benefits of a reduced probability of death.

Certain intangible benefits and costs simply cannot be measured. The safest approach is to exclude these in a cost-benefit analysis and then calculate how large intangibles must be to reverse the decision.

Despite the attention placed on procedures for cost-benefit analysis, actual discussions sometimes fall prey to several pitfalls:

Chain-reaction game—secondary benefits are included to make a proposal appear more favorable, without including the corresponding secondary costs.

Labor game—wages are viewed as *benefits* rather than *costs* of the project.

Double-counting game—benefits are mistakenly counted twice.

Distributional considerations are an unsettled area of cost-benefit analysis. Some analysts count dollars equally for all persons, while others apply weights which favor projects for selected population groups. Because of the potential for political manipulation, distributional weights must be introduced explicitly.

In uncertain situations, individuals favor less risky projects, other things being the same. In general, the costs and benefits of uncertain projects must be adjusted to reflect this.

DISCUSSION QUESTIONS

1. The Army Corps of Engineers frequently employs the cost-benefit ratio for evaluating public projects. In Senate hearings on a breakwater project, one Senator was impressed that the project had "an amazingly high 17 to 1 benefit-cost ratio" [U.S. Congress, 1973, p. 1]. If you were an assistant to the Senator, what would you have said?

2. The city of Sundown is considering a plan to build a convention center to revitalize the downtown area. The project requires hiring workers in the construction union. Because of unionization, the workers' wage rate is above the value which would be determined by supply and demand. However, city analysts have econometrically estimated the wage that would prevail if the labor market were competitive.

    a. If the convention center increases the total number of construction workers employed, what is the appropriate cost of labor?

    b. Suppose instead that total employment is unaffected; workers leave private projects to work in the convention center. Does your answer to **(a)** change? Why?

3. A project yields an annual benefit of $25 a year, starting next year and continuing forever. What is the present value of the benefits if the interest rate is 10 percent. [HINT: The infinite sum $x + x^2 + x^3 + \ldots$ is equal to $x/(1 - x)$, where x is a number less than 1.]

4. An outlay of $1,000 today yields an annual benefit of $80 beginning next year and continuing forever. There is no inflation and the market interest rate is 10 percent before taxes and 5 percent after taxes.

    a. What is the internal rate of return?

    b. Taxes levied to fund the project come entirely from consumer spending. Is the project admissible? Why? Suppose instead that taxes are collected by reducing private firms' investments. Is the project admissible in this case? Finally, suppose that consumers spend 60 cents of their last dollar and save 40 cents. Is the project admissible now? Explain your calculations.

    c. Suppose that the social discount rate is 4 percent. What is the present value of the project?

    d. Now suppose that 10 percent annual inflation is anticipated over the next 10 years. How are your answers to **(a)**, **(b)** and **(c)** affected?

5. Bill rides the subway at a cost of 75 cents per trip, but would switch if the price were any higher. His only alternative is a bus which takes five minutes longer, but costs only 50 cents. He makes 10 trips per year. The city is considering renovations of the subway system which would reduce the trip by 10 minutes, but fares would rise by 40 cents per trip to cover the costs. The fare increase and reduced travel time both take effect in one year and last forever. The interest rate is 25 percent.

    a. As far as Bill is concerned, what are the present values of the project's benefits and costs?

    b. The city's population consists of 55,000 "middle-class" people, all of whom are identical to Bill, and 5,000 "poor" people. Poor people are either unemployed or have jobs close to their homes, so they do not use any form of public transportation. What are the total benefits and costs of the project for the city as a whole? What is the net present value of the project?

    c. Some members of the city council propose an alternative project which consists of an immediate tax of $1.25 per middle-class person to provide "free" legal services for the poor in both of the following two years. The legal services are valued by the poor at a total of $62,500 per year.

(Assume this amount is received at the end of each of the two years.) What is the present value of the project?

  d. If the city must choose between the subway project and the legal services project, which should it select?

*e. What is the "distributional weight" of each dollar received by a poor person that would make the present values of the two projects just equal? That is, how much must each dollar of income to a poor person be weighted relative to that of a middle-class person? Interpret your answer.

SELECTED REFERENCES

Broome, J. "Trying to Value a Life." *Journal of Public Economics*, February 1978, pp. 91–100.

Klarman, Herbert E. "Syphilis Control Programs." In *Measuring Benefits of Government Investments*. ed. Robert Dorfman. Washington, D.C.: Brookings Institution, 1965, pp. 367–409.

McKean, R. N. "The Use of Shadow Prices." In *Cost-Benefit Analysis*. ed. Richard Layard. New York: Penguin Books, 1977, pp. 119–39.

Mishan, E. J. "Evaluation of Life and Limb: A Theoretical Approach." *Journal of Political Economy* 79, no. 4 (1971), pp. 687–705.

APPENDIX 9A
CALCULATING THE CERTAINTY
EQUIVALENT VALUE

This appendix shows how the certainty equivalent value of an uncertain project is calculated.

Consider Jones, whose current earnings are E dollars. He enters a job-training program with an unpredictable effect on his future earnings. The program will leave his annual earnings unchanged with a probability of $\frac{1}{2}$, or it will increase his earnings by y dollars, also with a probability of $\frac{1}{2}$.[25] The benefit of the program is the amount that Jones would be willing to pay for it, so the key problem here is to determine that amount. A natural answer is $\frac{1}{2}y$ dollars, the expected increase in his

---

* Difficult.

[25] In this analysis, probabilities of $\frac{1}{2}$ are used for simplicity. The general results hold regardless of the probabilities chosen. Incidentally, Kiefer's [1978] careful study of federally subsidized occupational-training programs suggests that in fact, they have little or no impact on subsequent employment or earnings.

earnings.[26] However, this value is too high, because it neglects the fact that the outcome is uncertain and therefore subjects Jones to risk. As long as Jones does not like risk, he would give up some income in return for gaining some security. When the benefits or costs of a project are risky, they must be converted into **certainty equivalents,** the amounts of *certain* income that the individual would be willing to trade for the set of uncertain outcomes generated by the project.

The notion of certainty equivalence is illustrated in Figure 9A.1. The horizontal axis measures Jones' income, and the vertical axis indicates

FIGURE 9A.1   Computing the Certainty Equivalent of a Risky Project

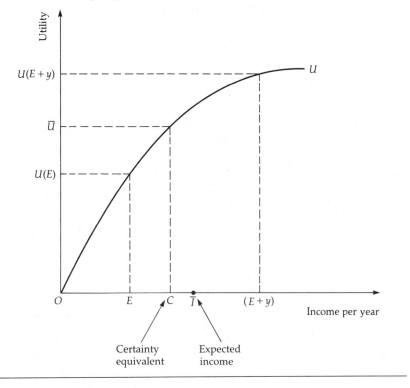

the amount of his utility. Schedule *OU* is Jones's utility function, which shows the total amount of utility associated with each income level. Algebraically, the amount of utility associated with a given income level, *I*, is *U(I)*. The shape of the schedule indicates that as income increases,

---

[26] Expected earnings are found simply by multiplying each possible outcome by the associated probability and then adding: $(\frac{1}{2} \times 0) + (\frac{1}{2} \times y) = \frac{1}{2}y$.

utility also increases, but at a slower rate—there is diminishing marginal utility of income.[27]

To find the amount of utility associated with any income level, simply go from the horizontal axis up to *OU*, and then off to the vertical axis. For example, if the training project yields no return so that Jones's income is *E*, then his utility is *U(E)*, as indicated on the vertical axis. Similarly, if the project succeeds so that Jones's income increases by *y*, then his total income is *(E + y)*, and his utility is *U(E + y)*.

Because each outcome occurs with a probability of ½, Jones's average or expected *income* is *E + y/2*, which lies halfway between *E* and *(E + y)* and is denoted $\bar{I}$. However, what Jones really cares about is not expected income, but expected *utility*.[28] Expected utility is just the average of the utilities of the two outcomes, or ½*U(E)* + ½*U(E + y)*. Geometrically, expected utility is halfway between *U(E)* and *U(E + y)*, and is denoted by $\bar{U}$.

We are now in a position to find out exactly how much certain money the job-training program is worth to Jones. All we have to do is find the amount of income that corresponds to utility level $\bar{U}$. This is shown on the horizontal axis as *C*, which is by definition the certainty equivalent. It is crucial to note that *C* is less than $\bar{I}$—the certainty equivalent of the job training program is *less* than the expected income. This is consistent with the intuition developed above. Jones is willing to pay a premium of $(\bar{I} - C)$ in exchange for the security of a "sure thing."

We have shown, then, that proper evaluation of the costs and benefits of an uncertain project requires more than finding the project's expected value. The latter must be reduced by a risk premium which depends upon the shape of the individual's utility function.

In a way, this is a disappointing outcome, because the computation of an expected value is relatively much more simple than that of a certainty equivalent. Fortunately, it turns out that in many cases the expected value is enough. Suppose that a new bomber is being considered, and because the technology is not completely understood, analysts are unsure of its eventual cost. The cost will be either $15 per family or $25, each with probability ½. Although in the aggregate a large amount of money is at stake, on a per-*family* basis, the sums involved are quite small compared to income. In terms of Figure 9A.1, the two outcomes are very close to each other on curve *OU*. As points on *OU* get closer and closer together, the expected value and certainty equivalent become virtually identical, other things being the same. Intuitively, people do

---

[27] If marginal utility were increasing, then all the results derived below would be reversed. Practically all economists believe that the assumption of diminishing marginal utility is more plausible.

[28] Those who are familiar with the theory of uncertainty will recognize the implicit assumption that individuals have "Von Neumann-Morgenstern utility functions." See Henderson and Quandt [1980].

not require a risk premium to accept a gamble that involves only a small amount of income.[29]

Thus, for projects which spread risk over large numbers of people, expected values can provide good measures of uncertain benefits and costs. But for cases in which risks are large relative to individuals' incomes, certainty equivalents must be computed.

---

[29] As the points on OU come closer together, the shape of the curve between them becomes approximately linear. When the utility function is linear, the risk premium is always zero, a fact that is easily verifiable diagramatically. See Arrow and Lind [1970].

CHAPTER 10

Government Behavior

*The hogs were really feeding. The greed level, the
level of opportunism, just got out of control.*
                                        David Stockman

Textbook discussions of market failures and their remedies tend to convey a rather rosy view of government. With a tax here, an expenditure there, the state can readily correct all market imperfections, meanwhile seeing to it that incomes are distributed in a way that reflects the community's ethical judgments. Such a view is at variance with apparent widespread public dissatisfaction with government performance. A poll taken in 1983 indicated that only 33 percent of Americans believed that the government in Washington can be trusted to do what is right most of the time [Clymer, 1983, p. 1]. President Ronald Reagan probably summarized the sentiments of many when he quipped, "When you get in bed with the government, you're going to get more than a good night's sleep." As suggested in the cartoon, the notion that government truly acts in the interests of its citizens is likely to be met with substantial cynicism.

It is possible that this is merely gratuitous whining on the part of individuals. As a matter of definition, in a democracy we get the government we want. Another possibility, however, is that it is inherently difficult for even democratically elected governments to respond to the "national interest."

To explore this possibility, we must recognize that although the notion of "government" is a useful abstraction, decisions are, in fact, made and influenced by *people*—politicians, bureaucrats, members of special interest groups, et al. This chapter discusses some theories of governmental action based on these agents' motivations and behavior. The

results are used to examine the important and perplexing question of the rapid growth of the public sector. Some institutional reforms to improve government performance are also discussed.

THE CAST OF CHARACTERS

The process of political decision making is clearly very complicated. Nevertheless, simple economic models of the behavior of some of the key agents involved provide useful insights.

Elected Politicians

In Chapter 6 we discussed various procedures by which members of a community can make decisions on fiscal matters. A key result was the **median voter rule:** If individual preferences are single peaked and can be represented along a single dimension, then the outcome of majority voting reflects the preferences of the median voter. In reality, direct referenda on fiscal matters are most unusual. It is far more common for citizens to elect representatives who make decisions on their behalf. Nevertheless, under certain assumptions, median voter theory can help explain how these representatives set their positions.

Consider an election between two candidates, Smith and Jones. Assume that voters have single-peaked preferences along the spectrum of political views. Voters cast ballots to maximize their own utility, and candidates seek to maximize the number of votes received.

What happens? Under these conditions, a vote-maximizing politician will adopt the preferred program of the median voter—the voter whose preferences are exactly in the middle of the distribution of preferences. To see this, assume that voters rank all positions on that basis of whether they are "conservative" or "liberal." Figure 10.1 shows a hypothetical distribution of voters who most prefer each point in the political spectrum. Suppose that Candidate Jones adopts position M, at the median, and Candidate Smith chooses position S to the right of center. Because each voter has single-peaked preferences and wants to maxi-

FIGURE 10.1   The Median Voter Rule for Elections

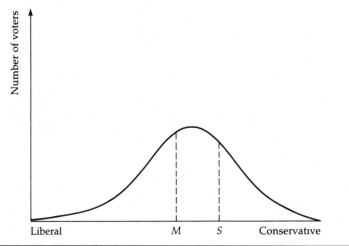

mize utility, he will support the candidate whose views lie closest to his own. Smith will win all the votes to the right of *S*, as well as some of the votes between *S* and *M*. Because *M* is the median, one half of the voters lie to the left of *M*. Jones will receive all of these votes and some of those to the right of *M*, guaranteeing him a majority. The only way for Smith to prevent himself from being "outflanked" is to move to position *M* himself. Therefore, it pays both candidates to position themselves as close as possible to the position of the median voter.

This model has two striking implications.

First, two-party systems tend to be stable in the sense that both parties stake out positions near the "center." In some respects, this is a good description of American political life. It appears, for example, that presidential candidates who are perceived as too far from the middle-of-the-road (Presidential candidates Barry Goldwater in 1964 and George McGovern in 1972) do not fare well with the electorate.[1]

Second, the replacement of direct referenda by a representative system will have *no* effect on the outcome. Both simply mirror the preferences of the median voter. Thus, government spending cannot be "excessive" because political competition for votes leads to a level of expenditure that is exactly in accord with the median voter's wishes.

Before taking these rather optimistic results too much to heart, however, several aspects of the analysis should be examined carefully.

---

[1] One of Goldwater's campaign slogans was "A choice, not an echo." The median voter theorem helps to explain why echoes are so prevalent.

Single Dimensional Rankings.   If all political beliefs cannot be ranked along a single spectrum, the median voter rule falls apart because the identity of the median voter will then depend upon the particular issue actually being considered. The median voter with respect to feminist questions may not be the same person as the median voter on atomic energy issues. Similarly, just as in the case of direct referenda (Chapter 6) if preferences are not single peaked, then there may not be a stable voting equilibrium at all.

Ideology.   While it is assumed that politicians are simple vote maximizers, they may care about more than just winning elections. Ideology can play an important role. After all, in 1850 Henry Clay said "Sir, I would rather be right than be president."

Issues Alone?   The assumption that voters' utilities depend only on issues may be unrealistic. In some cases, personalities may be more important in determining election outcomes. Some have argued, for example, that much of President Dwight D. Eisenhower's appeal was due to his "fatherly" personality.

Leadership.   In the model, politicians passively respond to voters' preferences. But these preferences may be influenced by the politicians themselves. This is just another way of saying that politicians provide "leadership." Indeed, at times in history, rational calculations of voter self-interest have apparently given way altogether to the appeals of charismatic politicians. "Politics is magic. He who knows how to summon forces from the deep, him they will follow."[2]

Decision to Vote.   The analysis assumes that every eligible citizen chooses to exercise his or her franchise. If the candidates' positions are too close, however, some people may become too apathetic to vote. Individuals with extreme views may fail to vote out of alienation. The model also ignores the costs of acquiring information and voting. A "rational" voter must make a determination on the suitability of a candidate's platform, the probability that the candidate will be able and willing to keep his or her promises, etc. The fact that these costs may be high together with the perception that a single vote will not influence the outcome anyway, may induce a self-interested citizen to abstain from voting. A free rider problem emerges—each individual has an incentive to not vote, but unless a sizable number of people exercise their franchise, a democracy cannot function [see Downs, 1957].

---

[2] Hugo von Hofmannsthal quoted in Schorske [1981, p. 172].

Although low voter-participation rates are often bemoaned (for example, in the 1980 presidential election, only 53.2 percent of the eligible voters cast a vote), in a way it is puzzling that the percentage is as high as it is. Part of the answer may be the success with which the educational system instills the idea that the citizen's obligation to vote transcends narrow self-interest.

Voting and Economic Performance.   As just noted, the median voter model does not consider how voters obtain information about the political candidates and their parties. One obvious way is by watching candidates' performance while in office. If the performance is satisfactory, then vote to reelect them. Otherwise, "throw the rascals out."

Fair [1982] based an econometric study of presidential election results on the notion that good economic performance enhances the probability that the incumbent party will remain in office. He estimated a regression equation[3] in which the Democratic proportion of the two-party presidential vote (which we denote D) is a function of the following explanatory variables:[4]

g = growth rate of real per capita gross national product in the second and third quarters of the year of the election, multiplied by -1 if the incumbent party is Republican. If voters reward parties whose presidents are associated with high growth rates, this variable should have a positive coefficient. The reason for the -1 is that if the Republicans do well, this should *decrease* the number of Democratic votes, other things being the same.

INF = rate of inflation, measured as the absolute value of the average growth rate of prices in the two-year period before the election multiplied by -1 if the incumbent party if Republican. If voters punish parties whose incumbents are associated with inflation, the coefficient on this variable should be negative.

DEM = 1 if there is a Democratic incumbent *and* he or she is running for reelection; -1 if there is a Republican incumbent who is running for reelection; zero otherwise. If incumbency produces an electoral advantage, the coefficient of this variable should be positive.

$INCUM$ = 1 if there is a Democratic incumbent; -1 if there is a Republican incumbent. If having a member of your party in

---

[3] The statistical technique of regression analysis is described in Chapter 3.

[4] Fair estimated a number of equations with other variables, as well. He also included in his equations a complicated measure of "vote-getting ability" which is not described here, and which is suppressed in reporting the results below. See Fair [1982] and [1978] for more details.

office during the election helps (even if the incumbent is not seeking reelection), the coefficient of this variable should be positive.

When Fair estimated the regression using data from the presidential elections of 1916 to 1980, he obtained the following result:

(10.1) $D = .478 + .0080\ g - .0096\ INF + .0479\ DEM + .0230\ INCUM$

The signs of the estimated parameters conform to expectations. The positive sign on g shows that a party associated with a high economic growth rate has enhanced prospects for capturing the White House. (Each 1 percent increase in the growth rate increases the proportion of the votes cast for Democrats by .008.) Inflation, on the other hand, diminishes a party's share of the vote. The coefficient on DEM indicates that merely by virtue of being an incumbent, a Democratic candidate can increase his or her fraction of the vote by about .047. The coefficient on $INCUM$ suggests that the party with the incumbent (even if he or she is not running) enjoys an advantage of 0.0230. Except for the coefficient on $INCUM$, all are *statistically significant,* i.e., it is unlikely that the results are a random fluke.

An interesting test of the equation's usefulness is to see how well it does at predicting election results. Consider the Carter-Reagan contest of 1980. In that year, g was -4.9, INF was 8.7, and both DEM and $INCUM$ were 1.0, because a Democratic incumbent (Carter) was running for office. Substituting these values into Equation (10.1), we obtain a prediction for Carter's fraction of the two-party vote of 0.426.[5] In fact, Carter received 0.447. Thus, the equation's prediction is off only by 0.021. Fair reports similar success in predicting most other elections.

Some comments about Fair's choices of variables to represent economic performance are required.

First, despite the fact that the unemployment rate is a widely quoted statistic, Fair finds that it has little or no explanatory power. This suggests that people's perceptions of economic performance are based more upon the growth of income than upon unemployment.

Second, note that g measures the income growth rate only for the *six months* preceding the election. Given that the incumbent party has held the presidency for almost four years by election time, it might be guessed that the growth rate measured over a longer period would be more appropriate. But this turns out not to be the case. Growth rates computed over longer horizons do a *worse* job at predicting election results. If this result is correct, it suggests that voters are extremely shortsighted; all they care about is the economy's behavior in the very

---

[5] $0.426 = 0.478 + 0.0080 \times (-4.9) - .0096 \times (8.7) + .0479 \times (1.0) + 0.0230 \times (1.0)$. If one uses the "vote getting ability variable," the predicted value is 0.438. See footnote 4.

recent past. This may help explain the often observed tendency of incumbents to increase government spending before elections to "pump up" the economy.[6] More generally, this finding is consistent with the notion that political decision making is inherently myopic. Politicians who are under pressure to produce favorable results by the next election have incentives to take actions that have high short-run payoffs but possibly detrimental long-run effects.

Finally, Fair's model does not include personalities, social issues, campaign spending, foreign affairs, etc. The fact that such a simple economic model can do so well at predicting elections is impressive. Nevertheless, other variables may also be important, and their inclusion could affect the results.[7] In any case, the use of economic models and econometrics to explain the behavior of voters and politicians is an active area of research which promises to provide many interesting insights.

Public Employees

The next group we consider is public employees, also referred to as bureaucrats. To understand their role, it is important to note that the legislation enacted by elected politicians is often vague. The precise way a program is run is in the hands of public employees. A classic example is the Internal Revenue Service, which makes rulings on hundreds of aspects of tax-code administration that are not considered by lawmakers. Similarly, important details in administration of welfare programs are often unspecified, so matters such as eligibility are left up to bureaucrats in the Department of Health and Human Services and other agencies. As Table 10.1 shows, the number of public employees is large and has been growing over time. Lately, bureaucrats have been the target of much bitter criticism. They are blamed for being unresponsive, creating excessive red tape, and intruding too much into the private affairs of citizens. Even a new wave rock group has joined in the attack:

> Red tape, I can see can't you see
> Red tape, do'in to you, do'in to me
> Red tape, bureaucracy in D.C.
> Red tape, killing you and killing me.
> Tax this, tax that, tax this, tax that.
> NO MORE RED TAPE.[8]

---

[6] It has been suggested that such behavior is an important cause of the business cycle. See Tufte [1978].

[7] For example, many believe that Carter lost the 1980 election because of the Iranian hostage crisis.

[8] From "Red Tape," words and music by Keith Morris and Greg Hetson of the Circle Jerks. © 1980, Irving Music, Inc., and Plagued Music (BMI). All rights reserved. International copyright secured.

TABLE 10.1   Government versus Private-Sector Employees

Year	All Governments* (000)	Federal* (000)	State and Local† (000)	All Private Industries (000)
1929	2,923	566	2,357	32,134
1939**	5,791	2,931	2,860	29,742
1949	5,561	1,967	3,594	39,577
1959	7,595	2,299	5,296	45,170
1969	11,031	2,863	8,168	56,638
1979	13,902	2,845	11,057	69,867
1981	14,009	2,855	11,154	70,510

Note: Employment is measured in "full-time equivalents." Hence, two half-time workers are counted as one employee.
* Does not include military.
† Includes education.
** Includes work relief.
Source: *Facts and Figures on Government Finance—22d Biennial Edition* (Washington, D.C.: Tax Foundation, 1983), p. 32.

It is important to remember, however, that a modern government simply cannot function without bureaucracy. Bureaucrats provide valuable technical expertise in the design and execution of programs. Moreover, the fact that their tenures in office often exceed those of elected officials provides a continuity in government that would otherwise be lacking.

On the other hand, it would be naive to assume a government bureaucrat's only aim is to interpret and passively fulfill the wishes of the electorate and its representatives. Having said this, we are still left with the problem of specifying the bureaucrats' goals. Niskanen [1971] argued that in the market-oriented private sector, an individual who wants to "get ahead" will do so by making his or her company as profitable as possible. When the firm's profits go up, so will the individual's salary. In contrast, bureaucrats tend to focus on such items as perquisites of office, public reputation, power, and patronage because opportunities for entreprenurial gains are minimal.[9] Niskanen suggested that all of these objectives are positively correlated with the size of the bureaucrat's budget, and hence concluded that the bureaucrat's objective is to maximize his or her budget.

To assess the implications of this hypothesis, consider Figure 10.2. The output of a bureaucracy, Q, is measured on the horizontal axis. Q might represent the number of units of public housing managed by the Department of Housing and Urban Development, or the quantity of

---

[9] Obviously, this distinction is blurred in the real world. Firm executives care about power and job "perks" as well as money. Nevertheless, the distinction is useful for analytical purposes.

FIGURE 10.2   Niskanen's Model of Bureaucracy

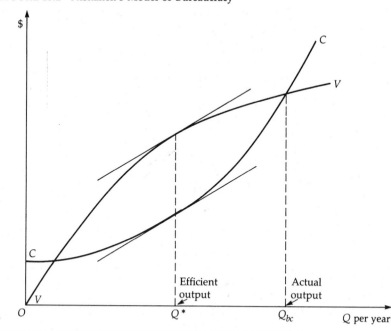

missiles stockpiled by the Department of Defense. Dollars are measured on the vertical axis. The curve *VV* represents the total value placed on each level of *Q* by the legislative "sponsor" who controls the budget. The slope of *VV* is the marginal social benefit of the output; it is drawn on the reasonable assumption of diminishing marginal benefit. The total cost of providing each output level is given by *CC*. Its slope measures the marginal cost of each unit of output. *CC* is drawn on the assumption of increasing marginal cost.

Suppose the bureaucrat knows that the sponsor will accept any project whose total benefits exceed total costs. Then the bureaucrat (*bc*) proposes Q_{bc}, the output level which maximizes the size of the bureau subject to the constraint that *CC* not be above *VV*. Q_{bc}, however, is an inefficient level of output. Efficiency requires that a unit of output be produced only as long as the additional benefit from that output exceeds the additional cost. Hence, the efficient output is that at which marginal cost equals marginal benefit, *not* total cost equals total benefit. In Figure 10.2 the efficient level is Q^*, where the *slopes* of *VV* and *CC* are equal. Thus, the bureaucrat's desire to build as large as "empire" as possible leads to an inefficiently large bureaucracy.

An important implication of Niskanen's model is that bureaucrats have incentives to expend effort on promotional activities to increase the sponsor's perceptions of the benefits of the bureau's output—to shift up the *VV* curve. This is analogous to the use of advertising in the private sector. If such efforts succeed, the equilibrium value of Q_{bc} moves to the right. Hence, Defense Department officials are expected to emphasize security threats, and their counterparts in Health and Human Services to promote awareness of the poverty problem. Note also that an unscrupulous bureaucrat may ask for more funds than needed to achieve a given output level and/or to overstate the benefits of his program. However, the tendency of bureaucracies to exceed their efficient size does not depend upon such outright trickery.

An obvious question is why the sponsor allows the bureaucrat to operate at Q_{bc} rather than Q^*. In essence, Niskanen assumes that the bureaucrat can present his output to the sponsor as an all-or-nothing proposition: take Q_{bc} or none at all. But, if the sponsor is well informed and cares about efficiency, he or she should require output Q^* and insist that it be produced at minimum cost. One impediment is that it may be difficult for the sponsor to know just what is going on. The process of producing the bureaucratic input is likely to be complicated and require specialized information which is not easily obtainable by the sponsor.[10] Just consider the technical expertise required to monitor production of electronic guidance systems for missiles.

Are government bureaucracies more likely to operate at points like Q_{bc} or Q^*? One way to find out would be to compare the costs and outputs of a government bureau to a private firm producing the same product. For example, hospital services are provided by both public and private institutions. Unfortunately, in many important cases like the Department of Defense, there is no private operation that corresponds to the public bureau. Moreover, government bureaucracies tend to produce outputs that are very hard to measure. (How can the quantity and quality of "health care" produced by a public or private hospital be measured?) Thus, the widespread suspicion that bureaucrats' main concern is empire building is hard to confirm or deny.

Bureaucrats' Salaries.   Another complaint about bureaucrats is that they are overpaid. It is argued that because government agencies are not subject to competitive pressures to minimize their costs, they pay more than private-sector firms. According to this view, overpayment is also encouraged by the fact that public employees and their families will vote for politicians who grant them big raises.

---

[10] This is an example of a more general issue in economics, the *principal-agent problem*. A principal (in our case, the legislative sponsor) needs some task completed by an agent (the bureaucrat). However, the principal cannot completely monitor the agent's behavior, so the principal cannot know for sure whether the agent is acting in the principal's interest. The question is what kind of incentive scheme maximizes the likelihood that the agent will act in the principal's interest. See Inman [1982].

TABLE 10.2   Average Annual Earnings per Employee in Public and Private Sectors

Year	All Government*	Federal*	State and Local†	All Private Industries
1929	$ 1,584	$ 1,917	$ 1,504	$ 1,416
1939**	1,348	1,244	1,476	1,269
1949	2,940	3,380	2,700	2,877
1959	4,695	5,538	4,329	4,715
1969	7,752	9,089	7,284	7,241
1979	15,037	19,365	13,923	14,334
1981	17,729	22,589	16,485	17,173

* Does not include military.
† Includes education.
** Includes work relief.
Source: *Facts and Figures on Government Finance, 22d Biennial Edition* (Washington, D.C.: Tax Foundation, 1983), p. 32.

Table 10.2 provides some data on the salaries of public-sector employees and those in the private sector. In recent decades, federal pay levels have substantially exceeded those in the private sector, while those for state and local employees have been slightly below. It would be erroneous to conclude immediately from these figures that federal employees are overpaid, because it may be that federal employment requires more skills (such as higher levels of education) than private employment. For the same reason, one cannot jump to the conclusion that state and local workers are underpaid. The salaries of public- and private-sector workers *with similar qualifications* must be compared. S. P. Smith [1977] analyzed the salaries of employees in both sectors, taking into account differences in education, work experience, marital status, sex, race, etc.[11] Using data from 1975, she found that employees of the federal government have wages 13 to 20 percent higher than equally qualified workers in the private sector. The magnitude of the differential varies with occupation, but it is always positive. On the other hand, Smith found that for state and local government employees, the pay relationship with comparable private-sector workers displays wide variation. In some occupations, private-sector employees are paid more, and in others less.

Special Interests[12]

We have been assuming so far that citizens who seek to influence government policy can act only as individual voters. In fact, people with

---

[11] Smith estimated a regression equation in which the dependent variable is the wage, and the explanatory variables include various worker characteristics and a public-employment variable. The public-employment variable is equal to one if the individual is employed in the public sector and is zero otherwise. The coefficient on this variable therefore gives the public-sector wage differential.

[12] Much of this section is based on the excellent treatment by Musgrave [1980].

common interests can exercise disproportionate power by acting together. The source of the group's power might be that its members tend to have higher voter participation rates than the population as a whole. Alternatively, members might be willing to use their incomes to make campaign contributions and/or pay bribes. As an example, in 1979–80, members of the House and Senate received $248.8 million in campaign contributions [U.S. Bureau of the Census, 1982, p. 495].

On what bases will these power groups be established? There are many possibilities.

Source of Income: Capital or Labor.   According to orthodox Marxism, people's political interests are determined by whether they are capitalists or laborers. This view is too simple to explain interest-group formation in the contemporary United States. Even though there is a tendency for those with high incomes to receive a disproportionate share of their income from capital, much of the income of the rich is also derived from labor. Thus, it is difficult to even identify who are the "capitalists" and the "laborers." Indeed, in the United States most of the inequality of total income is due to inequality in labor income, not to inequality in the distribution of capital [Musgrave, 1980, p. 370].

Size of Income.   On many economic policy issues, the rich and the poor will have different views, independent of the sources of their incomes. The poor favor redistributive spending programs and the rich oppose them. Similarly, each group supports implicit or explicit subsidies for goods they tend to consume intensively. Hence, the rich support subsidies for owner-occupied housing, while the poor favor special treatment for rental housing.

Source of Income: Industry of Employment.   Both workers and owners have a common interest in government support for their industry. In the tobacco industry, both groups lobby for federal tobacco subsidies. Similarly, both trucking companies and the Teamsters' Union worked intensively against a measure to deregulate trucking freight rates. (The union's methods took an extreme form—in 1982, its president was found guilty of conspiring to bribe a United States Senator.)

Region.   Residents of geographical regions often share common interests. Citizens of the Sun Belt are interested in favorable tax treatment of oil; Midwesterners care about agricultural subsidies; and Northeasterners lobby for expenditures on urban development.

Demographic and Personal Characteristics.   The aged support subsidized health care and generous retirement programs; young married couples are interested in good schools and low payroll taxes. Religious beliefs play a major role in debates over the funding of abortion and state aid to private schools. Ethnic groups differ on the propriety of government expenditure for bilingual education programs. Some analysts argue that sex is beginning to be an important basis for interest-group formation; in the 1982 congressional elections, women voted in disproportionately large numbers for Democrats, and much concern was expressed by Republicans over the "gender gap."

The list could go on indefinitely. Given the numerous bases upon which interest groups can be established, it is no surprise that people who are in opposition on one issue may be in agreement on another; "politics makes strange bedfellows" is more or less the order of the day.

This discussion has ignored the question of how individuals with common interests actually manage to organize themselves. Belonging to a group may require membership fees, donation of time, etc. Each individual has an incentive to let others do the work while he or she reaps the benefits, becoming a free rider. Stigler [1974] suggests that the probability that a group will actually form increases when the number of individuals is small, and it is possible to levy sanctions against nonjoiners. But perhaps the role of rational financial self-interest should not be relied upon too heavily as an explanation in this context. It is only necessary to observe the debate over the public funding of abortion to realize the influence of ideology and emotion on the decision to join a group.

The "Iron Triangle."   Let us now consider the interaction of interest groups with bureaucrats and elected representatives. In the view of some social commentators, this three-sided relationship—the *iron triangle*—is the most important aspect of modern American politics. [Will, 1981, p. 120] The idea is that the members of Congress who authorize a given program, the bureaucrats who administer it, and the special interests who benefit from it all tend to coalesce behind the program. Thus, we observe members of the construction, lumber, and electrical machinery industries joining with bureaucrats from the Department of Housing and Urban Development and Members of Congress with urban constituents to support public housing.

The obvious question to ask is how such bills are passed by a majority if they benefit only members of an iron triangle. There are two possible explanations.

The interest groups and bureaucrats may be well organized and armed with information, while those who will bear the costs are not organized and may not even be aware of what is going on. Even if those citizens who will bear the costs are well informed, it may not be worth their while to fight back. Because the costs of the program are spread over the population as a whole, any given citizen's share is low, and even if total costs exceed total benefits, it would not be worth the time and effort to organize opposition. In contrast, the benefits are relatively concentrated, making political organization worthwhile for potential beneficiaries.

The other reason for the success of such bills is that other representatives may be involved in their *own* iron triangles and therefore willing to trade votes to gain support for their pet projects. According to one member of the House of Representatives, the system works this way: each member brings his or her pet project to the chairman of the relevant committee, who incorporates it into a giant appropriations bill. "But there's one rule of thumb . . . You keep your mouth shut on all other projects in the bill." ["How Congress Slices the Pork," 1982, p. 18.]

As usual, it is not clear how much weight should be given to anecdotes. Determining the actual importance of the iron triangle phenomenon is a difficult task.

Other Actors

Without attempting to be exhaustive, we list a few other parties who affect government fiscal decisions.

The Judiciary.   Court decisions on the legality of various taxes have major effects upon government finance. One of the most famous Supreme Court rulings on taxation was the 1895 decision that a federal tax on personal incomes was unconstitutional. This was circumvented in 1913 by the 16th Amendment to the constitution. The judiciary also affects the expenditure side of the account. Judges have mandated public expenditures on items as diverse as bilingual education in the public schools and prison remodeling.

One of the reasons that judges have become deeply involved in public finance is laws are often so vaguely worded that it is difficult to determine congressional intent. In 1982, a furor was raised over the possibility that Bob Jones University, which practices racial discrimination, would be granted the preferential tax status to which private schools are generally entitled. When the issue went before the Supreme Court, one problem was that the Internal Revenue Code says nothing about racially discriminating private schools. In effect, the judges had to read the mind of Congress to determine what it wanted.

Journalists.   The ability to bring certain issues to public attention gives the press substantial influence. For example, the widespread publicity given to certain parts of the Reagan administration's plan to cut school lunches helped lead to their defeat in Congress. Politicians, bureaucrats, and special-interest groups often try to use the media to influence the outcomes of debates on fiscal issues. One attempt which received considerable attention surrounded the desire of an environmental interest group, the Sierra Club, to change the policies of the Interior Department. In a confidential memorandum leaked to the press, detailed plans were outlined for achieving maximum media coverage from a well-orchestrated political event which was supposed to look like a spontaneous grass-roots effort [Watts Ouster Planned, 1981].

Experts.   Information is potentially an important source of power. Legislative aids who gain expertise on certain programs often play important roles in drafting statutes. They can also affect outcomes by virtue of their ability to influence which items are put on legislative agenda. Of course, there are also experts outside the government. Many academic social scientists have sought to use their expertise to influence economic policy. Economists love to quote Keynes' [1965/1936, p. 383] famous dictum "the ideas of economists and political philosophers, both when they are right and when they are wrong, are more powerful than is commonly understood. Indeed, the world is ruled by little else." However, it is extremely difficult to determine whether social science research influences policy, and if so, through what channels this influence operates. In his careful study of the relationship between academic research and the formulation of Great Society programs during the administration of Lyndon Johnson, Aaron [1978, p. 9] observed that "in many cases, the findings of social science seemed to come after, rather than before, changes in policy, which suggests that political events may influence scholars more than research influences policy."

WHY HAS GOVERNMENT GROWN SO MUCH?

Much of the concern about whether government operates efficiently has been stimulated by the rate of growth in government. Table 10.3 reproduces from Chapter 2 data on total U.S. government and defense expenditures over time. (The expenditure figures include transfer payments.) As emphasized in Chapter 2, expenditures are far from perfect measures of government size. We focus upon annual government expenditures recognizing that they are merely a convenient yardstick.

Given the imprecision with which these numbers are measured, it does not make much sense to attach great importance to small changes in their magnitude. It is clear, however, that over the long run, both defense and nondefense expenditures have grown enormously both in absolute terms and proportionately. Interestingly, since the mid-1950s, the ratio of defense expenditures to GNP has fallen even as the total government ratio to GNP has gone up.

A growing public sector is not unique to the United States, as the figures for a few other Western countries in Table 10.4 indicate. Thus, as we search for explanations for the growth in government, care must be taken not to rely too heavily upon events and institutions that are pecu-

TABLE 10.3   State, Local, and Federal Government Expenditures (selected years)

	(1) Total Expenditures ($ billions)	(2) 1980 Dollars ($ billions)	(3) 1980 Dollars per Capita	(4) Percent of GNP	(5) National Defense as Percent of GNP
1902	$ 1.6	$ 17.6	$ 222	7.7%	0.7%
1938	17.7	107.9	830	20.9	1.2
1944	109.9	501.8	3,625	52.3	44.6
1950	70.3	233.6	1,539	24.7	6.4
1955	110.7	324.6	1,964	27.8	11.0
1960	151.3	389.9	2,158	30.0	10.0
1965	205.6	493.0	2,537	30.0	8.1
1970	333.0	655.5	3,199	34.0	8.6
1975	560.1	791.1	3,663	36.1	6.1
1980	958.7	958.7	4,210	36.5	5.6
1982	1,231.4	1,062.0	4,688	40.1	6.6

Source: For years prior to 1975, calculated from U.S. Bureau of the Census, *Historical Statistics of the United States, Colonial Times to 1970* (Washington, D.C.: U.S. Government Printing Office, 1975), p. 1120. For 1975 and 1980, calculated from U.S. Bureau of the Census, *Statistical Abstract of the United States: 1982–83*, 103d ed. (Washington, D.C.: U.S. Government Printing Office, 1982), p. 276. For 1982, from U.S. Bureau of the Census, *Governmental Finances in 1981–82* (Washington, D.C.: U.S. Government Printing Office, 1983), Table 1, p. 15.

TABLE 10.4   Ratio of Government Expenditures to GNP in Canada, Switzerland, and the United Kingdom (selected years 1900–1980)

Year	Canada	Switzerland	United Kingdom
1900	9.5	n.a.	14.4
1910	11.4	n.a.	12.7
1920	16.1	n.a.	26.2
1930	18.9 ·	15.9	26.1
1940	23.1	19.2	30.0
1950	22.1	19.9	39.0
1960	29.7	17.7	31.9
1970	31.2	21.3	33.2
1980	37.7	29.7	42.2

n.a.   Not available.
Source: Years prior to 1970 from Pommerehne, "Quantitative Aspects of Federalism: A Study of Six Countries," in *The Political Economy of Fiscal Federalism*, ed. Wallace Oates (Lexington, Mass.: D. C. Heath, 1977), p. 310. Years 1970 and 1980 computed from *National Accounts*, volume II (Paris: Organization for Economic Cooperation and Development, 1982).

liar to the U.S. experience. It should also be emphasized that the various explanations are not necessarily mutually exclusive. No single theory accounts for the whole phenomenon. Indeed, even taken together, they still leave much unexplained.

Some of the most prominent theories follow.

Citizen Preferences.   Growth in government expenditure is an expression of the preferences of the citizenry. Suppose that the median voter's demand for public sector goods and services (G) can be written as some function (f) of the relative price of public sector goods and services (P) and income (I):

$$G = f(P,I)$$

There are many different ways such a demand function can lead to an increasing proportion of income spent on public-sector goods and services.[13] Suppose that when income increases by a given percentage, the quantity demanded of public goods and services increases by a greater percentage—the income elasticity of demand is greater than one. If this is the case, then the process of income growth by itself will lead to an ever-increasing share of income going to the public sector, other things being the same.

Similarly, if the elasticity of G with respect to I is less than one but P falls fast enough over time, an increase in government's share of income will also occur.[14]

The important point is that the relative increase in the size of the public sector does not necessarily imply that something is "wrong" with the political process. Government growth could well be a consequence of the wishes of voters, who rationally take into account its opportunity cost in terms of foregone consumption in the private sector. There is indeed evidence from public opinion polls that most Americans favor a large and activist federal government. Aaron [1978, p. 161] suggests that it may not be the size of government per se that leads to griping, but rather the attempt of government to achieve hard-to-define and controversial objectives. (An example might be the pursuit of "equality" through affirmative action programs.)

Political-Economic Interaction.   According to some Marxist theories, the rise of state expenditure is viewed as inherent to the political-economic system.[15] In the Marxist model, the private sector tends to overproduce, so the capitalist-controlled government must expand expenditures to absorb this production. Typically, this is accomplished by augmenting military spending. At the same time, the state attempts to decrease worker alienation by increasing spending for social services.

---

[13] In this context, income redistribution should be thought of as a government "service."

[14] A number of attempts have been made to estimate the income elasticity of G by comparing public goods expenditures of various communities with different income levels. Most of the estimates suggest that it is less than one. See Inman [1979, pp. 286–88].

[15] These theories are surveyed by Musgrave [1980], upon which this discussion is based.

Eventually, rising expenditures outpace tax revenue capacity, and the government collapses.

Musgrave [1980] argues that the historical facts are inconsistent with this analysis. "There is little evidence . . . [that] expenses directed at appeasing social unrest [have] continuously increased" [p. 388]. It is also noteworthy that in Western Europe, the enormous increase in the size and scope of government in the post–World War II era has been accompanied by anything but a resurgence in militarism. The main contribution of this Marxist analysis is its explicit recognition of the links between the economic and political systems as sources of government growth.

Chance Events.   In contrast to the theories that view government growth as inevitable are those which consider it as the consequence of chance events [Peacock and Wiseman, 1967]. In "normal" periods there is only moderate growth in public expenditure. Occasionally, however, there are external shocks to the economic and social system which "require" higher levels of government expenditure and novel methods for financing them. Even after the shock disappears, higher levels continue to prevail because of inertia. Examples of candidates for such "shocks" are the Great Depression, World War II, the Great Society, the Vietnam War, etc.

Societal Attitudes.   In popular discussions, it is sometimes suggested that specific changes in societal attitudes have encouraged government growth. Lubar [1980] argued that social trends encouraging personal self-assertiveness lead people to make extravagant demands upon the political system.[16] At the same time, widespread television advertising has created unrealistically high expectations, leading to a "Santa Claus mentality" that causes people to lose track of the fact that government programs do have an opportunity cost.

However, it could just as well be argued that people misperceive the benefits of government projects instead of their costs. In this case, there would be a tendency for the public sector to be too small, not too big. More generally, although recent social phenomena might account for some movement in the growth of government expenditure, this expenditure has been going on for too many years and in too many places for this explanation to have much credibility.

Income Redistribution.   Government grows as a consequence of low-income individuals using the political system to redistribute income to-

---

[16] As evidence, Lubar notes that in 1980 a group appeared before the Democratic Party's Platform Committee demanding a plank calling for federal financing of sex-change operations.

ward themselves [see Meltzer and Richard, 1981]. The idea is that politicians can attract voters whose incomes are at or below the median by offering benefits that impose a net cost on those whose incomes are above the median. As long as average income exceeds the median, and the mechanisms used to bring about redistribution are not too detrimental to incentives, politicians have an incentive to increase the scope of government-sponsored income distribution. Suppose, for example, that there are five voters whose incomes are $5,000; $10,000; $15,000; $25,000; and $40,000. The median income is $15,000 and the average income is $19,000. A politician who supports government programs that transfer income to those with less than $25,000 will win in majority voting.

If this is the case, it must still be explained why the share of public expenditures increases *gradually* (as in Table 10.3). Why not a huge once-and-for-all transfer as the poor confiscate the incomes of the rich? Because in Western countries, property and/or status requirements for voting have *gradually* been abolished during the last century. In the United States, many of the remaining barriers to voting were removed by civil rights laws passed in the 1960s. Extension of the right to vote to those at the bottom of the income scale increases the proportion of voters likely to support politicians promising redistribution. Hence, it is the gradual extension of the franchise that leads to continuous growth in government, rather than a once-and-for-all increase.

One problem with this theory is that it fails to explain the methods used by government to redistribute income. If it is correct, most income transfers should go to the poor and should take the form that would maximize their welfare, i.e., direct cash transfers. Instead, as we saw in Chapter 5, transfers in the United States are often given in kind and many benefit those in the middle- and upper-income classes.[17]

An alternate view of the role of income redistribution focuses not on the poor, but on middle- and upper-income individuals. The idea is that government growth is a consequence of such individuals attempting to use the political system to redistribute income toward themselves. Via the "iron triangle" discussed above, coalitions of politicians, special-interest groups, and bureaucrats vote themselves programs of ever-increasing size.

Overview

There are very different hypotheses for explaining the growth of the state's economic role. Unfortunately, the chances for testing them econometrically seem remote. To begin with, it is very difficult to measure the size of government (see Chapter 2). In addition, it is hard to quantify many of the variables that are important in the politically ori-

---

[17] See Tullock [1978] for further discussion along these lines.

ented theories—how, for example, can "bureaucratic power" be measured? Thus, the relative importance of each theory is likely to remain open to question.

BRINGING GOVERNMENT "UNDER CONTROL"

As we have seen, substantial growth in the public sector need not imply that there is anything wrong with the political budgetary process. For those who believe that public sector fiscal behavior is more or less at the size desired by the median voter, bringing government under control is a nonissue.[18] On the other hand, for those who perceive growth in government as a symptom of flaws in the political process, bringing government under control is very much a problem.[19]

Two types of argument are made in the "controllability" debate.

One view is that the basic problem results from commitments made by government in the *past*, so there is very little current legislators and executives can do to change the rate of growth or composition of government expenditures. Pechman et al. [1981, p. 46] estimate that about three quarters of total federal outlays in fiscal year 1982 were uncontrollable in this sense. Entitlement programs which provide benefits to the retired, disabled, unemployed, sick, and others are the largest category of uncontrollable expenditure. (Chapters 5 and 8 provide descriptions of many of these programs.) Others include payments on the national debt, farm support programs, and certain defense expenditures.

There is some controversy over how uncontrollable these expenditures really are. If legislation created entitlement programs, it can take them away. In theory, then, many of the programs can be reduced or even removed. In reality, both moral and political considerations work against reneging on past promises to various groups in the population. Any serious reductions are likely to be scheduled sufficiently far into the future so that people who have made commitments based on current programs will not be affected.

According to the second argument, our political institutions are fundamentally flawed, and bringing things under control is more than just a matter of changing the entitlement programs. A number of remedies have been proposed.

Change Bureaucratic Incentives.   Niskanen, who views bureaucracy as a cause of unwarranted government growth, suggests that financial in-

---

[18] Of course, not only is the total size of government expenditure at issue, but so also is the composition of the expenditure. Some believe that defense expenditures are out of control, and social welfare expenditures are too small. Others argue just the contrary.

[19] Note that the judgment that government is currently inequitable or inefficient does not necessarily imply that government as an institution is "bad." People who like market-oriented approaches to resource allocation can nevertheless seek to improve markets. The same goes for government.

centives be created to mitigate bureaucrats' empire-building tendencies. For example, the salary of a government manager could be made to depend negatively upon changes in the size of his or her agency. A bureaucrat who *cut* the agency's budget would get a raise. (Similar rewards could be offered to budget-cutting legislators.) However, it is easy to imagine such a system leading to some undesirable results. To increase his or her salary, the bureaucrat might reduce the budget beyond the point at which marginal benefits equal marginal costs.

Niskanen also suggests expanding the use of private firms to produce public goods and services, although the public sector would continue to finance them. The idea here is that competition forces private firms to produce more efficiently than government bureaus do. For example, the state can provide parents with tuition money for their children's schooling, and the parents spend the money at the private institution of their choice. It has been argued that such an educational voucher scheme would lead to more effective provision of education than is done at present in the public schools.[20]

Change the Budget Process.   Most of the focus on bringing government spending under control has been on the budget-making process itself. Prior to the 1970s, the congressional procedure lacked coherence. The president submitted a budget message to Congress. Subcommittees concerned with different types of expenditure examined the budget independently. There was little coordination among committees, and decisions were made without considering a common budget total. It was as if a husband would make food decisions and a wife housing decisions, neither consulting the other or taking into account the size of the family income.

The Congressional Budget and Impoundment Control Act of 1974 was an attempt to improve this situation. A special budget committee was formed in each house, and a detailed calendar for the budget process was established. By May 15 each year, Congress must adopt a resolution that sets a floor under revenues and a ceiling on spending. The resolution also includes spending limits for major functions such as defense, agriculture, etc. After Congress completes work on the separate appropriations it customarily makes each year, it must pass a second resolution setting final binding targets by September 15. A *reconciliation resolution* may be needed to direct changes in various tax and expenditure provisions so that the limits of the second resolution are met. The new fiscal year begins on October 1.

---

[20] Vouchers are discussed by Gramlich and Koshel [1975]. Note that if a voucher system led to a smaller cost per unit of education, and if the price elasticity of demand for education exceeded one, then expenditure on education might actually increase.

The act also created a budgetary bureaucracy for the Congress, the Congressional Budget Office, with the job of providing the technical skill required to estimate costs of proposed legislation so that legislators can make sensible decisions.

Essentially, the purpose of the 1974 reform was to add some rationality to the budget process by forcing Congress to vote on totals, instead of just on individual items. Many believe that the reform has not been a success. In recent years, Congress simply has not been able to pass all appropriations before the start of the fiscal year. In 1982, for example, only 2 of 13 appropriations bills were passed before the new fiscal year began (so much for deadlines). In such cases, Congress passes a *continuing resolution*—a special authorization to fund departments that have not received regular appropriations. Critics of the process argue that it is about as undisciplined as ever.

Why the failure? One reason is technical. Budget making requires projections of revenues and expenditures over the course of the coming year. The precise size of revenues and expenditures depends upon events that are hard to predict. If unemployment is high, then unemployment insurance expenditures will be large and income tax receipts will be low. If interest rates increase, more funds will be needed to service the national debt. In such an environment, it is difficult to meet precise spending and revenue targets.

The second reason is that the new budget rules did nothing to change politicians' incentives to increase spending. "I've got to tell you that the mileage around here politically is still to be a giveaway artist," remarked the House Budget Committee Chairman in 1980 [Lubar, 1980, p. 85]. When the budget process gets in the way of incentives, legislators circumvent the process.

Institute Fiscal Limitations.   When the democratic process fails to control government, then alternative restrictions may be appropriate.[21] The idea is to put constraints on legislators that *force* them to hold down the size of government despite whatever incentives they may face. In recent years, voters in several states have imposed such restrictions. The most famous example occurred in 1978, when Californians approved Proposition 13, which restricts property taxation to no more than 1 percent of 1975 market values. Currently, about half the states have instituted some kind of spending- and/or tax-limitation legislation.

At the federal level, there has been considerable discussion of imposing fiscal limitations, either by statute or by constitutional amendment. (See Congressional Budget Office [1982b].) In 1982, a proposed constitu-

---

[21] Inman [1982] discusses conditions under which various kinds of restrictions are likely to be efficient.

tional amendment with the following provisions received much public attention:

1. Congress must adopt a budget statement "in which total outlays are no greater than total receipts."
2. Total receipts may not increase "by a rate greater than the rate of increase in national income."
3. "The Congress and President shall . . . ensure that actual outlays do not exceed the outlays set forth in the budget statement."
4. The provisions can be overridden in times of war.

Although the amendment received a lot of political support (including the president's), after a lengthy debate, it failed to get through Congress. Most economists of both liberal and conservative political persuasions believe that for several reasons the amendment was ill conceived.[22]

First, as noted earlier, adopting a statement of outlays and revenues requires making forecasts about how the economy will perform. This problem is sufficiently difficult that forecasters with complete integrity can arrive at very different estimates. How does the Congress choose among forecasts? If an incorrect forecast is chosen, Congress may be in violation of the law without realizing it! Things become even murkier when it is realized that some forecasts will be biased by political considerations. Those who want to expand expenditures, for example, would encourage forecasts that indicated a high rate of growth of tax revenues during the coming year and vice versa.

Second, the growth of total receipts is tied to "national income," but the amendment provides no definition. The official definition in the national income accounts goes on for several pages and is frequently revised. When the technical definition is revised, does the amount of revenue that the government can collect change? More generally, national income statistics are best regarded as rough and ready estimates of the economy's performance, not exact measures. To enshrine them as constitutional concepts is absurd.

Third and similarly, the amendment fails to define "outlays" and "receipts." By using suitable accounting methods, Congress could easily circumvent the law. For example, the government could simply create various agencies and corporations that were authorized to make expenditures and borrow. As noted in Chapter 2, such "off-budget" credit activity is already an important way of concealing the actual size of the budget. The Congressional Budget Office [1982b, p. 126] observes that among those states that have constitutional restrictions against borrowing, the more stringent the restrictions, the greater the number of such off-budget agencies and corporations.

---

[22] See Blinder [1982] and Penner [1982].

Finally, legal scholars have noted some important questions. What happens if there is a deficit? Is the entire Congress put in jail? Could Congress be sued for spending too much? Could a single citizen go to court and obtain an injunction to stop all government activity in the event of a deficit? One senator sarcastically suggested how the escape clause for times of war could be used. The idea would be to make an arrangement with a small country like Iceland. Every time a deficit appeared to be coming, the United States would declare war and then pay some kind of compensation to the Icelanders for having done so.

CONCLUSIONS

Government fiscal decisions are made in a complicated fashion that is not well understood. Contrary to simple models of democracy, there appear to be forces pulling government expenditures away from levels that would be preferred by the median voter. However, critics of the current budgetary process have not come up with a satisfactory alternative. The formulation of meaningful rules and constraints for the budgetary process, either at the constitutional or statutory level, is an important item on both the academic and political agendas for the years ahead.

SUMMARY

Explanations of actual government performance require studying the interaction of elected officials, public employees, and special-interest groups.

Under restrictive assumptions, the actions of elected officials will mimic the wishes of the median voter. However, it is unrealistic to assume that these assumptions are even approximately true.

Voters may respond to recent economic performance. If they do, the actions of elected politicians will be focused on favorably influencing the economy. Recent research indicates that near-term economic conditions are powerful predictors of voting behavior.

Public employees have an important impact upon the development and implementation of economic policy. One theory predicts that bureaucrats will attempt to maximize the size of their agency's budget, resulting in oversupply of the service.

Public employees are often suspected of being overpaid. Recent research suggests that federal government employees receive wages 13 percent to 20 percent higher than those paid equally qualified private-sector workers. However, state and local government employees may receive either more or less than private-sector employees.

Private citizens form groups to influence government activity. Special interests can form on the basis of income source, income size, industry, region, or personal characteristics.

The combined effects of elected officials, public bureaucrats, and special interests has been labeled the "iron triangle" and some consider it an important determinant of government action. Nonetheless, this view is hard to test empirically.

The growth of government has been rapid by any measure. Explanations of this phenomenon include:

Citizen preferences.

Marxist theories. Simple Marxism predicts that the public sector must expand to absorb private excess production.

Chance. Random events (such as wars) increase the growth of government, while inertia prevents a return to previous levels.

Societal attitudes. Unrealistic expectations have resulted in increasing demands which ignore the opportunity costs of public programs.

Income redistribution. Two theories are popular. One predicts that politicians form a coalition of the poor and redistribute in their favor. Another suggests that middle- and upper-income groups employ the "iron triangle" to increase their shares of income.

Proposals to "control" the growth in government include decentralization to reduce bureaucratic power, encouraging private-sector competition, reforming the budget process, and direct legislative restrictions. The most widely discussed form of the latter is a constitutional amendment requiring a balanced federal budget each fiscal year.

DISCUSSION QUESTIONS

1. Consider the situation in which there are seven voters who care only about the level of government spending. Their preferences are:

Voter	Preferred Amount
Alice	$ 500
Bill	1,000
Carla	300
Dan	500
Ethel	750
Fred	1,000
Gwendolyn	1,200

   a. Who is the median voter?
   b. Graph the distribution of preferences. If there are two candidates running for office, what level of government spending is likely? Why?
   c. Suppose that whenever a candidate proposes a level of spending more than $200 away from a voter's preferred level, the voter becomes "alien-

ated" and does not vote. Can you tell what level is now likely? Why or why not?

2. Industries in the country of Technologia invest in new equipment which annually increases productivity of private workers by 3 percent. Government employees do not benefit from similar technical advances.

   a. If wages in the private sector are set equal to the value of the marginal product, how much will they rise yearly?

   b. Government workers annually receive increases so that wages remain comparable to those in the private sector. What happens to the price of public services relative to privately produced goods?

   c. If the same quantity of public services is produced each year, what happens to the size of the government (measured by spending)?

3. Spending bills with many different programs are presented to the president either to sign or veto. Suppose that it is possible to assign benefits and costs to each individual program contained in the bill.

   a. Under what circumstances will the bill be signed?
   Suppose it is possible for the president to veto individual items within a bill.

   b. What decision criterion will determine the final composition of the bill?

   c. Do you expect government spending to change? Why? Is this result "good" or "bad"?

   d. What effect will the rule change have upon the strategies of members of Congress? Does this change the power of the president?

   e. Every president since Ulysses Grant has requested the "item veto." Why? Relate your answer to part d.

SELECTED REFERENCES

Congressional Budget Office. *Balancing the Federal Budget and Limiting Federal Spending: Constitutional and Statutory Approaches.* Washington, D.C.: U.S. Government Printing Office, 1982.

Fair, Ray C. "The Effect of Economic Events on Votes for President: 1980 Results." *Review of Economics and Statistics* 64, no. 2 (May 1982), pp. 322–24.

Greider, William. "The Education of David Stockman." *The Atlantic Monthly,* December 1981, pp. 27–54.

Musgrave, Richard A. "Theories of Fiscal Crises: An Essay in Fiscal Sociology." In *The Economics of Taxation,* ed. Henry J. Aaron and Michael J. Boskin. Washington, D.C.: Brookings Institution, 1980.

Tullock, Gordon. "The Rhetoric and Reality of Redistribution." *Southern Economic Journal* 47, no. 4 (April 1978), pp. 895–907.

Part Four

A Framework for
Tax Analysis

Both politicians and economists have long searched for a set of principles to guide tax policy. Several centuries ago, the French statesman Colbert suggested that "the art of taxation is the art of plucking the goose so as to get the largest possible amount of feathers with the least possible squealing" [Armitage-Smith, 1907, p. 36]. Modern economics takes a somewhat less cynical approach, emphasizing how taxes should be levied so as to enhance economic efficiency and to promote a "fair" distribution of income. These are the topics of the next three chapters. Although the discussion is illustrated with examples from the United States tax system, the main focus is a theoretical framework for thinking about tax policy. A more thorough discussion of U.S. tax institutions is deferred to Part Five.

CHAPTER 11

Taxation and Income Distribution

Struggle and contrive as you will, lay your taxes as
you please, the traders will shift it off from their own
gain.

John Locke

A simple way to determine how taxes change the income distribution is
to conduct a survey in which each person is asked how many dollars he
or she pays to the tax collector each year. Simple—but usually wrong.
An example demonstrates that assessing correctly the burden of taxation
is a complicated problem.

Suppose that the price of a bottle of wine is $10. The government
imposes a tax of $1 per bottle, to be collected in the following way: every
time a bottle is purchased the tax collector (who is lurking about the
store) takes a dollar out of the wine seller's hand before the money is put
into the cash register. A casual observer might conclude that the wine
seller is paying the tax.

However, suppose that a few weeks after its imposition, the tax induces a price rise to $11 per bottle. Clearly, the proprietor is receiving
the same amount per bottle as he did before the tax. The tax has apparently made him no worse off. The entire amount of the tax is being paid
by consumers in the form of higher prices. On the other hand, suppose
that after the tax the price only increases to $10.30. In this case, the
proprietor keeps only $9.30 for each bottle sold; he is worse off by 70
cents per bottle. Consumers are also worse off, however, because they
have to pay 30 cents more per bottle.[1] In this case, producers and con-

---

[1] Actually, the change in the prices faced by consumers and producers is only part of
the story. There is also a burden due to the tax-induced distortion of choice. See Chapter 12.

sumers share the burden of the tax. Yet another possibility is that after the tax is imposed, the price stays at $10. If this happens, the consumer is no worse off, while the seller bears the full burden of the tax.

The **statutory incidence** of a tax indicates who is legally responsible for the tax. All three cases in the preceding paragraph are identical in the sense that the statutory incidence is on the seller. But the situations differ drastically with respect to who is really bearing the burden. Because prices may change in response to the tax, knowledge of statutory incidence tells us *essentially nothing* about who is really paying the tax. In contrast, the **economic incidence** of a tax is the change in the distribution of private real income brought about by a tax.[2] Our focus in this chapter is on the forces that determine the extent to which statutory and economic incidence differ—the amount of **tax shifting.**

GENERAL REMARKS ON TAX INCIDENCE ANALYSIS

Only People Can Bear Taxes

Under the U.S. legal system, certain institutions are treated as if they were people. The most prominent example is the corporation. Although for many purposes this is a convenient fiction, it sometimes creates confusion. From an economist's point of view, people—stockholders, workers, landlords, consumers, etc.—bear taxes. A corporation cannot. Thus, when some politicians declare that "business must pay its fair share of taxes," it is not clear what, if anything, this means.

Given that only people can bear taxes, how should they be classified for purposes of incidence analysis? Often their role in production—what inputs they supply to the production process—is used. (Inputs are often referred to as *factors of production.*) Attention is then focused on how the tax system changes the distribution of income between capitalists, laborers, and landlords. This is referred to as the **functional distribution of income.**

Basing the analysis this way may seem a bit old-fashioned. In 18th-century England, it may have been the case that property owners never worked and workers owned no property. But in the contemporary United States, many people who derive most of their income from labor also have savings accounts and/or common stocks. (Often, these assets are held for individuals in pensions.) Similarly, there are people who own huge amounts of capital and also work full time. Thus it seems more relevant to study how taxes affect the way in which total income is distributed among people: the **size distribution of income.** Given information on what proportion of people's income is from capital, land, and labor, changes in the factor distribution can be translated into changes in

---

[2] Note the similarity to the problem of *expenditure incidence* introduced in Chapter 5.

the size distribution. For example, a tax that lowers the relative return on capital will tend to hurt those at the top of the income distribution because a relatively high proportion of the incomes of the rich is from capital.[3]

Other classification schemes might be interesting for particular problems. In the analysis of energy taxation, incidence by region is important. (Are people from the Northeast or the Sun Belt hurt more by a tax on fuel oil?) Alternatively, in a study of taxation of land in urban areas, it might be useful to look at incidence by race. It is easy to think of further examples based upon sex, age, etc.

Both Sources and Uses of Income Should Be Considered

In the wine tax example discussed in the introduction to this chapter, it is natural to assume that the distributional effects of the tax depend crucially upon people's spending patterns. To the extent that the price of wine increases, the people who tend to consume a lot of wine will be made worse off. Further thought suggests, however, that if the tax reduces the demand for wine, the factors employed in wine production may suffer income losses. Thus, the tax may also change the income distribution by affecting the sources of income. Suppose that poor people spend a relatively large proportion of their incomes on wine, but that vineyards tend to be owned by the rich. Then on the uses of income side, the tax redistributes income away from the poor, but on the sources side, it redistributes income away from the rich. The overall incidence depends upon how both the sources and uses of income are affected.

In practice, it is common for economists to ignore effects on the sources side when considering a tax upon a commodity, and to ignore the uses side when analyzing a tax upon an input. This procedure is appropriate if the most *systematic* changes of a commodity tax are on the uses of income and those of a factor tax on the sources of income. This assumption simplifies analyses, but its correctness must be considered for each case.

Incidence Depends upon How Prices Are Determined

We have emphasized that the incidence problem is fundamentally one of determining how taxes change prices. Clearly, different models of price determination may give quite different answers to the question of who really bears a tax. This chapter considers several different models, and compares the results.

---

[3] However, some low-income retirees also derive the bulk of their income from capital.

A closely related issue is the time dimension of the analysis. Incidence depends upon changes in prices, but change takes time. In most cases, it is expected that responses are larger in the long run than the short run. Thus, the short- and long-run incidence of a tax may differ, and the time frame that is relevant for a given policy question must be specified.

Incidence Depends upon the Disposition of Tax Revenues

Balanced-budget incidence computes the combined effects of levying taxes *and* the government spending financed by those taxes. In general, the distributional effect of a tax depends upon how the government spends the money. As an example, expenditures on missiles have a very different distributional impact than spending on hot lunches for school children. In some studies, it is assumed that the government spends the tax revenue exactly as the consumers would if they had received the money. This is equivalent to returning the revenue as a lump sum and letting consumers spend it.

In many cases, it is desirable to abstract from the question of how the government will spend the money. The idea is to examine how incidence differs when one tax is replaced with another, holding the government budget constant. This is called **differential tax incidence.** Because differential incidence looks at changes in taxes, it is useful to have a reference point. The hypothetical "other tax" used as the basis of comparison is often assumed to be a **lump sum tax**—a tax for which the individual's liability does not depend upon behavior. (For example, a 10 percent income tax is *not* a lump sum tax because it depends on how much the individual earns. But a head tax of $500 independent of earnings *is* a lump sum tax.)

Finally, **absolute tax incidence** examines the effects of a tax when there is no change in either other taxes or government expenditure. Absolute incidence is of most interest for macroeconomic models in which tax levels are changed to achieve some stabilization goal.

Tax Progressiveness Can Be Measured in Several Ways

Suppose that an investigator has managed to calculate every person's real share of a particular tax—the economic incidence as defined above. The "bottom line" of such an exercise is often to characterize the tax as proportional, progressive, or regressive. The definition of **proportional** is straightforward; it describes a situation in which the ratio of taxes paid to income is constant regardless of income level.[4]

---

[4] However, the definition of income is *not* straightforward; see Chapter 14.

It is not as easy to define progressive and regressive and, unfortunately, ambiguities in definition sometimes confuse public debate. A natural way to define these words is in terms of the **average tax rate,** the ratio of taxes paid to income. If the average tax rate increases with income, the system is **progressive;** if it falls, the tax is **regressive.**

Confusion arises because some people think of progressiveness in terms of the **marginal tax rate**—the *change* in taxes paid with respect to a change in income. To illustrate the distinction, consider the following very simple income tax structure. Each individual computes his or her tax bill by subtracting $3,000 from income and paying an amount equal to 20 percent of the remainder. (If the difference is negative, the individual gets a subsidy equal to 20 percent of the figure.) Table 11.1 shows the

TABLE 11.1   Tax Liabilities under a Hypothetical Tax System

Income	Tax Liability	Average Tax Rate	Marginal Tax Rate
$ 2,000	$-200	-0.10	0.2
3,000	0	0	0.2
5,000	400	0.08	0.2
10,000	1,400	0.14	0.2
30,000	5,400	0.18	0.2

amount of tax paid, the average tax rate, and the marginal tax rate for each of several income levels. The average rates increase with income. However, the marginal tax rate is constant at 0.2 because for each additional dollar earned, the individual pays an additional 20 cents, regardless of income level. People could disagree about the progressiveness of this tax system and each be right according to his or her own definition. It is therefore very important to make the definition clear when using the terms regressive and progressive. In the remainder of this book, it will be assumed that they are defined in terms of average tax rates.

Measuring *how* progressive a tax system is is even harder than defining progressiveness. Many reasonable alternatives have been proposed,[5] and we will consider two simple ones. The first says that the greater the increase in average tax rates as income increases, the more progressive the system. Algebraically, let T_0 and T_1 be the tax liabilities at income levels I_0 and I_1, respectively (I_1 is greater than I_0). The measurement of progressiveness, v_1 is

(11.1)
$$v_1 = \frac{\dfrac{T_1}{I_1} - \dfrac{T_0}{I_0}}{I_1 - I_0}.$$

[5] See Musgrave and Thin [1948].

Once the analyst has found the economic incidence of the tax as embodied in T_1 and T_0, the tax system with the higher value of v_1 is said to be more progressive.

The second possibility is to say that one tax system is more progressive than another if its elasticity of tax revenues with respect to income (i.e., the percentage change in tax revenues divided by percentage change in income) is higher. Here the expression to be evaluated is v_2, defined as

(11.2)
$$v_2 = \frac{(T_1 - T_0)}{T_0} \div \frac{(I_1 - I_0)}{I_0}$$

Now consider the following proposal: everyone's tax liability is to be increased by 20 pecent of the amount of tax he or she currently pays. This proposal would increase the tax liability of a person who formerly paid T_0 to $1.2 \times T_0$, and the liability which was formerly T_1 to $1.2 \times T_1$. Congressperson A says the proposal will make the tax system more progressive, while Congressperson B says that it has no effect on progressiveness whatsoever. Who is right? It depends on the progressivity measure. Substituting the expressions $1.2 \times T_0$ and $1.2 \times T_1$ for T_1 and T_0, respectively, in Equation (11.1), it is seen that v_1 increases by 20 percent. The proposal thus increases progressiveness. On the other hand, if the same substitution is done in Equation (11.2), the value of v_2 is unchanged. (Both the numerator and denominator are multiplied by 1.2 which cancels out the effect.) The lesson here is that even very intuitively appealing measures of progressiveness can give different answers.[6] Again, intelligent public debate requires that people make their definitions clear.

MODELS OF TAX INCIDENCE

With preliminaries out of the way, we turn now to the fundamental problem of this chapter: how taxes affect the income distribution. We have argued that the essence of the problem is that taxes induce changes in relative prices. Knowing how prices are determined is therefore a key ingredient in the analysis. In this section we analyze tax incidence using several different models of price determination.

Partial Equilibrium Models

Partial equilibrium models study only the market in which the tax is imposed and ignore the ramifications in other markets. This kind of

---

[6] Note also that v_1 and v_2 will, in general, depend upon the level of income. That is, even a single tax system does not usually have a constant v_1 and v_2. This further complicates discussions of the degree of progressiveness.

analysis is most appropriate when the market for the commodity taxed is relatively small compared to the economy as a whole.

Unit Taxes on Commodities.   We study first the incidence of a **unit tax,** so named because it is levied as a fixed amount per unit of a commodity sold. For example, the federal government imposes a tax on champagne of $3.40 per gallon and a tax on cigarettes of $8 per thousand.[7] Suppose that the price and quantity of champagne are determined competitively by supply (S_c) and demand (D_c) as in Figure 11.1. Prior to imposition of

FIGURE 11.1   **Price and Quantity Prior to Taxation**

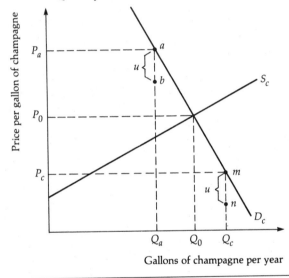

Gallons of champagne per year

the tax, the quantity demanded and price are Q_0 and P_0, respectively. Now suppose that a unit tax of $\$u$ per gallon is imposed on each purchase.

A key step in incidence analysis is to recognize that in the presence of a tax, the price paid by consumers and the price received by suppliers will differ. Previously, we could use a supply-demand analysis to determine the *single* market price. Now, this analysis must be modified to accommodate two different prices, one for buyers and one for sellers.

We begin by determining how the tax affects the demand schedule. Consider an arbitrary point a on the demand curve. Recall that this point indicates that the *maximum* price per gallon that people would be willing to pay for Q_a gallons is P_a. After the unit tax of u is imposed, the most

---

[7] As of April 1, 1983. See *Facts and Figures on Government Finance* [1983, p. 150].

that people would be willing to spend for Q_a *is still* P_a. There is no reason to believe that the tax affects the underlying valuation people place on champagne. However, when people pay P_a per gallon, the producer no longer receives the whole amount. Instead, he receives only $(P_a - u)$, an amount which is indicated as point *b* in Figure 11.1. In other words, after the unit tax is imposed, *a* is no longer a point on the demand curve as *perceived by suppliers*. Point *b* *is* on the demand curve as perceived by suppliers, because they realize that if Q_a is supplied, they will receive only $(P_a - u)$ per gallon. It is irrelevant to the suppliers how much consumers pay per gallon; all that matters to suppliers is the amount they receive per gallon.

Of course, point *a* was chosen arbitrarily. At any other point on the demand curve, the story is just the same. Thus, for example, after the tax is imposed, the price received by suppliers for output Q_c is at point *n*, which is found by subtracting a distance *u* from point *m*. If we repeat this process at every point along the demand curve, we generate a new demand curve, which is located exactly *u* dollars below the old one. In Figure 11.2, the demand curve so constructed is labeled D_c'. It is schedule

FIGURE 11.2   Incidence of a Unit Tax Imposed on the Demand Side

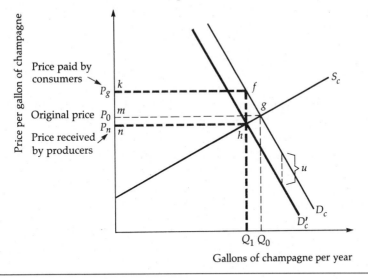

D_c' that is relevant to suppliers, because it shows how much they receive for each unit sold.

We are now in a position to find the equilibrium quantity of champagne after the unit tax is imposed. The equilibrium is where the supply equals demand as perceived by suppliers. In Figure 11.2, this takes place at output Q_1. Thus, the tax lowers the quantity sold from Q_0 to Q_1.

The next step is to find the new equilibrium price. As noted above, there are really two prices at the new equilibrium: the price received by producers, and the price paid by consumers. The price received by producers is at the intersection of their effective demand and supply curves, which occurs at P_n. The price paid by consumers is P_n *plus u*, the unit tax. To find this price geometrically, we must go up from P_n a vertical distance exactly equal to u. But by construction, the distance between schedules D_c and D_c' is equal to u. Hence, to find the price paid by consumers, we simply go up from the intersection of D_c' and S_c to the original demand curve D_c. The price so determined is P_g. Because P_g includes the tax, it is often referred to as the price *gross* of tax. On the other hand, P_n is the price *net* of tax.

Consumers are made worse off by the tax because P_g, the new price they face, is higher than the original price P_0. But the consumers' price has not increased by the full amount of the tax—$(P_g - P_0)$ is less than u. Producers also pay part of the tax in the form of a lower price received per gallon. Producers now receive only P_n, while before the tax they received P_0. Thus, both producers and consumers are made worse off by the tax.[8] By definition, revenues collected are the product of the number of units purchased, Q_1, and the tax per unit, u. Geometrically, Q_1 is the width of rectangle *kfhn* and u is its height, so tax revenues are the area of this rectangle.

This analysis has two important implications.

The Incidence of a Unit Tax Is Independent of whether It Is Levied on Consumers or Producers.   Suppose the same tax u had been levied on the suppliers of champagne instead of the consumers. Consider an arbitrary price P_i on the original supply curve in Figure 11.3. The supply curve indicates that for suppliers to produce Q_i units, they must receive at least P_i per unit. After the unit tax, suppliers still must receive P_i per unit. For them to do so, however, consumers must pay price $P_i + u$ per unit, which is shown geometrically as point j. It should now be clear where the argument is heading. To find the supply curve as it is perceived by consumers, S_c must be shifted up by the amount of the unit tax. This new supply curve is labeled S_c'. The post-tax equilibrium is at Q_1', where the schedules S_c' and D_c intersect. The price at the intersection, P_g', is the price paid by consumers. To find the price received by producers, we must *subtract* u from P_g', giving us P_n'. A glance at Figure 11.2

---

[8] In terms of surplus measures, consumers are worse off by area *mkfg* and producers are worse off by *mghn*. The loss of total surplus exceeds the tax revenues by triangle *fhg*; this is the *excess burden* of the tax, as explained in Chapter 12. Area *mghn* is the loss in producers' surplus. Just as consumers' surplus is the area between the demand curve and a horizontal line at the going price, producers' surplus is the area between the supply curve and a horizontal line at the going price. For a review of consumers' surplus, see Chapter 9.

FIGURE 11.3   Incidence of a Unit Tax Imposed on the Supply Side

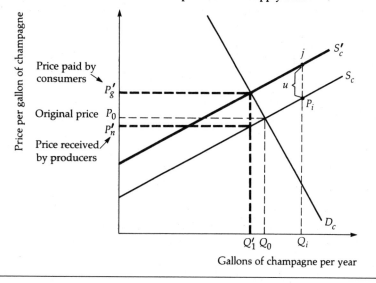

Gallons of champagne per year

indicates that $Q_1' = Q_1$, $P_g' = P_g$, and $P_n' = P_n$. Thus, the incidence of the unit tax is independent of the side of the market upon which it is levied.

This is the same as our statement that the statutory incidence of a tax tells us nothing of the economic incidence of the tax. It is irrelevant whether the tax collector (figuratively) stands next to the consumer and takes u dollars from him every time he pays for a gallon of champagne, or stands next to the seller and collects u dollars from him whenever he sells a gallon. Figures 11.2 and 11.3 prove that what matters is the size of the disparity the tax introduces between the price paid by consumers and the price received by producers, and not on which side of the market the disparity is introduced. The tax-induced difference between the price paid by consumers and the price received by producers is referred to as the **tax wedge.**

The Incidence of the Unit Tax Depends upon the Elasticities of Supply and Demand.   In Figure 11.2, consumers bear the brunt of the tax—the amount that they pay goes up much more than the amount received by producers goes down. This result is strictly a consequence of the way in which the demand and supply curves are drawn. In general, the more elastic the demand curve, the less the tax will be borne by consumers, *ceteris paribus.* Similarly, the more elastic the supply curve, the less the tax will be borne by producers, *ceteris paribus.* Intuitively, elasticity provides a rough measure of an economic agent's ability to "escape" the tax. The more elastic the demand, the "easier" it is for consumers to turn to other products when the price goes up, and therefore more of the tax must be borne by suppliers. Conversely, if consumers purchase the same amount regardless of price, then the whole burden can be shifted to them. Similar considerations apply to the supply side.

Two illustrations of extreme cases are provided in Figures 11.4A and 11.4B. In Figure 11.4A, commodity X is supplied perfectly inelastically.

FIGURE 11.4A   Tax Incidence When Supply Is Perfectly Inelastic

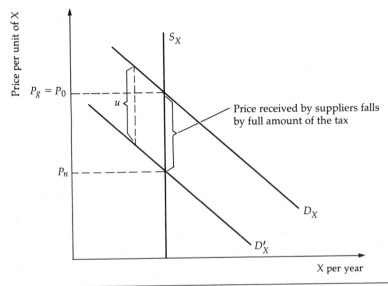

FIGURE 11.4B   Tax Incidence When Supply Is Perfectly Elastic

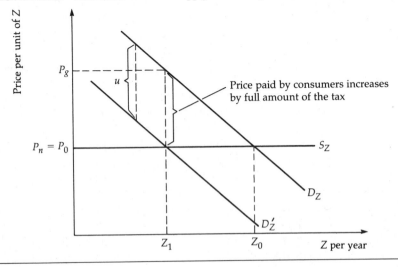

When a unit tax is imposed, the effective demand curve becomes D'_X. As before, the price received by producers is at the intersection of S_X and D'_X, which is P_n. Note that P_n is exactly u less than P_0. Thus, the price received by producers falls by exactly the amount of the tax. At the same time, the price paid by consumers, P_g $(= P_n + u)$, remains at P_0. When supply is perfectly inelastic, producers bear the entire burden.

Figure 11.4B represents an opposite extreme. The supply of commodity Z is perfectly elastic. Imposition of a unit tax leads to demand curve D'_Z. At the new equilibrium, quantity demanded is Z_1 and the price received by producers, P_n, is still P_0. The price paid by consumers, P_g, is therefore $P_0 + u$. In this case, consumers bear the entire burden of the tax.

Ad Valorem Taxes on Commodities.   We now turn to the incidence of an **ad valorem** tax, which is one with a rate given as a *proportion* of the price. Ad valorem taxes are quite common; for example, state and local taxes on food and clothing are usually levied as some proportion of sales price.

Luckily, the analysis of ad valorem taxes is very similar to that of unit taxes. The basic strategy is still to find out how the tax changes the effective demand curve and compute the new equilibrium. However, instead of moving the curve down by the same absolute amount for each quantity, the ad valorem tax lowers it in the same *proportion*. To show this, consider the demand (D_f) and supply (S_f) curves for food in Figure 11.5. In the absence of taxation, the equilibrium price and quantity are P_0 and Q_0, respectively. Now suppose that a tax of 25 percent of the gross price is levied on the consumption of food.[9] Consider point m on D_f. After the tax is imposed, P_m is still the most that consumers will pay for Q_m pounds of food; the amount that producers will receive is 75 percent of the vertical distance between point m and the horizontal axis, which is labeled point n. Hence, point n is one point on the demand curve perceived by producers. Similarly, the price at point r migrates down one quarter of the way between it and the horizontal axis to point s. When this exercise is repeated for every point on D_f, the effective demand curve facing suppliers is determined as D'_f in Figure 11.6. From here, the analysis proceeds in exactly the same way as in the unit tax case: The equilibrium is at the intersection of S_f and D'_f, with the quantity exchanged Q_1, the price received by food producers P_n, and the price paid by consumers P_g. As before, the extent to which the prices paid by

---

[9] There is a fundamental ambiguity involved in measuring ad valorem tax rates. Is the tax to be measured as a percentage of the net or gross price? In this example, the tax is 25 percent of the gross price, which is equivalent to a rate of 33 percent of net price. To see this, note that if the price paid by the consumer were $1, the tax paid would be 25 cents, and the price received by producers would be 75 cents. Expressing the 25 cents tax bill as a fraction of 75 cents gives us a 33 percent rate as a proportion of the net price.

FIGURE 11.5   Introducing an Ad Valorem Tax

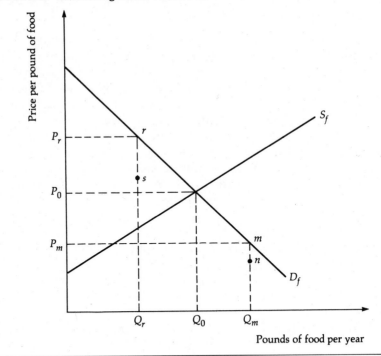

FIGURE 11.6   Incidence of an Ad Valorem Tax

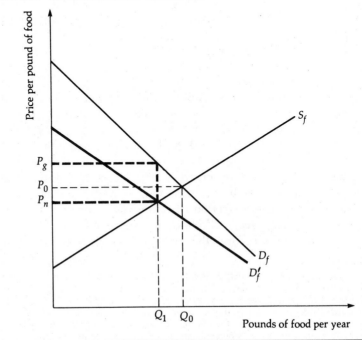

consumers and received by producers rise and fall, respectively, is determined by the elasticities of supply and demand.

So far we have discussed taxes on goods, but the analysis can also be applied to factors of production. Consider the payroll tax used to finance the social security system. As noted in Chapter 8, a tax equal to 7.0 percent of workers' earnings must be paid by their employers, and a tax at the same rate paid by the workers themselves—a total of 14.0 percent.[10] This division has a long history and is a consequence of our lawmaker's feeling that the payroll tax should be shared equally by employers and employees. It is important to realize that the *statutory distinction between workers and bosses is irrelevant.* As noted earlier, the incidence of this tax on labor is determined only by the wedge that the tax puts between what employees receive and employers pay.

This point is illustrated in Figure 11.7, where D_L is the demand for labor and S_L is the supply of labor. For purposes of illustration, S_L is assumed to be perfectly inelastic. Prior to taxation, the wage is w_0. The ad valorem tax on labor moves the effective demand curve to D'_L. As

FIGURE 11.7   Incidence of a Payroll Tax with an Inelastic Supply of Labor

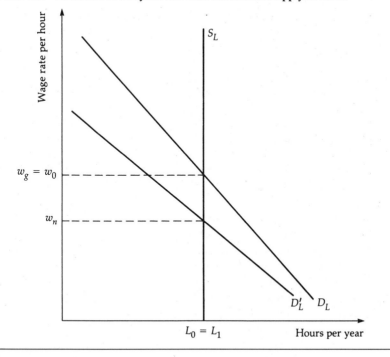

---

[10] After earnings of $37,800, the payroll tax rate becomes zero. These figures are for the year 1984. They are scheduled to rise throughout the 1980s.

usual, the distance between D'_L and D_L reflects the difference between what is paid for an item and what is received by those who supply it. After the tax is imposed, the wage received by workers falls to w_n. On the other hand, w_g, the price paid by employers, stays at w_0. In this example, despite the statutory division of the tax, the wage rate received by workers falls by exactly the amount of the tax—they bear the entire burden.

Of course, we could have gotten just the opposite result by drawing the supply curve as perfectly elastic. The key point to remember is that nothing about the incidence of a tax can be known without information on the relevant behavioral elasticities. In fact, there is some evidence that the elasticity of the total supply of hours of work in the United States is about zero.[11] At least in the short run, labor probably bears most of the payroll tax, despite the intense congressional debates on the "fair" distribution of the burden.

Commodity Taxation in the Absence of Competition.   The assumption of competitive markets has played a key role in our analysis. We now discuss how the results might change under alternative market structures.

Monopoly.[12]   The polar opposite of competition is monopoly—one seller. Figure 11.8 depicts a monopolist which produces commodity X. Prior to any taxation, the demand curve facing the monopolist is D_X, and the associated marginal revenue curve is MR_X. The marginal cost curve for the production of X is MC_X, and the average total cost curve, ATC_X. As usual, the condition for profit maximization is that production be carried to the point where marginal revenue equals marginal cost. This occurs at output X_0 where the price charged is P_0. Economic profit per unit is the difference between average revenue and average total cost, distance ab. The number of units sold is db. Hence, total profit is ab times db, which is the area of rectangle $abdc$.

Now suppose that a unit tax of u is levied on X. For exactly the same reasons as before, the effective demand curve facing the producer shifts down by a vertical distance equal to u.[13] In Figure 11.9, this demand curve is labeled D'_X. At the same time the marginal revenue curve facing the firm also shifts down by distance u because the firm's incremental revenue for each unit sold is reduced by the amount of the tax. The new effective marginal revenue curve is labeled MR'_X.

---

[11] See Rosen and Quandt [1978].

[12] See Baumol and Blinder [1982, Chapter 25] for a review of price and output determination under monopoly.

[13] Alternatively, we could have the marginal cost curve shift up by u. The final outcomes are identical.

FIGURE 11.8   Equilibrium of a Monopolist

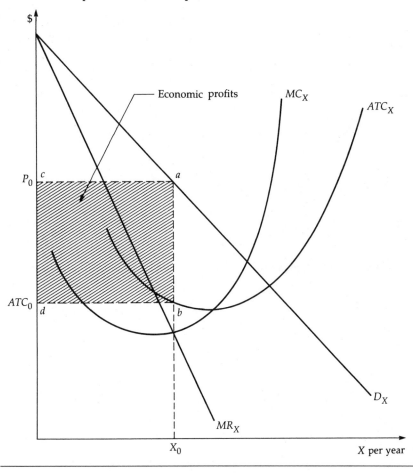

The profit-maximizing output is found at the intersection of MR'_X and MC_X, which occurs at output X_1. Using output X_1, we find the price received by the monopolist by going up to D'_X, the demand curve facing him, and locate price P_n. The price paid by consumers is determined by adding u to P_n, which is shown as price P_g on the diagram. After-tax profit per unit is the difference between the price *received by the monopolist* and average total cost, distance fg. Number of units sold is if. Therefore, monopoly economic profits after tax are measured by area $fghi$.

What are the effects of the tax? Quantity demanded goes down ($X_1 < X_0$); the price paid by consumers goes up ($P_g > P_0$); and the price received by the monopolist has gone down ($P_n < P_0$). Note that monopoly profits are lower under the tax—area $fghi$ in Figure 11.9 is smaller than area $abcd$ in Figure 11.8. Despite its market power, a monopolist is

FIGURE 11.9   Imposition of a Unit Tax on a Monopolist

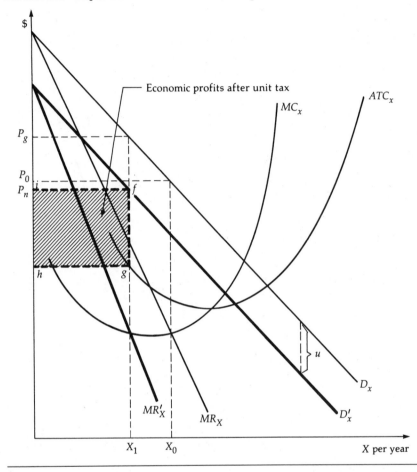

in general made worse off by a unit tax on the product it sells. In public debate it is often assumed that a firm with market power can simply "pass on" all taxes to consumers. This analysis shows that even a completely greedy and grasping monopolist must bear some of the burden. As before, the precise share of the burden borne by consumers depends upon the elasticity of the demand schedule.

It is straightforward to repeat the exercise for an ad valorem tax on the monopolist (D_X and MR_X pivot instead of moving down in a parallel fashion); this is left as an exercise for the reader.

Oligopoly.   Between the polar extremes of perfect competition and monopoly is the oligopoly market structure in which there are a "few" sellers. Unfortunately, there is no well-developed theory of tax incidence in oligopoly. The reason for this embarrassing fact is simple: incidence depends primarily upon how relative prices change when taxes are imposed, but there is no generally accepted theory of how oligopolistic prices are determined. Depending upon your view of how oligopolists function, practically anything can happen when a tax is imposed.

Suppose first that any single oligopolist believes that if he raises his price in response to a tax, the other firms in the industry will not follow. According to this belief, raising your price will lead to a substantial loss of customers to the other firms [see Musgrave, 1959, p. 281]. If every oligopolist shares the same belief, then none will raise price in response to the tax. The price paid by the consumer remains constant, and the entire burden of the tax falls on producers.

However, a different story about oligopoly behavior can lead to the opposite prediction. Suppose that the imposition of a tax serves as a signal to the members of the oligopoly that they can all raise prices together, without having to fear that any one firm will leave its price low. In this case, much of the tax might be shifted to consumers. Yet another possibility is that oligopolistic firms engage in *markup pricing*— they set their prices as some fixed percentage in excess of their costs. To the extent that taxes on their output are regarded as part of costs, they will be reflected in higher prices paid by consumers.

As economic behavior under oligopoly becomes better understood, improved models of incidence will be developed. In the meantime, most economists feel fairly comfortable in relying on the predictions produced by competitive models, although they realize that these are only approximations.

Profits Taxes.   So far we have been discussing taxes based upon sales. Firms can also be taxed upon their **economic profits,** defined as the return to owners of the firm in excess of the opportunity costs of the factors used in production. (Economic profits are also referred to as "supernormal" or "excess" profits.) We now show that as long as firms are profit maximizing, a tax on economic profits cannot be shifted—it is borne only by the owners of the firm.

Consider first a perfectly competitive firm in short-run equilibrium. The firm's output is determined by the intersection of its marginal cost and marginal revenue schedules. A tax of a given rate on economic profits changes neither marginal cost nor marginal revenue. Therefore, no firm has the incentive to change its output decision. Because output does not change, neither does the price paid by consumers, so they are no worse off. The tax is completely absorbed by the firms. Another way to get to the same result is this: If the tax rate on economic profits is t_p, the firm's objective is to maximize after-tax profits, $(1 - t_p)\pi$, where π is the pretax level of economic profits. But it is just a matter of arithmetic that whatever strategy maximizes π is identical to the one that maximizes $(1 - t_p)\pi$. Hence, output and price faced by consumers stay the same, and the firm bears the whole tax.

In long-run competitive equilibrium, a tax on economic profits has no yield, because economic profits are zero—they are all competed away. For a monopolist, there may be economic profits even in the long run. But for reasons exactly the same as those given in the preceding paragraph, the tax is borne by the owners of the monopoly. If a firm is profit maximizing before the profits tax is imposed, then the tax cannot be shifted.[14]

Because they distort no economic decisions, taxes on economic profits might appear to be very attractive policy alternatives. However, they have received very little support from public finance specialists. Probably the main reason for this is tremendous problems in making the theoretical notion of economic profits operational. For example, excess profits are often computed by examining the rate of return that a firm makes on its capital stock and comparing it to some "basic" rate of return set by the government. Clearly, how the capital stock is measured will be important. Should the original cost be used, or the cost of replacing it? And what if the rate of return is high not because of excess profits, but because the enterprise is very risky and investors have to be compensated for this risk? Considerations like these lead to major difficulties in administration and compliance.[15]

In this context, it should be noted that many taxes popularly referred to as "profits taxes" *do not in any way* resemble taxes on economic profits. For example, the so-called windfall profits tax on oil that created so much controversy when introduced during the Carter administration is essentially a complicated *sales tax* on crude oil.[16] Unlike a tax on economic profits, such a tax would certainly be expected to affect production incentives and to be shifted (by an amount determined by the relevant elasticities) to consumers.

General Equilibrium Models

A great attraction of partial equilibrium models is their simplicity—examining only one market at a time is a relatively uncomplicated affair. In some cases, however, ignoring feedback into other markets leads to an incomplete picture of a tax's incidence. Suppose, for example, that a tax is levied on all capital used in the construction of housing. Partial

---

[14] On the other hand, if the firm is following some other goal, then it may raise the price in response to a profits tax. One alternative to profit maximization is revenue maximization; firms try to make their sales as large as possible, subject to the constraint that they earn a "reasonable" rate of return.

[15] See Gillis and McLure [1979] for further details.

[16] See Meiselman [1979].

equilibrium analysis of this tax would involve analyzing only the supply and demand curves for housing capital. But suppose that the tax induces some people who formerly invested in housing to invest their capital in the manufacturing sector instead. As new capital flows into the manufacturing sector, the rate of return to capital employed there will fall. Thus, capitalists in the manufacturing sector may end up bearing part of the burden of a tax imposed on the housing sector.

More generally, when a tax is imposed on a sector that is "large" relative to the economy, looking only at the market where the tax is imposed may not be enough. The purpose of **general equilibrium analysis** is to take into account the ways in which various markets are interrelated. Before turning to the specifics of general equilibrium analysis, it is important to note that the fundamental lesson from partial equilibrium models still holds: because of relative price adjustments, the statutory incidence of a tax generally tells *nothing* about who is really bearing its burden.

Tax Equivalence Relations.   The idea of dealing with tax incidence in a general equilibrium framework at first appears daunting. After all, there are thousands of different commodities and inputs traded in the economy. How can we keep track of all of their complicated interrelations? Luckily, it turns out that for many purposes useful general equilibrium results can be obtained from models in which there are only two commodities, two factors of production, and no savings. For illustration, call the two commodities food (F) and manufactures (M), and the two factors capital (K) and labor (L). There are nine possible ad valorem taxes in such a model:

t_{KF} = a tax on capital used in the production of food.

t_{KM} = a tax on capital used in the production of manufactures.

t_{LF} = a tax on labor used in the production of food.

t_{LM} = a tax on labor used in the production of manufactures.

t_F = a tax on the consumption of food.

t_M = a tax on consumption of manufactures.

t_K = a tax on capital in both sectors.

t_L = a tax on labor in both sectors.

t = a general income tax.

The first four taxes, which are levied on a factor in only some of its uses, are referred to as *partial factor taxes.*

Certain combinations of these taxes are equivalent to others. One of these equivalences is already familiar from the theory of the consumer.[17]

---

[17] The theory of the consumer is outlined in the Appendix at the end of the book.

Taxes on food (t_F) and manufactures (t_M) at the same rate are equivalent to an income tax (t).[18] To see this, just note that equiproportional taxes on all commodities have the same effect on the consumer's budget constraint as a proportional income tax. Both create a parallel shift inward.

Now consider a proportional tax on both capital (t_K) and labor (t_L). Because in this model all income is derived from either capital or labor, it is a simple matter of arithmetic that taxing both factors at the same rate is also equivalent to an income tax (t).

Perhaps not so obvious is the fact that partial taxes on both capital and labor in the food sector at a given rate $(t_{KF} = t_{LF})$ are equivalent to a tax on food (t_F) at the same rate. Because capital and labor are the only inputs to the production of food, making each of them more expensive by a certain proportion is equivalent to making the food itself more expensive in the same proportion.

More generally, any two sets of taxes which generate the same changes in relative prices will have equivalent incidence effects. All the equivalence relations that can be derived using similar logic are summarized in Table 11.2. For a given ad valorem tax rate, the equivalences are

TABLE 11.2   Tax Equivalence Relations

t_{KF}	and	t_{LF}	are equivalent to	t_F
and		and		and
t_{KM}	and	t_{LM}	are equivalent to	t_M
are equivalent to		are equivalent to		are equivalent to
t_K	and	t_L	are equivalent to	t

Source: Charles E. McLure, Jr., "The Theory of Tax Incidence with Imperfect Factor Mobility," *Finanzarchiv* 30 (1971), p. 29.

shown by reading across the rows or down the columns. To determine the incidence of all three taxes in any row or column, only two have to be analyzed in detail. The third can be determined by addition or subtraction. For example, from the third row, if we know the incidence of taxes on capital and labor, then we also know the incidence of a tax on income.

In the next section, we will discuss the incidence of four taxes: a food tax (t_F), an income tax (t), a general tax on labor (t_L), and a partial tax on capital in manufacturing (t_{KM}). With results on these four taxes in hand, the incidence of the other five can be determined by using Table 11.2.

---

[18] Note that given the assumption that all income is consumed, an income tax is also equivalent to a tax on consumption expenditure.

Assumptions of the Model.   The pioneering work in applying general equilibrium models to public finance is Harberger's [1974c]. The principal assumptions of his model are as follows:

1. Technology.   Firms in each sector use capital and labor to produce their outputs. The technologies in each sector are such that a simultaneous doubling of both inputs leads to a doubling of output, *constant returns to scale*.[19] However, there is no requirement that the production technologies be the same in each sector. In general, the production technologies will differ with respect to the ease with which capital can be substituted for labor (the **elasticity of substitution**) and the ratios in which capital and labor are employed. For example, it has been calculated that the capital-labor ratio in the production of food is about 1.3 times that used in the production of appliances.[20] The industry in which the capital-labor ratio is relatively high is characterized as **capital intensive;** the other is **labor intensive.**

2. Behavior of Factor Suppliers.   Suppliers of both capital and labor maximize total returns. Moreover, capital and labor are perfectly mobile—they can freely move across sectors according to the wishes of their owners. Consequently, the net marginal return to capital must be the same in each sector, and so must the net marginal return to labor. Otherwise, it would be possible to reallocate capital and labor in such a way that total net returns could be increased.[21]

3. Market Structure.   Firms are competitive and maximize profits. Therefore, factors are fully employed, and the return paid to each factor of production is the value of its marginal product—the value to the firm of the output produced by the last unit of the input.

4. Total Factor Supplies.   The total amounts of capital and labor available to the economy are fixed. But, as suggested above, both factors are perfectly free to move between sectors.

5. Consumer Preferences.   All consumers have identical preferences. A tax therefore cannot generate any distributional effects by affecting people's uses of income. This assumption allows us to concentrate on the effect of taxes on the sources of income.

---

[19] It is also assumed that the production function is homogeneous, a technical condition which means that each ratio of factor prices is uniquely associated with a given ratio of capital to labor.

[20] See Devarajan, Fullerton, and Musgrave [1980, p. 167].

[21] To see why maximizing behavior results in an allocation in which marginal returns are equal, see the Appendix to this book.

6.   Tax Incidence Framework.   The framework for the analysis is differential tax incidence: we consider the substitution of one tax for another.
Therefore, approximately the same amount of income is available before
and after the tax, so it is unnecessary to consider how changes in aggregate income may change demand and factor prices.

Clearly, these assumptions are somewhat restrictive, but they serve
to simplify the analysis considerably. Later in this chapter, we will consider the consequences of dropping some of them. In the meantime, we
employ the assumptions to analyze several different taxes.

Analysis of Various Taxes.   *A Commodity Tax (t_F).*   When a tax on
food is imposed, its relative price increases (although not necessarily by
the amount of the tax). Consumers are thereby induced to substitute
manufactures for food. Consequently, less food and more manufactures
are produced. As food production falls off, some of the capital and labor
that formerly were used in food production are forced to find employment in manufacturing. Because the capital-labor ratios probably differ
between the two sectors, the relative prices of capital and labor have to
change for manufacturing to be willing to absorb the unemployed factors from food production. For example, assume that food is the capital-
intensive sector. (U.S. agriculture does, in fact, use relatively more
capital equipment—tractors, reapers, etc.—than many types of
manufacturing.) Therefore, relatively large amounts of capital must be
absorbed in manufacturing. The only way for all of this capital to find
employment in the manufacturing sector is for the relative price of capital to fall—including capital already in use in the manufacturing sector.
In the new equilibrium, then, *all* capital is relatively worse off, not just
capital in the food sector. More generally, a tax on the *output* of a particular sector will induce a decline in the relative price of the *input* used
intensively in that sector.
    To go beyond such qualitative statements, additional information is
needed. The greater the elasticity of demand for food, the more dramatic
will be the change in consumption from food to manufactures, which
will ultimately induce a greater decline in the return to capital. The
greater the difference in factor proportions between food and manufactures, the greater must be the decrease in capital's price for it to be
absorbed into the manufacturing sector. (If the capital-labor ratios for
food and manufactured goods were identical, neither factor would suffer relative to the other.) Finally, the harder it is to substitute capital for
labor in the production of manufactures, the greater the decline in the
rate of return to capital needed to absorb the additional capital.
    Thus, on the sources side of the budget, the food tax tends to hurt
people who receive a proportionately large share of their incomes from
capital. Given that all individuals are identical (assumption 5), there are

no interesting effects on the uses side. However, were we to drop this assumption, then clearly those people who consumed proportionately large amounts of food would tend to bear relatively larger burdens. The total incidence of the food tax then depends upon both the sources and uses sides. For example, a capitalist who eats a lot of food is worse off on both counts. On the other hand, a laborer who eats a lot of food is better off from the point of view of the sources of income, but worse off on the uses side.

An Income Tax (t).   As noted above, an income tax is equivalent to a set of taxes on capital and labor at the same rate. Since factor supplies are completely fixed (assumption 4), this tax cannot be shifted. It is borne in proportion to people's initial incomes. The intuition behind this result is similar to the analogous case in the partial equilibrium model; since the factors cannot "escape" the tax (by opting out of production), they bear the full burden.

A General Tax on Labor (t_L).   A general tax on labor is a tax on labor in *all* its uses, in the production of both food and manufactures. As a result, there are no incentives to switch labor use between sectors. Further, the assumption of fixed factor supplies implies that labor must bear the entire burden.

A Partial Factor Tax (t_{KM}).   When capital used in the manufacturing sector *only* is taxed, there are two initial effects: (1) The price of manufactures tends to rise, which decreases the quantity demanded by consumers. (2) As capital becomes more expensive in the manufacturing sector, producers there use less capital and more labor. Mieszkowski [1969] refers to the first as the **output effect,** and the second as the **factor substitution effect.** A flow chart for tracing the implications of these two effects is presented in Figure 11.10.

The output effect is described on the left side. As its name suggests, the output effect is a consequence of reductions in the production of manufactures. When the price of manufactures increases and less is demanded, capital and labor are released from manufacturing and must find employment in the production of food. If the manufacturing sector is labor intensive, then (relatively) large amounts of labor have to be absorbed in the food sector, and the relative price of capital increases. If, on the other hand, the manufacturing sector is capital intensive, the relative price of capital falls. Thus, the output effect is ambiguous with respect to the final effect on the relative prices of capital and labor.

This ambiguity is not present with the factor substitution effect, as depicted in the right-hand side of Figure 11.10. As long as substitution between capital and labor is possible, an increase in the price of capital

FIGURE 11.10   Incidence of a Partial Factor Tax

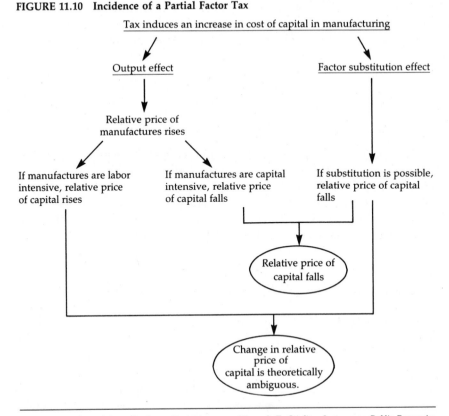

Source: Adapted from Anthony B. Atkinson and Joseph E. Stiglitz, *Lectures on Public Economics* (New York: McGraw-Hill, 1980), p. 173.

induces manufacturers to use less capital and more labor, tending to decrease the demand for capital and its relative price.

Putting the two effects together, we see that if manufacturing is capital intensive, both effects work in the same direction, and the relative price of capital must fall. But if the manufacturing sector is labor intensive, the final outcome is theoretically ambiguous. Even though the tax is levied on capital, it can make labor worse off! More generally, as long as factors are mobile between uses, a tax on a given factor in *one* sector ultimately effects the return to *both* factors in *both* sectors. Such results cannot be obtained with the partial equilibrium models discussed earlier in this chapter.

Much of the applied research on incidence in general equilibrium models has focused on the corporation income tax. In such work, it is assumed that the two sectors are "corporate" and "noncorporate," and that the corporation income tax is an ad valorem tax on capital only on its use in the corporate sector.[22] Given the theoretical ambiguity of the effect of a partial factor tax on the demand for capital, empirical work is required to find its incidence. Using plausible values for the key parameters of the model, Shoven [1976] estimated that capital bears the full burden of the corporation tax.

Some Qualifications.   We now discuss how changes in the assumptions underlying the general equilibrium model can modify its implications for tax incidence.

Differences in Individuals' Tastes.   By assumption 5, all consumers have the same preferences for two goods. When they do not, tax-induced changes in the distribution of income change aggregate spending decisions and hence relative prices and incomes. Consider a general tax on labor. As noted above, in the model with fixed factor supplies, this is borne entirely by laborers. However, if laborers consume different commodities than capitalists, those commodities favored by laborers will face a decrease in demand. Resources will then be allocated away from these commodities, and the factor used intensively in their production will receive a lower return. If laborers tend to consume capital-intensive goods disproportionately, capital can end up bearing part of the burden of a general tax on labor.

More than Two Sectors.   The division of the economy into two sectors is an enormously useful abstraction that keeps the analysis both conceptually and mathematically tractable. Nevertheless, this assumption can lead to misleading results. For example, the noncorporate sector lumps together such diverse enterprises as agriculture, real estate, crude oil, and gas. To the extent that taxes induce substitutions *within* each of the two sectors, there are potentially important effects on the income distribution that are ignored in the two-sector model. Shoven [1976] analyzed corporation tax incidence for the United States in a model with 12 sectors. Interestingly, he found results quite similar to those obtained in the two-sector case.[23] There is currently a good deal of research in progress to refine the computation of incidence in general equilibrium models.

Immobile Factors.   By assumption 2, resources are free to flow between sectors, seeking the highest rate of return possible. However, for institutional or technological reasons, some factors may be immobile. For example, if certain land is zoned for residential use, it cannot be used in manufacturing, no matter what the rate of return. Abandoning perfect

---

[22] As we shall see in Chapter 16, this is a somewhat controversial view.

[23] However, there have also been studies in which multisector approaches yield significantly different results. See Fullerton, Henderson, and Shoven [1982].

mobility can dramatically affect the incidence implications of a tax. For example, we showed above that if factors are mobile, the incidence of a partial factor tax is ambiguous, depending upon the outcome of several conflicting effects. If the factor is immobile, however, the incidence result is clear-cut: the taxed factor bears the whole burden. Intuitively, this is because the factor cannot "escape" taxation by migrating to the other sector [see McLure, 1971]. Note also that because the return to the taxed immobile factor falls by just the amount of the tax, the prices of capital and labor in the untaxed sectors are unchanged, as is the price of the good in the taxed sector.

Variable Factor Supplies. By assumption 4, the total supplies of both factors are fixed. In the long run, however, the supplies of both capital and labor to the economy are variable. Allowing for growth can turn conclusions from the static model completely on their heads. Consider a general factor tax on capital. When the capital stock is fixed, this tax is borne entirely by the capital's owners. In the long run, however, less capital may be supplied due to the tax.[24] To the extent this occurs, the economy's capital-labor ratio will decrease, and the return to labor will fall. (The wage falls because labor has less capital with which to work, and hence is less productive, *ceteris paribus*.) Thus, labor can be made worse off as a result of a general tax on capital.

Because the amount of calendar time that must elapse before the long run is reached may be substantial, short-run effects should not be regarded as inconsequential. On the other hand, intelligent policy also requires consideration of the long-run consequences of taxation.

An Applied Incidence Study. In an influential study, Pechman and Okner [1974] used the theory of tax incidence as a framework to estimate how the U.S. system of federal, state, and local taxation affects the distribution of income.[25] It should by now be clear that all incidence results depend crucially upon the underlying models. Pechman and Okner examined tax burdens using several alternative models and compared the results. In some of their computations, for example, it was assumed that markets are competitive, and capital flows freely between sectors. In other variants, it was assumed that capital is essentially immobile between sectors, so that, for example, corporate capital bears the entire burden of the corporation income tax.

Using data from 1966, Pechman and Okner found that most of the population faces roughly the same average tax rate, about 32 percent. Hence, the tax system does not have much of an effect on the distribution of income. This is even true under the assumption that the corpora-

---

[24] However, the supply of capital will not necessarily decrease. See Chapter 15.

[25] Their analysis is based upon individual's annual incomes. Some measure of lifetime income would be more appropriate. See Chapter 5.

tion tax is borne by the owners of capital, which would be expected to generate a progressive outcome.

It is important to note that in *all* their analyses, Pechman and Okner assumed there is no shifting of the personal income tax, and that general commodity taxes are borne by consumers in proportion to their consumption of the taxed items. These assumptions help simplify the problem considerably. But the theory of tax incidence suggests that they are extremely questionable, especially in the long run. Empirical results on the distributive implications of taxation can only be as solid as the incidence theories that underlie them. As economists learn more about the long-run incidence of taxation, Pechman and Okner's conclusions may be modified considerably.

Tax Incidence and Capitalization

We now consider special issues that arise when land is taxed. For these purposes, the distinctive characteristics of land are that it is fixed in supply and it is durable.[26] Suppose the annual rental rate on land is R_0 this year. It is known that the rental will be R_1 next year, R_2 two years from now, etc. How much should someone be willing to pay for the land? If the market for land is competitive, the price of land is just equal to the present discounted value of the stream of the rents. Thus, if the interest rate is i, the price of land (P_R) is

(11.3) $$P_R = \$R_0 + \frac{\$R_1}{(1 + i)} + \frac{\$R_2}{(1 + i)^2} + \cdots + \frac{\$R_T}{(1 + i)^T}$$

where T is the last year the land yields its services (possibly infinity).

Now assume that it is announced that a tax of u_0 will be imposed on land now, u_1 next year, u_2 two years from now, etc. From Figure 11.4 we know that because land is fixed in supply, the annual rental received by the owner will fall by the full amount of the tax. That means that the landlord's return initially will fall to $(R_0 - u_0)$, in year 1 to $(R_1 - u_1)$, in year 2 to $(R_2 - u_2)$, etc. Prospective purchasers of the land take into account the fact that if they purchase the land, they buy a future stream of tax liabilities as well as a future stream of returns. Therefore, the most a purchaser will be willing to pay for the land after the tax is announced (P_R'), is

(11.4) $$P_R' = \$(R_0 - u_0) + \frac{\$(R_1 - u_1)}{1 + i} + \frac{\$(R_2 - u_2)}{(1 + i)^2} + \cdots$$
$$+ \frac{\$(R_T - u_T)}{(1 + i)^T}$$

---

[26] Hence, the analysis of this section applies to any commodity or input with these characteristics.

Comparing Equations (11.4) and (11.3), we see that as a consequence of the tax, the price of land falls by an amount equal to

$$u_0 + \frac{u_1}{1 + i} + \frac{u_2}{(1 + i)^2} + \cdots + \frac{u_T}{(1 + i)^T}$$

Thus, at the time the tax is imposed, the price of the land falls by the present value of *all future tax payments.* This process by which a stream of taxes becomes incorporated into the price of an asset is referred to as **capitalization.**[27]

As a consequence of capitalization, the person who bears the full burden of the tax *forever* is the landlord at the time the tax is levied. To be sure, *future* landlords make payments to the tax authorities, but such payments are not really a "burden" because they just balance the lower price paid at purchase. Capitalization complicates attempts to assess the incidence of a tax on a durable item that is fixed in supply. Knowing the identities of current owners is not sufficient—one must know who the landlords *were* at the time the tax was imposed.[28]

To the extent that land is *not* fixed in supply, the preceding analysis must be qualified. For example, at the fringes of urban areas that are adjacent to farmland, the supply of urban land can be extended. Similarly, in some areas the amount of land can be increased by landfills. In such cases, the tax on land is borne both by landlords and the users of land, in proportions that depend upon the elasticities of demand and supply.[29]

INCIDENCE IN AN INTERGENERATIONAL SETTING: THE BURDEN OF THE DEBT

Up to now, we have focused attention on how taxation affects the incomes of people who live during a given time period without considering how government financial policies might change the distribution of income across generations. This issue crops up most often in discussions of whether or not there is a "burden" to the public debt. Specifically, suppose the government has the option of financing a project either by taxation or by borrowing. If the latter option is chosen, is the burden shifted to the members of future generations, who have to pay off the loan?

---

[27] More generally, capitalization refers to the incorporation of any change in the revenue stream into the price.

[28] If a land tax is anticipated before it is levied, then presumably it is borne at least in part by the owner at the time the anticipation becomes widespread. In theory, then, even finding out the identity of the landowner at the time the tax was imposed may not be enough.

[29] In the same way, if imposition of the land tax somehow leads to changes in the discount rate, i, then the results will change.

TABLE 11.3   Gross Debt (all levels of government)

	(1) Total Debt ($ millions)	(2) Per Capita Debt	(3) Debt/GNP Ratio	(4) Federal Share (percent)
Year				
1902	$ 3,285	$ 41	0.15	35.9%
1927	33,393	281	0.35	55.4
1940	63,251	479	0.63	67.9
1946	285,339	2,037	1.36	94.4
1950	281,445	1,853	0.98	91.4
1955	381,641	1,930	0.96	86.1
1960	356,286	1,980	0.70	80.4
1965	416,786	2,154	0.61	76.1
1970	514,489	2,524	0.52	72.1
1975	764,055	3,586	0.49	71.2
1980	1,249,919	5,501	0.47	73.2
1982	1,542,817	6,663	0.50	74.3

Source: *Facts and Figures on Government Finance—22nd Biennial Edition* (Washington, D.C.: Tax Foundation, 1983), pp. 30–31.

As Table 11.3 indicates, this is not merely an academic issue. Over time, government debt has grown enormously, both in absolute (column 1) and per capita (column 2) terms.[30] To keep these figures in perspective, however, they should be compared to some measure of the country's productive capacity, such as gross national product. Column 3 indicates that the ratio of debt to gross national product has more or less stayed constant in recent years, after having fallen from the peaks associated with World War II. Also, in the postwar period, the federal share of the total government debt declined until recent years (column 4).

Whether or not the existence of all this debt will lower the welfare of our descendants has been debated furiously by both politicians and economists.[31] We will see that just as with other incidence problems, the answer depends upon the assumptions made about economic behavior.

Lerner's View.   Assume that the government borrows from its own citizens—the obligation is an **internal debt.** According to Lerner [1948], an internal debt creates no burden for the future generation. Members of the future generation simply owe it to each other. When the debt is paid off, there is a transfer of income from one group of citizens (those who do not hold bonds) to another (bondholders). However, the future generation as a whole is no worse off in the sense that its consumption level is the same as it would have been.

---

[30] In interpreting these figures, however, keep in mind the difficulties in measuring the size of the government budget. See Chapter 2.

[31] The macroeconomic implications of debt (does it affect the unemployment and inflation rates?) are equally controversial, but are not discussed here.

The story is quite different when a country borrows from abroad to finance current expenditure. This is referred to as an **external debt**.[32] Suppose that the money borrowed from overseas is used to finance current consumption. In this case, the future generation certainly bears a burden, because its consumption level is reduced by an amount equal to the loan plus the accrued interest[33] which must be sent to the foreign lender. If, on the other hand, the loan is used to finance capital accumulation, the outcome depends upon the project's productivity. If the marginal return on the investment is greater than the marginal cost of funds obtained abroad, then the combination of the debt and capital expenditure actually makes the future generation better off. To the extent that the project's return is less than the marginal cost, the future generation is worse off.

The view that an internally held debt does not burden future generations dominated the economics profession in the 1940s and 1950s. There is now widespread belief that things are considerably more complicated.

An Overlapping Generations Model.[34]   In Lerner's model, a "generation" consists of everyone who is alive at a given time. Perhaps a more sensible way to define a generation is everyone who was born at about the same time. Using this definition, at any given time several generations coexist simultaneously, as an **overlapping generations model** takes into account. Analysis of a simple overlapping generations model shows how the burden of a debt can be transferred across generations.

Assume that the population consists of equal numbers of "young," "middle-aged," and "old" people. Each generation lasts 20 years, and each person has a fixed income of $12,000 over the 20-year period. There is no private saving—everyone consumes their entire income. This situation is expected to continue forever. Income levels for three representative people for the period 1984 to 2004 are depicted in row (1) of Figure 11.11.

Now assume that the government decides to borrow $12,000 to finance public consumption. The loan is to be repaid in the year 2004. Only the young and the middle-aged are willing to lend to the government—the old are unwilling because they will not be around in 20 years to obtain repayment. Assume that half the lending is done by the young and half by the middle-aged, so that consumption of each person is reduced by $6,000 during the period 1984 to 2004. This fact is recorded in row (2) of Figure 11.11. However, with the money obtained from the

---

[32] In the United States, internal debt is more important than external debt; in 1982, only 13 percent of the federal debt was held by foreign investors. (Computed from *Facts and Figures on Government Finance*, 1983, p. 164.)

[33] If the loan is refinanced, only the interest must be paid.

[34] This argument is based on Bowen, Davis, and Kopf [1960].

FIGURE 11.11   An Overlapping Generations Model

		The Period 1984–2004		
		Young	*Middle-Aged*	*Old*
(1)	Income	$ 12,000	$ 12,000	$12,000
(2)	Government borrowing	−6,000	−6,000	
(3)	Government-provided consumption	4,000	4,000	4,000

			The Year 2004	
		Young	*Middle-Aged*	*Old*
(4)	Government raises taxes to pay back the debt	$−4,000	$−4,000	$−4,000
(5)	Government pays back the debt		+6,000	+6,000

loan, the government provides an equal amount of consumption for all—each person receives $4,000. This is noted in line (3).

Time passes, and the year 2004 arrives. The generation that was old in 1984 has departed from the scene. The formerly middle-aged are now old, the young are now middle-aged, and a new young generation has been born. The government has to raise $12,000 to pay off the debt. It does so by levying a tax of $4,000 on each person. This is recorded in line (4). With the tax receipts in hand, the government can pay back its debt holders, the now middle-aged and old (row 5). (It is assumed for simplicity that the rate of interest is zero, so all the government has to pay back is the principal. Introducing a positive rate of interest would not change the substantive result.)[35]

The following results now emerge from Figure 11.11: (1) as a consequence of the debt and accompanying tax policies, the generation that was old in 1984 to 2004 has a lifetime consumption level $4,000 higher than it otherwise would have had; (2) those who were young and middle-aged in 1984 to 2004 are no better or worse off from the point of view of lifetime consumption; and (3) the young generation in 2004 has a lifetime consumption stream that is $4,000 lower than it would have been in the absence of the debt and accompanying fiscal policies. In effect, $4,000 has been transferred from the young of 2004 to the old of

---

[35] The assumption of a zero interest rate also means that there is no need to discount future consumption to find its present value.

1984. To be sure, the debt repayment in 2004 involves a transfer between people who are alive at the time, but the young are at the short end of the transfer because they have to contribute to repaying a debt from which they never benefited. Note also that the internal-external distinction that was key in Lerner's model is of no relevance here; even though the debt is all internal, it creates a burden for the future generation.

Of course, the model of Figure 11.11 is highly restrictive—there is no private saving, no growth, and no economic response on the part of individuals to government fiscal policies. However, even in more complicated models, intergenerational burden shifting remains a real possibility.

Models Including Economic Behavior. The intergenerational models discussed so far do not allow for the fact that economic decisions can be affected by government debt policy, and changes in these decisions have consequences for who bears the burden of the debt. Instead, it has been assumed that the taxes levied to pay off the debt affect neither work nor savings behavior when they are imposed. If taxes distort these decisions, real costs are imposed on the economy. (See Chapter 12.)

More importantly, we have ignored the potentially important effect that debt finance can have upon capital formation. When the government initiates a project, whether financed by taxes or borrowing, resources are removed from the private sector. It is usually assumed that when tax finance is used, most of the resources removed come at the expense of consumption. On the other hand, when the government borrows, it competes for funds with individuals and firms who want the money for their own investment projects. Hence, it is generally assumed that debt has most of its effect upon private investment.[36] To the extent that these assumptions are correct, debt finance will leave the future generation with a smaller capital stock, *ceteris paribus.*[37] Its members will therefore be less productive and have smaller real incomes than otherwise would have been the case. Thus, even in Lerner's model, the debt can have a burden. The mechanism through which it works is the reduction of capital formation.

Finally, the models also have ignored the potential importance of individuals' *intentional* transfers across generations. Suppose that when the government borrows, members of the "old" generation realize that their heirs will be made worse off. Suppose further that the old care about the welfare of their descendants and therefore do not want their

---

[36] Debt finance can also have an impact on consumption. For example, if government competition for funds drives up the interest rate, then consumers might be induced to channel more of their incomes into saving, *ceteris paribus.*

[37] One of the things that is "held equal" here is the public-sector capital stock. As suggested above, to the extent that the public sector undertakes productive investment with the resources it extracts from the private sector, the *total* capital stock increases.

descendants' consumption levels reduced. What can the old do about this? One possibility is simply to increase their bequests by an amount sufficient to pay the extra taxes that will be due in the future. Private individuals thus can undo the intergenerational effects of government debt policy. The form of government finance here is totally irrelevant.[38]

Although intergenerational bequests certainly are important, it is hard to believe that they are arranged in exactly the way just suggested. After all, information on the implications of current deficits for future tax burdens is not easy to obtain. Moreover, given the considerable uncertainty that exists concerning one's date of death, it is difficult to arrange a bequest of exactly the right size. Finally, there may not be all *that* much altruistic feeling between generations.

We conclude that the burden of the debt is hard to pin down. First of all, it is not even obvious how "burden" should be defined. One possibility is to measure it in terms of the lifetime consumption possibilities of a group of people of about the same age. Another is in terms of the consumption available to all people alive at a given point in time. Even when we settle on a definition, the existence of a burden depends on the answers to several questions. Is it internal or external? How are various economic decisions affected by debt policy? What kind of projects are financed by the debt? Empirical examination of some of these decisions has been attempted, but so far no consensus has emerged [see Buiter and Tobin, 1979].

Finally, we turn to the normative question of whether or not one generation *ought* to pass a burden on to another. To the extent that one generation uses government debt to finance activities that create returns for a future generation, it may be appropriate for the future generation to bear a commensurate burden. As an example, is it unfair for the current generation of young people to help pay for World War II? In addition, income distribution considerations suggest that shifting burdens across generations might be called for. Suppose that due to technological progress, our grandchildren will be richer than we are. If it makes sense to transfer income from rich to poor people within a generation, why shouldn't we transfer income from rich to poor generations? Of course, if future generations are expected to be poorer than we are (due, say, to the exhaustion of irreplaceable resources) then this logic would lead to just the opposite conclusion.

CONCLUSIONS

We began this chapter with an innocent question: "Who bears the burden of tax?" It led us to an analysis of the sometimes complicated rela-

---

[38] See Barro [1974] and Buiter and Tobin [1979] for further details.

tionships between various markets, both at a given point in time and across time periods. We have seen that price changes are the key to finding the burden of a tax, but that price changes depend on a lot of things: market structure, elasticities of supply and demand, movements of factors of production, and so on. At this stage, an obvious question is: "What do we really know?"

For taxes that may reasonably be analyzed in isolation, the answer is "Quite a bit." To do a partial equilibrium incidence analysis, the economist needs only to know the market structure and the shapes of the supply and demand curves. In cases other than a clear-cut monopoly, the competitive market paradigm has proved to be a sensible choice of market structure. Estimates of supply and demand curves can be obtained using the empirical methods discussed in Chapter 3. Incidence analysis is on firm ground.

Even in general equilibrium models, incidence analysis is equally suitable for analyzing taxes on immobile factors. Here the incidence of the tax is straightforward—it is borne entirely by the taxed factor. More generally, though, if a tax affects many markets, incidence depends upon the reactions of numerous supply and demand curves for goods and inputs. The answers are correspondingly less clear.

Unfortunately, it seems that many important taxes such as the corporate tax fall in the last category. Why is this? It may be for the very reason that the incidence is hard to find. What are the political chances of a tax that will clearly hurt some important group in the population? "Complicated" taxes may actually be simpler for a politician, because no one is sure who actually ends up paying them.

In any case, the models in this chapter tell us exactly what information is needed to understand the incidence even of very complex taxes. To the extent that this information is currently unavailable, the models serve as a measure of our ignorance. This is not altogether undesirable. As St. Jerome noted, "It is worse still to be ignorant of your ignorance."

SUMMARY

Statutory incidence refers to the legal liability for a tax, while economic incidence shows the actual sacrifice of income due to the tax. Knowledge of the legal incidence usually tells us little about economic incidence.

Economic incidence is determined by the way price changes when a tax is imposed. The incidence of a tax ultimately falls on individuals via both their sources and uses of income.

Neither incidence nor progressiveness are unambiguous concepts. Depending on the policy being considered, it may be appropriate to examine balanced budget, differential, or absolute incidence. Similarly, progressiveness may be measured in reference to either the average or the marginal tax rate.

Most partial equilibrium incidence studies assume that markets are competitive. In these models, tax incidence depends upon the elasticities of supply and demand. The same general approach can be used to study incidence in a monopolized market. For oligopoly, however, there is no single accepted framework for tax analysis.

General equilibrium incidence analysis is often conducted using a two-sector, two-factor model in which all consumers are assumed to have identical tastes. In this framework, there are nine possible taxes. Certain combinations of these taxes are equivalent to others.

Taxing a single factor in its use only in a particular sector changes relative factor prices, and hence, the distribution of income. The particular outcome depends upon factor intensities, ease of substitution in production, mobility of factors, and elasticities of demand for outputs.

Due to capitalization, the burden of future taxes may be borne by *current* owners of an inelastically supplied durable commodity such as land.

The burden of public finance can be shifted through time by using public debt. Overlapping generations models show changes in lifetime consumption patterns under alternative schemes of debt and tax finance.

DISCUSSION QUESTIONS

1. In 1983, the federal unit tax on gasoline was increased by 5 cents per gallon. An industry analyst predicted that the increase would be entirely passed on to consumers: "The dealers who try to eat this tax will be few and far between" ["Gas Tax Rise," 1983, p. D1]. Construct a model in which you evaluate this prediction. Under what circumstances is it likely to be correct?

2. **a.** Suppose that the federal government imposes a 6 percent ad valorem tax on toothpaste. Discuss the incidence of the tax.
   b. Now assume that Peoria, Illinois, levies a 6 percent ad valorem tax on toothpaste, but no one else does. Discuss the incidence of the tax, and compare your answer to part **(a).** (Hint: How do the supply curves of toothpaste for the country as a whole and for Peoria differ?)

3. "In a two-sector general equilibrium model, the distributional effects of a combined income and capital tax can be achieved just as well by a subsidy to labor in both sectors." Comment.

4. Assume that the capital-labor ratios are identical in all sectors of the economy. What determines the incidence of a tax on the output of any single sector?

SELECTED REFERENCES

Bowen, William G.; Richard Davis; and David Kopf. "The Public Debt: A Burden on Future Generations?" *American Economic Review* 50, no. 4 (September 1960), pp. 701–6.

Devarajan, S.; D. Fullerton; and R. Musgrave. "Estimating the Distribution of Tax Burdens: A Comparison of Alternative Approaches." *Journal of Public Economics* 13 (1980), pp. 155–82.

Mieszkowski, Peter M. "Tax Incidence Theory: The Effects of Taxes on the Distribution of Income." *Journal of Economic Literature* 7 (1969), pp. 1103–24.

Pechman, Joseph A.; and Benjamin A. Okner. *Who Bears the Tax Burden?* Washington, D.C.: Brookings Institution, 1974.

CHAPTER 12

Taxation and Efficiency

Waste always makes me angry.
Rhett Butler in
Gone With the Wind

Taxes impose a cost upon the taxpayer. It is tempting to view the tax burden as the amount of money that individuals hand over to the tax collector. However, a simple example indicates that this is just part of the story.

Consider Mr. Breyer Dazs, a citizen who typically consumes 10 ice-cream cones each week, at a price of 80 cents per cone. The government levies a 25 percent tax on his consumption of ice-cream cones, so that Dazs now faces a price of $1.[1] In response to the price hike, Dazs reduces his ice-cream cone consumption to zero, and he spends the $8 per week on other goods and services. Obviously, because Dazs consumes no ice-cream cones, the ice-cream tax yields zero revenue. Do we want to say that Dazs is unaffected by the tax? The answer is no. Dazs is worse off because the tax has induced him to consume a less desirable bundle of goods than previously. We know that the after-tax bundle is less desirable because, prior to tax, Dazs had the option of consuming no ice-cream cones. Since he chose to buy 10 cones weekly, this must have been preferred to spending the money on other items. Thus, despite the fact that the tax raised zero revenue, it made Dazs worse off.

This example is a bit extreme. Normally, we expect that an increase in price will diminish the quantity demanded, but not drive it all the way to zero. Nevertheless, the basic result holds: because a tax distorts eco-

---

[1] As emphasized in Chapter 11, the price paid by the consumer generally will not rise by the full amount of the tax. This assumption, which is strictly correct only if the supply curve is horizontal, is made here only for convenience.

nomic decisions, it brings about an **excess burden**—a loss of welfare above and beyond the tax revenues collected. Excess burden is sometimes referred to as *welfare cost* or *deadweight loss*. In this chapter we discuss the theory and measurement of excess burden.

EXCESS BURDEN IN A SIMPLE MODEL

Ruth has a fixed income of I dollars, which she spends on only two commodities: barley and corn. The price per pound of barley is P_b and the price per pound of corn is P_c. There are no taxes or "distortions" like externalities or monopoly in the economy, so the prices of the goods reflect their social marginal costs. For convenience, these social marginal costs are assumed to be constant with respect to output. In Figure 12.1, Ruth's consumption of barley is measured on the horizontal axis and her consumption of corn on the vertical. Her budget constraint is the line AD, which has slope $-P_b/P_c$ and horizontal intercept I/P_b.[2] Assuming

FIGURE 12.1   Effect of a Tax on the Budget Constraint

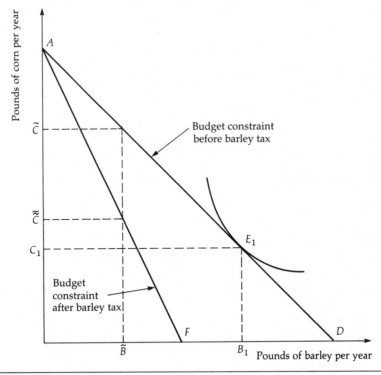

---

[2] The construction of budget constraints and the interpretation of their slopes and intercepts are discussed in the Appendix at the end of the book.

that Ruth maximizes a utility function characterized by standard indifference curves (convex to the origin), she chooses a point like E_1, where she consumes B_1 pounds of barley and C_1 pounds of corn.

Now suppose that the government levies a tax at a percentage rate of t_b on barley so that the price Ruth faces becomes $(1 + t_b)P_b$. (The before-tax price is unchanged because of our assumption of constant marginal social costs.) Imposition of the tax changes Ruth's budget constraint. It now has a slope of $-[(1 + t_b)P_b/P_c]$ and horizontal intercept $I/[(1 + t_b)P_b]$. This is represented in Figure 12.1 as line AF. (Because the price of corn is still P_c, lines AF and AD have the same vertical intercept.)

Note that for any given consumption level of barley, the vertical distance between AD and AF shows Ruth's tax payments measured in terms of corn. To see this, consider an arbitrary quantity of barley $\tilde{B}$ on the horizontal axis. Before the tax was imposed, Ruth could have both $\tilde{B}$ pounds of barley and $\tilde{C}$ pounds of corn. After the tax, however, if she consumed $\tilde{B}$ pounds of barley, the most corn she could afford would be $\tilde{\tilde{C}}$ pounds. The difference (distance) between $\tilde{C}$ and $\tilde{\tilde{C}}$ must therefore represent the amount of tax collected by government measured in pounds of corn. If we choose, we can convert tax receipts to dollars by multiplying the distance $\tilde{C}\tilde{\tilde{C}}$ by the price per pound of corn, P_c. For convenience, we can choose to measure corn in units such that $P_c = 1$. In this case, the distance $\tilde{C}\tilde{\tilde{C}}$ measures tax receipts in corn *or* dollars.

So far we have not indicated which point Ruth chooses on her new budget constraint, AF. Figure 12.2 shows that her most preferred bundle is at E_2 where her consumption of barley is B_2, her consumption of corn is C_2, and her tax bill is the associated vertical distance between AD and AF, GE_2. Note that if the tax authorities had erroneously assumed that Ruth would maintain her barley consumption at B_1 after the tax, they would have estimated tax receipts greater than the amount actually collected. In general, failure to account for the fact that taxes affect economic behavior leads to incorrect revenue predictions.

Clearly, Ruth is worse off at E_2 that she was at E_1. Presumably, any tax would have put her on a lower indifference curve.[3] The important question is whether there is a way that the government could have extracted GE_2 from Ruth which would have left her better off than at E_2. By definition, such a tax would have a lower excess burden.

A **lump sum tax** is *independent* of the taxpayer's behavior; i.e., a certain amount must be paid regardless of what the taxpayer does. The barley tax that we have been discussing is not a lump sum tax, because the revenue yield ultimately depends upon Ruth's barley consumption. Suppose now that the government levies upon Ruth a lump sum tax of E_2G. In Figure 12.3, the budget line associated with the lump sum tax is HI; it is generated simply by subtracting E_2G from each point along the

---

[3] This ignores benefits that might be obtained by the expenditures financed by the tax.

FIGURE 12.2   Effect of a Tax on the Consumption Bundle

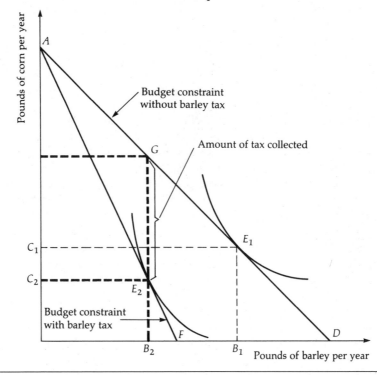

initial budget line AD. Because the lump sum tax does not change relative prices, HI is parallel to AD. Note that by construction, HI must pass through point E_2. If Ruth were faced with the lump sum tax, she would maximize utility at a point like E_3, and consume B_3 pounds of barley and C_3 pounds of corn.

Figure 12.3 suggests a rather remarkable result. Even though the lump sum tax collects the same revenue as the barley tax, it leaves Ruth better off—E_3 is on a higher indifference curve than E_2. This leads to a more precise definition of *excess burden*; it is the reduction of utility in excess of that which would have occurred had the tax been collected as a lump sum.[4] In Figure 12.3, it is the difference in utility levels associated with points E_2 and E_3.

The skeptical reader may suspect that this result is merely an artifact of the particular way the indifference curves are drawn in Figure 12.3. This is not the case. It can be shown that as long as the indifference

---

[4] There are alternative ways to define excess burden, but they are all very similar conceptually. See Auerbach and Rosen [1980].

FIGURE 12.3   Excess Burden of the Barley Tax

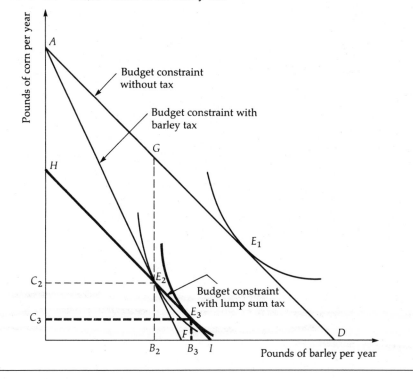

curves have the usual shape, a tax that changes relative prices generates an excess burden.[5] Alternatively, a tax that changes relative prices is inefficient in the sense that it lowers individual utility more than is necessary to raise a given amount of revenue.

This discussion raises some important questions.

If Lump Sum Taxes Are So Efficient, Why Aren't They Widely Used?
Lump sum taxation is an unattractive policy tool for several reasons. Suppose the government announced every person's tax liability was $2,000 per year. This is a lump sum tax, but most people would consider it unfair for everyone to pay the same tax regardless of their economic circumstances. As an alternative, suppose that people were made to pay different lump sum taxes depending upon their incomes. A rich person might be required to pay $20,000 annually, independent of his economic

---

[5] For a proof see Diamond and McFadden [1974]. For the more general case in which marginal social costs are not constant, the analogous result is that any tax which creates an inequality between the ratio of prices and the ratio of marginal social costs generates an excess burden.

decisions, while a poor person would pay only $500. The problem with this proposal is that people entering the work force would soon realize that their eventual tax burden depended upon their incomes. They would then adjust their work and savings decisions accordingly. In short, since the amount of income an individual earns, and hence his tax liability, is at least in part under his control, the income-based tax is not a lump sum tax.

Ultimately, to achieve an equitable system of lump sum taxes, it would be necessary to base the tax on some underlying "ability" characteristic which measured individuals' *potential* to earn income. In this way, high- and low-potential people could be taxed differently. Because the base is "potential," an individual's tax burden would not depend upon his behavior. Even if such an ability measure existed, however, it could not possibly be observed by the taxing authority. Thus, individual lump sum taxes are best viewed as standards of efficiency, but not as major policy options in a modern economy.

Are There Any Results from Welfare Economics that Would Help Us Understand Why Excess Burdens Arise?   Recall from Chapter 4 that a necessary condition for a Pareto efficient allocation of resources is that the marginal rate of substitution of barley for corn in consumption (MRS_{bc}) equal the marginal rate of transformation of barley for corn in production (MRT_{bc}). Under the barley tax, consumers face a price of barley of $(1 + t_b)P_b$. Therefore they set

$$(12.1) \qquad\qquad MRS_{bc} = \frac{(1 + t_b)P_b}{P_c}$$

Equation (12.1) is the algebraic characterization of the equilibrium point E_2 in Figure 12.3.

Producers make their decisions by setting the marginal rate of transformation equal to the ratio of the prices *they receive*. Even though Ruth pays $(1 + t_b)P_b$ per pound of barley, the barley producers receive only P_b—the difference goes to the tax collector. Hence, profit-maximizing producers set

$$(12.2) \qquad\qquad MRT_{bc} = \frac{P_b}{P_c}$$

Clearly, as long as t_b is not zero, MRS_{bc} exceeds MRT_{bc}, and the necessary condition for an efficient allocation of resources is violated.

Intuitively, when MRS_{bc} is greater than MRT_{bc}, the marginal utility of substituting barley consumption for corn consumption exceeds the change in production costs necessary to do so. Thus, utility would be raised if such an adjustment were made. However, in the presence of the barley tax there is no *financial* incentive to do so. The excess burden is just a measure of the utility loss. The loss arises because the barley tax creates a disparity between what the consumer pays and what the producer receives (i.e., a tax wedge). In contrast, under a lump sum tax, the price ratios faced by consumers and producers are equal. There is no wedge, so the necessary conditions for Pareto efficiency are satisfied.

Does an Income Tax Entail an Excess Burden?   In Figure 12.3, the imposition of a lump sum tax was shown as a downward parallel movement from AD to HI. This movement could just as well have arisen via a tax which took some proportion of Ruth's income. Like the lump sum tax, an income reduction moves in the intercepts of the budget constraint, but leaves its slope unchanged. Perhaps, then, lump sum taxation and income taxation are equivalent. In fact, if income were fixed, then an income tax *would* be a lump sum tax. However, once we explicitly consider choices with respect to income, it becomes clear that an income tax is *not* generally equivalent to a lump sum tax.

Think of Ruth as consuming *three* commodities, barley, corn, and leisure time, l. (We could draw indifference surfaces in three dimensions, but this is not essential for our argument.) Ruth gives up leisure (supplies labor) to earn income which is spent on barley and corn. In the production sector, Ruth's leisure is an input to the production of the two goods. The rate at which her leisure time can be transformed into barley is MRT_{lb}, and into corn MRT_{lc}. Just as a utility maximizing individual sets the marginal rate of substitution between two commodities equal to their price ratio, the MRS between leisure and a given commodity is set equal to the ratio of the wage (the price of leisure) and the price of that commodity.

Again appealing to the theory of welfare economics, the necessary conditions for a Pareto efficient allocation of resources in this three-commodity case are

$$MRS_{lb} = MRT_{lb}$$
$$MRS_{lc} = MRT_{lc}$$
$$MRS_{bc} = MRT_{bc}$$

A proportional income tax, which is equivalent to a tax at the same rate on barley and corn, leaves the third equality unchanged, because producers and consumers still face the same *relative* prices for barley and corn. However, it introduces a tax wedge in the first two conditions. To see why, suppose that Ruth's employer pays her a before-tax wage of w, and the income tax rate is t. Ruth's decisions depend upon her after-tax wage, $(1 - t)w$. Hence, she sets $MRS_{lb} = (1 - t)w/P_b$. On the other hand, the producer's decisions are based on the wage rate he or she pays, the before-tax wage, w. Hence, the producer sets $MRT_{lb} = w/P_b$. Consequently, $MRS_{lb} \neq MRT_{lb}$. Similarly, $MRS_{lc} \neq MRT_{lc}$. In contrast, a lump sum tax leaves all three equalities intact. Thus, income and lump sum taxation are generally not equivalent.

The fact that the income tax breaks up two equalities while taxes on barley and corn at different rates break up all three is in itself irrelevant for determining which system is more efficient. Once *any* of the equalities fails to hold, a loss of efficiency results, and the sizes of the welfare losses cannot be compared merely by counting wedges. Rather, the excess burdens associated with each tax regime must be computed and then compared. There is no presumption that income taxation is more efficient than a system of commodity taxes at different rates—*differential commodity taxation*. It *may* be true, but this is an empirical question that cannot be answered on the basis of theory alone.[6]

If the Demand for a Commodity Does Not Change When It Is Taxed, Does This Mean that There Is No Excess Burden?   The intuition behind excess burden is that it results from distorted decisions. If there is no change in the demand for the good being taxed, it might be concluded that there is no excess burden. This conjecture is examined in Figure 12.4. Naomi, the individual under consideration, begins with the same income as Ruth and faces the same prices and taxes. Hence, her initial budget constraint is AD, and after the barley tax, it is AF. However, as was not true in Ruth's case, the quantity of barley demanded by Naomi is unchanged by the barley tax—$B_1 = B_2$. The tax revenues are $E_1 E_2$. Is there an excess burden? If $E_1 E_2$ had been collected as a lump sum, so that Naomi faced budget line JK, her level of utility would be at E_3. This is a higher level of utility than at E_2. Hence, even though Naomi's barley consumption is unchanged by the barley tax, it still creates an excess burden.

The explanation of this paradox begins with the observation that even though Naomi's barley consumption doesn't change, her corn consumption does (from C_1 to C_2). When the barley tax changes the relative price, the marginal rate of substitution is affected, and the composition of the commodity *bundle* is distorted.

A more rigorous explanation requires that we distinguish between two types of responses to the barley tax. The movement from E_1 to E_2 is the **uncompensated response.** It shows how consumption changes because of the tax and incorporates effects due to both losing income and the tax-induced change in relative prices. In contrast, the movement from E_1 to E_3 shows the effect on consumption of a lump sum tax. This change is due solely to the loss of income (which by construction is the same as the loss from the barley tax) because relative prices are unaffected. In effect, then, the movement from E_3 to E_2 is strictly due to the change in relative prices. It is generated by giving Naomi enough in-

---

[6] It turns out that income taxation is necessarily more efficient than differential commodity taxation only when the underlying structure of consumer preferences has a very particular property. See Sandmo [1976].

**FIGURE 12.4   Excess Burden of a Tax on a Commodity Whose Ordinary Demand
Curve Is Perfectly Inelastic**

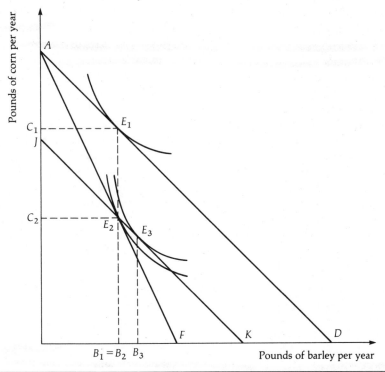

come to afford bundle E_2 even as barley's price rises due to the tax.
Because Naomi is being "compensated" for the rising price of barley
with additional income, the movement from E_3 to E_2 is called the **compensated response.**[7]

It is the compensated response which is important to the calculation
of excess burden. Why? By construction, the same tax revenue is collected via the barley tax (at E_2) and the lump sum tax (at E_3). As a result,
the loss in utility beyond the income lost in taxes—the excess burden—
is due *solely* to the movement from E_3 to E_2. This is precisely the compensated response. Note also that it is only in moving from E_3 to E_2 that the
marginal rate of substitution is affected. As shown above, it is this

_____

[7] The compensated response is often referred to as the *substitution effect* of a price
change, and the movement from E_1 to E_3 as the *income effect*. See the appendix to the book
for further discussion of substitution and income effects.

In some treatments of the problem, the substitution effect is measured by the *utility-
compensated* response in consumption—the response when prices change and income is
simultaneously adjusted to keep the individual at the same utility level. For small changes
in tax rates, the income and utility-compensated measures are equivalent. See Auerbach
and Rosen [1980].

change which violates the necessary conditions for a Pareto efficient allocation of commodities.

An ordinary demand curve depicts the uncompensated change in the quantity of a commodiity demanded when price changes. A **compensated demand curve** shows how the quantity demanded changes when price changes *and* simultaneously income is compensated. (Sometimes it is referred to as an *income-compensated demand curve*.) A way of summarizing this discussion is to say that excess burden depends upon movements along the compensated rather than the ordinary demand curve.

Although these observations may seem like theoretical nit-picking, they are actually quite important. In many policy discussions, attention is focused on whether or not a given tax influences observed behavior, with the assumption that if it does not, then there is necessarily no serious efficiency problem. For example, some would argue that if hours of work do not change when an income tax is imposed, then the tax has no adverse efficiency consequences. We have shown that such a notion is fallacious. A substantial excess burden may be incurred even if the uncompensated response of the taxed commodity is zero.

ANALYSIS OF EXCESS BURDEN USING DEMAND CURVES[8]

The concept of excess burden can be reinterpreted using (compensated) demand curves.[9] This interpretation relies heavily on the notion of consumers' surplus—the difference between what people would be *willing to pay* for a commodity and the amount they actually have to pay. As shown in Chapter 9, consumers' surplus is measured by the area between the demand curve and the horizontal line at the market price. Assume that the compensated demand curve for barley can be represented by the straight line D_b in Figure 12.5. For convenience, we continue to assume that the social marginal cost of barley is constant at P_b, so that the supply curve is the horizontal line marked S_b.[10] In equilibrium, b_1 pounds of barley are consumed. Consumers' surplus, the area between the price and the demand curve, is *aih*.

Again suppose that a tax at percentage rate, t_b, is levied on barley, so the new price, $(1 + t_b)P_b$, is associated with supply curve S'_b. Supply and demand now intersect at output b_2. Observe the following characteristics of the new equilibrium:

1. Consumers' surplus is reduced to the area between the demand curve and S'_b, *agf*.

---

[8] This section is based on Harberger [1974a].

[9] Compensated demand curves are discussed in the Appendix at the end of the book.

[10] The analysis is easily generalized to the case when the supply curve slopes upward. See footnote 11 on p. 286.

2. The revenue yield of the barley tax is rectangle *gfdh*. This is because tax revenues are equal to the product of the number of units purchased *(hd)* and the tax paid on each unit: $(1 + t_b)P_b - P_b = gh$. But *hd* and *gh* are just the base and height, respectively, of rectangle *gfdh*, and hence their product is its area.
3. The sum of post-tax consumers' surplus and tax revenues collected (area *hafd*) is less than the original consumers' surplus *(ahi)* by area *fid*. In effect, even if we returned the tax revenues to barley consumers as a lump sum, they would still be worse off by triangle *fid*. The triangle, then, is the excess burden of the tax.

This analysis provides a convenient framework for computing an actual dollar measure of excess burden. The area of triangle *fid* is one

FIGURE 12.5   Excess Burden of a Commodity Tax

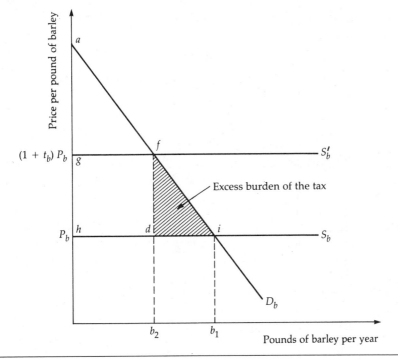

half the product of its base (the tax-induced change in the quantity of barley) and height (the tax per pound). Some simple algebra leads to the conclusion that this product can be written:

(12.3) $\frac{1}{2}\eta P_b b_1 t_b^2$

where η is the absolute value of the compensated price elasticity of demand for barley.[11] (A proof is provided in Appendix 12A.)

A high (absolute) value of η indicates that the compensated quantity demanded is quite sensitive to changes in price. Thus, the presence of η in Equation (12.3) makes intuitive sense—the more the tax distorts the (compensated) consumption decision, the higher the excess burden. $P_b \times b$ is the total revenue expended on barley initially. Its inclusion in the formula shows that the greater the initial expenditure on the taxed commodity, the greater the excess burden. Finally, the presence of t_b^2 suggests that as the tax rate increases, excess burden goes up with its square. Doubling a tax quadruples its excess burden, other things being the same.

Preexisting Distortions.   This analysis has assumed that there are no distortions in the economy other than the tax under consideration. In reality, when a new tax is introduced, there are already other distortions: monopolies, externalities, and preexisting taxes. In such a situation, the analysis of excess burden becomes more complicated.

Suppose that consumers regard gin and rum as substitutes. Suppose further that rum is currently being taxed, creating an excess burden "triangle" similar to that depicted in Figure 12.5. Now the government decides to impose a tax on gin. What is the excess burden of the gin tax? In the gin market, the gin tax creates a wedge between what gin consumers pay and gin producers receive. As usual, this creates an excess burden. But the story is not over. If gin and rum are substitutes, the rise in the consumers' price of gin induced by the gin tax increases the demand for rum. As a consequence, the quantity of rum demanded increases. Now, because rum was taxed under the status quo, "too little" of it was being consumed. The increase in rum consumption induced by the gin tax helps move rum consumption back toward its efficient level. There is thus an efficiency gain in the rum market that helps offset the excess burden imposed in the gin market. In theory, the gin tax could actually lower the *overall* excess burden. (A more rigorous graphical discussion of this phenomenon is contained in Appendix 12B.)

---

[11] The formula holds strictly only for an infinitesimally small tax levied in the absence of any other distortions. Therefore, it should be viewed only as an approximation. When the supply curve is upward sloping rather than horizontal, the excess-burden triangle contains some producers' surplus as well as consumers' surplus. The formula for excess burden then depends upon the elasticity of supply as well as the elasticity of demand. Bishop [1968] shows that in this case, the excess burden is

$$\frac{1}{2} \frac{P_b b}{\dfrac{1}{\eta} + \dfrac{1}{\varepsilon}} t_b^2$$

where ε is the elasticity of supply. Note that as ε approaches infinity, this expression collapses to Equation (12.3). This is because an ε of infinity corresponds to a horizontal supply curve as in Figure. 12.5.

We have shown, then, that the efficiency impact of a given tax or subsidy cannot be considered in isolation. To the extent that there are other markets with distortions, and the goods in these markets are related (either substitutes or complements), then the overall efficiency impact depends on what is going on in *all* the markets.[12] To compute the overall efficiency impact of a set of taxes and subsidies, it is generally incorrect to calculate separately the excess burdens in each market and then add them up. The aggregate efficiency loss is not equal to the "sum of its parts."

This result can be quite discomfitting because strictly speaking, it means that *every* market in the economy must be studied to assess the efficiency implications of *any* tax or subsidy. In most cases, practitioners simply assume that the amount of interrelatedness between the market of their concern and other markets is sufficiently small that cross-effects can safely be ignored.[13] Although this is clearly a convenient assumption, its reasonableness must be evaluated in each particular case.

The Excess Burden of a Subsidy: Too Much of a Good Thing?   Commodity subsidies are important components of the fiscal systems of many countries. In effect, a subsidy is just a negative tax, and like a tax, it is associated with an excess burden. To illustrate the calculation of the excess burden of a subsidy, we will consider the subsidy for owner-occupied housing which is provided by the federal government via certain provisions of the personal income tax. (See Chapter 14 for details of the law.)

Assume that the demand for owner-occupied housing services is the straight line D_h in Figure 12.6. Supply is horizontal at price P_h, which measures the marginal social cost of producing housing services. Initially, the equilibrium quantity is h_1. Now suppose that the government provides a subsidy of s percent to housing consumers. The new price for housing services is then $(1 - s)P_h$ and the associated supply curve is S_h'. The subsidy increases the quantity of housing services consumed to h_2. If the purpose of the subsidy was to increase housing consumption, then it has succeeded. But if its goal was to maximize social welfare, is it an appropriate policy?

Prior to the subsidy, consumers' surplus was area mno. After the subsidy, consumers' surplus is mqu. The benefit to housing consumers is the increase in their surplus, area $nouq$. But at what cost is this benefit obtained? The cost of the subsidy program is the quantity of housing

---

[12] This is an example of the "theory of the second best"; in the presence of existing distortions, policies that in isolation would increase efficiency can decrease it and vice versa.

[13] There are exceptions. Ballard, Shoven, and Whalley [1982] examined the overall excess burden of the U.S. tax system in 1973, taking into account interactions between various markets. Depending on the assumptions used in the calculations, they found excess burdens ranging from 12 percent to 22 percent of revenues [p. 26].

FIGURE 12.6   Excess Burden of a Housing Subsidy

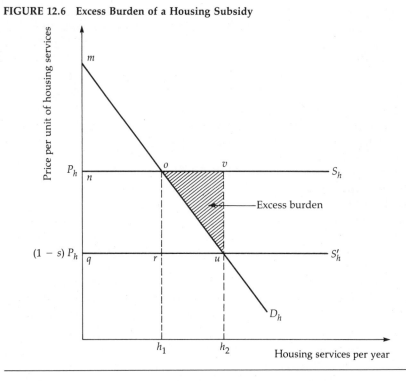

services consumed, *qu*, times the subsidy per unit, *nq*, or rectangle *nvuq*.[14] Thus, the cost of the subsidy actually exceeds the benefit—there is an excess burden equal to the difference between areas *nvuq* and *nouq*, which is the shaded area *ovu*.

How can a "good thing" like a subsidy be inefficient? Recall that any point on the demand curve for housing services measures how much people value that particular level of consumption. To the right of h_1, although individuals do derive utility from consuming more housing, its value is less than P_h, the marginal cost to society of providing it. In other words, the subsidy induces people to consume housing services that are valued at less than their cost—hence, the inefficiency.[15] Rosen [1979]

---

[14] It is assumed that the funds for the subsidy are raised with lump sum taxes. To the extent this is not the case, the cost will be even greater because raising the funds to provide the subsidy will create another excess burden. In addition, this analysis ignores any administrative costs of the program. For further details, see Laidler [1969].

[15] Another way to look at this is that after the subsidy, the marginal rate of substitution in consumption depends upon $(1 - s)P_h$, while the marginal rate of transformation in production depends upon P_h. Hence, the marginal rate of transformation is unequal to the marginal rate of substitution, and the allocation of resources cannot be efficient. Of course, if there were a positive externality associated with housing, then a subsidy might enhance efficiency. See Chapter 7.

estimated that in the United States for the year 1970, the excess burden of the subsidy on owner-occupied housing was about $107 per household annually.

A very important policy implication follows from this analysis. It is often proposed that some group be helped by subsidizing a commodity that its members tend to consume heavily. We have shown that this is an inefficient way to aid people. Less money could raise them to the same utility level if it were given to them as a direct grant. In terms of Figure 12.6, people would be indifferent between a housing subsidy program costing *nvuq* and a direct grant of *nouq,* even though the subsidy program costs the government more money.[16] This is one of the reasons many economists of all political persuasions prefer direct income transfers to commodity subsidies.[17]

Humorist Russell Baker never uses the term *excess burden* in the column reproduced below. Nevertheless, it is an excellent description of the phenomenon.

*American Way of Tax**

NEW YORK—The tax man was very cross about Figg. Figg's way of life did not conform to the way of life several governments wanted Figg to pursue. Nothing inflamed the tax man more than insolent and capricious disdain for governmental desires. He summoned Figg to the temple of taxation.

"What's the idea of living in a rental apartment over a delicatessen in the city, Figg?" he inquired. Figg explained that he liked urban life. In that case, said the tax man, he was raising Figg's city sales and income taxes. "If you want them cut, you'll have to move out to the suburbs," he said.

To satisfy his local government, Figg gave up the city and rented a sub-

urban house. The tax man summoned him back to the temple.

"Figg," he said, "you have made me sore wroth with your way of life. Therefore, I am going to soak you for more federal income taxes." And he squeezed Figg until beads of blood popped out along the seams of Figg's wallet.

"Mercy, good tax man," Figg gasped. "Tell me how to live so that I may please my government, and I shall obey."

The tax man told Figg to quit renting and buy a house. The government wanted everyone to accept large mortgage loans from bankers. If Figg complied, it would cut his taxes.

Figg bought a house, which he did

---

* By Russell Baker, *International Herald Tribune,* April 13, 1977, page 14. © 1977 by The New York Times Company. Reprinted by permission.

---

[16] This result is very similar to that obtained when we examined in-kind subsidy programs in Chapter 5.

[17] For a discussion of why commodity subsidies nevertheless remain politically popular, see Chapter 5.

not want, in a suburb where he did not want to live, and he invited his friends and relatives to attend a party celebrating his surrender to a way of life that pleased his government.

The tax man was so furious that he showed up at the party with blood-shot eyes. "I have had enough of this, Figg," he declared. "Your government doesn't want you entertaining friends and relatives. This will cost you plenty."

Figg immediately threw out all his friends and relatives, then asked the tax man what sort of people his government wished him to entertain. "Business associates," said the tax man. "Entertain plenty of business associates, and I shall cut your taxes."

To make the tax man and his government happy, Figg began entertaining people he didn't like in the house he didn't want in the suburb where he didn't want to live.

Then was the tax man enraged indeed. "Figg," he thundered, "I will not cut your taxes for entertaining straw bosses, truck drivers, and pothole fillers."

"Why not?" said Figg. "These are the people I associate with in my business."

"Which is what," asked the tax man.

"Earning my pay by the sweat of my brow," said Figg.

"Your government is not going to bribe you for performing salaried labor," said the tax man. "Don't you know, you imbecile, that tax rates on salaried income are higher than on any other kind?"

And he taxed the sweat of Figg's brow at a rate that drew exquisite shrieks of agony from Figg and little cries of joy from Washington, which already had more sweated brows than it needed to sustain the federally approved way of life.

"Get into business, or minerals, or international oil," warned the tax man, "or I shall make your taxes as the taxes of 10."

Figg went into business, which he hated, and entertained people he didn't like in the house he didn't want in the suburb where he did not want to live.

At length the tax man summoned Figg for an angry lecture. He demanded to know why Figg had not bought a new plastic factory to replace his old metal and wooden plant. "I hate plastic," said Figg. "Your government is sick and tired of metal, wood, and everything else that smacks of the real stuff, Figg," roared the tax man, seizing Figg's purse. "Your depreciation is all used up."

There was nothing for Figg to do but go to plastic, and the tax man rewarded him with a brand new depreciation schedule plus an investment credit deduction from the bottom line.

An Example: Calculating the Excess Burden of Income Taxation. The theory of excess burden that we have developed for taxing commodities applies just as well to factors of production. In Figure 12.7, Jacob's hours of work are plotted on the horizontal axis and his hourly wage on the vertical. Jacob's compensated labor supply curve, which shows the smallest wage that would be required to induce him to work each additional hour, is labeled S_L. Initially, Jacob's wage is w and the associated hours of work L_1. In the same way that consumers' surplus is measured as the area between the demand curve and the market price, workers' surplus is the area between the supply curve and the market wage rate. When the wage is w, Jacob's surplus is therefore area adf.

FIGURE 12.7   Excess Burden of a Tax on Labor

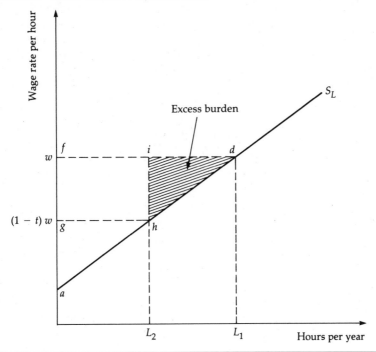

Now assume that an income tax at a rate t is imposed. The after-tax wage is then $(1 - t)w$, and given supply curve S_L, the quantity of labor supplied falls to L_2 hours. Jacob's surplus after the tax is agh, and the government collects revenues equal to *fihg*. The excess burden due to the tax-induced distortion of the work choice is the amount by which Jacob's loss of welfare *(fdhg)* exceeds the tax collected: area *hid* $(=fdhg -fihg)$. In analogy to Equation (12.3), area *hid* is approximately

(12.4) $\frac{1}{2}\varepsilon w L_1 t^2$

where ε is the compensated elasticity of hours of work with respect to the wage.

Recent calculations suggest that for an American married male, a reasonable value for ε is about 1.7.[18] For illustrative purposes, suppose that prior to taxation, Jacob works 2,000 hours per year at a wage of $6 per hour. A tax on earnings of 25 percent is then imposed. Substituting these figures into Equation (12.4), the excess burden of the tax is about $637 annually. One way to put this figure into perspective is to note that

---

[18] See Hausman [1981]. Note that this is the *compensated* response. Hausman's estimate of the uncompensated response is close to zero.

it is approximately one fifth the value of tax revenues. Thus, on average, each additional dollar of tax collected creates an excess burden of 20 cents. Of course, wage rates, tax rates, and elasticities vary across members of the population, so different people are subject to different excess burdens. Using data from 1975, Hausman [1981] calculated that the excess burden for the typical married man is about 22 percent of tax revenues collected. For married women, the comparable figure is 58.1 percent.[19]

DIFFERENTIAL TAXATION OF INPUTS[20]

In the income tax example just discussed, it was assumed that labor income was taxed at the same rate regardless of the market to which the labor was supplied. But sometimes the tax levied on a factor of production depends on where it is employed. For instance, because of the corporate income tax, some argue that capital employed in the corporate sector faces a higher rate than capital in the noncorporate sector. Another example is the differential taxation of labor in the household and market sectors. If an individual does housework, valuable services are produced, but they are not taxed.[21] On the other hand, if the same individual works in the market, the services are subject to the income and payroll taxes. The fact that labor is taxed in one sector and untaxed in another distorts people's decisions on how much time to spend on each. The efficiency cost can be measured using a model developed by Harberger [1974b]. In Figure 12.8A, hours of work in the household sector are measured on the horizontal axis, and dollars are measured on the vertical. Now define the **value of the marginal product** *(VMP)* of hours worked in the household sector as the dollar value of the *additional* output produced for each hour worked. The schedule VMP_x in Figure 12.8A represents the value of the marginal product of household work. It is drawn sloping downward, reflecting the reasonable assumption that as more hours are spent in the home, the incremental value of those hours decreases. This is just an example of the law of diminishing marginal returns.

Similarly, schedule VMP_z in Figure 12.8B shows the value of the marginal product of hours worked in the market sector. Although we also expect VMP_z to slope downward, there is no reason to expect that its shape will be identical to that of VMP_x.

---

[19] These calculations do not take into account the excess burden of the income tax on unearned income—interest, dividends, rent, etc.

[20] This section is relatively difficult, and can be skipped without loss of continuity.

[21] The value of housework was expressed nicely by a biblical author who wrote during an era in which it was assumed that homes were managed only by females. In Proverbs 31, he discusses in detail the many tasks performed by the women who "looketh well to the ways of her household" (*v.* 27). His general conclusion is that "her price is far above rubies." (*v.* 10). Unfortunately, price data on rubies during the biblical era are unavailable.

FIGURE 12.8   The Allocation of Time between Housework and Market Work

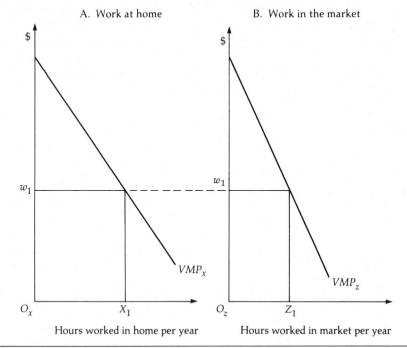

For simplicity assume that the total number of hours of work available is fixed, so that the only question is how to divide the work between the market and household sectors. Assume further that individuals allocate their time between housework and market work so as to maximize their total incomes. As a result of this allocation process, the value of the marginal product of labor will be the same in both sectors. If it were not, it would be possible for people to reallocate labor between the sectors so as to increase their incomes.[22] In Figure 12.8, the initial equilibrium occurs where X_1 hours are devoted to housework and Z_1 hours to market work. The value of the marginal product of labor in both sectors is w_1 dollars. Competitive pricing ensures that the wage in the market sector is equal to the value of the marginal product.

Now assume that a tax of t is levied on income from market work, but the return to housework is untaxed. Immediately after the tax is levied, the *net* return to market work declines to $(1 - t)w_1$. The original allocation is no longer desirable to individuals because the return to the last hour of work in the household (w_1) exceeds the comparable rate in the

---

[22] For further discussion of why this must be true, see the Appendix at the end of the book.

market, $(1 - t)w_1$. As a result, people begin working less in the market and more at home. As individuals devote less time to the market sector, VMP_z begins to rise; as they enter the household sector, VMP_x falls. Equilibrium is reached when the *after-tax* value of marginal product in the market sector equals the value of marginal product in the household sector. In Figure 12.9, this occurs when people work X_2 hours in the

FIGURE 12.9   Differential Factor Taxation

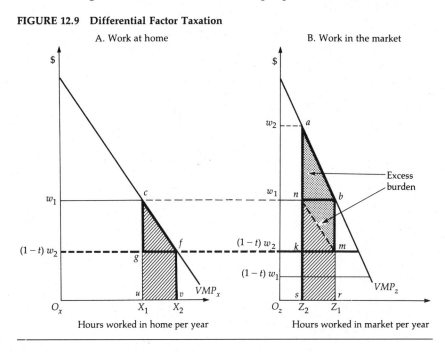

A. Work at home

B. Work in the market

Hours worked in home per year

Hours worked in market per year

home and Z_2 hours in the market. Because the *total* hours of work are fixed, the increase in hours in the household sector exactly equals the decrease in the market sector—distance X_1X_2 equals distance Z_2Z_1.

At the new equilibrium, the after-tax VMPs in the two sectors are both equal to $(1 - t)w_2$. However, the *before-tax* VMP in the market sector, w_2, is greater than the VMP in the household sector $(1 - t)w_2$. This means that if more labor were supplied to the market sector, the increase in income there (w_2) would exceed the loss of income in the household sector, $(1 - t)w_2$. But there is no incentive for this reallocation to occur, because individuals are sensitive to the returns they receive *after tax*, and these are already equal. The tax thus creates a situation in which there is "too much" housework being done, and "not enough" work in the market. In short, the tax leads to an inefficient allocation of resources in the sense that it distorts incentives to employ inputs in their most productive uses. The resulting decrease in real income is the excess burden of the tax.

To measure its size, we must analyze Figure 12.9 closely. Begin by observing that as a result of the exodus of labor from the market, output there goes down by an amount whose value is area *abrs*, the area under VMP_z between Z_1 and Z_2.[23] On the other hand, as labor enters the household sector, output increases by an amount whose value is *cfvu*, the area under the VMP_x curve between X_1 and X_2. Therefore the excess burden is area *abrs* minus area *cfvu*. Because $X_1 X_2 = Z_2 Z_1$ (remember, the total supply of hours is fixed), it follows that area *cfvu* equals area *nmrs*. Hence, the difference between *abrs* and *cfvu* is simply *abmn*. This area, which is the excess burden of the tax, has a convenient algebraic representation:

$$\tfrac{1}{2}(\Delta Z)tw_2$$

where ΔZ is the change in hours worked in the market sector.[24] The greater the change in the allocation of labor (ΔZ) and the greater the tax wedge (tw_2), the greater the excess burden.

In general, whenever a factor is fixed in total supply and is taxed differently in different uses, a misallocation of factors between sectors and hence an efficiency loss is generated. In the case of housework versus market work just discussed, Boskin [1975] estimated that the cost of the distortion was between $22 billion and $45 billion in 1972, about 6 to 13 percent of tax revenues.

DOES EFFICIENT TAXATION MATTER?

Every year both public- and private-sector organizations publish dozens of documents relating to the details of government spending and taxation. You would look in vain, however, for an "excess burden budget," detailing the distortionary impact of government fiscal policies. The reason for this is not hard to understand. Excess burden does not appear in anyone's bookkeeping system. It is conceptually a rather subtle notion and is not easy to make operational. Nevertheless, although the losses in real income associated with tax-induced changes in behavior are hidden, they are real, and according to some estimates, they are very large. We have emphasized repeatedly that efficiency considerations alone are never enough to determine policy. As Chief Justice Warren Burger remarked in a different context, "Convenience and efficiency are not the primary objectives—or the hallmarks—of democratic government." Still, it is unfortunate that policymakers often seem to ignore efficiency altogether.

---

[23] The vertical distance between VMP and the horizontal axis at any level of input gives the value of *marginal* product for that level of input. Adding up all these distances gives the value of the *total* product. Thus, the area under VMP gives the value of total product.

[24] Proof: Area *abmn* is the sum of two triangles *abn* and *nbm*. Triangle $abn = \tfrac{1}{2}(nb)(an) = \tfrac{1}{2}\Delta Z(an)$. Triangle $nbm = \tfrac{1}{2}(nb)(bm) = \tfrac{1}{2}(\Delta Z)(bm)$. Their sum is $\tfrac{1}{2}(\Delta Z)(an + bm) = \tfrac{1}{2}(\Delta Z)tw_2$.

The fact that a tax generates an excess burden is not necessarily "bad." One hopes, after all, that the tax will be used to obtain something beneficial for society either in terms of purchase of public goods or income redistribution. But to determine whether or not the supposed benefits are large enough to justify the costs, intelligent policy requires that excess burden be included in the calculation. Providing such information is an important role for the economist.

SUMMARY

Taxes generally impose an excess burden—a cost beyond the tax revenue collected.

Excess burden is caused by tax-induced distortions in behavior. It may be examined using either indifference curves or compensated demand curves.

Lump sum taxes do not cause distortions, but are unattractive as policy tools. Nevertheless, they are an important standard against which the excess burdens of other taxes can be compared.

Excess burden may result even if observed behavior is unaffected, because it is the compensated response to a tax that determines its excess burden.

When a single tax is imposed, the excess burden is proportional to the compensated elasticity of demand, and to the square of the tax rate.

Excess-burden calculations typically assume that there are no other distortions. If other distortions exist, it is possible that an additional tax will reduce the welfare cost. In effect, such a new tax restores incentives distorted by the original tax.

Subsidies also create excess burdens because they encourage people to consume goods valued less than the marginal social cost of production.

An important application of excess burden analysis is the impact on efficiency of differential taxation of inputs. In this instance, inputs are used "too little" in taxed activities and "too much" in untaxed activities.

DISCUSSION QUESTIONS

1. a. Using a simple example in which there are only two goods, sketch a set of indifference curves which exhibit the property that the income-compensated effect of taxing one of the goods is zero.
    b. Draw the compensated demand curve corresponding to your answer to part **(a)** and contrast it with a situation in which there is a large compensated response. Be sure to show the equilibrium before and after the tax, the tax revenues, and the excess burden. Can you relate your results to Equation (12.3)?

2. Which of the following is likely to impose a large excess burden?
    a. A tax on land.
    b. A subsidy for personal computers.
    c. A tax on interest from accounts at savings and loan associations only.
    d. A subsidy for food consumption.
    e. A tax on economic profits.

3. "In the formula for excess burden given in Equation (12.3), the tax is less than one. When it is squared, the result is smaller, not bigger. Thus, having t^2 instead of t in the formula makes the tax less important." Comment.

4. Convert the formula for excess burden to a formula for the burden as a percentage of tax revenues. Interpret your result.

5. Recall Harberger's general equilibrium model which was presented in Chapter 11. In that model, there are two commodities and two factors of production, and the total supply of each factor of production is fixed. What is the excess burden of a proportional income tax?

6. Suppose there are two commodities, R and S. When a tax on R alone is imposed, the excess burden is χ_R. When a tax on S alone is imposed, the excess burden is χ_S. When the two taxes are imposed simultaneously, the overall excess burden is *greater* than $\chi_R + \chi_S$. Explain how this might happen.

SELECTED REFERENCES

Boskin, Michael J. "Efficiency Aspects of the Differential Tax Treatment of Market and Household Economic Activities." *Journal of Public Economics* 4 (1975), pp. 1–25.

Harberger, Arnold C. "Taxation, Resource Allocation, and Welfare." In *Taxation and Welfare*, ed. Arnold C. Harberger. Boston: Little, Brown, 1974, pp. 25–62.

Sandmo, Agnar. "Optimal Taxation—An Introduction to the Literature." *Journal of Public Economics* 6 (1976), pp. 37–54.

APPENDIX 12A
FORMULA FOR EXCESS BURDEN

This appendix shows how the excess burden triangle *fdi* of Figure 12.5 may be written in terms of the compensated demand elasticity. The triangle's area, χ, is given by the formula:

(12A.1)
$$\chi = \tfrac{1}{2} \times \text{base} \times \text{height}$$
$$= \tfrac{1}{2} \times (di) \times (fd)$$

fd is just the change in the price (ΔP_b) due to the tax:

(12A.2) $fd = \Delta P_b = (1 + t_b) \times P_b - P_b = t_b \times P_b$

di is the change in the quantity (Δb) as a result of the price rise:

(12A.3) $di = \Delta b = \Delta b \left(\dfrac{\Delta P_b}{\Delta P_b}\right) = \dfrac{\Delta b}{\Delta P_b} (\Delta P_b)$

Now, note that the definition of the price elasticity, η, is:

$$\eta \equiv \frac{\Delta b}{\Delta P_b} \frac{P_b}{b}$$

so that

(12A.4) $\dfrac{\Delta b}{\Delta P_b} = \eta \left(\dfrac{b}{P_b}\right)$

Now, put (12A.4) into (12A.3) to get:

(12A.5) $di = \eta \times \left(\dfrac{b}{P_b}\right) \times (\Delta P_b)$

and use (12A.2) in (12A.5) so that:

(12A.6) $di = \eta \times \dfrac{b}{P_b} \times (t_b P_b) = \eta \times b \times t_b$

Finally, substitute both (12A.6) and (12A.2) into (12A.1) to get:

$$\begin{aligned} \chi &= \tfrac{1}{2}(di)(fd) \\ &= \tfrac{1}{2}(\eta\, b t_b) \times (t_b P_b) \\ &= \tfrac{1}{2} \times \eta \times P_b \times b \times (t_b)^2 \end{aligned}$$

as in the text.

APPENDIX 12B
TAX WEDGES IN SEVERAL MARKETS

This appendix discusses the measurement of excess burden when a tax is imposed in the presence of a preexisting distortion. The analysis is based upon Harberger [1974a].

In Figure 12B.1 we consider two goods, gin and rum, whose demand schedules are D_g and D_r, and whose before-tax prices are P_g and P_r, respectively. (The prices represent marginal social costs, and are assumed to be constant.) Rum is currently being taxed at a percentage rate t_r so its price is $(1 + t_r)P_r$. This creates an excess burden in the rum market, triangle *abc*. Now suppose that a tax on gin at rate t_g is introduced, creating a wedge between what gin consumers pay and gin producers receive. This creates an excess burden in the gin market of *efd*.

FIGURE 12B.1 Excess Burden of a Tax in the Presence of an Existing Tax

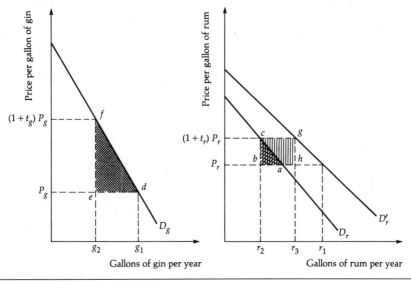

But this is not the end of the story. If gin and rum are substitutes, the increase in the consumers' price of gin induced by the gin tax shifts the demand curve for rum to the right, say to D_r'. As a consequence, the quantity of rum demanded increases from r_2 to r_3, distance cg. For each bottle of rum purchased between r_2 and r_3, the amount that people pay $[(1 + t_r)P_r]$ exceeds the social cost (P_r) by distance cb. Hence, there is a social gain of cb per bottle of rum times cg bottles, or area $cbhg$.

To summarize: given that the tax on rum was already in place, the tax on gin creates an excess burden of efd in the gin market *and* simultaneously decreases excess burden by $cbhg$ in the rum market. If $cbhg$ is sufficiently large, the tax can actually reduce overall excess burden.

This discussion is a special case of the result that the excess burden of a *set* of taxes generally depends upon the whole set of tax rates, as well as on the degree of substitutability and complementarity between the various commodities. Specifically, suppose that n commodities are subject to taxation. Let P_i be the before-tax price of the ith commodity; t_i the ad valorem tax on i^{th} commodity; and S_{ij} be the compensated response in the demand of the ith good with respect to a change in the price of the jth good. Then it can be shown [see Tresch, 1981, Chapter 15] that the overall excess burden is

$$\frac{1}{2} \sum_{i=1}^{n} \sum_{j=1}^{n} t_i P_i t_j P_j S_{ij}$$

For example, in the two-good case discussed above, where the goods are g and r, the overall excess burden is

$$\frac{1}{2}(t_r^2 P_r^2 S_{rr} + 2t_r P_r t_g P_g S_{rg} + t_g^2 P_g^2 S_{gg}).$$

CHAPTER 13

Efficient and Equitable Taxation

A nation may fall into decay through taxation in two ways. In the first case, when the amount of the taxes exceeds the powers of the nation and is not proportioned to the general wealth. In the second case, when an amount of taxation, proportioned on the whole to the powers of the nation, is viciously distributed.

Pietro Verri

The last two chapters have focused on the positive questions: "How do taxes affect the distribution of income and economic efficiency?" We turn now to the normative question: "How should a tax system be designed if it is to yield efficient and fair outcomes?" Our goal is to establish a set of criteria that can be used to evaluate real-world tax systems.

OPTIMAL COMMODITY TAXATION

Consider a simple society composed of a group of identical taxpayers. Assume that government spending decisions have been made. As a result, the government requires a certain amount of revenue. Suppose further that the revenue must be raised by taxes on various commodities—lump sum levies are ruled out. The theory of optimal commodity taxation outlines how these taxes should be imposed to minimize excess burden.

In addition to the above, assume that each individual consumes only two commodities, X and Y, as well as leisure, l. The price of X is P_x, the price of Y is P_y, and the wage rate (which is the "price" of leisure) is w.

The maximum number of hours per year that the individual can work—his **time endowment**—is fixed at $\bar{T}$. (Think of $\bar{T}$ as the amount of time left over after sleep.) It follows that hours of work are $(\bar{T} - l)$—whatever time is not spent on leisure is devoted to work. Income is the product of the wage rate and hours of work—$w(\bar{T} - l)$. Assuming that all income is spent on commodities X and Y (there is no saving), then the budget constraint is

(13.1)
$$w(\bar{T} - l) = P_xX + P_yY$$

The left-hand side gives total earnings, and the right-hand side shows how the earnings are spent.

Equation (13.1) can be rewritten as

(13.2)
$$w\bar{T} = P_xX + P_yY + wl$$

The left-hand side of (13.2) is the value of the time endowment. It shows the income that could be earned if the individual worked every waking hour.

Now, suppose that it is possible to tax X, Y, *and* l at the same ad valorem rate, t. The tax raises the effective price of X to $(1 + t)P_x$, of Y to $(1 + t)P_y$, and of l to $(1 + t)w$. Thus, the individual's after-tax budget constraint is

(13.3)
$$w\bar{T} = (1 + t)P_xX + (1 + t)P_yY + (1 + t)wl$$

Dividing through Equation (13.3) by $(1 + t)$, we have

(13.4)
$$\frac{1}{1 + t} w\bar{T} = P_xX + P_yY + wl$$

Comparison of (13.3) and (13.4) points out the following fact: a tax on all commodities *including leisure*, at the same percentage rate, t, is equivalent to reducing the value of the time endowment from $w\bar{T}$ to $[1/(1 + t)] \times w\bar{T}$. For example, a 25 percent tax on X, Y, and l is equivalent to a reduction of the value of the time endowment by 20 percent. However, because w and $\bar{T}$ are fixed, their product, $w\bar{T}$, is also fixed; for any value of the wage rate, the individual cannot change the value of his time endowment. Therefore, a tax that reduces the value of the time endowment is in effect a lump sum tax. From Chapter 12 we know that lump sum taxes have no excess burden. We conclude that a tax at the same rate on all commodities, *including leisure*, is equivalent to a lump sum tax and has no excess burden.

In practice, putting a tax on leisure time is impossible (see Chapter 12.) The only *available* tax instruments are taxes on commodities X and Y. Therefore, *some* excess burden generally is inevitable. The goal of optimal commodity taxation is to select tax rates on X and Y in such a way that the excess burden of raising the required tax revenue is as low as possible. It is popular to suggest that the solution to this problem is to tax X and Y at the same rate—so-called **neutral taxation.**[1] We shall see that in general, neutral taxation is *not* efficient.

The Ramsey Rule

To develop some intuition for the theory of optimal taxation, suppose that X and Y are unrelated commodities—they are neither substitutes nor complements for each other. Hence, a change in the price of either commodity affects only its own demand, and not the demand for the other. Figure 13.1A shows the compensated demand for X, D_x, and

FIGURE 13.1

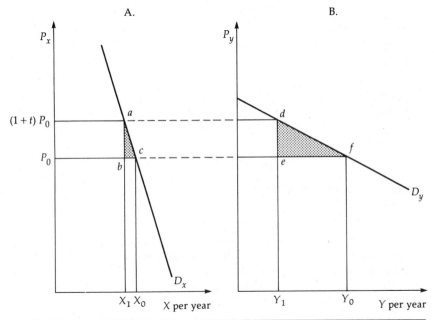

Figure 13.1B shows the compensated demand for Y, D_y. For convenience, it is assumed that the initial starting price for each commodity is the same, P_0. The consumer can buy all of each commodity he wants at price P_0, so the supply curves are horizontal. Also, units are defined in such a way that the initial quantities, X_0 and Y_0, are equal.

Suppose that an ad valorem tax of t is levied on both goods, so the price goes up to $(1 + t)P_0$. As a consequence, the quantity demanded for X falls to X_1, and the quantity demanded for Y falls to Y_1. The methods

---

[1] Note that in this model, a tax on X and Y at the same rate is equivalent to an income tax.

developed in Chapter 12 indicate that the excess burden of the tax on X is *abc*, and the excess burden of the tax on Y is *def*.

As shown, a tax of t percent on Y creates a much larger excess burden than a t percent tax on X. This is no surprise—D_y is more elastic than D_x, and the more elastic the demand for a good, the larger the excess burden of a tax, *ceteris paribus*. [Recall Equation (12.3).]

It would seem, then, that if we want to minimize the overall excess burden of collecting the tax revenues, it would make sense to put more of the tax on good X than on good Y. This intuition is formalized in the so-called **inverse elasticity rule:** if t_x is the percentage tax rate on good X, and t_y is the tax rate on good Y, then to minimize excess burden, we require:

(13.5) $$\frac{t_x}{t_y} = \frac{\eta_y}{\eta_x}$$

where η_y and η_x are the compensated elasticities of Y and X, respectively. As long as goods are unrelated in consumption, tax rates should be inversely proportional to elasticities.[2]

The intuition behind the inverse elasticity rule is straightforward. An efficient set of taxes should distort decisions as little as possible. The potential for distortion is greater the more elastic the demand for a commodity. Therefore, efficient taxation requires that relatively high rates of taxation be levied on relatively inelastic goods. Indeed, if the compensated demand for a commodity were perfectly inelastic, efficient taxation would require that all revenues be raised by taxes on that good, since no distortion would arise at all.[3]

If we cross multiply in Equation (13.5), we find $t_x\eta_x = t_y\eta_y$. Now, $t_x\eta_x$ is the percentage change in the price times the percentage change in the compensated quantity demanded when the price increases by 1 percent. Hence, $t_x\eta_x$ is the percentage reduction in the compensated demand for X. Similarly, $t_y\eta_y$ is the proportional reduction in Y. Thus, Equation (13.5) implies that total excess burden is minimized when the taxes are

---

[2] A more careful demonstration requires a little calculus. Recall from Equation (12.3) that the excess burden on commodity X is $\frac{1}{2}\eta_x P_x X t_x^2$. Similarly, the excess burden on Y is $\frac{1}{2}\eta_y P_y Y t_y^2$. Then the total excess burden is $\frac{1}{2}\eta_x P_x X t_x^2 + \frac{1}{2}\eta_y P_y Y t_y^2$. (We can just add up the two expressions because by assumption, X and Y are unrelated.) Now, suppose the required tax revenue is R. Then t_x and t_y must satisfy the relation $P_x X t_x + P_y Y t_y = R$. Our problem is to choose t_x and t_y to minimize $\frac{1}{2}\eta_x P_x X t_x^2 + \frac{1}{2}\eta_y P_y Y t_y^2$ subject to $R - P_x X t_x - P_y Y t_y = 0$. Set up the Lagrangian expression

$$\mathcal{L} = \tfrac{1}{2}\eta_x P_x X t_x^2 + \tfrac{1}{2}\eta_y P_y Y t_y^2 + \lambda[R - P_x X t_x - P_y Y t_y]$$

where λ is the Lagrange multiplier. (The method of Lagrangian multipliers is reviewed in Henderson and Quandt [1980, pp. 381–83].) Taking $\partial\mathcal{L}/\partial t_x$ yields $\eta_x t_x = \lambda$ and $\partial\mathcal{L}/\partial t_y$ yields $\eta_y t_y = \lambda$. Hence, $\eta_x t_x = \eta_y t_y$, and Equation (13.5) follows immediately. For a more rigorous proof which also allows goods to be substitutes and/or complements, see Sandmo [1976].

[3] In terms of indifference curve analysis, a perfectly inelastic compensated demand curve means that the "substitution effect" is zero. See the Appendix to the book.

imposed such that the proportional reduction in X is equal to the proportional reduction in Y. This result, called the **Ramsey Rule** (after its discoverer, Frank Ramsey [1927]) also holds even for cases when X, Y, and l are related goods—substitutes or complements.

But why should efficient taxation induce equiproportional changes in quantities demanded rather than equiproportional changes in price? Because excess burden is a consequence of distortions in *quantities*. To minimize total excess burden requires that all these changes be in the same proportion.

Corlett and Hague [1953] showed that efficient taxation requires taxing the good that is complementary to leisure at a relatively high rate. To understand why, recall that *if* it were possible to tax leisure, then a "first-best" result would be obtainable—revenues could be raised with no excess burden. Although the tax authorities cannot tax leisure, they *can* tax goods that tend to be consumed jointly *with* leisure, indirectly lowering the demand for leisure. If yachts are taxed at a very high rate, people will consume fewer yachts and spend less time at leisure. In effect, then, taxing complements to leisure at high rates provides an indirect way to "get at" leisure, and hence, move closer to the perfectly efficient outcome that would be possible if leisure were taxable.[4]

Equity Considerations

At this point the reader may suspect that efficient tax theory has unpleasant policy implications. For example, the inverse elasticity rule says that inelastically demanded goods should be taxed at relatively high rates. Is this fair? Do we really want a tax system that collects the bulk of its revenue from taxes on insulin?

Of course not. Unlike the model discussed so far, in the real world, people are not all the same. Efficiency thus becomes only one criterion for evaluating a tax system; fairness is just as important. In particular, it is widely agreed that a tax system should have **vertical equity**: it should distribute burdens fairly across people with different ability to pay. The Ramsey Rule has been modified to consider the distributional consequences of taxation. Suppose that:

1. The poor spend a greater proportion of their income on commodity X than do the rich, and vice versa for commodity Y. X might be bread, and Y caviar.
2. The social welfare function puts a higher weight on the utilities of the poor than on those of the rich (see Chapter 5).

Then even if X is more inelastically demanded than Y, optimal taxation may require a higher rate of tax on Y than X [Diamond, 1975]. True,

---

[4] As Auerbach [1982] notes, what is "special" about leisure in this model is that it is the only good with an endowment $(\bar{T})$ that cannot be taxed independently of its consumption.

a high tax rate on Y will create a relatively large excess burden, but it will also tend to redistribute income toward the poor. Society may be willing to pay the price of a higher excess burden in return for a more equal distribution of income. In general, the extent to which it makes sense to depart from the Ramsey Rule depends upon:

1. The strength of society's egalitarian preferences. If society cares only about efficiency—a dollar to one person is the same as a dollar to another, rich or poor—then it may as well strictly follow the Ramsey Rule.
2. The extent to which the consumption patterns of the rich and poor differ. If the rich and the poor consume both goods in the same proportion, then taxing the goods at different rates can have no effect on the distribution of income. Even if society *has* a distributional goal, it cannot be achieved by differential taxation of X and Y.

Overview

If lump sum taxation were available, then taxes could be raised without any excess burden at all. Optimal taxation would need to focus only upon distributional issues. Lump sum taxes are not available, however, so the problem becomes how to collect a given amount of tax revenue with as small an excess burden as possible. In general, minimizing excess burden requires that taxes be set so that the (compensated) demands for all commodities are reduced in the same proportion. In the case of unrelated goods, this implies that tax rates should be set in inverse proportion to the demand elasticities. However, if society has distributional goals, departures from efficient taxation rules may be appropriate.

An Application of Optimal Commodity Taxation: Taxing the Family Unit[5]

Under current federal income tax law, the fundamental unit of income taxation is the family. The family's tax base is the sum of the husband's and wife's incomes. Regardless of whether the wife or the husband earns an extra dollar, it is taxed at the same rate.[6] Is this efficient? In other words, is the family's excess burden minimized by taxing each spouse's income at the same rate?

Imagine the family as a unit whose utility depends upon the quantities of three "commodities": total family consumption, husband's hours of work, and wife's hours of work. Family utility increases with family

---

[5] This section is based upon Boskin and Sheshinski [1979].

[6] Under recent changes in the tax law, this statement does not hold exactly for some families. See Chapter 14.

consumption, but decreases with each spouse's hours of work. Each spouse's hours of work depend upon his or her wage rate, among other variables. A tax on earnings distorts the work decision, creating an excess burden. (See Chapter 12.) How should tax rates be set so that the *family's* excess burden is as small as possible?

Assume for simplicity that the husband's and wife's hours of work are approximately "unrelated goods"—an increase in the husband's wage rate has very little impact on the wife's work decision and vice versa. This assumption is consistent with much empirical research.[7] Then application of the inverse elasticity rule suggests that a higher tax should be levied upon the "commodity" which is relatively inelastically supplied. To enhance efficiency, whoever's labor supply is relatively inelastic should bear a relatively high tax rate. Numerous econometric studies suggest that the husband's supply of labor is considerably less elastic than that of the wife.[8] Efficiency could therefore be gained if the current tax law were modified so as to give husbands higher marginal tax rates than wives.

Again, it must be emphasized that efficiency is only one consideration in tax design. However, it is interesting that this result is consistent with the claims of some who have argued that on equity grounds the relative tax rate on the earnings of working wives should be lowered.[9]

OPTIMAL USER FEES

So far we have assumed that all production takes place in the private sector. The government's only problem is to set the tax rates which determine consumer prices. Sometimes, the government itself is the producer of a good or service. If so, the government must then directly choose a **user fee**—a price paid by users of a good or service provided by the government. As usual, we would like to determine the "best" possible user fee. Analytically, the optimal tax and user fee problems are closely related. In both cases, the government sets the final price paid by consumers. In the optimal tax problem, this is done indirectly by choice of the tax rate, while in the optimal user fee problem, it is done directly.

When does the government choose to produce a good instead of purchasing it from the private sector? Government production is likely when the production of some good or service is subject to continually decreasing average costs—the greater the level of output, the lower the cost per unit. Under such circumstances, it is unlikely that the market for the service will be competitive. A single firm can take advantage of

---

[7] See Hausman [1983] for a review of econometric studies on taxes and labor supply.

[8] See Hausman [1983].

[9] See, for example, Munnell [1980] and Chapter 14.

economies of scale and supply the entire industry output, at least for a sizable region. This phenomenon is often called **natural monopoly.**[10] Examples are highways, bridges, electricity, and television. In some cases, these commodities are produced by the private sector and regulated by the government (electricity), and in others they are produced by the public sector (highways). Here we will study public production, but many of the important insights apply to regulation of private monopolies.

FIGURE 13.2   A "Natural Monopoly"

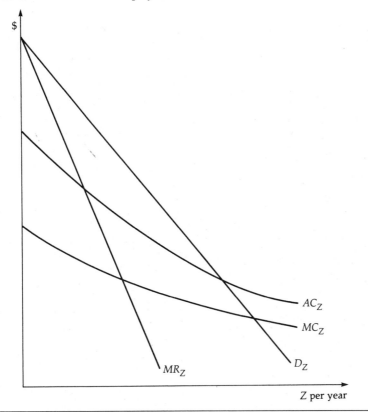

Figure 13.2 measures the output of the natural monopoly, Z, on the horizontal axis, and dollars on the vertical. The average cost schedule is denoted AC_z. By assumption, it decreases continuously over all relevant ranges of output. Because average cost is decreasing, marginal cost must

---

[10] It is also possible that the industry will end up as an oligopoly (few sellers). We focus on the analytically more simple case of monopoly.

be less than average. Therefore, the marginal cost *(MC$_z$)* curve, which shows the incremental cost of providing each unit of Z, lies below *AC$_z$*. The demand curve for Z is represented by *D$_z$*. The associated marginal revenue curve is *MR$_z$*. It shows the incremental revenue associated with each level of output of Z.

To illustrate why decreasing average costs often lead to public sector production or regulated private sector production, consider what would happen if Z were produced by an unregulated monopolist. If the monopolist seeks to maximize profits, it will produce up to the point that marginal revenue equals marginal cost. In Figure 13.3, this occurs at

FIGURE 13.3   Alternative Pricing Schemes for a Natural Monopoly

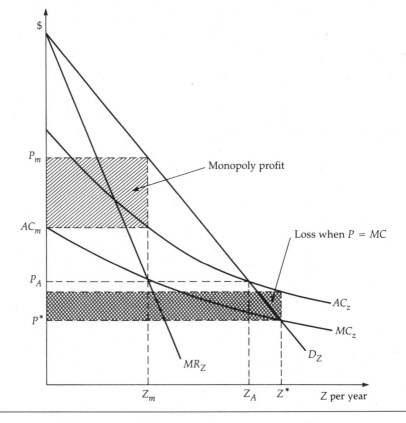

output level *Z$_m$*. The associated price, *P$_m$*, is found by going up to the demand curve, *D$_z$*. Monopoly profits are equal to the product of number of units sold times the profit per unit, and are represented geometrically by the diagonally striped rectangle.

Is output Z_m efficient? According to the theory of welfare economics, efficiency requires that price equal marginal cost—the value that people place on the good must equal the incremental cost to society of producing it. At Z_m, price is *greater* than marginal cost. Hence, Z_m is inefficient. This inefficiency, plus the fact that society may not approve of the existence of the monopoly profits, provide a possible justification for government taking over the production of Z.[11]

The obvious policy prescription seems to be for the government to produce up to the point where price equals marginal cost. In Figure 13.3, the output at which $P = MC$ is denoted Z^*, and the associated price is P^*. There is a problem, however: at output Z^*, the price is less than the average cost. Price P^* is so low that the operation cannot cover its costs, and it continually suffers losses. The total loss is equal to the product of the number of units sold, Z^*, times the loss per unit, measured as the vertical distance between the demand curve and AC_z at Z^*. Geometrically, the loss is the crosshatched rectangle in Figure 13.3.

How should the government confront this dilemma? Several solutions have been proposed.

Average Cost Pricing.   To set price equal to average cost, find the intersection of the demand and average cost schedules. At this point, output is Z_A in Figure 13.3 and price is P_A. By definition, when price equals average cost, there are neither profits nor losses—the enterprise just "breaks even." The operation no longer has to worry about a deficit. However, note that Z_A is less than Z^*. Although average cost pricing leads to more output than at the profit-maximizing level, it still falls short of the efficient amount.

Marginal Cost Pricing with Lump Sum Taxes.   Charge $P = MC$, and make up the deficit by levying lump sum taxes. Charging $P = MC$ ensures efficiency in the market for Z; financing the deficit with lump sum taxes on the rest of society guarantees that no new inefficiencies are generated by meeting the deficit. However, there are two problems with this solution.

First, as noted above, lump sum taxes are generally unavailable. It is more likely that the deficit will have to be financed by distorting taxes, such as income or commodity taxes. If so, it is possible that the distortion in the market where the tax is levied will more than outweigh the efficiency gain in the market for Z.

Second, there is a widespread belief that fairness requires consumers of a publicly provided service to pay for it—the so-called **benefits-**

---

[11] The usual caveat applies: just because government intervention can improve the status quo does not mean that it will.

received principle. If this principle is taken seriously, it is unfair to make up the deficit by general taxation. Why should people who don't use a bridge have to pay for it?

Two-Part Tariff.   A **two-part tariff** involves a lump sum charge to gain permission to use the service, plus a price equal to marginal cost for each unit of the service consumed. To see how this works, suppose there are 1,000 users of service Z. Under the simplest version of the scheme, each user would be charged 1/1,000 of the deficit just for the privilege of having the option to purchase Z. Once this lump sum "entrance fee" was paid, Z could be freely purchased at a price equal to its marginal cost. Hence, the deficit is made up by a nondistorting tax on the users of the service, who are then given incentives to consume it in efficient quantities. Two-part tariffs may seem like a peculiar idea, but they are really fairly common. Just think of the telephone company, which charges each user a monthly fee plus an additional fee for each minute of calling time.[12]

The two-part tariff is not a perfect solution, however, because having to pay the entrance fee may deter some users so that consumption falls below the efficient level. Whether this is an empirically important problem depends upon the commodity in question. In a country like the United States, it is not likely to be important for natural monopolies like water and electricity.

Another problem is that the entrance fee is essentially an equal lump sum tax on all users, rich and poor alike. If society cares about income distribution, this will be undesirable. Feldstein [1972] shows how the two-part tariff can be modified when society has distributional objectives. Suppose that Z is consumed in disproportionately high amounts by the rich and that society places a relatively high weight on the welfare of the poor. Then it is optimal to set the price per each unit of Z *above* marginal cost. When the price is greater than marginal cost, the deficit is less than the crosshatched area in Figure 13.3. Because the rich consume Z in proportionately large amounts, it is they who account for the bulk of the reduction of the deficit. Thus, by charging a price above marginal cost, some efficiency is lost, but some equity is gained. There is an obvious similarity to the optimal tax problem discussed above. In both cases, departures from full efficiency may be appropriate in the presence of distributional objectives.

Of the various possibilities for dealing with decreasing costs, which has the United States chosen? In most cases, average cost pricing has been selected whether for a publicly owned or a regulated private enterprise. Tresch [1981, pp. 203–06] argues that although average cost pric-

---

[12] This is not to imply that the structure of the telephone company's two-part tariff is necessarily optimal.

ing is inefficient, it is probably a reasonable compromise. It has the virtue of being fairly simple and adheres to the popular benefits-received principle.[13] Some economists, however, argue that more reliance on two-part tariffs would be desirable.

OPTIMAL INCOME TAXATION

Thus far, we have assumed that a government can levy taxes on all commodities and factors of production. We now turn to the question of how to design systems in which tax liabilities are based on people's incomes. Income taxation is an obvious candidate for special attention because of its importance in the revenue structures of most developed countries. In addition, some argue that income is an especially appropriate tax base because it is the best measure of an individual's ability to pay. For the moment, we merely assume that society has somehow decided that income taxation is desirable, and ask what is the optimal way to structure an income tax. In subsequent chapters, we will discuss whether income really is a particularly desirable tax base.

Edgeworth's Model

At the end of the 19th century, Edgeworth [1959/1897] examined the question of optimal income taxation using a simple model based upon the following assumptions.

1. Subject to the revenues required, the goal is to make the sum of individual's utilities as high as possible. Algebraically, if U_i is the utility of the ith individual and W is social welfare, then the tax system should maximize

(13.6) $$W = U_1 + U_2 + \cdots + U_n$$

where n is the number of people in the society.

2. Individuals have identical utility functions which depend only upon their levels of income. These utility functions exhibit diminishing marginal utility of income; as an individual's income increases, he becomes better off, but at a decreasing rate.

3. The total amount of income available is fixed.

The reader will recognize that these are virtually identical to the assumptions behind the optimal income distribution model presented in Chapter 5. It was shown there that with these assumptions, maximization of social welfare requires that each person's marginal utility of income be the same. But if utility functions are identical, equal marginal utilities of income occur only at equal levels of income. The implications

---

[13] There are problems in administering average cost pricing in regulated industries. See Tresch [1981, Chapter 10].

for tax policy are clear: Taxes should be set in such a way that the after-tax distribution of income is as equal as possible. In particular, income should be taken first from the rich because the marginal utility lost is smaller than that of the poor. If the government requires more revenue even after complete equality has been reached, then the additional tax burden should be evenly distributed.

Edgeworth's model, then, implies a radically progressive tax structure—incomes are leveled off from the top until complete equality is reached. However, as stressed in Chapter 5, each of the assumptions underlying this analysis is subject to question. Beginning in the 1970s, a number of studies were done to ascertain how Edgeworth's results change when certain of the assumptions are relaxed.

Modern Studies

One of the most vexing problems with Edgeworth's analysis is the assumption that the total amount of income available to society is fixed. Confiscatory tax rates are assumed to have no effect upon the amount of output produced. More realistically, suppose that individuals' utilities depend not only upon income, but upon leisure, as well. Then income taxes will distort work decisions and create excess burdens. A society with a utilitarian social welfare function thus faces an inescapable dilemma. On the one hand, it desires to allocate the tax burden so as to equalize the after-tax distribution of income. However, in the process of doing so, it reduces the total amount of real income available. Design of an optimal income tax system must take into account the costs (in terms of excess burden) of achieving more equality. In Edgeworth's model, the cost of obtaining more equality is zero, which explains the prescription for a perfectly egalitarian outcome.

How much is Edgeworth's result changed when work incentives are taken into account? Stern [1976] studied a model similar to Edgeworth's, except that individuals make choices between income and leisure. To simplify the analysis, Stern assumed that the amount of tax revenues collected from a person is given by

(13.7)   Revenues $= -\alpha + t \times$ Income

where α and t are positive numbers. For example, suppose that $\alpha = \$3,000$ and $t = .25$. Then a person with income of $20,000 would have a tax liability of $2,000 ($= -\$3,000 + .25 \times \$20,000$). A person with an income of $5,000 would have a tax liability of *minus* $1,500 ($= -\$3,000 + .25 \times \$6,000$). Such a person would receive a $1,500 grant from the government.

The significance of Equation (13.7) is best understood by graphing it. In Figure 13.4, income is measured on the horizontal axis and tax revenues on the vertical. When income is zero, the individual's "tax burden"

FIGURE 13.4   A Linear Income Tax

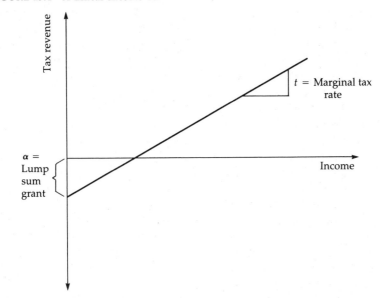

is negative—he receives a lump sum grant from the government of α dollars. Then, for each dollar of income, the individual must pay t dollars to the government. Thus, t is the **marginal tax rate**, the proportion of an additional dollar that must be paid in tax. Because the geometric interpretation of (13.7) is a straight line, it is referred to as a **linear income tax schedule.** In popular discussions, a linear income tax schedule is often referred to as a **flat tax.** It is important to note that even though the marginal tax rate for a linear tax schedule is constant, the schedule is progressive in the sense that the higher an individual's income, the higher the proportion of income paid in taxes.[14] Just how progressive depends on the precise values of α and t. Greater values of t will be associated with more progressive tax systems. However, at the same time that high values of t lead to more progressiveness, they create larger excess burdens. The optimal income tax problem is to find the "best" combination of α and t—the values that maximize social welfare [Equation (13.6)] subject to the constraint that a given amount of revenue be collected.

Stern [1976] finds that allowing for a modest amount of substitution between leisure and income,[15] and with required government revenues

---

[14] See the discussion of the definition of "progressive" in Chapter 11.

[15] Specifically, the result reported here assumes that the elasticity of substitution between leisure and income is 0.6.

equal to about 20 percent of income, a value of t of about 19 percent maximizes social welfare. This is considerably less than the value of 100 percent implied by Edgeworth's analysis. It is, incidentally, also much smaller than the actual marginal tax rates found in many Western countries. Even quite modest incentive effects appear to have important implications for optimal marginal tax rates.

More generally, Stern showed that the more elastic the supply of labor, the lower the optimal value of t, other things being the same. Intuitively, the "cost" of redistribution is the excess burden it creates. The more elastic the supply of labor, the greater the excess burden from taxing it. [See Equation (12.4).] More elastic labor supply therefore means a higher cost to redistribution, so that less should be done.

Stern also investigated how alternative social welfare functions affect the results, focusing on the impact of giving different social weights to the utilities of the rich and the poor. In terms of Equation (13.6), more egalitarian preferences are represented by assigning the utilities of poor people higher weights than utilities of the rich.[16] An interesting extreme case is the maximin criterion, according to which the only individual who receives any weight in the social welfare function is the person with the minimum utility (see Chapter 5). Stern found that the maximin criterion calls for a marginal tax rate of about 80 percent. Not surprisingly, if society has extremely egalitarian objectives, high tax rates are called for. Even here, though, the rates fall short of 100 percent.

We noted earlier that Stern restricted himself to studying linear income tax schedules. There have also been analyses of tax schedules which allow nonconstant marginal tax rates; t can either increase or decrease with income. One of the most surprising results is that maximization of social welfare requires the marginal tax rate to be *zero* at the very top of the income scale.

To see why, suppose that the richest person is Mr. Hughes, who currently has an income of exactly $1 billion, and who faces a positive marginal tax rate on his billion and first dollar. Now suppose the marginal tax rate on the billion and first dollar is reduced to zero. Knowing that if he earns another dollar he will get to keep it all, Hughes may decide to do so. If he does, it makes him better off. The government is no worse off, because it still collects the same amount of revenue as before. Similarly, no other taxpayer is made worse off. In short, Hughes is better off, and no one else's welfare has decreased. Social welfare, which is the sum of utilities, has therefore increased. Of course, Hughes may choose not to earn the extra dollar. In that case, no harm is done—the status quo is simply maintained.

Note that this result pertains to the *marginal* tax rate facing the richest individual. It says nothing about the *average* tax rate. It is possible to

---

[16] See Chapter 5.

collect very high taxes from an individual on income earned before the last dollar, and thus have a high average rate even though the marginal rate is very low.

The contrast between this result and real-world income tax systems is striking. Far from having zero marginal tax rates at the highest incomes, actual tax systems tend to tax these incomes at the highest marginal rates. Under the U.S. personal income tax, the highest marginal income tax rate is currently 50 percent; at times it has been 90 percent.

The theory and computation of optimal tax rates has continued to be the subject of great interest for economists. The basic models have been expanded to see how optimal tax rates are affected by new complications.[17] This literature cannot be expected to produce a blueprint of "the" optimal tax system. As has been shown, the answer depends to a large extent upon value judgments, and the tools of economics do not provide definitive answers to ethical questions. The contribution of the literature on optimal taxation is to systematically draw out the implications of alternative ethical and behavioral assumptions, thus allowing a coherent discussion of tax policy.

POLITICS AND OPTIMAL TAXATION

Optimal taxation is a purely normative theory. It does not purport to predict what real-world tax systems look like, or to explain how these tax systems emerge. The theory pays little attention to the institutional and political setting in which tax policy is made. Brennan and Buchanan [1977] argued that actual tax systems may look more reasonable when political realities are taken into account than they do from an optimal tax point of view.

Assume that in a certain society, there are three commodities, X, Y, and leisure. Labor is totally fixed in supply, and therefore, income is fixed. Currently, this society levies a tax on X, but its constitution forbids taxing Y. Viewing this situation, a student of optimal tax theory might say something like: "You are running an inefficient tax system. Because labor is fixed in supply, you could have no excess burden if you taxed X and Y at equal rates—an income tax. I recommend that you lower the tax on X and impose a tax at the same rate on Y. Set the rates so that the same amount of revenue is collected as before."

Suppose, however, that the citizens suspect that if they allow Y to be taxed, their politicians and bureaucrats will *not* lower the tax rate on X. Rather, they will simply take advantage of the opportunity to tax some-

---

[17] Boskin and Sheshinski [1978] examined the implications of *interdependent utilities*, i.e., the utility of each individual depends not only on his own income, but upon the incomes of other individuals. Eaton and Rosen [1980a] studied how people's uncertainties about their future incomes affect optimal tax rates.

thing new to make tax revenues as large as possible. As we saw in Chapter 10, there are indeed theories of the public sector suggesting that those who run the government can and will maximize tax revenues despite the wishes of the citizenry. Therefore, by constitutionally precluding the taxation of Y, the citizens may be rationally protecting themselves against an inefficiently large public sector. In other words, what looks inefficient from the point of view of optimal commodity taxation may be efficient in a larger setting.

As we emphasized in Chapter 10, it is hard to establish just what the goals of the people who run the government are, and whether these are likely to coincide with these of the voters. In any case, care must be taken to understand the political setting before making recommendations based upon optimal tax theory.

OTHER CRITERIA FOR EVALUATING TAX SYSTEMS

As we have seen, optimal taxation depends upon the trade-off between "efficiency" and "fairness." However, the use of these concepts in optimal tax theory does not always correspond closely to lay usage. In the context of optimal tax theory, a fair tax is one that guarantees a socially desirable distribution of the tax burden; an efficient tax is one with a small excess burden. In public discussion, on the other hand, a fair tax is often one which imposes equal liabilities on people that have the same ability to pay, and an efficient tax system is one that keeps down administrative and compliance expenses. These alternative notions of fairness and efficiency in taxation are the subject of this section.

Horizontal Equity

A traditional criterion for good tax design is **horizontal equity:** "people in equal positions should be treated equally" [Musgrave, 1959, p. 160]. Horizontal equity appeals to a fundamental sense of justice. However, to use this notion, "equal position" must be defined. Customarily, some observable index of ability to pay, such as income, expenditure, or wealth, is used to define equal position.

Unfortunately, these measures represent the *outcomes* of people's decisions, and are not really suitable measures of equal position. Consider two individuals, both of whom can earn $10 per hour. Mr. A chooses to work 1,500 hours each year, while Ms B works 2,200 hours each year. A's income is $15,000 and B's is $22,000, so that in terms of income, A and B are not in "equal positions." In an important sense, however, A and B *are* the same, because their earning capacities are identical—B just happens to work harder. Thus, because work effort is at least to some extent under people's control, two individuals with different incomes may actually be in equal positions. Similar criticism would apply to expenditure or wealth as criteria for measuring equal positions.

These arguments suggest that the individual's wage *rate* rather than income be considered as a candidate for measuring equal positions, but there are two major problems with this idea.

First, investments in "human capital"—education, on-the-job training, health care, etc.—can influence the wage rate. If Mr. A had to go to college to earn the same wage that Ms B is able to earn with only a high school degree, is it fair to treat them the same?

Second, computation of the wage rate requires division of total earnings by hours of work, but the latter is not easy to measure. (How should time spent on coffee breaks, etc., be counted?) Indeed, for a given income, it would be worthwhile for a worker to exaggerate hours of work so as to be able to report a lower wage rate and pay fewer taxes. Presumably, bosses could be induced to collaborate with their employees in return for a share of the tax savings.

As an alternative to measuring equal position either in terms of incomes or wage rates, Feldstein [1976a] suggests that it be defined in terms of utilities. Hence, the **utility definition of horizontal equity:** *(a)* if two individuals would be equally well off (have the same utility level) in the absence of taxation, they should also be equally well off if there is taxation; and *(b)* taxes should not alter the utility ordering—if A is better off than B before taxation, he should be better off after.

To assess the implications of Feldstein's definition, first assume that all individuals have the same preferences, i.e., identical utility functions. In this case, individuals who consume the same commodities (including leisure) should pay the same tax, or equivalently, all individuals should face the same tax schedule. Otherwise, individuals with equal before-tax utility levels would have different after-tax utilities.

Now assume that people have diverse tastes. For example, let there be two types of individuals, Gourmets and Sunbathers. Both groups consume food (which is purchased using income) and leisure, but Gourmets put a relatively high value on food, as do Sunbathers on leisure time. Assume further that prior to any taxation, Gourmets and Sunbathers have identical utility levels. If the same proportional income tax is imposed on everybody, Gourmets are necessarily made worse off than Sunbathers, because the former need relatively large amounts of income to support their food habits. Thus, even though this income tax is perfectly fair judged by the traditional definition of horizontal equity, it is not fair according to the utility definition. Indeed, as long as tastes for leisure differ, *any* income tax will violate the utility definition of horizontal equity.

Of course, the practical difficulties involved in measuring individuals' utilities preclude the possibility of having a "utility tax." Nevertheless, the utility definition of horizontal equity has some provocative policy implications. Assume again that all individuals have the same preferences. Then it can be shown that *any* existing tax structure does not violate the utility definition of horizontal equity *if* individuals are free to choose their activities and expenditures.

To see why, suppose that in one type of job a large part of compensation is in the form of "amenities" which are not taxable. These might include items like pleasant offices, access to a swimming pool, etc. In another occupation, compensation is exclusively monetary, all of which is subject to income tax. According to the traditional definition, this situation is a violation of horizontal equity, because a person in the job with a lot of amenities has "too small" a tax burden. But, if both arrangements coexist and individuals are free to choose, then the net after-tax rewards (including amenities) must be the same in both jobs. Why? Suppose that the net after-tax reward is greater in the jobs with amenities. Then individuals will migrate to these jobs to take advantage of them. But the increased supply of workers in these jobs will depress their wage. The process continues until the *net* returns are equal. In short, although people in the different occupations pay unequal taxes, there is no horizontal inequity because of adjustments in the *before-tax* wage.

It is sometimes suggested that certain tax advantages that are available only to the rich are sources of horizontal inequity.[18] According to the utility definition, this notion is wrong. If these advantages are open to everyone with high income, and all high-income people have identical tastes, then the advantages may indeed reduce tax progressiveness, but they have no effect whatsoever on horizontal equity.

We are lead to a striking conclusion: given common tastes, a preexisting tax structure cannot involve horizontal inequity. Rather, all horizontal inequities arise from *changes* in tax laws. This is because individuals make commitments based on the existing tax laws which are difficult or impossible to reverse. For example, people may buy larger houses because of the preferred tax treatment for owner-occupied housing.[19] When the tax laws are changed, their welfare goes down, and horizontal equity is violated. These observations give new meaning to the dictum, "The only good tax is an old tax."

The fact that tax changes may generate horizontal inequities does not necessarily imply that they should not be undertaken. After all, tax changes may lead to improvements from the points of view of efficiency and/or vertical equity. However, the arguments suggest that it might be appropriate to somehow ease the transition to the new tax system. For example, if it is announced that a given tax reform is not to go into effect until a few years subsequent to its passage, people who have based their

---

[18] A number of such tax provisions are discussed in Chapter 14.

[19] The tax treatment of owner-occupied housing is discussed in Chapter 15.

behavior on the old tax structure will be able to make at least some adjustments to the new regime. The problem of finding fair processes for changing tax regimes **(transitional equity)** is very difficult and not many results are available on the subject.

The very conservative implications of the utility definition of horizontal equity should come as no great surprise, because implicit in the definition is the notion that the status quo has special ethical validity. (Otherwise, why be concerned about changes in the ordering of utilities?) A more general feature of the utility definition is its focus on the *outcomes* of taxation. In contrast, some have suggested that the essence of horizontal equity is to put constraints on the *rules* which govern the selection of taxes, rather than to provide criteria for judging their effects. Thus, horizontal equity excludes capricious taxes, or taxes based on irrelevant characteristics. For example, we can imagine the government levying special lump sum taxes on people with red hair, or putting very different taxes on angel food and chocolate cakes. The **rule definition** of horizontal equity would presumably exclude such taxes from consideration, *even* if they somehow had desirable efficiency or distributional effects. In this sense, provisions in the U.S. Constitution that rule out certain kinds of taxes can be interpreted as an attempt to guarantee horizontal equity (see Chapter 2).

However, identifying the permissible set of characteristics on which to base taxation is a problem. Most people would agree that religion and race should be irrelevant for purposes of determining tax liability. On the other hand, there is considerable disagreement as to whether or not marital status should influence tax burdens (see Chapter 14). And even once there is agreement that certain characteristics are legitimate bases for discrimination, the problem of how much discrimination is appropriate still remains. Everyone agrees that serious physical impairment should be taken into account in determining personal tax liability. But how much must your vision be impaired before you are eligible for special tax treatment as blind? And by what amount should your tax bill be reduced?

We are forced to conclude that horizontal equity, however defined, is a rather amorphous concept. Yet it continues to have enormous appeal as a principle of tax design. Notions of fairness among equals, regardless of their vagueness, will continue to play an important role in the implementation of tax policy.

Costs of Running the Tax System

Most optimal tax models assume that collecting taxes is a costless activity. However, gathering taxes requires the consumption of resources by the taxing authorities. At the same time, taxpayers incur costs in complying with the tax system. These include outlays for accountants and tax lawyers, as well as the value of taxpayers' time spent on filling out tax returns and keeping records.

The costs of administering the income tax in the United States are fairly low. In 1981, for example, the Internal Revenue Service expended only 41 cents to raise each $100 in taxes [Commissioner of Internal Revenue, 1982, p. 55]. However, the compliance costs of personal income taxation are quite substantial. On the basis of survey evidence, Slemrod and Sorum [1983] estimated that in 1982, the average U.S. household devoted about 29 hours to state and federal tax preparation, and spent about $53 for professional advice. If the value of time is approximated at about $10.70 per hour, then the total resource cost per household is about $364. Multiplying this by the 97 million taxpaying units in 1982 gives a total resource cost of $35.3 billion, about 9 percent of total federal and state income tax revenue.

Clearly, the choice of tax and subsidy systems should account for administrative and compliance costs. Even systems that appear fair and efficient (in the excess burden sense) might be undesirable because they are excessively complicated and expensive to administer. Consider the possibility of taxing output produced in the home—housecleaning, child care, etc. As suggested in Chapter 12, the fact that market work is taxed but housework is not creates a sizable distortion in the allocation of labor. Moreover, an argument could be made that taxing differentially on the basis of choice of workplace violates some notions of horizontal equity. Nevertheless, the difficulties involved in valuing household production would create such huge administrative costs that the idea is infeasible.

Unfortunately, in many cases, administrative problems receive insufficient attention. For example, a number of cities grant special tax rebates to building developers to stimulate growth. It sounds like a good idea—if the administrators can determine correctly where the rebates should be targeted and in what amounts. A study of such a program in New York City indicated that it was a failure. City officials gave rebates without knowing whether they stimulated growth and without obtaining any information on whether they would increase employment. Indeed, no one even knew for sure how much the program cost [Goodwin, 1983, p. 1]. Now, part of the problem may have been incompetence of the particular administrators involved. But the inherent difficulties in administering such a complicated tax program had a major effect on the outcome.

Obviously, no tax system is costless to administer; the trick is to think carefully about whether or not the administrative costs are worth the benefits. To make this notion more concrete, assume that the government can potentially levy a large number of commodity taxes, some of which are more costly to administer than others.[20] Now, the more of the

---

[20] This analysis is based upon Yitzhaki [1979].

taxes that the government levies, the smaller the excess burden of collecting a given amount of tax revenue. This is due to the fact that when a commodity is excluded from taxation, in effect its tax rate is set as zero. In general, however, we expect the Ramsey Rule to imply nonzero tax rates on each commodity. Hence, as each commodity becomes subject to taxation, its tax rate can be set at the efficient level, and excess burden decreases.[21] Intuitively, excess burden decreases because the tax burden is "spread over" more commodities.

Now suppose that we can rank taxes on the basis of cost of administration, with the cheapest to administer first. By definition, as we move from taxes that are easy to administer to those that are difficult, the cost of administration rises. In Figure 13.5, the horizontal axis measures the

FIGURE 13.5   Optimal Size of Tax Administration

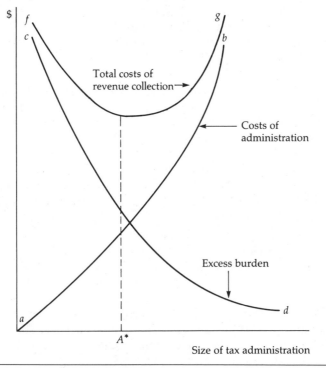

number of taxes used, which can be thought of as the "size of tax administration." The vertical axis measures dollars. The direct relationship between size of administration and the cost of administration is depicted by the upward sloping schedule *ab*.

---

[21] More precisely, the excess burden cannot increase with the number of possible taxes provided that as more taxes are introduced, each tax rate is reset so that the Ramsey Rule holds.

On the other hand, as the size of administration increases, the excess burden of the tax system decreases. This inverse relationship is represented by schedule *cd*. The total cost of revenue collection is the sum of the excess burden and administration costs, given by schedule *fg*. The optimal size of tax administration is where the total cost of tax collection is a minimum, at point A^*. Even though a move to the right of A^* would lower the excess burden of the tax system, the associated administrative costs are too high to merit doing so. Similarly, a move to the left of A^* would make the system cheaper to administer, but this advantage would be offset by the increased excess burden.

Tax Evasion

We now turn to one of the most important problems that faces any tax administration—cheating. First, it is important to distinguish between tax avoidance and tax evasion. **Tax avoidance** is changing your behavior in such a way as to reduce your legal tax liability. There is nothing illegal about tax avoidance:

> Over and over again courts have said that there is nothing sinister in so arranging one's affairs so as to keep taxes as low as possible. Everybody does so, rich or poor; and all do right, for nobody owes any public duty to pay more than the law demands. . . . To demand more in the name of morals is mere cant. (Judge Learned Hand [*Commissioner* v. *Newman*, 1947])

In contrast, **tax evasion** is failing to pay taxes which are legally due. If a tax on mushrooms is levied and you sell fewer mushrooms, it is tax avoidance. If you fail to report your sales of mushrooms to the government, it is tax evasion.

Tax evasion is not a new problem. Centuries ago Plato observed, "When there is an income tax, the just man will pay more and the unjust less on the same amount of income." In recent years, however, the phenomenon of tax evasion has received an especially large amount of public attention. A March 28, 1983 *Time* magazine cover showing a taxpayer hiding thousands of dollars behind his back is typical. The headline read "Tax Cheating—Bad and Getting Worse."

By its very nature tax cheating is very difficult to measure. The Internal Revenue Service estimated that in 1976 between $100 and $135 billion of taxable income was not reported by individuals on their tax returns.[22] If this estimate is even approximately correct, it suggests that evasion is a very important issue.

---

[22] See Simon and Witte [1980, p. 71]. They also discuss evasion of taxes other than those on income.

There are several common ways to commit tax fraud:[23]

1. Keep two sets of books to record business transactions. One records the actual business and the other is shown to the tax authorities. Some evaders use two cash registers.
2. Moonlight for cash. Of course, there is nothing illegal in working an extra job. In many cases, however, the income received on such jobs is paid in cash rather than by check. Hence, there is no legal record, and the income is not reported to the tax authorities.
3. Barter. "I'll fix your car if you bake me five loaves of bread." When you receive payment in kind instead of money, it is legally a taxable transaction. However, such income is seldom reported.
4. Under report tips. Tips paid to hotel and restaurant workers, parking lot attendants, and the like are subject to taxation. Only the recipient knows for sure how much is received, however, and under reporting is common.
5. Deal in cash. Paying for goods and services with cash and checks made out to "cash" makes it very difficult for the Internal Revenue Service to trace transactions.

Public perception of the tax evader has changed over time. As Sandmo [1981] notes, whereas previously tax evasion was associated with income from capital hidden in Swiss bank accounts, the current image of a tax evader may well be a repairer who gets a substantial amount of income from "unofficial" work which is not reported for tax purposes. There is widespread feeling that "everyone is doing it."

We will first discuss the positive theory of tax evasion, and then turn to the normative question of how public policy should deal with it.

Positive Analysis of Tax Evasion.[24]   Assume that Al cares only about maximizing his expected income. He has a given amount of earnings, and is trying to choose R, the amount that he will hide from the tax authorities. Suppose that Al's marginal income tax rate is 0.3. Then for each dollar shielded from taxable income, his tax bill falls by 30 cents. This is the marginal benefit to him of hiding a dollar of income from the tax authorities. More generally, if Al faces a marginal income tax rate t, then the marginal benefit of each dollar shielded from taxation is t.

The tax authority does not know Al's true income, but it randomly audits all taxpayers' returns. As a result, there is some probability, π, that Al will be audited. If he is caught cheating, Al pays a penalty which increases with R at an increasing rate. Note that if it were costless to monitor Al every second of every day, then there would be no opportu-

---

[23] For further examples, see Lohr [1981, p. 1].

[24] This model is similar in structure to those that have been used to describe criminal behavior in general. See Becker [1968].

nities for evasion. The fact that such monitoring is infeasible is the fundamental source of the problem.

Assuming that Al knows the value of π and the penalty schedule, he makes his decision by comparing the marginal costs and benefits of cheating. In Figure 13.6 the amount of income not reported is measured

FIGURE 13.6   Optimal Tax Evasion Is Positive

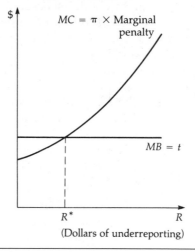

(Dollars of underreporting)

on the horizontal axis, and dollars on the vertical. The marginal benefit *(MB)* for each dollar not reported is *t*, the amount of tax saved. The expected marginal cost *(MC)* is the amount by which the penalty goes up for each dollar of cheating (the marginal penalty) times the probability of detection. For example, if the additional penalty for hiding the thousandth dollar is $1.50 and the probability of detection is 1 in 3, then the *expected* marginal penalty is 50 cents. The "optimal" amount of cheating is where the two schedules cross, at *R**. *R** is optimal in the sense that *on average* it is the policy that maximizes Al's income. In a world of uncertainty, finding the best policy in this "expected value" sense is a reasonable way to proceed. It is possible, of course, that it will be optimal not to cheat at all. For the individual in Figure 13.7, the marginal cost of cheating exceeds the marginal benefit for all positive values of *R*, so the optimum is equal to zero.

The model implies that cheating will increase when marginal tax rates go up. This is because a higher value of *t* increases the marginal benefit of evasion, shifting up the marginal benefit schedule so that the intersection with marginal cost occurs at a higher value of *R*.[25] Also, cheating

---

[25] This prediction is borne out by the econometric work of Clotfelter [1983], who estimated that the elasticity of underreported income with respect to the marginal tax rate is about 0.84.

FIGURE 13.7   Optimal Tax Evasion Is Zero

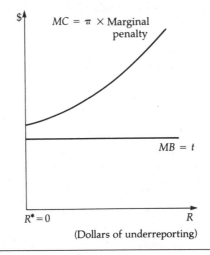

(Dollars of underreporting)

will decrease when the probability of detection goes up, and will decrease when the marginal penalty rate increases. Both of these steps raise the expected marginal cost of cheating.

Although this model yields useful insights, it ignores some potentially important considerations.

Psychic Costs of Cheating.   Simply put, tax evasion may make people feel guilty. One way to model this phenomenon is by adding psychic costs to the marginal cost schedule. For some very honest people the psychic costs are so high that they would not cheat even if the expected marginal penalty were zero.

Risk Aversion.   In Figures 13.6 and 13.7, it is assumed that people care only about expected income, and that risk per se does not bother them. To the extent that individuals are risk averse, their decisions to engage in what is essentially a gamble may be modified. (See the appendix to Chapter 9 for a discussion of choice under uncertainty.)

Work Choices.   The model assumes that the only decision is how much income to report. The type of job and the amount of before-tax income are taken as given. In reality, the tax system may affect how much time is spent at work and what kinds of jobs people take. For example, high marginal tax rates might induce people to choose occupations that provide substantial opportunities for evading taxation,[26] the so-called

------

[26] However, this is not necessarily the case. See Sandmo [1981].

underground economy. This includes economic activities that are legal but easy to hide from the tax authorities (home repairs) as well as work that is criminal per se (prostitution, robbery). The cartoonist's comment on this phenomenon is salient.

Sidney Harris. Reprinted with permission.

"THE MONEY WE GET FROM STOLEN PROPERTY — DO WE LIST THAT AS WAGES OR CAPITAL GAINS?"

Changing Probabilities of Audit.   In our simple analysis, the probability of an audit is independent of both the amount evaded and the size of income reported. However, in the United States audit probabilities depend upon occupation and the size of reported income. This complicates the model, but does not change its essential aspects.

It is clear, then, that cheating is a more complicated phenomenon than Figures 13.6 and 13.7 suggest. Nevertheless, the model provides us with a useful framework for thinking about the factors that influence the decision to evade. Unfortunately, little empirical work has been done on tax evasion. It is not known whether high fines or frequent audits are more effective ways of deterring cheating. It is not even known whether a previous audit experience decreases the likelihood that an individual will cheat again. For some people, it appears, the audit experience is so negative that it increases their desire to cheat the tax collector in the future [Simon & Witte, 1980, p. 75].

Normative Analysis of Tax Evasion.   An assumption in much public discussion is that the existence of the underground economy is a bad thing and that policy should be designed to reduce its size. Although this proposition may be correct, it is worth careful scrutiny.

An important question in this context is whether or not we care about the welfare of tax evaders. In the jargon of welfare economics, are the utilities of participants in the underground economy to be included in the social welfare function? Assume for the moment that they are. Then under certain conditions, the existence of an underground economy raises social welfare. For example, if the supply of labor is more elastic to the underground economy than to the regular economy, optimal tax theory suggests that the former be taxed at a relatively low rate. This is simply an application of the inverse elasticity rule, Equation (13.5). Alternatively, suppose that participants in the underground economy tend to be poorer than those in the regular economy. Then to the extent society has egalitarian income redistribution objectives, it might be desirable to leave the underground economy intact.

Of course, there is no proof that either of these assertions is correct. The important point is that analysis of the usual utilitarian welfare criteria leads to ambiguous results about the desirability of an underground economy.[27]

Consider now the policy implications when evaders are not given any weight in the social welfare function, and the goal is simply to eliminate cheating at the lowest administrative cost possible. Figure 13.6 suggests a fairly straightforward way to accomplish this objective. The expected marginal cost of cheating is the product of the penalty rate and the probability of detection. The probability of detection depends upon the amount of resources devoted to tax administration; if the Internal Revenue Service has a big budget, it can catch a lot of cheaters. However, even if the tax authorities have a small budget so that the probability of detection is low, the marginal cost of cheating can still be made arbitrarily high if the penalty is large enough. If only one tax evader were caught each year, but he was publicly hung for his crime, the *expected* cost of tax evasion would deter many people. The fact that such a draconian policy has never been seriously proposed in the United States is

---

[27] For further discussion along these lines, see Sandmo [1981].

indicative of the fact that existing penalty systems try to take into account the notion of "just retribution."[28] Contrary to the assumptions of the utilitarian framework, society cares not only about the end result (getting rid of cheaters), but also the rules by which the result is achieved.

The development of the underground economy raises several broader issues for society. Some have argued, for example, that cheating is habit-forming; once people become accustomed to evading taxation, they will continue to do so, even if marginal tax rates are lowered in the future. (See Lindbeck, [1980b].) There is no econometric evidence for this assertion, but it is very troubling. There are also fears that growth of the underground economy will *force* some people into cheating. Suppose that tax evasion becomes prevalent in sectors of the economy dominated by small businesses whose activities are particularly difficult to monitor. Then firms that eschew cheating will be at a competitive disadvantage because of higher costs. The only choices for these firms are to cheat or to go out of business.

More generally, in a system that relies to an important extent on self-assessment by taxpayers, a high marginal tax rate is in some sense a tax on honesty. Honesty is obviously a desirable quality for ethical reasons. It is also important for the functioning of the economy. Just imagine what would happen to efficiency if for every economic transaction, you had to take precautions against being cheated. The fact that our tax system is making it ever more expensive to be honest has consequences that are impossible to quantify, but which may be significant.

OVERVIEW

Traditional analysis of tax systems elucidated several "principles" of tax design: taxes should have horizontal and vertical equity, be "neutral" with respect to economic incentives, be administratively easy, etc. In recent years, public finance economists have integrated these somewhat ad hoc guidelines with the principles of welfare economics. The optimal tax literature *derives* the criteria for a good tax using an underlying social welfare function.

On some occasions, optimal tax analysis has corrected previous errors. For example, it may *not* be efficient for all tax rates to be the same (neutral). More frequently, however, the benefit has been to clarify the trade-offs between efficiency and equity in tax design. As a by-product, the various definitions of "equity" have been scrutinized carefully.

The result of this work is not a "blueprint" for building a tax system, if for no other reason than the economic theory forming the basis for

---

[28] Other nations have not been so constrained in enforcing economic honesty. In 1982, China announced the execution of a local official for embezzlement.

optimal tax theory has its own problems (see Chapter 4). In this context two comments are cogent: (1) Optimal tax theory generally ignores political and social institutions. An "optimal" tax may easily be ruined by politicians or be overly costly to administer. (2) While the optimal tax approach points out that the concept of horizontal equity is difficult to make operational, the fact remains that "equal treatment of equals" is an appealing ethical concept. Horizontal equity is difficult to integrate with optimal tax theory because of the latter's focus on outcomes rather than processes.

Thus, optimal tax theory has used the tools of welfare economics to add analytical strength to the traditional discussion of the goals of tax design. Nevertheless, it is wedded to the utilitarian welfare approach in economics. As such, it is open to criticisms concerning the adequacy of this description of the world.

SUMMARY

Efficient commodity tax theory studies the methods by which a given amount of revenue may be raised while creating a minimum excess burden.

For unrelated goods, the Ramsey Rule stipulates that relative tax rates be inversely related to compensated elasticities. While this ensures maximum efficiency, the rule may be modified to achieve distributional goals.

When goods are related and leisure cannot be taxed, minimization of excess burden requires that complements to leisure be relatively more heavily taxed than substitutes. In this way, a commodity tax system can be brought closer to the results of lump sum taxation.

Choosing optimal user fees for government-produced services is quite similar to choosing optimal taxes. In particular, there are efficiency and distributional considerations in choosing an optimal two-part tariff.

Income taxation is a major source of revenue in developed countries. Edgeworth's early study of optimal income taxes stipulated that after-tax incomes be equal. However, when the excess burden of distorting the leisure/income trade-off is included, marginal tax rates of far less than 100 percent are optimal. A surprising result of optimal income tax theory is that if marginal tax rates are allowed to vary, in general, the marginal tax rate on the highest income should be zero.

Tax systems may be evaluated by standards other than those of optimal tax theory. Horizontal equity, the costs of administration, incentives for tax evasion, and political constraints all affect the design of tax systems.

Traditional definitions of horizontal equity rely upon income as a measure of "equal position" in society. However, it is not clear that income as conventionally measured does an adequate job. The utility definition is more precise, but leads to radically different policy provisions and contains an inherent bias toward the status quo. Other definitions of horizontal equity focus on the rules by which taxes are chosen.

The costs of running a tax system are ignored in most theoretical analyses. However, administrative and compliance costs will affect the choice of tax base, tax rates, and the amount of tax evasion.

DISCUSSION QUESTIONS

1. "If the compensated demand for a single commodity is completely inelastic, the most socially desirable ad valorem tax rate on this commodity will be higher than the tax rates on other commodities." Comment.

2. Describe a simple situation in which on efficiency grounds only, it is possible that the optimal tax system will subsidize one good and tax another.

3. Give an example of a tax schedule with high average tax rates on high incomes and with a zero marginal tax rate on the last dollar earned.

4. "If tips must be reported as taxable income, restaurants will go out of business; costing jobs. In addition, it's too hard to find out how much in tips waiters and waitresses actually receive. Besides, most of the people who earn tips have low incomes and shouldn't be taxed anyway." Discuss the equity and efficiency aspects of the problem of taxing tips.

SELECTED REFERENCES

Brennan, Geoffrey, and James M. Buchanan. "Towards a Tax Constitution for Leviathan." *Journal of Public Economics* 8, no. 3 (December 1977), pp. 255–74.

Simon, Carl P., and Ann D. Witte. "The Underground Economy: Estimates of Size, Structure and Trends." In *Special Study on Economic Change.* Vol. 5, *Government Regulation: Achieving Social and Economic Balance.* Washington, D.C.: U.S. Government Printing Office, 1980, pp. 70–120.

Sandmo, Agnar. "Optimal Taxation—An Introduction to the Literature." *Journal of Public Economics* 6 (1976), pp. 37–54.

Slemrod, Joel. "Do We Know how Progressive the Income Tax System Should Be?" *National Tax Journal* 36, no. 3 (September 1983), pp. 361–70.

Part Five

" WHOOPEE... MY TAX CUT. WHERE WILL I SPEND IT? "

The United States Tax System

The next five chapters are devoted to description and analysis of the major taxes in the U.S. fiscal system. This involves some bad news and some good news. The bad news is that it is hard to know just how long the descriptive material will be correct. Major changes in the tax system are under consideration, and it is likely that a number of "reforms" will be made in the future. The good news is that after seeing the tools of public finance applied to the existing tax institutions, the reader will be in a position to analyze any new taxes that may arise. Moreover, for each tax we will discuss some of the major proposed modifications.

Describing each tax individually seems to be the only feasible expositional technique. Nevertheless, keep in mind that the various taxes do interact. For example, your federal income tax liability depends in part upon the amount of property tax paid to local government. More generally, as the cartoon indicates, failure to consider more than one tax at a time gives a misleading picture of the overall magnitude of the tax burden.

CHAPTER 14

The Personal Income Tax

It was true as taxes is. And nothing's truer than them.

Charles Dickens,
David Copperfield

The personal income tax is the basic workhorse of the federal revenue system. In 1981, 95.3 million tax returns were filed, which generated $332 billion in revenue, accounting for 70.4 percent of federal tax revenues and 51.1 percent of tax receipts raised by *all* levels of government.[1] The income tax is as unpopular as it is important—recent public opinion polls suggest that Americans find it the least fair of all taxes they pay. Reforming the income tax always occupies an important place on the public agenda.

This chapter discusses problems associated with designing a personal income tax system, how the United States has dealt with them, and the efficiency and equity of the results. The tax code is incredibly complicated, and an army of accountants and lawyers exists just to interpret its provisions. Our exposition of the legal issues is therefore necessarily sketchy. Fortunately, an understanding of the general structure of the tax system is sufficient for our purposes.

BASIC STRUCTURE

Each year on April 15, Americans file a tax return which computes their tax liability for the previous year. The calculation requires a series of

---

[1] Computed from *Facts and Figures on Government Finance* [1983, pp. 23, 138].

FIGURE 14.1   Computation of Federal Personal Income Tax Liability

1. *Add* together income from all
      taxable sources: wages, rents, interest, etc.
   Subtract business expenses
   Exclude employers' contributions to
      pensions, 60 percent of capital gains,
      interest from tax-exempt bonds, etc.

   ↓

   ADJUSTED GROSS INCOME (AGI)

2. *Subtract* personal exemptions.
   Subtract itemized deductions:
      charitable donations,
      interest payments, certain
      medical expenses, etc. *or*
   Subtract the standard deduction (zero bracket amount).

   ↓

   TAXABLE INCOME

3. *Apply* the rate schedule.
   Subtract tax credits.

   ↓

   TAX LIABILITY

---

steps summarized in Figure 14.1. The first step is to compute **adjusted gross income (AGI).** AGI is defined as total income from all taxable sources less certain expenses incurred in earning that income. Taxable sources include (but are not limited to) wages, dividends, interest, business and farm profits, rents, royalties, prizes, and even the proceeds from embezzlement.

Not all of AGI is subject to tax. The second step is to convert AGI to **taxable income**—the amount of income that is subject to tax. This is done by subtracting various amounts called **exemptions** and **deductions** from AGI. Deductions and exemptions are discussed more carefully below.

The final step is to calculate the amount of tax due. A **rate schedule** indicates the tax liability associated with each level of taxable income. Different types of taxpayers face different rate schedules. For example, husbands and wives who file tax returns together—**joint returns**—have different rates than single people.

For most taxpayers, during the year some tax is withheld out of each paycheck. The amount that actually has to be paid on April 15 is the difference between the tax liability and the accumulated withholding payments. If more has been withheld than is owed, the taxpayer is entitled to a refund.

It sounds pretty straightforward, but in reality, complications arise in every step of the process. We now discuss some of the major problems.

DEFINING INCOME: CONCEPTUAL ISSUES[2]

Clearly, the ability to identify "income" is necessary to operate an income tax. A natural way to begin this section would be to discuss and evaluate the definition of income that appears in the tax law. However, the statutes provide no definition. The constitutional amendment that introduced the tax merely says "The Congress shall have power to lay and collect taxes on incomes, from whatever source derived." While the tax law does provide examples of items that should be classified as income—wages and salaries, rents, dividends, etc.—the words "from whatever source derived" do not really provide a standard that can be used to decide whether or not the exclusion of certain items from taxation is appropriate.

Public finance economists have traditionally used their own standard, the so-called **Haig-Simon (H-S) definition:**[3] income is the money value of the net increase to an individual's power to consume during a period. This is equal to the amount actually consumed during the period plus net additions to wealth. Net additions to wealth—saving—must be included in income because they represent an increase in *potential* consumption.

It must be emphasized that the H-S criterion requires the inclusion of *all* sources of potential increases in consumption, regardless of whether the actual consumption takes place, and regardless of the form in which the consumption occurs. At the same time, the H-S criterion requires that any decreases in an individual's potential to consume should be subtracted in determining income. For example, if certain expenses have to be incurred to earn income, these should be subtracted. If the gross revenues from an individual's business are $100,000, but business expenses were $95,000, then the individual's potential consumption has only increased by $5,000.

The H-S definition encompasses those items that are ordinarily thought of as income: wage and salary receipts, business profits, rent and royalty income, and dividend and interest receipts.[4] However, the criterion also includes certain "unconventional" items.

Employer Contributions to Pensions and Other Retirement Plans.   Such payments, even though not made directly to the recipient, represent an increase in an individual's potential to consume.

Employer Contributions for Employees' Insurance.   The fact that compensation is paid to an employee in the form of a certain commodity (in

---

[2] Much of the discussion in this and the following section is based upon Pechman [1977a], which should be consulted for further details.

[3] Named after Robert M. Haig and Henry C. Simons, economists who wrote in the first half of the 20th century. Goode [1977] discusses some alternative income definitions.

[4] Again, these must all be measured net of the expenses required to earn them.

this case, an insurance policy) rather than in cash does not make it any less income.

Transfer Payments, Including Social Security Retirement Benefits, Unemployment Compensation, and Aid to Families with Dependent Children. Any receipt, be it from the government or an employer, is income.

Capital Gains. Increases in the value of an asset are referred to as **capital gains,** decreases as **capital losses.** Suppose that Brutus owns some shares of IBM stock which increase in value from $10,000 to $12,500 over the course of a year. Then he has enjoyed a capital gain of $2,500. This $2,500 represents an increase in potential consumption, and hence, belongs in income.[5]

If Brutus sells the IBM stock at the end of the year, the capital gain is said to be **realized,** otherwise it is **unrealized.** From the H-S point of view, it is strictly irrelevant whether a capital gain is realized or unrealized. It represents potential to consume and hence, is income. If Brutus does not sell his IBM stock, in effect he chooses to save by reinvesting the capital gain in IBM. Because the H-S criterion does not distinguish between different uses of income, the fact that Brutus happens to reinvest is irrelevant.

All the arguments for adding in capital gains apply to subtracting capital losses. If Casca's Kodak stock decreases in value by $4,200 during a given year, this $4,200 should be subtracted from other sources of income.

Income in Kind. Some people may receive part or all of their incomes in kind—in the form of goods and services rather than cash. Farmers often provide field hands with food, corporations give employees subsidized lunches or access to a company car, etc. One important form of income in kind is the annual rental value of owner-occupied homes. A homeowner receives a stream of services from his dwelling. The net monetary value of these services—**imputed rent**—is equal to the rental payments the owner would have received had he chosen to rent the house out, after subtracting maintenance expenses, taxes, etc.

In all these cases, from the H-S point of view, it makes no difference whether benefits are received in monetary form, or in the form of goods and services. They are all income.

Some Practical and Conceptual Problems. A number of difficulties arise in attempts to use the Haig-Simons criterion as a basis for constructing a tax system.

---

[5] It is the *real* value of capital gains that constitutes income, not gains due merely to inflation. This issue is discussed below.

First, the criterion makes it clear that only income *net of business expenses* increases potential consumption power. But it is often hard to distinguish between expenditures that are made for consumption and those that are costs of obtaining income. What portion of a "three-martini lunch" designed to woo a client is consumption and what portion is business? If Calpurnia buys a desk to use while working at home, but the desk is also a beautiful piece of furniture, to what extent is the desk a business expense?

Second, capital gains and losses may be very difficult to measure, particularly when they are unrealized. For assets that are traded in active markets, the problem is fairly manageable. Even if Brutus does not sell his shares of IBM common stock, it is easy to determine their value at any point in time by consulting the financial section of the newspaper. It is not nearly as easy to measure the capital gain on a piece of art that has appreciated in value. One possibility would be to find a comparable piece that had recently been sold, a task which would be difficult if there were not many sales being made. Alternatively, art owners could be required to hire professional appraisers to value their collections each year, but this would be expensive and different appraisers might produce different estimates.

Third, imputed income from durables presents measurement difficulties. For example, it may be hard to estimate what the market rent of a particular owner-occupied dwelling would be. Similarly, measuring the imputed rental streams generated by other durables such as cars, stereos, and food processors is not feasible.

Finally, in-kind services are hard to value. One important example is the income produced by people who do housework rather than participate in the market. These services—housecleaning, cooking, child care, etc.,—are clearly valuable. However, even though markets exist for purchasing these services, it would be difficult to estimate whether a given homemaker's services were equal to that market value. Another important example is the value of government goods and services received by an individual. As stressed in Chapter 6, the value that people place on public goods is inherently difficult to measure. In theory, the services each citizen receives from the defense department represent consumption, but how do you put a dollar value on this consumption?

Evaluation: Who's Afraid of Haig and Simons?   Numerous additional examples of the difficulties involved in implementing the H-S criterion can be provided, but the main point is clear. No definition of income can make the administration of an income tax simple and straightforward. Arbitrary decisions about what should be included in income are inevitable. Nevertheless, the Haig-Simons criterion has often been regarded as an ideal toward which the tax system should strive: income should be defined as broadly as is feasible, and all sources of income received by a particular person should be taxed at the same rate.

There are two reasons for the attractiveness of the H-S criterion.

First, the criterion appeals to a sense of justice. Recall the traditional definition of horizontal equity from Chapter 13—people with equal incomes should pay equal taxes. For this dictum to make any sense, *all* sources of income must be included in the tax base. Otherwise, two people with identical abilities to pay could end up with different tax liabilities.

On the other hand, Feldstein [1976a] has argued that as long as people's abilities to earn income differ, the H-S criterion will *not* produce fair outcomes. Suppose that Popeye is endowed with a lot of "brains," and Bluto with a lot of "brawn." Suppose further that the work done by brawny people is less pleasant than that available to brainy individuals. In that case, if Bluto and Popeye have the same *income*, then Popeye has more *utility*. Is it fair to tax them as equals?

The second reason for the appeal of the Haig-Simons criterion is efficiency. Defenders of the criterion argue that it has the virtue of *neutrality*—it treats all forms of income the same, and hence, does not distort the pattern of economic activity. Following this reasoning, it is argued that the failure to tax imputed rent from owner-occupied housing leads to excessive investment in housing.

It is doubtless true that many departures from the Haig-Simons criterion have led to inefficiencies. But it does *not* follow that equal tax rates on all income, regardless of source, would be most efficient. Consider income from rent on unimproved land. The supply of such land is perfectly inelastic, and hence, no excess burden would be created by taxing it at a very high rate.[6] An efficient tax system would tax the returns to such land at higher rates than other sources of income, and *not* tax all sources at the same rate, as dictated by the Haig-Simons criterion. More generally, the optimal tax literature discussed in Chapter 13 suggests that as long as lump sum taxes are ruled out, efficiency is enhanced when relatively high tax rates are imposed on those activities with relatively inelastic supply. "Neutrality", in the sense of equal tax rates on all types of income, generally does *not* minimize excess burden.

Where does this leave us? Sunley [1977, p. 272] points out that we cannot be sanguine about the possibilities for using optimal tax theory as a framework for designing the tax base: "If one follows this efficiency logic, . . . one would end up with a highly differentiated tax system that would strike most people as unjust, unworkable, and having no obvious appeal." It would be unwise, therefore, to abandon the Haig-Simons criterion altogether. On the other hand, there is no reason to

---

[6] This fact has long been recognized. See George [1914].

regard the criterion as sacred. Departures from it should be considered on their merits, and should not be viewed prima facie as unfair and inefficient.

EXCLUDABLE FORMS OF MONEY INCOME

We have seen that some income sources which would be taxable according to the Haig-Simons criterion are omitted from the tax base for practical reasons. In addition, several forms of income that would be administratively quite easy to tax are partially or altogether excluded.

Interest on State and Local Bonds

The interest earned by individuals on bonds issued by states and localities is not subject to federal tax. From the H-S point of view, this exclusion makes no sense—interest from these bonds represents no less an addition to potential consumption than any other form of income. The exclusion was originally a consequence of the opinion that it would be unconstitutional for one level of government to levy taxes upon the securities issued by another level of government. However, many constitutional experts now believe that such taxation would be permissible [see Pechman, 1977b, p. 115].

In the absence of legal restrictions, the exclusion of state and local interest might be justified as a powerful tool for helping states and localities to raise revenues. If investors do not have to pay federal tax on interest from state and local bonds, then they should be willing to accept a lower before-tax rate of return than they receive on taxable bonds. Suppose that Caesar faces a tax rate of 50 percent on additional income, and that the rate of return on taxable securities is 16 percent. Then as long as the rate of return on state and local securities exceeds 8 percent, Caesar prefers them to taxable securities, other things being the same.[7] Hence, state and local governments can borrow funds at rates lower than those prevailing on the market. In effect, the revenue foregone by the treasury subsidizes borrowing by states and localities.

Unfortunately, tax-exempt bonds are an expensive way to help state and local governments. To see why, assume there are two taxpayers, Caesar, who faces a 50 percent tax rate on additional income, and Brutus, who faces a 25 percent rate. If the market rate of return on taxable bonds is 16 percent, then Caesar's after-tax return is 8 percent and Brutus' is 12 percent. To induce *both* Caesar and Brutus to buy something other than taxable bonds, the net rate of return must therefore be at least 12 percent. Suppose a town issues tax-exempt bonds yielding just slightly more than 12 percent, and both Caesar and Brutus purchase the bonds. The key thing to note is that some of the tax break is

---

[7] In particular, it is assumed that the two types of securities are perceived as being equally risky. The demand for assets whose risks differ is discussed in the next chapter.

"wasted" on Caesar—he would have been willing to buy the bond at any yield greater than 8 percent, yet he receives 12 percent.[8]

What is the net effect on government revenues? Suppose that the town borrows $100 from Brutus at the interest rate of 12 percent instead of the market rate of 16 percent. This saves the town $4 in interest payments. On the other hand, the treasury loses $4 (= .25 × $16) in income tax revenue. In effect, the treasury has provided a $4 subsidy to the town. On the other hand, if the town borrows $100 from Caesar it still saves only $4. But the Treasury loses $8 (= .5 × $16) in tax revenues. Thus, $4 of the tax break is "wasted."

In short, the net effect of tax-exempt bonds is zero only for those investors who are just on the margin of choosing tax-exempt versus taxable securities. For all others, the subsidy to the state and local borrower is outweighed by the revenue lost at the federal level.

Why not eliminate the interest exclusion and simply have the federal government make direct grants to states and localities? The main reason such a proposal has never generated much enthusiasm is probably political. A direct subsidy to states and localities would be just another item in the federal budget, an item whose existence might be jeopardized by the vagaries of the political climate. Indeed, if the subsidy were made explicit, rather than buried in the tax law, voters might decide that it was not worthwhile. Hence, state and local officials have lobbied intensively—and successfully—to maintain this exclusion.

Capital Gains

Another important departure from the Haig-Simons criterion is the tax treatment of capital gains. There are several important provisions.

Only Realizations Taxed.   Unless a capital gain is actually realized—the asset is sold—no tax is levied. In effect, then, the tax on a capital gain is deferred until the gain is realized. The mere ability to postpone taxes may not seem all that important, but its consequences are enormous.[9] Consider Cassius, who purchases an asset for $100,000 that increases in value by 12 percent each year. After the first year, it is worth $100,000 × (1 + .12) = $112,000. After the second year, it is worth $112,000 (1 + .12) = $100,000 × (1 + .12)^2 = $125,440. Similarly, by the end of 20 years, it is worth $100,000 (1 + .12)^{20} = $964,629. If the asset is sold at the end of 20 years, Cassius realizes a capital gain of $864,629 (= $964,629 − $100,000). Assume that the tax rate applied to *realized* capital gains is 25 percent. Then Cassius' tax liability is $216,157 (= $864,629 × .25), and

---

[8] Note that the individual with the higher tax rate enjoys a greater increase in income due to the tax-exempt status of the state and local bonds. As we argued in Chapter 13, this is not necessarily a violation of horizontal equity.

[9] At this point, it may be useful to review the discussion of interest compounding from Chapter 9.

his net gain (measured in terms of dollars 20 years from now) is $648,472 (= $864,629 − $216,157).

Now assume that the 25 percent capital gains tax is levied *as the capital gains accrue,* regardless of whether they are realized. At the end of the first year, Cassius has $109,000 [= $100,000 × (1 + .09)]. (Remember, $3,000 of the $12,000 gained go to the tax collector.) Assuming that the $9,000 after-tax gain is reinvested in the asset, at the end of two years, Cassius has $109,000 (1 + .09) = $100,000 × $(1.09)^2$ = $118,810. Similarly, by the end of 20 years, he has $100,000 × $(1.09)^{20}$ = $560,441. Cassius' after-tax capital gain is $460,441 (= $560,441 − $100,000). Comparing this to the gain of $648,472 above makes clear that the seemingly innocent device of letting the gains accrue without tax makes a big difference. This is because the deferral allows the investment to grow geometrically at the before-tax rather than the after-tax rate of interest. In effect, the government gives the investor an interest-free loan on the taxes the investor has due.

It should now be clear why a favorite slogan among tax accountants is "taxes deferred are taxes saved." Many very complicated tax shelter plans are nothing more than devices for deferring payment of taxes.

Because only realized capital gains are subject to tax, taxpayers who are considering switching or selling capital assets must take into account that doing so will create a tax liability. As a consequence, they may be less likely to make changes in their portfolios. This phenomenon is referred to as the **lock-in effect,** because the tax system tends to lock investors into their current portfolios. There have been several econometric studies of the tax treatment of capital gains realizations. Auten and Clotfelter [1982] found that cuts in capital gains tax rates would significantly increase the realization of long-term capital gains.

Partial Exclusion of Realized Gains.   When a capital gain is realized, only 40 percent of its value is counted as income, provided that the asset has been held for at least 12 months. Capital gains on assets held this length of time are called **long-term capital gains. Short-term capital gains** are taxable at the same rates as ordinary income. The basis of this long/short distinction is the view that short-term capital gains are the fruit of "speculation," and speculation has harmful effects upon the economy. The evidence that speculation is destabilizing or otherwise bad is far from overwhelming, however, and many economists do not find this distinction very meaningful.[10]

Capital Losses.   Capital losses—decreases in the value of an asset— can be offset against capital gains. Suppose that Antony realizes a gain of $6,000 on asset A, but a loss of $2,000 on asset B. Then Antony is

---

[10] See, for example, Baumol and Blinder [1982, Chapters 24 and 38].

treated as if his capital gains are only $4,000. Moreover, 50 percent of capital losses in excess of capital gains (up to a limit of $3,000) can be subtracted from ordinary income. Suppose that in the example just given, asset B had lost $8,200. Then Antony could reduce his capital gains liability to zero and still have $2,200 in losses left over. He could subtract half of this amount, $1,100, from his ordinary income.

Death.   Capital gains are not taxed at death. Suppose Octavius purchases an asset for $1,000. During Octavius' lifetime, he never sells the asset, and at the time he dies, it is worth $1,200. Under U.S. law, the $200 capital gain is *not* subject to tax when Octavius dies. Moreover, when Octavius, Jr. (Octavius' heir) gets around to selling the asset, his computation of capital gains is made as if the purchase price were $1,200, not $1,000. In effect, then, capital gains on assets held to death of the owner are never taxed. Death and taxes may both be inevitable, but the former helps your heirs escape the latter.

Evaluation.   We conclude that in terms of the Haig-Simons criterion, the current tax treatment of capital gains is pretty much a disaster. The criterion requires that all capital gains be taxed, whether realized or unrealized. In fact, the tax system gets only at the realized gains, and these are taxed at 40 percent the rate of ordinary income. If the asset is held until death of the owner, capital gains escape taxation altogether. Neither does the optimal tax literature provide any justification for preferential treatment of this form of capital income.[11]

A number of rationalizations have been proposed for preferential treatment of capital gains. Some argue that capital gains are not regular income, but rather windfalls which occur unexpectedly. Fairness requires that such unexpected gains not create a tax liability. Moreover, because investing requires the sacrifice of abstaining from consumption, it is only fair to reward this sacrifice. However, it could just as well be asserted that *labor* income should be treated preferentially, because it involves the unpleasantness of work, while those who receive capital gains need only relax and wait for their money to flow in. Ultimately, it is impossible to argue convincingly that production of one source of income or another requires more "sacrifice" and should therefore be treated preferentially.

Another justification for preferential taxation of capital gains is that it is needed to stimulate capital accumulation and risk taking. In the next chapter, we deal at some length with the question of how taxation affects saving and risk-taking incentives. For now, we merely note that it is not at all clear that special treatment for capital gains does increase

---

[11] However, under certain conditions, optimal tax theory suggests that *no* forms of capital income should be taxed. See Chapter 17.

saving and risk taking. If the goal is to stimulate these activities, there are probably more efficient ways to do so.

Some promote preferential treatment of capital gains because it helps counterbalance the effects that inflation has on increasing the effective rate at which capital gains are taxed. As we shall see below, under existing tax rules, inflation does indeed produce an especially heavy burden upon capital income. But arbitrarily taxing capital gains at a different rate is not the best way to deal with this problem.

The fact that capital gains are taxed relatively lightly gives private investors incentives to put their money in assets with returns that come in the form of capital gains. Most economists agree that such distortions in the pattern of investment are undesirable and that capital gains should be taxed at the same rate as other forms of capital income such as interest and dividends. But there is considerable disagreement as to what this rate should be. Some argue that the tax system should be brought more into line with the Haig-Simons criterion. Realized capital gains should be taxed the same as ordinary income, and unrealized capital gains should be taxed at death of the owner. Others have argued that the situation would be improved if the tax rates on *all* capital income were set equal to zero. This controversial suggestion is discussed in Chapter 17.

Finally, it must be stressed that a full picture of the tax treatment of capital income requires taking into account that much of this income is generated by corporations, and corporations are subject to a separate tax system of their own. The overall rate of tax on capital income thus depends upon the personal *and* corporate rates. The effect of the corporation tax upon the return to capital is discussed in Chapter 16.

Two Hundred Dollars Worth of Dividends

Also contrary to the Haig-Simons criterion, husbands and wives who choose to be taxed on their joint incomes can exclude from taxation up to $200 of dividends. For those who file as individuals, the sum is $100. Neither Haig-Simons nor optimal tax criteria justify this exclusion. It simply represents a small bonus to people who happen to have dividend income. One possible justification is to encourage saving. Note, however, that for couples who already have more than $200 in dividends, there is no impetus to save *additional* amounts.

Employer Contributions to Pensions and Medical Insurance Plans

Income paid by an employer that is put into an employee's retirement fund is not subject to tax. Neither does the government tax the interest that accrues on the pension contributions over time. Only when the pension is paid out at retirement are the principal and interest subject to taxation. Similarly, employer contributions to medical insurance plans are not included in income.

As argued above, pensions and health insurance represent additions to potential consumption, and hence, should be counted as income according to the Haig-Simons criterion. Similarly, the interest on pension funds should be taxable as it accrues.

Workers can also engage in tax-favored pension saving for themselves. Using an **individual retirement account (IRA),** any worker can deposit up to $2,000 per year in a **qualified account.** (A qualified account includes most of the usual forms of saving: savings accounts, money market funds, etc.) A person with a spouse who does not engage in market work can deposit $2,250. The money so deposited is deductible from adjusted gross income. Just as in an employer-managed pension fund, the interest that accrues is untaxed. Tax is due only when the money is paid out at retirement.[12] In 1982, $28.4 billion were contributed to IRAs [Internal Revenue Service, 1984, p. 62].

Another type of retirement account, a **Keogh plan,**[13] is available only to self-employed individuals. As of 1983, such individuals could exclude from taxation 15 percent of their net business income (up to $15,000) if the money was deposited into a qualified account. Again, participants are allowed the powerful advantage of tax-free accrual of interest. In 1982, $2.5 billion were contributed to Keogh plans [Internal Revenue Service, 1984, p. 62].

IRAs and Keogh plans were introduced partly to give more people the option to accumulate retirement wealth in tax-favored funds. Part of the motivation was also to stimulate saving. However, it is not clear how aggregate saving will be affected. People may merely shuffle around their portfolios, reducing their holdings of some assets and depositing them into retirement accounts. It will be possible to assess the impact of such accounts only as experience accumulates. It is clear, however, that their existence represents another important departure from the H-S criterion.

Gifts and Inheritances

Despite the fact that gifts and inheritances represent increases in the beneficiaries' potential consumption, these items are not subject to the federal income tax. Instead, there are separate tax systems to cover gifts and estates. These are discussed in Chapter 18.

---

[12] Penalties are imposed if money is withdrawn early.

[13] Named after the member of Congress who proposed the idea.

EXEMPTIONS AND DEDUCTIONS

In terms of Figure 14.1, we have now completed the first step in the computation of income taxes, figuring adjusted gross income. Once adjusted gross income is determined, certain subtractions are made to find taxable income. The two principal types of subtractions are exemptions and deductions, which we discuss in turn.

Exemptions

Basically, a family is allowed an exemption of $1,000 for each of its members. For example, a husband and wife with three dependent children may claim five exemptions and subtract $5,000 from its AGI. Blind individuals receive an extra exemption, as do individuals who are 65 years of age or older. Consider a household where spouse I is 68 years old and blind, and spouse II is 62 years old and can see. Spouse I is entitled to three exemptions and spouse II to one, so the family as a whole can claim four.

Why are there exemptions? Some argue that they adjust ability to pay for the presence of children. Raising children involves certain nondiscretionary expenses, and taxable income should be adjusted accordingly. Others do not take the view of the personal exemption as a child allowance very seriously. As most parents will tell you, if the exemption is really there to compensate for the expenses of child rearing, $1,000 is much too little. Moreover, it is not clear why expenses involving children should be considered nondiscretionary in the first place. Given the wide availability of contraceptive methods, many would argue that raising children is undertaken as the result of conscious choice [see Becker and Lewis, 1973]. If one couple wishes to spend its money on European vacations while another chooses to raise a family, why should the tax system reward the latter?[14] On the other hand, the religions of certain people rule out contraception, and for them, children are not a "choice" as the term is conventionally defined.

Although exemptions are sometimes viewed as a kind of child allowance, it is also important to note their role as a method of providing tax relief for those at the bottom of the income scale. The higher the exemption, the greater adjusted gross income must be before *any* income tax is due. Consider a family of four with an AGI of $4,000 or less. When this family's $4,000 in exemptions is subtracted from AGI, the family is left

---

[14] If there are positive externalities involved in raising children, then a subsidy might be appropriate (see Chapter 7). Some would argue that because the world is overcrowded, additional children create negative externalities, and hence, should be *taxed*. In China, families with more than one child forfeit certain government benefits. In effect, this is a tax on children.

with zero taxable income, and hence, no tax liability. More generally, the greater is the exemption level, the greater will be the progressiveness with respect to average tax rates.

Deductions

The other type of subtraction allowed from AGI is a deduction. There are two kinds. **Itemized deductions** are subtractions for specific expenditures which are cited in the law. The taxpayer must list each item separately on the tax return and be able to prove (at least in principle) that the expenditures have been made. In lieu of itemizing deductions, the taxpayer can take a **standard deduction** (also referred to as the **zero-bracket amount**), which is a fixed amount for all taxpayers, and which does not require documentation. The taxpayer can choose whichever type of deduction minimizes his or her tax liability.

Digression: Deductibility and Relative Prices.   Before cataloging the expenditures that can be itemized, it is useful to consider the relationship between deductibility of expenditures on an item and its relative price. Suppose that expenditures on commodity Z are tax deductible. The price of Z is \$10 per unit. Suppose further that Cleopatra's marginal tax rate is 40 percent. Then, whenever Cleopatra purchases a unit of Z, it only costs her \$6. Why? Because expenditures on Z are deductible, purchasing a unit lowers Cleopatra's taxable income by \$10. Given a 40 percent marginal tax rate, \$10 less of taxable income saves Cleopatra \$4 in taxes. Hence, her effective price of a unit Z is \$10 minus \$4, or \$6.

More generally, if the price of Z is P_Z and the individual faces a marginal tax rate of t, then allowing deduction of expenses on Z lowers Z's effective price from P_Z to $(1 - t)P_Z$. This analysis brings out two important facts: (1) because deductibility changes the relative price of the commodity involved, in general, we expect the quantity demanded to change; and (2) the higher the individual's value of t, the greater the value to the individual of a given dollar amount of deductions and the lower the effective price of the good.[15]

Itemized Deductions.   We now discuss some of the major itemized deductions. The list is far from inclusive, and the tax code should be consulted for further details.

---

[15] Note that observations (1) and (2) apply more generally to expenditures on any items that are excluded from the tax base, not just deductions. For example, the value of excluding interest from municipal bonds increases with the marginal tax rate, other things being the same.

Unreimbursed Medical Expenses that Exceed 5 percent of AGI.   In 1981, a total of $15.5 billion in medical expenses were deducted.[16] The justification is that large medical expenses are nondiscretionary and therefore do not really contribute to an individual's ability to pay. It is hard to say to what extent health-care expenditures are under an individual's control. A person suffering a heart attack does not have much in the way of choice. On the other hand, individuals can choose how often to visit their doctors, whether to visit expensive or moderately priced practitioners, and whether or not to have elective surgery. Moreover, it may be possible for individuals to substitute preventive health care (good diet, exercise, etc.) for formal medical services.

Finally, insurance to pay for medical care can be obtained on the private market. Under typical private insurance plans, the first portion of medical expenses is met entirely by the insured, but after a point, some proportion is paid by the insurance company and the rest by the individual. In effect, by allowing deduction of some medical expenses, the tax system provides a kind of social health-care insurance. The terms of this "policy" are that the amount that the individual pays entirely on his own is 5 percent of AGI, and after that the treasury pays a share equal to the marginal tax rate. The pros and cons of providing social insurance were already discussed in Chapter 8.

State and Local Taxes.   These include state and local income taxes, real estate taxes, and general sales taxes.[17] Such payments, which accounted for $79.7 billion worth of deductions in 1981, are supposed to represent nondiscretionary decreases in ability to pay. The appropriateness of this deduction depends on the nature of state and local taxes. One view is that they are simply user fees. A person pays local taxes in return for locally provided benefits such as public schools, police protection, etc. Some people choose to live in communities which provide a lot of such services, and they pay relatively high amounts of tax; others opt for low-service, low-tax communities. To the extent this is an accurate description of reality, there is no particular reason to allow deductibility of state and local taxes. If some people want to purchase a lot of local public services while others choose to buy privately provided goods, why should the former receive a deduction?

On the other hand, if state and local taxes are not user fees, it may be appropriate to regard them as decreases in ability to pay.[18] Unfortu-

---

[16] At that time, expenses in excess of 3 percent of AGI were allowed. All figures on values of deductions in this section are from Internal Revenue Service [U.S. Department of the Treasury, 1983a, pp. 53–54].

[17] Certain state and local taxes are not deductible, including those on gasoline, liquor, and tobacco.

[18] But not necessarily! If the taxes are capitalized into the value of property, then the current owners may not be bearing any of their burden. See Chapter 11.

nately, it is very difficult to determine what proportion of state and local taxes are best viewed as user fees for public services.

This deduction can also be considered as a way to help state and local governments finance themselves. For people who itemize on their federal tax returns, deduction lowers the effective cost of state and local tax payments. Knowledge of this fact may increase the likelihood that people will support tax increases at the state and local levels. Why isn't a more direct method of subsidy used? As in the case of the interest exemption for state and local bonds, political considerations are an important part of the explanation. A subsidy hidden in the tax code may be easier to maintain than an explicit subsidy.

Interest Expenses.   Interest payments on business loans are deductible from taxable income. In addition, individuals can deduct interest payments on home mortgages, charge accounts, and installment contracts on personal property such as cars and televisions.[19] In the context of the Haig-Simons criterion, it is perfectly appropriate to deduct interest payments because they represent decreases in an individual's potential consumption. In 1981, $108.7 billion in interest deductions were taken, most of them for home mortgages.

The deductibility of interest together with the exemption of certain types of capital income from taxation can lead to lucrative opportunities for smart investors. Assume that Caesar, who has a 50 percent tax rate, can borrow all the money he wants from the bank at a rate of 16 percent. Given the tax deductibility of interest, for every dollar of interest paid, his tax bill is reduced by 50 cents. Hence, Caesar's effective borrowing rate is only 8 percent. Suppose that the going rate of return on tax-exempt state and local bonds is 9 percent. Then Caesar can borrow from the bank at 8 percent and lend to states and localities at 9 percent. The tax system appears to have created a "money machine" which can be cranked to generate infinite amounts of income. The process of taking advantage of such opportunities is referred to as **tax arbitrage.**

The example just given overstates the potential returns to tax arbitrage, because in real-world capital markets people cannot borrow arbitrarily large sums of money.[20] Still, opportunities for gain are clearly present. The tax authorities realized this many years ago and made it

---

[19] There is no limit on the amount of mortgage interest that can be deducted. Other forms of interest are limited to the sum of certain forms of property income plus $10,000. (See U.S. Department of the Treasury, Internal Revenue Service, Form 4952, *Investment Interest Expense Deductions.*)

[20] Moreover, there will be a tendency for competition among those who engage in tax arbitrage to reduce the return to that activity. For example, as more and more arbitrageurs buy municipal bonds, their rate of return will go down. If everyone had a 50 percent marginal tax rate, in equilibrium we would expect the return on municipals to fall until it was exactly one half the rate on taxable bonds. At that point, there would be no net advantage to owning municipals.

illegal to deduct interest from loans whose proceeds are used to purchase tax-exempt bonds. But it is not easy to prove that someone is breaking this rule. Given that money can be used for many different purposes, how can it be proved that a given amount of borrowing was "for" municipal bond purchases rather than for some other purpose?

This very simple "scam" illustrates some important general lessons:

1. Interest deductibility in conjunction with preferential treatment of certain kinds of capital income can create important money-making opportunities.
2. High-income individuals will be more likely than their low-income counterparts to benefit from these opportunities. This is because they tend to face higher tax rates, and to have better access to borrowing.
3. The tax authorities can certainly declare various tax arbitrage schemes to be illegal, but it is hard to enforce these rules. Moreover, clever lawyers and accountants are always on the lookout for new tax arbitrage opportunities.[21] The Internal Revenue Service is usually right behind them trying to plug the loopholes. In the process, many inefficient investments are made, and a lot of resources are spent on tax avoidance and tax administration.

Charitable Contributions.   Individuals can deduct the value of contributions made to religious, charitable, educational, scientific, or literary organizations. Gifts of property are deductible, but personal services are not. In most cases, total charitable deductions cannot exceed 50 percent of adjusted gross income. In 1981, individuals recorded charitable deductions of $30.8 billion.

Some argue that charitable donations constitute a reduction in taxable capacity, and hence, should be excluded from taxable income. However, as long as the contributions are made voluntarily, this argument is unconvincing. If people don't receive as much utility from charity as from their own consumption, why should they give to charity in the first place? Probably the best way to understand the presence of the deduction is as an attempt by the government to encourage charitable giving.

Has the deduction succeeded in doing so? The deductibility provision changes an individual's "price" for a dollar's worth of charity from $1 to $(1 - t)$, where t is his marginal tax rate. The effectiveness of the deduction as a means for encouraging giving therefore depends upon the price elasticity of demand for charitable contributions. If the price elasticity is zero, charitable giving is unaffected. In this case, the deduction is just a bonus for those who would give anyway. If the price elasticity exceeds zero, then giving is actually encouraged.

---

[21] For some complicated possibilities, see Stiglitz [1981].

A number of attempts have been made to estimate the elasticity of charitable giving with respect to its after-tax price. Typically, a regression is estimated in which the dependent variable is the amount of charitable donations, and the explanatory variables are: *(a)* the "price" of charitable donations (one minus the marginal tax rate); *(b)* income; and *(c)* personal characteristics of individuals that might influence their decisions to give, such as age and marital status. Several studies have suggested that the price elasticity of demand for donations exceeds one.[22] The implications of this result are striking. Consider an individual with a marginal tax rate of 30 percent. The deductibility of charitable donations lowers his price of giving from $1 to 70 cents, a reduction of 30 percent. If the elasticity exceeds one, he increases his charitable giving by *more* than 30 percent. Hence, charitable organizations gain more than the treasury loses.

Although there is disagreement with respect to the precise value of the elasticity, the consensus is that the demand for charitable contributions has been stimulated substantially by the deductibility provisions. This is not to say that the deduction is uncontroversial. Whether the government should be subsidizing gifts to private charities can be questioned. Some opponents point to the fact that allowing deduction of contributions to churches and synagogues constitutes a violation of the principle of separation of church and state.

Others object to the fact that the effective price reduction depends upon a person's marginal tax rate. Indeed, for those who don't itemize, until very recently, no deduction for charitable contributions was allowed at all. In 1981 special provisions for nonitemizers were introduced. For tax years 1982 and 1983, an individual who did not itemize was permitted to deduct 25 percent of his first $100 of annual charitable contribution, thus allowing a maximum of $25 each year. For years after 1983, the size of the deduction is set to increase until 1986, when it is scheduled to terminate.

The Standard Deduction (zero-bracket amount).   Itemized deductions are listed separately on the individual's tax return, and in principle each one requires documentation (such as receipts) to prove that the expenditure has indeed been made. All this record-keeping increases the administrative cost of the system. To simplify tax returns, the standard deduction was introduced in 1944. The standard deduction currently is a fixed amount available to all taxpayers. Each household can choose between taking the standard deduction or itemizing, depending on which offers the greater advantage. In 1982, about 65 percent of all returns filed used the standard deduction [Internal Revenue Service, 1984, p. 62].

Recently, the standard deduction was renamed the **zero-bracket**

---

[22] Clotfelter and Steuerle [1981] review these studies.

amount. This label draws attention to the fact that no tax is due for households whose incomes fall below it. Currently, the zero-bracket amount is $3,400 for spouses who file tax returns together, and $2,300 for people who file separately.

Deductions versus Credits.   As already noted, the higher an individual's marginal tax rate, the greater the value of a deduction of a given dollar amount. In contrast, a **tax credit** is a subtraction from the tax liability (*not* taxable income), and hence, its value is independent of the individual's marginal tax rate. A tax credit of $100 reduces an individual's tax liability by $100 whether his tax rate is 14 percent or 50 percent. Under current law, credits are allowed for certain child-care expenses, contributions to candidates for public office, installation of energy-saving items in personal residences, the use of alcohol fuel, and a number of other expenditures.[23]

Some argue that deductions and exemptions should be converted into credits. For example, the deduction of interest payments would be changed to a credit for some percentage of the value of interest paid. With a 20 percent interest credit, each individual could subtract from his tax bill an amount equal to one fifth of his interest payments. Proponents of credits argue that they are more fair than deductions. Under a regime of tax deductions, a poor person (with a low marginal tax rate) benefits less than a rich person (with a high marginal tax rate) even if they both have identical interest expenses. With a credit, the dollar benefit is the same.

The choice between deductions and credits should depend at least in part on the purpose of the exclusion. If the motivation is to correct for the fact that a given expenditure reduces ability to pay, then a deduction seems appropriate. If the purpose is mainly to encourage certain types of behavior, it is not at all clear whether credits or deductions are superior. A credit reduces the effective price of the favored good by the *same* percentage for all individuals; a deduction decreases the price by *different* percentages for different people. If people differ with respect to their elasticities of demand, it may make sense to present them with different effective prices. For example, it is ineffective to give *any* subsidy to someone whose elasticity of demand for the favored good is zero. The subsidy is "wasted" because it encourages no new demand. In this context it is interesting to note that Clotfelter and Steuerle [1981] estimated that the greater a household's income, the higher the price elasticity of demand for charitable donations. On the average, a given percentage decrease in price stimulates more charitable giving by a high- than a low-income household.

---

[23] For details, see U.S. Department of the Treasury, Internal Revenue Service, *1040 Federal Income Tax Forms and Instructions*, 1983.

Impact on the Tax Base.   To what extent has the presence of exemptions and deductions influenced the size of the tax base? In 1981, adjusted gross income was $1,773 billion dollars. After completing all the subtractions from AGI, taxable income was only $1,411 billion dollars, a reduction of about 20 percent.[24] As discussed below, a number of reforms have been proposed to reduce the amount of "erosion of the tax base."

Tax Expenditures

Failure to include a particular item in the tax base results in a loss to the treasury. Suppose that as a consequence of excluding item Z from the tax base, the treasury loses a billion dollars. Compare this to a situation in which the government simply hands over $1 billion of general revenues to those who purchase item Z. In a sense, these activities are equivalent as both subsidize purchases of item Z. It just so happens that one transaction takes place on the expenditure side of the account and the other on the revenue side. The former is a **tax expenditure,** defined in the Congressional Budget Act of 1974 as a revenue loss "attributable to provisions of the federal tax laws which allow a special exclusion, exemption, or deduction from gross income or which provide a special credit, a preferential rate of tax, or a deferral of tax liability" [Goode, 1977, p. 26]. The list of tax expenditures for 1984 had over 100 items. A few of the major ones are listed in Table 14.1. Some estimates of the total revenue loss from tax expenditures exceed $253.5 billion [Congressional Budget Office, 1982c, p. 61].

The law requires that an annual tax expenditure budget be compiled by the Congressional Budget Office. A major intent of the law was to

TABLE 14.1   Selected Tax Expenditure Items for Fiscal Year 1984 ($ millions of foregone taxes)*

Exclusion of pension contributions and earnings (employer plans)	$56,560
Partial exclusion of capital gains	14,320
Deductibility of mortgage interest on owner-occupied homes	27,945
Deductibility of property taxes on owner-occupied homes	9,535
Deductibility of medical expenses	2,630
Exclusion of social security benefits	22,210
Deductibility of charitable contributions (education)	840

* These are projections based on data available in 1983.
   Source: Congressional Budget Office, *Tax Expenditures: Current Issues and Five-Year Budget Projections for Fiscal Years 1984–1988* (Washington, D.C.: U.S. Government Printing Office, 1983), pp. 48–58.

---

[24] It should be recalled that AGI itself is substantially less than the amount of income that would be included with the Haig-Simons definition. When credits are taken into account, the reduction is much larger yet. See U.S. Department of the Treasury [1983a, p. 2].

raise public consciousness of the symmetry between a *direct* subsidy for an activity via an expenditure and an *implicit* subsidy through the tax system. However, the notion of a tax expenditure budget has been subject to several criticisms.

First, a serious technical problem arises in the way the computations are made. It is assumed that in the absence of a deduction for a given item, all the expenditures currently made on it would flow into taxable income. Given that people are quite likely to adjust their behavior in response to changes in the tax system, this is not a good assumption, so the tax expenditure estimates may be quite far off the mark.

Second, the tax expenditure budget is simply a list of items that are exempt from taxation. However, to characterize an item as "exempt," you must first have some kind of criterion for deciding what "ought" to be included. As we saw above, there exists no rigorous set of principles for determining what belongs in income. One person's "loophole" may be regarded by another as an appropriate adjustment of the tax base. Hence, considerable arbitrariness is inevitably involved in deciding what to include in the tax expenditure budget.

Finally, the concept of tax expenditures has been attacked on philosophical grounds:

> The tax expenditures concept implies that all income belongs of right to the government, and that what government decides, by exemption or qualification, not to collect in taxes constitutes a subsidy. This . . . violates a widely held conviction, basic to the American polity, that government is the servant and not the master of the people; and that the income earned by the people belongs to them, not the government. They agree, through their representatives, on what portion of their income they will pay as taxes, but income not paid in taxes is definitely not a subsidy from the government [Jones, 1978, p. 53].

Defenders of the tax expenditure concept have argued that the concept does not really carry these ideological implications. It is merely an attempt to force recognition of the fact that the tax system is a major method for subsidizing various activities. Moreover, the fact that the estimates are not exact does not mean that they are useless for assessing the implications of tax policy.

An assumption in much public debate is that when government subsidies are proper at all, they are best provided by direct government expenditure:

> Wouldn't it be more honest with the taxpayer to take [tax expenditures] out of hiding and put a price tag on them. . . . That way we know how much each social policy costs each year, and we are more inclined to curtail tax expenditures that presently go on and on, unexamined [Safire, 1982, p. A31].

However, Feldstein [1980] has pointed out that under certain conditions, a tax expenditure may be a more effective way for the government to stimulate a given activity than is a direct payment. Assume that the government wants to stimulate the activities of charitable organizations. One possible method is a tax expenditure. As noted above, if the price elasticity of demand for charitable donations exceeds 1, each dollar foregone by the treasury generates more than a dollar in charitable giving. Now suppose that instead, the government implements a direct subsidy using the funds which were previously foregone because of the charitable deduction. One possibility is that each government dollar spent on charity "crowds out" a private dollar—when citizens see public support for charity, they reduce their own. In this case, the government would have to spend *more* than the estimated revenue loss to provide the equivalent total expenditure on charity.

Of course, we do not expect that in most cases every dollar of public spending will replace exactly a dollar of private spending. Nor can it be assumed that the price elasticity of demand for each preferred item exceeds unity. But this simple example illustrates the basic point: In general, whether a tax expenditure or a direct subsidy is effective will depend upon the amount of crowding out that takes place, and on how responsive the demand for the preferred item is with respect to its after-tax price. It is an empirical question which must be answered on a case-by-case basis.

Calculation of the Tax Base: Administrative and Compliance Issues. We have seen that calculation of the tax base is no simple matter. Certain types of income are taxed at lower rates than others or excluded altogether. Similarly, certain types of expenditure receive favorable tax treatment. All of these special cases are bound to create administrative complexities, because rules must be made to determine just what items qualify, how taxpayers must document that they qualify, and where on the tax return these items must be recorded.

In 1983, the set of instructions for filing the basic personal tax return (Form 1040) was 52 pages long. There were 25 possible schedules to fill out. As noted in Chapter 13, the costs of dealing with this complexity are probably high, but difficult to estimate. As the poem by Russell Baker indicates, the tax system has become for many a bad joke. Later we will discuss some proposals that have been made for simplification.

Ode to the I.R.S.*

I've got this form here.
It's called Ten Forty.
It's the long form, not the shorty.
The long form's for the sporty
and it comes with Schedule E.

I love a schedule. I'm so precise.
That's why I think the I.R.S. is nice.
To offer Schedule E
—how much sweeter could they be?
But not just Schedule E

* By Russell Baker. *The New York Times Magazine*, April 8, 1984, page 24. Copyright © 1984 by The New York Times Company. Reprinted by permission.

—Schedules A, B, C, and D!
It makes me wish that I could pay
  them twice.

Here's W-2. Oh, how they'll love it.
It'll give them something more to
  covet.
Last year, it shows, they left me
  dough for beer.
I'm sorry about those suds.
If they don't take my duds this year
I'll rise above it.

And yes, yes, here's 1040 ES. It requires you to guess,
1040 ES, and guessing I hate.
"Come press your fate,"
says 1040 ES. "Come, estimate."

I guess what I'll owe next year.
It can be amended later if you've got
  the proper form.
They seldom jail you if the guess is
  warm,
I guess. And the proper form
must be somewhere here.

Let's see: I've got depreciation and
  sworn declaration.
I've got wage estimation and amortization.
What I'd like to have and haven't got
is Alternative Minimum Tax Computation.
No, they said, you are not
permitted Alternative Minimum Tax
  Computation
unless you are very, very rich.

Why does a man with Form Ten Forty
  long;
a man entitled to Schedules A, B, C, D
  and E;
a man who has W-2 and 1040 ES,
a man with access to depreciation,
sworn declaration,
wage estimation,
wage amendment estimation
and amortization
—why does such a man want Alternative Minimum Tax Computation?

Because then they'd give me Form
  6251 to attach.
I love attaching. It's such a gas.
And attaching Form 6251 has so much
  class.
I'll tell you why: It can be attached to
  Form 990 T.
Alas for you and me, chances are we'll
  die and never know the pleasure of
  attaching to Nine-nine-zero T.

Thank God for Cuomo* good Mario
  Cuomo,
and jolly Mayor Koch* of high Manhattan.
Their tax forms on my desk out-top
  the Duomo
and I batten
with delight upon the skill with which
  they fatten
on the man who loves attaching
until he's sealed in thatching
made of forms he's been attaching,
attaching night and day, forevermore.
Quoth the Cuomo, "Attach some
  more."

* *Author's note:* Cuomo is the governor of New York, and Koch is mayor of New York City. Baker is referring here to his state and city income tax problems. In New York State, the maximum marginal income tax rate is 14 percent; for New York City, the figure is 4.3 percent.

RATE STRUCTURE

Basic Description

We have now arrived at the third step in Figure 14.1, calculating the amount of tax that must be paid on a given amount of taxable income. Under U.S. law, a bracket system is used to define tax rates. The income scale is divided into segments, and the law specifies the tax rate that applies to income on that segment. Actually, there are four different rate schedules, one each for married couples who file together (joint returns), married people who file separately, unmarried people, and single people who are "heads of households." (A head of household maintains a home which includes a dependent.) Table 14.2 shows the 1984 tax schedule for married individuals who file joint returns.

TABLE 14.2   Tax Rate Schedule for Married Individuals
Filing Joint Returns (1984)

Taxable Income	Marginal Tax Rate (percent)
$ 0– 3,400	0%
3,400– 5,500	11
5,500– 7,600	12
7,600– 11,900	14
11,900– 16,000	16
16,000– 20,200	18
20,200– 24,600	22
24,600– 29,900	25
29,900– 35,200	28
35,200– 45,800	33
45,800– 60,000	38
60,000– 85,600	42
85,600–109,400	45
109,400–162,400	49
162,400–	50

Source: Computed from Pub. L. 97-34 (August 31, 1981), Economic Recovery Tax Act of 1981, 95 Stat. 172.

Consider the Smiths, whose joint taxable income is $8,000. They pay no tax on their first $3,400; 11 percent on each dollar between $3,400 and $5,500 ($231); 12 percent on each dollar between $5,500 and $7,600 ($252); and 14 percent on each of the $400 in excess of $7,600 ($56). Their total tax liability is therefore $539 (= $231 + $252 + $56). The Smiths' *marginal* tax rate is 14 percent. The *average* tax rate with respect to taxable income is 6.7 percent (= $539/$8,000).

Averaging.   The fact that marginal tax rates increase with income can lead to difficulties when people's incomes are highly variable over time. Consider two households, one which has a taxable income of $30,000 in each of two successive years, and the other which has taxable income of $10,000 the first year, and $50,000 the second. Using Table 14.2, the tax liability of the first family over the two-year period is $9,636 and that of the second is $12,199. Thus, the tax burdens are quite different even though for the two-year period as a whole, the taxable capacities of the families are very similar.[25] More generally, under a tax system with increasing marginal tax rates, families with uneven income streams tend to pay more tax than those with steady streams. To mitigate this effect, the tax allows for **income averaging.** The actual procedure is too complicated to summarize in a simple formula.[26] Basically, it permits a tax reduction for a household whose income in a given year is considerably higher than its average income over the previous four years.

Trends in Tax Rates over Time

Table 14.2 demonstrates that the statutory tax rates on high incomes are quite substantial. It is often hard for people to comprehend how low income tax rates used to be. When the federal income tax was introduced in 1913, the bracket rates ranged from 1 percent to 7 percent. As late as 1939, half the taxpayers faced marginal rates below 4 percent. With the advent of World War II, rates went up substantially. By 1945, the lowest bracket rate was 23 percent, and the highest 94 percent.

There is widespread belief that tax rates increased substantially during the 1960s and 1970s. However, because of the bracket system, at any given time different marginal tax rates apply to different levels of income. It is therefore possible for tax rates on some ranges of income to increase from one year to another, while those on another range decrease. Thus, there exists no neat and comprehensive way to characterize how tax rates change from year to year. One simple measure is the average value of the marginal tax rate. According to Barro and Sahasakul [1983], in 1961 this figure was 17.2 percent, and in 1980, 20.0 percent.

Another informative measure is the fraction of the number of returns whose marginal rate exceeded some relatively high figure. Barro and Sahasakul compute that in 1961 only 1.2 percent of the returns had marginal tax rates exceeding 35 percent, while in 1980, the comparable figure was 10.1 percent. By these measures, at least, tax rates rose between 1961 and 1980. Although comparable calculations have not yet been done for subsequent years, there is evidence that the tax reductions implemented at the beginning of the Reagan administration reduced somewhat the percentage of households subject to relatively high marginal tax rates. [See Clotfelter, 1984, p. 150.]

Rates for Low Income Individuals

Every household is allowed to subtract from income its exemptions (roughly equal in value to the number of household members times

---

[25] They are not identical because their present values are not the same (see Chapter 9). This consideration is minor in the present context, and will be ignored in the rest of this discussion.

[26] For details, see Department of the Treasury, Internal Revenue Service, *Individual Income Tax Return, Form 1040, Schedule G.*

$1,000) and a standard deduction (zero-bracket amount) of $3,400 for husbands and wives who file together, and $2,300 for individuals who file separately.[27] Therefore, a family of four with an adjusted gross income under $7,400 has no tax liability at all. Obviously, families with a larger number of exemptions can earn larger incomes and still be subject to a zero average tax rate.

In addition, low income families with dependents benefit from the **earned income credit.** A tax credit equal to 10 percent of all wage and salary income up to $5,000 is allowed.[28] To help guarantee that only the poor benefit from the credit, it is reduced by 10 percent of adjusted gross income in excess of $5,000. For example, an individual with $5,000 of earnings and an AGI of $7,500 would be entitled to a credit of $250. If the credit exceeds the tax liability, then the difference is refunded. Thus, some very low income households actually have negative income tax liabilities.

The combination of exemptions, the standard deduction, and the earned income credit has succeeded fairly well in sheltering the very poor from the personal income tax. Over the years, the tax-exempt levels for a family of four have tended to coincide quite closely with official government poverty levels [Steuerle and Hartzmark, 1981].

Rates for High Income Individuals

As noted earlier, certain types of income' such as capital gains are treated preferentially by the tax system. It is therefore possible for some households to have rather high incomes, yet pay little or no tax. The **minimum tax,** introduced in 1969, is an attempt to ensure that people who benefit from some of these preferences pay at least some tax. The calculation for the minimum tax requires taking AGI and adding to it some of the income not taxed at ordinary rates.[29] For example, the deduction for capital gains and the dividend exclusion must be added back in. Then certain deductions are permitted, but on a more limited basis than under the ordinary tax. Next, an exemption is provided—$30,000 can be subtracted for individuals, and $40,000 for married couples. The remainder is subject to the minimum tax rate of 20 percent. When this amount is less than the individual's ordinary income tax, the ordinary income tax is paid. Otherwise, the minimum tax is paid.

Clearly, the minimum tax is an ad hoc method for adjusting the tax

---

[27] More precisely, the rate schedule is set so that the tax due on the first $3,400 for joint returns is zero. See Table 14.2.

[28] The earned income tax credit does not apply to capital income.

[29] More precisely, there are *two* minimum taxes. The one described in this paragraph is the *alternative minimum tax.* The other is called the *add-on minimum tax,* which is a 15 percent tax levied on certain preference items (after various deductions are subtracted).

burdens of upper income individuals. Its presence is another demonstration of the general lack of coherence in the tax system's design.

Effective Tax Rates and the Theory of Taxation: A Reminder

At this point it is important to recall the distinction between statutory and effective tax rates. In this section, we have been discussing the former, the legal rates established by the law. In general, there will differ from effective tax rates for at least three reasons.

First, because the tax system treats certain types of income preferentially, taxable income may be considerably lower than some more comprehensive measures of income. The fact that tax rates rise rapidly with *taxable* income does not by itself tell us much about how taxes vary with "actual" income.

Second, even in the absence of loopholes, the link between statutory and effective tax rates is weak. As was emphasized in Chapter 11, taxes can be shifted, so there is no reason to believe that income taxes will really be borne by the people who pay the money to the government. The economic incidence of the income tax is determined by the market responses when the tax is levied, and there is still considerable uncertainty as to the true pattern of the burden.

Finally, the tax system imposes decreases in utility that exceed revenue collections. Excess burdens arise because taxes distort behavior away from patterns that otherwise would have occurred (see Chapter 12). Similarly, the costs of compliance with the tax code, in terms of taxpayers' own time as well as explicit payments to accountants and lawyers, must be taken into account.

In this connection it is important to note that, contrary to the impression sometimes received in popular discussions, the existence of items like tax-exempt bonds does not, in general, allow the rich to entirely "escape" the burden of taxation. Consider again Caesar, whose marginal tax rate is 50 percent, and who can buy taxable assets which pay a return of 16 percent. Suppose that the going rate on municipal bonds is 9 percent. We expect that other things being the same, Caesar will buy municipals because their 9 percent return exceeds the after-tax return of 8 percent on taxable securities. To be sure, Caesar pays no tax. But the tax system has nevertheless made him worse off, because in its absence, he would have been able to make a return of 16 percent. In general, there is a tendency for the rate of return on tax-preferenced items to fall by an amount which reflects the tax advantage. Galper and Toder [1982] estimate that because of this tendency, the *effective* tax rate on capital income actually increases with an individual's income, despite the availability of tax-preferred assets.

Thus, examination of statutory rates alone probably tells us little about the progressiveness of the current system. Conceivably, a statute with lower marginal tax rates but a broader base would lead to a system with incidence as progressive as that of the current system, and perhaps even more so.[30] At the same time, a system with lower marginal tax rates would reduce excess burden and perhaps lower tax evasion. Such considerations have prompted a number of proposals to restructure the income tax dramatically. One plan that has received a lot of public attention is called the **flat tax.** A flat tax has two attributes: (1) it applies the same rate of tax to everyone and to each component of the tax base; and (2) to arrive at the tax base, there are no deductions from total income except personal exemptions and strictly defined business expenses.[31]

Assuming that a certain amount of tax revenue must be collected, under a flat tax, the key trade-off is between the size of the personal exemption and the marginal tax rate. A higher exemption may be desirable to secure relief for those at the bottom of the income schedule and to increase progressiveness (with respect to average tax rates.) But a higher exemption means that a higher marginal tax rate must be applied to maintain revenues.[32] According to one calculation, a tax rate of 19 percent together with a personal exemption of $6,200 for a married couple filing jointly and $3,800 for single taxpayers, would have satisfied the revenue requirements in 1982.[33]

Proponents of the flat tax claim that lowering marginal tax rates would reduce both the excess burden of the tax system and the incentive to cheat. Moreover, the simplicity gained would cut down on administrative costs and improve taxpayer morale. And all of this could be achieved without a serious cost in terms of equity because, as just noted, the flat tax can be made as progressive as desired by suitable choice of the exemption level.

Opponents of the flat tax believe that it will probably redistribute more of the tax burden from the rich to the middle classes. It is hard to evaluate this claim because of the usual difficulties involved in doing tax incidence analysis (Chapter 11). Critics also note that the whole range of conceptual and administrative problems involved in defining income will not disappear merely by declaring that business expenses are to be strictly defined. There will *never* be a simple tax code.

Claims of perfection for a flat tax must certainly be taken with a grain of salt. But perfection is not a useful criterion for evaluating real-world

---

[30] This, of course, does not mean that the current system *should* be more progressive. For a discussion of the determinants of optimal tax progressiveness, see Chapter 13.

[31] In essence, then, a flat tax is just a linear income tax, as defined in Chapter 13.

[32] This assumes that at such tax rates, increasing marginal rates will increase tax revenues, an assumption consistent with empirical evidence. (See Chapter 15.)

[33] See Hall and Rabushka [1983].

policies. Proposals that attempt to simplify the current system deserve serious consideration.

CHOICE OF UNIT[34]

We have discussed at length problems that arise in defining "income" for taxation purposes. Yet, even very careful definitions of income give little guidance with respect to choosing *who* should be taxed on the income. Should each person be taxed separately on his or her own income? Or should individuals who live together in a family unit be taxed on their joint incomes? Public debate of this question has been intense. In this section, we discuss some of the issues surrounding the controversy.

Background

To begin our discussion, it is useful to consider the following three propositions:

1. The income tax should involve increasing marginal tax rates.
2. Families with equal incomes should, other things being the same, pay equal taxes.
3. Two individuals' tax burdens should not change when they marry; the tax system should be **marriage neutral.**

Although a certain amount of controversy surrounds these propositions (particularly the first), it is probably fair to say that they reflect a broad consensus as to desirable features of a tax system.

Despite the appeal of these principles, a problem arises when it comes to implementing them: In general, no tax system can adhere to all three simultaneously. This point is made most easily with an arithmetic example. Assume the existence of the following simple progressive tax schedule: a taxable unit pays in tax 10 percent of all income up to $6,000, and 50 percent of all income in excess of $6,000. The first two columns of Table 14.3 show the incomes and tax liabilities of four individuals, Lucy,

TABLE 14.3   Tax Liabilities under a Hypothetical Tax System

	Individual Income	Individual Tax	Family Tax with Individual Filing	Joint Income	Joint Tax
Lucy	$ 1,000	$ 100 ⎫	$12,200	$30,000	$12,600
Ricky	29,000	12,100 ⎭			
Ethel	15,000	5,100 ⎫	10,200	30,000	12,600
Fred	15,000	5,100 ⎭			

---

[34] Much of this discussion is based upon Rosen [1977].

Ricky, Fred, and Ethel. (For example, Ricky's tax liability is $12,100 (= .10 × $6,000 + .50 × $23,000).) Now assume that romances develop—Lucy marries Ricky, and Ethel married Fred. In the absence of joint filing, the tax liability of each individual is unchanged. However, two families with the same income ($30,000) will be paying different amounts of tax. (The Lucy-Ricky's pay $12,200 while the Ethel-Fred's pay only $10,200, as noted in the third column.) Suppose instead that the law views the family as the taxable unit, so that the tax schedule applies to joint income. In this case, the two families pay equal amounts of tax, but now tax burdens have been changed by marriage. Of course, the actual change in the tax burden depends upon the difference between the tax schedules applied to individual and joint returns. This example has assumed for simplicity that the schedule remains unchanged. But it does make the main point: given increasing marginal tax rates, we cannot have both (2) and (3).

What choice has the United States made? Over time, it has changed.[35] Prior to 1948, the taxable unit was the individual, and principle (2) was violated. In 1948, **income splitting** was introduced. Under income splitting, a family with an income of $50,000 is taxed as if it were two individuals with incomes of $25,000. Clearly, with increasing marginal tax rates, this can be a major advantage. Note also that under such a regime, an unmarried person with a given income will find his or her tax liability reduced substantially if he or she marries a person with little or no income. Indeed, under the 1948 law, it was possible for an individual's tax liability to fall drastically when the person married—a violation of principle (3).

The differential between a single person's tax liability and that of a married couple with the same income was so large that Congress created a new schedule for unmarried people in 1969. Under this schedule, a single person's tax liability could never be more than 20 percent higher than the tax liability of a married couple with the same taxable income. (Under the old regime, differentials of up to 40 percent were possible.)

Unfortunately, this decrease in the single/married differential was purchased at the price of a violation of principle (3) in the opposite direction: in many cases it was now possible for persons' tax liabilities to increase when they married. In effect, the personal income tax levied a tax upon marriage. In 1981, Congress attempted to reduce the "marriage tax" by introducing a new deduction for two-earner married couples. Two-earner families now receive a deduction equal to 10 percent of the lower earning spouse's wage income, but no more than $3,000. The effect of this change is not major. For a two-earner family in the 50 percent bracket, the most this deduction can possibly be worth is $1,500 a year. Table 14.4 shows some estimates of the "marriage tax" for 1983.

---

[35] For a comprehensive history of the tax treatment of the family, see Bittker [1975].

TABLE 14.4   The "Marriage Tax" by Adjusted Gross Income of Each Spouse (estimates for 1983)

Husband's Income	Wife's Income				
	$0–5,000	$5–10,000	$10–20,000	$20–30,000	$30,000+
$ 0–10,000	$ −22	$ 169	$ −89	$−471	$−871
10–20,000	−298	255	331	598	702
20–30,000	−754	139	474	1,050	1,690
30–40,000	−1,270	−8	627	1,460	2,300
40–50,000	−1,730	7	1,120	2,550	2,650
50,000+	−3,240	−1,250	209	1,300	2,980

Source: Daniel Feenberg, *The Tax Treatment of Married Couples under the 1981 Tax Law*, National Bureau of Economic Research, Working Paper no. 872, April 1982, p. 14.

Negative entries indicate that taxes go down with marriage (a "tax dowry"); other entries indicate that taxes increase. The table indicates that a substantial marriage penalty still exists for many, and that it tends to be highest when both spouses have similar earnings. On the other hand, when there are considerable differences in their earnings, the tax code provides a bonus for marriage.

Analysis of the Marriage Tax

The economist surveying this scene is likely to ask the usual two questions—is it equitable and is it efficient? Much of the public debate focuses on the equity issue: is it fairer to tax individuals or families? One argument favoring the family as the choice is that it allows a more fair treatment of nonlabor income (dividends, interest, profits). There are fears that with individual filing, high-earnings spouses would transfer property to their mates to lower family tax bills *(bedchamber transfers of property)*. It is difficult to predict whether or not this would occur on a massive scale. The view implicit in these fears is that property rights within families are irrelevant.[36] However, given current high rates of divorce, turning property over to a spouse just for tax purposes may be a risky strategy, and there is no strong evidence that such transfers would occur in massive amounts.

The family can also be defended as the appropriate unit of taxation on a more philosophical level:

> [T]he family is today, as it has been for many centuries, the basic economic unit in society. . . . Taxation of the individual in . . . disregard of his inevitably close financial and economic ties with the other members of the

[36] Moreover, it is not obvious that lowering the effective rate of tax on capital income would be a bad thing. It depends upon the considerations raised in Chapter 13.

basic social unit of which he is ordinarily a member, the family, is in our view [a] striking instance of [a] lack of a comprehensive and rational pattern in . . . [a] tax system [*Report of the Royal Commission*, 1966, pp. 122–23].

The case for the family unit is not as compelling as the quotation suggests. Bittker [1975, p. 1398] argued

If married couples are taxed on their consolidated income, for example, should the same principle extend to a child who supports an aged parent, two sisters who share an apartment, or a divorced parent who lives with an adolescent child? Should a relationship established by blood or marriage be demanded, to the exclusion, for example, of unmarried persons who live together, homosexual companions, and communes?

Clearly, beliefs concerning the choice of the fairest taxable unit will be influenced by value judgments and by attitudes toward the role of the family in society. The debate continues to be lively.

When we turn to the efficiency aspects of the problem, the question is whether the marriage tax distorts individuals' behavior. As far as marriage decisions go, it is hard to construct a very strong case against the current law on efficiency grounds. Although the tax system changes the "price of marriage," there is no statistical evidence that this has distorted people's decisions to marry. However, anecdotes about postponed marriage, divorce, or separation for tax reasons are becoming common. Couples are increasingly asking why if corporations can merge and diverge strictly for tax benefits, couples should be treated any differently?

An efficiency concern that is easier to document surrounds the impact of joint filing upon labor supply decisions. It was shown in Chapter 13 that because married women tend to have more elastic labor supply schedules than their husbands, efficient taxation requires taxing wives at a relatively lower rate. Under joint filing, both spouses face identical marginal tax rates upon their last dollars of income. Hence, joint filing is inefficient.

It is hard to imagine Congress implementing separate income tax schedules for wives and husbands. This does not mean, however, that it is impossible to move family taxation in the direction of greater efficiency. One possible reform would be simply to eliminate joint filing and have all people file as individuals. This would not only enhance efficiency, but it would produce more marriage neutrality than under the current system.

Unfortunately, individual filing would lead to a violation of principle (2): equal taxation of families with equal income. This brings us back to where we started. No tax system can satisfy all three criteria, so society must decide which have the highest priority.

TAXES AND INFLATION

Lenin is alleged to have said, "The way to crush the bourgeoisie is to grind them between the millstones of taxation and inflation." Although the interaction of taxes and inflation in the United States has not created quite such drastic effects, there is widespread agreement that it has produced serious distortions. In economics, it is customary to distinguish between "anticipated" and "unanticipated" inflation. The latter is generally viewed as being much more detrimental to efficiency, because it does not allow people to adjust their behavior optimally to price level changes. In this section, we show that in the presence of an income tax system of the kind that exists in the United States, even perfectly anticipated inflation causes distortions. Some methods for eliminating these distortions are also discussed.

How Inflation Affects Taxes

The most popularly understood way in which inflation affects taxes is the phenomenon known as **bracket creep.** Suppose that an individual's earnings and the price level both increase at the same rate over time. Then his **real income** (the amount of actual purchasing power) is unchanged. However, the tax system is based upon the individual's **nominal income**—the number of dollars he receives.[37] As nominal income increases, the individual is pushed into tax brackets with higher marginal tax rates. Hence, the proportion of income that is taxed increases despite the fact that real income stays the same. Even individuals who are not pushed into a higher bracket find more of their incomes taxed at the highest rate to which they are subject. In effect, then, inflation brings about an automatic increase in the real tax burden without any legislative action.

Another effect of inflation occurs because exemptions and the standard deduction are set in nominal terms. Hence, increases in the price level decrease their real value. Again, the effective tax rate increases as a consequence of inflation.

The Congressional Budget Office [1980] estimated the effect of inflation upon the tax burdens of several hypothetical taxpayers. Tax liabilities for the year 1980 were calculated before and after a 13.3 percent inflation rate. (This was the rate being predicted for 1980.) The results are shown in Table 14.5. Note that for both low and high income taxpayers, the percentage increase in tax liabilities exceeds the inflation rate—real tax burdens rise for all. However, the magnitude of the increase differs across individuals, indicating that inflation acts to redistribute real income.

---

[37] At least this is the case until 1985. See below.

TABLE 14.5 Inflation and Tax Liability for Some Hypothetical Taxpayers: 1980 (joint return with two dependents)

Adjusted Gross Income	Current Tax	Tax after 13.3 Percent Inflation	Tax Increase as a Percent of Original Tax Liability	Percent of Decrease in Real After-Tax Income
$ 10,000	$ 374	$ 587	57.0%	1.5%
15,000	1,233	1,527	23.8	0.8
25,000	2,901	3,556	22.6	1.1
50,000	9,323	11,525	23.6	2.1
100,000	27,714	32,732	18.1	1.6

Source: Congressional Budget Office, *Indexing the Individual Tax* (Washington, D.C.: U.S. Government Printing Office, 1980), p. 6.

As usual, the particular estimates are based on fairly restrictive assumptions and may not be exactly correct. But the main qualitative result is almost certainly true—because of bracket creep, inflation increases real tax liabilities and induces capricious changes in the distribution of income.

It turns out, however, that even with a simple proportional income tax without exemptions, deductions, or increasing bracket rates, inflation would distort tax burdens. To be sure, under such a system, general inflation would not affect the real tax burden on wage and salary incomes. If a worker's earnings during a year doubled, so would his taxes, and there would be no real effects. But inflation would change the real tax burden on *capital* income.

Suppose Calpurnia buys an asset for $5,000. Three years later, she sells it for $10,000. Suppose further that during the three years, the general price level doubled. In real terms, the change in Calpurnia's income is zero. However, capital gains liabilities are based on the difference between the *nominal* selling and buying prices. Hence, Calpurnia incurs a tax liability on $5,000 of illusory capital gains. In short, because the inflationary component of capital gains is subject to tax, the real tax burden depends upon the inflation rate.

Given the magnitudes of historical inflation rates, this phenomenon is quite important as an empirical matter. Feldstein and Slemrod [1978] found that in 1973, individuals paid tax on $4.6 billion of capital gains on corporate stocks. However, when the prices of these securities at sale are corrected for increases in the general price level since the time they were purchased, the $4.6 billion gain turned out to be a real *loss* of nearly $1 billion.

Those who receive taxable interest income are similarly affected. Suppose that the **nominal interest rate** (the rate observed in the market) is 16 percent. Suppose further that the anticipated rate of inflation is 12 percent. Then for someone who lends at the 16 percent nominal rate, the

real interest rate is only 4 percent, because that is the percentage by which the lender's real purchasing power is increased. However, taxes are levied on nominal, not real, interest payments. Hence, tax must be paid on receipts which represent no gain in real income.

It is useful to consider this argument from an algebraic point of view. Call the nominal interest rate i_n. Then the after-tax nominal return to lending for an individual with a marginal tax rate of t is $(1 - t)i_n$. To find the *real* after-tax rate of return, we must subtract the expected rate of inflation, $\dot{p}$. Hence, the real after-tax rate of return i, is

(14.1) $$i = (1 - t)i_n - \dot{p}$$

Suppose $t = .25$, $i_n = 16$ percent, and $\dot{p} = 10$ percent. Then although the **nominal interest rate is 16 percent, the real after-tax return is only 2 percent.**[38]

Now suppose that any increase in the expected rate of inflation increases the nominal interest rate by the same amount; if inflation increases by four points, the nominal interest rate increases by four points.[39] It might be expected that the two increases would cancel out, leaving the real after-tax rate of return unchanged at 2 percent. But Equation (14.1) indicates that this is not so. If $\dot{p}$ goes from 10 percent to 14 percent and i_n goes from 16 percent to 20 percent, then with t equal to 0.25, i decreases to 1 percent. Inflation, even though it is perfectly anticipated, is not "neutral." This is a direct consequence of the fact that nominal rather than real interest payments are taxed.

So far we have been considering the issue from the point of view of lenders. Things are just the opposite for borrowers. In the absence of the tax system, the real rate paid by borrowers is the nominal rate minus the anticipated inflation rate. However, the tax law allows deductibility of nominal interest payments from taxable income. Thus, debtors can subtract from taxable income payments that represent no decrease in their real incomes. The tax burden on borrowers is decreased by inflation.

Coping with the Tax/Inflation Problem

Inflation leads to unlegislated increases in the real burden of the income tax. Historically, these effects have been mitigated by a series of ad hoc reductions in statutory rates. Such tax cuts were enacted in 1969, 1971, 1975, 1976, 1977, and 1981. These ad hoc adjustments have been partially successful in undoing some effects of inflation [see Aaron, 1976, p. 21].

---

[38] In the 1970s it was common for people to earn *negative* real rates of return even before tax—the inflation rate exceeded their nominal before-tax rate of return.

[39] There is some controversy as to whether this proposition holds exactly, but it is a useful approximation for our purposes. See Tanzi [1980].

Nevertheless, a number of legislators and academics view this process unfavorably. Each tax cut offsets inflation only for a short time. After a while, it becomes necessary to make changes all over again. The whole business has tended to increase public cynicism about the tax-setting process. Many citizens have learned that the tax "reductions" about which their legislators boast are nothing of the kind when measured in *real* terms.

An alternative to ad hoc adjustments would be to *index* the tax system. The idea of indexing is to legislate a formula which *automatically* removes the influence of inflation from real tax liabilities.[40] Indexing is already an important feature of many contracts throughout the economy. For example, social security benefits are indexed. So are many wage and business contracts in the private sector.

A number of technical issues must be settled to index the tax system.[41] The most difficult question is just which tax provisions should be adjusted. The more provisions adjusted, the more immune the system becomes to inflation, but the greater its administrative complexity. It would be relatively straightforward to index bracket widths so that as prices increased, the brackets would increase by the same percentage. This would end bracket creep. Similarly, indexing the size of personal exemptions and the zero bracket amount would be easy. On the other hand, dealing with the problems of measuring capital income would be difficult. For example, as suggested above, increases in inflation generate real gains for debtors, because the real value of the amounts they have to repay decreases. In a fully indexed system, such capital gains would have to be measured and taxed, a task that would certainly be complex.

There is considerable controversy over the desirability of indexing.[42] Opponents emphasize the administrative difficulties involved in developing adequate measures of real capital income.[43] They also argue that the system of periodic ad hoc adjustments is a good thing because it allows the legislature to examine and revise other aspects of the tax code

---

[40] Indexing is an important part of the tax systems of such countries as Chile and Brazil which have experienced chronic inflation at high rates.

[41] See Congressional Budget Office [1980] for further details.

[42] See, for example, Pechman [1982].

[43] We have been dealing with this debate from a microeconomic standpoint. There is also considerable disagreement about the macroeconomic consequences of indexing. Opponents argue that it would remove an important tool for conducting macroeconomic policy. For example, if more fiscal restraint is needed during an inflationary period, this is *automatically* generated by increases in tax revenues. In contrast, voting tax increases and/or expenditure cuts takes time. On the other hand, indexing proponents argue that the automatic rise in federal revenues may simply encourage legislators to spend more, and hence have no stabilizing effect. Indeed, they argue that a nonindexed system creates incentives for legislators to pursue inflationary policies, because these policies tend to increase the real quantity of resources available to the public sector.

that may need changing. Proponents of indexing argue that reducing the opportunities for revising the tax code may itself be a benefit, because it is desirable to have a stable and predictable tax law. Moreover, fewer opportunities to change the law also mean fewer chances for legislative mischief. Certainly the most important argument of those who favor indexing is that it would eliminate unlegislated increases in real tax rates. They believe that allowing the real tax schedule to be changed systematically by a nonlegislative process is antithetical to democratic values.

With legislation passed in 1981, the United States made its first move toward a system of indexing. Beginning in 1984 (with respect to 1985 taxes), the tax rate schedule will be widened annually to prevent bracket creep. The percentage change in the brackets will be determined by the change in the consumer price index. In addition, the $1,000 personal exemption will also be subject to adjustments for indexing. It remains to be seen whether this experiment in indexing will be successful, and whether the role of indexing will be expanded.[44]

STATE INCOME TAXES

The role of individual income taxes in state revenue systems has been growing rapidly.[45] In 1960, 12.2 percent of state tax collections were from individual income taxes; by 1982, the figure was 28.1 percent [*Facts and Figures on Government Finance*, 1983, p. 254]. As of April 1983, 40 states and the District of Columbia had an individual income tax [*Facts and Figures on Government Finance*, 1983, pp. 260–61].[46]

State income taxes tend to be similar in structure to the federal tax. The tax base is found by subtracting various deductions and exemptions from gross income, and tax liability is determined by associating a marginal tax rate with each of several income brackets. The marginal rates are much lower than those of the federal system. In 1983, for about half the states which levied an income tax the highest bracket rate was 8 percent or below. (The maximum was 16 percent in Minnesota.)

The states differ considerably with respect to rules governing deductions and exemptions. Some rule out practically all deductions, while others follow rules similar to the federal system. As noted above, state income taxes, like most state and local taxes, are deductible from federal tax liability. However, in only about 16 states is the federal income tax deductible. Just as the federal government cannot tax interest on state and local bonds, the state governments cannot tax interest on obligations issued by the federal government.

---

[44] Indeed, at the time of this writing, efforts are being made to repeal indexing.

[45] For local governments, income taxes are generally not of much importance in the revenue structure, although in some of the larger cities, they play a significant role.

[46] A few other states taxed only some components of income such as capital gains.

REFORMING THE FEDERAL INCOME TAX

In this chapter, we have discussed many problems with the personal income tax. In an editorial titled "Tax Reform, Tra-La," the *New York Times* asked

> What's wrong with the Federal Income Tax? Just count the ways. The system is so complicated that it requires armies of accountants and lawyers just to figure out who owes what. It's so inequitable that the rich often pay a smaller percentage of their incomes in taxes than the struggling middle classes. It's so irrational that two wage earners with the same income rarely pay the same tax, and so inefficient that it leads people to buy houses when they'd rather rent apartments, to be unemployed when they'd like to work, to invest in cattle ranches and shopping centers when they'd be better off with a savings account ["Tax Reform, Tra-La," 1980, p. A22].

Given that paying taxes simply is not fun, it is hard to imagine a citizenry ever speaking in glowing terms about its tax system. Nevertheless, this chapter suggests that much of the discontent cannot be dismissed as mere griping. If there is so much wrong with the system, why isn't it reformed?[47]

One problem is that in many cases, even fairly disinterested experts disagree about what direction reform should take. For example, we noted earlier that even though there is a consensus that differentially taxing various types of capital income is undesirable, there is disagreement with respect to how this should be remedied. What one person views as a "reform" can be perceived by another as an undesirable change.

Another difficulty is that attempts to change specific provisions are likely to encounter fierce political opposition from those whom the changes will hurt. Heads of religious and educational institutions, for example, would be expected to lobby ferociously against the removal of the charitable deduction. In Chapter 10 we discussed some theories which suggested that in the presence of special-interest groups, the political process can lead to expenditure patterns that are suboptimal from society's point of view. The same theories might explain the persistent failure of attempts to reform the tax system. One member of the House Ways and Means Committee, Andrew Jacobs, summed it up this way: "If you evade your taxes, you go to the penitentiary. If you want to avoid taxes, you go to the U.S. Congress—and see what they can do for you" [*Tax Policy Guide*, 182, p. 5].

---

[47] For a detailed discussion of the problems involved in implementing tax reform, see Break and Pechman [1975].

However, we should add that not only organized lobbies are likely to impede reform. In many cases, once a tax provision is introduced, "ordinary" people modify their behavior on its basis and are likely to lose a lot if it is changed. For example, many families have purchased larger houses than they otherwise would have because of the provisions for deducting mortgage interest and property taxes. Presumably, if these provisions were eliminated, house values would fall. Homeowners would not take this lying down. Indeed, some notions of horizontal equity suggest that it is unfair to change provisions which have caused people to make decisions that are costly to reverse (see Chapter 13).

Some have argued that attempts to make broad changes in the tax system are likely to be more successful than attempts to modify specific provisions on a piecemeal basis. If *everyone's* ox is being gored, people are less apt to fight for their particular loophole. This view seems overly optimistic. It appears more likely that general changes will earn the simultaneous opposition of all those who would lose by them. William Safire discussed what happened when a general change in the form of a flat tax was proposed to former President Richard Nixon:

> The President was intrigued, "I'm a lawyer, and I can't make head or tail out of the current form," he said. But John Connally, then treasury secretary and the resident political sage in the administration, shook his silver-maned head, "It'll never fly," he opined. "Every special interest group in the country will shoot it down." President Nixon glumly nodded and told his aids to chuck the charts [Safire, 1982, p. A31].

Break and Pechman [1975] point out an additional impediment to broad changes in the tax system. Such modifications create uncertainty for many people with respect to how their liabilities will change. If, on one hand, I lose my mortgage interest deduction, but on the other hand, face lower tax rates, will I be better off on balance? Reasoning that "the devil you know is better than the devil you don't know," many people prefer the status quo. We conclude that one cannot be optimistic about the possibilities for improvement.

SUMMARY

Computation of federal individual income tax liability has three major steps: measuring "total" income (adjusted gross income), converting total income to taxable income, and calculating taxes due.

A traditional benchmark measure of income is the Haig-Simons definition: income during a given period is the net change in the individual's power to consume.

Implementation of the Haig-Simons criterion is confounded by several difficulties:

Income must be measured net of the expenses of earning it.

Unrealized capital gains are not easily gauged.

The imputed income from durable goods is not directly observable.

It is difficult to measure the value of in-kind receipts.

The Haig-Simons criterion is viewed by many public finance economists as the ideal toward which real-world tax systems should strive. However, critics note that the criterion does not necessarily guarantee either fair or efficient outcomes.

Several sources of income are excluded from the U.S. income tax base. These include:

Interest on state and local bonds.

Certain proportions of capital gains and losses, depending upon the length of ownership of the asset and other factors.

A fixed amount of dividend income.

Employer contributions to pension and medical plans.

Gifts and inheritances.

These mark serious departures from the Haig-Simons criterion.

The conversion of adjusted gross income (AGI) to taxable income involves subtracting allotted exemptions and deductions.

Exemptions are fixed amounts per family member, with special consideration for the blind and elderly. Exemptions are subtracted from AGI and may be viewed as compensation for the cost of child rearing or as a method of setting the progressiveness of the tax system.

Deductions are either standard or itemized. A standard deduction reduces taxable income by a fixed amount. Alternatively, taxpayers may choose to itemize their deductions from AGI.

Itemized deductions are permitted for expenditures on particular goods and services. Itemized deductions change after-tax relative prices. Economic theory and empirical evidence indicate that this often affects economic behavior.

The major itemized deductions in the U.S. tax code include:

Unreimbursed medical expenses in excess of 5 percent of AGI.

State and local taxes.

Interest expenses.

Charitable contributions.

Tax credits are direct reductions in tax liability instead of reductions in taxable income. In general, there is no obvious means by which to choose between deductions and credits.

Tax expenditures are the revenues foregone due to preferential tax treatment. In some instances a tax expenditure may be the most effective way to stimulate a particular private activity. Empirical research is necessary to determine whether a direct subsidy or tax expenditure is most appropriate.

The final step in determining tax liability is to apply a schedule of rates to taxable income. Currently there are four different schedules, each of which is characterized by a series of increasing marginal tax rates.

With increasing marginal tax rates, uneven income streams are taxed more heavily than steady incomes. Income averaging attempts to mitigate this phenomenon.

Over time, statutory tax rates have risen, a minimum tax has been introduced, zero-bracket levels have been changed, and the percentage of individuals in higher tax brackets has risen. However, these observations by themselves provide little information about the effective rate of taxation or the excess burden associated with it.

A flat or linear income tax has been proposed to simplify the tax code while maintaining the desired progressiveness through the choice of the personal exemption and tax rate. While tax computations are eased, conceptual problems of measuring taxable income are still present.

The fundamental problem in the tax treatment of the family is that no tax system can simultaneously achieve increasing marginal tax rates, tax burdens unchanged upon marriage, and equal taxes for families with equal incomes. The U.S. tax code has been changed several times in attempts to satisfy each of these conflicting goals.

Under the current system, inflation affects real personal income tax burdens in several ways. First, it increases the proportion of real income taxed via *bracket creep* and reduces the value of exemptions and credits. Second, inflation results in taxation of nominal capital gains even when real incomes are unchanged. Finally, inflation lowers the real after-tax return to lending and the real after-tax cost of borrowing.

Income tax systems are becoming more important as revenue raisers for the states. State income taxes have lower rates than the federal system and vary widely in their exact provisions.

DISCUSSION QUESTIONS

1. Suppose that you are asked to implement an income tax which uses the Haig-Simons criterion of income as the tax base.
    a. If social security (SS) is simply a transfer program, what is the appropriate treatment of SS taxes paid and SS benefits received?
    b. If, instead, SS is viewed as an insurance program, what is the appropriate treatment? Compare your answer to (a) and explain any differences.
    c. How should your tax system treat changes in the value of labor skills? In particular, suppose that darts becomes a popular and lucrative spectator sport. The anticipated future earnings of skilled darts players will rise dramatically. How does this affect tax liability? (Hint: What happens to the value of a player's "human capital"? Compare to the tax treatment of "physical capital.") Also, what treatment should be applied to medical care of wrist injuries to dart players? What happens to tax liability if the dart boom suddenly collapses?

2. Discuss:
   a. "Like medical expenditures, food expenditures are nondiscretionary. Therefore, food expenditure should be deductible from adjusted gross income."
   b. The Reagan administration proposed taxing employer contributions to medical insurance plans.

3. If Rafael, a painter, donates his work to a museum, he is permitted to deduct only the value of the canvas, ink, etc. If he sells the painting to Hughes who donates the painting, then Hughes may deduct the purchase price. Does this make sense? Is it fair to the painter? Explain carefully.

*4. Jones, who has a federal personal income tax rate of 50 percent, holds an oil stock which appreciates in value by 10 percent each year. He bought the stock one year ago. Jones' stockbroker now wants him to switch the oil stock for a gold stock that is equally risky. Jones has decided that if he holds on to the oil stock, he will keep it only one more year and then sell it. If he sells the oil stock now, he will invest all the (after-tax) proceeds of the sale in the gold stock and then sell the gold stock one year from now. What is the minimum rate of return that the gold stock must pay for Jones to make the switch? Relate your answer to the *lock-in effect*.

5. Public education in the United States is financed mostly by state and local taxes. Suppose that: (1) the "typical" taxpayer has a marginal federal income tax rate of 30 percent, and (2) the elasticity of demand for public education is −0.8. How would removing federal deductions for state and local taxes affect public education?

6. Suppose that a "typical" taxpayer has a marginal personal income tax rate of 40 percent. The nominal interest rate is 13 percent, and the expected inflation rate is 8 percent.
   a. What is the real after-tax rate of interest?
   b. Suppose that the expected inflation rate increases by 3 percentage points to 11 percent, and the nominal interest rate increases by the same amount. What happens to the real after-tax rate of return?
   *c. If the inflation rate increases as in part **(b)**, by how much would the nominal interest rate have to increase so as to keep the real after-tax interest rate at the same level as in part **(a)**? Can you generalize your answer using an algebraic formula?

SELECTED REFERENCES

Aaron, Henry J. "Inflation and the Income Tax: An Introduction." In *Inflation and the Income Tax*, ed. Henry J. Aaron. Washington, D.C.: Brookings Institution, 1976, pp. 1–31.

---

* Difficult.

Bittker, Boris. "Federal Income Taxation and the Family." *Stanford Law Review* 27 (July 1975), pp. 1392–1463.

Pechman, Joseph A., ed. *Comprehensive Income Taxation.* Washington, D.C.: Brookings Institution, 1977.

Steuerle, Eugene, and Michael Hartzmark. "Individual Income Taxation, 1947–79." *National Tax Journal* 34 (June 1981), pp. 145–66.

CHAPTER 15

Personal Taxation and Behavior

Putting on the spectacles of science in expectation of finding the answer to everything looked at signifies inner blindness.

J. Frank Dobie

The theory of taxation makes clear that ultimately the efficiency and equity of taxes depend on how they affect behavior. The impact of taxes on behavior is a matter of intense debate, both among academics and politicians. Some argue that taxes have very little effect: "disincentives, like the weather, are much talked about, but relatively few people do anything about them" [Break, 1957, p. 549]. Others suggest that taxes are really important:

> Today people are taxed at unprecedented high rates on any additional income that they earn, either from work effort, saving, or upgrading their skills. The *inevitable* results of little reward for extra effort are worsening work attitudes, high absenteeism rates, reluctance to work overtime and to assume risks, and the lowest personal saving rate in anyone's memory" [italics added] [Roberts, 1981, p. 26].

As was suggested in Chapter 14, the income tax affects incentives for a myriad of decisions—everything from the purchase of medical services to the amount of charitable donations. We choose to focus on four particularly important topics which have been the subject of much investigation—the effects of taxation on labor supply, saving, portfolio decisions, and housing consumption.

377

LABOR SUPPLY

Theoretical Considerations[1]

Hercules is trying to decide how much of his time to devote each week to work and how much to leisure. In Figure 15.1, the horizontal axis measures the number of hours devoted to leisure. Even if Hercules does not work at all, there is an upper limit to the amount of leisure he can consume, because there are just so many hours in a week. This number of hours, referred to as the **time endowment,** is shown by the distance OT in Figure 15.1. We assume that all time not spent on leisure is devoted to work in the market.[2] Any point on the horizontal axis therefore simultaneously indicates hours of leisure and hours of work. For example, at point a, Oa hours are devoted to leisure, and the difference between that and the time endowment, OT, represents time spent at work, aT.

Our first problem is to illustrate how Hercules' income, which is measured on the vertical axis, varies with his hours of work. Assume that he can earn a wage of $\$w$ per hour. Then his earnings for any number of hours worked are just the product of $\$w$ and the number of hours. Suppose, for example, Hercules does not work at all. If labor is his only source of income, his income is simply zero. This option of zero work and zero income is represented by point T.

If Hercules works one hour each week, by definition he consumes leisure equal to his time endowment minus one hour. This point is one hour to the left of T on the horizontal axis. Working one hour gives him a total of $\$w$. The combination of one hour of work with a total income of $\$w$ is labeled point b. If Hercules works two hours—moves two hours to the left of T—his total income is $2 \times \$w$ which is labeled point c. If we continue to compute the income associated with each number of hours of work, we trace out all the leisure/income combinations that are available to Hercules—the straight line TD, whose slope, in absolute value, is the wage rate. TD is the analog of the "budget constraint" in the usual analysis of the choice between two goods. (See the Appendix to the book.) Here, however, the "goods" are income and leisure. The "price" of an hour of leisure is its *opportunity cost* (the income foregone by not working that hour), which is just the wage.

To know which point on TD Hercules chooses, we need information on his tastes. In Figure 15.2 we reproduce the budget constraint TD. Assume that preferences for leisure and income can be represented by

---

[1] A verbal discussion of the theory of labor supply was provided in Chapter 3. The reader may want to consult that discussion before proceeding with the graphical exposition provided here.

[2] A more general model allows for three uses of time: leisure, work in the market, *and* housework.

FIGURE 15.1   Budget Constraint for the Leisure/Income Choice

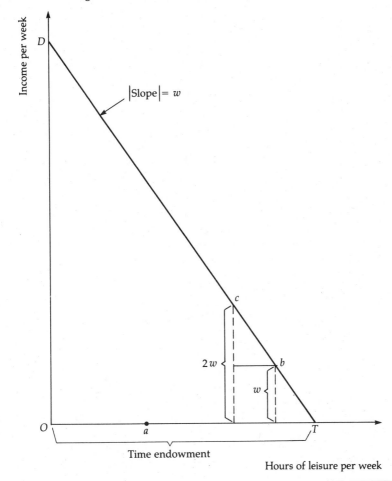

normal, convex-to-the-origin indifference curves. Three such curves are labeled *i*, *ii*, and *iii* in Figure 15.2. Utility is maximized at point E_1, where Hercules devotes *OF* hours to leisure, works *FT* hours, and earns income *OG*.

Now suppose that the government levies a tax on earnings at rate *t*. The tax reduces the reward for working an hour from $\$w$ to $\$(1 - t)w$. When Hercules consumes an hour of leisure he now gives up only $\$(1 - t)w$, not $\$w$. In effect, the tax reduces the opportunity cost of an hour of leisure. This observation is represented in Figure 15.3. The budget constraint facing Hercules is no longer *TD*. Rather, it is the flatter line, *TH*, whose slope in absolute value is $(1 - t)w$. Because of the tax,

FIGURE 15.2   Utility Maximizing Choice of Leisure and Income

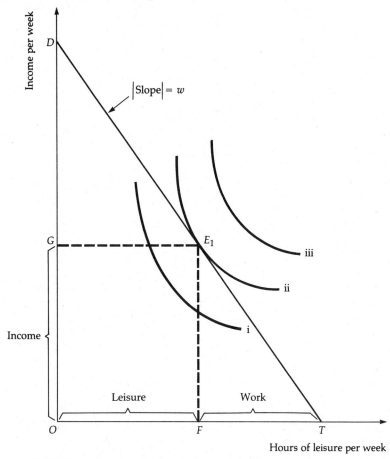

the original income/leisure choice, E_1, is no longer attainable. Hercules must choose a point somewhere along the after-tax budget constraint TH. In Figure 15.3, this is E_2, where Hercules consumes OI hours of leisure, works IT hours, and has an after-tax income of OG'. The tax has lowered Hercules' labor supply from FT hours to IT hours.

Can we therefore conclude that a "rational" individual will *always* reduce labor supply in response to a proportional tax? To answer this question, consider Theseus, who faces exactly the same before and after-tax budget constraints as Hercules, and who chooses to work the same number of hours *(FT)* prior to imposition of the tax. As indicated in Figure 15.4, when Theseus is taxed, he *increases* his hours of work from FT to JT. There is nothing "irrational" about this. Depending upon a

FIGURE 15.3   Leisure/Income Choice under a Proportional Income Tax

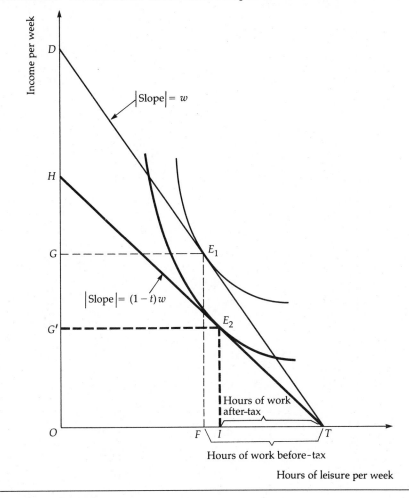

person's tastes, it is possible to want to work more, less, or the same amount after being subject to a tax.

The source of the ambiguity is the conflict between two effects generated by the tax, the *substitution effect* and the *income effect*. When the tax reduces the take-home wage, the opportunity cost of leisure goes down, and there is a tendency to substitute leisure for work. This is the substitution effect, and it tends to decrease labor supply. At the same time, for any number of hours worked, the tax reduces the individual's income. Assuming that leisure is a "normal good," for any number of hours worked, this loss in income leads to a reduction in consumption of

FIGURE 15.4   Example of a Proportional Income Tax Increasing Hours of
Labor Supplied

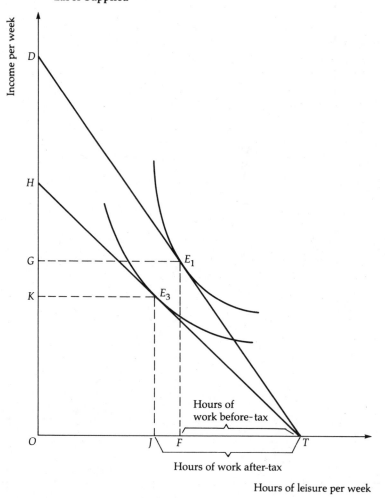

leisure, other things being the same. But a decrease in leisure means an
increase in work. The income effect therefore tends to induce an individual to work more. Thus, the two effects work in opposite directions. It is
simply impossible to know on the basis of theory alone whether the
income effect or substitution effect will dominate. For Hercules, shown
in Figure 15.3, the substitution effect dominates. For Theseus, shown in
Figure 15.4, the income effect is more important.[3]

---

[3] For a more general discussion of income and substitution effects, see the Appendix to
the book.

The analysis of a progressive tax system is very similar to that of a proportional tax. Suppose that Hercules is now confronted with increasing tax rates; t_1 on his first $5,000 of earnings, t_2 on his second $5,000 of earnings, and t_3 on all income above $10,000.[4] As before, prior to the tax the budget line is TD, which is depicted in Figure 15.5. After tax, the budget constraint is the kinked line $TLMN$. Up to $5,000 of income, the opportunity cost of an hour of leisure is $(1 - t_1)w$, which is the slope (in absolute value) of segment TL. On segment ML, which lies between

FIGURE 15.5   Leisure/Income Choice under a Progressive Income Tax

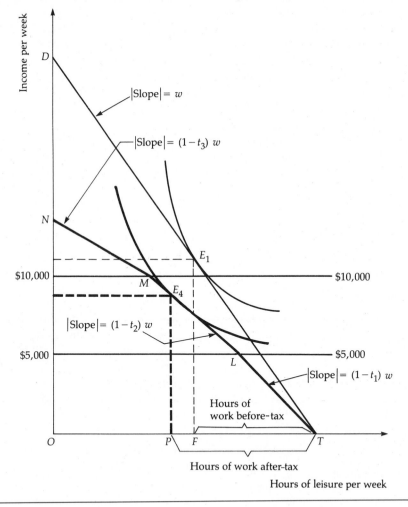

[4] Note that this rate structure is similar in essentials to that of the U.S. income tax. See Chapter 14.

$5,000 and \$10,000, the absolute value of the slope is $(1 - t_2)w$. *ML* is flatter than *TL* because t_2 is greater than t_1. Finally, on segment *MN* which lies above \$10,000, the slope is $(1 - t_3)w$, which is even flatter. Depending on his preferences, Hercules can end up anywhere on *TLMN*. In Figure 15.5, he maximizes utility at E_4 where he works *PT* hours.[5]

Empirical Findings

The theory just discussed suggests that an individual's labor supply decision depends upon: *(a)* variables that affect the position of the budget constraint, especially the after-tax wage;[6] and *(b)* variables that affect the individual's indifference curves for leisure and income, such as age, sex, and marital status. Econometricians have estimated regression equations in which they seek to explain annual hours of work as a function of such variables.[7] Although considerable differences in estimates arise due to inevitable differences in samples, time periods, and statistical techniques, it would be fair to say that the following two important general tendencies have been observed:[8] (1) For males between roughly the ages of 20 and 60, the effect of changes in the net wage upon hours of work is small in absolute value and is often statistically insignificant. (2) The hours of work and labor force participation decisions of married women are quite sensitive to changes in the net wage. Although estimates differ widely, a number of investigators have found that the elasticity of hours worked with respect to the net wage is in excess of 1.0.

Some Caveats

The theoretical and empirical results just described are certainly more useful than the uninformed guesses often heard in political debates. Nevertheless, we should be aware of some important qualifications.

Demand-Side Considerations.   The analyses above ignore effects that changes in the supply of labor might have on the demand side of the market. Suppose that taxes on married women were lowered in such a

---

[5] An issue that has received substantial attention is the effect on hours of work of replacing a proportional tax with a progressive tax that yields the *same* tax revenue. Hemming [1980] has shown that the outcome depends upon the shape of the indifference curves and exactly how "progressive" is defined.

[6] Another important determinant of the budget constraint is nonlabor income: dividends, interest, transfer payments, etc. Nonlabor income causes a parallel shift in the budget constraint; there is a constant addition to income at every level of hours worked.

[7] See Chapter 3 for an explanation of regression analysis.

[8] See, for example, Hausman [1983].

way that their net wages increased by 10 percent. With a labor supply elasticity of 1.0, their hours of work would increase by 10 percent. If firms could absorb all of these hours of the new net wage, that would be the end of the story. More typically, as more hours of work are offered, there is a tendency to bid down the *before*-tax wage. This mitigates the original increase in the *after*-tax wage, so that the final increase in hours of work would be less than originally guessed.

The situation becomes even more complicated when we realize that major changes in work decisions could influence consumption patterns in other markets. The resulting relative price changes might feed back upon labor market decisions. For example, if married women increased their hours of work, the demand for child care would probably increase. To the extent this raised the price of child care, it might discourage mothers of small children from working, at least in the short run. Clearly, tracing through these general equilibrium implications is a complicated business. Most investigators are willing to assume that the first-round effects are a reasonable approximation to the final result.

Individual versus Group Effects.   Our focus has been on how much an individual will work under alternative tax regimes. Musgrave [1959] points out that it is difficult to use such results to predict how the total hours of work supplied by a *group* of workers will change. When the tax schedule is changed, incentives will be changed differently for different people. For example, in a move from a proportional to a progressive tax, low-income workers may find themselves facing lower marginal tax rates while just the opposite may be true for those with high incomes. It is quite possible, then, that the labor supplies of the two groups will move in opposite directions, making the overall outcome difficult to predict.

Other Dimensions of Labor Supply.   The number of hours worked annually is an important and interesting indicator of labor supply. But the *effective* amount of labor supplied by an individual depends upon more than the number of hours elapsed at the workplace. A highly educated, healthy, well-motivated worker presumably is more productive than a counterpart who lacks these qualities.

As indicated at the beginning of the chapter, some fear that taxes induce people to invest too little in the acquisition of skills. Economic theory yields surprising insights into how taxes might affect the accumulation of human capital—investments that people make in themselves to increase their productivity. Consider Hera, who is contemplating entering an on-the-job training program. Suppose that over her lifetime, the program will increase Hera's earnings by an amount whose present value is B. However, participation in the program reduces the amount of time currently available to Hera for income-producing activity, and hence costs her some amount, C, in terms of foregone wages. If she is sensible, Hera makes her decision using the investment criterion described in Chapter 9, and enters the program only if the benefits exceed the costs:

(15.1) $B - C > 0$

Now suppose that Hera's earnings are subjected to a proportional tax at rate t. Part of the higher wages earned by virtue of participation in the training program will be taxed away. One might guess that the tax therefore lowers the likelihood that she will participate. This reasoning is misleading. To see why, assume for the moment that after the tax Hera continues to work the same number of hours as she did before.[9] The tax does indeed reduce the benefits of the training program from B to $(1 - t)B$. But at the same time, it reduces the costs. Recall that the costs of the program are the foregone wages. Because these wages would have been subject to tax, Hera gives up not C, but only $(1 - t)C$. The decision to enter the program is based on whether after-tax benefits exceed after-tax costs:

(15.2) $(1 - t)B - (1 - t)C = (1 - t)(B - C) > 0$

A glance at Equation (15.2) indicates that it is exactly equivalent to (15.1). Any combination of benefits and costs that was acceptable before the earnings tax is acceptable afterward. In this model, a proportional earnings tax reduces benefits and cost in the same proportion, and therefore has *no* effect on the human capital investment.

This unambiguous result is a consequence of the assumption that labor supply is constant after the tax is imposed. Suppose instead that as a result of the earnings tax, Hera increases her supply of labor. (The income effect predominates.) In this case, the tax will lead to an increase in human capital accumulation.[10] In effect, the after-tax labor supply is the "utilization rate" of the human capital investment. The more hours a person works, the greater the payoff to an increase in the wage rate from a given human capital investment. Therefore, if the tax induces more work, it will make human capital investments more attractive, other things being the same. Conversely, if the substitution effect predominates so that labor supply decreases, human capital accumulation will be discouraged.

Of course, the framework in which we have been discussing this problem is very simple. It ignores the important fact that the returns to a human capital investment usually cannot be known with certainty. Moreover, for some types of human capital, costs other than foregone

---

[9] In terms of our earlier discussion, the income and substitution effects just offset each other.

[10] See Eaton and Rosen [1980a].

earnings are important. College tuition is an obvious example. Finally, when the tax system is progressive, the benefits and costs of human capital investments may be taxed at different rates. However, when such factors are considered, the basic result is confirmed—from a theoretical point of view, the effect of earnings taxation upon human capital accumulation is ambiguous. At this time, unfortunately, little empirical work on this important question is available.

The Expenditure Side. The standard analysis of labor supply and taxation ignores the disposition of the tax receipts. However, at least some of the revenues are used to purchase public goods, the availability of which can affect work decisions. If the tax money is used to provide recreational facilities such as national parks, we expect the demand for leisure to increase, *ceteris paribus*. On the other hand, expenditure on child-care facilities for working parents might increase labor supply. Ideally, we should examine the labor supply consequences of the entire budget, not just the tax side [see Lindbeck, 1980a]. In practice, it has been difficult for empirical investigators to learn about how public expenditures affect work decisions. The difficulty stems from the fact that it is hard to determine how much of a public good a given household actually consumes, a problem which we have already discussed in several different contexts. (See Chapters 5 and 6.)

Relation to the Welfare System

Our focus so far has been the impact of explicit taxes upon the labor supply. Now, the poor face fairly low federal income tax rates. However, the welfare system imposes very high *implicit* tax rates on the earnings of low-income individuals. This occurs because various benefits are *means-tested*—they are reduced when the authorities learn that a welfare recipient has earned some income. For example, after earnings of $30 per month, Aid to Families With Dependent Children (AFDC) is reduced by about 67 cents for each dollar earned. Similarly, under certain circumstances, foodstamps are reduced by some fraction (.82 in 1983) of each dollar of additional income. Suppose that whenever a welfare recipient earns one more dollar, his benefits are reduced by 90 cents. In effect, this is equivalent to a 90 percent marginal tax rate, because the recipient comes out only 10 cents ahead for each additional dollar earned.

As an extreme case, consider a regime under which each dollar earned results in relief payments being reduced by one dollar—a 100 percent marginal tax rate on earnings.[11] The consequences of such a

---

[11] Under current welfare laws, for some recipients, the implicit marginal tax rate actually exceeds 100 percent—the loss in all benefits (AFDC plus foodstamps, etc.) exceeds the gain in income.

FIGURE 15.6   Budget Constraint under a Welfare System with a 100 Percent Marginal Tax Rate

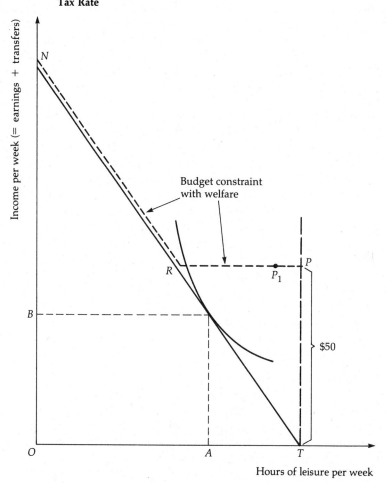

system are assessed in Figure 15.6, a standard leisure/income choice diagram. Prior to the introduction of the welfare system, Zeus faces a wage given by the absolute value of slope of his budget line, *TN*, and chooses to work *TA* hours, giving him earnings of *OB*. Suppose now that the welfare authorities announce that Zeus is eligible to receive a grant of $50 per week, but the grant will be reduced by $1 for each dollar he earns. How does introduction of the program modify the budget constraint?

Clearly, one option available is point *P*, which is associated with zero hours of work and an income of $50 from welfare. Now suppose that Zeus works one hour. Graphically, this is represented by a one-hour movement to the left from P. When Zeus works one hour, he receives a wage of $\$w$ from his employer, *but* simultaneously his welfare is reduced by the same amount. The hour of work has netted him nothing—his total income is still $50. This is shown by point P_1, where there is one hour of work and total income is still $50. Additional hours of work continue to produce no net gain in income, so the budget constraint is flat. This continues until point R, at which point Zeus' earnings exceed $50, so that he is out of the welfare system altogether. Beyond that point, each hour of work raises his income by $\$w$.[12] Thus, the budget constraint is the kinked line PRN, whose segment PR has zero slope, and whose segment RN has a slope equal to the absolute value of w.

How will Zeus respond to such incentives? Figure 15.7 shows one distinct possibility: he maximizes utility at point P, at which no labor is supplied. On the other hand, if the indifference curves are flat enough, Zeus may select a point along segment RN. But in no case will a rational person work between zero and PR hours. This should come as no surprise. Why should someone work if he can receive the same income by not working?

Although for many recipients the system is less extreme than depicted in Figure 15.7, there is considerable evidence that the welfare system has substantially reduced the labor supply of recipients.[13] There is a consensus that presenting able-bodied welfare recipients with such unfavorable work incentives is socially undesirable.[14]

A welfare system which has gained substantial support from economists is a **negative income tax.** Under this scheme, individuals who do not work receive some basic grant. But welfare recipients who enter the labor market have their grants reduced only by some fraction of their earnings, rather than by 100 percent. For example, suppose that the basic weekly grant is $200 and the system has a marginal tax rate of 25 percent. If Zeus earns $100, the basic grant is reduced by $25 (= .25 × $100), to $175. Total weekly income is then the sum of $175 (from relief) plus $100 (from earnings), or $275.

Figure 15.8 illustrates this scheme. As before, in the absence of welfare, Zeus works AT hours and earns OB. In the presence of the negative income tax, one option is point Q, where no labor is supplied and Zeus receives $200 from welfare. If Zeus works one hour, he receives w from his employer. Simultaneously, his grant is reduced by $\frac{1}{4}w$. This still leaves him ahead by $\frac{3}{4}w$. Thus, another point on the budget constraint is U, which is one hour to the left of Q, and $\frac{3}{4}w$ above it. Similarly, Zeus continues to receive an effective hourly wage of $\frac{3}{4}w$ until he works VT

---

[12] Of course, if Zeus becomes subject to the income tax, his take-home wage will be less than $\$w$.

[13] See Danziger, Haveman, and Plotnick [1981] or Williams [1975].

[14] For example, the 1980 platform of the Republican Party noted disapprovingly that "for those on welfare, our nation's policies provide a penalty for getting a job."

**FIGURE 15.7   Work Decision under a Welfare System with a 100 Percent Marginal
Tax Rate**

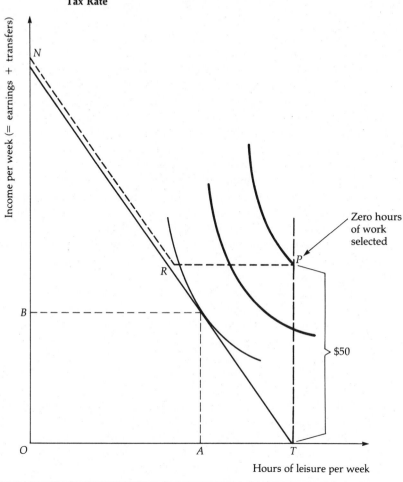

hours, at which point his earnings are high enough that he receives no
welfare.[15] Thus, the budget constraint is the kinked line *QSN*. Segment
QS has a slope in absolute value of ¾*w*, segment *SN* a slope of *w*.

---

[15] At point *S*, Zeus is earning $800 weekly. He receives no welfare at this, or any
higher, level of earnings because the amount "taxed" away exhausts the basic grant of
$200. Algebraically, the benefit received *(B)* is related to the basic grant *(G)*, tax rate *(t)*, and
level of earnings *(E)* by:

$$B = G - tE$$

Using this, it follows that the benefit is zero *(B = 0)* when:

$$E = G/t$$

or at any higher level of *E*.

FIGURE 15.8   Budget Constraint under a Negative Income Tax

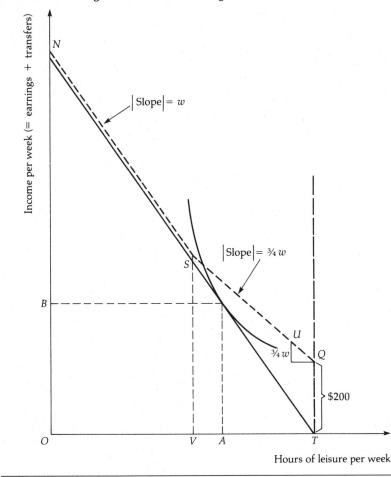

As usual, the ultimate work decision depends upon the shapes of the individual's indifference curves. As drawn in Figure 15.9, Zeus works less than he did before the negative income tax (BT hours, as opposed to AT before). However, unlike the situation depicted in Figure 15.7, he does not opt out of the labor force altogether. To be sure, we could also draw indifference curves at which the maximum utility is reached at zero hours of work. But because the implicit tax rate is less than 100 percent, this outcome is less likely under the negative income tax.

The fundamental dilemma in designing a negative income tax is the trade-off between the size of the basic grant and the marginal tax rate. For a given program cost, the larger the basic grant, the larger must be the marginal tax rate. A system with "good" work incentives might

FIGURE 15.9   Labor Supply Decision under a Negative Income Tax

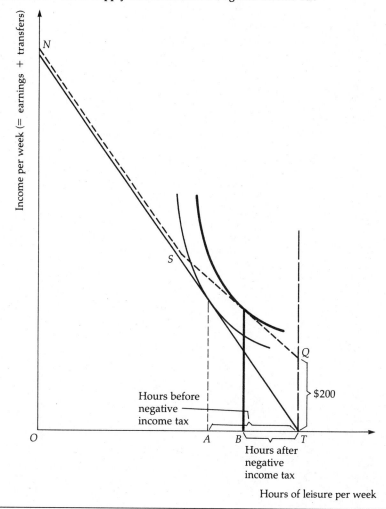

provide little money for those who are *unable* to work, such as the severely disabled.[16]

Most proponents of negative income taxes argue that the program should be universal—available to all people who qualify on the basis of income. In contrast, current welfare programs are often targeted at particular groups. For example, in many states, a family cannot receive AFDC payments if the father is present. It is widely believed (although

---

[16] The negative income tax could be supplemented with a system of special grants for such individuals. This would, of course, complicate administration considerably.

there is not much proof) that this has reduced the stability of low-income families. If this is the case, then moving to a negative income tax might have a desirable effect on family stability. On the other hand, some have expressed fears that introduction of such a universal negative income tax would lead to widespread withdrawals from the labor force.[17] To investigate this possibility, the federal government sponsored a major social experiment in the 1960s. A sample of low income individuals were allowed to participate in a negative income tax program. The behavior of members of a control group who did not participate was also monitored. The results of the experiment are still being analyzed. However, the preliminary evidence indicates that a negative income tax does not induce substantial reductions in work effort.[18] Of course, such results must be interpreted cautiously, due to the problems with social experiments discussed in Chapter 3. These findings do suggest, however, that the negative income tax is a policy option worth taking seriously.

Overview. Public concern over how much welfare recipients work may be somewhat misplaced. True, an important aspect of any welfare system is the incentive structure it creates. But if the goal of welfare policy were only to maximize work effort, the government could simply force the poor into workhouses, a policy actually implemented at times in British history. As suggested in Chapter 13, designing good transfer systems requires a careful balancing of efficiency and equity considerations.

Labor Supply and Tax Revenues

So far, our emphasis has been on finding the amount of labor supply associated with any given tax regime. We now explore the related issue of how tax collections vary with the tax rate.

Consider the supply curve of labor S_L depicted in Figure 15.10. It shows the optimal amount of work for each after-tax wage, other things being the same.[19] As it is drawn, hours of work increase with the net wage—the substitution effect dominates throughout the range of wages being considered. The argument presented below could be repeated using a labor supply curve for which the income effect is dominant.

The before-tax wage, w, is associated with L_0 hours of work. Obviously, since the tax rate is zero, no revenue is collected. Now suppose a proportional tax at rate t_1 is imposed. The net wage is $(1 - t_1)w$, and

---

[17] "We categorically reject the notion of a guaranteed annual income, no matter how it may be disguised, which would destroy the fiber of our economy and doom the poor to perpetual dependence." (1980 platform of the Republican Party.)

[18] See Rees [1974].

[19] The labor supply curve (or equivalently, the leisure demand curve) can be derived from the individual's indifference map. See the Appendix at the end of the book.

FIGURE 15.10   Tax Rates, Hours of Work, and Tax Revenue

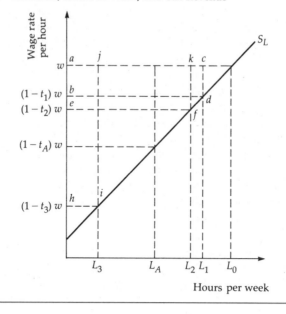

Hours per week

labor supply is L_1 hours. Tax collections are equal to the tax per hour worked (*ab*) times the number of hours worked (*ac*), or rectangle, *abdc*. Similar reasoning indicates that if the tax rate were raised to t_2, tax revenues would be *eakf*. Given the shape of supply curve S_L, *eakf* exceeds *abdc*—a higher tax rate leads to greater revenue collections. Does this mean that the government can always collect more revenue by increasing the tax rate? No. For example, at tax rate t_3, revenues *haji* are less than those at the lower rate t_2. Although the tax collected *per hour* is very high at t_3, the number of hours has decreased so much that the product of the tax rate and hours is fairly low. Indeed, as the tax rate approaches 100 percent, people stop working altogether and tax revenues fall to zero.

All of this is summarized compactly in Figure 15.11, which shows the tax rate on the horizontal axis and tax revenue on the vertical. At very low tax rates, revenue collections are low. As tax rates increase, revenues increase, reaching a maximum at rate t_A. For rates exceeding t_A, revenues begin to fall, eventually diminishing to zero. Note that it would be absurd for the government to choose any tax rate exceeding t_A, because tax rates could be reduced without the government suffering any revenue loss.

Hard as it may be to believe, Figure 15.11 has been the center of a major political controversy. This is largely due to the well-publicized assertion by economist Arthur B. Laffer that the United States currently

FIGURE 15.11   Tax Rates versus Tax Revenue

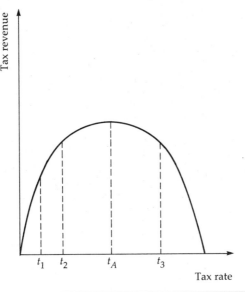

is operating to the right of t_A [see Laffer, 1979]. Indeed, in the popular press, the tax rate–tax revenue relationship is known as the **Laffer curve.** The notion that tax rate reductions would create no revenue losses became an important tenet of the "supply-side economics" espoused by the Reagan administration.[20]

The popular debate surrounding the Laffer curve has been confused and confusing.[21] A few points are worth making.

First, the shape of a Laffer curve is determined by the elasticity of labor with respect to the net wage. For any change in the tax rate, there is a corresponding percentage change in the net wage. Whether tax revenues rise or fall is determined by whether changes in hours worked offset the change in the tax rate. This is precisely the issue of the elasticity of labor supply investigated by public finance economists.

Second, some critics of supply-side economics argue that the *very idea* that tax rate reductions can lead to increased revenue is absurd. However, the discussion surrounding Figure 5.10 suggests that in principle, lower tax rates can indeed lead to higher revenue collections.

Third, it is therefore an empirical question whether or not the economy is actually operating to the right of t_A. A careful study of this issue

[20] Supply-side economics is just as concerned with the taxation of savings as of labor, and all the arguments made here apply to savings, as well.

[21] For a good summary, see Fullerton [1982].

suggests that given all plausible estimates of the elasticity of labor supply, the economy is *not* operating in this range [see Fullerton, 1982]. Tax-rate reductions are unlikely to be self-financing in the sense of unleashing so much labor supply that tax revenues do not fall.

Finally, it does *not* follow from this observation that tax rate reduction is necessarily undesirable. As emphasized in previous chapters, determination of the optimal tax system depends upon a wide array of social and economic considerations. Those who believe that the government sector is too large should presumably be quite happy to see tax revenues reduced. In this connection, we should note the unfortunate tendency of some "supply siders" to attribute important normative properties to tax rate t_A.[22] As should be clear from the theory of optimal income taxation, the fact that revenues are maximized at rate t_A tells us *nothing* about whether it is the most desirable tax rate from either an equity or an efficiency perspective.

Overview

In 1983, over 100 million Americans worked an average of about 35 hours per week and received total compensation of roughly $2 trillion, approximately 75 percent of national income [*Economic Report of the President*, 1984, pp. 244, 256, 264]. How labor supply is determined and whether taxes affect it are clearly important issues. Economic theory tells us what variables to examine, but provides no firm answers. Econometric work indicates that for prime age males, hours of work are not much affected by taxes. For married women, on the other hand, taxes probably reduce labor force participation rates and hours of work.

However, two important qualifications are necessary: (1) the welfare system presents many poor people with very high *implicit* marginal tax rates, which discourage their working; and (2) the effect of taxes on other dimensions of labor supply, such as educational and job-training decisions, is not well understood.

Some politicians have suggested that if tax rates were cut, such large amounts of labor supply would be unleashed that the treasury would suffer no revenue loss. Although this is a theoretical possibility, there is no reliable empirical evidence that it would happen.

SAVING

A second behavioral area that may be affected by taxation is saving. Most modern theoretical and empirical work on saving decisions is

---

[22] One influential supply sider, Jude Wanniski, argued that the peak of the curve "is the point at which the electorate desires to be taxed" [1978, p. 98]. There is absolutely no theoretical or empirical basis for this statement.

based on the **life-cycle model** that says individuals' consumption and savings decisions during a given year are the result of a planning process which considers their lifetime economic circumstances.[23] That is, the amount you save each year depends not only on your income that year, but also on the income that you expect in the future and the income you have had in the past. This section uses a simple life-cycle model to explore the impact of taxes on savings decisions.

Consider Scrooge, who expects to live two periods: "now" (period 0) and the "future" (period 1). Scrooge has an income of I_0 dollars in the present period, and knows that his income will be I_1 dollars in the future period. (It might be useful to think of "now" as "working years," when I_0 is labor earnings; and the "future" as retirement years, when I_1 is fixed pension income.) His problem is to decide how much to consume in each period. When Scrooge decides how much to consume, he simultaneously decides how much to save or borrow. If his consumption this period exceeds his current income, he must borrow. If his consumption is less than current income, he saves. We now show how the saving and borrowing decisions are made, and how they are affected by the introduction of a tax.

The first step is to depict the possible combinations of present and future consumption available to Scrooge—his budget constraint. In Figure 15.12, the amount of current consumption, c_0, is measured on the horizontal axis, and the amount of future consumption, c_1, is measured on the vertical axis. One option available to Scrooge is to consume all his income just as it comes in—to consume I_0 in the present and I_1 in the future. This bundle, which is called the **endowment point,** is denoted by A in Figure 15.12. At the endowment point, Scrooge neither saves nor borrows.

Another option is to save out of current income to be able to consume more in the future. Suppose that Scrooge decides to save S dollars this period. If he invests his savings in an asset with a rate of return of i, he can increase his future consumption by $(1 + i)S$—the principal S plus the interest iS. In other words, if Scrooge decreases present consumption by S, he can increase his future consumption by $(1 + i)S$. Graphically, this possibility is represented by moving S dollars to the left of the endowment point A, and $(1 + i)S$ dollars above it—point D in Figure 15.12

Alternatively, Scrooge can consume more than I_0 in the present if he can borrow against his future income. Assume that Scrooge can borrow money at the same rate of interest, i, at which he can lend. If he borrows B dollars to add to his present consumption, how much does his future

---

[23] See Modigliani and Brumberg [1955]. Modern empirical work suggests that about 75 percent of the population behaves in a manner that is consistent with a life-cycle perspective. See King [1983].

FIGURE 15.12   Budget Constraint for Present and Future Consumption

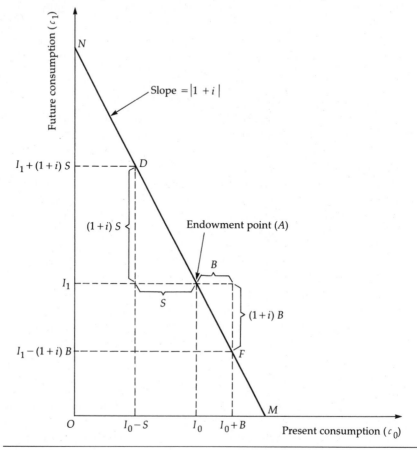

consumption have to be reduced? When the future arrives, Scrooge must pay back B *plus* interest of iB. Hence, Scrooge can increase present consumption by B only if he is willing to reduce future consumption by $B + iB = (1 + i)B$. Graphically, this process involves moving B dollars to the right of the endowment point, and then $(1 + i)B$ dollars below it—point F in the Figure 15.12.

By repeating this process for various values of S and B, we can determine how much future consumption is feasible given any amount of current consumption. In the process of doing so, we trace out budget line MN, which passes through the endowment point A, and has a slope of absolute value $1 + i$. As always, the slope of a budget line represents the opportunity cost of one good in terms of the other. Its slope of $1 + i$ indicates that the cost of $1 of consumption in the present is $1 + i$ dollars of foregone consumption in the future.[24] Because MN shows the trade-off between consumption across periods, it is referred to as the **intertemporal budget constraint.**

To determine which point along MN is actually chosen, we introduce Scrooge's preferences for future as opposed to present consumption. It is assumed that these preferences can be represented by conventionally shaped indifference curves. In Figure 15.13 we reproduce Scrooge's

FIGURE 15.13   Utility Maximizing Choice of Present and Future Consumption

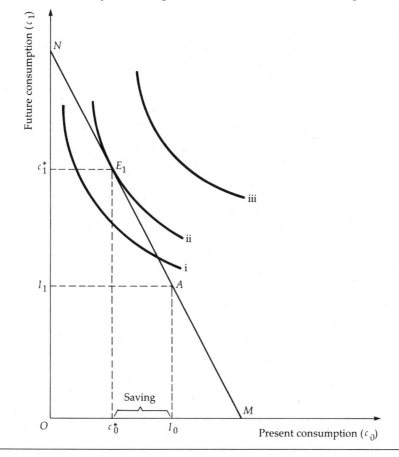

[24] Budget line MN has a convenient algebraic representation. The fundamental constraint facing Scrooge is that the present value of his consumption equals the present value of his income. (See Chapter 9 for an explanation of present value.) The present value of his consumption is $c_0 + c_1/(1 + i)$, while the present value of his income stream is $I_0 + I_1/(1 + i)$. Thus, his selection of c_0 and c_1 must satisfy $c_0 + c_1/(1 + i) = I_0 + I_1/(1 + i)$. The reader can verify that viewed as a function of c_0 and c_1, this is a straight line whose slope is $-(1 + i)$, and which passes through the point (I_0, I_1).

budget constraint, MN, and superimpose a few indifference curves labeled i, ii, and iii. Under the reasonable assumption that more consumption is preferred to less consumption, curves further to the northeast represent higher levels of utility.

Subject to budget constraint MN, the point at which Scrooge maximizes utility is E_1. At this point, Scrooge consumes c_0^* in the present and c_1^* in the future. With this information, it is easy to find how much Scrooge saves. Because present income, I_0, exceeds present consumption, c_0^*, then by definition the difference, $I_0 - c_0^*$, is saving.

Of course, this does not prove that it is always rational to engage in saving. If the highest feasible indifference curve had been tangent to the budget line below point A, then present consumption would have exceeded I_0, and Scrooge would have been a borrower. The analysis of taxation below assumes that Scrooge is a saver, but none of the important implications changes if he is a borrower.

We now consider how the amount of saving changes when a proportional tax on interest income at rate t is introduced.[25] It is assumed that interest payments received by savers are subject to tax, and interest payments made by borrowers are tax deductible. This is in conformity to actual practice under the U.S. tax code (see Chapter 14). How does such a tax regime change the budget line? Figure 15.14 reproduces the before-tax constraint MN from Figure 15.12. The first thing to note is that the after-tax budget constraint must also pass through the endowment point (I_0, I_1), because interest tax or no interest tax, Scrooge always has the option of neither borrowing nor lending. The tax reduces the rate of interest received by savers from i to $(1 - t)i$. Therefore, the opportunity cost of consuming a dollar in the present is only $[1 + (1 - t)i]$ dollars in the future.

At the same time, for each dollar Scrooge borrows, he can deduct one dollar from taxable income. This is worth $\$t$ to him in terms of lower taxes. Hence, the effective rate that has to be paid for borrowing is $(1 - t)i$. Therefore, the cost of increasing current consumption by one dollar, in terms of future consumption, is only $[1 + (1 - t)i]$ dollars. Together, these facts imply that the after-tax budget line has a slope (in absolute value) of $[1 + (1 - t)i]$.

The budget line which passes through I_0, I_1 and has a slope of $[1 + (1 - t)i]$ is drawn as PQ in Figure 15.14. As long as the tax rate is positive, it is necessarily flatter than the pretax budget line MAN.

To complete the analysis, we draw in indifference curves. The new optimum is at E^t, where present consumption is c_0^t, and future consumption is c_1^t. As before, saving is the difference between present consumption and present income, distance $c_0^t I_0$. Note that $c_0^t I_0$ is less than $c_0^* I_0$, the

---

[25] We could consider an *income* tax with a base of both labor and capital income, but this would complicate matters without adding any important additional insights.

FIGURE 15.14 An Interest Tax that Decreases Saving

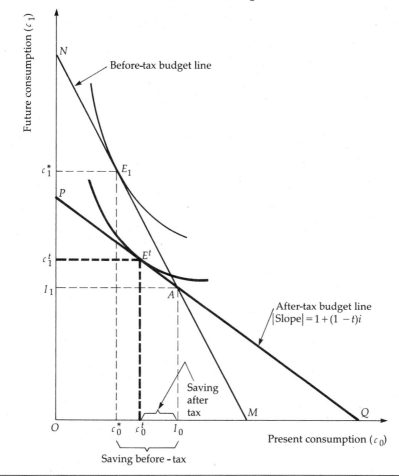

amount that was saved before the tax was imposed. Imposition of the interest tax thus lowers saving by an amount equal to distance $\hat{c}_0^* \hat{c}_0^t$.

However, this result does not follow as a general rule. For a counterexample, consider Figure 15.15. The before- and after-tax budget lines are identical to their counterparts in Figure 15.14 as is the before-tax equilibrium at point E_1. But the tangency of an indifference curve to the after-tax budget line occurs at point $\tilde{E}$, to the left of E_1. Consumption in the present is $\tilde{c}_0$, and in the future, $\tilde{c}_1$. In this case, a tax on interest actually increases saving, from $\hat{c}_0^* I_0$ to $\tilde{c}_0 I_0$. Thus, depending upon the individual's preferences, taxing interest can either increase or decrease saving.

FIGURE 15.15   An Interest Tax that Increases Saving

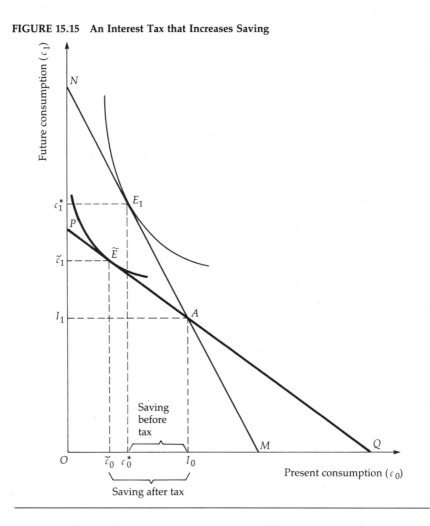

The source of this ambiguity is the conflict between two different effects. On one hand, taxing interest reduces the opportunity cost of present consumption, which tends to increase c_0 and lower saving. This is the substitution effect, which comes about because the tax changes the price of c_0 in terms of c_1. On the other hand, the fact that interest is being taxed makes it harder to achieve any future "consumption goal"—it is necessary to save more to attain any given level of future consumption.[26]

[26] This second effect is well illustrated by the extreme case of the "target saver" described by Musgrave [1959]. Suppose an individual's only goal is to have a given amount of consumption in the future—no more and no less. If the net rate of return goes down, the only way for the individual to reach his target is to increase saving. Similarly, if the net rate of return goes up, the individual's target can be met with smaller saving. Thus, for the target saver, saving and the net interest rate always move in opposite directions.

This is the income effect, which arises because the tax lowers real income. If present consumption is a normal good, then a decrease in income lowers c_0, and hence raises saving. Just as in the case of labor supply, whether the substitution or income effect dominates cannot be known on the basis of theory alone.

This simple two-period model ignores some important real-world complications.

First, as usual, the analysis is couched in real terms—it is the *real* net rate of return that governs behavior. As was emphasized in Chapter 14, care must be taken to correct the *nominal* rates of return observed in the market for inflation.

Second, in the model there is one vehicle for saving, and the returns to saving are taxed at a single rate. In reality, there are numerous assets, each with its own before-tax rate of return. Moreover, as observed in the last chapter, the returns to different assets are taxed at different rates. It is therefore an oversimplification to speak of how changes in "the" after-tax rate of return influence saving.

Third, the model focuses only on private saving. For many purposes, the important variable is social saving, defined as the sum of government and private saving. For example, if the government were to save a sufficiently high proportion of tax receipts from an interest tax, social saving could go up even if private saving decreased.

Finally, the possibility that individuals may choose to leave bequests is ignored in the model. Neither does the model allow for the facts that the rates for borrowing and lending may differ, and that there may be uncertainty concerning what these rates will be. (For example, when an individual purchases common stock, he does not know for sure how much it will increase in value, or even if the price will rise at all.)

Incorporating these points explicitly would make the model both richer and more complicated. In no case, however, would doing so change the basic result that the effect of taxation on saving cannot be predicted without empirical work.

Econometric Studies of Saving

Several econometric studies have estimated the effect of taxation upon saving. In a typical study, the quantity of saving is the left-hand variable and the explanatory variables are the rate of return to saving, disposable income, and other variables that might plausibly affect saving. If the coefficient on the rate of return is positive, the conclusion is that increases in taxes (which decrease the rate of return) depress saving and vice versa.

Prior to the late 1970s, investigators typically concluded that taxes did not have much of an impact on saving.[27] However, most of these early

---

[27] Boskin [1978] provides a review.

analyses failed to correct market rates of return for inflation and/or taxes. As noted above, theoretical considerations suggest that it is the after-tax, inflation-corrected rate of return that governs saving decisions. In general, when a variable in a regression is mismeasured, there is a tendency for its coefficient to be smaller (in absolute value) than is really the case. Hence, it is no surprise that early studies failed to uncover any effect of the net rate of return upon saving.

More recently, Boskin [1978] claimed that the rate of return, when properly measured, has an important effect upon the amount of saving. Boskin used annual U.S. data from 1929 to 1969 to estimate how per capita real saving[28] varies with current and previous year disposable private income, wealth, the rate of unemployment, and the real after-tax return on capital. Depending on the precise estimation technique used, he found an elasticity of saving with respect to the net real interest rate between 0.2 and 0.4. This suggests that lowering the tax rate on capital income would induce substantial amounts of saving.[29]

Boskin's results have been the subject of considerable controversy. Much of the discussion has centered on his computation of the real rate of return.[30] As noted in Chapter 14, this is done by correcting the before-tax rate of return for taxes and then subtracting the expected inflation rate. Several problems arise in implementing this procedure.

First, because there are many assets in the economy, there is no unique before-tax interest rate. Should the rate of return on corporate bonds be used? What about common stock or passbook accounts in commercial banks? An arbitrary choice must be made, and the substantive results may depend upon the decision.

In addition, correcting market returns for inflation requires measuring the *expected* inflation rate. Presumably, people's expectations are based on past experience plus anticipation of the future, but no one knows for sure how expectations are formed. Boskin calculated the expected inflation rate as a complicated weighted average of past inflation rates. In another study, Howrey and Hymans [1980] used the results from surveys in which people were actually asked about their expectations, which led to econometric results quite different from Boskin's. Howrey and Hymans found that the real rate of return does not have much of an impact upon saving at all.

At this time, then, the difficulties involved in estimating the impact of

---

[28] Actually, Boskin's dependent variable is per capita consumption. Because by definition, income is the sum of consumption and saving, anything that increases consumption by a given amount must reduce saving by the same amount. Hence, the coefficients from a regression that explains consumption can be used to predict how changes in the right-hand side variables would affect saving.

[29] However, this response is not nearly large enough to imply that tax reductions on the return to saving would be self-financing. See the discussion of the Laffer curve above.

[30] For further discussion of the controversy, see McLure [1980b].

taxes on saving have defied the efforts of economists to reach a consensus. Research along these lines will no doubt continue.

Taxes and the "Capital Shortage"

As a political issue, the taxation of capital income has been the subject of at least as much public discussion as the taxation of wages. Much of the debate has centered on the proposition that by discouraging saving, the tax system has lead to a *capital shortage*—there is not enough capital around to meet our national "needs." Reduction of taxes on capital is therefore needed to end the so-called *productivity crisis*.[31]

A major problem with this line of reasoning is that, as we have just shown, it is not at all obvious that taxation has reduced the supply of saving. Let us assume, for the sake of argument, that saving has indeed declined as a consequence of taxes. Nevertheless, as long as the capital market is competitive, a decrease in saving will not create a gap between the demand for investment funds and their supply. Instead, the interest rate will adjust to bring supply and demand into equality.[32] However, it is true that the new equilibrium will, other things being equal, involve a lower rate of investment, possibly leading to lower productivity growth.

But to look only at these issues is unfair. Taxation of *any* factor may reduce the equilibrium quantity. Just as in any other case, the important efficiency question is whether taxation of capital income has led to large excess burdens compared to other ways of raising tax revenues. We defer to Chapter 17 a discussion of whether economic efficiency would be enhanced if taxes on capital were eliminated. In the meantime, we conclude by noting that there is no reason a high rate of investment alone is a desirable objective. In a utilitarian framework, at least, capital accumulation is a means of enhancing individual welfare, not an end in itself.

PORTFOLIO COMPOSITION

Taxes may affect not only the total amount of wealth that people accumulate, but also the assets in which that wealth is held. Some argue that taxes have discouraged people from holding risky assets. For example, in 1980, a bipartisan Committee to Fight Inflation, whose members included a number of former treasury secretaries, suggested that Congress could encourage risk taking if it would schedule substantial reductions in business taxes. Intuitively, this proposition seems plausible. Why take a chance on a risky investment if your gains are going to be grabbed

---

[31] See, for example, Ruhm [1981, p. 21].

[32] See Feldstein [1977] for a discussion of other fallacies that have arisen in discussions of the capital shortage.

by the tax collector? It turns out, however, that the problem is considerably more complicated than this line of argument suggests.

Most modern theoretical work on the relationship between taxes and portfolio composition is based upon the path-breaking analysis of Tobin [1958]. Here we summarize the intuition behind Tobin's results, and present a graphical analysis in the appendix to this chapter.

In Tobin's model, individuals make their decisions about whether to invest in an asset on the basis of two characteristics—the expected return on the asset, and how risky that return is. Other things being the same, investors prefer assets which are expected to yield high returns. At the same time, investors are assumed to dislike risk; other things being the same, investors prefer safer assets.

Suppose that there are two assets. The first is perfectly safe, but it yields a zero rate of return. (Imagine holding money in a world with no inflation.) The second is a bond which *on average* yields a positive rate of return, but it is risky—there is some chance that the price will go down, so that the investor incurs a loss.

Note that the investor can adjust the return and risk on the entire portfolio by holding different combinations of the two assets. In one extreme case he or she could hold only the safe asset—there is no return, but no risk. On the other hand, the investor could hold only the risky asset—his or her expected return rises, but so does the risk involved. The typical investor holds a combination of both the risky and safe assets to suit tastes concerning risk and return.

Now assume that a proportional tax is levied on the return to capital assets. Assume also that the tax allows for **full loss offset**—individuals can deduct all losses from taxable income. (To a considerable extent, this reflects actual practice in the United States. See Chapter 14.) Because the safe asset has a yield of zero, the tax has no effect on its rate of return— the return is still zero. In contrast, the risky asset has a positive expected rate of return, which is lowered by the presence of the tax. It seems that the tax reduces the attractiveness of the risky asset compared to the safe asset.

However, at the same time that the tax lowers the return to the risky asset, it lowers its riskiness as well. Why? In effect, introduction of the tax turns the government into the investor's "silent partner." If the investor "wins" (in the sense of receiving a positive return), then the government shares in the gain. But because of the loss-offset provision, if the individual loses, the government also shares in the loss. Suppose, for example, that an individual loses $100 on an investment. If his or her tax rate is 25 percent, then the ability to subtract the $100 from taxable income lowers the tax bill by $25. Thus, even though the investment lost $100, the investor loses only $75. In short, introduction of the tax tightens the dispersion of returns—the highs are less high and the lows are less low—and hence, reduces the risk. Thus, although the tax makes the risky asset *less* attractive by reducing its expected return, it simultaneously makes it *more* attractive by decreasing its risk. If the second effect dominates, taxation can on balance make the risky asset more desirable.

An important assumption behind this discussion is the existence of a perfectly riskless asset. This is not a very realistic assumption. In a world where no one is sure exactly what the inflation rate will be, even the "return" on money is risky. But the basic reasoning still holds. Because taxes decrease risk as well as returns, the effect of taxes on portfolio choice is ambiguous [see Feldstein, 1969 for a demonstration].

Resolving this ambiguity econometrically is very difficult. A major problem is that it is hard to obtain reliable information on just what assets people hold. Individuals may not accurately report their holdings to survey takers because they are not exactly sure of the true values at any point in time. Alternatively, people might purposely misrepresent their asset positions because of fears that the information will be reported to the tax authorities. In one study using a fairly reliable data set from the early 1960s, Feldstein [1976c] found that other things being the same, people in higher tax brackets hold a higher proportion of their portfolios in common stock, which is quite risky, than in relatively safe assets like money and bonds. This finding lends at least tentative support to the notion that taxation increases risk taking. But the issue is far from being resolved.

HOUSING DECISIONS

Another area that may be affected by taxation is housing decisions. How this happens can best be illustrated with an example. Macbeth owns a house and decides to rent it out for profit. Being a landlord entails certain annual costs. An important one is the opportunity cost *(OC)* of the funds invested in the house. For example, if Macbeth has invested $200,000 in the house and the going rate of interest is 12 percent, then the annual opportunity cost is the $24,000 of foregone interest. If he has borrowed money to purchase the house, the interest payments on the mortgage *(Mi)* are also costs. In addition, expenditures for maintenance *(MA)* and property taxes *(PT)* must be incurred. Finally, some costs arise due to changes in the value of the house. If the dwelling depreciates in value during the year due to wear and tear, this is as much a cost of renting it out as any of those listed above. On the other hand, if the house increases in value, then Macbeth has enjoyed a capital gain, which should be counted as a "negative cost." We will denote the value of capital gains by ΔV. (A negative value of ΔV, then, indicates that the house has decreased in value.)

Adding up these items, the total annual cost *(A)* is

(15.3) $$A = OC + Mi + MA + PT - \Delta V$$

For example, suppose that Macbeth's annual mortgage interest payments are $12,000; his maintenance expenditures $3,000; his property taxes $2,500; and his expected appreciation on the house $4,000 per year. Then his total annual cost (including opportunity cost) is $37,500 (= $24,000 + $12,000 + $3,000 + $2,500 − $4,000).

As long as the market for housing is competitive, the rental income received by the landowner will be bid down to the point at which it just equals the cost. Hence, Macbeth's yearly rental income from the house is *A*. Under a Haig-Simons income tax system, Macbeth must include *A* in his taxable income. If his marginal tax rate is 50 percent, the rental income creates a tax liability of $18,750 (= .5 × $37,500).[33]

Now suppose that instead of renting the house out, Macbeth and his wife choose to live in it themselves. By virtue of living in the house, they derive services from it that have a market value of *A*. Of course, they do not literally receive *A* dollars—the income is in kind. However, under a comprehensive income tax system, the form in which income is received is irrelevant, and the "imputed rent" from owner occupied housing is a part of taxable income. Moreover, any increase in the value of the house is income, just like any other asset. (Decreases in house value lower income.)

Under U.S. law, the imputed rent from owner-occupied housing is *not* subject to tax, despite the fact that mortgage interest payments and property taxes are deductible. Moreover, housing capital gains are generally exempt from taxation.[34] If the Macbeths' marginal tax rate is *t* and they itemize their deductions,[35] then these tax provisions lower the effective cost of owner-occupied housing from Equation (15.3)[36] to

(15.4) $OC + Mi + MA + PT - \Delta V - t(Mi + PT)$

The last term in Equation (15.4) reflects the value to the owner of being able to deduct mortgage interest and property taxes. In effect, then, the federal income tax implicitly subsidizes owner-occupied housing. Because marginal tax rates tend to increase with income, the subsidy is worth more to high-income people, other things being the same. It has been estimated that the deduction of mortgage interest and property tax payments lowered tax revenues by about $37 billion in fiscal year 1984.[37]

---

[33] Of course, the landlord would be able to deduct the costs incurred in earning this income.

[34] Capital gains from the sale of a principal residence are excluded when another residence costing at least as much is purchased within two years. In addition, for taxpayers 55 years of age and older, there is a one-time housing capital gains exclusion of $125,000.

[35] Not all homeowners itemize the deductions; about 50 percent simply deduct mortgage payments.

[36] If the individual took the standard deduction as a renter, he would gain the itemized deductions at the expense of the standard deduction. In this case, Equation (15.4) must be increased by the value to the individual of taking the standard deduction.

[37] See Chapter 14, Table 14.1.

The size of the implicit subsidy has been affected by inflation. Higher inflation rates lead to both higher nominal interest rates (including mortgage rates) *and* to higher nominal housing capital gains. Because interest rates are a cost and capital gains are a benefit, one might guess that the two effects would cancel each other. Equation (15.4) indicates that this is not the case because interest payments are tax deductible, while the housing capital gains are untaxed. On balance, inflation *increases* the attractiveness of owner occupation. This is another example of how inflation affects *real* incentives in the presence of the existing tax structure. (See Chapter 14.) It is difficult to say just how much inflation has increased the attractiveness of housing, because the effect of inflation on nominal interest rates is an unresolved question.

Still, it is generally agreed that by lowering its effective price, the federal income tax increases the demand for owner-occupied housing. The precise size of the increase depends upon the price elasticity of demand for such housing. Using data from 1970, Rosen [1979] estimated a price elasticity of about −1.0 and calculated that removal of the favorable tax provisions for housing would in the long run, reduce the quantity consumed by about 14 percent.

The implicit subsidy affects not only how much housing people purchase, but also whether they become owners or renters in the first place. At the end of World War II, 48 percent of U.S. households resided in owner-occupied housing; by 1980, the figure had grown to 66 percent. Over this period, increasing marginal tax rates tended to enhance the attractiveness of the implicit subsidy to owner occupation. Of course, other factors were changing that might have influenced housing patterns; for example, incomes rose considerably. However, according to an econometric study by Hendershott and Shilling [1980], about one quarter of the increase in the proportion of homeowners since World War II is attributable to tax considerations.

Proposals for Changing the Tax Treatment of Housing.   In Chapter 7, we discussed the pros and cons of providing a subsidy for owner-occupied housing. The point made there was that from an externality point of view, the subsidy does not have much merit. And since the subsidy's value increases with income, one can hardly claim that it equalizes the income distribution. In light of these facts, a number of proposals have been made to reform the federal tax treatment of housing. Probably the most radical change would be to include net imputed rent in taxable income.[38] Such a move might create administrative problems, because the authorities would have to determine the potential market rental

---

[38] The imputed income from owner-occupied housing was taxed in the United Kingdom until 1963. This practice is still followed to some extent in a number of European countries. See Fainstain [1980].

value of each house. In many cases this is difficult because it is hard to find a comparable dwelling that has recently been on the rental market.[39]

Moreover, taxing imputed rent does not appear politically feasible. Homeowners are more likely to perceive their house as endless drains on their financial resources than as revenue producers. It would not be easy to convince homeowners—who comprise more than half the electorate—that taxation of imputed rental income is a good idea.

A number of alternative reform proposals have focused upon reducing the value of mortgage interest and property tax deductions to upper income individuals. One possibility would be to put upper limits on the dollar amounts that can be deducted. Another would be to convert these deductions into credits: each homeowner would be allowed to subtract the *same* proportion of interest and property tax payments from his tax liability. In terms of Equation (15.4), the marginal tax rate, t, would be replaced by some number—say 0.25—independent of the household's tax status. In this way, those with higher marginal tax rates would not enjoy an advantage, other things being the same.

Questions of administrative feasibility lessen the attractiveness of deduction limitations. For example, some taxpayers could simply secure mortgate loans on other assets and legally deduct the interest costs. More generally, it is difficult to evaluate all such proposals because it is not clear what their objectives are and what other policy instruments are assumed to be available. For example, if a more equal income distribution is the goal, why bother with changing from deductions to credits? It would make more sense just to adjust the rate schedule appropriately.

Finally, we should note that much of the debate over the tax treatment of housing implicitly assumes that full taxation of imputed rent would be the most efficient solution. Recall from the theory of optimal taxation (Chapter 13) that if lump sum taxes are excluded, the efficiency maximizing set of tax rates is generally a function of the elasticities of demand and supply for all commodities. Only in very special cases do we expect efficiency to require equal rates for all sources of income. On the other hand, it is also highly improbable that the efficient tax rate on imputed rental income is zero. Determining the appropriate rate is an important topic for further research.

CONCLUSION: A NOTE ON POLITICS AND ELASTICITIES

Despite much investigation, the effect of income taxation upon several important kinds of behavior is not known for sure. Different "experts"

---

[39] However, similar problems have been dealt with by local tax authorities who levy taxes based on the value of real property. See Chapter 18.

are therefore likely to give policymakers different pieces of advice. In this situation, it is almost inevitable that policymakers will adopt those behavioral assumptions that enhance the perceived feasibility of their goals. Although it is always dangerous to generalize, liberals tend to believe that behavior is not very responsive to the tax system, while conservatives take the opposite view. Liberals prefer low elasticities because they can raise large amounts of money for public sector activity without having to worry too much about charges that they are "killing the goose that laid the golden egg." In contrast, conservatives like to assume high elasticities because this limits the volume of taxes that can be collected before serious efficiency costs are imposed on the economy. Thus, when journalists, politicians, and economists make assertions about how taxes affect incentives, it is prudent to evaluate their claims in light of what their "hidden agendas" might be.

SUMMARY

The U.S. personal income tax affects a myriad of economic decisions, including the amount of labor supplied, the level of saving, the choice of assets held in portfolios, and the amount of residential housing consumed.

For labor supply, saving, and choice of portfolio, the *direction* of the effects of taxation is theoretically ambiguous. Further, in each area, the *size* of tax-induced behavioral changes may be determined only by empirical investigation. For these reasons, the effect of taxation is among the most contended of all areas of public policy.

Econometric studies of labor supply indicate that prime age males vary their hours only slightly in response to tax changes, while hours of married women are quite sensitive to variations in the after-tax wage rate.

Earnings taxes can increase, decrease, or leave unchanged the attractiveness of human capital investments. The outcome depends in part on how taxes affect hours of work.

The welfare system imposes high implicit tax rates on the poor and is generally considered to reduce their labor supply. An alternative popular among economists is a negative income tax. Preliminary evidence from social experiments indicates that the negative income tax does not introduce strong work disincentives.

The effect of tax rates upon tax revenues depends upon the responsiveness of personal behavior to changes in tax rates. It is theoretically possible that tax-rate reductions may increase tax revenues, but there is no evidence that this is currently the case for the United States.

The effect of taxes on saving may be analyzed using the life-cycle model which assumes that people make their annual consumption and saving decisions keeping in mind their lifetime resources. Taxing interest income lowers the opportunity cost of and thereby creates incentives to increase present consumption—i.e., lowers saving. However, this substitution effect may be offset by the fact that the tax reduces total lifetime resources which tends to *reduce* present consumption,—i.e., increase saving. The net effect on saving may be determined only by empirical observation.

Analysis of the impact of taxes on saving is complicated by the existence of numerous interest rates, each of which must be adjusted for inflation. Further, total saving includes the net saving by government which may offset changes in private saving. Finally, contrary to the simple life-cycle model, individuals may choose not to consume all of their income, but rather to leave a bequest.

Econometric studies of saving behavior have foundered on both conceptual and practical difficulties. As a result there is no consensus opinion on the effects of taxation on saving.

The theoretical effects of taxation on portfolio composition are ambiguous. Taxes reduce the expected return on a risky asset but also lessen its riskiness. The net effect of these conflicting tendencies has not been empirically resolved.

The personal income tax unambiguously provides incentives to increase consumption of owner-occupied housing. This affects both the percentage of those choosing to own their homes and the quantity of owner-occupied housing.

Proposals to modify the tax treatment of housing include taxing imputed rent at the personal income tax rate, limiting the deduction for mortgage interest, or converting the deduction to a tax credit. Each proposal should be evaluated by the standards of optimal tax theory.

DISCUSSION QUESTIONS

1. Using a supply-demand diagram, illustrate the effects upon hours of work of imposing a proportional wage tax under each of the following circumstances:
   a. The income effect dominates the market labor supply curve; labor demand is perfectly elastic.
   b. The substitution effect dominates the market labor supply curve; labor demand is perfectly elastic.
   c. The substitution effect dominates the market labor supply curve; labor demand is negatively related to the wage rate.
   Discuss the differences.

2. Consider the following two negative income tax programs:
   a. Recipients are given a basic annual benefit of $7,500 which is reduced by 75 cents for each dollar earned outside the program.
   b. Recipients are given a basic grant of $2,500 which is reduced by 25 cents for each dollar earned outside the program.

    i. At what level of earnings does a recipient break even with respect to each system?

    ii. Discuss the labor supply consequences of each program.

*3. In 1981, the United States Savings and Loan League urged Congress to increase the exclusion of interest and dividend income from $200 to $1,000 per individual. Using the simplified two-period diagram and assuming that there is a proportional tax on interest income:

    a. Sketch the intertemporal budget constraints when there is no tax, when the exclusion is $100, and when the exclusion is raised. (Assume all interest expenses on loans are deductible.)

    b. Illustrate circumstances in which personal saving is raised, reduced, and unchanged.

    c. Does such a program provide any additional incentive to save?

4. Discuss: "The capital gains tax is another instance of antiproducer taxation. It is aimed directly at the enterprise and risk taking needed in an economy where investment decisions are made by individuals and not by the state." [Wallich, 1979, p. 26].

5. The *New York Times* (October 17, 1982, p. 1) reported that:

> Time and time again, families choose one community over another simply because of the reputation of the schools. They will pay vastly more for a house that is no more desirable than another because they want their children in one school system rather than another.

    a. How does this enter into the issue of the tax deductible status of property taxes?

    b. If tax deductibility were eliminated, how would the effective cost of owner-occupied housing be changed?

    c. What impact would this have on the demand for owner-occupied housing? Why?

SELECTED REFERENCES

Feldstein, Martin S. "The Effects of Taxation on Risk Taking." *Journal of Political Economy* 77 (1969), pp. 755–64.

Fullerton, Don. "On the Possibility of an Inverse Relationship between Tax Rates and Government Revenues." *Journal of Public Economics* 19, no. 1 (October 1982), pp. 3–22.

McLure, Charles E., Jr. "Taxes, Saving, and Welfare: Theory and Evidence." *National Tax Journal* 33, no. 3 (September 1980), pp. 311–20.

Rees, Albert. "An Overview of the Labor-Supply Results." *The Journal of Human Resources* 9, no. 2 (Spring 1974), pp. 158–80.

---

* Difficult.

APPENDIX 15A
TAXATION AND PORTFOLIO COMPOSITION

This appendix summarizes Tobin's [1958] discussion of how a tax on the return to capital can increase the share of risky assets in an individual's portfolio.

Suppose that there are only two assets available for purchase.[40] The first offers a zero rate of return with complete certainty. The other asset is risky—it provides a positive rate of return *on average*, but there is a possibility that it may produce a loss. The problem is to determine how much of each asset the individual buys, and how the introduction of a tax changes that decision.

We assume that the investor has expectations concerning how the risky asset will perform. Consider asset *A* in Figure 15A.1. Our investor

FIGURE 15A.1   Calculating Expected Value

	Expected Increase (percent)	
Probability	*Asset A*	*Asset B*
$\frac{1}{3}$	−2%	−5%
$\frac{1}{3}$	5	5
$\frac{1}{3}$	12	15
Expected Value	5%	5%

believes that it will increase in value by 12 percent with a probability of one in three, increase by 5 percent with probability of one in three, and decrease by 2 percent with probability of one in three. *On average*, the asset is expected to produce a return of 5 percent ($= \frac{1}{3} \times 12\% + \frac{1}{3} \times 5\% - \frac{1}{3} \times 2\%$). We will denote this **expected value** as μ.

Now consider asset *B*, which yields returns of 15 percent, 5 percent, and −5 percent, each with probability of one in three. Its expected value is also 5 percent. However, *B* is more risky than *A* in the sense that there is greater dispersion of possible outcomes around the expected value. We denote as σ the amount of dispersion of the distribution around its expected value. In the language of statistics, σ is referred to as the **standard deviation** of the distribution. More precisely, the standard deviation of a set of *N* outcomes, $x_1, \ldots, x_N$, is defined as

$$\sqrt{\frac{1}{N-1} \sum_{i=1}^{N} (x_i - \mu)^2}$$

---

[40] See Mossin [1968] for a generalization to the case where there are many assets.

where μ is the expected value. Thus, for example, for distribution A

$$\sigma = \sqrt{\tfrac{1}{2}[(-2 - 5)^2 + (5 - 5)^2 + (12 - 5)^2]} = 7$$

and for asset B,

$$\sigma = \sqrt{\tfrac{1}{2}[(-5 - 5)^2 + (5 - 5)^2 + (15 - 5)^2]} = 10$$

It is assumed that investors make their decisions about holdings of an asset on the basis of its values of μ and σ.[41] Other things being the same, people prefer high values of μ to low values. To the extent people do not like to subject themselves to risk, they prefer low values of σ to high values, other things being the same.

Let us now return to the case where one asset is risky and the other is riskless. Denote the expected value and standard deviation of the risky asset as μ_R and σ_R, respectively, and the proportion of the individual's portfolio held in the risky asset as λ. Because there are only two assets, the proportion held in the safe asset must be $(1 - \lambda)$. The expected return on the portfolio, μ, is a weighted average of the expected value of the safe asset (zero) and the expected value of the risky asset (μ_R), with the weights being the proportions held:

(15A.1) $\mu = (1 - \lambda) \times 0 + \lambda \times \mu_R = \lambda\mu_R$

Thus, if a person holds one fourth of his portfolio in an asset with an expected return of 8 percent, and the rest of the portfolio in an asset with an expected return of zero, then the expected return on the portfolio is 2 percent ($.75 \times 0 + .25 \times 8\%$). Note that the greater the share held in the risky asset, the greater the expected return on the portfolio.

In the same way, the risk of portfolio σ is a weighted average of the risks of the two assets:

(15A.2) $\sigma = (1 - \lambda) \times 0 + \lambda \times \sigma_R = \lambda\sigma_R$

Taken together, (15A.1) and (15A.2) implicitly summarize all the risk and return opportunities available to the individual. We need only substitute any value of λ into (15A.1) and (15A.2) to find the values of μ and σ for the associated portfolio. For example, if $\lambda = 0$ is chosen, according to (15A.1) and (15A.2), both μ and σ equal zero. This makes sense intuitively, because $\lambda = 0$ is the case where the whole portfolio is in the safe asset. If $\lambda = \tfrac{1}{3}$ is chosen, then $\mu = \tfrac{1}{3}\mu_R$ and $\sigma = \tfrac{1}{3}\sigma_R$. If $\lambda = 1$ is selected, then the characteristics of the portfolio are identical to those of the risky asset: $\mu = \mu_R$ and $\sigma = \sigma_R$.

Figure 15A.2 summarizes this discussion graphically. The horizontal axis measures σ, the riskiness of the portfolio, and the vertical axis measures μ, its expected return. Straight line OA represents all the

---

[41] It is only under rather special conditions that the characteristics of assets can be summarized by these two parameters alone. See Mossin [1968] for details.

FIGURE 15A.2 **Possible Combinations of Risk and Return**

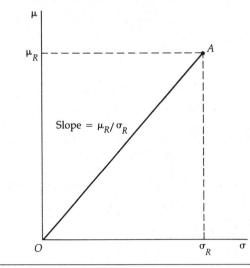

possible values that μ and σ can take as λ varies from zero to one.[42] In effect, *OA* is the "budget constraint" because it shows the most return that can be obtained for any level of risk. The slope of *OA* is μ_R/σ_R.[43] Note that point *A* corresponds to the portfolio where $\lambda = 1$ and hence has $\sigma = \sigma_R$ and $\mu = \mu_R$.

The particular point on line *OA* chosen by an individual depends upon his attitudes toward risk. Some individuals are not too worried about sustaining a loss. We would expect them to choose a portfolio near point *A*. Others are more cautious, and would be expected to locate closer to point *O*. A natural way to model these preferences is by drawing indifference curves between risk and return. Three typical indifference curves are drawn in Figure 15A.3 and labeled *i, ii,* and *iii.* Unlike "typical" indifference curves, they slope *upward.* This reflects the assumption that risk is perceived as undesirable. Therefore, if an individual is subjected to more risk, the only way to maintain a constant utility level is to compensate him with more return. The arrow in the diagram indicates the direction of increasing utility. Indifference curve *iii* repre-

---

[42] λ can actually exceed one if investors are allowed to "sell short," but this is a complication that need not be considered here.

[43] To prove that the slope is μ_R/σ_R, divide equation (15A.1) by equation (15A.2) to obtain

$$\frac{\mu}{\sigma} = \frac{\mu_R}{\sigma_R}$$

Therefore $\mu = (\mu_R/\sigma_R)\sigma$. Whenever σ increases by one unit, μ increases by μ_R/σ_R units, and by definition, the slope is μ_R/σ_R.

FIGURE 15A.3   Optimal Choice of Risk and Return

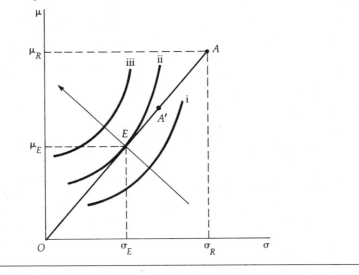

sents a higher level of utility than curve *ii* because the former allows the possibility of a higher expected value with no more risk.

Utility is maximized at the point where budget constraint *OA* is tangent to an indifference curve. In Figure 15A.3, this occurs at point *E*. The optimal portfolio has return μ_E and risk σ_E.

How much of the risky asset must be purchased to obtain a portfolio with these characteristics? To answer this question, turn to either Equation (15A.1) or (15A.2) which tell us exactly what proportion of the portfolio has to be invested in the risky asset to achieve any given expected value for the overall portfolio. Specifically, by substituting μ_E into (15A.1), we find that the optimal proportion to hold in the risky asset, λ_E, is given by

(15A.3) $\lambda_E = \mu_E / \mu_R$

[The same value of λ_E is found by substituting σ_E into equation (15A.2)].

Now suppose that the government levies a 25 percent proportional income tax. Assume that the tax allows for full-loss offset, so that individuals deduct losses from taxable income.[44] As usual, to find the effect of the tax on behavior, we must see how it changes the individual's opportunity locus. For the riskless asset, the after-tax value of μ is identical to the before-tax value for the simple reason that a proportional tax on a zero return yields no revenue. The story is different for the risky

---

[44] The analysis can also be done assuming a tax system with increasing marginal tax rates and/or the absence of full-loss offset. These assumptions complicate the model considerably.

asset. The tax lowers the expected value from μ_R to $(1 - t)\mu_R$. At the same time, however, the tax lowers standard deviation from σ_R to $(1 - t)\sigma_R$. This can be shown mathematically by using the definition of σ presented above. When each of the possible returns is multiplied by $(1 - t)$, the value of σ is also reduced by a factor of $(1 - t)$. The intuitive explanation for why the tax reduces σ is given in the text of this chapter.

Algebraically, after imposition of the tax, the relations described in (15A.1) and (15A.2) become

(15A.4) $$\mu = \lambda(1 - t)\mu_R$$

(15A.5) $$\sigma = \lambda(1 - t)\sigma_R$$

With equations (15A.4) and (15A.5) in hand, we can generate the after-tax opportunity locus by substituting various values of λ and graphing the results on a diagram with σ and μ on the axes. Doing so indicates that the locus: (a) passes through the origin, when $\lambda = 0$; (b) passes through the point $[(1 - t)\sigma_R], (1 - t)\mu_R]$, when $\lambda = 1$; and (c) has a slope equal to μ_R/σ_R.[45] But these are exactly the same as the characteristics of the before-tax budget line, except that the after-tax line does not extend all the way up to point A. In effect, each point on the before-tax budget constraint just migrates along OA by an amount equal to 25 percent of the distance between itself and the origin. Thus, the after-tax budget line, denoted OA' in Figure 15A.3, coincides with the before-tax budget line up to point A'.

If the opportunity locus stays the same, then so does the point of utility maximization, E.[46] You might be tempted to argue, then, that the tax has no effect on the individual's portfolio. But this is incorrect. The diagram shows only the expected return and risk of the optimal portfolio, *not* how the investor divides his wealth between the two assets. To find the latter information, we have to go back either to Equation (15A.4) or (15A.5) to find the value of λ now required to attain μ_E and σ_E. Substituting μ_E into Equation (15A.4), we find the after-tax proportion held in the risky asset, λ_t, is $\mu_E/[\mu_R(1 - t)]$. Comparing this to equation (15A.3), we see that $\lambda_t > \lambda_E$. The proportion of the portfolio in the risky asset has actually increased. To understand this result intuitively, consider the problem of maintaining an *after-tax* expected return of μ_E on a portfolio after a 50 percent tax is levied. The only way to do so is to double the share of the risky asset.

Tobin's analysis thus turns the popular view right on its head—taxation *encourages* risk taking, not the other way around. The key to this

---

[45] To see that this is the case, simply divide (15A.4) by (15A.5), and follow the argument given in footnote 43.

[46] If λ is constrained to be between zero and one, then an exception occurs if the before-tax equilibrium was somewhere between A' and A. In this case, the original equilibrium would be infeasible under the tax, and the new optimum would be at A'.

outcome is the realization that the tax reduces not only the expected return on the risky asset but the risk, as well.

This unambiguous result is a consequence of some special features of the model. If any one of several of the assumptions behind Figure 15A.3 is modified, the theoretical effect of taxation on risk taking becomes ambiguous. Assume, for example, that the safe asset has a positive return, μ_S, rather than zero as before. (It might be a savings account which offers a guaranteed real rate of 5 percent.) In this case, the rate of return on the portfolio is

(15A.6) $$\mu = (1 - \lambda)\mu_S + \lambda\mu_R$$

The risk of the portfolio is still proportional to the share held in the risky asset

(15A.7) $$\sigma = \lambda\sigma_R$$

As before, by substituting all possible values of λ into (15A.6) and (15A.7), we can derive the opportunity locus, which is straight line PB in Figure 15A.4. Unlike OA in Figure 15A.3, it does not pass through the origin. This is because even if λ is 0, the portfolio earns a positive return of μ_S.[47] Given opportunity locus PB, the individual optimizes at a point

FIGURE 15A.4   Portfolio Choice When the Safe Asset Has a Positive Return

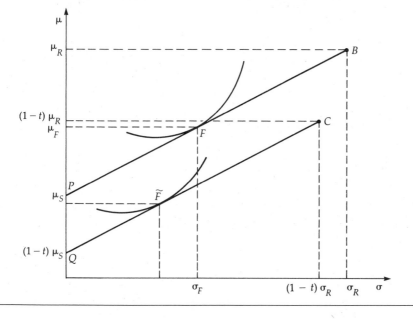

---

[47] The slope of PB is $[(\mu_R - \mu_S)/\sigma_R]$. To see this, solve (15A.7) for λ, substitute into (15A.6), and solve for μ as a function of σ. This yields $\mu = \mu_S + \sigma[(\mu_R - \mu_S)/\sigma_R]$, with an intercept of μ_S, and a slope of $(\mu_R - \mu_S)/\sigma_R$.

like F. He then uses equations (15A.6) and (15A.7) to choose λ so as to attain a portfolio with expected return μ_F and risk σ_F.

When a tax with full-loss offset is levied, the equations defining the budget constraint become

(15A.8) $\mu = (1 - \lambda)(1 - t)\mu_S + \lambda(1 - t)\mu_R$

(15A.9) $\sigma = \lambda(1 - t)\sigma_R$

The budget constraint implied by these equations has the same slope as PB, but its intercept is lower.[48]

The new locus is represented by QC in Figure 15A.4. Exactly where the investor locates along the new budget constraint depends upon his indifference map. If a tangency occurs at a point like $\bar{F}$, then he might decrease the share of his portfolio in the risky asset. We conclude that when the riskless asset has a positive rate of return, imposition of a tax can increase or decrease the proportion of the portfolio held in the risky asset.[49]

---

[48] To see this, solve (15A.9) for λ, substitute into (15A.8), and solve for μ as a function of σ. This yields $\mu = (1 - t)\mu_S + \sigma[(\mu_R - \mu_S)/\sigma_R]$. This has the same slope as the equation in footnote 47, but its intercept is $(1 - t)\mu_S$ instead of μ_S.

[49] A similar ambiguity arises if it is assumed that *neither* asset is perfectly safe. In this case, the opportunity locus between σ and μ turns out to be curved. See Feldstein [1969].

CHAPTER 16

The Corporation Tax

*I'll probably kick myself for having said this, but
when are we going to have the courage to point out
that in our tax structure, the corporation tax is very
hard to justify?*

Ronald W. Reagan

In 1983, $1,918.4 billion or 58 percent of the gross domestic product originated in nonfinancial corporations alone. A **corporation** is a form of business organization created by a specific state through its approval of a corporate charter. While the charter is filed by the founders of the corporation, a corporation is owned by its stockholders, with ownership usually represented by transferable stock certificates. The stockholders have limited liability for the acts of the corporation. This means that their liability to the creditors of the corporation is limited to the amount they have invested in the corporation.

Corporations are independent legal entities and as such are often referred to as artificial legal persons. A corporation may make contracts, hold property, incur debt, sue, and be sued. And just like any other person, a corporation must pay tax upon its income. The present chapter explains the structure of the federal corporation income tax and analyzes its effects upon the allocation of resources.

The relative importance of the federal corporation tax has fallen in recent decades. In 1950, the tax accounted for 27.9 percent of all federal tax collections. By 1983, this figure was down to 5.8 percent [*Facts and Figures on Government Finance*, 1981, p. 117; *Facts and Figures on Government Finance*, 1983, p. 129]. There might be a temptation, then, to dismiss the tax as not being worthy of much attention. This would be a mistake for two reasons. First of all, the absolute amount of corporation tax revenues is still large. In 1982, about 2.95 million returns were filed and $66 billion collected [U.S. Department of the Treasury, 1983b, pp. 7–8]. Second, the theory of excess burden suggests that a tax may create efficiency costs that are far out of proportion to the revenues yielded. There is some evidence that the corporation tax is an example of this important phenomenon.

WHY TAX CORPORATIONS?

Before undertaking a careful description and analysis of the tax, we should ask whether it makes sense to have a special tax system for corporations in the first place. To be sure, from a *legal* point of view, corporations are people. But from an economic standpoint, this notion makes little sense. As we have seen in Chapter 11, only real people can pay a tax. If this is the case, why should corporate activity be subject to a special tax? Is it not sufficient to tax the incomes of the corporation *owners* via the personal income tax?

A number of justifications for a separate corporation tax have been proposed.

First, contrary to the view just stated, corporations—especially very big ones—really are distinct entities. Large corporations have thousands of stockholders, and the managers of such corporations are controlled only very loosely, if at all, by the stockholder/owners. Most economists would certainly agree that there is separation of ownership and control in large corporations, and this creates important problems for understanding just how corporations function. Nevertheless, it does not follow that the corporation should be taxed as a separate entity.

Second, the corporation receives a number of special privileges from society, the most important of which is limited liability of the stockholders. The corporation tax can be viewed as a user fee for this benefit. However, the tax is so structured that there is no reason to believe that the revenues paid approximate the benefits received.

Finally, the corporation tax protects the integrity of the personal income tax. Suppose that Karl's share of the earnings of a corporation during a given year is $10,000. According to the standard definition of income (Chapter 14) this $10,000 is income whether the money happens to be retained by the corporation or paid out to Karl. If the $10,000 is paid out, it is taxed in an amount which depends upon his personal income tax rate. In the absence of a corporation tax, the $10,000 creates no tax liability if it is retained by the corporation. Hence, unless corporation income is taxed, Karl can reduce his tax liability by accumulating income within the corporation.[1]

---

[1] Of course, the money will be taxed when it is eventually paid out, but in the meantime, the full $10,000 grows at the before-tax rate of interest. Remember from Chapter 14, "taxes deferred are taxes saved."

It is certainly true that if corporate income goes untaxed, opportunities for personal tax avoidance are created. But a special tax on corporations is not the only way to include earnings accumulated in corporations. An alternative method which is viewed as superior by many economists is discussed at the end of this chapter.

STRUCTURE

Under current law, corporate taxable income in excess of $100,000 is taxed at a rate of 46 percent. Income below $100,000 is taxed at lower rates. Since roughly 90 percent of all corporate income is taxed at the 46 percent rate, for our purposes, the system can safely be presented as a flat rate of 46 percent.

As in the case of the personal income tax, knowledge of the rate applied to taxable income by itself gives relatively little information about the effective burden. We must know exactly what deductions from before-tax corporate income are allowed to compute taxable income. Accordingly, we now discuss the rules for defining taxable corporate income.[2]

Wage Payments Excluded

As we saw in Chapter 14, a fundamental principle in defining personal income is that income should be measured net of the expenses incurred in earning it. The same logic applies to the measurement of corporate income. One important business expense is labor, and wages paid to workers are excluded from taxable income.

Interest Payments Excluded

When corporations borrow, interest payments to lenders are excluded from taxable income. Again, the justification is that business costs should be deductible. However, when firms finance their activities by issuing stock, the dividends paid to the stockholders are *not* deductible from corporate earnings. The consequences of this asymmetry in the treatment of interest and dividends are discussed below.

Depreciation Excluded[3]

Suppose that during a given year the XYZ corporation makes two purchases: *(a)* $1,000 worth of stationery, which is used up within the

---

[2] The definition of corporate income occupies many hundreds of pages, and there is no attempt here to be inclusive. For further detail, see *Economic Recovery Tax Act of 1981* [1981]. Note also that many of these rules apply to noncorporate businesses, as well.

[3] Understanding the impact of depreciation allowances requires the concept of present value. Readers may wish to review the relevant material in Chapter 9.

year, and (b) a $1,000 drill press, which will last for 10 years. Should there be any difference in the tax treatment of these expenditures?

From the accounting point of view, these are very different items. Because the stationery is entirely consumed within the year of its purchase, its entire value is deductible from that year's corporate income. But the drill press is a durable good. It is not entirely used up during the year. To be sure, during its first year of use, some of the machine is "used up" by wear and tear, which decreases its value. This process is called **economic depreciation.** But at the end of the year, the drill press is still worth something to the firm, and in principle could be sold to some other firm at that price.

We conclude that during the first year of the life of the drill press, a consistent definition of income requires that only the economic depreciation experienced that year be subtracted from the firm's before-tax income. Similarly, the economic depreciation of the machine during its second year of use should be deductible from that year's gross income, and so on for as long as the machine is in service.

It is a lot easier to state this principle than to apply it. In practice, the tax authorities do not know exactly how much a given investment asset depreciates each year, or even what the useful life of the machine is. The tax law has rules which indicate for each type of asset what proportion of its acquisition value can be depreciated each year, and over how many years the depreciation can be done—the **tax life** of the asset. These rules, which often fail to reflect true economic depreciation, are discussed below.

Calculating the Value of Depreciation Allowances. Assume that the tax life of the $1,000 drill press is 10 years, and a firm is allowed to depreciate ⅟₁₀th the machine's value each year. How much is this stream of depreciation allowances worth to the XYZ corporation?[4]

At the end of the first year, XYZ is permitted to subtract ⅟₁₀th the acquisition value, or $100 from its taxable income. With a corporation income tax rate of 46 percent, this $100 deduction saves the firm $46. Note, however, that XYZ receives this benefit a year after the machine is purchased. The *present value* of the $46 is found by dividing it by $(1 + i)$, where i is the opportunity cost of funds to the firm.

At the end of the second year, XYZ is again entitled to subtract $100 from taxable income, which generates a saving of $46 that year. Because this saving comes two years in the future, its present value is $46/(1 + i)^2$. Similarly, the present value of depreciation taken during the third year is $46/(1 + i)^3$, during the fourth year, $46/(1 + i)^4$,

---

[4] We assume for now that the general level of prices stays fixed over time. The impact of inflation is discussed later.

etc. The present value of the entire stream of depreciation allowances is

$$\frac{\$46}{1 + i} + \frac{\$46}{(1 + i)^2} + \frac{\$46}{(1 + i)^3} + \cdots + \frac{\$46}{(1 + i)^{10}}$$

For example, if $i = 10\%$, this expression is equal to $282.70. In effect, then, the depreciation allowances lower the price of the drill press from $1,000 to $717.30 ($= \$1,000 - \$282.70$). Intuitively, the effective price is below the acquisition price because the purchase leads to a stream of tax savings in the future.

More generally, suppose that the tax law allows a firm to depreciate a given asset over T years, and the proportion of the asset that can be "written off" against taxable income in the nth year is $D(n)$. [In the example above, T was 10, and $D(n)$ was equal to $\frac{1}{10}$th every year. There are, however, several depreciation schemes for which $D(n)$ varies across years.] Consider the purchase of an investment asset which costs $1. The amount which can be depreciated at the end of the first year is $D(1)$ dollars, the value of which to the firm is $\theta \times D(1)$ dollars, where θ is the corporation tax rate. (Because the asset costs $1, $D(1)$ is a fraction.) Similarly, the value to the firm of the allowances in the second year is $\theta \times D(2)$. The present value of all the tax savings generated by a $1 purchase, which we denote ψ, is given by

(16.1) $$\psi = \frac{\theta \times D(1)}{1 + i} + \frac{\theta \times D(2)}{(1 + i)^2} + \cdots + \frac{\theta \times D(T)}{(1 + i)^T}$$

Because ψ is the tax saving for one dollar of expenditure, it follows that if the acquisition price of an asset is q, the presence of depreciation allowances lowers the effective price to $(1 - \psi)q$. For example, a value of $\psi = 0.25$ indicates that for each dollar spent on an asset, 25 cents worth of tax savings are produced. Hence, if the machine cost $1,000 ($q = \$1,000$) the effective price is only 75 percent of the purchase price, or $750.

Equation (16.1) suggests that the tax savings from depreciation depend critically upon the value of T and the function $D(n)$. In particular, the tax benefits are greater: (1) the shorter the time period over which the machine is written off—the lower is T; and (2) the greater the proportion of the machine's value that is written off at the beginning of its life—the larger the value of $D(n)$ when n is small. Schemes that allow firms to write off assets faster than true economic depreciation are referred to as **accelerated depreciation**.[5] An extreme possibility is to allow

---

[5] Note also that depreciation allowances are not worth anything unless there is some income from which to deduct them. Some have argued that this discriminates against firms that are just starting out and tend to have small cash flows. Under the tax law passed in 1981, firms with low incomes were able to "sell" their depreciation allowances to firms which could use them. However, opportunities for doing so were substantially curtailed in 1982.

the firm to deduct from taxable income the full cost of the asset at the time of acquisition. This is referred to as **expensing.**

Until the 1980s, the tax lives of assets—values of T—were chosen so as to roughly approximate the actual useful lives. For example, trucks were depreciated over 7 years, while commercial structures had a tax life of 37 years [Gravelle, 1982, p. 8]. The **Accelerated Cost Recovery System (ACRS)** introduced in 1981, represents a departure from this tradition. Under ACRS, only an extremely weak attempt is made to relate values of T to useful lives of assets. Every depreciable asset is assigned to one of only four categories, with respective tax lives of 3, 5, 10, or 15 years. Autos and light-duty trucks have a three-year tax life, and most other equipment five years. A value of T equal to 10 is assigned to relatively short-lived public utility property, and a value of 15 granted to other public utility property and most structures.[6] For most assets, the ACRS tax lives are considerably shorter than those stipulated previously. This change has potential consequences for corporate investment behavior, which we discuss below.

With respect to the rate at which assets can be depreciated, basically two methods are currently relevant.

Straight-Line Method.   This is the method we have been using for our examples so far. If the tax life of the asset is T years, the firm can write off 1/Tth of the cost each year. Thus, for a $1,000 asset which may be depreciated over five years, $200 is deducted each year.

One-Hundred-Fifty-Percent   Method. One-and-one-half   times   the straight-line percentage is deductible in the first year, and in each successive year, the same percentage is applied to the amount that remains undepreciated as of that year.[7] Consider again a $1,000 asset with a tax life of five years. One-and-one-half times the straight-line percentage is 30 percent. Thus, the firm can deduct .30 × $1,000 = $300 during the first year. During the second year, the undepreciated balance is $700, so the allowance is .30 × $700 = $210 and so forth. The firm can switch to straight line when the amount deductible under that method exceeds the amount from the 150 percent method. Compared to straight-line depreciation, the 150 percent method always produces tax savings with a higher present value.[8]

---

[6] Further details on the system are provided in King and Fullerton [1982].

[7] This applies to equipment. For structures, one-and-three-quarters times the straight-line percentage is allowed.

[8] Under current practice, firms do not have to do the calculation themselves. Instead, the Internal Revenue Service provides tables which show the proportion of acquisition cost that can be deducted each year, assuming that the switch-over to straight-line depreciation is done optimally.

Depreciation Allowances and Tax Shelters.   When tax depreciation is faster than economic depreciation, tax arbitrage opportunities are created. These opportunities are most dramatic in the case of assets which are legally depreciable for tax purposes, but actually *appreciate* in value over time. This is especially attractive if the capital gain realized at the time of sale is taxed at rates below those on ordinary income. Complicated tax shelter plans involving investments in real estate, cattle, and timber have been based upon this principle. The use of such shelters is widespread, as the cartoon suggests.

From *The Wall Street Journal*, with permission of Cartoon Features Syndicate.

"I have the necessities—food, clothing, and tax shelter."

A nice example is provided by baseball. If you buy a baseball team, part of the "product" you receive is the players' contracts. Normally, the amount allocated to player contracts is a large proportion of the acquisition cost of the team. These contracts are viewed as a depreciable asset. Since the tax life of contracts is relatively short, the amount allowed as a deduction in the early years generally exceeds the income generated by the team for those years. This produces an accounting loss that can be used to reduce the owners' taxable income from other sources. However, when the team is sold, if it has increased in value, the gain is taxed preferentially as a capital gain.[9] No wonder that an owner once claimed that you can never lose money on a baseball team!

_____
[9] Specifically, that part of the capital gain attributable to the value of owning the franchise itself (as opposed to the contracts) is treated as a capital gain.

Depreciation Allowances and Inflation.   Like the personal income tax, the corporation tax was designed at a time when inflation was not an important phenomenon. As a consequence, little thought was given to how the real corporate tax burden would change with inflation. It turns out that the real value of depreciation allowances is quite sensitive to the rate of inflation. Recall that until recently, depreciation allowances were set so as to approximate the costs due to physical wear and tear. The amount that could be depreciated in any period was some portion of the original or **historic purchase price.** In periods of inflation, however, the historic purchase price may be substantially less than the actual replacement cost. Thus, inflation lowers the real value of depreciation allowances.

For example, suppose that XYZ purchases a $4,000 asset and takes straight-line depreciation over a period of eight years—$500 per year. Suppose further that after the asset is purchased, the price level doubles. Then, the $500 that is deductible each year represents only 1/16th of the real replacement cost of the asset, not the 1/8th that was intended.

Now, if the real value of depreciation allowances goes down, then other things being the same, the effective tax rate on corporate capital goes up. Feldstein and Summers [1979, p. 449] estimated that in 1977, depreciation schedules based upon historic purchase price led to corporate taxes that were $19.1 billion higher than they would have been in the absence of inflation. This figure amounts to a third of the taxes actually paid.

Two methods of dealing with this problem have received considerable attention.

Index Depreciation Allowances.   The value of depreciation allowances each year could be adjusted for the rise in the capital goods price index over the previous year.

Shorten the Number of Years over Which the Asset Can Be Depreciated. Allowing assets to be depreciated more rapidly tends to counteract the decline in real value of the amounts being written off.

Indexing complicates tax administration. For example, if all assets do not increase in price at the same rate, it might be necessary to design different price indexes for different types of assets. In contrast, shortening the tax lives of assets is quite simple and easy to administer. However, any particular shortening of tax lives, even if it adjusts perfectly for the *current* rate of inflation, will necessarily be inappropriate if the inflation rate changes in the future. If inflation were to decrease, the allowances based on the current rate would be too generous and vice versa. Considering the substantial variability of inflation rates that the United States has experienced, this is a serious drawback. For this reason, most economists prefer indexing. Nevertheless, with the adoption of ACRS in 1981, the United States has clearly cast its lot with shortening asset lives rather than indexing.

Investment Tax Credit Allowed

Another important aspect of the tax treatment of corporations is the **investment tax credit (ITC),** which permits a firm to subtract some portion of the purchase price of an asset from its tax liability at the time the asset is acquired. If a drill press costs $1,000, and if the XYZ firm is allowed an investment tax credit of 10 percent, the purchase of a drill press lowers XYZ's tax bill by $100. The effective price of the drill press (before depreciation allowances) is thus $900. More generally, if the investment tax credit is k and the acquisition price is q, then the effective price of the asset is $(1 - k)q$. In contrast to depreciation allowances, the value to the firm of an ITC does not depend upon the corporate income tax rate. This is because the credit is subtracted from tax liability rather than taxable income. As of 1981, equipment with a tax life of three years is eligible for a 6 percent credit, and all equipment with a longer life is entitled to a credit of 10 percent. Most structures are not entitled to an investment tax credit.

Note that in principle, the taxes paid by a firm on its gross income from a particular asset can be less in present value than the present value of tax savings from ACRS depreciation allowances and the ITC. In essence, the tax system subsidizes the asset—the "tax rate" is negative.[10] As we shall see below, this is not a mere theoretical curiosity. Under current law, the corporation tax is actually a subsidy for many new investments.

"Inflation Profits" Taxed

Suppose that at the end of 1984, XYZ has an inventory of 100 widgets acquired for $1,000 each. (Widgets do not depreciate over time.) During 1985, the firm acquires 50 identical widgets at a cost of $1,500 each. Then an opportunity arises for XYZ to sell 25 of the widgets for $2,000 a piece. If XYZ takes advantage of this opportunity, what are its profits?

The answer depends upon what cost is assigned to the widgets that are sold. One possibility is to value them at their 1984 cost. This is referred to as **first-in, first-out (FIFO)** accounting, because the widgets acquired first are the ones treated as having been sold first. Under FIFO, profits are 25 × ($2,000 − $1,000) = $25,000. Alternatively, the firm can

---

[10] This requires that the corporation have other income against which the various deductions can be offset. Under current law, if a corporation's deductions exceed its income, it is not entitled to a "negative tax," that is, a subsidy.

value the widgets at the cost of those obtained most recently. Now the *last* widgets acquired are viewed as the first being sold. Under **last-in, first-out (LIFO)** accounting, profits are $25 \times (\$2,000 - \$1,500) = \$12,500$.

This example illustrates that in periods of rising prices, FIFO leads to larger accounting profits than LIFO. But higher accounting profits mean higher corporate taxes. Thus, FIFO firms are taxed on profits that are due to illusory increases in inventory value. Feldstein and Summers [1979, p. 449] estimated that in 1979, those firms that used FIFO paid $7 billion in excess taxes because of inflation.[11]

Dividends and Retained Earnings Treated Differently

So far we have been focusing on taxes directly payable by the corporation. For many purposes, however, the important issue is not the corporation's tax liability per se, but rather the total tax rate on income generated in the corporate sector. As noted in Chapter 14, corporate income received by individuals is subject to the personal income tax. It is important to discuss how the corporate and personal tax structures interact.

Corporate profits may either be retained by the firm or paid out to stockholders in the form of dividends. Dividends paid are *not* deductible from corporation income and hence are subject to the corporation income tax. At the same time, stockholders who receive dividends must treat them as ordinary income and pay personal income tax in an amount that depends upon their marginal tax rates. In effect, then, such payments are taxed twice—once at the corporation level, and again when distributed to the shareholder. Eliminating **double taxation** is a prime objective of many tax reformers, and is discussed below.

To assess the tax consequences to the stockholder of retained earnings is a bit more complicated. Suppose that XYZ retains $1 of earnings. To the extent that the stock market accurately values firms, the fact that the firm now has one more dollar will cause the value of XYZ stock to increase by $1.[12] But as we saw in Chapter 14, income generated by increases in the value of stock—capital gain—is treated preferentially for tax purposes. The gain received by a typical XYZ stockholder is not taxed at all until it is realized, and even upon realization, it is taxed at rates below those on ordinary income. The tax system thus creates sub-

---

[11] Why don't firms switch to LIFO? This is somewhat of a mystery. It has been conjectured that some managers prefer FIFO because it makes profits appear higher (as long as prices are increasing), and hence presents a more favorable picture of the firm to stockholders and potential creditors.

[12] This considerably oversimplifies the complicated relationship between share values and retained earnings. Bradford [1981] argues that under plausible conditions, less than each dollar of retained earnings will be reflected in stock values. Although this question is still in dispute, we adopt the traditional assumption that share values and retained earnings rise on a one-for-one basis.

stantial incentives for firms to retain earnings rather than pay them out as dividends.

Summary: Effective Tax Rate on Corporate Capital

We began this section by noting that the statutory tax rate on capital income in the corporate sector is currently 46 percent. It should now be clear that it would be most surprising if this were the effective rate as well. At the corporate level, computing the effective rate requires taking into account the effects of interest deductibility, depreciation allowances, tax credits, and inflation. Moreover, as just noted, corporate income in the form of dividends and realized capital gains is also taxed at the level of the personal income tax. Finally, some corporate income is subject to state corporation taxes and locally levied property taxes.

Allowing for all these considerations, King and Fullerton [1982] computed that in 1982, the effective overall marginal tax rate on capital income was 31.5 percent. Interestingly, they found that if the corporation tax system had been eliminated, this 31.5 percent would have gone *up* to 35 percent. We observed earlier that theoretically the tax benefits from accelerated depreciation, the ITC, etc. could exceed the tax liabilities associated with the corporation tax. King and Fullerton's calculation suggests that this indeed happened. Overall, the marginal investment was subsidized rather than taxed at the corporate level.

Of course, any such calculation must be based upon assumptions concerning items such as the appropriate choice of discount rate [i of Equation (16.1)], the expected rate of inflation, the extent of true economic depreciation, etc. It is therefore likely that investigators using other assumptions would generate a somewhat different figure. It is unlikely, however, that alternative methods would much modify the dramatic difference between statutory and effective marginal tax rates.[13]

INCIDENCE AND EXCESS BURDEN OF THE CORPORATION TAX

Computing effective tax rates is only the first step in an analysis of the corporation tax. We still must determine who ultimately bears the burden of the tax and measure the costs of any inefficiencies it induces. The economic consequences of the corporation tax are among the most controversial subjects in public finance. An important reason for the con-

---

[13] It must also be emphasized that the marginal and average tax rates are expected to differ. For instance, to the extent that the new rules for depreciation are more generous than their predecessors, the marginal tax rate on new investment is lower than the average rate. This is because the average rate takes into account the higher taxes being paid on previous investments.

troversy is disagreement with respect to just what kind of tax it is. We can identify several views.

Economic Profits Tax.   The corporation tax can be considered a tax on economic profits.[14] This view is based on the observation that the tax base is determined by subtracting costs of production from gross corporate income, leaving only "profits." As we explained in Chapter 11, analyzing the incidence of a tax on economic profits is straightforward. As long as a firm maximizes economic profits, then a tax on them induces no adjustments in firm behavior—all decisions regarding prices and production are unchanged. Hence, there is no way to shift the tax, and it is borne by the owners of the firm.[15] Moreover, by the very fact that the tax leaves behavior unchanged, it generates no misallocation of resources. Hence, the excess burden is zero.

Modeling the corporation tax as a simple tax on economic profits is almost certainly wrong. Recall that the base of a pure profits tax is computed by subtracting from gross earnings the value of *all* inputs, *including* the opportunity cost of the inputs supplied by the owners. In fact, no such deduction for the capital supplied by shareholders is allowed, so the base of the tax includes elements other than economic profits.

Tax on Capital Employed in the Corporate Sector.   Since the opportunity cost of capital is included in the tax base, it appears reasonable to view the corporation tax as a tax upon capital that is used in the corporate sector. In terms of the classification scheme developed in Chapter 11, the corporation tax is a partial factor tax. This is the view that predominates in most writing on the subject.[16]

In a general equilibrium model of the type developed by Harberger (Chapter 11), the tax on corporate capital leads to a migration of capital from the corporate sector until after-tax rates of return are equal throughout the economy. In the process, the rate of return to capital in the noncorporate sector is depressed so that ultimately *all* owners of capital, not just those in the corporate sector, are affected. The reallocation of capital between the two sectors also affects the return to labor. As shown in Chapter 11, the extent to which capital and labor bear the ultimate burden of the tax depends upon the technologies used in production in each of the sectors, as well as the structure of consumers' demands for corporate and noncorporate goods. Using what he con-

---

[14] Atkinson and Stiglitz [1980, p. 132] note that this view had some adherents in the 1920s.

[15] If firms are not profit maximizing initially, the story may be quite different. See Chapter 11.

[16] For example, it is the view which underlies the effective tax calculations of King and Fullerton [1982] presented above.

sidered to be plausible values for the relevant technological and behavioral parameters, Harberger [1974c] concluded that capital bears the entire burden of the tax.

Turning now to efficiency aspects of the problem, computation of the excess burden of a partial factor tax was discussed in Chapter 12. By inducing less capital accumulation in the corporate sector than otherwise would have been the case, the corporation tax diverts capital from its most productive uses and creates an excess burden. Ballard, Shoven, and Whalley [1982, p. 23] estimated that the increase in excess burden when one more dollar is raised via the corporation tax—the marginal excess burden—is 49 cents.

The Harberger model assumes perfect competition and profit-maximizing behavior. Without these conditions, a tax on corporate capital may have quite different incidence and efficiency implications. Moreover, the model is static—the total amount of capital to be allocated between the corporate and noncorporate sectors is fixed. Suppose that over time, the tax on corporate capital changes the total amount of capital available to the economy. If the tax lowers the total amount of capital, the marginal product of labor, and hence the wage rate, will fall. Thus, labor will bear a greater share of the burden than otherwise would have been the case. If the tax increases the amount of capital, just the opposite will result.[17] Hence, even if we accept the view of the corporation tax as a partial factor tax, its efficiency and incidence effects are not at all clear.

Economic Profits Tax—Again. Stiglitz [1973] argued that viewing the corporation tax as a partial factor tax ignores the crucial institutional feature of interest deductibility. He showed that under certain conditions, as long as the corporation is allowed to deduct interest payments made to its creditors, the corporation tax is equivalent to a tax on economic profits.

To understand the reasoning behind Stiglitz's result, consider a firm that is contemplating the purchase of a machine costing $1. Suppose that the before-tax value of the output which will be produced by the machine is known with certainty to be G dollars. It is also known that the machine will experience economic depreciation equal to δ dollars. To finance the purchase, the firm borrows $1, and must pay an interest charge of i dollars. In the absence of any taxes, the firm will buy the machine if the net return (total revenue minus depreciation minus interest) is positive. Algebraically, the firm purchases the machine if

(16.2) $$G - \delta - i > 0.$$

---

[17] As shown in Chapter 15, whether a tax on the return to capital increases or decreases capital accumulation is logically indeterminate.

Now assume that a corporation tax with the following features is levied: *(a)* net income is taxed at rate θ; and *(b)* in the computation of net income, the firm is allowed to subtract interest costs and economic depreciation from total revenue. How does such a tax influence the firm's decision about whether to undertake the project? Clearly, the firm must make its decision on the basis of the *after*-tax profitability of the project. In light of feature *(b)*, the firm's taxable income is $G - \delta - i$. Given feature *(a)*, the project therefore creates a tax liability of $\theta(G - \delta - i)$, so the after-tax profit on the project is $(1 - \theta)(G - \delta - i)$. The firm will do the project only if the after-tax profit is positive; that is, if

(16.3) $(1 - \theta)(G - \delta - i) > 0.$

Now note that any project that passes the after-tax criterion (16.3) also satisfies the before-tax criterion (16.2). [Just divide Equation (16.3) through by $(1 - \theta)$ to get Equation (16.2)]. Hence, imposition of the tax leaves the firm's investment decision completely unchanged—anything it would have done before the tax, it will do after. The owners of the firm continue to behave exactly as they did prior to the tax; they simply lose some of their profit on the investment to the government. In this sense the tax is equivalent to an economic profits tax. And like an economic profits tax, its incidence is on the owners of the firm, and it creates no excess burden.

This conclusion depends critically upon the underlying assumptions, and these can easily be called into question. Stiglitz's analysis assumes that firms deduct economic depreciation. As we have seen, statutory allowances generally do not even approximate economic depreciation. In addition, the argument assumes that firms will choose to finance their additional projects by borrowing. There are several reasons why they might instead raise money by selling shares or using retained earnings. For example, firms may face constraints in the capital market and be unable to borrow all they want. Alternatively, if a firm is uncertain about what the return on the project will be, it might be reluctant to finance the project by borrowing. If things go wrong, the greater a firm's debt, the higher the probability of bankruptcy, other things being the same.

However, the fact that its assumptions are not met perfectly does not mean that Stiglitz' analysis yields no insights with respect to the impact of the corporation tax. Empirical work is required to determine its relevance. In the meantime, the incidence and efficiency effects of the corporation tax remain as much a puzzle as ever.

EFFECTS ON BEHAVIOR

The corporation tax influences a wide range of corporate decisions. In this section we will discuss three important types: *(a)* the total amount of physical investment (equipment and structures) to make; *(b)* the types of physical assets to purchase; and *(c)* the way to finance these investments.[18] In a sense, it is artificial to discuss these decisions separately because presumably the firm makes them simultaneously. However, each of the issues is sufficiently complicated that it would be extremely difficult to analyze them jointly.

Physical Investment

A firm's net investment in a given period is the increase in physical assets during that time.[19] The main question is whether features of the corporate tax structure such as accelerated depreciation and the investment tax credit have stimulated investment demand, as was intended. The question is important. According to the Congressional Budget Office [1982c, pp. 56–57], in 1983 accelerated depreciation and the investment tax credit cost the treasury approximately $12.4 billion and $18.7 billion, respectively. Is the country getting its "money's worth" in terms of a greater capital stock?

The answer depends in part upon your view of how corporations make their investment decisions. Many different models have been proposed, and there is no agreement on which is the best. We will discuss two investment models that have received substantial attention.

The Accelerator Model.   Suppose that production techniques are such that the ratio of capital to output is fixed. For example, production of every unit of output requires three units of capital. Then for each unit increase in output, the firm must increase its capital stock—invest—three units of capital. Thus, the main determinant of the amount of investment is changes in the level of output.

This theory, which is sometimes referred to as the **accelerator model,** implies that depreciation allowances and ITCs are for the most part *irrelevant* when it comes to influencing physical investment. It is only the quantity of output that influences the amount of investment, because technology dictates the ratio in which capital and output must be used. In other words, tax benefits for capital may make capital cheaper, but in the accelerator model this does not matter, because the demand for capital does not depend on its price.[20]

---

[18] In addition, the tax code has numerous special provisions affecting other aspects of firm behavior—everything from discouraging compliance with the Arab boycott of firms that do business with Israel to encouraging compliance with health and safety regulations. On the former, see *The Operation and Effect of the International Boycott Provisions of the Internal Revenue Code* (Washington, D.C.: Dept. of the Treasury, December 1980). On the latter, see Office of Tax Analysis, *The Use of Tax Subsidies for the Cost of Compliance with Safety and Health Regulations* (Washington, D.C.: Department of the Treasury, January 1981).

[19] Firms acquire assets both to add new plant and equipment and to replace old plant and equipment. Replacement investment is not dealt with here.

[20] These tax provisions may stimulate an increase in demand for output, and thus *indirectly* increase investment demand via the accelerator model.

The Neoclassical Model.   A less extreme view of the investment process is that the ratio of capital to output is not technologically fixed. Rather, the firm can choose between alternative technologies. But how does it choose? According to Jorgenson's [1963] **neoclassical model,** a key variable is the firm's **user cost of capital**—the opportunity cost that the firm incurs as a consequence of owning an asset. If the user cost of capital is relatively high, other things being the same, the firm will choose a less capital-intensive technology and vice versa. Thus, to the extent that tax policy reduces the user cost of capital, it can increase the amount of capital that firms desire, and hence, increase investment.

All of this leaves open two important questions: (1) how do changes in the tax system change the user cost of capital; and (2) just how sensitive is investment to changes in the user cost of capital? To examine these points, we must first calculate the user cost of capital.

Calculation of the User Cost of Capital.[21]   Assume first that there are no taxes, no depreciation, no inflation, and the firm can borrow and lend at the market rate of interest, i_g. (The subscript g reflects the fact that this is the gross or before-tax rate of interest.) Suppose the firm purchases an asset for q dollars. Because the asset does not depreciate, the firm can sell it back for exactly q at the end of a year. Then the only cost to the firm of owning the asset is the money it could have made if it had lent the g dollars instead of tying the money up in the asset. Specifically, the firm could have earned $i_g \times q$ dollars, which is the user cost of capital in this simple example.

Notice that the firm will purchase the asset only if the value of the product produced during the year is at least as great as the user cost. Thus, in the neoclassical model, firms desire to invest up to the point where the marginal return to capital assets just equals the opportunity cost of owning them.

Now assume that the asset experiences economic depreciation at an annual rate δ. For example, if a machine is worth \$100 at the beginning of the year ($q = \$100$) and economic depreciation is 12 percent per year ($\delta = 0.12$) then it will be worth \$88 at the end of the year. Depreciation thus costs the firm \$12, or more generally, $\delta \times q$ dollars. Adding this to the interest cost above, the user cost of capital, C, is

(16.4) $$C = i_g q + \delta q = (i_g + \delta)q$$

Using our example with $q = \$100$, $\delta = 0.12$, and assuming $i_g = 0.08$, the user cost is \$20. The firm will purchase assets until the marginal revenues per asset are \$20—just sufficient to cover the opportunity cost.

Now enters the corporation tax, which we will assume is 40 percent ($\theta = 0.40$). What, now, does it cost the firm to earn the same \$20 as

---

[21] This section is relatively difficult. Readers may skip to the next section without serious loss of continuity.

before? Note that the firm must generate more before-tax revenue, $33.33, to end up with $20. The increase from $20 to $33.33—a factor of 1.67—is just sufficient to offset the tax. More generally, because the tax collector is leaving the corporation only $(1 - \theta)$ of each dollar earned, then *before*-tax revenues must increase by a factor of $1/(1 - \theta)$ for *after*-tax revenue to stay unchanged. But if the firm needs to increase revenue by a factor of $1/(1 - \theta)$, it requires an asset whose productivity is higher by a factor of $1/(1 - \theta)$, which in turn, will have a price that is higher by a factor of $1/(1 - \theta)$. In terms of our example, because the initial acquisition cost was $100, the firm now needs to purchase an asset with a value of $166.67 $(= \$100 \times 1/(1 - .4))$ to receive the same $20 that it formerly received from a $100 asset. In short, if an asset costing $\$q$ was initially required to produce a given amount of revenue, now an asset costing $q/(1 - \theta)$ is required.

What is the opportunity cost of acquiring this $166.67 asset? As before, there is an interest component and a depreciation component. Since interest received by the corporation is taxed (or, equivalently, interest payments are tax deductible) the opportunity cost of interest foregone is not the market rate of 8 percent, but rather the market rate times one minus the firm's marginal tax rate. Algebraically, the effective interest rate is $(1 - \theta)i_g$, where i_g is the before-tax rate of interest.[22] Recalling that the effective asset cost is now $q/(1 - \theta)$, it follows that the interest component of the opportunity cost is

$$[(1 - \theta)i_g] \times \left[\frac{q}{1 - \theta}\right] = i_g q$$

In terms of our numerical example, this is $8.

Turning now to the depreciation component, we note that economic depreciation is computed as the depreciation rate of 12 percent times the asset cost of $166.67, or about $20. Algebraically, the depreciation component is now:

$$[\delta] \times \left[\frac{q}{1 - \theta}\right]$$

Thus, the user cost in this example is now $28 $(= \$8 + \$20)$ which is the result of adding together the interest and economic depreciation components:

(16.5)
$$C = \underbrace{[(1 - \theta)i_g] \times \left[\frac{q}{1 - \theta}\right]}_{\substack{\text{interest} \\ \text{component}}} + \underbrace{[\delta] \times \frac{q}{(1 - \theta)}}_{\substack{\text{depreciation} \\ \text{component}}}$$

$$= [(1 - \theta)i_g + \delta] \times \left[\frac{q}{1 - \theta}\right]$$

[22] Earlier we defined i as the opportunity cost of funds to the firm. Hence, in this model, $i = (1 - \theta)i_g$.

According to (16.5), the corporation income tax raises the user cost of capital by forcing firms to purchase more expensive assets than otherwise needed to generate the same after-tax revenue. These more expensive assets raise the value of the sum of foregone interest and economic depreciation.

We are not yet done, however, because the tax also affects the user cost of capital via depreciation allowances and the investment tax credit. In Equation (16.1) we defined ψ as the present value of the depreciation allowances that flow from an asset whose acquisition cost is \$1. If depreciation allowances lower the cost of a \$1 investment to $(1 - \psi)$ dollars, then they lower the cost of a q dollar asset to $(1 - \psi)q$ dollars. Similarly, we showed that an investment tax credit (ITC) at rate k reduces the cost of a \$1 acquisition to $(1 - k)$ dollars. Putting the depreciation allowances and the investment tax credit together, the effective acquisition cost of a q dollar asset is lowered from q dollars to $(1 - \psi - k)q$ dollars.[23] Hence, Equation (16.5) must be adjusted to

(16.6) $$C = [(1 - \theta)i_g + \delta] \times \left[\frac{q}{1 - \theta}\right] \times (1 - \psi - k)$$

In summary, the corporate tax system influences the firm's user cost of capital in several ways. By taxing corporate income, the tax makes devoting resources to capital investment more expensive, other things being the same. However, depreciation allowances and ITCs tend to lower the user cost. Any change in the corporation tax system will influence some combination of θ, ψ, and k, and hence change the user cost of capital.

Effect of User Cost on Investment.   Even if how changes in the tax system influence the user cost of capital is determined, how changes in the user cost of capital influence investment must still be ascertained. If the accelerator model is correct, even drastic reductions in the user cost have no impact on investment. On the other hand, if investment is relatively responsive to the user cost of capital, then depreciation allowances and ITCs will be relatively powerful tools for influencing investment.

Jorgenson [1963] estimated a regression equation in which the right-hand side variables include (among others) the user cost of capital. The exact form taken by the regression is fairly complicated, and is discussed in the appendix to this chapter. Jorgenson's basic conclusion is that the amount of investment is indeed quite sensitive to tax-induced changes in the cost of capital. For example, the parameters from one equation based on Jorgenson's model imply that without accelerated depreciation

---

[23] This assumes that the basis used to compute depreciation allowances is not reduced when the firm takes the ITC. If the basis is reduced, then the expression must be modified.

and the investment tax credit, investment in 1977 would have been about 40 percent lower than the actual level [Chirinko and Eisner, 1983].

Substantial controversy has swirled around Jorgenson's conclusion that accelerated depreciation and investment tax credits are potent inducements to investment. His analysis has been criticized on a number of grounds. One of the most important is that it takes no account of the importance of expectations. Compare scenario 1, in which firms expect the investment tax credit to be raised considerably *next* year, and scenario 2, in which investors expect it to be reduced. According to Jorgenson's model, the amount of capital that firms desire depends *only* upon the user cost of capital *this* period. Therefore, the value of C is identical under both scenarios. This result is implausible; if firms expect the investment tax credit to go up next period, it would make sense to defer some investment until then and vice versa. The fact is that we cannot observe individuals' expectations, and as of now there is no really satisfactory way for estimating how expectations affect behavior. Given that different assumptions concerning expectation formation can have quite different implications for the effectiveness of tax policy, the validity of Jorgenson's results is thrown into question.

Other criticisms of Jorgenson's model are discussed in the appendix to the chapter. The key point of the critics is that when some of Jorgenson's assumptions are modified in reasonable ways, the implications for tax policy can differ dramatically. Chirinko and Eisner [1983] used five well-known models to predict the extent to which investment in equipment would have fallen in 1977 if the investment tax credit then in effect had been removed. The estimates ranged from $1.4 billion to $12.9 billion. Although the results of the different models differ dramatically, it is difficult to choose between them on the basis of standard statistical criteria. Apparently, the sheer complexity of the investment process has stymied attempts to reach a consensus with respect to how sensitive investment is to tax incentives.[24]

Types of Asset

So far our focus has been the total volume of investment spending without much attention to its composition. It is likely, though, that the tax system affects the types of assets purchased by firms. For example, the fact that the investment tax credit on equipment is 10 percent while most structures receive no tax credit will tend to encourage investment in favor of equipment, other things being the same.

King and Fullerton [1982] computed the effective marginal tax rates on various assets under the pre-1981 system and the Accelerated Cost

---

[24] Surveys of various findings are included in Jorgenson [1971] and Chirinko and Eisner [1983].

Recovery System (ACRS) as it applied in 1982. Some of the results are reported in Table 16.1. The most striking features of the table are that both systems are characterized by higher tax rates on structures than equipment,[25] and ACRS has decreased marginal tax rates on both types of assets.

TABLE 16.1   Effective Marginal Tax Rates by Asset Type

	1980*	1982(ACRS)*
Equipment	17.6%	11.0%
Structures	41.1	33.2

* Computations assume a 6.7 percent inflation rate.

Source: Mervyn A. King and Don Fullerton, eds., *The Taxation of Income from Capital: A Comparative Study of the U.S., U.K., Sweden and West Germany,* Woodrow Wilson School, Princeton University, Discussion Paper no. 37 (Princeton, N.J.), figs. 6.20, 6.28.

Clearly, the tax system biases investment in favor of equipment and against structures. In this context, note that by itself the overall marginal tax rate on capital under ACRS (about 31.5 percent) provides essentially no information about its distorting impact on investment. To assess the system's efficiency effects requires knowledge of the effective tax rate on each type of asset, not just some average of the rates. Indeed, it is conceivable that even if the overall system turned out to yield zero revenue (the subsidies to some assets just balanced the taxes on others), there would still be significant excess burden because of tax-induced distortions in the pattern of investment. Using methods of excess burden calculation very similar to those introduced in Chapter 12, Gravelle [1982] estimated that the 1981 version of the ACRS led to an efficiency cost of about $3.8 billion in 1980 dollars.

As emphasized earlier, computations like those in Table 16.1 require making a number of assumptions. For example, the value of depreciation allowances depends upon the discount rate used by firms [see Equation (16.1)], and different values lead to different answers. Similarly, given historic cost depreciation, assumptions about the future rate of inflation have an important impact on effective tax rates. Hence, it is possible that different investigators might find results somewhat different from those in the table. There is little doubt, however, that the qualitative picture suggested in the table is correct. The corporation tax system distorts investment incentives.

---

[25] Under the 1981 version of ACRS, the effective marginal tax rate on equipment was actually negative. See King and Fullerton [1982, Figure 6.27].

Corporate Finance

In addition to "real" decisions concerning physical investment, the owners of a firm must determine how to finance the firm's operations and whether to distribute profits or retain them. The effects of taxes upon these financial decisions are discussed in this section.

Why Do Firms Pay Dividends?   Profits earned by a corporation may be either distributed to shareholders in the form of dividends or retained by the company. If it is assumed that: (1) outcomes of all investments are known in advance with certainty; and (2) there are no taxes, then the owners of a firm are indifferent in choosing between a dollar of dividends and a dollar of retained earnings. Provided that the stock market accurately reflects the firm's value, $1 of retained earnings increases the value of the firm's stock by $1. This $1 capital gain is as much income as a $1 dividend receipt. Under the assumptions given above, then, stockholders do not care whether profits are distributed.[26]

Of course, in reality, considerable uncertainty surrounds the outcomes of economic decisions, and corporate income *is* subject to a variety of taxes. As noted above, when dividends are paid out, the shareholder incurs a tax liability, while retained earnings generate no concurrent tax liability. True, the retention creates a capital gain for the stockholder, but no tax is due until the gain is realized, and even then, it is taxed at rates below those on ordinary income.

On the basis of these observations, it appears that paying dividends is more or less equivalent to giving away money to the tax collector, and we would expect firms to retain virtually all of their earnings. Surprise! During the period 1967 to 1981, on average 45 percent of real after-tax corporate profits were paid out as dividends [Feldstein, 1982c, p. 10]. This phenomenon continues to baffle students of corporate finance.

One possible explanation is that dividend payments serve as a signal concerning the firm's financial strength. If investors perceive firms that regularly pay dividends as in some sense "solid," then paying dividends will enhance the value of the firms' shares. In the same way, a firm that reduces its dividend payments may be perceived as being in financial straits. However, although it is conceivable that the owners of a firm would be willing to pay some extra taxes to provide a positive signal to potential shareholders, it is hard to imagine that the benefits gained are worth the huge sums sacrificed. After all, there are certainly ways other than dividend policy for potential investors to obtain information about a firm's status.

Another explanation centers on the fact that not all investors have the same marginal tax rate. High-income individuals currently face rates up

---

[26] For a rigorous discussion of this argument, see Fama and Miller [1972, pp. 80–81].

to 50 percent, while untaxed institutions (such as pension funds and universities) face a rate of zero. Those with low marginal tax rates would tend to put a relatively high valuation on dividends, and it may be that some firms "specialize" in attracting these investors by paying out dividends. Feldstein and Green [1983] proposed a model in which there are two types of investors, taxable individuals and untaxed institutions. They show that if stock returns are known in advance with certainty, taxable individuals will only purchase shares of firms that pay no dividends, while the untaxed institutions will invest exclusively in firms that pay out all dividends. This is referred to as a **clientele effect,** because firms set their financial policies to cater to different clienteles. In the real world, of course, such dramatic segmentation of stockholders is not observed. According to Feldstein and Green, the reason for this is that stock returns are not known with certainty in advance. Even if your tax rate on dividends is high, you will not invest exclusively in low-dividend firms, because when there is uncertainty, it is bad policy to put all your eggs in one basket.

The notion that firms specialize in attracting shareholders with particular tax situations has stimulated empirical research. Studies in this area are hindered by the lack of data on just who owns shares in what firms. Auerbach [1982] conducted an indirect test for the presence of clientele effects by examining the behavior of stock prices on the *ex-dividend day*—the first day that a new owner of a stock is not entitled to a previously declared dividend. Consider the ex-dividend day behavior of stock prices in each of the following situations.

No Taxes.   In this case, on the ex-dividend day the price of stock decreases by exactly the amount of the previously declared dividend. For example, if people were willing to pay $100 for a share in anticipation of a $10 dividend payment, then after the dividend is paid, new buyers should be willing to pay only $90, other things being the same.

Tax System with Constant Marginal Tax Rate.   If everyone faces the same marginal tax rate on dividends, then on the ex-dividend day, the stock should drop in value only by the *after-tax* value of the dividend. In the example just given, if dividends are taxed at a rate of 30 percent, the $10 dividend is worth only $7 to stockholders. Therefore, immediately after the point at which the $10 dividend is paid, the stock is worth only $7 less to them.

Tax System with Increasing Marginal Tax Rates.   With increasing marginal tax rates, the decline in stock value will be a weighted average of the marginal tax rates of the firm's stockholders. If the stockholders tend to have high marginal tax rates, on ex-dividend days the price of the stock will not fall by very much and vice versa. This observation is the basis for Auerbach's test. If firms do specialize in different types of stockholders, this should be revealed in the varying performances of stocks on their ex-dividend days. Auerbach found that there does seem to be systematic differences in ex-dividend day behavior that can be explained by clientele effects.

The Effect of Taxes on Dividend Policy.   Since the tax system appears to bias firms against paying dividends (although it by no means discourages them completely), the natural question is how corporate financial policy would change if the tax treatment of dividends vis-à-vis retained earnings were modified. Suppose that for whatever reasons, firms want to pay *some* dividends as well as retain earnings. One factor that will determine the desired amount of retained earnings is the opportunity cost in terms of after-tax dividends paid to stockholders. For example, if there were no taxes, then the opportunity cost of $1 of retained earnings would be $1 of dividends. On the other hand, if the stockholder faces a 40 percent marginal income tax rate, then the opportunity cost of retaining a dollar in the firm is only 60 cents of dividends.[27] In effect, then, the current tax system lowers the opportunity cost of retained earnings.

Over the last several decades, there have been a number of shifts in British tax policy which have had the effect of generating dramatic changes in the opportunity cost of retained earnings in terms of dividends. Data from the United Kingdom therefore provide an excellent opportunity for examining the impact of taxes upon firm dividend policy. Feldstein [1970] used British data to estimate a regression in which the dependent variable is the proportion of corporate income paid out as dividends, and the independent variables include the opportunity cost of retained earnings. He found that when the opportunity cost of retained earnings increases by 10 percent, the ratio of dividends to corporate income goes up by about 9 percent.

If this result extends to the United States, it suggests that the tax system has substantially increased the amount of earnings retained by corporations. Some argue that this is desirable because increasing retained earnings makes more money available for investment. Now, it is true that retained earnings represent saving. However, it may be that shareholders take corporate saving into consideration when making their personal financial decisions. Specifically, if owners of the firm perceive that the corporation is saving a dollar on their behalf, then they may simply reduce their personal saving by that amount. Thus, although the composition of overall saving has changed, its total amount

---

[27] A more careful calculation would take into account the effective capital-gains tax liability that is eventually generated by the retention. This is ignored for purposes of illustration.

is just the same as before the retention. There is indeed some econo-metric evidence that personal and corporate saving are approximately offsetting.[28] This analysis illustrates once again the pitfalls of viewing the corporation as a separate person with an existence apart from the stockholders.

Debt Versus Equity Finance. Another important financial decision for a corporation is how to raise money. The firm has basically two options. It can borrow money (issue debt). However, the firm must pay interest on its debt, and inability to meet the interest payments or repay the principal may have serious consequences. A firm can also issue shares of stock (equity) and stockholders *may* receive dividends on their shares.

Recall that under the U.S. tax system, corporations are permitted to deduct payments of interest from taxable income, but are not allowed to deduct dividends. The tax law therefore builds in a bias toward debt financing.[29] It is difficult to precisely estimate the impact that this bias has had on the debt-equity choice. Between 1960 and 1981, corporate debt increased by a factor of about 7.6, while corporate profits (before tax) rose only by a factor of 4.7.[30] Many economists have argued that taxes are an important factor in explaining the growth in the use of debt finance.

Indeed, we might wonder why firms do not use debt financing exclusively. Part of the answer lies in the fact that the outcomes of a firm's decisions are not known with certainty. There is always some possibility of a very bad outcome, and therefore a fear of bankruptcy. The more a firm borrows, the higher its debt payments, and the greater the proba-bility of bankruptcy, other things being the same. It has been argued that by encouraging the use of debt, the tax system has had the undesir-able effect of increasing probabilities of bankruptcy above levels that otherwise would have prevailed.

STATE CORPORATION TAXES

As of 1983, 46 states levied their own corporation income taxes, and in 1982, corporate tax revenues accounted for about 8.6 percent of total state tax collections [*Facts and Figures on Government Finance*, 1983, pp. 251, 265]. As is the case with state personal income taxes, state corporate tax systems differ substantially with respect to rate structures and rules for defining taxable income.

---

[28] See Feldstein [1973].

[29] It turns out that in the absence of taxation and given complete uncertainty with respect to investment outcomes, firms are indifferent between debt and equity finance. This is often referred to as the "Modigliani-Miller Theorem" after the authors who first proved it. See Modigliani and Miller [1958]. For a careful intuitive exposition, see Fama and Miller [1972].

[30] Computations based on U.S. Bureau of the Census [1982, pp. 535, 545].

All of the complications that arise in analyzing the incidence and efficiency effects of the federal corporation income tax also bedevil attempts to understand the state systems. McLure [1981b] points out that the variation in rates across state lines gives rise to a set of possibly even more intractable questions. If a given state levies a corporation tax, how much of the burden will be "exported" to citizens of other states? How is the portion that is not exported shared by the residents of the state?[31]

Preliminary answers to these questions may be obtained by applying the theory of tax incidence (Chapter 11).[32] Recall the general intuitive proposition that immobile factors of production are more likely to end up bearing a tax than mobile factors, other things being the same. This means, for example, that if capital is easier to move to another state than labor, there will be a tendency for the incidence of a state corporation tax to fall on labor. Thus, analyzing a system of varying corporate tax rates requires that the effects of interstate mobility be added to the already formidable list of factors that come into play when studying the federal corporation tax. Research on this issue is at a formative stage.

CORPORATION TAX REFORM: INTEGRATION WITH THE PERSONAL TAX?

Toward the beginning of this chapter we observed that if corporation income were untaxed, individuals would be able to avoid personal income taxation by accumulating income within corporations. Evidently, this would lead to serious equity and efficiency problems. The government's response has been to construct a system which taxes corporate income twice: first at the corporate level, where the statutory tax rate is 46 percent, and again at the personal level, where distributions of dividends are taxed as ordinary income (currently at a maximum rate of 50 percent).

A number of proposals have been made to integrate personal and corporate income taxes into a single system. The most radical approach is the **partnership method,** sometimes also referred to as **full integration.** Under this approach, all earnings of the corporation during a given year, whether they are distributed or not, are attributed to stockholders just as if the corporation were a partnership.[33] Each shareholder is then

---

[31] There are also difficult administrative questions. When a corporation does business in several states, how should its income be apportioned among states for tax purposes? What if the corporation does business abroad? In 1983, the Supreme Court ruled that states could tax the overseas earnings of multinational corporations in their jurisdictions. As of 1983, a dozen states allowed such worldwide taxation, and many more were considering it.

[32] For additional details, see McLure [1981b].

[33] The **dividend relief approach** is less extreme. With it, the corporation can deduct dividends paid to stockholders just as it now deducts interest payments to bondholders. Although this plan would eliminate the double taxation of dividends, it would still maintain the corporation tax as a separate entity.

liable for personal income tax on his share of the earnings. Thus, if Karl owns 2 percent of the shares of IBM, each year his taxable income includes two percent of IBM's taxable earnings. The corporation tax as a separate entity is eliminated.

There has been considerable debate with respect to whether adopting the partnership method or some close variant would be a desirable step for the United States. The discussion has focused on several issues.

Nature of the Corporation.   Those who favor full integration emphasize that a corporation is, in effect, merely a "conduit" for transmitting earnings to shareholders. It makes more sense to tax the people who receive the income than the institution that happens to pass it along. Those who oppose full integration argue that in large modern corporations, it is ridiculous to think of the shareholders as "partners," and that the corporation is best regarded as a separate entity.

Administrative Feasibility.   Opponents of full integration stress the administrative difficulties that it would create.[34] How are corporate earnings imputed to individuals who hold stock for less than a year? Would shareholders be allowed to deduct the firm's operating losses from their personal taxable income? Proponents of full integration argue that a certain number of fairly arbitrary decisions must be made to administer any complicated tax system. The administrative problems here are no worse than those that have arisen in other parts of the tax code, and can probably be dealt with satisfactorily.

Effects on Efficiency.   Those who favor integration point out that the current corporate tax system imposes large excess burdens on the economy, many of which would be eliminated or at least lessened under full integration. Feldstein and Frisch [1977] argue that the economy would benefit from four types of efficiency gains.

First, the misallocation of resources between the corporate and noncorporate sectors would be eliminated.

Second, to the extent that integration lowered the rate of taxation on the return to capital, tax-induced distortions in savings decisions would be reduced.[35]

Third, integration would remove the incentives for "excessive" retained earnings that characterize the current system. Firms with substantial amounts of retained earnings do not have to enter capital markets to finance new projects. Without the discipline that comes from

---

[34] Administrative issues are discussed carefully by McLure [1979].

[35] As suggested in Chapter 12, lowering taxes on the return to saving could enhance efficiency even if the volume of savings stayed the same or actually fell when the tax decreased.

having to convince investors that projects are worthwhile, such firms may invest inefficiently.

Finally, integration would remove the bias toward debt financing that occurs in the present system, because there would be no separate corporate tax base from which to deduct payments of interest. High ratios of debt to equity increase the probability of bankruptcy. This increased risk and the actual bankruptcies that do occur lower welfare without any concomitant gain to society.

Opponents of full integration point out that given all the uncertainties concerning the operation of the corporation tax, it is hard to quantify the supposed efficiency gains, or even to verify that they exist. For example, as discussed above, to the extent that Stiglitz's view of the tax as equivalent to a levy on pure profits is correct, the tax induces no distortion whatsoever between the corporate and noncorporate sectors. Similarly, there is no solid evidence that corporations invest internal funds less efficiently than those raised externally.

Effects on Saving.   It is sometimes argued that full integration would lower the effective tax rate on capital and therefore lead to more saving.[36] As we saw in Chapter 15, this is a nonsequitur. From a theoretical point of view, the volume of saving may increase, decrease, or stay the same when the tax rate on capital decreases. Econometric work has not yet provided a definitive answer.

Effects on the Distribution of Income.   The introduction of full integration would probably have a substantial impact upon the distribution of income. At least in the short run, those stockholders whose personal tax rates were higher than the corporate tax rate would tend to lose by a move to the partnership method and vice versa. This tendency is illustrated by Feldstein and Frisch's [1977] estimates of the impact of full integration upon tax liabilities. As the data are shown in Table 16.2, negative signs correspond to tax decreases. The figures indicate a modest cut for taxpayers at the lower range of the income distribution, and substantial increases for those at the top.

Feldstein and Frisch [1977] note that these figures must be interpreted with caution for at least two reasons:

The computations are based on the assumption of no behavioral response to the new tax regime. However, it is likely that full integration

---

[36] There are at least two other ways in which national saving might be affected by full integration. As noted above, it would probably lower retained earnings. To the extent that shareholders failed to compensate by increasing personal savings, the total volume of saving would decrease. And full integration would lead to redistribution of income across income classes (see the next section). To the extent that individuals differ in their propensities to save out of additional income, the total amount of saving would change. Feldstein and Frisch [1977] argue that both these effects would probably be small.

TABLE 16.2   Distributional Effects of Introducing Full Integration (1973 data)

Adjusted Gross Income Class ($000)	Change in Tax	Change in Tax as a Percentage of Current Total Tax
$ 0–5	$ −56.1	−37.17%
5–10	−118.6	−13.93
10–15	−91.0	−5.98
15–20	−142.3	−5.70
20–30	−254.8	−5.93
30–50	−489.3	−4.91
50–100	−132.5	0.51
100–500	8,415.8	8.59
500–1,000	78,125.3	12.95
1,000+	241,184.5	12.33

Source: Martin Feldstein and Daniel Frisch, "Corporate Tax Integration: The Estimated Effects on Capital Accumulation and Tax Distribution of Two Integration Proposals," *National Tax Journal* 30 (March 1977), p. 47.

would eventually induce changes in behavior. For example, investors might alter the proportions of their portfolios devoted to corporate and noncorporate assets. Such changes would affect before-tax rates of return on productive factors, which in turn, would induce further changes in the income distribution.

Moreover, full integration would lead to a fall in overall tax revenues. If the authorities wished to keep total revenues constant, then taxes would have to be raised elsewhere. The ultimate effect of integration upon tax progressiveness would depend upon how such revenues were raised.

The discussion in this section makes it clear that there is considerable uncertainty surrounding the likely impact of full integration. This simply reflects our imperfect knowledge of the workings of the current system of corporate taxation. There is by no means unanimous agreement that introducing the partnership method would be a good thing. However, on the basis of the existing and admittedly imperfect evidence, many economists have concluded that both efficiency and equity would be enhanced if the personal and corporate taxes were fully integrated.

SUMMARY

Corporations are subject to a separate federal income tax. While this tax is no longer a leading source of revenue, it has the potential to generate large efficiency losses.

Prior to applying the 46 percent tax rate, firms may deduct wage payments, interest payments, and depreciation allowances. These are meant to measure the cost of producing revenue. Dividends, the cost of acquiring equity funds, are not excluded.

Because depreciation allowances are based upon historic cost their real value declines with inflation. In principle, this effect might be offset by either indexing depreciation allowances, or by shortening tax lives and increasing the proportion of value allocated to early years.

Investment Tax Credits (ITCs) are deducted from the firm's tax bill when particular physical capital assets are purchased.

Due to illusory changes in the value of inventories, first-in, first-out (FIFO) accounting exaggerates corporate profits and tax burdens under inflation. Last-in, first-out (LIFO) accounting eliminates this effect, but not all firms have adopted LIFO.

The corporate tax has been viewed either as an economic profits tax or as a partial factor tax. In the former case, the tax is borne entirely by owners of firms, while in the latter the incidence depends upon capital mobility between sectors, substitution of factors of production, the structure of consumer demand, and the sensitivity of capital accumulation to the net rate of return.

The effect of the corporate tax system on physical investment depends upon: (a) its effect on the user cost of holding capital goods; and (b) the sensitivity of investment to changes in the user cost. In the accelerator model, investment depends only on output, making the user cost irrelevant. The neoclassical model incorporates both effects.

In the neoclassical investment model, the user cost of capital is given by:

$$C = [(i_g(1 - \theta) + \delta)] \times \left[\frac{q}{1 - \theta}\right] \times (1 - k - \psi)$$

where C is the user cost, i_g the before-tax interest rate, δ the economic depreciation rate, θ the corporation tax rate, k the ITC, ψ the present value of depreciation allowances per dollar, and q the purchase price of the asset. Thus, corporate taxation raises the user cost, while the ITC and depreciation allowances reduce it.

Estimates of the effect of the user cost on investment vary greatly. One reason is the critical role played by unobservable changes in expectations.

Effective tax rates vary greatly between equipment and structures, creating substantial efficiency losses.

Due to combined corporate and personal income taxation of dividends, it is somewhat of a mystery why firms pay dividends. Dividends may serve as a signal of the firm's financial strength, or be used to cater to particular "clienteles."

Interest deductibility provides a strong incentive for debt finance. However, increasing the proportion of debt may lead to larger bankruptcy costs.

Forty-six states have corporate income taxes. The possibilities for tax exporting and interstate mobility of factors of production complicate analysis of these taxes.

One possible corporate tax reform is full integration of the corporate and personal income taxes. Owners of stock would be taxed on their share of corporate income as if they were partners. The corporation tax as a separate entity would cease to exist.

DISCUSSION QUESTIONS

1. Which of the following expenditures do you feel should be deductible prior to corporate taxation? Explain your reasoning.
    a. Travel expenses for the corporate president to speak at his alma mater.
    b. Long-distance telephone calls.
    c. Payments to advisers on foreign contracts.

2. Suppose you were asked to calculate the economic depreciation on your new car. How might this be done? Would the task be more difficult for your new food processor?

*3. Consider Equation (16.6), which shows the user cost of capital.
    a. Suppose that depreciation allowances may only be taken on that portion of the acquisition cost not covered by the ITC. What is the user cost of capital. That is, how must Equation (16.6) be modified?
    b. Suppose that inflation is anticipated to occur steadily at a rate of $\dot{p}$ percent per year. What is the user cost of capital in these circumstances?

SELECTED REFERENCES

Feldstein, Martin, and Daniel Frisch. "Corporate Tax Integration: The Estimated Effects on Capital Accumulation and Tax Distribution of Two Integration Proposals." *National Tax Journal* 30 (March 1977), pp. 37–52.

Gravelle, Jane G. "Effects of the 1981 Depreciation Revisions on the Taxation of Income From Business Capital." *National Tax Journal* 35, no. 1 (March 1982), pp. 1–20.

King, Mervyn A., and Don Fullerton, eds. *The Taxation of Income from Capital: A Comparative Study of the U.S., U.K., Sweden and West Germany.* Woodrow Wilson School, Princeton University, 1982. Discussion Paper no. 37.

McLure, Charles E., Jr. *Must Corporate Income Be Taxed Twice?* Washington, D.C. Brookings Institution, 1979.

---

* Difficult.

APPENDIX 16A
THE NEOCLASSICAL INVESTMENT MODEL

The purpose of this appendix is to outline the structure of Jorgenson's [1963] neoclassical model of investment. Jorgenson assumes that in any given period n, each firm decides upon an optimal capital stock, K_n^*—the *total amount* of equipment and structures that it would like to have on hand. If the firm's actual capital stock is not equal to the optimum, it orders enough machines to eliminate the discrepancy. The number of new orders placed each period is therefore the difference between the optimum that period and the optimum in the prior period. Algebraically, this is just $K_n^* - K_{n-1}^*$.

If capital goods were always delivered immediately upon order, then the amount the firm invested each period would be $K_n^* - K_{n-1}^*$. But in fact, delivery lags occur. Suppose that only two thirds of each order is delivered immediately, and the remaining one third arrives the next period. In this case, the firm's actual investment during the period would be the sum of two amounts. The first would be $\frac{2}{3}(K_n^* - K_{n-1}^*)$, which represents the amount of this period's orders that arrive this period. The second is $\frac{1}{3}(K_{n-1}^* - K_{n-2}^*)$, which represents the amount of *last* period's orders that are *delivered* this period. Hence, if INV_n is the amount of net investment done during period n, then $INV_n = \frac{2}{3}(K_n^* - K_{n-1}^*) + \frac{1}{3}(K_{n-1}^* - K_{n-2}^*)$.

In practice, econometric investigators do not know for sure how many periods it takes for all orders to be delivered. Generally, it is necessary to experiment with different figures and see which value does the best job of explaining the data. For the sake of concreteness, let us assume that the process is completed in three periods. Define β_1 as the (unknown) proportion of orders that is delivered immediately, β_2 as the proportion delivered next period, and β_3 as the proportion delivered two periods hence. Then,

(16A.1) $\quad INV_n = \beta_1(K_n^* - K_{n-1}^*) + \beta_2(K_{n-1}^* - K_{n-2}^*) + \beta_3(K_{n-2}^* - K_{n-3}^*)$

As Equation (16A.1) stands, the βs cannot be estimated econometrically, because the K_n^*s are *desired*, not *actual* capital stocks, and are therefore unobservable. We require a theory that relates K_n^* to observable variables. Jorgenson assumes that K_n^* is related to the firm's level of output during period n, Q_n, the price at which it can sell that output, P_n, and the user cost of capital, C_n, by the equation

(16A.2) $$K_n^* = \alpha \left(\frac{P_n}{C_n}\right) Q_n$$

where α is constant. [The variable C is defined in Equation (16.6).] In words, the amount of capital desired by a firm in a given period is directly proportional to the amount of output it produces and the price at which it can sell that output, but inversely proportional to the user cost of capital.[37]

Substituting (16A.2) into (16A.1) we find

(16A.3) $$INV_n = \beta_1\left(\frac{\alpha P_n}{C_n} Q_n - \frac{\alpha P_{n-1}}{C_{n-1}} Q_{n-1}\right)$$

$$+ \beta_2\left(\frac{\alpha P_{n-1}}{C_{n-1}} Q_{n-1} - \frac{\alpha P_{n-2}}{C_{n-2}} Q_{n-2}\right)$$

$$+ \beta_3\left(\frac{\alpha P_{n-2}}{C_{n-2}} Q_{n-2} - \frac{\alpha P_{n-3}}{C_{n-3}} Q_{n-3}\right)$$

Equation (16A.3) looks intimidating, but it is just a complicated version of the basic regression model introduced in Chapter 3. The reason it appears so complex is that each of the right-hand side variables is a combination of different variables (Q, P, and C) instead of a single one. However, the basic idea is the same. If we can estimate the βs and α, then we can predict how any tax induced changes in a right-hand side variable will affect investment.

Estimation of Equation (16A.3) requires observations on INV_n, P_n, C_n, and Q_n. Figures on INV_n, P_n, and Q_n are fairly straightforward to obtain. The user cost of capital, C_n, is not directly observable. However, it can be constructed using Equation (16.6). Hence, Jorgenson is able to estimate the parameters of the equation.

One of the chief criticisms of equation (16A.3) is the fact that the specification for K_n^* given in Equation (16A.2) *imposes* the result that whenever the user cost of capital goes up by a given percentage, the optimal capital stock goes down by exactly the same percentage. (For example, if C_n doubles, then K_n^* goes down by half.) The model *assumes* a substantial responsiveness of investment demand with respect to changes in C_n independent of the data. In some studies which allow the data to determine the responsiveness of K_n^* to C_n, investigators have found a considerably smaller effect [see, for example, Eisner & Nadiri, 1968]. Contrary to Jorgenson, these studies imply that "tax breaks" for business have failed to stimulate capital accumulation. As noted in the text, the impact of taxes on investment remains an unresolved question.

---

[37] Those who are familiar with the theory of production will recognize that (16A.2) is the profit-maximizing amount of capital (given the level of output) when the underlying production function is Cobb-Douglas.

CHAPTER 17

Taxes on Consumption

But when the impositions, are laid upon those things
which men consume, every man payeth equally for
what he useth: nor is the common wealth defrauded by
the luxurious waste of private men.

Thomas Hobbes

The base of an income tax is the value of inputs that an individual sells for use in *production*. Taxes can also be based on the value (or quantity) of commodities that are sold to a person for use in *consumption*. In the United States today, retail taxes are levied on purchases of a wide variety of commodities (see Table 17.1). These taxes account for about 13 percent of the revenues collected by all levels of government. This chapter begins with a discussion of the existing structure of sales taxes.

Two proposals for substantially expanding the role of consumption-based taxes in the U.S. revenue system have been receiving increased attention. Both involve fairly novel tax bases, at least in the context of U.S. fiscal experience. The first is a value-added tax (VAT), and the second a personal consumption tax. The pros and cons of each are discussed later in the chapter.

SALES TAXES

Background

Under a sales tax, the purchase of a commodity creates a tax liability. A **general sales tax** imposes the same tax rate on the purchase of all commodities. A **selective sales tax,** also referred to as an **excise tax,** or a **differential commodity tax,** is levied at different rates on the purchase

**TABLE 17.1   Sales Tax Revenues by Source and Level of Government, 1981
($ millions)**

	Total	Federal	State	Local
General sales tax	$ 55,641	$ 0	$ 46,412	$ 9,229
Motor fuel	14,537	4,678	9,734	125
Tobacco	6,631	2,584	3,893	154
Alcoholic beverages	8,487	5,667	2,613	206
Public utilities	9,038	2,326	4,296	2,417
Other	32,038	25,145	5,803	1,089
Customs duties	8,161	8,161	0	0
Total sales taxes	$ 134,532	$ 48,561	$ 72,751	$ 13,220
Total revenue from own sources	$1,075,387	$658,955	$240,042	$176,391
Percent of revenue from sales taxes*	12.5%	7.1%	31.6%	7.5%

* Computed by the author.
Source: *Facts and Figures on Government Finance—22nd Biennial Edition* (Washington, D.C.: Tax Foundation, 1983), p. 23.

of different commodities. (Some of those rates can be zero.) Sales taxes generally take one of two forms. A **unit tax** is a given amount for each unit purchased. For example, most states levy a tax on motor fuel which is a certain number of cents per gallon.[1] In contrast, an **ad valorem** tax is computed as a percentage of the value of the purchase. For example, the federal excise tax rate on bows and arrows is 11 percent [*Facts and Figures on Government Finance*, 1983, p. 150].

Table 17.1 summarizes the role of sales taxes in the U.S. revenue structure. At the federal level, sales taxes are not very important—only 7.1 percent of total revenues. There is currently no federal general sales tax. Sales taxes play a more important role in the revenue systems of state governments. In 1983, 45 states plus the District of Columbia had general sales taxes with rates that varied from 2 to 7.5 percent [*Facts and Figures on Government Finance*, 1983, p. 267]. (Slightly over half the states exempt food from tax, and virtually all exempt prescription drugs.) In about half the states, municipalities and counties levy their own general sales taxes. As of 1981, the highest combined county, city, and state sales tax rate was 8.25 percent in New York City [*Facts and Figures on Government Finance*, 1983, p. 321].

Rationalizations

Administrative Considerations.   Perhaps the main attraction of sales taxes is ease of administration. The sales tax is collected from sellers at the retail level. In comparison to the situation with an income tax, there

---

[1] In 1983, motor fuel taxes ranged from 4 cents per gallon in Florida to 16 cents in Minnesota [*Facts and Figures on Government Finance*, 1983, p. 269].

are relatively few individuals whose behavior has to be monitored by the tax authorities. This is not to say that administration of a sales tax is without complications. Many difficulties arise because it is unclear whether a given transaction creates a tax liability. In Kentucky, candy is not subject to sales tax, but cookies are. Are Twinkies and Suzy-Q's cookies or candy? In Illinois, your tax liability for a meal ordered on a train depends on whether the meal is consumed totally within the borders of the state. The point is that defining the base for a sales tax involves making arbitrary distinctions, as was true in the case of the personal and corporate income taxes. Moreover, just as is true for other taxes, tax evasion can be a real problem. For example, officials in New York State estimated that evasion of gasoline sales taxes costs the state about $100 million annually ["State Finds Evasion of Sales Tax on Gas," 1983, p. B1].

Nevertheless, sales taxes are probably easier to administer than income taxes. Sales taxation is therefore a particularly attractive option in less developed countries, where individual record-keeping is not widespread, and where the resources available for tax administration are quite limited.

Optimal Tax Considerations.   In countries with high literacy and good record-keeping, these administrative arguments do not seem very compelling. Are there any other justifications? In particular, what role is there for differential taxes on various commodities given that an income tax is already in place? A natural framework for examining this question is the theory of optimal taxation. Atkinson and Stiglitz [1980] showed that if the income tax schedule is chosen optimally, then under fairly reasonable conditions, social welfare cannot be improved by levying differential commodity taxes.[2] However, if for some reason the income tax is not optimal, then differential commodity taxes can improve welfare. For example, if society has egalitarian goals, social welfare can be improved by taxing "luxury goods" at relatively high rates.

A related question is how the rates should be set, given that it has been decided to have differential commodity taxes. Obviously, the answer depends upon the government's objectives. According to optimal tax theory, if the goal is to collect a given amount of revenue as efficiently as possible, then tax rates should be set so that the compensated demand for each commodity is reduced in the same proportion (see Chapter 13). When the demand for each good depends only upon its own price, this is equivalent to the rule that tax rates be inversely related

---

[2] Suppose the utility function of each individual is a function of his consumption of leisure and a set of other commodities. Then as long as the marginal rate of substitution between any two commodities is independent of the amount of leisure, differential commodity taxation cannot improve social welfare in the presence of an optimal earnings tax [Atkinson & Stiglitz, 1980, p. 437].

to compensated price elasticities of demand. Goods with inelastic demand are taxed at relatively high rates and vice versa. It seems unlikely that efficiency will require a general sales tax with the same tax rate for each commodity.

If the government also cares about equity as well as efficiency, optimal tax theory suggests that departures from the inverse elasticity rule are appropriate. As noted in Chapter 13, if price-inelastic commodities make up a high proportion of the budgets of the poor, we expect governments with egalitarian objectives to tax such goods lightly or not at all. This may help explain why many states exempt food from sales taxation, a phenomenon noted above.

Within the conventional welfare economics framework, another justification for a sales tax is the presence of externalities. If consumption of a commodity generates costs which are not included in its price, then in general, efficiency requires a tax upon the use of that good (see Chapter 7). The high tax rate on tobacco is sometimes rationalized in this way. Smokers impose costs upon others by polluting the atmosphere, so a tax on tobacco may enhance economic efficiency.

In some cases, sales taxes can be viewed as substitutes for user fees. It is infeasible to charge motorists a fee for every mile driven, even though the process of driving creates costs in terms of road damage, congestion, etc. Because the amount of road use is related to gasoline consumption, road use can be taxed indirectly by putting a tax on gasoline. Of course, the correspondence is far from perfect: some cars are more fuel efficient than others, some do more damage than others, etc. Still, an approximately correct user fee may be more efficient than none at all.

Other Considerations.   Several rationalizations for differential commodity taxation lie outside the framework of conventional economics. Certain excises can be regarded as taxes on "sin." A particular commodity, such as tobacco or alcohol, is deemed to be bad per se, and its consumption is therefore to be discouraged by the state. Such commodities are just the opposite of "merit goods" (see Chapter 4), which are viewed as being good per se. In both cases, the government is essentially imposing its preferences upon those of the citizenry.

Some argue that politicians are attracted to sales taxes because they are included in the final price of the commodity, and are hence relatively easy to hide. However, it is hard to determine whether citizens really are less sensitive to sales taxes than to other types of taxes.

Efficiency and Distributional Implications

From an efficiency point of view, the fundamental question is whether actual sales tax rates are set so as to minimize excess burden. As pointed out in Chapter 12, when a group of commodities is being taxed, the overall excess burden depends not only upon the elasticities of each good, but also upon the degree to which the goods are complementary and substitutable. At this time, values of all the relevant elasticities are not known with any degree of certainty. Therefore, no definitive judgment as to the efficiency of the existing pattern of sales taxes is available.

As noted earlier, setting all rates equal is almost certainly not efficient. On the other hand, given that the information required to determine fully efficient taxes is not presently available (and perhaps never will be), uniform tax rates may not be a bad approach. This is particularly likely if departures from uniformity open the door to tax rate differentiation based on political rather than equity or efficiency considerations.[3]

The conventional view of the distributional effects of general sales taxes is that they are regressive.[4] It is well known that as annual income rises, the proportion of household income devoted to consumption expenditures falls. Hence, under a general sales tax, the amount of tax paid is a higher proportion for low income than for high income households.

There are two problems with this line of reasoning. First, it looks at the tax as a proportion of *annual* income. In the absence of severe credit market restrictions, *lifetime* income is probably more relevant, and there is reasonably strong evidence that the proportion of lifetime income devoted to consumption is about the same at all levels.[5] Second, and perhaps more fundamentally, the conventional view totally ignores the theory of tax incidence. Implicitly, it is assumed that the taxes on a good are borne entirely by the consumers of that good. As emphasized in Chapter 11, however, a commodity tax generally is shifted in a complicated fashion that depends upon the supply and demand responses when the tax is imposed. The effect of sales taxes upon the distribution of income is still an open question.[6]

The incidence of selective sales tax systems depends crucially upon which goods are taxed at low rates or exempted altogether. By exempting those goods consumed intensively by the poor, the after-tax income

---

[3] In New York, Broadway theatre tickets are exempt from tax, but baseball tickets are not. Purchase of a flag is subject to tax—unless it is a New York State flag. It is hard to believe that the legislators who approved these rules were much concerned with optimal taxation.

[4] See Due and Friedlaender [1977, p. 382].

[5] See, e.g., Friedman [1957].

[6] In the United States, analyzing the incidence of sales taxes is further complicated by the fact that the rate on a given good varies from jurisdiction to jurisdiction. This may induce citizens from one jurisdiction to make purchases in another, so it is hard to tell just who is paying the tax. In New York, clothing is taxed; in New Jersey, it is not. Not surprisingly, many New Yorkers who live near New Jersey do their clothes shopping in the latter. Similarly, it is not unknown for Massachusetts citizens to buy their alcohol in New Hampshire, where the tax rate on liquor is relatively low.

distribution can be made more equal, other things being the same. But problems can arise with attempts to achieve equality in this way. Even if it is true that food expenditures on average play an especially important role in the budgets of the poor, there are still many upper income families whose food consumption is proportionately very high. Moreover, exempting certain commodities creates administrative complexities, because it is not always clear whether certain goods belong in the favored category. Are soft drinks "food"? If so, how much syrup has to be added to carbonated water before it becomes a soft drink? In New York State, at one time *hot* nuts were deemed to be food, and not subject to tax, but *cold* nuts were not exempted. In several states, if you buy a sandwich and eat it in the store, it is subject to an excise tax on "restaurant meals." If you buy the same sandwich in the same store but take it out, the sandwich is "food," and therefore exempt from tax.

We conclude that the use of selective sales taxation is a fairly clumsy way to achieve egalitarian goals, particularly if a progressive income tax system is already in place.

VALUE-ADDED TAX[7]

Typically, goods are produced in several stages. Consider a simple model of bread production. The farmer grows wheat and sells it to a miller who turns it into flour. The miller sells the flour to a baker who transforms it into bread. The bread is purchased by a grocer who sells it to consumers. A hypothetical numerical example is provided in Table 17.2. Row 1 shows the sale value at each stage of production, and row 2

TABLE 17.2   Implementation of a Value-Added Tax (VAT)

	Farmer	Miller	Baker	Grocer	Total
1. Sales	$400	$700	$950	$1,000	$3,050
2. Purchases	0	400	700	950	2,050
3. Value added	400	300	250	50	1,000
4. VAT at 20 percent rate	80	60	50	10	200

shows the purchases made by the producer at each stage. For example, the miller pays $400 to the farmer for wheat, and sells the processed wheat to the baker for $700. The **value added** at each stage of production is the difference between the firm's sales and the purchased material inputs used in production. Because the baker paid $700 for the wheat and sold the bread for $950, his value added is $250. The value added at

---

[7] For excellent descriptions of how value-added taxes work, see Aaron [1981] and McLure [1981a], upon which much of this section is based.

each stage of production is computed by subtracting purchases from sales, and is shown in row 3.[8]

A **value-added tax (VAT),** then, is a percentage tax on value added applied at each stage of production. For example, if the rate of the VAT is 20 percent, the grocer would pay $10, which is 20 percent of $50. Row 4 shows the amount of VAT liability at each stage of production. The total revenue created by the VAT is found by summing the amounts paid at each stage, and equals $200.

The identical result could have been generated by levying a 20 percent tax at the retail level, that is, by a tax of 20 percent on the value of sales made to consumers by the grocer. In essence, then, a VAT is just an alternative method for collecting a sales tax.[9]

Implementation Issues

The United States has never had a national VAT, but this method of raising revenue is quite popular in Europe. The European experience indicates that certain administrative decisions have a major outcome on a VAT's ultimate economic effects.

First, it must be decided how purchases of investment assets by firms will be treated in the computation of value added. There are three possibilities:

1. The purchase of an investment good is treated like any other material input. Its full value is subtracted from sales in the computation, despite the fact that it is a durable good. This is referred to as a **consumption-type VAT** because the tax base excludes investment and involves only consumption.
2. Each period, firms may deduct only the amount by which investment goods depreciate. The tax base is thus total income net of depreciation, which is why this is characterized as a **net income–type VAT.**
3. Firms are allowed no deductions at all for investment and depreciation. This is called a **gross income–type VAT.**

Thus, by making different provisions with respect to the treatment of investment goods, a VAT can be transformed into three distinct taxes, each of which presumably has different efficiency and distributional effects. A VAT does not *necessarily* have to be a tax on consumption. In fact, however, most European VATs are of the consumption type [Aaron, 1981, p. 3].

---

[8] By definition, value added must equal the sum of factor payments made by the producer: wages, interest, rent, and economic profits.

[9] Note that in this example, net income is $1,000, the same as value added. Hence, the VAT is equivalent to a proportional income tax. As we see below, this is not always true.

In addition, a procedure for collection must be devised. European countries use the **invoice method,** which can be illustrated in terms of the hypothetical example in Table 17.2. Each firm is liable for tax on the basis of its *total* sales, *but* it can claim the taxes already paid by its suppliers as a credit against this liability. For example, the baker is liable for taxes on his \$950 in sales, giving him a tax obligation of \$190 (= .20 × \$950). However, he can claim a credit of \$140 (the sum of taxes paid by the farmer and the miller), leaving him a net obligation of \$50. The catch is that the credit is allowed only if supported by invoices provided by the baker and the miller. This system provides an incentive for the producers to police themselves against tax evasion, e.g., whatever taxes the farmer and miller evade must be paid by the baker. The invoice method cannot eliminate evasion completely. For example, producers can collude to falsify invoices. Nevertheless, there appears to be some evidence that multistage collection has cut down on fraud.

Finally, a rate structure must be established. In our simple example, all commodities are taxed at the same rate. In Europe, commodities are taxed differentially. Food and health care products are taxed at low rates, presumably because of equity considerations. For reasons of administrative feasibility, very small firms are exempted altogether in some countries. Similarly, banking and finance institutions escape taxation because they tend to provide services in kind, and it is therefore difficult to compute value added. The consumption of services generated by owner-occupied housing is exempt from tax for the same reasons that it is usually exempted from income taxation (see Chapter 15).

Nonuniform taxation increases administrative complexity, especially when firms produce multiple outputs, some of which are taxable and some of which are not. But the system can work, as evidenced by the European experience. For the United States, then, the question is not whether a national VAT is feasible, but whether its introduction would be an improvement over the status quo.

The Desirability of a VAT for the United States

The VATs suggested for the United States are usually of the European consumption type, and hence essentially general sales taxes. Therefore, the arguments regarding the efficiency and equity of sales taxes made earlier in this chapter are applicable, and there is no need to repeat them. The fundamental problem is the same: Attempts to obtain additional equity by exempting various goods may increase the excess burden of the tax system as a whole, and certainly lead to greater administrative complexity.

More generally, the desirability of a national VAT can be determined only if we know what tax (or taxes) it would replace, how the revenues would be spent, etc. For example, many public finance economists believe that the corporation income tax is undesirable in practically all respects and would be happy to see a VAT replace it, other things being the same. However, they would probably not be as well disposed toward replacing the personal income tax with a VAT.[10]

In this context, it is useful to note that in a number of European countries, the VAT replaced a **turnover tax,** which has as its base the *total* value of sales at each level of production. In terms of Table 17.2, under a 20 percent turnover tax, the farmer's liability is $80, the miller's $140, the baker's $190, and the grocer's $200. The total yield is $610. Now suppose that the farmer, miller, baker, and grocer merge into one firm. Then there is only one "stage" of production, which has sales of $1,000, and hence a liability of only $200. Thus, the yield of the turnover tax depends arbitrarily upon the number of stages of production. Virtually all notions of efficient and equitable taxation suggest that such a system is inferior, and a VAT is certainly an improvement.

Introduction of a national VAT to the United States would create transitional problems, the precise nature of which would depend upon the exact form of the VAT, and what it was replacing. For example, if a consumption-type VAT were to replace the personal income tax, members of the older generations would suffer during the transition period. During their working years, they accumulated wealth to consume during retirement. The interest, dividends, and realized capital gains that they received along the way were subject to the personal income tax. A reasonable expectation for such people is that when they reached retirement, their consumption would not be subject to new taxes. If a consumption-type VAT were suddenly introduced, however, these expectations would be disappointed. Clearly, equity—not to mention political feasibility—requires some method for compensating the elderly during the transition.

McLure [1981a] has argued convincingly that if the United States decides to go the way of a national general sales tax, transition problems would be fewer if a conventional retail sales tax were adopted instead of a VAT. Unlike the nations of Europe, the United States has little experience with multistage taxes, but it has a good deal of experience with retail taxes. There is no good reason to throw out all this experience in return for a tax which is virtually identical from a substantive point of view.

Finally, we must consider the political implications of introducing a VAT. Once it is in place, each percentage point increase in the VAT would yield roughly $21.6 billion in tax revenues, measured in 1983

---

[10] The only serious attempt to introduce a VAT in the United States was the unsuccessful Tax Restructuring Act of 1979. According to this bill, revenues from the VAT would have been used to reduce the social security and income taxes, to liberalize depreciation allowances for business firms, and increase certain welfare payments, among other things. (See McLure [1980a] for details.) It is hard to predict the effects of such a hodgepodge.

dollars.[11] In a world where political institutions accurately reflect the wishes of the citizenry, this observation may not be of much significance. But for those who believe that at least to some extent the interests of the government differ from those of the public (see Chapter 10), the revenue potential of a VAT is frightening. Some fear that the VAT might be used to sneak by an increase in the size of the government sector:

> Because it would be collected by business enterprises, VAT would be concealed in the total price the consumer paid and hence not perceived as a direct tax burden. That is its advantage to legislators—and its major defect to the taxpayers. [Friedman, 1980, p. 90]

As shown in Table 17.3, in virtually all countries with a VAT, the rate has increased over time, as has the share of gross domestic product

TABLE 17.3   The Value-Added Tax (VAT) in Selected European Countries

Country	Year of Introduction	General Rate		VAT Receipts as Percent of Total Revenues (1978)	Total Revenues as Percent of Gross Domestic Product	
		Year of Introduction	1980		Year of Introduction	1978
Denmark	1967	10.0%	22.0%	21.2%	36.1%	43.6%
France	1968	16.7	17.6	21.6	36.3	39.7
Germany	1968	10.0	13.0	15.1	33.9	37.8
Netherlands	1969	12.0	18.0	16.0	39.9	46.8
Luxembourg	1970	8.0	10.0	10.4	34.3	49.9
Belgium	1971	16.0	16.0	17.6	36.5	44.2
Ireland	1972	16.4	20.0	19.5	31.5	33.4
Italy	1973	12.0	14.0	14.2	28.3	32.6
United Kingdom	1973	10.0	15.0	9.0	35.5	34.4
Sweden	1969	11.1	23.5	13.2	41.0	53.5
Norway	1970	20.0	20.0	20.4	42.4	46.9
Austria	1973	16.0	18.0	19.7	38.4	41.4

Source: Henry J. Aaron, ed., *The Value-Added Tax—Lessons from Europe* (Washington, D.C.: Brookings Institution, 1981), p. 14. Used with permission.

devoted to taxes. Of course, this does not prove that the VAT was "responsible" for a larger government sector. On the other hand, one would not expect to be successful in assuaging the fears expressed above by appealing to the European experience.

---

[11] This is a rough approximation made by multiplying personal consumption expenditures in 1983 by 0.01. A more careful estimate would require taking into account behavioral changes generated by the tax.

PERSONAL CONSUMPTION TAX

A major objection to both sales taxes and VATs is that they do not allow personal circumstances to be taken into account when determining tax liabilities. In particular, it is very difficult to differentiate between people on the basis of ability to pay.

In contrast, a personal tax based on total consumption expenditures during a given period allows the tax authorities to take individual characteristics into account in determining tax liability. Under a **personal consumption tax** (also referred to as an **expenditure tax**), each household files a return which reports its consumption expenditures during the year. Just as under the personal income tax, various exemptions and deductions can be taken to allow for special circumstances such as extraordinary medical expenses. Each individual's tax bill is then determined by applying a rate schedule to the adjusted amount of consumption. The rate schedule can be as progressive as desired by the legislature.

To see precisely how the base of such a personal consumption tax differs from that of an income tax, recall from Chapter 14 the Haig-Simons definition of income: the increase in potential consumption during a period. Potential consumption has two components, actual consumption, and changes in wealth. Algebraically,

(17.1) $I = c + \Delta\omega$

where I is income, c is consumption, and $\Delta\omega$ is net additions to wealth.[12] The base for a comprehensive income tax is I, while the base for a personal consumption tax is $c = I - \Delta\omega$. Thus, unconsumed additions to wealth are exempt from taxation. An alternative expression for c is found by noting that income is the sum of labor income, E, and income from capital. But income from capital is just the product of the interest rate, i, and the amount of wealth, ω. Hence,

(17.2) $c = E + i\omega - \Delta\omega$

In words, consumption is just the difference between all cash receipts $(E + i\omega)$ and the amount of unconsumed additions to wealth.

Some argue that if the income tax were replaced by a consumption tax, efficiency, equity, and administrative simplicity would be enhanced. The defenders of the income tax have argued that the case for expenditure taxation is seriously flawed. The remainder of this chapter discusses the controversy.[13]

---

[12] $\Delta\omega$ can be positive or negative. Note that "net additions to wealth" is just another way of defining "saving"—whatever is not consumed becomes part of wealth.

[13] For a good discussion of the pros and cons, see Pechman [1980].

Efficiency Issues

The efficiency implications of personal consumption versus income taxation can be examined using the simple two-period model of consumption and saving that was introduced in Chapter 15. In Figure 17.1, the horizontal axis measures the amount of Friedrich's present consumption, c_0, and the vertical axis measures the amount of his future consumption, c_1. Assume that prior to taxation, Friedrich earns wages of I_0 in period zero, and I_1 in period 1. For the moment it is assumed that labor supply is fixed, so that the before-tax earnings levels I_0 and I_1 are

FIGURE 17.1   Effect of a 25 Percent Income Tax on the Budget Constraint for Present and Future Consumption

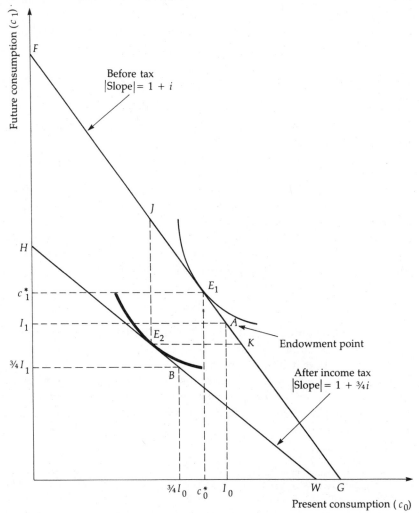

unaffected by taxes. The combination I_0 and I_1 is Friedrich's endowment point, and is marked by an A in Figure 17.1. If Friedrich can borrow and lend at the market rate of return i, his budget line is straight line FG, which passes through point A and has a slope equal in absolute value to $(1 + i)$. Utility is maximized at point E_1, where Friedrich consumes c_0^* in the present and c_1^* in the future.

Suppose that a 25 percent income tax is levied, and interest payments are deductible. How does this affect Friedrich's budget constraint? We know that after-tax labor income in the initial period becomes $\frac{3}{4}I_0$, and after-tax labor income in period 2 becomes $\frac{3}{4}I_1$. This point is marked B in Figure 17.1. Point B must lie on Friedrich's after-tax budget line, because he always has the option of consuming exactly the amount of his after-tax labor income each period—to neither save nor to borrow. If he does choose to lend or borrow, he now faces an effective rate of return of $\frac{3}{4}i$ rather than i.[14] Hence, the after-tax budget line passes through point B and has a slope in absolute value of $(1 + \frac{3}{4}i)$. It is drawn as line HW in Figure 17.1. Friedrich maximizes utility at point E_2. The amount of tax collected is equal to E_2J if measured in terms of future consumption, or E_2K if measured in terms of present consumption.[15]

Now suppose that the same amount of revenue had been collected as a consumption tax. The key thing to note in this context is that the consumption tax leaves the market rate of return available to Friedrich unchanged. If he can earn a rate of return i before a consumption tax, he can earn it after, because receiving income by itself does not create a tax liability—only consuming it does. Hence, after the consumption tax, the budget constraint has a slope (in absolute value) of $1 + i$, and is parallel to the original budget constraint, FG.

To fix the position of the new budget constraint, recall that we want to analyze a consumption tax that yields the *same revenue* as the income tax. Therefore, the new constraint must pass through point E_2. In Figure 17.2, line LM passes through E_2, is parallel to FG, and is therefore the budget line after the consumption tax is imposed. Note that by construction, any point on LM yields tax revenues of E_2K, just the amount generated by the income tax.

Given budget line LM, Friedrich maximizes utility at point E_3. Point E_3 lies on a higher indifference curve than E_2. In this model, a consumption tax leaves the individual at a higher level of utility than would an equal-yield income tax, and hence is to be preferred on efficiency grounds.

The intuition behind this result is familiar from Chapter 12 on excess

---

[14] If he saves a dollar and earns i, the government taxes away one quarter, leaving him with only $\frac{3}{4}i$. If he borrows a dollar, the interest payments are deductible, so the cost of borrowing is reduced to $\frac{3}{4}i$.

[15] In Chapter 12, we discussed at greater length how to measure tax liabilities from an indifference curve diagram. Students may find it useful to review that material.

FIGURE 17.2   Comparison of Equal-Yield Consumption and Income Taxes

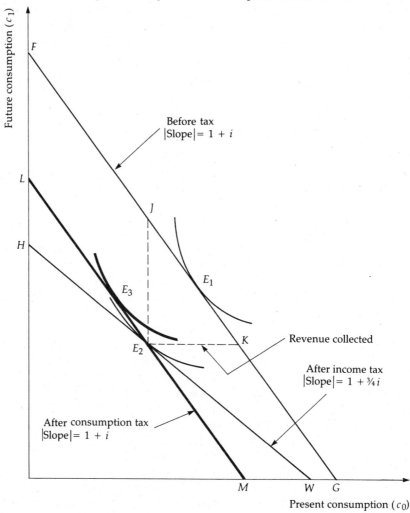

burden. The income tax, by changing the rate of return, distorts individual decisions between future and present consumption. In contrast, the consumption tax leaves the rate of return unchanged, and hence does not distort the relative "price" of consumption in the present and in the future. In other words, the income tax acts like a distorting excise tax, while the consumption tax is equivalent to a nondistorting lump sum tax.

Is this result general, or is it a consequence of some special assumptions of this model? The reader will recall that in Chapter 12 a similar argument was used to "prove" that taxes at equal rates on all commodities are always more efficient than differential rates on different commodities. We showed there the fallacy in that argument. Once it is recognized that even an equiproportional tax distorts the choice between leisure and each of the taxed commodities, it is no longer clear that taxing all commodities at the same rate is efficient. The same consideration applies here. Figures 17.1 and 17.2 are built on the *assumption* that the supply of labor is fixed. Once the possibility that labor supply decisions are choices is raised, it is no longer true that the consumption tax is necessarily more efficient than an income tax.

True, unlike the income tax, the consumption tax leaves unchanged the rate at which Friedrich can trade off consumption between the two periods. However, in general, the consumption tax *does* distort the rate at which Friedrich can trade off leisure against consumption. Suppose that his wage rate is w. Prior to the consumption tax, Friedrich can trade off one hour of leisure for w dollars worth of consumption. If consumption is taxed at rate t_c, however, surrendering one hour of leisure allows him only $w/(1 + t_c)$ dollars worth of consumption. Thus, the consumption tax distorts the decision between work and consumption.

In short, as long as labor supply is a matter of choice, both income and consumption taxes distort some decisions. Therefore, *both* systems induce an efficiency cost, and only empirical work can determine for which tax the cost is smaller.

Several studies have suggested that given what is known about labor supply and saving behavior, a consumption tax creates a smaller excess burden than an income tax, even when labor supply distortions created by both taxes are taken into account. For example, Fullerton, Shoven, and Whalley [1982, p. 28] estimate that the efficiency gain from moving to a consumption tax would be about 2 to 3 percent of national income each year. However, such results are quite sensitive to assumptions about the responsiveness of consumption to changes in the interest rate. As we saw in Chapter 15, this is notoriously hard to measure. As research on saving behavior progresses, our understanding of the efficiency aspects of income versus consumption taxation will improve.

Equity Issues

Progressiveness. As noted earlier, there is a widespread assumption that sales taxes are regressive. Whatever the merits of this view, there is an unfortunate tendency to assume that it applies to any tax with consumption as a base. This is simply wrong. Given that the base of the tax being considered here is *personal* consumption expenditures, the structure can be made as progressive as desired. In 1977, the Department of the Treasury estimated that a personal consumption tax with marginal rates ranging from 10 percent to 40 percent could raise the same amount of revenue as the corporate and personal income taxes [U.S. Department of the Treasury, 1977, p. 169]. Under this scheme, average tax rates with respect to before-tax consumption would range from 2.1 percent for those whose before-tax consumption is less than $5,000 to 35.7 percent for those whose before-tax consumption levels exceeded $100,000, as shown in Table 17.4.

TABLE 17.4   Effective Tax Rates under a Model Consumption Tax (1976 levels)

Gross Consumption Class (thousands of dollars)	Effective Tax Rate* (percentage)
$ 0–5	2.1%
5–10	7.7
10–15	11.9
15–20	15.1
20–30	18.3
30–50	23.1
50–100	30.3
100 or more	35.7

* As a percentage of gross consumption.
Source: U.S. Department of the Treasury, *Blueprints for Basic Tax Reform* (Washington, D.C.: U.S. Government Printing Office, 1977), p. 171.

Ability to Pay.   Those who favor the income base argue that *actual* consumption is merely one component of *potential* consumption. It is the power to consume, not necessarily its exercise, that is relevant. They point out that under a consumption tax, it would be possible for a miserly millionaire to have a smaller tax liability than a much poorer person. In response, some proponents of consumption taxes suggest that it is more fair to tax an individual according to what he "takes out" of the economic system, in the form of consumption, than what he "contributes" to society, as measured by income. As the 17th-century philosopher Thomas Hobbes said:

> For what reason is there, that he which laboureth much, and sparing the fruit of his labour, consumeth little, should be more charged, than he that liveth idly, getteth little, and spendeth all he gets; seeing the one hath no more protection from the commonwealth than the other. [1651/1963, p. 303]

From this point of view, if the miserly millionaire chooses not to consume very much, that is all to the good, because the resources he saves become available to society for capital accumulation.

A related question is whether or not an income tax results in "double taxation" of interest income. Some argue that an income tax is unfair because it taxes capital income twice: once when the original income is earned, and again when the investment produces a return.[16] As Goode [1980, p. 54] notes, the logic of income taxation impels that the return to saving be taxed. Whether or not this is fair depends, as usual, upon value judgments. The debate is likely to continue.

Annual versus Lifetime Equity.   It is widely agreed that events which influence a person's economic position for only a very short length of time do not provide an adequate basis for determining ability to pay. Indeed, some have argued that ideally tax liabilities should be related to lifetime income. Proponents of consumption taxation point out that an annual income tax leads to tax burdens that can differ quite substantially even for people who have the same lifetime wealth.

To see why, consider Mr. Grasshopper and Ms Ant, both of whom live for two periods. In the present, they have identical fixed labor incomes of I_0, and in the future, they both have labor incomes of zero. (The assumption of zero second-period income is made solely for convenience.) Grasshopper chooses to consume heavily early in life because he is not very concerned about his retirement years. Ant chooses to consume most of her wealth later in life, because she wants a lavish retirement.

Define Ant's present consumption in the presence of a proportional income tax as c_0^A, and Grasshopper's as c_0^G. By assumption, $c_0^G > c_0^A$. Ant's future income before tax is the interest she earns on her savings: $i(I_0 - c_0^A)$. Similarly, Grasshopper's future income before tax is: $i(I_0 - c_0^G)$.

Now, if the proportional income tax rate is t, in the present Ant and Grasshopper have identical tax liabilities of tI_0. However, in the future, Ant's tax liability is $ti(I_0 - c_0^A)$, while Grasshopper's is $ti(I_0 - c_0^G)$. Because $c_0^G > c_0^A$, Ant's future tax liability is higher. Solely because Ant has a greater taste for saving than Grasshopper, her lifetime tax burden (the discounted sum of her tax burdens in the two periods) is greater than Grasshopper's.

In contrast, under a proportional consumption tax, lifetime tax burdens are *independent* of tastes for saving, other things being the same.[17] To prove this, all we need to do is write down the equation for each taxpayer's budget constraint. Because all of Ant's noncapital income (I_0) comes in the present, its present value is simply I_0. Now, the present value of lifetime consumption must equal the present value of

---

[16] "The fundamental bias against capital formation in our tax system results from the multiple taxation of income which is saved and invested" [Meiselman, 1977, p. 30].

[17] However, when marginal tax rates depend upon the level of consumption, this may not be the case.

lifetime income. Hence, Ant's consumption pattern must satisfy the relation

(17.3)
$$I_0 = c_0^A + \frac{c_1^A}{1 + i}$$

Similarly, Grasshopper is constrained by

(17.4)
$$I_0 = c_0^G + \frac{c_1^G}{1 + i}$$

Equations (17.3) and (17.4) say simply that the lifetime value of income must equal the lifetime value of consumption.

If the proportional consumption tax rate is t_c, then Ant's tax liability the first period is $t_c c_0^A$; her tax liability the second period is $t_c c_1^A$; and the present value of her lifetime consumption tax liability, R_c^A is

(17.5)
$$R_c^A = t_c c_0^A + \frac{t_c c_1^A}{1 + i}$$

Similarly, Grasshopper's lifetime tax liability is

(17.6)
$$R_c^G = t_c c_0^G + \frac{t_c c_1^G}{1 + i}$$

By comparing Equations (17.5) and (17.3), we see that Ant's lifetime tax liability is equal to $t_c I_0$. [Just multiply Equation (17.3) through by t_c.] Similar comparison of Equations (17.4) and (17.6) indicates that Grasshopper's lifetime tax liability is also $t_c I_0$. We conclude that under a proportional consumption tax, two people with identical lifetime incomes always pay identical lifetime taxes (where "lifetime" is interpreted in the present value sense). This stands in stark contrast to a proportional income tax, where the pattern of lifetime consumption influences lifetime tax burdens.

A related argument in favor of the consumption tax centers on the fact that there is a tendency for income to fluctuate more than consumption. In years when income is unusually low, individuals may draw upon their savings or borrow to smooth out fluctuations in their consumption levels. The point is that annual consumption is likely to be a better reflection of lifetime circumstances than is annual income.

Opponents of consumption taxation would question whether a lifetime point of view is really appropriate. There is too much uncertainty in both the political and economic environments for a lifetime perspective to be very realistic. Moreover, the "consumption smoothing" required for the lifetime arguments requires that individuals be able to save and borrow freely at the going rate of interest. Given that capital markets are imperfect—individuals often face constraints on the amounts they can borrow—it is not clear how relevant the lifetime arguments are. Although a considerable body of empirical work suggests that the life-cycle model is a good representation for most households (see King [1983]), this argument still deserves some consideration.

Administrative Advantages and Disadvantages

In discussions of personal consumption taxation, administrative issues are of more than usual interest. This is because such a tax system has never been implemented successfully.[18] Indeed, for many years a consumption tax has been viewed mostly as an intellectual curiosity rather than a realistic policy option. But recently, a number of economists and lawyers have suggested that a consumption tax is quite feasible and not as different from the current income tax system as one might think.

If the only way to compute annual consumption were to add up all expenditures made over the course of a year, taxpayers would have to keep records and receipts for every purchase. This would be infeasible from an administrative point of view. All taxpayers simply cannot be expected to maintain complete balance sheets.

Andrews [1974] and others have suggested that instead consumption be measured on a **cash-flow basis,** meaning that it would be calculated simply as the difference between all cash receipts and savings. To keep track of saving, qualified accounts would be established at savings banks, savings and loan associations, security brokerage houses, and other types of financial institutions. Funds that were certified by these institutions as having been deposited in qualified accounts would be exempt from tax.[19] Most of the record-keeping responsibility would be met by these institutions, and would not involve more paperwork than exists already. As long as capital gains and interest from such accounts were retained, they would not be taxed. Such qualified accounts already exist in the forms of Keogh plans and Individual Retirement Accounts (Chapter 14). One way to look at a consumption tax is simply as an expansion of the opportunities to invest in such accounts.

A potentially important administrative problem concerns the valuation of the consumption benefits produced by durable goods. The purchase of a durable is an act of saving, and hence would be deductible under a consumption tax. Over time, the durable generates consumption benefits, which are subject to tax. But here the usual problems of imputing consumption streams arise. How do we measure the annual flow of benefits produced by a house or a car?

Proponents of a consumption tax argue that this problem is avoidable if a **tax prepayment approach** for durables is used. When the original

---

[18] India and Sri Lanka were the only two countries to adopt a consumption tax, and both nations soon abandoned it.

[19] For further details, see U.S. Department of the Treasury [1977].

durable investment is made, it is taxed as if it were consumption. There is no attempt later to tax the returns generated by the investment. Thus, imputation problems are avoided. But does prepayment yield the appropriate amount of tax? In present value terms, tax prepayment does indeed yield the same amount as would have been collected if the consumption were taxed when it actually occurred, as long as the tax rate is fixed. To see why, suppose that the durable lasts for T years, and produces expected consumption benefits of c_1 in year 1, c_2 in year 2, etc. In equilibrium, the price of the durable, V, just equals the present value of the stream of consumption the durable generates:

(17.7)
$$V = \frac{c_1}{1 + i} + \frac{c_2}{(1 + i)^2} + \cdots + \frac{c_T}{(1 + i)^T}$$

where i is the interest rate. Now, if consumption is taxed at rate t_c, then revenue collections under the tax prepayment approach are $t_c V$. On the other hand, if consumption is taxed when it occurs, the present value of the tax proceeds (R_c) is

(17.8)
$$R_c = \frac{t_c c_1}{1 + i} + \frac{t_c c_2}{(1 + i)^2} + \cdots + \frac{t_c c_T}{(1 + i)^T}$$

Examining Equations (17.7) and (17.8) together, we note that R_c is exactly equal to $t_c V$. Hence, the same amount of tax is collected in present value terms.

Although many people have become convinced that consumption taxation is practical, many others believe it would be an administrative nightmare. We now catalog some advantages and disadvantages of consumption taxation relative to income taxation, and also note a few problems that are common to both.

Advantages of a Consumption Tax. *No Need to Measure Capital Gains and Depreciation.*   Some of the most vexing problems in administering an income tax arise from difficulties in measuring additions to wealth—$\Delta\omega$ of Equation (17.1). For example, a comprehensive measure of $\Delta\omega$ requires calculation of capital gains and losses even on those assets that are not sold during the year, a task so difficult that it is not even attempted under the current system. Similarly, for those who have income produced by capital equipment, $\Delta\omega$ must be lowered by the amount the equipment depreciates during the year. But as we noted in Chapter 16, very little is known about actual depreciation patterns. Andrews [1983] views the inability of real-world income tax systems to measure and tax $\Delta\omega$ as their fatal flaw:

> A comprehensive income tax ideal with an immediate concession that taxation is not to be based on actual value is like a blueprint for constructing a building in which part of the foundation is required to be located in

quicksand. If the terrain cannot be changed, the blueprint had better be amended. [p. 282]

Under a consumption tax, all such problems *simply disappear* because $\Delta\omega$ is no longer part of the tax base.

Fewer Problems with Inflation.   In the presence of a nonindexed income tax, inflation creates important distortions. Some of these are a consequence of a progressive rate structure, but some would occur even if the tax were proportional. These distortions occur because computing capital income requires the use of figures from years which have different price levels. For example, if an asset is sold, calculation of the capital gain or loss requires subtracting the value in the year of purchase from its value in the current year. In general, part of the change in value will be due to inflation, so that individuals are taxed on gains that do not reflect increases in real income.[20] As noted in Chapter 14, setting up an appropriate scheme for indexing income generated by investments is very complicated, and has not been attempted in the United States.

In contrast, under a consumption tax, calculation of the tax base involves only current-year transactions. Therefore, any distortions associated with inflation are likely to be much less of a problem.

No Need for Separate Corporation Tax.   Some argue that implementation of a consumption tax would allow removal of the corporation tax, at least in theory. Recall from Chapter 16 that one of the main justifications of the corporation tax is to get at income that people accumulate in corporations. If accumulation per se were no longer part of the personal income tax base, this would not be necessary. Elimination of the corporation tax would probably enhance efficiency.

Advocates of the consumption tax often point out that adoption would not be as radical a move as first appearances might suggest. In some respects, the present system *already* looks very much like a consumption tax:

1. Income is exempt from taxation when it is saved in certain forms such as Keogh plans, IRAs, and pensions.
2. Unrealized capital gains on financial assets are untaxed, as are virtually all capital gains on housing.
3. Realized capital gains are taxed preferentially and are free of all taxation at the death of the owner.

---

[20] Suppose, for example, that Smith buys an asset for $100. After a year, the asset is worth $200, but the price level has also doubled. In real terms, there has been no increase in income, yet Smith nevertheless has incurred a tax liability.

4. Accelerated depreciation and investment tax credits reduce the amount of investment purchases included in the tax base.

In light of these considerations, characterizing the status quo as an "income tax" is a serious misnomer; it is more a hybrid between income and consumption taxation.

Disadvantages of a Consumption Tax. *Administrative Problems.* An important consideration raised by opponents of consumption taxation is that monitoring and accounting costs would be larger than at present. They argue that even if the cash-flow method were adopted, people would have to keep more records with respect to their asset positions.

It is also argued that a consumption tax would create significant incentives for people to falsify the prices at which capital transactions take place. Of course, such incentives exist under the current system; if a person claims to have sold an asset for a lower price than the actual one, his capital gains tax liability will be lower. But the incentive to lie is somewhat mitigated by the fact that the tax rate on capital gains is low. Under a consumption tax, unless the proceeds from a sale are reinvested, the full amount is subject to tax. Hence, there are potentially large payoffs to cheating.[21]

The tax prepayment approach, which is central to the taxation of durables under a consumption tax, has also been criticized. Equation (17.7) indicates the relation between the *expected* benefits of an investment and its cost. But these returns cannot be known with certainty. If the stream of c's turns out to be higher than expected, then the tax prepayment plan will result in a tax liability that is lower than it would be otherwise. Similarly, if the c's are lower, tax prepayment results in higher liabilities. Critics argue that taxes should be based on outcomes, not expectations, so that the tax prepayment approach is fundamentally unfair.

Transitional Problems. Critics have also argued that despite already existing elements of consumption taxation in the present system, the switch to a consumption tax would be a major one, and would be accompanied by enormous transitional problems. During the transition, people would have incentives to conceal their assets, and to liquidate them later without reporting the proceeds. Moreover, during the transition, the elderly generation would be hurt by moving to a consumption tax. In a sense, they would be subject to double jeopardy—in their working years, when they were accumulating wealth for retirement, their capital income was subject to tax. Then, when they reach retirement, they have

---

[21] Other examples of tax dodges that might be available under a consumption tax are discussed by Graetz [1980].

to pay tax on the consumption itself. This kind of problem arises in any major tax reform—people who have made commitments on the basis of the existing system are likely to be hurt when it changes. Fairness would seem to require that the elderly be compensated for the losses they would incur during the transition. Those advocating the consumption tax have proposed a number of rules for alleviating transitional problems [see Department of the Treasury, 1977].

Problems with Both Systems.   Even the most enthusiastic proponents of the consumption tax recognize that its adoption would not usher in an era of perfection in revenue raising. Several of the most intractable problems inherent in the income tax system would also plague any consumption tax. These include, but are not limited to:

1. Distinguishing consumption commodities from commodities used in production. (Should a desk purchased for use at home be considered consumption or a business expense?)
2. Defining consumption itself. (Are health-care expenditures part of consumption, or should they be deductible?)
3. Choosing the unit of taxation, determining an appropriate rate structure, and integrating the system with gift and estate taxes.
4. Valuing fringe benefits of various occupations. (If a job gives a person access to the company swimming pool, should the consumption benefits be taxed? If so, how can they be valued?)
5. Determining a method for averaging across time if the schedule has increasing marginal tax rates.
6. Taxing production that occurs in the home.
7. Discouraging incentives to avoid taxes altogether by participating in the underground economy.

Finally, it must be emphasized that it is not quite fair to compare an *ideal* consumption tax to the *actual* income tax. Historically, special interests have been very effective at persuading politicians to tax certain types of income preferentially. Adoption of a consumption tax could hardly be expected to eliminate political corruption of the tax structure. It is hard to predict whether a real-world consumption tax would be better than the current system.

SUMMARY

Sales taxes may be levied per unit or as a percentage of purchase value (ad valorem), on all (general sales tax) or specific (excise tax) purchases. General sales and excise taxes are important revenue sources at the state and local levels.

A major attraction of sales taxes is that they are relatively easy to administer. Some sales taxes can be justified as correctives for externalities or as substitutes for user fees.

Typically sales taxes are viewed as regressive. However, this is based on calculations involving annual rather than lifetime income. This view also assumes that the incidence of the tax lies with the purchaser.

The value-added tax (VAT) is quite popular in Europe, but is not used in the United States. The VAT is levied on the difference between sales revenue and cost of purchased commodity inputs. Different treatment of input costs leads to a consumption-type, net income-type, or gross income-type VAT.

The base of a personal consumption tax is found by subtracting additions to wealth from income. Optimal tax theory indicates that a consumption tax is *necessarily* more efficient than an income tax when labor supply decisions are independent of the allocation of consumption over time. Otherwise, the relative efficiency of consumption and income taxes can only be determined by empirical work.

Proponents of the personal consumption tax argue that it eliminates double taxation of interest income, promotes lifetime equity, taxes individuals on the basis of the amount of economic resources they use up, may be adjusted to achieve any desired level of progressiveness, and is administratively feasible. In particular, it eliminates difficult problems involved in measuring the changing value of assets.

Opponents of the personal consumption tax point out difficult transition problems, argue that income better measures ability to pay, feel that it is administratively burdensome, and oppose taxation of durables on the basis of expected, not actual, outcomes.

DISCUSSION QUESTIONS

1. "Because the tax base includes the purchase of necessities, both general sales taxes and personal consumption taxes are regressive." Discuss.

2. Under what circumstances is a VAT equivalent to a comprehensive income tax?

3. The simple life-cycle model in this chapter assumes that lifetime income just equals lifetime consumption. In contrast, some people set aside part of their lifetime income for bequests. If you were to devise a comprehensive income tax, how would bequests be treated? Would the treatment differ under a personal consumption tax? If so, how and why?

4. "Movement from income to consumption taxation would increase personal saving, and hence promote economic efficiency." Comment.

SELECTED REFERENCES

Aaron, Henry J., ed. *The Value-Added Tax—Lessons from Europe.* Washington, D.C.: Brookings Institution, 1981, pp. 1–18.

McLure, Charles E., Jr. "Tax Restructuring Act of 1979: Time for an American Value-Added Tax?" *Public Policy* 28, no. 3 (Summer 1980), pp. 301–22.

Pechman, Joseph A., ed. *What Should Be Taxed: Income or Expenditure?* Washington, D.C.: Brookings Institution, 1980.

CHAPTER 18

Wealth Taxes

The love of wealth is therefore to be traced, as either a principal or accessory motive, at the botton of all that the Americans do; this gives to all their passions a sort of family likeness.

Alexis de Tocqueville

The taxes we have discussed so far are levied on items such as income, consumption, and sales. In the jargon of economics, these are known as **flow variables** because they are associated with a time dimension. For instance, income is a flow, because the concept is meaningful only when put in the context of some time interval. If you say "My income is $10,000," it means nothing unless one knows whether it is over a week, month, or year. A **stock variable,** on the other hand, has no time dimension. It is a quantity at a point in time, not a rate per unit of time. Wealth is a stock, because it refers to the value of the assets an individual has accumulated as of a given time.

This chapter involves taxes that are levied on the stock of wealth. Our focus is on the property tax imposed upon owners of certain kinds of wealth, and upon gift and estate taxes levied when wealth is transferred from one owner to another.

WHY TAX WEALTH?

Before turning to the specifics of each tax, we might ask what justifications there are for using wealth as a tax base. Several answers have been proposed.

First, wealth taxes help to correct for certain (inevitable) problems that arise in the administration of a comprehensive income tax. Recall that *all* capital gains, realized or not, belong in the tax base of a comprehensive income tax. In practice, it is impossible to tax unrealized capital gains. By taxing the wealth of which these gains become a part, perhaps this situation can be remedied. Now, it is true that wealth at a given point in time includes the sum of capital gains and losses from all earlier years. However, there is no reason to believe that the yield from an annual wealth tax will approximate the revenues that would have been generated by full annual taxation of unrealized capital gains.

Second, the higher an individual's wealth, the greater his or her ability to pay, other things—including income—being the same. Therefore, wealthy individuals should have a higher tax liability. Suppose that a miser has accumulated a huge hoard of gold that yields no income. Should he be taxed on the value of the hoard? Some believe that as long as the miser was subject to the income tax while the hoard was accumulating, it should not be taxed again. Others would argue that the gold per se generates utility and should be subject to tax. In any case, note that the logic of the ability to pay argument requires that if wealth is to be taxed, it must be *net* wealth—assets minus debts. If Cain and Abel both own $100,000 houses, but Cain has a $75,000 mortgage while Abel owns his house outright, then it is absurd to treat them as having identical amounts of wealth. As we will see below, property taxes in the United States do not allow deductions for liabilities.

Third, wealth taxation reduces the concentration of wealth, which is desirable socially and politically. As we saw in Chapter 5, although it is difficult to measure income precisely, the best estimates suggest that the distribution of income in the United States is quite unequal. The quality of data on wealth is even less precise. What information there is suggests that the distribution of wealth is very unequal. One study using data from the early 1960s indicated that the top 6 percent of families owned 57 percent of all wealth.[1] The desirability of such inequality turns on a complicated set of ethical issues that are quite similar to those discussed in Chapter 5 in connection with the distribution of income. A related issue is whether a highly concentrated distribution of wealth is likely to lead to corruption of democratic political processes. While this is a vitally important question, it is beyond our scope. Note that this whole line of argument *assumes* that wealth taxation does indeed lead to a more equal distribution of wealth. It is shown below that this is not necessarily the case.

Finally, wealth taxes are payments for benefits that wealth holders receive from government. Society, after all, protects the wealth of citizens, and some payment is deserved in return. In addition, government makes certain expenditures that are likely to especially benefit wealth holders. If the state builds and maintains a road that goes by my store,

---

[1] Brittain [1978, Chapter 1] discusses this and a number of other studies.

then it confers a benefit upon me for which I should pay. Although the notion of basing taxes on benefits has some appeal, it is not clear that any feasible wealth tax can achieve this goal. A lawyer arguing the case for the property tax asked rhetorically, "[I]sn't it true that one with twice as much house receives twice as much benefit from . . . police and fire services rendered to property?" [Hagman, 1978, pp. 42]. Contrary to what he apparently believed, the answer is "probably not." The value to a given household of most services provided by local government depends upon factors other than house size. For example, the value of education depends upon the number of children. Even the value of fire and police services depends upon how much furniture is in the house and how much insurance protection has been purchased. If benefit taxation is the goal, a system of user fees for public services would be more appropriate than a wealth tax.

To summarize, wealth taxes have been rationalized on both ability-to-pay and benefit grounds. Neither set of arguments is very convincing. As we shall see, the main justification for the U.S. system of wealth taxation may be more political than economic. We now turn to a discussion of that system.

PROPERTY TAX[2]

Background

At the turn of the 20th century, the property tax accounted for 42 percent of tax revenues raised by all levels of government [U.S. Bureau of the Census, 1975, p. 1119]. By 1981, this figure was down to 11.5 percent. Of the $75.0 billion raised by property taxes that year, $3.0 billion was collected by the states (2 percent of their tax revenues) and $72.0 billion by localities (76 percent of their tax revenues) [*Facts and Figures on Government Finance*, 1983, p. 23]. There is no federal property tax. Although it is not as important as many other taxes when viewed from a national perspective, the property tax clearly plays a key role in local public finance.

To understand how the actual system of property taxes works, it is useful to consider a hypothetical system in which all forms of wealth are taxed at a uniform rate. The base of such a tax would include the value of homes, automobiles, land, property used for business purposes, etc. In contrast, in the United States, literally thousands of jurisdictions operate their property tax systems more or less independently.[3] No jurisdiction

---

[2] For further details, see Aaron [1975], upon which much of this discussion is based.

[3] As of 1983, if counties, municipalities, townships and towns, school districts, and special districts are included, there were over 82,600 local governments. About 80 percent of them had the power to levy property taxes. See *Facts and Figures on Government Finance*, 1983, p. 14.

includes a comprehensive measure of wealth in its tax base, but there are major differences with respect to just what types of property are excludable and what rates are applied. Some jurisdictions tax farm property at low rates. Property owned by religious and nonprofit institutions make "voluntary" contributions in lieu of taxes. Some communities tax new business plants preferentially, presumably to attract more commercial activity. Few areas tax personal wealth other than homes so that items like cars, jewels, and stocks and bonds are usually exempt. Typically, structures and the land upon which they are built are subject to tax. But the rates differ substantially across jurisdictions. Table 18.1 shows residential property tax rates in selected large cities in 1980.

TABLE 18.1   Residential Property Tax Rates in Selected Cities (1980)

City	Effective Tax Rate*
Boston	4.60%
Detroit	4.01
Chicago	2.73
Atlanta	2.21
San Antonio	2.05
Los Angeles	1.13
New Orleans	0.94
Phoenix	0.66

* Effective rates take into account the fact that properties are not taxed at their full market values. See the discussion of "assessment ratios" in this chapter.

Source: U.S. Bureau of the Census, *Statistical Abstract of the United States: 1982–83* (Washington, D.C.: U.S. Government Printing Office, 1982), p. 302.

Although we will continue to describe the subject matter of this section as "the" property tax, it should now be clear that there is no such thing. The fact that there are many different property taxes is crucial to assessing the economic effects of the system as a whole.

The picture is complicated further by the fact that even within a jurisdiction, the tax rate on a given kind of property may not be constant. An individual's property tax liability is the product of the tax rate and the property's **assessed value**—the value the jurisdiction assigns to the property. In most cases, jurisdictions attempt to make assessed values correspond to market values. However, if a piece of property has not been sold recently, the tax collector does not know its market value and must therefore make an estimate. This estimate is based in part on the market values of comparable properties that have been sold recently.

Market and assessed values will diverge to an extent that depends on the accuracy of the jurisdiction's estimating procedure. The ratio of the assessed value to market value is called the **assessment ratio.** If all properties have the same statutory rate and the same assessment ratio, then their effective tax rates will be the same. Suppose, however, that assessment ratios differ across properties. Ophelia and Hamlet both own properties worth $100,000. Ophelia's property is assessed at $100,000 and Hamlet's at $80,000. Clearly, even if they face the same statutory rate (say 2 percent), Ophelia's effective rate of 2 percent (= $2,000/100,000) is higher than Hamlet's 1.6 percent (= $1,600/$100,000). In fact, in many communities, tax authorities have done a very poor job of assessing property values so that properties with the same statutory rate differ drastically with respect to effective rates.

Incidence and Efficiency Effects

There is considerable controversy with respect to the question of who ultimately bears the burden of the property tax. We will discuss three different views and then try to reconcile them.

Traditional View: The Property Tax as an Excise Tax.   The traditional view is that the property tax is an excise tax that falls on land and structures. Incidence of the tax is determined by the shapes of the relevant supply and demand schedules in precisely the manner explained in Chapter 11. The shapes of the schedules are different for land and structures. Each is discussed in turn.

Land.   As long as the amount of land cannot be varied, by definition its supply curve is perfectly vertical. A factor with such a supply curve bears the entire burden of a tax levied upon it. Intuitively, because its quantity is fixed, land cannot "escape" the tax. This is illustrated in Figure 18.1. $S_{\mathscr{L}}$ is the supply of land. Prior to the tax, the demand curve is $D_{\mathscr{L}}$, and the equilibrium rental value of land is $P_0^{\mathscr{L}}$. The imposition of an ad valorem tax on land pivots the demand curve (see Chapter 11). The after-tax demand curve is $D'_{\mathscr{L}}$. The rent received by suppliers of land (landowners) is found at the intersection of the supply curve with $D'_{\mathscr{L}}$, and is given by $P_n^{\mathscr{L}}$. The rent paid by the users of land is found by adding the tax per acre of land to $P_n^{\mathscr{L}}$, giving $P_g^{\mathscr{L}}$. As expected, the rent paid by the users of the land is unchanged ($P_0^{\mathscr{L}} = P_g^{\mathscr{L}}$); the rent received by landowners falls by the full amount of the tax. Landowners bear the entire burden of the tax.

As discussed in Chapter 11, under certain circumstances the tax is capitalized into the value of the land. Prospective purchasers of the land take into account the fact that if they buy the land, they also buy a future stream of tax liabilities. This lowers the amount that they are willing to pay for the land. Therefore, the person who bears the full burden of the tax is the landlord at the time the tax is levied. To be sure, future

FIGURE 18.1   Incidence of a Tax on Land

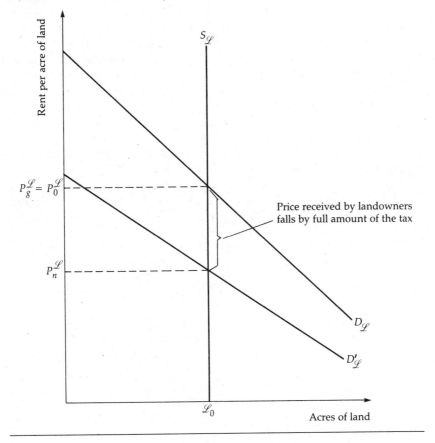

landlords make payments to the tax authorities, but such payments are not really a "burden" because they just balance the lower price paid at purchase. Capitalization complicates attempts to assess the incidence of the land tax. Knowing the identities of current owners is not sufficient; we must know who the landlords *were* at the time the tax was imposed.

To the extent that land is *not* fixed in supply, then the preceding analysis does not hold. For example, the supply of urban land can be extended at the fringes of urban areas that are adjacent to farmland. Similarly, the amount of land can be increased if landfills are possible, or if reclamation of wasteland is feasible. In such cases, the tax on land is borne both by landlords and the users of land, in proportions that depend upon the elasticities of demand and supply. But it is usually assumed that a vertical supply curve for land is a good approximation of reality.

Structures.   To understand the traditional view of the tax on structures, we begin by considering the national market for capital. Capital can be used for many purposes: construction of structures, equipment for manufacturing, public sector projects like dams, etc. At any given time, capital has some price which rations the capital among alternative uses. According to the traditional view, in the long run, the construction industry can obtain all the capital it demands at the market price. Thus, the supply curve of structures is perfectly horizontal—a higher price is not required to obtain more of them.

The market for structures under these conditions is depicted in Figure 18.2. Prior to the tax, the demand for structures by tenants is D_B, and the supply curve, S_B, is horizontal at the going price, P_0^B. At price P_0^B the quantity exchanged is B_0. Upon imposition of the tax, the demand curve pivots to D_B', just as the demand for land pivoted in Figure 18.1. But the outcome is totally different. The price received by the suppliers of struc-

FIGURE 18.2   Incidence of a Tax on Structures

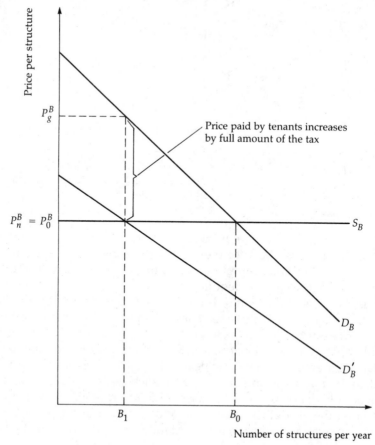

tures, P_n^B, is the same as the price before the tax was imposed ($P_n^B = P_0^B$). Demanders of structures pay a price, P_g^B, which exceeds the original price, P_0^B, by precisely the amount of the tax. Hence, the burden is shifted entirely to tenants. This result, of course, is a consequence of the assumption that the supply curve is horizontal. Intuitively, the horizontal supply curve means that capital will not stay in the housing sector if it does not receive a return of at least P_0^B. But if the price received by the suppliers of capital cannot be lowered, then the tax must be borne entirely by tenants.

We can summarize the traditional view of the property tax as follows: the part of the tax on land is borne by landowners (or, at least the landowners at the time the tax is levied); the tax on structures is passed on to tenants. Therefore, the land part of the tax is borne by people in proportion to the amount of rental income they receive, and the structures part of the tax is borne by people in proportion to the amount of housing they consume.

Implications for Progressiveness.   With these observations in mind, we can assess the distributional implications of the traditional view of the property tax. The effect of the land part of the tax on progressiveness hinges on whether or not the share of income from land ownership tends to rise with income. There is fairly widespread agreement that it does, so that this part of the tax is progressive.

Similarly, the progressiveness of the tax on structures depends critically on whether the proportion of income devoted to housing rises or falls as income increases. If it falls, then the structures part of the tax will tend to be regressive and vice versa.

An enormous amount of econometric work has been done to estimate how housing expenditures actually do respond to changes in income. The ability to reach a consensus has been impeded by disagreement over what concept of income to use. Some investigators use *yearly* income. They tend to find that the proportion of income devoted to housing falls as income increases, suggesting that the tax is regressive. Other investigators believe that some measure of *normal* or *permanent* income is more relevant to understanding housing decisions. According to this view, the fact that a family's annual income in a given year happens to be higher or lower than its normal income should not have much of an impact on that year's housing consumption. Housing decisions are made in the context of the family's long-run prospects, not yearly variations.

Of course, those who believe that permanent income is the appropriate variable must find some way to estimate it. One approach is to define permanent income as the average of several year's annual incomes.[4]

---

[4] See, for example, Carliner [1973].

Investigators who use such measures to explain housing expenditures tend to find higher responsiveness of housing expenditures to income changes than do those who use annual income. Indeed, although the results are mixed, it appears reasonable to say that based on the evidence, housing consumption is roughly proportional to permanent income. Hence, the structures part of the tax is probably neither regressive nor progressive. Nevertheless, housing demand estimates based on annual income, which suggest the tax is regressive, have tended to have the greater influence on public discussion of the tax.

The New View: The Property Tax as a Capital Tax. The traditional view uses a standard partial equilibrium framework. As we noted in Chapter 11, although partial equilibrium analysis is often useful, it may produce misleading results for taxes that are "large" relative to the economy. The "new" view of the property tax proposed by Mieszkowski [1972] involves a general equilibrium perspective and generates some surprising conclusions.

According to the new view, it is best to think of the property tax as a general wealth tax with some assets taxed below the average rate, and some taxed above. Both the average level of the tax and the deviations from that average have to be taken into account.

General Tax Effect. Assume for the moment that the property tax can be approximated as a uniform tax on all capital. Then the property tax is just a general factor tax on capital. Now assume further that the supply of capital to the economy is fixed. As shown in Chapter 11, when a factor is fixed in supply, it bears the full burden of a general tax levied upon it. Hence, the property tax falls entirely on owners of capital. And since the proportion of income from capital tends to rise with income, a tax on capital tends to be progressive. Thus, the property tax is progressive, a conclusion that turns the traditional view exactly on its head!

Excise Tax Effects. As noted earlier, the property tax is emphatically not a uniform tax. Rates vary according to the type of property and the jurisdiction in which the property is located. Some rates are higher than average, and some are lower. Hence, the property tax is a set of excise taxes on capital. According to the new view, there is a tendency for capital to migrate from areas where it faces a high tax rate to those where it is low.[5] In a process reminiscent of that used in the Harberger model (Chapter 11), as capital migrates into low-tax-rate areas, its before-tax rate of return there tends to get bid down. At the same time, the before-

---

[5] There have been some attempts to estimate how responsive business location decisions are to local property tax rates, but the evidence is mixed. See Small [1981] for a survey.

tax rate of return in high-tax areas increases as capital leaves. The process continues until after-tax rates of return are equal throughout the economy. In general, as capital moves, returns to other factors of production also change. The impact on the other factors depends in part upon their mobility. Land, which is perfectly immobile, cannot shift the tax. (In this conclusion, at least, the new and old views agree.) Similarly, the least-mobile types of capital are most likely to bear the tax.

As is usually the case in general equilibrium models, the ultimate incidence depends upon how production is organized, the structure of consumer demand, and the extent to which various factors are mobile.

Long-Run Effects.   In our discussion of the general tax effect of the property tax, it was assumed that the amount of capital available to the economy is fixed. However, in the long run, the supply of capital may be sensitive to the tax rate. If the property tax decreases the supply of capital, the productivity of labor, and hence the real wage, will fall. If the tax increases capital accumulation just the opposite occurs.

Summary of the New View.   The property tax is a general tax on capital with some jurisdictions and types of capital taxed at rates above the average, others below. The general effect of the tax is to lower the return to capital, which tends to be progressive in its impact on income distribution. The differentials in tax rates create excise effects, which tend to hurt immobile factors in highly taxed jurisdictions. The adjustment process set in motion by these excise effects is very complicated, and not much is known about their effects on progressiveness. Neither can much be said concerning the importance of long-term effects created by changes in the size of the capital stock. If the excise and long-run effects do not counter the general effect too strongly, then the overall impact of the property tax is progressive.

The Property Tax as a User Fee.   The discussion so far has ignored the fact that property taxes are often used by communities to purchase public services such as education and police protection. Suppose that individuals are free to move to that community with the mix of public services they most prefer. Then people who do not care very much about public services will live in communities with a small public sector and low property tax levies, while those who have a strong taste for public services will select communities with a large public sector and high property taxes. In this kind of model, the property tax is just the cost of purchasing public services, and each individual buys exactly the amount he or she desires.[6] Thus, the property tax is really not a tax at all;

---

[6] The structure of such models is discussed more carefully in the next chapter.

it is more like a user fee for public services. This view has three important implications:

1. The notion of the "incidence of the property tax" is meaningless because the levy is not a tax in the normal sense of the word.
2. The property tax creates no excess burden. As Hamilton [1975a, p. 13] points out, "If consumers treat the local property tax as a price for public services, then this price should not distort the housing market any more than the price of eggs should distort the housing market."
3. By allowing the deduction of property tax payments, the federal income tax in effect subsidizes the consumption of local public services (see Chapter 14). As long as the demand for local public services slopes downward, the deduction increases the size of the local public sector, other things being the same.

As noted earlier, the link between property taxes and services received is often tenuous, so we should not take the notion of the property tax as a user fee too literally. Nevertheless, this line of reasoning has some interesting implications. For example, if people care about the public services they receive, we expect that the depressing effects of high property taxes on housing values may be counteracted by the public services financed by these taxes. In an important paper, Oates [1969] constructed an econometric model of property value determination. In his model, the value of homes in a community depends positively upon the quality of public services in the community and negatively upon the tax rate, *other things being the same.* Of course, across communities, factors that influence house prices do differ. These include physical characteristics of the houses, such as number of rooms, and characteristics of the communities themselves, such as distance from an urban center. These factors must be taken into account when trying to sort out the effects of property taxes and local public goods on property values. Oates used multiple regression analysis to do so.

Specifically, he obtained 1960 data on 53 municipalities located within the New York metropolitan area, and estimated a regression with the community's median house value as the dependent variable, and the following independent variables: the effective property tax rate, school expenditures per pupil, the distance from the community to midtown Manhattan, the median number of rooms per owner-occupied house, the percentage of houses built since 1950, median family income, and percentage of families with less than $3,000 in income.[7] School expenditures per pupil are supposed to represent the quality of the community's

---

[7] The tax rate, per-pupil expenditures, and distance to Manhattan are entered as natural logarithms.

local public services, the idea being the more that is spent, the better the public education.

When the regression was estimated, the parameter multiplying the tax-rate variable had a negative sign, and that of the per-pupil expenditure variable had a positive sign. Moreover, the parameter values implied that the increase in property values created by expanding school expenditures approximately offset the decrease generated by the property taxes raised to finance them.

Oates' results need to be interpreted with caution. For one thing, expenditure per pupil may not be an adequate measure of local public services. Localities provide many public services other than education, such as crime protection, parks, and libraries. Furthermore, even if education were the only local public good, expenditure per pupil might not be a good measure of educational quality. It is possible, for example, that expenditures in a given community are high because the community has to pay a lot for its teachers, its schools are not administered efficiently, or its students are more difficult to educate.

Subsequent to Oates' study, a number of other investigators have examined the relationship between property values, property taxes, and local public goods using data from different geographical areas and employing different sets of explanatory variables. Although the results are a bit mixed, Oates' general conclusion seems to be valid—property taxes and the value of local public services are capitalized into housing prices.[8] Thus, if two communities have the same level of public services, but the first has higher taxes than the second (perhaps because its cost of providing the services is greater), then we expect the first to have lower property values, other things being the same. More generally, these results imply that to understand how well off members of a community are, we cannot look at property tax rates in isolation. Government services and property values must also be considered.

Reconciling the Three Views.   It is a mistake to regard the three views of the property tax as mutually exclusive alternatives. As Aaron [1975] emphasizes, which one is valid depends upon what question is being asked. If, for example, we want to find the consequences of eliminating all property taxes and replacing them with a national sales tax, then the "new view" is appropriate because a change that affects all communities requires a general equilibrium framework. On the other hand, if a given community is considering lowering its property tax rate and making up the revenue loss from a local sales tax, then the "traditional" view offers the most insight. This is because a single community is so small relative to the economy that its supply of capital is essentially perfectly horizontal, and Figure 18.2 applies. Finally, when taxes and benefits are jointly

---

[8] For a recent example using California data, see Rosen [1982].

changed and there is sufficient mobility for people to pick and choose communities, the "user fee view" is useful.[9]

Why Do People Hate the Property Tax So Much?

On June 7, 1978, the voters of California approved a statewide property tax limitation initiative known as Proposition 13. Its key provisions[10] were (a) to put a 1 percent ceiling on the property tax rate that any locality could impose, (b) to limit the assessed value of property to its 1975 value,[11] and (c) to forbid state and local governments to impose any additional property taxes without approval by a two-thirds majority local vote. Proposition 13 was the most famous of a number of tax limitation statutes, and is typical in its focus on property tax finance. Indeed, the higher a state's property tax revenue per dollar of personal income in 1974, the higher the probability that it imposed some sort of new fiscal controls in the 1970s [Ladd, 1978]. Why is the property tax so unpopular? Several explanations have been advanced.

First, Aaron [1975, p. 12] emphasizes that more than any other major tax, "The impact of the property tax depends on the vagaries of administration." Because housing market transactions typically do not occur frequently, the tax must be levied on an estimated value. To the extent that this valuation is done incompetently (or corruptly), the tax will be perceived as unfair.

Second, the property tax is highly visible. Under the federal income and payroll taxes, payments are withheld from each of the worker's paychecks, and the employer sends the proceeds to the government. In contrast, the property tax is often paid directly by the taxpayer. Moreover, the payments are typically made on a quarterly or an annual basis, so each payment comes as a large shock. It is hard to know how seriously to take this argument. Even those citizens who are somehow oblivious to the fact that federal income and payroll taxes are withheld during the year receive a pointed reminder of how much they have paid every April. There may be enough rage in that one month to last a whole year.

Third, the property tax is perceived as being regressive. This perception is partly a consequence of the fact that the "traditional view" of the property tax continues to dominate public debate. It is reinforced by the fact that some property owners, particularly the elderly, may not have enough cash to make property tax payments, and are therefore forced to

---

[9] A more precise characterization of the conditions under which the user fee approach is appropriate is given in the next chapter.

[10] For further details, see Rosen [1982].

[11] For property transferred after 1975, the assessed value was defined as the market value at which the transaction took place.

sell their homes. Some states have responded to this phenomenon by introducing **circuit breakers** that provide benefits to taxpayers (usually in the form of a refund on state income taxes) which depend upon the excess of residential property tax payments over some specified proportion of income.[12] A more appropriate way of dealing with this problem would be to defer tax payments until the time when the property is transferred.

Fourth, taxpayers may dislike other taxes as much as the property tax, but they feel powerless to do anything about the others. It is relatively easy to take aim at the property tax, which is levied locally. In contrast, mounting a drive against (say) the federal income tax would be very difficult, if for no other reason than a national campaign would be necessary and hence involve large coordination costs.

Finally, some argue that the particular circumstances of the 1970s contributed to discontent over the property tax. These years were characterized by high inflation rates, and housing prices rose even faster than the general price level. Given a constant ad valorem property tax rate, this led to an increased real burden, which was not perceived as being accompanied by an increase in benefits. The result was a lot of angry taxpayers [see Oakland, 1979].

In light of the widespread hostility toward the tax, it is natural to ask whether there are any ways to improve it. A very modest proposal is to improve assessment procedures. The use of computers and modern valuation techniques can make assessments more uniform.[13] Compared to the current system of arbitrary tax rates within a jurisdiction, uniform tax rates would probably enhance efficiency. The equity issues are more complicated. On one hand, it seems a violation of horizontal equity for two people with identical properties to pay different taxes on them. However, the phenomenon of capitalization requires that we distinguish carefully between the owners at the time the tax is levied and the current owners. A property with an unduly high tax rate can be expected to sell for a lower price, other things being the same. Thus, an individual who buys the property after tax is imposed is not necessarily worse off due to the high tax rate. Indeed, movement to equal assessment ratios could generate a whole new set of horizontal inequities.

A more ambitious reform of the property tax would be to convert it into a **personal net worth tax.** The base of such a tax is the difference between the market value of all the taxpayer's assets and his liabilities.[14]

---

[12] See Aaron [1975, pp. 72–79] for a discussion of how circuit breaker rules vary across states.

[13] Aaron [1975] cites evidence that assessment procedures have generally been getting better over time, but suggests that there is still a lot of room for improvement.

[14] Some version of net worth tax is used in several European countries. See Aaron [1975, pp. 90–91].

An advantage of such a system over a property tax is that by allowing for deduction of liabilities, it provides a better index of ability to pay. Moreover, because it is a personal tax, exemptions can be built into the system and the rates can be varied in as progressive or regressive a manner as desired.

The administrative problems associated with a net worth tax are formidable. We indicated earlier the difficulties that arise in valuing housing for property tax purposes. These pale in comparison to valuing many other types of assets. (Think of trying to value paintings, antiques, or Persian rugs.) Moreover, while a house is difficult to conceal, other types of assets are relatively easy to hide from the tax collector. Note also that because individuals can have assets and liabilities in different jurisdictions, a net worth tax would undoubtedly have to be administered by the federal government.

This brings us to what many people consider to be the main justification for the current system of property taxation. Whatever its flaws, the property tax can be administered locally without any help from the federal or state governments. Hence, it provides local government with considerable fiscal autonomy. As one observer put it, "Property taxation offers people in different localities an instrument by which they can make local choices significant" [Harris, 1978, p. 38]. According to this view, elimination of the property tax would ultimately destroy the economic independence of local units of government. There is certainly some overstatement here; localities do, after all, have access to other tax bases. Nevertheless, the political role of the property tax needs to be taken seriously in any discussion of its reform.

ESTATE AND GIFT TAXES

Property taxes are levied at regular intervals. In contrast, estate and gift taxes are levied only upon the occurrence of certain events—the estate tax upon the death of the wealth holder **(decendent),** and the gift tax when property is transferred between the living *(inter vivos).* Both federal and some state governments levy taxes on gifts and estates. At neither level are the taxes very important as revenue raisers. Death and gift taxes account for about 1.3 percent of the revenues raised by both federal and state governments from their own sources [*Facts and Figures on Government Finance*, 1983, p. 23]. The federal tax does not touch the lives of most citizens. In 1982, only 135,000 federal estate tax returns were filed [Internal Revenue Service, 1983b, p. 7]. Some have suggested that the role of estate and gift taxes should be expanded. The arguments for and against doing so are explored in this section.

We begin by describing the rationales for estate and gift taxation, and then discuss briefly the system as it operates in the United States. At the end, several suggestions for change are considered.

Rationalizations

Estate taxes have been around a long time, but they are very controversial. The following issues have been raised in the debate over their desirability.[15]

Payment for Services.   First, it is argued that the government protects property rights and oversees the transfer of property from the decedent to his or her heirs. As compensation for providing these services, the state is entitled to a share of the estate. Those who oppose the estate tax argue that provision of such services is a fundamental right that does not have to be paid for. Moreover, it seems arbitrary to pick out property transfers as special objects of taxation. If Moe spends $10,000 on a trip to Europe, Curly spends $10,000 on his daughter's college education, and Larry leaves $10,000 to his son, why should Larry face a special tax?

Reversion of Property to Society.   In addition, it is claimed that ultimately, all property belongs to society as a whole. During an individual's lifetime, society permits him to dispose of the property he has managed to accumulate as he wishes. But at death, the property reverts to society, which can dispose of it at will. As the reader will recall from Chapter 5, many controversial value judgments lie behind such claims. Some suggest it is fundamentally wrong to argue that a person holds wealth only at the pleasure of "society," or that "society" ever has any valid claim upon personal wealth.

Incentives.   Some suggest that estate taxes are good for incentives. Perhaps the most famous statement of this theme is attributed to Andrew Carnegie: "The parent who leaves his son enormous wealth generally deadens the talents and energies of the son, and tempts him to lead a less useful and less worthy life than he otherwise would" [Pechman, 1977a, p. 221]. By taxing away estates, the government can prevent this from happening.

The incentive problem is much more complicated than that suggested by Carnegie, because we must take into account the behavior of the donor as well as the recipient. Consider Lear, an individual who is motivated to work hard during his lifetime to leave a big estate to his daughters. The presence of an estate tax might discourage Lear's work effort. ("Why should I work hard if my wealth is going to the tax collector instead of my daughters?") On the other hand, in the presence of an estate tax, a greater amount of wealth has to be accumulated to leave a given *after-tax* bequest. Thus, the presence of an estate tax might induce Lear to work harder to maintain the net value of his estate. Conse-

---

[15] This discussion ignores gift taxes for the most part. They are discussed subsequently.

quently, whether or not an estate tax will induce a donor to work more or less is logically indeterminate.[16] Even if Carnegie was right and estate taxation induces potential heirs to work more, it might also generate incentives for donors to work less. On balance, we cannot know on the basis of theory alone which tendency dominates.

Similarly, we cannot predict how an estate tax will affect the donor's saving behavior. It is easy to describe scenarios in which he saves less and in which he saves more.

In this context, observe that the presence of an estate tax can affect not only the amount of wealth that is transferred across generations, but also the form in which the transfers take place. A tax on bequests of physical capital creates incentives to transmit wealth in the form of human capital. Thus, instead of giving each daughter $40,000 worth of stocks and bonds, Lear might spend $40,000 on each of their college educations. An estate tax could thus lead to overinvestment in human capital.

Unfortunately, there is very little in the way of empirical evidence to settle any of these incentive issues. A thorough study requires lifetime data on the labor supply and saving behavior of a group of individuals and their heirs. Economists have had to settle for rather more fragmentary sources of data, and no definitive results exist.

Relation to Personal Income Tax.   Estate and gift taxation is necessary, it can be argued, because receipts of gifts and inheritances are excluded from the recipient's personal income tax base. A natural response to this observation is to ask why gifts and estates are not included in adjusted gross income in the first place. After all, they constitute additions to potential consumption, and by the conventional definition are therefore income to the recipient. However, there has always been a strong aversion to including inheritances and gifts in the income tax base.[17] Such receipts simply are not perceived as being in the same class as those from wages, interest, etc. It is not necessarily the case, though, that a tax on gifts and estates is the best remedy for this omission. A possible alternative is discussed below.

Income Distribution.   An estate tax is a valuable tool for creating a more equal distribution of income. Let us leave aside the normative question of whether or not the government ought to pursue a more equal income distribution and consider the positive issue of whether or

---

[16] The reader will recognize that the ambiguity arises because of the familiar conflict between substitution and income effects. See Chapter 15.

[17] One possible explanation is that taxing estates and gifts under a progressive tax system would be unfair because these forms of income tend to come in large lumps. However, it would surely be possible to develop an appropriate averaging scheme to mitigate such effects.

not an effective system of estate taxation is likely to achieve this goal. Certainly the prevailing assumption is that it would; "the one aim of a death tax that stands scrutiny is its redistributive or anticoncentration aim" [Jantscher, 1977, p. 517]. However, Stiglitz [1978] has suggested several reasons that banning inheritances might backfire and create a less equal distribution of income.

He argues that if the estate tax reduces saving, there will be less capital. This will lead to a lower real wage for labor, and under certain conditions, a smaller share of income going to labor.[18] To the extent that capital income is more unequally distributed than labor income, the effect will be to increase inequality.

In addition, *within* a generation, it is likely that most individuals transfer wealth only to others who are worse off than they are. Such transfers clearly tend to enhance equality. Eliminating such voluntary transfers could well lead to more inequality than otherwise would have been the case.

Finally, suppose that parents whose earnings capacities are much higher than average produce children whose earnings capacities are closer to the average level. (This phenomenon is known as *regression toward the mean*.) If well-off parents wish to compensate their children for their lesser earnings capacity by making bequests, it will tend to reduce inequality *across* generations. Conversely, banning such transfers will increase intergenerational inequality.

Although the view that estate taxation enhances equality dominates most discussions, Stiglitz's provocative observations remind us that there are many facets to this problem.

Provisions

It should be noted at the outset that gift taxation and estate taxation are inextricably bound. Suppose that estates are taxed and gifts are not. If Lear desires to pass his wealth on to his daughters and knows that it will be taxed at his death, then he can avoid tax by making the transfer as a gift *inter vivos*. Similar opportunities would arise if there were a gift tax but no estate tax. Since 1976, the gift and estate taxes in the United States have been integrated, and are officially referred to as the **unified transfer tax.**

The unified transfer tax is similar in basic structure to the personal income tax. First the gross estate is calculated, then various deductions and exemptions are subtracted, leaving the taxable estate. The tax liabil-

---

[18] When the wage rate decreases, the quantity of labor demanded increases. Thus, what happens to labor income—the product of the wage and the quantity demanded—depends on the elasticity of demand for labor. This in turn, depends upon the ease with which capital may be substituted for labor (the elasticity of substitution of capital for labor) [see Henderson and Quandt, 1980, pp. 111–14].

ity is determined by applying a progressive rate schedule to the taxable estate.

Computing the Taxable Base.   The **gross estate** consists of all property owned by the decedent at the time of death. This includes real property, stocks, bonds, and insurance policies. It also includes gifts made during the decedent's lifetime. To find the **taxable estate,** deductions are allowed for funeral expenses, costs of settling the estate (lawyers' fees), and any outstanding debts of the estate. Gifts to charity are deductible without limit.

The following deductions are available under legislation passed in 1981.[19]

1.   For 1985, each estate is allowed a lifetime exemption of $400,000. For 1986, the figure is $500,000; and for 1987 and after, it is $600,000. No federal estate tax is levied on estates which are less than the lifetime exemption.
2.   All qualified transfers to spouses—by gift or bequest—are deductible in arriving at the taxable base.[20] Thus, in 1985 the estate of a multimillionairess who leaves $400,000 to her children and the rest to her husband bears no tax liability.
3.   Each individual is qualified for an annual gift exclusion of $10,000 per recipient. (The recipient need not be a relative.) Consider a family with three children. Each year Mom can give $10,000 to each child, as can Dad. Together, then, the couple can give their three children annually $60,000 tax-free. Interestingly, there is some evidence that wealthy people do not fully exploit the tax advantages of distributing wealth before death [See Pechman, 1977a, p. 231]. Why? There is a story about a rich man who gave each of his children $1 million when they reached the age of 21. When asked why he did so, the millionaire explained that he wanted his children to be able to tell him to "go to hell"—to have total financial independence. It appears that most people would just as soon *not* have their children be able to tell them to go to hell. These people therefore keep control of their wealth as long as possible, even at the cost of a larger-than-necessary tax liability.

Rate Structure.   For 1985 and thereafter, the taxable base is subject to marginal rates ranging from 18 percent (on the first $10,000) to 50 percent (for amounts over $2.5 million). Whether or not these rates are efficient in the sense of optimal tax theory is hard to say. As usual, the

---

[19] For further details, see *Economic Recovery Tax Act of 1981* [1981].

[20] Special rules apply to **terminable interests,** which are transfers that can be revoked under specified conditions. For example, a woman might leave her husband certain property on the condition that he not remarry.

answer depends upon the responsiveness of behavior to changes in the tax rate. But as indicated above, little is known about how economic decisions are affected by estate and gift taxes.

Special Problems.   A number of difficulties arise in the administration of an estate and gift tax.

Jointly Held Property.   Suppose a husband and wife own property together. For purposes of estate taxation, should this be considered one estate or two? The philosophical problems concerning whether the family or the individual should be the unit of taxation were discussed in Chapter 14, and there is no need to do so again here. Under current law, one half of the value of jointly held property is now included in the gross estate of the first spouse to die, regardless of the relative extent to which the spouses contributed to the accumulation of the property.[21]

Closely Held Businesses.   Suppose Lear wants to bequeath his business, which is the only asset he owns, to his daughters. Because there is no cash in Lear's estate, it may happen that the daughters have to sell the business to pay the estate tax due. To reduce the likelihood of such an event, the law allows the estate taxes on closely held businesses to be paid off over a period as long as 15 years, at favorable rates of interest. Moreover, in computing the gross estate, the fair market value of family farms can be reduced by $750,000.[22] Such provisions reflect a value judgment that there is something socially desirable per se in having the same family control a given business for several generations.

Trusts.   An implicit goal of the estate tax is to tax wealth at least once a generation. In the past, it was relatively straightforward for an individual to arrange his estate so that one or more generations of his descendants would avoid the tax. The vehicle for such **generation skipping** was a **trust.** This is an arrangement whereby a person or institution known as a **trustee** holds legal title to assets with the obligation to use them for the benefit of another party. The trustee can be a relative, friend, attorney, or bank.

Consider the following simple version of how trusts might be used to avoid estate tax. Lear puts his estate into trust, at which time an estate tax is paid. He assigns his daughters the income from the trust for as long as they live. Although the daughters receive income from the trust,

---

[21] More precisely, this rule holds for joint property owned with **right of survivorship,** meaning that upon the death of one owner, the property automatically passes to the other owner.

[22] This provision applies to individuals dying in 1983 and thereafter. The rule would seem to create incentives for wealthy people to invest heavily in agricultural property, but there is currently no evidence that this has taken place.

legally they do not own the assets. When the trust terminates, the property is legally transferred to some other parties, say Lear's grandchildren.[23] Tax is not due until the grandchildren transfer the property. Because the property was never legally transferred to the daughters, they never incurred an estate tax liability. Hence, their generation was "skipped."

In 1976, the laws on the tax treatment of trusts were tightered so as to make generation skipping more difficult. Nevertheless, complicated trust maneuvers are still available for avoiding estate taxation. One legal scholar recently opined that "for those who do not want to contribute their estates to the government (or to charity), there is an impressive array of strategies for moving wealth from one generation to another outside the purview of estate and gift taxation" [Cooper, 1979, p. 4]. We must add, of course, that even in cases where the tax generates no revenues, it may create excess burdens and/or compliance costs for people who modify their behavior to avoid it.

Charitable Foundations.   In general, there is no limit placed on deduction of charitable donations from the gross estate. (In contrast, the personal income tax limits charitable deductions to 50 percent of adjusted gross income.) In 1981, charitable bequests from estates amounted to about $3.5 billion [U.S. Bureau of the Census, 1982, p. 346].

Charitable bequests can be used to set up nonprofit foundations with the purpose of serving the "public good." The Rockefeller and Ford Foundations are famous examples. It is easy to imagine how the opportunity to set up such foundations could be abused. For example, the foundation might use its funds to make low-interest loans to members of the establishing family, who could then use the proceeds for personal purposes. Although such antics were never really epidemic, enough horror stories reached public attention that a number of regulations were instituted in 1969. The available evidence suggests that these regulations have been largely successful in preventing abuses of nonprofit foundations [Pechman, 1977a, p. 239].

State Taxes.   In addition to the federal estate and gift tax, wealth transfers at death are also taxed by most states.[24] Many states levy **inheritance taxes.** While estate taxes are imposed upon the wealth itself, inheritance taxes are levied upon the individual receiving the wealth. The inheritance tax schedule faced by a recipient depends upon his relationship to the decedent. In general (but not in all states), a spouse, child, or parent faces lower rates than a brother or sister, who in turn, has a lower

---

[23] It might be asked why the property would not be kept in trust forever. There are laws which prohibit this and make the effective life of most trusts less than 100 years.

[24] For a list, see *Facts and Figures on Government Finance* [1983, pp. 246–79].

rate than a nonrelative. Complications in estate taxation arise when a decedent's wealth is held in more than one state. In some states, the estates of nonresidents are taxed according to the amount of their property located in the state.

Given that the rates tend to vary considerably across states, a natural question is whether elderly citizens make their residential decisions in such a way as to lower the tax burden on their bequests. It is sometimes suggested that the choice of Florida as a retirement place for those from the Northeast is influenced by such considerations. Obviously, many factors determine locational decisions, and the relative importance of differential estate taxation is not known.

Reforming Estate and Gift Taxes

For those who wish to expand the role of estate and gift taxes, the most straightforward approach would be to lower the lifetime exemption. However, if the estate tax is ever to play an important part in the revenue system, then methods for dealing with avoidance via trusts and other such instruments must be devised.

A popular reform among many tax theorists is integrating the estate- and gift-tax system into the personal income tax. Gifts and inheritances would be taxed as income to the recipients. As noted earlier, such receipts are income, and according to conventional notions, should therefore be included in adjusted gross income. To account for the fact that income in this form tends to be "lumpy," some form of averaging would have to be devised.

There is, however, popular resistance to taxing gifts and inheritances as ordinary income. A somewhat different method of changing the focus of estate and gift taxation from the donor to the recipient has been suggested. Specifically, under an **accessions tax,** each individual would be taxed on his total lifetime acquisitions from inheritances and gifts. The rate schedule could be made progressive and include a zero-bracket amount, if so desired. The attraction of such a scheme is that it relates tax liabilities to the recipient's ability to pay rather than to the estate. Administrative difficulties would arise from the need for taxpayers to keep records of all sizable gifts and estates. But if it is ever decided to put more of an emphasis on taxing wealth transfers, an accessions tax deserves serious consideration.

SUMMARY

Wealth taxes are assessed on a tax base which is a stock of assets instead of a flow such as income, sales, etc.

Wealth taxes have been rationalized as a way to correct the income tax for unrealized capital gains, as a way to reduce the concentration of wealth, and as compensation for benefits received by wealth holders. It is also argued that wealth by itself is a good index of ability to pay and should therefore be subject to tax.

Property taxes in the United States are levied by state and local governments. Tax liabilities are computed by multiplying the tax rate by the assessed value of the property. Both tax rates and the assessment ratio—the ratio of assessed value to market price—vary greatly across jurisdictions. This fact greatly complicates measuring the incidence and efficiency effects of the property tax.

The incidence and efficiency effects of the property tax are generally viewed in one of three, not mutually exclusive, ways:

The "traditional view" is that the property tax is an excise tax on land and structures. The tax on land is borne by landowners and is roughly progressive. The tax on structures is borne by tenants and is roughly regressive, at least with respect to annual income. This partial equilibrium approach is most useful when analyzing tax changes for a single community.

The "new view" is that the property tax is a general tax on all capital with rates that vary across jurisdictions and different types of capital. Incidence depends upon the general equilibrium response of mobile factors of production. This view is most appropriate for analyzing possible changes in the entire system of property taxation.

The "user fee view" regards property taxes as payment for local public services. An implication is that the tax has no excess burden.

The property tax is one of the most unpopular taxes. One possible improvement is to upgrade the quality of assessment procedures. A more sweeping proposal is to institute a personal net worth tax in which the tax base is the difference between the market value of assets and liabilities. However, this is administratively complex and may undermine the most appealing aspect of the property tax—local administration.

Estate and gift taxes are levied upon the value of wealth transfers, either from a decedent or from another living individual. Neither is a major revenue source at any level.

Possible rationalizations for estate and gift taxes are as a payment for protection of property rights, as a means by which society allocates "its" property, as an incentive for the young to work, as a corrective for certain inadequacies in the personal income tax, and as a method to equalize the distribution of income.

While these arguments figure prominently in debates, there is little empirical evidence on the incentive effects or incidence of estate and gift taxes.

Major proposals for reform of estate and gift taxes are either to incorporate these transfers in the personal income tax system or to institute an accessions tax (a tax based on total lifetime gifts and bequests received).

DISCUSSION QUESTIONS

1. "When Batman makes a gift to Robin, the gift is not included in Robin's taxable income. However, this is not a flaw in the income tax system, because the gift is not deductible from Batman's income." Comment. Your answer should include a discussion of whether gift giving reduces the donor's "ability to pay."

2. David and Jonathan own identical homes. David has owned his home for many years and paid $100,000 for it. Jonathan purchased his home after a recent property tax increase and paid $80,000. Should the local assessor change the assessed value of Jonathan's home to maintain horizontal equity? (Assume that there has been no inflation in housing prices since David purchased his home, and that David and Jonathan value equally all public services provided in the local community.) In your answer, carefully define all key concepts.

3. "Estate taxes are an efficient and equitable means for raising revenues." What evidence would be required to evaluate the validity of this assertion?

SELECTED REFERENCES

Aaron, Henry J. *Who Pays the Property Tax? A New View.* Washington, D.C.: Brookings Institution, 1975.

Cooper, George. *A Voluntary Tax? New Perspectives on Sophisticated Estate Tax Avoidance.* Washington, D.C.: Brookings Institution, 1979.

Mieszkowski, Peter M. "The Property Tax: An Excise Tax or a Profits Tax?" *Journal of Public Economics* 1 (1972), pp. 73–96.

Oates, Wallace. "The Effects of Property Taxes and Local Spending on Property Values: An Empirical Study of Tax Capitalization and the Tiebout Hypothesis." *Journal of Political Economy* 77 (1969), pp. 957–71.

Part Six

Multigovernment Public Finance

For many purposes it is useful to think of public finance decisions as being made by a single government. In the United States, however, an astounding number of entities have the power to tax and spend. As of the early 1980s, there were over 82,000 governmental jurisdictions: 1 federal, 50 state, 3,041 county, 19,083 municipality, 16,748 township, 15,032 school district, and 28,733 special district.[1] The interaction of state, local, and federal governments plays a crucial role in the U.S. fiscal system. Thus, in Chapter 19 we examine the public finance issues that arise in federal systems.

Although in many situations state and local governments can act independently, of course, they are not sovereign. A whole new set of issues arises when we consider the interactions of tax and expenditure policies among independent nations. Chapter 20 examines the problems involved in the international coordination of public finance.

---

[1] From *Monthly Tax Features* [October 1982, p. 3]. "Special districts" generally perform a single function or oversee some specific area of responsibility.

CHAPTER 19

Public Finance in a Federal System

*The larger the society, provided it be within a
practical sphere, the more duly capable it will be of
self-government. And happily for the republican
cause, the practicable sphere may be carried to a very
great extent, by a judicious modification and mixture
of the federal principle.*

James Madison

In the summer of 1982, the city of Glen Cove, Long Island, banned
Soviet diplomats who lived there from using its tennis courts and other
recreational facilities. The stated reason for the ban was the fact that the
property being inhabited by the Russians was exempt from local property taxes.[1] Glen Cove's action caused an international furor, and the
State Department requested that the city desist from meddling in foreign
affairs. But the mayor responded, "Unless the State Department wants
to pay up all the property taxes the Soviets have never had to pay like
other Glen Cove residents, then the Russians will have to stay off the
tennis courts."

This incident highlights three areas that surround the operation of the
U.S. system of public finance.

First, subfederal units of government function with considerable autonomy. Attempts from the outside to change their behavior are likely to
be met with active or passive resistance. Is decentralized decision making desirable?

---

[1] Note, however, that the ban originated after federal officials said that the Russians
had installed eavesdropping equipment in their mansion. The controversy was finally
settled in 1984, when the Russians agreed to make some payment for city services.

Second, different types of public services are customarily provided by different levels of government. The reason that the Glen Cove incident received so much attention—and created such amusement (diplomats excepted)—was the incongruity of a local level of government in effect making foreign policy. International relations "belong" to the central government. On the other hand, decisions on the quantity and type of recreational facilities "belong" to localities. How should different functions be allocated to different levels of government?

Finally, the story illustrates the crucial role of property taxes in the finance of U.S. local governments: no property taxes, no tennis. Are locally raised taxes a good way for the services provided by municipalities to be financed? Or should the money come from the state and federal governments?

These are important issues in the United States where, as noted earlier, there are a multitude of governmental jurisdictions. The appropriate division of power among them has been a matter of controversy since the founding of the nation. This chapter examines the normative and positive aspects of public finance in a federal system.

BACKGROUND

Oates [1972, p. 17] provides a useful economic definition of **federal government:**

> A public sector with both centralized and decentralized levels of decision making in which choices made at each level concerning the provision of public services are determined largely by the demands for those services of the residents of (and perhaps others who carry on activities in) the respective jurisdictions.

We can imagine situations in which a single government controls all aspects of economic activity, or the opposite extreme in which each community operates with total autonomy. It is best, however, to think of the extent of federalism as a continuum rather than an either-or proposition. Between the polar cases, one system is characterized as being more centralized than another when more of its decision-making powers are in the hands of authorities with a larger jurisdiction.

When is one system more centralized than another? The most common measure is the **centralization ratio,** the proportion of total direct government expenditures made by the central government. ("Direct" government expenditure comprises all expenditure except transfers made to other governmental units.) The centralization ratio is by no means a foolproof indicator. Suppose that states make expenditures for highways, but the money comes in the form of grants from the federal government. Congress decides that no state will receive highway grants unless it mandates a 55-mile-per-hour speed limit. Every single state complies. Who is really in charge? The point is that if local and state government spending behavior is constrained by the central government, then the centralization ratio underestimates the true extent of centralization in the system. Conversely, if states and localities effectively lobby the federal government to achieve their own ends, then the centralization ratio may underestimate the degree of decentralized economic power.

With these qualifications in mind, we present in Table 19.1 some centralization ratios for the United States and a number of other devel-

TABLE 19.1   Percentage of All Direct Expenditures by Central Government (1976–1980)*

Australia	51%
Canada	41
France	84
Germany (West)	57
Sweden	57
Switzerland	47
United Kingdom	71
United States	55

* The centralization percentage for each country represents the latest year from the period 1976–1980 for which the needed observation was available.
Source: The foreign data were kindly provided by Professor Wallace Oates. Figure for the United States is from U.S. Bureau of the Census, *Statistical Abstract of the United States: 1982–83* (Washington, D.C.: U.S. Government Printing Office, 1982), p. 274.

oped countries. The United States appears to be in the lower third of this group with respect to the percent of total direct expenditures by central government.

Table 19.2 shows how the distribution of United States government expenditure by level of government has been changing over time. The long-run trend has been for the centralization ratio to increase, although the movement upward has not been steady.

Table 19.3 shows the division of public spending by level of government for various government functions. The figures indicate that a number of activities that have an important impact on the quality of life are in the hands of state and local governments. In the context of the current debate over "who should pay for welfare," it is noteworthy that 70 percent of public welfare expenditures are made by state and local governments. This figure gives a somewhat exaggerated view of the importance of decentralized redistribution for two reasons:[2] (1) most of the

---

[2] See Ladd and Doolittle [1982] for further details.

TABLE 19.2   Distribution of All Government Expenditure
by Level of Government in the United States
(1900–1981)

	Federal	State	Local
1900	34.1%	8.2%	57.7%
1910	30.1	9.0	60.9
1920	39.7	9.8	50.5
1930	32.5	16.3	51.2
1938	45.5	16.2	38.3
1950	59.3	15.2	26.5
1960	57.6	13.8	28.6
1971	48.4	18.6	33.0
1980	54.9	18.1	27.0
1981	56.3	17.9	25.8

Source: Werner Pommerehne "Qualitative Aspects of Federalism: A Study of Six
Countries," in *The Political Economy of Fiscal Federalism*, ed. W. Oates (Lexington,
Mass.: D.C. Heath, 1977), p. 311, except
for 1980 figure, which is computed from
U.S. Bureau of the Census, *Statistical Abstract of the United States: 1982–83*
(Washington, D.C.: U.S. Government
Printing Office, 1982), p. 274, and 1981
figure, from *Facts and Figures on Government—22nd Biennial Edition* (Washington,
D.C.: Tax Foundation, 1983), p. 18.

TABLE 19.3   Percentage of Expenditures by Selected Functions and Level of
Government (fiscal year 1981)

	Federal	State	Local
National defense and international relations	100.0%	0%	0%
Education	7.7	25.1	67.20
Highways	0.9	59.3	39.90
Public welfare	30.0	51.7	18.30
Hospitals	18.1	39.5	42.40
Health	35.9	35.0	29.10
Police	11.3	13.5	75.20
Housing and urban renewal	49.0	2.9	48.10
Unemployment compensation	1.4	98.1	0.01
Social Security	100.0	0	0

Source: Computed from *Facts and Figures on Government Finance—22nd Biennial Edition* (Washington, D.C.: Tax Foundation, 1983), p. 18. Percentages may not add to 100%
due to rounding.

financing (about three quarters) of these expenditures is done by the
federal government; and (2) much of the spending is subject to federal
standards on eligibility and benefit levels. Food stamps is an example of
a program with extensive federal guidelines. On the other hand, in
setting the benefit levels for a number of welfare programs such as Aid

to Families with Dependent Children, states may act with substantial autonomy.

Be this as it may, we are left with a critical question: Is the division of powers reflected in Table 19.3 sensible? In other words, what is the optimal allocation of economic responsibilities in a federal system?

OPTIMAL FEDERALISM

The principal goal here is to determine the proper division of activities among the levels of government. Let us first briefly consider macroeconomic functions. There is virtually universal agreement that spending and taxing decisions intended to affect the levels of unemployment and inflation should be made by the central government. No state or local government is large enough to affect the overall level of economic activity. It would not make sense, for example, for each locality to issue its own money supply and pursue an independent monetary policy.[3] Now, some macroeconomists have suggested that it may not be possible for even a central government to pursue effective policies to counter the business cycle. This issue is beyond the scope of this text.[4] We merely note that to the extent a stabilization policy is feasible and desirable, it should be done at the national level.

With respect to the microeconomic activities of enhancing economic efficiency and modifying the income distribution, there is considerably more controversy. Posed within the framework of welfare economics, the question is whether a centralized or decentralized system is more likely to maximize social welfare. For simplicity, most of our discussion assumes that there are just two levels of government, "central" and "local." No important insights are lost with this assumption.

Disadvantages of a Decentralized System

Consider a country composed of a group of small communities. Each community government makes decisions so as to maximize a social welfare function depending only upon the utilities of its members—outsiders do not count.[5] How do the results compare to those that would emerge if a national social welfare function that took into account all citizens' utilities were maximized? We consider first efficiency and then equity issues.

Efficiency Issues. *Externalities.* We define a public good with benefits that accrue only to members of a particular community as a **local**

---

[3] Under the Articles of the Confederation, states did issue their own monies.

[4] See Baily [1982] for a discussion.

[5] We ignore for now the questions of how the social welfare function is determined and whether the people who run the government will actually try to maximize it.

public good. For example, the public library in Idaho Falls has little effect on the welfare of people in Baton Rouge. However, in many real-world situations, local public goods and services purchased by one community may affect the utility levels of people in other communities. If one town provides good public education for its young people and some of them eventually emigrate, then members of other communities may benefit from having a better-educated work force. Or if one town's sewage-treatment plant pollutes a river that passes by other communities downstream, people in the downstream communities will be made worse off. In short, communities impose externalities (both positive and negative) upon each other. If each community cares only about its own members, these externalities will be overlooked. Hence, according to the standard argument (see Chapter 7), an inefficient allocation of resources will result.[6]

Scale Economies in Provision of Public Goods.   For certain public services, it may be that the more people who use them, the lower the cost per person. If several communities coordinated their use of such services, the members of all participating communities could be made better off because each person would need to pay less for the service. Thus, for example, it might make sense for neighboring communities to run their police departments jointly and so avoid the costs of acquiring duplicates of certain types of equipment. Communities that operate with complete independence lose such opportunities for cost savings.

Of course, different activities are subject to different scale economies. The optimal scale for the provision of library services might differ from that for fire protection. And both surely differ from the optimal scale for national defense. This observation, incidentally, helps rationalize a system of overlapping jurisdictions—each jurisdiction can handle those services with scale economies that are appropriate for the jurisdiction's size.

Inefficient Tax Systems.   Roughly speaking, efficient taxation requires that inelastically demanded or supplied goods be taxed at relatively high rates and vice versa.[7] Suppose that the supply of capital to the entire country is fixed, but capital is highly mobile between communities. Each community realizes that if it levies a substantial tax upon capital, the capital will simply move somewhere else, thus making the community worse off. In such a situation, a rational community will tax capital very lightly, if at all. In contrast, from a national point of view, efficiency requires a very high tax on capital, because it is inelastic in total supply.

---

[6] Of course, if the actions of individual citizens impose externalities upon members of other communities, the same type of problem arises.

[7] See Chapter 13.

In reality, of course, the total capital stock is not fixed in supply. Nor is it known just how responsive firms' locational decisions are to differences in local tax rates.[8] However, the basic point remains: taxes levied by decentralized communities are unlikely to be efficient from a national point of view. Instead, communities are likely to select taxes on the basis of whether they can be "exported" to outsiders. For example, if a community has the only coal mine in the country, there is a reasonable chance that the incidence of a locally imposed tax on coal will fall largely on coal users outside the community.[9] A coal tax would be a good idea from the community's point of view, but not necessarily from the viewpoint of the nation.[10] Phares [1980] estimated that about 17 percent of state taxes are exported to residents of other states, a substantial proportion.

An important implication of tax shifting is that communities may purchase local public goods in inefficiently large amounts. Efficiency requires that local public goods be purchased up to the point where their marginal social benefit equals marginal social cost. If communities can shift some of the burden to other jurisdictions, the community's perceived marginal cost will be less than marginal social cost. This will induce them to purchase local public goods with marginal social benefit equal to the perceived marginal cost, but which fall short of the marginal social cost. The result is an inefficiently large amount of local public goods.

Scale Economies in Tax Collection.   Individual communities may not be able to take advantage of scale economies in the collection of taxes. Each community has to devote resources to tax administration, and savings may be obtained by having a joint taxing authority. Why not split the costs of a single computer to keep track of tax returns, rather than have each community purchase its own?[11] Carrying this argument to its extreme, taxation should be done only by the central government, and the revenues returned to individual communities for community use. This actually describes some aspects of the U.S. system of intergovernmental grants discussed below.

Equity Issues.   In a utilitarian philosophical framework, the maximization of social welfare may require income transfers to the poor. Suppose that a particular community adopts an expenditure-tax pattern favorable to its low income members. If there are no barriers to movement between communities, we expect an in-migration of the poor from the rest of the country. As the poor population increases, so does the cost of the redistributive fiscal policy. At the same time, the town's upper income people may decide to exit. Why should they pay high taxes for the poor when they can move to another community where the expenditure pattern is to their own benefit? Thus, the demands on the community's tax base increase while its size decreases. Eventually the redistributive program has to be abandoned.

This argument relies heavily on the notion that people's decisions to locate in a given community are influenced by the available tax-welfare package. Whether or not that is true is an empirical matter, and econometric evidence is scanty.[12] Nevertheless, on the basis of casual observation, most economists would argue that substantial income redistribution cannot be carried out by decentralized communities.

Advantages of a Decentralized System

Tailoring Outputs to Local Tastes.   Some people want expensive computers used in the education of their children; others believe that this is unnecessary. Some people enjoy parks; others do not. A centralized government tends to provide the same level of public services throughout the country, regardless of the fact that people's tastes differ. As de Tocqueville observed, "In great centralized nations the legislator is obliged to give a character of uniformity to the laws, which does not always suit the diversity of customs and of districts [Oates, 1972, p. 31]." Clearly it is inefficient to provide individuals with more or less of a public good than they desire if the quantity they receive can be more closely tailored to their preferences. It is often argued that under a decentralized system, individuals with similar tastes for public goods will group together, so that communities will provide the types and quantities of public goods desired by their inhabitants.

A closely related notion is that local government's greater proximity to the people will make it more responsive to citizens' preferences than central government.[13] This is especially likely to be the case in a large country where the costs of obtaining and processing information on everybody's tastes are substantial. As a political stance, this view has always been influential in the United States. (Just think about the issue

---

[12] For a careful econometric study suggesting that the location decisions of the poor are indeed influenced by welfare programs, see Blank [1983].

[13] However, if one believes that the preferences of members of some communities are wrong, then this advantage turns into a disadvantage. For example, a community might decide to legalize slavery. Under what circumstances should the central government be able to overrule state and local governments? This is a fundamental issue beyond our scope.

of "states' rights.") We will examine it from an economic perspective more carefully later.

In the same way, economic regulations enacted at the national level may not make sense in every community. Consider the Fair Labor Standards Act, which sets national rules for wages, hours, and working conditions. Certain provisions of the act prohibit *industrial homework*— doing factory work in the home. The idea is to eliminate sweatshop conditions that were once common in big cities and that might become a problem again in industrial areas. But in 1983, a federal judge ruled that the act also applied to Vermont farmers who knit ski caps at home to supplement their incomes. The ruling created a furor: "Tell them to do their work down in Washington and leave us alone, and let us do our work up here," said one 63-year-old Vermonter [Clendinen, 1983, p. 8]. The story shows how a regulation that is sensible in some areas might not be in others. Why not let each state decide for itself, rather than impose uniformity?

Fostering Intergovernment Competition.   Many theories of government behavior focus on the fact that those who run the governments may lack incentives to act efficiently (see Chapter 10). If the managers of private firms behave inefficiently, they are eventually driven out of business. In contrast, government managers can continue to muddle along. However, if citizens can choose among communities, then substantial mismanagement may cause citizens simply to choose to live elsewhere. This threat may produce incentives for government managers to act more efficiently.

Experimentation and Innovation in Locally Provided Goods and Services.   What is the "best" way to run a school system? Some argue that extra pay for superior teachers helps motivate teachers to do a better job. Others suggest that good teachers are not motivated by money: "Good teaching is truly a vocation. It isn't the same as selling used cars" [Stark, 1983, p. A3]. In this view, merit pay merely creates dissension.

No one is certain what the "right" answer is, or even whether there is a single method that is best in all situations. One way to find out is to let each community choose its own way, and then compare the results. For example, Los Angeles has adapted a merit pay system, and other communities are closely watching the outcome.[14]

More generally, a system of diverse governments enhances the chances that new methods will be tried. As Supreme Court Justice Brandeis once observed, "It is one of the happy incidents of the Federal

---

[14] It is interesting to note that in San Marino, a suburb of Los Angeles, a merit pay scheme was recently dropped after 25 years. While the program provided incentives for better instruction, it resulted in divisive teacher-administration relations.

system that a single courageous state may, if its citizens choose, serve as a laboratory, and try moral, social, and economic experiments without risk to the rest of the country."

Implications

The foregoing discussion makes it clear that a purely decentralized system cannot be expected to maximize social welfare. Efficiency requires that those commodities with spillovers that affect the entire country—"national" public goods—be provided at the national level. Defense is a classic example. On the other hand, it seems perfectly appropriate for local public goods to be provided locally.[15]

This leaves us with the in-between case of community activities that create spillover effects which are not national in scope. One possible solution would be to put all the communities that affect each other under a single regional government. In theory, this government would take into account the welfare of all its citizens, and hence, internalize the externalities. However, a larger governmental jurisdiction carries the cost of less responsiveness to local differences in tastes. Moreover, there is some evidence that attempts at "regional government" to correct externalities have not worked very well.[16]

An alternative method for dealing with externalities would be a system of Pigouvian taxes and subsidies. In Chapter 7 it was shown that efficiency can be enhanced when the government taxes activities that create negative externalities and subsidizes activities that create positive externalities. We can imagine the central government using similar devices to influence the decisions of local governments. For example, if primary and secondary education create benefits that go beyond the boundaries of a jurisdiction, then the central government can provide communities with educational subsidies. Local autonomy is maintained, yet the externality corrected. We will see later that some federal grants to communities follow this model.

Our theory suggests a fairly clean division of responsibility for public good provision—local public goods by localities, and national public goods by the central government. In practice, there is considerable interplay between levels of government. For example, although localities have primary responsibility for education and public transportation, there are numerous federal regulations which they must obey. Given that localities might act inappropriately in the absence of such regulations, the presence of regulations may improve welfare. However, some

---

[15] This is subject to the usual proviso that the various levels of government are actually capable of providing goods efficiently (see Chapter 6).

[16] See Ackerman, Ackerman, Sawyer, and Henderson [1974] for a discussion of the Delaware River Basin Commission, which was established to deal with environmental problems faced in common by Delaware, New Jersey, New York, and Pennsylvania.

believe that the system of federal regulation over subfederal governmental units has become so complicated that it may be difficult to determine which level of government has responsibility for what. Recently, proposals have been made to reform the U.S. federal system to clarify division of responsibilities. These proposals are discussed below.

If a division of responsibilities is appropriate from an efficiency point of view, does the same hold for income distribution? As noted earlier, states and localities have a substantial amount of responsibility for the administration of welfare programs. President Ronald Reagan's "New Federalism" program calls for shifting even more responsibility for welfare policy back to the states. Under Reagan's program, both Aid to Families with Dependent Children (AFDC) and food stamps would be run by the states.[17]

Most economists believe that the mobility considerations discussed above rule out relying heavily upon local governments to achieve distributional aims. An individual jurisdiction that attempts to do so is likely to find itself in financial trouble. This is probably one of the reasons New York City nearly went bankrupt in the late 1970s [See Gramlich, 1976]. Even if it were possible for certain states and communities to redistribute income to *their* poor citizens, this would do nothing to help the poor outside those areas. If the country decides that it wants income redistribution, the program must be national in scope.

COMMUNITY FORMATION

Thus far, the discussion has focused on the appropriate role for existing local jurisdictions. Additional insights are gained by considering why these communities were originally formed. In this context, it is useful to think of a community as a **club**—a voluntary association of people who band together to share some kind of benefit. In this section a theory of clubs is developed and used to explain how the size of a community and its provision of public goods are determined.[18]

Consider a group of people who wish to band together to purchase land for a public park. For simplicity, assume that all members of the group have identical utility functions and that they will share equally the use of the park and its costs. The "community" can costlessly exclude all nonmembers, and it operates with no transaction costs. Given the assumption of identical tastes, we need consider only the desires of a representative member. Two decisions must be made: how large a park to acquire and how many members to have in the community.

---

[17] In return, responsibility for Medicaid would be assumed by the federal government.

[18] Most club models are based on the work of Buchanan [1965]. For a survey of this area, see Sandler and Tschirhart [1980].

To show how the community makes these decisions, first consider the relationship between the total cost per member and the number of members, *given* that a certain size park is selected. For the moment, suppose that the park is 400 acres. Clearly, the larger the community, the more people there are to shoulder the expense of purchasing a 400-acre park, and the smaller the required contribution per member. But if the per capita cost continually decreases with membership size, why not simply invite an infinite number of people to join? The problem is that as more people join the community, the public park becomes congested. The "marginal congestion cost" measures the dollar cost of the incremental congestion created by each new member. We assume that marginal congestion cost increases with the number of members.[19]

The community should expand its membership as long as the marginal decrease in the membership fee exceeds the marginal increase in congestion costs. Call this optimal membership size for a 400-acre park N_{400}. In Figure 19.1, membership is measured on the horizontal axis, size of park on the vertical, and point *a* indicates that when the park is 400 acres, optimal community size is N_{400}.

This whole analysis was done for a 400-acre park, and may just as well be repeated for a 500-acre park. The strategy is the same. For each level of membership, determine marginal cost savings and marginal congestion costs, and find the point at which they are equal. It is reasonable to assume that the total cost of the 500-acre park is greater than that of the 400-acre park, so that when a new member joins, the incremental cost saving will be greater. On the other hand, because the facility is larger, the incremental congestion cost due to a new member will be smaller than before. These considerations suggest that N_{500}, the optimal number of members for a 500-acre park, will exceed N_{400}. This is represented by point *b* in Figure 19.1.

This exercise can be done repeatedly to find the optimal membership for a park of any size. The information obtained from doing so is summarized in Figure 19.1 by schedule *NN*, which shows the optimal number of members for each size of park.

Schedule *NN* shows only how many members the community should have for each amount of acreage; it does not indicate what the acreage should be. To find the optimal amount, we have to take into account the costs and benefits of acquiring acreage. Assume for a moment that the community has 5,000 members. It is reasonable to believe that the higher the amount of acreage, the greater the *total* benefit to each member. (More acreage means that the park can have more gardens, accom-

---

[19] It might be the case that for low membership levels, marginal congestion costs are negative—new members are welcomed because of the company they provide. For simplicity, we ignore this possibility.

FIGURE 19.1   Optimal Community Membership for Each Acreage

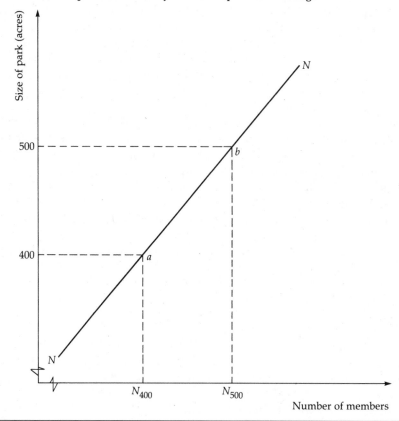

Every point on *NN* shows, for each acreage, the membership at which the marginal congestion cost of the last member just equals the marginal decrease in the membership fee.

modate more diverse activities, etc.) However, if space in parks is subject to diminishing marginal utility, then the *marginal* benefit declines with acreage. To find the optimal acreage, we must compare these marginal benefits with the marginal cost of an acre. What is the marginal cost?

Assume that the community can purchase all the land that it wants at the going price, say $10,000 an acre. Then the marginal cost for the community is constant at $10,000 per acre. Given that costs are divided equally among the members, the marginal cost for each member is constant at $10,000/5,000 = $2. Thus, a community with 5,000 members should purchase land until the marginal benefit per person equals the marginal cost per person of $2. Denote the acreage at which this equality holds as A_{5000}. In Figure 19.2, the fact that A_{5000} is the optimal acreage for a 5,000-member club is recorded at point *c*.

FIGURE 19.2   Optimal Acreage for Each Community Membership

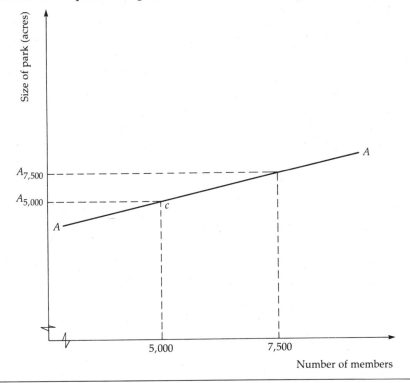

Every point on *AA* shows, for each membership, the acreage at which the marginal benefit of acquiring another acre just equals the marginal acquisition cost.

What is the optimal acreage for a community with more than 5,000 people? Again, we compute marginal benefits and marginal costs of each acre of land. We expect that with more members, the marginal benefit to an existing member of each additional acre of park land will be greater than previously. This is because under crowded conditions, people will put a higher value on additional land. On the cost side, the marginal cost to the *community* of an additional acre is still constant at $10,000, but now it is being shared by more people. For example, if the club has 7,500 members, the marginal cost per member falls to $1.33. If the marginal benefits rise and the marginal costs of acreage fall when the community is larger, then the optimum acreage will increase. In Figure 19.2, A_{7500}, the optimal acreage for a 7,500-member club, exceeds A_{5000}.

We can continue in this manner to find the optimal acreage for each membership size. The results obtained from doing so are summarized as schedule *AA* in Figure 19.2.

There is now enough information to solve the club's problem. In Figure 19.3 we impose schedule *AA* upon *NN*. The overall "best" must be at a point where acreage is optimal given membership, *and* membership is optimal given acreage. That is, the optimum must lie on both *AA*

FIGURE 19.3   Optimal Community Membership and Optimal Acreage

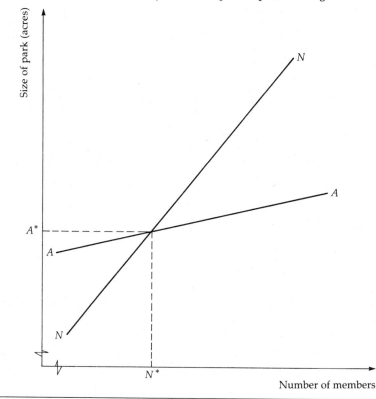

and *NN*, and hence, is defined by their intersection, where membership is N^* and acreage is A^*.

Although this club model is very simple, it highlights the crucial aspects of the community-formation process. Specifically, it suggests how community size will depend upon the type of public goods the people want to consume, the extent to which these goods are subject to crowding, and the costs of obtaining them, among other things. However, viewing communities as clubs leaves unanswered several important questions that are relevant for understanding local public finance:

1. How are the public services to be financed? A country club can charge a membership fee, but a community normally levies taxes to pay for public goods.

2. A club can exclude nonmembers and so eliminate the free rider problem. How can communities achieve this end?
3. When people throughout the country organize themselves into many different clubs (communities), will the overall allocation of public goods prove to be equitable and efficient?

These questions are taken up in the next section.

THE TIEBOUT MODEL

"Voting with Feet"

"Love it or leave it." When people who oppose U.S. federal government policy are given this advice, it is generally about as constructive as telling them to "drop dead." Only in extreme cases do we expect people to leave their country because of government policy.[20] Because of the large pecuniary and psychic costs of emigrating, a more realistic option is to stay home and try to change the policy. On the other hand, most citizens are not as strongly attached to their local communities. If you dislike the policies being followed in Skokie, Illinois, the easiest thing to do may be to move a few miles away to Evanston. This section discusses the relationship between intercommunity mobility, voluntary community formation, and the efficient provision of public goods.

Chapter 6 examined the idea that markets generally fail to provide public goods efficiently. The root of the problem is that the market does not force individuals to reveal their true preferences for public goods. Everyone has an incentive to be a free rider. The usual conclusion is that some kind of government intervention is required.

In an important article, Charles Tiebout [1956] (rhymes with "me too") argued that the ability of individuals to move among jurisdictions produces a market-like solution to the local public goods problem. Individuals "vote with their feet" and locate in the community that offers the bundle of public services and taxes they like best. Much as Jones satisfies his desire for private goods by purchasing them on the market, he satisfies his desire for public goods by the appropriate selection of a community in which to live and pays taxes for the services. In equilibrium, people distribute themselves across communities on the basis of their demands for public goods. Each individual receives his or her desired level of public goods and cannot be made better off by moving (or else the individual would). Hence, the equilibrium is Pareto efficient, and there is no "market failure." Government action is not required to achieve efficiency.

---

[20] For example, in the 1960s a number of young men left the country to evade military service in Vietnam.

More Rigorous Statement

Tiebout's provocative assertion that a quasi-market process can solve the public goods problem has stimulated a large amount of research.[21] Much of that research has been directed toward finding a precise set of sufficient conditions under which the ability of citizens to vote with their feet will lead to efficient public goods provision. Some of the conditions are listed below.[22]

1.   There are no externalities arising from local government behavior. As emphasized above, to the extent there are spillover effects between communities, the allocation of resources will be inefficient.

2.   Individuals are assumed to be completely mobile. Each person can travel costlessly to a jurisdiction with a bundle of public services that is best for him. The location of an individual's place of employment puts no restriction on where he resides.

3.   People have perfect information with respect to the public services they will receive in each community and the taxes they will have to pay.

4.   There are enough different communities so that each individual can find one with public goods meeting his demands.

5.   The cost per unit of public services is assumed to be constant, which implies that if the quantity of public services doubles, then the total cost also doubles. In addition, the technology of public good provision is such that if the number of residents is doubled, the quantity of the public good provided must be doubled. To see why these conditions are required for a Tiebout equilibrium to be efficient, imagine instead that the cost per unit of public services fell as the scale of provision increased. In that case, there would be scale economies of which independently operating communities might fail to take advantage (see above).

Note that assumption 5 makes the public good essentially a publicly provided private good. "Pure" public goods (such as national defense) do not satisfy this assumption. However, many local public services such as education and garbage collection appear to fit this description to a reasonable extent.

6.   Public goods are also assumed to be financed by a proportional property tax. The tax rate can vary across communities.[23]

7.   Communities can enact **exclusionary zoning laws**—statutes that prohibit certain uses of land. Specifically, they can require that any house purchased be of some minimum size. To see why this assumption

---

[21] See the papers in Zodrow [1983].

[22] Hamilton [1975a] and Bewley [1981] provide more detail. Note that not all of these conditions were included in Tiebout's original article.

[23] Tiebout [1956] assumed finance by head taxes. The more realistic assumption of property taxation is from Hamilton [1975a].

is crucial, recall that in Tiebout equilibrium, communities are segregated on the basis of their members' demands for public goods. To the extent that income is positively correlated with the demand for public goods, community segregation by income will result. In high income communities, the *level* of property values will tend to be high, and hence, the community will be able to finance a given amount of public spending with a relatively low property tax *rate*. In the absence of exclusionary zoning, low income families have an incentive to move into rich communities and build relatively small houses. Because of the low tax rate, low income families will have relatively small tax liabilities, but nevertheless be able to enjoy the high level of public goods provision. As more low income families get the idea and move in, the tax base per family in the community perceptibly falls. Tax rates must be increased to finance the expanded level of public goods required to serve the increased population.

Since we assume perfect mobility, there is no reason for the rich to put up with this. They can just move to another community. But what stops the poor from following them? In the absence of constraints on mobility, nothing. Clearly, it is possible for a game of "musical suburbs" to develop in a Tiebout model. Exclusionary zoning is a way of preventing this phenomenon and thus maintaining a stable Pareto efficient equilibrium.

Tiebout and the Real World

Exactly meeting the list of conditions required for the Tiebout model is unlikely. People are not perfectly mobile; there are probably not enough communities so that each family can find one with a bundle of services that suits it perfectly, and so on. Moreover, contrary to what the Tiebout model implies, we observe many communities within which there are massive income differences. Just consider any major city.

However, we should not dismiss the Tiebout mechanism too hastily. There is a lot of mobility in the American economy—in 1980, over 45 percent of Americans had different residences than they had in 1975 [U.S. Bureau of the Census, 1982, p. 14].[24] Moreover, within most metropolitan areas, there is a wide range of choice with respect to type of community. As White [1975, p. 52] notes,

> The salient fact about location choice in a large American metropolis is that households have a wide choice of places to live. Within a 20-mile radius they generally have a choice of one or more central cities and up to several hundred suburbs.

---

[24] The figure is for persons over 5 years of age.

Certainly, casual observation suggests that across suburbs there is considerable residential segregation by income, and that exclusionary zoning is practiced widely. In addition, it is not hard to find popular accounts of classic Tiebout-type behavior:

> Police departments in California are in a bind: Crime is increasing, but after Proposition 13 took its toll of local property taxes, they are running out of money.[25] So some communities are turning to the "police tax."
>
> State law allows two thirds of the voters of any community to override the limits of Proposition 13 and pass a supplemental assessment for police services. In affluent suburban communities, this works well. "We all gained huge savings as homeowners from Proposition 13," explains a member of the Atherton City Council. So paying up to $200 a year to help the police protect expensive homes from increasingly active burglars seems a good investment.
>
> But in larger, poorer cities, the idea did not fare well. Los Angeles and Oakland voters turned down police taxes. With lower property values, they have gained less from Proposition 13, and didn't consider a new tax so affordable. They also have less faith in police, and don't see how extra money would help.
>
> Despite the attention that it receives from politicians and the media, the fear of crime is evidently not absolute; it's just another part of life, factored in with all the others. ["Relative Crime," *New York Times,* June 22, 1981]

It appears that communities' decisions with respect to public good provision sometimes can be explained on the basis of the tastes and incomes of their members.

There have been several formal empirical tests of the Tiebout hypothesis. One type of study looks at whether the values of local public goods and taxes are capitalized into local property values. The idea is that if people move in response to local packages of taxes and public services, then differences in these packages should be reflected in property values.[26] A community with better public services should have higher property values, other things (including taxes) being the same. These capitalization studies were already discussed in Chapter 18. As noted there, capitalization does appear to be a widespread phenomenon.

Another interesting test was done by Gramlich and Rubinfeld [1982]. They analyzed responses to survey questions in which individuals were asked about their desired levels of local public expenditures. If the Tiebout mechanism is operative, we would expect to find substantial homogeneity of demands within suburbs located near many other communities, because, in such a setting, the model suggests that those who are dissatisfied with current spending levels will simply move else-

---

[25] Proposition 13 is discussed in Chapter 18.

[26] Actually, there are some circumstances under which the Tiebout hypothesis does not imply that capitalization necessarily will occur. See Rubinfeld [1983].

where. On the other hand, in areas where there are not a lot of other communities nearby, it is less easy to exit if you are not happy. In such areas, people with very different demands for public goods may be lumped together in a single community. Gramlich and Rubinfeld found that compared to areas where there is not much scope for choice, there are indeed relatively smaller differences in tastes for public goods within communities that are located in large metropolitan areas.

Gramlich and Rubinfeld's results must be regarded with caution because they are based on survey questions regarding the demand for public goods. What people *say* they want is not necessarily what they really want. Nevertheless, the study suggests that, at least in some settings, the Tiebout model is a good depiction of reality.

Relation to the "Urban Crisis"

Many American cities are experiencing major social and economic difficulties. The urban problem has many dimensions: loss of population, physically decaying neighborhoods, inability to pay for public services, and a high proportion of residents on public assistance, among others. There is no dearth of theories to explain the cities' difficulties. In one recent survey, about 40 possible explanations were listed![27] Our purpose here is to discuss how the U.S. system of local public finance may have contributed to the urban crisis.

Imagine a situation where low income households in a city gain political power and use this power to establish a "pro-poor" pattern of expenditures and taxes. Provided that they are sufficiently mobile, those high income individuals who do not wish to support such a fiscal pattern can leave for the suburbs. The poor are unable to follow them, either because their personal circumstances make them less mobile, or because of exclusionary zoning in the suburbs. As a consequence, the proportion of low income families in the city increases. At the same time, the city's income- and property-tax bases fall because of the exit of the middle and upper classes.

In this extremely simple model of urban decline, the villain is the fragmented system of local public finance. If an entire metropolitan area had a unified government, fiscal decisions would apply uniformly to the entire jurisdiction. As a consequence, there would be less incentive for those with relatively high incomes to leave the central city behind.

Bradford and Oates [1975] used data on a group of New Jersey cities and suburban communities to estimate the potential effects of moving to a metropolitan-wide system of local public finance. As expected, they found that in the long run, the central cities would have a greater pro-

---

[27] See Bradbury, Downs, and Small [1982], who also provide an excellent treatment of the methodological problems involved in attempts to measure and explain urban decline.

portion of high income families under the unified system than under the status quo. However, it is hard to say what the distributional consequences of moving to a unified system would be. Changes in both the patterns of taxation and expenditure must be considered.

Imposing uniform property tax rates throughout the metropolitan area would create substantial capital losses for those property owners whose tax rates were formerly lower than average and vice versa (other things being the same). Would these changes tend to make the distribution of wealth more or less equal? To answer this question, we need information on the initial wealth positions of city landlords, among other things. If the move to a unified system ended up lowering tax rates in the city, and urban landlords were wealthy to begin with, then there would be a tendency for the distribution of wealth to become more unequal. If it turned out that urban landlords were less wealthy then their suburban counterparts, just the opposite conclusion would emerge. Unfortunately, little information on the wealth of inner-city landlords is available. Therefore, it is hard to guess what the redistributive impact of the changing tax rates would be.

On the expenditure side of the account, Bradford and Oates found that guaranteeing equal school expenditures for each pupil in the metropolitan area would tend to redistribute real income from high to low income people. This is because under the current system, communities with more income tend to spend greater amounts on education than do those communities with less. Interestingly, if expenditures on *all* public services were equalized throughout the metropolitan area, it might work to the disadvantage of poorer central city residents, because smaller suburban communities often provide fewer public sector services than the cities provide. A small suburb, for example, may have a volunteer fire department and leave garbage collection to private firms. Requiring equal expenditure everywhere would benefit such communities, other things being the same.

A major problem with a unified system is that community autonomy would be severely limited. As noted earlier, the ability of communities to make their own decisions has certain efficiency advantages. After considering both distributive and efficiency issues, Bradford and Oates concluded that there is simply not enough information to say which system is superior. In any case, metropolitan consolidation has received very little political support in the United States.[28] In practice, the main method for dealing with urban fiscal problems has been grants-in-aid from federal and state governments, a subject to which we now turn.

---

[28] A partial exception is the Minneapolis–St. Paul metropolitan area, which has adopted a system that permits some tax-base sharing. See Bradbury, Downs, and Small [1982].

INTERGOVERNMENTAL GRANTS

Grants from one level of government to another are the main method for changing fiscal resources within a federal system. Table 19.4 indicates that in the last few decades, grants from the federal government have

TABLE 19.4   Relation of Federal Grant-in-Aid Outlays to Federal, State, and Local Expenditures (selected fiscal years)

Fiscal Year	Total Grants ($ billions)	Grants as a Percent of Total Federal Outlays	Grants as a Percent of State and Local Expenditures
1950	$ 2.3	5.3%	10.4%
1960	7.0	7.7	14.7
1970	24.0	12.3	19.2
1980	91.5	15.9	26.2
1982	88.2	12.1	22.1

Source: Office of Management and Budget, *Special Analyses, Budget of the United States Government Fiscal Year 1984* (Washington, D.C.: U.S. Government Printing Office, 1983), p. H-16.

increased both in dollar amount and as a proportion of total federal outlays. Grants as a percentage of state and local expenditures have also increased over the long run. The importance of grants as an element in local public finance is particularly striking. Table 19.5 indicates that by the early 1980s, grants from federal and state government were about three quarters of the amount that localities raised from their own taxes.

TABLE 19.5   Federal and State Grants to Local Government (selected fiscal years)

	State and Federal Aid	
Fiscal Year	Amount ($ billions)	Percent of Local General Revenue*
1955	$ 6.3	43.1%
1960	10.1	44.2
1965	15.2	46.9
1970	29.5	57.5
1975	62.0	73.4
1980	102.4	78.8
1981	111.4	76.5

* Figures in this column are expressed as a percentage of revenues the localities raised on their own.
Source: Advisory Commission on Intergovernmental Relations, *Significant Features of Fiscal Federalism 1981–1982 Edition* (Washington, D.C.: U.S. Government Printing Office, 1983), p. 67.

Grants are used to finance activities that run practically the entire gamut of government functions. In 1982, the greatest proportion of federal grant outlays (46 percent) went for programs relating to income security and health [Congressional Budget Office, 1983a, p. 27]. Grants were also used for education, development of infrastructure, transportation, general fiscal assistance, and other purposes.

Why have intergovernmental transfers grown so much? This question is closely related to why government spending in general has increased. As we saw in Chapter 10, the answer is far from clear. One explanation for the growth of grants emphasizes that over the last several decades, the demand for the types of services traditionally provided by the state and local sector—education, transportation, police protection, etc.—has been growing rapidly. However, the state and local revenue structures, which are based mainly on sales and property taxes, have not provided the means to keep pace with the growth of desired expenditures. In contrast, federal tax revenues have tended to grow automatically over time, largely due to the progressive nature of the federal personal income tax and inflation. Hence, there is a "mismatch" between where tax money is collected and where it is demanded. Grants from the central government to states and localities provide a way of correcting this mismatch.[29]

Types of Grants

The form of a grant can have an important influence upon its economic impact. There are basically two types, conditional and unconditional. Each is discussed in turn.

Conditional Grants.   These are sometimes called **categorical grants.** The donor specifies, to some extent, the purposes for which the recipient can use the funds. As of 1982, about 93 percent of federal grants were for specific purposes.[30] The ways in which conditional grant money must be spent are often spelled out in minute detail. In 1982, the U.S. House of Representatives decided to try to discourage drunken driving and voted to give money to states that established anti-drunk driving programs. The House specified everything from the percent of blood-alcohol concentration that would be the criterion for intoxication to the length of time the driver's license would be suspended for a first offense. This is not atypical. According to one count, as of the mid-

---

[29] See Tresch [1981, pp. 614–15] for further details. A major problem with the "mismatch theory" is that it fails to explain why states and localities cannot raise their tax *rates* to keep up with increases in the demand for local public goods and services.

[30] Computed from Congressional Budget Office [1983a, p. 25].

1970s, the federal government imposed 1,259 spending mandates upon states and localities.[31]

There are several types of conditional grants.

Matching Grants.   For every dollar given by the donor to support a particular activity, a certain sum must be expended by the recipient. For example, a grant might indicate that whenever a community spends a dollar on education, the federal government will contribute a dollar, as well.

A useful way to understand the effects of a matching grant is by taking advantage of the standard theory of rational choice. In Figure 19.4, the horizontal axis measures the quantity of local government out-

FIGURE 19.4   Analysis of a Matching Grant

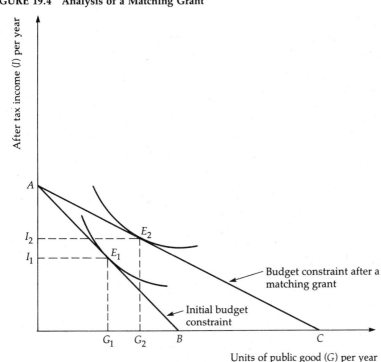

put, G, consumed by the residents of the town of Smallville. The vertical axis measures Smallville's total after-tax income, I. Assume for simplicity that units of G are defined so that the price of one unit is \$1. Then Smallville's budget constraint between I and G is a straight line whose

---

[31] Claude Barfield, quoted in Ornstein [1982, p. 12].

slope in absolute value is one.[32] The unitary slope indicates that for each dollar Smallville is willing to spend, it can obtain one unit of public good. The budget constraint is denoted AB in Figure 19.4.

Suppose that Smallville's preferences for G and I can be represented by a set of conventionally shaped indifference curves.[33] Then the town will choose the combination of I and G that maximizes its utility subject to budget line AB. In Figure 19.4, this bundle is at point E_1, where public good consumption is G_1 and community after-tax income is I_1.

Now suppose that a matching grant regime of the sort described above is instituted. The federal government will match every dollar that Smallville spends. When Smallville gives up \$1 of income, it can obtain \$2 worth of G—one of its own dollars, and one from the federal government. The slope (in absolute value) of Smallville's budget line therefore becomes one half. In effect, the matching grant halves the price of G. It is an ad valorem subsidy on consumption of the public good. The new budget line is drawn in Figure 19.4 as AC.

At the new equilibrium, Smallville consumes G_2 public goods and has I_2 available for private consumption. Note that not only is G_2 greater than G_1, but I_2 is greater than I_1. Smallville uses part of the grant to buy more of the public good, and part to reduce its tax burden. It would be possible, of course, to draw the indifference curves so that I_2 equals I_1, or even so that I_2 is less than I_1. Nevertheless, there is a distinct possibility that part of the grant meant to stimulate public consumption will be used not to buy more G, but to obtain tax relief. In an extreme case, the community's indifference curves might be such that $G_2 = G_1$—the community consumes the same amount of the public good and uses the entire grant to reduce taxes. Thus, theory alone cannot indicate how a matching grant affects a community's expenditure on a public good. It depends upon the responsiveness of demand to changes in price.[34]

A matching grant is a sensible way to correct for the presence of a positive externality. As explained in Chapter 7, when an individual or a firm generates a positive externality, an appropriate subsidy can enhance efficiency. The same logic is supposed to apply to a community. Of course, all the problems that arise in implementing the subsidy scheme are still present. In particular, the central government has to be able to measure the actual size of the externality.

---

[32] Details on the construction of budget constraints are provided in the Appendix at the end of the book. The model in this chapter ignores the deduction of state and local property taxes in the federal income tax system. If taxpayers itemize deductions and the marginal federal income tax rate is t, then the absolute value of the slope of AB is $(1 - t)$.

[33] Of course, this supposition ignores all the problems—and perhaps the impossibility—of preference aggregation raised in Chapter 6. We return to this issue later.

[34] The existing econometric work on the demand for local services suggests that they are price inelastic—a 1 percent decrease in their effective price leads to a less than 1 percent increase in quantity demanded. See Inman [1979].

Matching Closed-Ended Grant.   With a matching grant, the cost to the donor ultimately depends upon the recipient's behavior. If Smallville's consumption of G is very stimulated by the program, then the central government's contributions will be quite large and vice versa. To put a ceiling on the cost, the donor may specify some maximum amount that it will contribute. Such a closed-ended matching grant is illustrated in Figure 19.5. As before, prior to the grant, Smallville's budget line is AB,

FIGURE 19.5   Analysis of a Closed-Ended Matching Grant

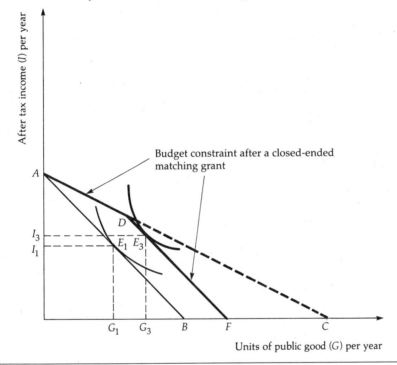

and the equilibrium is at point E_1. With the closed-ended matching grant, the budget constraint is the kinked line segment ADF. Segment AD has a slope of minus one half, reflecting the one-for-one matching provision. But after some point D, the donor will no longer match dollar for dollar. Smallville's opportunity cost of a unit of government spending again becomes \$1, which is reflected in the slope of segment DF.

The new equilibrium at E_3 involves more consumption of G than under the status quo, but less than under the open-ended matching grant. The fact that the grant "runs out" limits its ability to stimulate expenditure on the public good. Note, however, that in some cases the closed-endedness can be irrelevant. If desired community consumption of *G* involves an expenditure below the ceiling, then the presence of the ceiling simply does not matter. In graphical terms, if the new tangency had been along segment *AD* of Figure 19.5, then the fact that points along *DC* are not available is irrelevant.

Nonmatching Grant.   In this case, the donor gives a fixed sum of money with the stipulation that it be spent on the public good. Figure 19.6

FIGURE 19.6   Analysis of a Nonmatching Conditional Grant

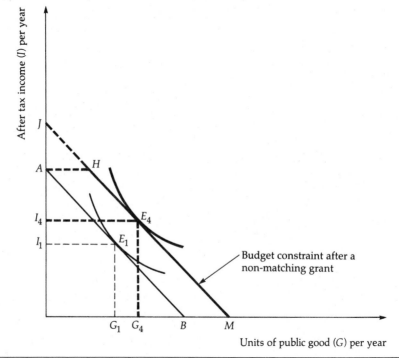

depicts a nonmatching grant to buy *AH* units of G. At each level of community income, Smallville can now buy *AH* more units of the public good than it did before. Thus, the new budget constraint is found by adding a horizontal distance *AH* to the original budget constraint *AB*. The result is the kinked line *AHM*.

Smallville maximizes utility at point E_4. Note that although public good consumption goes up from G_1 to G_4, the difference between the two is less than the amount of the grant, *AH*. Smallville has followed the stipulation that it spend the entire grant on G_1, *but* at the same time, it has reduced its own expenditures for the public good. If the donor expected expenditures to be increased by exactly *AH*, then Smallville's reaction has frustrated these hopes. It turns out that the situation depicted in Figure 19.6 is a good description of reality. Communities often use some portion of nonmatching conditional grant money to reduce their own taxes [see Inman, 1979].

Observe from Figure 19.6 that budget line *AHM* looks *almost* as if it were created by giving the community an unrestricted lump sum grant of *AH* dollars. Such a grant would have lead to a budget line *JM*, which is just segment *MH* extended to the vertical axis. Smallville happens to behave exactly the same way facing constraint *AHM* as it would have if it had faced *JM*. In this particular case, then, *the conditional grant could just as well have been an unrestricted lump sum grant*. Intuitively, as long as the community wants to consume at least an amount of the public good equal to the grant, then the fact that the grant is conditional is irrelevant. In contrast, if the community wanted to consume less of the public good than *AH* (if the indifference curves are such that the optimum along *JM* is to the left of *H*), then the conditional nature of the grant actually affects behavior.[35]

Unconditional Grants.   These are sometimes referred to as **revenue sharing.** An unconditional grant places no restrictions on the use of funds. In effect, it is a lump sum grant to the community. As illustrated in Figure 19.7, an unconditional grant generates a shift parallel to the original budget line, say from *AB* to *KL*. The new equilibrium is at point E_5. Part of the unconditional grant is used to purchase the public good, and part for tax relief.[36]

Why should the central government be in the business of giving unconditional grants to states and localities? The usual response is that such grants can be used to equalize the income distribution. It is not clear that this argument stands up under close scrutiny. Even if it is a goal of public policy to help poor *people*, it does not follow that the best way to do so is to help poor *communities*. After all, the chances are that a community with a low average income will probably have some relatively rich members and vice versa. If the goal is to help the poor, why not give them the money directly?

One possible explanation is that the central government is particularly concerned that the poor consume a greater quantity of the publicly provided good. An important example is education. This is a kind of commodity egalitarianism (Chapter 5) applied to the output of the public sector. However, as we just demonstrated, with unconditional grants we cannot know for sure that all the money will ultimately be spent on

---

[35] Note the similarity to analysis of in-kind transfer programs discussed in Chapter 5.

[36] Because the community can locate anywhere along *KL*, there is a theoretical possibility that the new equilibrium could involve less *G* than under the status quo. However, this is not likely because most empirical work suggests that local public goods are "normal"—an increase in income increases the quantity demanded, *ceteris paribus*. See Inman [1979].

FIGURE 19.7   Analysis of an Unconditional Grant

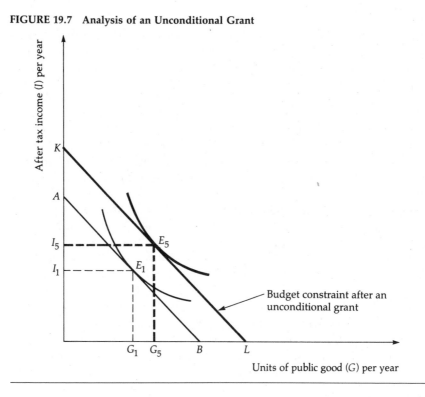

the favored good. (Indeed, the same is generally true for conditional grants as well.)

Measuring Need.   In any case, an unconditional grant program requires that the donor determine which communities "need" money and in what amounts.[37] Federal allocations are based on complicated formulas established by Congress. The amount of grant money received by a state depends upon such factors as per capita income, the size of its urban population, and the amount of its state income tax collections. The allocations to localities are not only functions of such conventional economic factors, but can also depend upon items like the ethnicity of the population.[38]

An important factor in determining how much a community receives is its **tax effort,** normally defined as the ratio of tax collections to tax capacity. The idea is that communities that try hard to raise taxes but still cannot finance a very high level of public services are worthy of receiving

---

[37] In some cases, eligibility for conditional grants is also based upon need.

[38] Allocations are made first to some tribes of Native Americans [Break, 1980, p. 148].

a grant. Unfortunately, it is quite possible that this and related measures will yield little or no information about a community's true effort. Suppose that Smallville is in a position to "export" its tax burden in the sense that the incidence of any taxes it levies will fall on outsiders. Then a hight tax rate tells us nothing about how much the members of the community are sacrificing.[39]

More fundamentally, the tax effort approach may be rendered totally meaningless because of the phenomenon of capitalization. Consider two towns, Sodom and Gomorrah. They are identical except for the fact that Sodom has a brook which provides water at essentially zero cost. In Gomorrah, on the other hand, it is necessary to dig a well and pump out the water.

Gomorrah levies a property tax to finance the water pump. If there is a tax in Gomorrah and none in Sodom, and the communities are otherwise identical, why should anyone live in Gomorrah? As people migrate to Sodom, property values increase there (and decrease in Gomorrah) until there is no net advantage to living in either community. In short, property values are higher in Sodom to reflect the presence of the brook.

For reasons discussed above, we do not expect the advantage to necessarily be 100 percent capitalized into Sodom's property values. Nevertheless, capitalization compensates at least partially for the differences between the towns. Just because Gomorrah levies a tax does *not* mean that it is "trying harder" than Sodom, because the Sodomites have already paid for their water in terms of a higher price for living there. We conclude that conventional measures of tax effort may not be very meaningful.

Grants and Spending Behavior

The "community indifference curve" analysis given above begs a fairly fundamental question: *whose* indifference curves are they? According to median voter theory (Chapter 10), the answer is that the preferences are those of the community's median voter. Bureaucrats and elected officials play a passive role in implementing the median voter's wishes.

A straightforward implication of the median voter rule is that a $1 increase in community income has exactly the same impact upon public spending as receipt of a $1 unconditional grant. In terms of Figure 19.7, both events generate identical parallel outward shifts of the initial budget line. If the budget line changes are identical, then the changes in public spending levels must also be identical.

---

[39] Recall that the property tax plays an important role in local public finance, but the incidence of that tax is a matter of some controversy (Chapter 18).

A considerable amount of econometric work has been done on the determinants of local public spending. (Many of these studies are summarized in Inman [1979].) Contrary to what one might expect, a conclusion common to virtually all studies is that a dollar received by the community in the form of a grant results in *greater* public spending than a dollar increase in community income. This phenomenon has been dubbed the **flypaper effect,** because the money seems to stick in the sector where it initially hits.

Some explanations of the flypaper effect focus on the role of bureaucrats. In the model of Filimon, Romer, and Rosenthal [1982], bureaucrats are interested in maximizing the sizes of their budgets. As budget maximizers, the bureaucrats have no incentive to inform citizens about the true level of grant funding being received by the community. By concealing this information, the bureaucrats may "trick" citizens into voting for a higher level of funding than would otherwise have been the case. According to this view, the flypaper effect is a consequence of the fact that citizens are unaware of the true budget constraint. To support their theory, Filimon et al. [1982, p. 57] noted that in states which have direct referenda on spending questions, ballots often contain information about the tax base but rarely have data on grants.

Project Grants.   We have been assuming up to now that whether a community receives a grant is largely outside the community's control. However, so-called **project grants** are awarded to communities on the basis of submitted proposals which specify how the funds will be used. At times, such grants have accounted for up to a fifth of federal grant expenditures [Break, 1980, p. 76]. The existence of project grants puts a premium on "grantsmanship." Those communities with grant writers who know what kind of projects will appeal to Washington and how the proposals should be written, will have a better chance of receiving grants, other things being the same.

The fact that a community's receipts of grant money may depend on its own efforts complicates the already difficult task of determining how grants affect spending behavior. Does a community spend a lot on public services because it has a large grant, or does it apply for a large grant because it has a strong taste for public services? As a statistical matter, sorting out the direction of causality is a difficult matter.

Grants and Politics

Under President Reagan's suggested New Federalism program, all major federal grants would be consolidated into a few broad **block grants,** which are essentially nonmatching conditional grants. (As of 1982, such block grants accounted for only 12.3 percent of total federal grants).[40] Within a given "block" of programs, states have much more choice on spending priorities than is the case with the typical conditional grant. In return for cutting federal strings, which presumably would lower the states' administrative costs, the level of federal grants would be reduced quite dramatically. Like the other parts of Reagan's New Federalism program discussed earlier, the plan to restructure grants created a political storm.

Why are the particular forms taken by grants of such intense public interest? We might begin by asking why conditional grants are so prevalent in the first place. Economic theory gives us one possible rationalization—externalities. But those familiar with politics suggest another—members of Congress simply do not trust the states to use the money "appropriately," and they therefore want to attach as many restrictions as possible.

A related point is that a conditional grant gives Congress the opportunity to regulate behavior that has nothing whatsoever to do with the ostensible purpose of the grant. For example, grants are unabashedly used to influence actions on civil rights:

> [M]ost of the enforcement of federal civil rights laws hinges on the allocation of federal dollars. For example, Title VI of the Civil Rights Act of 1964 states, in part, that "no person in the United States shall on the ground of race, color, or national origin, be excluded from participation in, be denied the benefits of, or be otherwise subjected to discrimination under any program or activity receiving federal financial assistance." Such a guarantee is plainly irrelevant when the source of financial assistance is a state or municipal government rather than the federal government. [Davidson, 1982, p. A31]

This discussion draws attention to the fundamental political problem of a federal system. If the central and local governments disagree on spending priorities, whose view will prevail? In this context, it becomes easier to understand why conservatives like President Reagan tend to favor block grants with no strings, while liberals like to attach a lot of conditions:

> The stated purpose of the block grants is not just to improve efficiency, but to further conservative ideals. . . . The block strategy flows partly from a deeply held Republican belief that Washington contains a powerful network of liberal political centers. . . . Dispersing decision-making responsibility to the states . . . would undermine such forces, and thus change the priorities of government [Steven V. Roberts quoted in Ornstein, 1982, pp. 13–14].

---

[40] Computed from Office of Management and Budget [1983, p. H-20].

THE COURTS AND THE REFORM OF LOCAL PUBLIC FINANCE[41]

Tiebout-type behavior leads to a situation in which different communities may provide very disparate levels of public goods to their members. Some view unequal provision of local public goods as undesirable, especially for items like education and police protection. One way to change the status quo is through a system of grants. However, the grant system created by Congress has not had enough of an impact to satisfy the critics. A substantial effort has been mounted to bypass the legislative process altogether and achieve more intercommunity equality through the judicial system.[42]

Courts have been particularly active in the area of school finance. The basic issue is whether it is legal to finance education only by local taxes when such funding leads to unequal spending across communities. In *Serrano* v. *Priest*, the Supreme Court of California invalidated that state's system of public education finance, which was based upon local property taxes. The decision emphasized that reliance on local property taxation, because of widely varying tax bases per pupil, had resulted in unacceptably large differentials in expenditure per pupil.[43] The court left the problem of coming up with a better system to the state legislature.

How might a legislature faced with this judicial mandate react? Some possibilities are given below.

Do Nothing. In New Jersey, after receiving an edict from the state supreme court to reform school finance, the legislature produced a plan that still substantially relied on local funding and therefore had large intercommunity differentials [Inman & Rubinfeld, 1979, p. 1747]. Of course, when the legislature comes up with an unacceptable plan, the courts can order them to develop another one. But in the meantime, implementation of the court's wishes can be delayed for years.

Institute Statewide Control of Educational Finance. In principle, the state could then distribute funds in any manner it wished. Of course, this would severely diminish local autonomy over spending decisions, and thereby create potential problems of economic efficiency, as well as change the balance of political power.

---

[41] This section is based on the excellent review by Inman and Rubinfeld [1979].

[42] A number of cases have also dealt with equality of public-service provision *within* communities. See Inman and Rubinfeld [1979].

[43] Not all state courts have concurred. In 1982, New York's highest court declared that neither the state nor the United States constitutions require that spending be equal across school districts (*Board of Education* v. *Nyquist*).

Develop a Less Extreme Method for Transferring Funds from Wealthy to Less-Wealthy Communities.   A method known as **district power equalization (DPE)** has gained some attention. Under DPE, if a community's property tax collections exceed a certain amount, then some proportion of the difference is taken by the state, which then distributes the money to communities whose collections are smaller than that amount.[44]

At first glance, it appears that a program like DPE would substantially increase equality in spending per student. However, the theory of local public finance suggests that the ultimate increase in equality might not be all that great. When DPE is instituted, some of the taxes in high income communities are siphoned off to other communities. Therefore, in the high income communities, the level of public services associated with any given level of tax collections falls. The community becomes a less desirable place to live, and hence its property values go down. (Recall the discussion of capitalization above.) Now that the tax *base* is lower in the high income community, a higher tax rate is required to finance any given level of public services. Similar reasoning suggests that in low income communities, property values increase, and the tax rate needed to finance any given level of services falls.

These tax-base changes tend to undo some of DPE's initial equalization of educational spending levels. Under DPE, the decrease in the high income community's tax base means that for each dollar of educational spending, less is taken away by the state. This effect will tend to *increase* educational spending in high-income communities toward pre–DPE levels. Likewise, the low income community's effective price of education increases, which tends to decrease its educational spending in the direction of the pre–DPE figure. In short, there is a tendency for educational spending to move back to the levels under the status quo. Inman and Rubinfeld [1979, p. 1735] estimated that the effects of property value changes would cut the initial increase in spending equality almost in half.

Finally, we should note that most of the courts' attention has been on educational *spending* per pupil. Presumably, what society cares about is the *quality* of education received. Unfortunately, the link between schooling expenditures and the quality ultimately received is not clear. For example, some claim that the home background of students is the chief determinant of educational success; spending does not matter much.[45] In 1983, President Ronald Reagan argued that major improvements in educational quality could be obtained without increased funds if the curriculum were appropriately changed ("back to basics"). Some

---

[44] Specifically, suppose the certain amount is B^*, the community's actual tax base is B, and its tax rate as a fraction of B^* is t. Then aid received from DPE is $t(B^* - B)$. If $B > B^*$, "aid" is negative—the community has money taken away from it. For further details, see Inman and Rubinfeld [1979, pp. 1707, 1715.])

[45] The controversy is discussed in Aaron [1978, Chapter 3].

of his critics suggested that to the contrary, a massive infusion of money was needed.

Social science research has not provided a definitive set of answers. It is safe to say, however, that measuring output by input is a mistake: twice as much spending does not necessarily mean twice as much quality. Hence, even if the courts obtained their goal of equality in spending, it is not clear that their real objectives would be achieved.

More generally, our discussion of court intervention in local public finance suggests that attempts to create a given distribution of local public goods by judicial fiat may not be successful. The effects of judicial edicts can be partially undone either by passive resistance on the part of legislators and bureaucrats, or by economic decisions of the citizenry. To find rules that "work" requires an understanding of how people will react to them.

OVERVIEW

At the beginning of this chapter we posed some questions concerning federal systems: is decentralized decision making desirable; how should responsibilities be allocated; and how should local governments finance themselves? We have seen that economic reasoning suggests federalism is a sensible system. Allowing local communities to make their own decisions very likely enhances efficiency in the provision of local public goods. However, efficiency and equity are also likely to require a significant economic role for a central government. In particular, a system in which only local resources are used to finance local public goods is viewed by many as inequitable.

While our focus has naturally been on economic issues, questions of power and politics are never far beneath the surface in discussions of federalism. The dispersion of economic power is generally associated with the dispersion of political power. How should power be allocated? Is your image of subfederal government a racist governor keeping black students out of the state university, or a town hall meeting in which citizens democratically make collective decisions? When you think of the central government, do you picture an uncaring and remote bureaucrat imposing bothersome regulations, or a justice department lawyer seeing to it that the civil rights of all citizens are maintained? The different images coexist in most of our minds, creating conflicting feelings about the proper distribution of governmental power.

SUMMARY

In a federal system, different governments provide different services to overlapping jurisdictions. The U.S. federal system includes the federal government, states, counties, townships, cities, school districts, and special districts.

One possible measure of the degree of centralized government power is the ratio of central government to total government direct expenditure—the centralization ratio. However, use of this ratio is fraught with potential error.

Disadvantages of decentralization are intercommunity externalities, foregone scale economies in the provision of local public goods, inefficient taxation, and loss of scale economies in tax collection.

Advantages of decentralization are the ability to alter the mix of public services to suit local tastes, the beneficial effects of competition between local governments, and the potential for low cost experimentation at the subfederal level.

The issue of why communities form may be analyzed using the club model. People unite to provide a level of local public goods at which the marginal cost per person is just offset by the per capita marginal benefit of the public good. Simultaneously, individuals are permitted to enter the group until the marginal savings in cost per person are offset by the increased congestion. The club model indicates that community size and quantity of public goods will depend upon: tastes for public goods, costs of providing public services, and the costs of crowding.

The Tiebout model emphasizes the key roles of mobility, property tax finance, and zoning rules in local public finance. Under certain conditions, "voting with the feet"—moving to one's preferred community—will result in a Pareto efficient allocation of public goods.

The requirements necessary for Pareto efficiency are unlikely to be met exactly, but various empirical studies indicate that Tiebout-like sorting does occur to some extent.

Interjurisdictional mobility has been isolated as a factor in the urban crisis because high income households leave urban areas to avoid income redistribution. One solution is to unify the tax base of metropolitan areas, but this is not popular and its efficacy is unclear. Another solution is use of intergovernmental grants.

Intergovernmental grants have become more important over time. One explanation is that demand for public services rises most rapidly at the local level, while revenues rise most rapidly at the federal level. Grants "correct" this mismatch.

Grants may be either conditional (categorical) or unconditional (lump sum). Conditional grants may be open-ended matching, closed-ended matching, or nonmatching. Each type of grant embodies different incentives for local governments. In all cases, the final mix of increased expenditure versus lower local taxes depends upon the preferences dictating local choices.

An important issue is whose preferences dictate local fiscal decisions. If the median voter model is correct, increasing the median voter's income by a dollar and increasing an unconditional grant to the community by a dollar have the same effect upon public good expenditure. Empirical studies contradict this prediction, instead indicating a *flypaper effect*—an increase in grant money induces greater spending on public goods than does an equivalent increase in local income. Models which emphasize the importance of bureaucrats' preferences explain this phenomenon as the result of incomplete citizen information about budget constraints.

Grants are provided to communities partly on the basis of "need." Local tax effort—the ratio of tax revenues to tax capacity—is also taken into account. Unfortunately, conventional measures of tax effort may be a poor reflection of true community sacrifice.

Politics are an important factor in the design of intergovernmental grants. Congress favors the control inherent in conditional grants, but the New Federalism proposed by President Ronald Reagan favors a move to block grants which allow more local autonomy.

Judicial rulings are an important factor in local finance, especially school expenditure. However, judicial demands for equal school expenditures regardless of location may be undone either by legislative indifference or by the behavioral responses of the citizenry.

DISCUSSION QUESTIONS

1. For each of the following, decide whether the activity should be under the control of the federal, state, or local government, and explain why.
   a. Auto air-pollution control regulations.
   b. Fishing licenses for the Colorado River.
   c. Provision of weather satellites.
   d. Public refuse collection.

*2. Using the club model apparatus, indicate the effect on optimal community size when marginal costs of acquiring the facility increase with the size of the facility. (Hint: Does the change affect the AA schedule, the NN schedule, or both?)

3. Illustrate the following circumstances using community indifference curves and the local government budget constraint:
   a. An unconditional grant increases both the quantity of public goods purchased and local taxes.
   b. A matching grant leaves provision of the public good unchanged.
   c. A closed-ended matching grant has the same impact as a conditional nonmatching grant.
   d. A closed-ended matching grant leaves local taxes unchanged.

4. In 1982, Lew Lehrman ran for Governor of New York on a platform that advocated substantial cuts in state personal income taxes.
   a. If New York's personal income taxes were cut, how would this affect the number of people employed in New York State? Why? Would your answer differ if all other states cut taxes in the same manner?
   b. Would the cut in personal income taxes raise the personal saving rate? If so, does this ensure that capital formation in New York State would be enhanced?
   c. What would you expect the effect of the tax cut to be on New York State

---

* Difficult.

property values? Does your answer change if school expenditures are cut to offset the lost revenue?

SELECTED REFERENCES

Buchanan, James N. "An Economic Theory of Clubs." *Economica* 32 (February 1965), pp. 1–14.

Inman, Robert P., and Daniel L. Rubinfeld. "The Judicial Pursuit of Local Fiscal Equity." *Harvard Law Review* 92 (1979), pp. 1662–750.

Oates, Wallace E. *Fiscal Federalism.* New York: Harcourt Brace Jovanovich, 1972.

Tiebout, Charles. "A Pure Theory of Local Expenditures." *Journal of Political Economy* 64 (1956), pp. 416–24.

CHAPTER 20

Some International Issues

Just as there is no uncomplicated personal relationship between individuals, so, I think, there is no international relationship between sovereign states which is without its elements of antagonism, its competitive aspects.

George F. Kennan

Thus far, this book's focus has been on public finance in a *national* context. Things can just as well be viewed from a *world* perspective. At a purely formal level, this change introduces no major difficulties. We begin by specifying a social welfare function that includes the utilities of everyone on earth. The problem is then to determine whether the operation of the world economy is likely to result in attaining a maximum of this function subject to technological constraints. A familiar set of potential difficulties emerges.

Public Goods. Some individuals or governments provide goods (or "bads") that are public from a world point of view. Investment in agricultural research is an example.

Externalities. One country's citizens can influence the welfare of citizens in another country through channels that are external to the international market. For instance, manufacturing in the United States creates pollution which falls on Canada as acid rain.

Monopoly. A country or group of countries may have enough market power to raise the price of some commodity above the competitive level. In recent years, the most prominent example has been the Organization of Petroleum Exporting Countries (OPEC).

Income Distribution.   The worldwide distribution of income is extremely unequal. In 1981, per capita gross national product in wealthy countries like the United States and Denmark was in the $13,000 range. In comparison, Zaire's figure was $210, and Chad's was $110 [World Bank, 1983, pp. 148–49].[1] Using an egalitarian world social welfare function, the status quo would be unacceptable on equity grounds, even if the world economy were perfectly efficient.

Our earlier analysis suggests that under certain circumstances government can help to remedy such problems. The obvious question is: "*What* government?" Clearly, no worldwide government exists, so there is no authority to take on the taxation and expenditure programs that might be appropriate. To be sure, organizations like the United Nations and the International Monetary Fund play some role in this context. But the inability of such bodies to coerce funds from their members severely limits their efficacy. At the moment, despite a great number of social science papers on "the new international economic order," the prospects for the emergence of an effective worldwide system of public finance are unpromising.[2] As a result, not much research has been devoted to the establishment of global tax and expenditure systems.

However, considerable attention has been focused on the interaction of national tax systems. People who do business in foreign countries may very well find their incomes and the products they sell subject to taxation in more than one nation. Given the huge volume of world trade (about $2 trillion by 1981) [U.S. Bureau of the Census, 1982, p. 880] and its importance to the U.S. economy (exports were about $350 billion in 1982) [*Economic Report of the President*, 1983, p. 163], the equity and efficiency aspects of alternative tax treatments of international transactions are of considerable interest. This chapter deals with both international income and commodity taxation.

TAXATION OF FOREIGN SOURCE INCOME

We begin with problems surrounding the taxation of individuals who earn income in foreign countries, and then turn to corporations.

Individuals

U.S. Provisions.   Income earned by an individual outside his or her nation of citizenship is potentially of interest to the tax authorities of the citizen's home and host governments. U.S. law recognizes the principle

---

[1] These figures give a false sense of precision. National income estimates in less developed countries are notoriously unreliable, and international comparisons of standards of living are always difficult. There is no doubt, however, that the disparities between rich and poor countries are enormous.

[2] See Doyle [1983] for a survey.

that the host country has the primary right to tax income earned within its borders. At the same time, the United States adheres to the notion that an American citizen, wherever he or she earns money, has a tax obligation to the native land. To avoid double taxation of foreign source income, the United States taxes income earned abroad, but allows a credit for tax paid to foreign governments.[3] Suppose that Smith's U.S. tax liability on her income earned in Germany is $7,000, and she has paid $5,500 in German income taxes. Then $5,500 can be taken as a credit on Smith's U.S. tax return, so that she need pay only $1,500 to the Internal Revenue Service. A U.S. citizen's total tax liability, then, is based upon *global* income.

Prior to 1981, under certain conditions, citizens residing abroad were allowed to deduct excess costs created by foreign residence. The rationalization is the usual one—business costs should be excluded from taxable income. The tax law passed in 1981 went a step further. To encourage U.S. citizens to work abroad, it introduced an outright exclusion of some portion of foreign earned income. The amounts involved are quite substantial—after 1985, a qualified individual is entitled to an annual exclusion of $95,000.[4] In addition to the exclusion, certain foreign housing expenses are also deductible.

Global versus Territorial Systems.[5]   The philosophical premise of the U.S. system is that equity in taxation is defined on a citizenship basis. If you are a U.S. citizen, the total amount of tax you pay should be roughly independent of whether you earn your income at home or abroad. We will refer to this as a **global system.** In contrast, virtually every other country adheres to a **territorial system**—a citizen earning income abroad need pay tax only to the host government. The only other country on the U.S. system is the Philippines [See Bhagwati, 1982, p. 286]. Which system is better? It is hard to build a case for the superiority of one system over the other on either equity or efficiency grounds. The points below expand on the problem.

Equity.   John, a citizen of the United Kingdom, and Sam, a U.S. citizen, both work in Hong Kong and have identical incomes. Because the United Kingdom has a territorial system, John pays tax only to Hong Kong. Sam, on the other hand, also owes money to the United States (provided that his U.S. tax bill is higher than his Hong Kong tax payment). Thus, Sam pays more tax than John, even though they have the

---

[3] The credit cannot exceed what the U.S. tax on the foreign income would have been.

[4] An individual qualifies for the exclusion if he or she is a foreign resident for at least an entire taxable year, or is physically present in the country at least 330 days out of a period of 12 months in a row. See *The Economic Recovery Tax Act of 1981—A Summary and Analysis* [1981, pp. 18–19] for further details.

[5] Much of this discussion is based on Bhagwati [1982, pp. 286–87].

same income. Although a global system produces equal treatment for citizens of the same country, it can lead to substantially different treatments for citizens of different countries. Should horizontal equity be defined on a national or world basis? Each principle has some merit, but in general, no system of international tax coordination can satisfy both.

Efficiency. The global system may distort international production decisions. Suppose that American firms operating abroad have to pay the U.S. income tax for their American employees. French firms, which operate under the territorial system, have no analogous obligation. Other things being the same, then, the U.S. companies may end up paying more for their labor, and hence be at a cost disadvantage.[6] French firms could conceivably win more contracts than the American firms, even if the latter are more technologically efficient.

On the other hand, a territorial system can produce a different kind of distortion—in people's locational decisions. Citizens of a given country may find their decision to work abroad influenced by the fact that their tax liability depends upon where they live. Under a global regime, you cannot escape your country's tax collector unless you change citizenship. Hence, there is less incentive to relocate just for tax purposes.

Thus, the global system may distort production decisions, and the territorial system residential decisions. It is hard to know which kind of distortion creates a larger efficiency cost.

Relation to the "Brain Drain."   In the United States, the tax treatment of personal foreign source income has not been a prominent issue in public policy debates. Concerns that the foreign income exclusion is too big or too little are periodically expressed, but the issue does not occupy an important place on most tax reform agendas. In contrast, the problem occupies center stage in many less developed countries. It arises in discussions of the **brain drain,** the emigration of highly skilled citizens of these nations to more developed countries.

Because the less developed countries (like practically all other countries) use the territorial system, once a citizen of such a nation leaves his or her country, the country has no claim on the citizen's earnings. Some argue that less developed countries should tax the incomes of their citizens who are successful abroad. Doing so might discourage some of the society's more productive members from leaving. And the taxes collected from those who still chose to emigrate could be used to help benefit those left behind. The basic justification is that "one should

---

[6] This assumes that: (*a*) the incidence of the U.S. tax falls on employers rather than employees, and (*b*) American companies cannot respond simply by hiring French workers. The validity of assumption (*a*) depends on the elasticity of supply of U.S. workers to U.S. firms abroad. To the extent the supply curve is not horizontal, employees will bear part of the tax. See Chapter 11.

reject . . . citizenship without the obligation to pay the income tax"
[Bhagwati, 1982, p. 285].

The idea of taxing citizens employed abroad raises a number of difficult philosophical questions. What relationship is there between social
responsibilities and place of birth? Why should an Indian practicing
medicine in Chicago owe more to India than an American practicing
medicine in Chicago? Does the answer hinge on the amount of Indian
resources that were devoted to the Indian's education? Should a citizen
who wishes to leave a country be required to pay back the money that
the country has invested in him? What is the trade-off between the
personal freedom to move and social responsibility?

Let us assume that the government of a less developed country has
somehow worked its way through these questions and come to the
conclusion that taxing emigrants on their foreign earnings is justifiable.
Assume further that it is administratively feasible for that country to
collect the tax. The country must then reformulate its optimal income tax
schedule in light of this new opportunity. As noted in Chapter 13, the
determination of an optimal income tax requires the specification of a
social welfare function. Here a knotty question arises: Should the utilities of the emigrants be included? On one hand, the emigrants are still
citizens, and their utilities should therefore be given weight. On the
other hand, they have "abandoned ship," and therefore severed their
relationship to the community. There is no obvious solution, but our
discussion here follows Bhagwati and Hamada [1982], who assume that
the less developed country's social welfare depends only on the utilities
of those left behind after emigration.[7]

In the standard optimal income tax problem, higher tax rates allow
more income redistribution, but they lower economic efficiency. The
idea is to find the tax schedule associated with just the right combination
of efficiency and equity. Here, the basic setup is the same, but for a
country on the territorial system, "efficiency" must include not only
distortions in work decisions, but losses to the nation when highly productive people emigrate to escape taxation.

Bhagwati and Hamada [1982] showed that under reasonable conditions, the opportunity to tax emigrants raises the optimal tax rate. Allowing the taxation of emigrants puts more resources at the less developed country's disposal, so that it can pursue a more redistributive
policy than would otherwise have been possible. Alternatively, the ability to tax emigrants makes the effective labor supply in the home country more inelastic, because workers cannot escape tax by moving

---

[7] This assumption introduces a technical complication because the number of those left
behind in general depends upon the tax policy chosen. Bhagwati and Hamada solved this
problem by assuming that social welfare depends only upon the utilities of individuals
who would stay behind under any feasible tax regime.

abroad. As shown in Chapter 13, the more inelastic the supply of labor, the higher the optimal marginal tax rate, other things being the same.

We observed at the outset that the entire argument rests on the assumption that it is administratively feasible to tax emigrants. The problem of enforcing tax compliance is never easy (see Chapter 13), and it is harder when the taxpayers are abroad. Even if an effective method were somehow devised, some emigrants might respond by changing their citizenship. The possibility that a country may create a class of "tax exiles" needs to be taken into account when it sets policy.

Corporate Income

U.S. Provisions.   U.S. tax treatment of foreign source corporate income is similar to treatment of individuals. U.S. multinational corporations are subject to tax at the standard rate on total taxable income, including income earned abroad. A credit is then allowed for foreign taxes paid. The credit cannot exceed the amount that would have been owed under U.S. tax law. However, a number of considerations complicate the taxation of foreign source corporate income.

Subsidiary Status.   Taxation of the income from a foreign enterprise can be deferred if the operation is a **subsidiary**. (A foreign subsidiary is a company owned by a U.S. corporation but incorporated abroad, and hence, a separate corporation from a legal point of view.) Profits earned by a subsidiary are included only if returned **(repatriated)** to the parent company as dividends. Thus, for as long as the subsidiary exists, earnings retained abroad can be kept out of reach of the U.S. tax system. Frisch [1981, p. 7] estimated that in 1972, if deferral had not been allowed, taxable foreign source income of U.S. firms would have increased by 56 percent. It is hard to say how much tax revenue was lost because of deferral. Given the credit system, the answer depends upon the tax rate levied abroad. If all foreign countries had tax rates greater than that of the United States, no additional tax revenue would have been gained by this country. However, to the extent that a foreign country taxes corporate income less heavily than does the United States, deferral makes the country attractive to U.S. firms as a "tax haven."[8]

Income Allocation.   It is often difficult to know how much of a multinational firm's total income to allocate to its operations in a given country. The procedure now used for allocating income between domestic and

---

[8] A few countries such as the Dutch Antilles have intentionally structured their laws to allow U.S. firms to abuse the tax system. There are some provisions to limit the tax savings from these true tax havens, but they have not had much impact.

foreign operations is the **arm's length system.** Essentially the domestic and foreign operations are treated as separate enterprises doing business independently ("at arm's length"). The taxable profits of each entity are computed as its own sales minus its own costs.

The problem is that certain factors of production are like public goods from the firm's point of view.[9] Suppose, for example, that all research and development (R&D) is done at the firm's head office. The results of R&D are available to all the company's operations and hence serve as an "input" for all of them. But under a strict application of the arm's length system, the operation at headquarters deducts all of the R&D expenditures.

This procedure does not make sense, but it is not at all clear how the R&D expenditures should be allocated across operations. For practical purposes, some fairly arbitrary rules have been devised. According to Internal Revenue Service regulations issued in 1977, certain head office charges can be allocated among operations using a formula based on the sales and assets of each operation. Essentially, the greater a given operation's share of total company assets and sales, the greater the proportion of company public goods it can deduct. This is known as the **shares allocation** approach.

A potential problem arises if different governments have different rules for allocating incomes between home and foreign operations. International tax treaties usually indicate that countries will try to coordinate their rules.

Royalties. Multinational oil companies have presented U.S. tax makers with a special set of problems. These stem from the fact that in many countries, the host governments are essentially the owners of the oil. Formerly, these governments charged the multinationals royalty fees for exploiting their oil.

The problem from the oil companies' point of view was that unlike foreign tax payments, which are a tax *credit*, royalties are allowed only as a tax *deduction*. As we saw in Chapter 14, a deduction of a given amount is worth less to a taxpayer than a credit of the same size. At the request of the oil companies, many of the host countries simply declared that their royalty fees were now income taxes. Some of these "taxes" are levied at rates well above the U.S. level. In addition, they often exceed the host country's tax rate on other corporate activities. Operating on the premise that such tax payments are a sham, over the years Congress has developed a very complicated set of rules for the taxation of oil income. The rules substantially reduce the advantages of treating royalties as taxes.

---

[9] Of course, all the standard problems that arise in computing domestic corporate taxable income are still present. See Chapter 16.

Discussion.   An evaluation of the U.S. tax treatment of multinational firms requires a careful statement of the policy goal. One possible objective is to maximize worldwide income, another is to maximize national income.

Maximization of World Income.   The maximization of world income requires that the before-tax rate of return on the last dollar invested in each country—the marginal rate of return—be the same.[10] To see why this is true, imagine a situation in which marginal returns are not equal. Then it would be possible to increase world income simply by taking capital from a country where its marginal return was low and moving it to one where the marginal return was high.[11] Algebraically, if $i_{U.S.}$ is the marginal rate of return in the U.S. and i_f is the marginal rate of return in a given foreign country, then worldwide efficiency requires

(20.1) $$i_f = i_{U.S.}$$

What kind of tax system will induce profit-maximizing firms to allocate their capital so that the outcome is consistent with Equation (20.1)? The answer hinges on the fact that investors make their decisions on the basis of *after*-tax returns. They therefore allocate their capital across countries so that the after-tax marginal return in each country is equal. If $t_{U.S.}$ is the U.S. tax rate and t_f is the foreign tax rate, then a firm allocates its capital so that

(20.2) $$(1 - t_f)i_f = (1 - t_{U.S.})i_{U.S.}$$

Clearly, condition (20.1) is satisfied if and only if t_f equals $t_{U.S.}$. Intuitively, if we want capital allocated efficiently from a global point of view, capital must be taxed at the same rate wherever it is located.

The policy implication seems to be that if the United States cares about maximizing world income, it should devise a system that makes its firms' tax liabilities independent of their location. A *full* credit against foreign taxes paid (with no deferral) would do the trick. However, as noted above, the U.S. system allows a tax credit *only* up to the amount that U.S. tax on the foreign earnings would have been.

Why is the credit limit present? Our model implicitly assumes that the behavior of foreign governments is independent of U.S. government actions. Suppose that the United States announces it will pursue a policy of allowing a full foreign tax credit to its multinational firms. Then foreign governments have an incentive to raise their own tax rates on U.S. corporations virtually without limit. Doing so will not drive out the foreign countries' American firms, because the tax liability for their do-

---

[10] As usual, we refer here to rates of return after differences in risk are taken into account.

[11] For further discussion of this principle, see the appendix at the end of the book.

mestic operations is reduced by a dollar for every dollar foreign taxes are increased.[12] Essentially, the program turns into a transfer from the United States to foreign treasuries. Limiting the credit is an obvious way to prevent this from happening.

Maximization of National Income.   At the outset, we noted the importance of defining the objectives of tax policy on foreign source corporate income. Some have argued that tax policy should be set so as to maximize not world income, but national income.[13] Some care must be taken in defining national income here. It is the sum of *before*-tax domestically produced income and foreign source income *after* foreign taxes are paid. This is because taxes paid by U.S. firms to the U.S. government, although not available to the firms themselves, are still part of U.S. income. Thus, domestic income is counted before tax. However, taxes paid to foreign governments are not available to U.S. citizens, so foreign income is counted after tax.

National income maximization requires a different condition than that shown in Equation (20.1). The difference arises because marginal rates of return must now be measured from the U.S. point of view. According to the U.S. perspective, the marginal rate of return abroad is $(1 - t_f)i_f$—foreign taxes represent a cost from the U.S. point of view and hence are excluded in valuing the rate of return. The marginal return on investments in the United States is measured at the before-tax rate, $i_{U.S.}$. Hence, maximization of national income requires

(20.3) $(1 - t_f)i_f = i_{U.S.}$

A comparison with Equation (20.1) suggests that under a regime of world income maximization, investments are made abroad until $i_f = i_{U.S.}$, while if national income maximization is the goal, foreign investment is made until $i_f = i_{U.S.}/(1 - t_f)$. In words, if national income maximization is the goal, the before-tax marginal rate of return on foreign investment is higher than it would be if global income maximization were the goal. [As long as t_f is less than one, $i_{U.S.} < i_{U.S.}/(1 - t_f)$.] But under the reasonable assumption that the marginal return to investment decreases with the amount of investment, a higher before-tax rate of

---

[12] The amount the foreign government can extract in this way is limited to the firm's tax liability to the United States on its domestic operations. Suppose that the firm's tax liability on its U.S. operations is $1,000. If the foreign government levies a tax of $1,000, under a full credit, the firm's U.S. tax liability is zero. If the foreign government raises the tax to $1,001, the firm's domestic tax liability cannot be reduced any further (assuming that there is no negative income tax for corporations).

[13] In terms of our normative framework, this view implies that only the utilities of U.S. citizens appear in the relevant social welfare function. The conflict between a "world" and a "national" point of view is analogous to the clash of "national" and "community" perspectives that arises in federal systems. (See Chapter 19.)

return means less investment. In short, from a national point of view, world income maximization results in "too much" investment abroad.

What kind of tax system will induce American firms to allocate their capital so that Equation (20.3) is satisfied? Suppose that multinational firms are allowed to *deduct* foreign tax payments from their U.S. taxable income. Given that foreign tax payments are deductible, a firm's overseas return of i_f increases its taxable U.S. income by $i_f(1 - t_f)$. Therefore, after U.S. taxes, the return on the foreign investment is $t_f(1 - t_f)(1 - t_{U.S.})$. At the same time, the after-tax return on investments in the United States is $i_{U.S.}(1 - t_{U.S.})$. Assuming that the investors equalize after-tax marginal returns at home and abroad,

(20.4) $$i_f(1 - t_f)(1 - t_{U.S.}) = i_{U.S.}(1 - t_{U.S.})$$

Clearly, Equations (20.4) and (20.3) are equivalent. [Just divide both sides of 20.4) by $(1 - t_{U.S.})$.] Because Equation (20.3) is the condition for national income maximization, this implies that deduction of foreign tax payments leads to a pattern of investment that maximizes U.S. income.

Such reasoning has lead to some political support for replacing credits for foreign taxes paid with deductions. One important problem with the case for deductions is the analysis assumes that the capital-exporting country can impose the tax rate which maximizes its income, while the capital-importing foreign countries passively keep their own tax rates constant. Feldstein and Hartman [1977] analyzed a model in which the capital-exporting country takes into account the possibility that changes in its tax rate may induce changes in the host countries' tax rates. Suppose, for example, that if the United States lowers its tax rate on capital invested abroad, host governments will do the same. In this case, it may be worthwhile for the United States to preferentially tax income earned abroad. Of course, it is also possible that host governments will choose to raise their tax rates when the U.S. rate goes down. The point is that when interdependent behavior is allowed, the national income-maximizing tax system will generally not consist of a simple deduction for foreign taxes paid. The effective tax rate on foreign-source income can be either larger or smaller than that associated with deductibility.

Finally, we should note that our whole discussion of the treatment of foreign-source corporate income has assumed that the United States exports capital to the rest of the world. Hartman [1982, p. 1] points out that this may no longer be a very good description of reality. In 1979, net direct investment by foreigners in their U.S. affiliates was $11.9 billion, or about 15 percent of net plant and equipment expenditures in the United States. This fact requires a rethinking of certain domestic tax-policy issues. For example, discussions of domestic tax incentives for investment usually ignore the foreign sector. However, policymakers will underestimate the stimulating effects of such incentives if they fail to account for the fact that the policies may increase the amount of investment at home at the expense of investment abroad. On the other hand, tax policies to encourage *saving* by lowering the tax rate on capital income could lead to less domestic *investment* than one might guess, if part of the increased saving is used to finance investment abroad.

As noted in Chapters 15 and 16, econometric evidence concerning the effects of tax policy on saving and investment is far from clear. Taking into account international considerations complicates the picture further, and there is not much quantitative evidence concerning the importance of such considerations.[14]

COMMODITY TAXES

We now turn from the problems of taxing income to those surrounding commodities. To understand the effects of various taxes levied on internationally traded goods, we require some understanding of why international trade occurs in the first place. By definition, in the absence of trade, each country has to produce all the goods and services that it consumes. Even if Norway's climate is not very well suited for growing grapes, it would have to do so if Norwegians wanted to drink wine. According to the **theory of comparative advantage,** each country specializes in that good which it produces with the greatest relative efficiency and trades with the rest of the world to obtain other commodities. Trade allows each country to specialize in doing what it does best, and hence allows everyone to be better off.[15]

Countries do not completely specialize. Even if the United States has a comparative advantage in the production of food, we do not expect it to produce only food and nothing else. If the United States specialized completely in food production, presumably every bit of land in production would be devoted to agriculture, but not all of the land is well suited for this purpose, and the cost of food produced on ill-suited land would be quite high. At some point, the cost would become so high that it would be cheaper to obtain food abroad. Thus, a comparative advantage in the production of a commodity does not necessarily extend to all levels of output. It is quite possible, therefore, that a country will simultaneously domestically produce and import some commodities.

We now consider how various kinds of taxes can distort the pattern of trade away from that associated with comparative advantage. To do so, we consider a simple model in which there are only two commodities, computers and shoes, produced by a single factor, labor. The United States has a comparative advantage in computers, which it exports. It imports shoes, although some shoes are produced at home. Assume

---

[14] For some preliminary econometric work along these lines, see Hartman [1982].

[15] The theory of comparative advantage is described in more detail in Caves and Jones [1981].

also that the United States is a *price taker* on the world market, i.e., U.S. production and consumption of these commodities is sufficiently small that the nation cannot affect world prices. For simplicity, we also assume that the costs of transporting goods are negligible.

Tariffs

A **tariff** is an excise tax levied on imported goods. As is true with any commodity tax, one reason for levying a tariff is to raise revenue. In the early years of the United States, tariffs were the single most important source of federal government revenue. As late as 1902, they accounted for 37 percent of federal revenues.[16] Tariffs are no longer major money raisers. In 1983, they accounted for only about 1.5 percent of federal tax revenues.[17] Today, in most developed countries the main reason for tariffs is protection.[18] As an example, if a tariff on imported shoes is imposed, it obviously puts foreign producers at a disadvantage in the U.S. market. Consequently, more shoes are produced in the United States and fewer abroad than is consistent with efficiency. Although U.S. shoe producers are better off, American consumers are worse off because of the higher shoe prices they have to pay. On the basis of such reasoning, most economists regard protective tariffs as undesirable.[19]

Origin and Destination Taxes

We now turn to taxes on traded goods that do not involve discrimination on the basis of whether the goods are imported. It is customary to distinguish between taxes levied in the country in which the goods are consumed (the **destination principle**), and taxes levied on goods in the country in which they are produced (the **origin principle**). A tax on all shoes consumed in the United States, regardless of whether they are domestic or imported, satisfies the destination principle. A tax on all computers produced in the United States, regardless of where they are eventually consumed, satisfies the origin principle.

Our discussion of the two principles will continue to make use of the assumption that the United States is a price taker in world markets. However, the important results are true in the case in which U.S. production is large enough to influence world prices. In addition, we make

---

[16] Calculated from U.S. Bureau of the Census [1975, p. 1122].

[17] Calculated from *Facts and Figures on Government Finance* [1983, p. 129].

[18] In poorer countries tariffs are more important as revenue raisers because tariffs are relatively cheap to administer.

[19] A number of defenses for protective tariffs have been attempted, but few of them stand careful scrutiny. See Baumol and Blinder [1982, pp. 716–27] for a discussion. As usual, in the presence of other distortions, the claim that protective tariffs are undesirable may have to be modified.

the simplifying assumption that the supply of labor is fixed, so that there is no need to consider inefficiencies that arise when taxes distort leisure/income choices.

Destination Taxes. Suppose that the world price of computers is P_c, and the world price of shoes is P_s. Producers in the United States make their decisions about how many shoes and computers to produce on the basis of the price ratio, P_c/P_s. Specifically, the production decision is characterized by the condition that the marginal rate of transformation between computers and shoes equals P_c/P_s. Similarly, consumers decide how much to buy by setting P_c/P_s equal to their marginal rates of substitution.[20]

Suppose that the United States levies a tax of t_s on each shoe purchased within its borders. Given that the United States is a price taker on the world market, the price received by foreign producers cannot fall as a result of the tax. If the price were to fall below P_s, foreign producers would simply sell elsewhere. Similarly, if U.S. producers cannot get P_s in their home market, they will sell their output abroad. If the price received by producers has to remain at P_s, then the price paid by consumers must rise by the exact amount of the tax. Hence, as a consequence of the tax, the price ratio faced by American consumers becomes $P_c/(P_s + t_s)$.[21] The price ratio facing producers remains P_c/P_s.

On the basis of this analysis, we make two observations on the efficiency effects of a destination tax: (1) The tax distorts the relative prices facing consumers, and hence creates an excess burden for them. (2) However, production decisions are unchanged because the relative prices facing producers are unchanged. Unlike tariffs, then, destination taxes do not distort the international pattern of production.[22]

Origin Taxes. Now suppose that the United States levies a tax on all computers produced within its borders, whether they are eventually consumed domestically or abroad. Under our assumptions, the price paid by consumers of American computers cannot rise. If the price were to go above P_c, consumers would simply purchase foreign brands. If the price paid by consumers does not rise, then the price received by American producers must fall by exactly the amount of the tax. If the tax is t_c per computer, then the price ratio facing producers becomes $(P_c - t_c)/P_s$.

---

[20] These results are discussed in the Appendix to the book.

[21] The fact that the United States is a price taker means that the supply of shoes to the United States is perfectly elastic at the world price. Thus, this analysis is consistent with the result from Chapter 11: the incidence of a tax on a commodity that is perfectly elastic in supply falls entirely on consumers.

[22] If a destination tax is levied at the same ad valorem rate on all commodities, it does not create an excess burden even on the consumption side. In this case, the prices of both goods increase by the same proportion, so their ratio is unchanged. Note that this argument depends crucially on the assumption that labor is totally fixed in supply. (See Chapter 12.)

American producers now set their marginal rates of transformation equal to $(P_c - t_c)/P_s$ instead of P_c/P_s. Because producers face distorted prices, they no longer produce the "right" combination of commodities. Intuitively, the tax on computers produced in America induces firms to produce a smaller number of computers than is consistent with America's comparative advantage. We conclude that an origin tax levied on a particular commodity distorts the pattern of international production.

Under certain conditions, it may be possible for the United States to undo the distorting effects of the tax on computers if it rebates the tax on exports of computers. The notion that export rebates of production taxes can enhance efficiency has been built into the **General Agreement on Tariffs and Trade (GATT),** which regulates international trade practices.[23] According to GATT, a country can grant an export rebate equal to the value of taxes that are included in the costs of production.

A major implementational problem is deciding just which taxes enter the costs of production and are therefore eligible for rebate. For example, according to GATT rules, the corporation tax is borne by profits. Therefore, it is not a cost of production and does not qualify for a rebate. In essence, the GATT rule decrees an answer to the question of the incidence of the corporation tax. Unfortunately, there is no reason to believe that GATT's answer is necessarily correct. (See Chapter 16.) If in fact, the corporation tax is included in the price of goods produced in the corporate sector, then in some sense American producers do not receive the rebate to which they are "entitled." On the other hand, to the extent that accelerated depreciation and investment tax credits lower the price of goods produced by the corporate sector, Americans receive an "advantage" compared to foreign producers, *ceteris paribus*. It is no wonder that GATT's rules concerning rebates have been a source of some friction among trading partners.

In principle, the framework provided by optimal tax theory provides a better way for determining rebates. With information on the shapes of supply and demand schedules and data on preexisting taxes, we could calculate the set of rebates that maximize world income. Although the problem is simple to pose, it would be very difficult to solve. The GATT procedures, though somewhat arbitrary, may provide a satisfactory practical solution.

CONCLUSION

At a purely theoretical level, it is easy to extend the welfare economics framework to an international setting. Just make social welfare a function of everyone in the world's utilities and determine what policies are required to maximize social welfare. It is not clear how useful this ap-

---

[23] GATT was introduced after World War II. Under the agreement, the approximately 100 member countries agree to meet periodically to negotiate on various trade issues.

proach is. First of all, there is no world government. Second, the problems involved in democratically adopting a social welfare function—difficult enough within a single nation—are virtually intractable in a worldwide context.

Nevertheless, the standard tools do provide insight into the practical problems that arise in coordinating the tax systems of various nations. In particular, the analysis shows clearly how the goals being pursued by a country will determine its optimal policies with respect to the international tax treatment of income and commodities. As the volume of international trade increases, these issues become ever more important.

SUMMARY

Most research in international public finance focuses on the interaction of national systems for taxing personal incomes, corporate incomes, and commodities.

Tax treatment of personal income may follow either a global or territorial system. Under a global system, the total tax due is independent of where it is earned. The United States roughly follows a global system by allowing tax credits for foreign income taxes paid. Under a territorial system, taxes are paid to the country in which the income is earned and total taxes depend upon the geographical distribution of earnings.

Neither the global nor the territorial system is obviously superior. A global system allows horizontal inequities between citizens of different countries, while a territorial system results in disparities between citizens of the same country. Similarly, the global system may distort world production decisions, but a territorial system may distort labor location decisions.

A prominent issue in less developed countries has been the relation between tax treatment of foreign personal income and the "brain drain." The opportunity to tax emigrants raises a country's optimal marginal tax rate because labor is less able to "escape" the tax.

In principle, U.S. taxation of corporate income earned outside the country is quite similar to taxation of personal income in that tax credits are permitted for taxes paid to foreign governments. However, complications arise due to tax deferral using foreign subsidiaries, allocation of net income to countries in which a multinational firm operates, and the correct treatment of royalties paid by oil companies.

Evaluation of U.S. tax treatment of corporate income earned abroad hinges on the assumed policy goal. Maximization of world income requires that U.S. and foreign effective tax rates be identical. National income maximization requires equating the foreign after-tax rate of return with the before-tax domestic rate of return.

In an international framework, commodity taxes may take the form of tariffs, origin taxes, or destination taxes. Tariffs are levied on imports, origin taxes on goods in the country of production, and destination taxes on goods in the country of consumption.

Tariffs were once a major source of revenue for the United States; however, they are presently used primarily to protect particular domestic producers. While tariffs help some producers, they are a burden to consumers and are generally deemed undesirable by economists.

Destination taxes distort relative prices facing consumers but leave production decisions unaffected. Origin taxes do the reverse.

DISCUSSION QUESTIONS

1. Under what circumstances would global and territorial tax treatment of personal income have identical effects on economic efficiency?

2. "A U.S. tax on pure economic profits does not affect the international allocation of resources." Comment.

3. "Origin taxes are preferable to destination taxes because they are less regressive." Comment, taking advantage of the theory of tax incidence.

SELECTED REFERENCES

Bhagwati, Jagdish N. "Introduction." *Journal of Public Economics* 18, no. 3 (August 1982), pp. 285–90.

Feldstein, Martin S., and David Hartman. *The Optimal Taxation of Foreign Source Investment Income.* Harvard Institute of Economic Research, Discussion Paper no. 563 (Cambridge, Mass., July 1977).

APPENDIX

Some Basic Microeconomics

He who has choice also has pain.
German Proverb

Certain tools of microeconomic theory are used throughout the text. They are briefly reviewed in this appendix. Readers who have had an introductory course in microeconomics will likely find this review sufficient to refresh their memories. Those who are confronting the material for the first time will find it worthwhile to consult one of the standard introductory texts.[1]

The subjects covered are demand and supply, consumer choice, marginal analysis, and production decisions.

DEMAND AND SUPPLY

The demand and supply model shows how the price and output of a commodity are determined in a competitive market. We discuss in turn the determinants of demand, supply, and their interaction.

---

[1] See Baumol and Blinder [1982] or Samuelson [1980].

Demand

What factors influence people's decisions to consume a certain good? To make the problem concrete, let us consider the specific case of coffee. A bit of introspection suggests that the following factors affect the amount of coffee that people want to consume during a given period of time:[2]

Price.   We expect that as the price goes up, the quantity demanded goes down.

Income.   Changes in income modify people's consumption opportunities. It is hard to say a priori, however, what effect such changes will have upon consumption of a given good. One possibility is that as incomes go up, people use some of their additional income to purchase more coffee. On the other hand, it may be that as incomes increase, people consume less coffee, perhaps spending their money on cognac instead. We expect that changes in income will affect demand one way or the other, but in some cases it is hard to say what the direction of the change will be. If an increase in income increases the demand (other things being the same), the good is called a **normal** good. If an increase in income decreases demand (other things being the same) the good is called an **inferior** good.

Prices of Related Goods.   Suppose the price of tea goes up. If people can substitute coffee for tea, this increase in the price of tea will increase the amount of coffee people wish to consume. Now suppose the price of cream goes up. If people tend to consume coffee and cream together, this would tend to decrease the amount of coffee consumed. Goods like tea and coffee are called **substitutes;** goods like coffee and cream are called **complements.**

Tastes.   The extent to which people "like" a good will affect the amount they demand. Presumably, less coffee is demanded in Mormon communities because that religion prohibits its consumption. Often, it is realistic to assume that consumers' tastes stay the same over time, but this is not always the case. For example, the announcement made by some scientists that coffee might cause birth defects presumably changed the tastes of pregnant women for coffee.

We see, then, that a wide variety of things can affect demand. However, it is often useful to focus on the relationship between the quantity of a commodity demanded and the price. Suppose that we fix income, the

---

[2] Depending on the good under consideration, other items could be added to the list.

prices of related goods, and tastes. We can imagine varying the price of coffee and seeing how the quantity demanded changes under the assumption that the other relevant variables stay at their fixed values. A **demand schedule** (or **demand curve**) is the relation between the market price of a good and the quantity demanded of that good during a given time period, other things being the same. (Economists often use the Latin for "other things being the same," *ceteris paribus.*)

A hypothetical demand schedule for coffee is represented graphically by line D_c in Figure A.1. The horizontal axis measures pounds of coffee

FIGURE A.1   A Hypothetical Demand Curve for Coffee

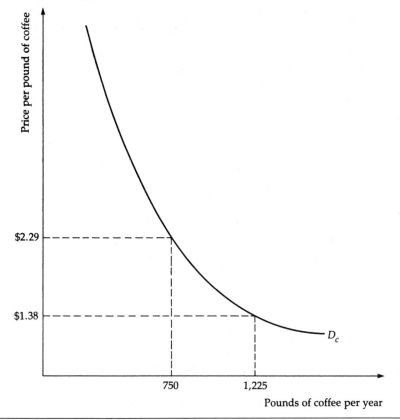

per year in a particular market, and the price per pound is measured on the vertical. Thus, for example, if the price is $2.29 per pound, people are willing to consume 750 pounds; when the price is only $1.38, they are willing to consume 1,225 pounds. The downward slope of the demand schedule reflects the reasonable assumption that when the price goes up, the quantity demanded goes down.

The demand curve can also be interpreted as an approximate schedule of "willingness to pay," because it shows the maximum price that people would pay for a given quantity. For example, when people purchase 750 pounds per year, they value it at $2.29 per pound. At any price **above $2.29, they would not willingly consume 750 pounds per year. If** for some reason people were able to obtain 750 pounds at a price below $2.29, this would in some sense be a "bargain."

As stressed above, the demand curve is drawn on the assumption that all other variables that might affect quantity demanded do not change. What happens if one of them does? Suppose, for example, that the price of tea increases, and as a consequence, people want to buy

FIGURE A.2   Effect of an Increase in the Price of Tea upon the Demand for Coffee

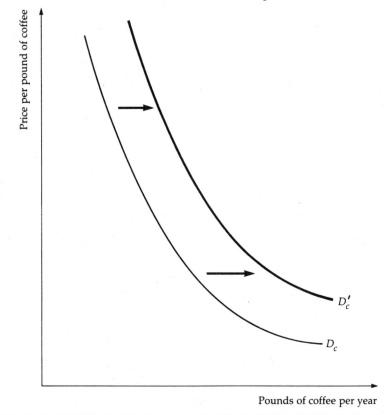

more coffee. In Figure A.2, schedule D_c from Figure A.1 (before the increase) is reproduced. As a consequence of the increase in the price of tea, at *each price* of coffee people are willing to purchase more coffee than they did previously. In effect, then, an increase in the price of tea shifts each point on D_c to the right. The collection of new points is D_c'. Because D_c' shows how much people are willing to consume at each price *(ceteris paribus)*, it is by definition the demand curve.

More generally, a change in any variable that influences the demand for a good—except its own price—shifts the demand curve.[3] (A change in a good's own price induces a movement *along* the demand curve.)

Supply

Now consider the factors that determine the quantity of a commodity that firms supply to the market. We will continue using coffee as our example.

Price.   In many cases, it is reasonable to assume that the higher the price per pound of coffee, the greater the quantity that profit-maximizing firms will be willing to supply.

Price of Inputs.   Coffee producers have to use inputs to produce coffee—labor, land, fertilizer, etc. If their input costs go up, the amount of coffee that they can profitably supply at any given price goes down.

Conditions of Production.   The most important factor here is the state of technology. If there is a technological improvement in coffee production, the supply increases. Other variables also affect production conditions. For agricultural goods, weather is important. Several years ago, for example, flooding in Latin America seriously reduced the coffee crop.

As with the demand curve, it is useful to focus attention on the relationship between the quantity of a commodity supplied and the price, holding the other variables at fixed levels. The **supply schedule** is the relation between market prices and the amount of a good that producers are willing to supply during a given period of time, *ceteris paribus*.

A supply schedule for coffee is depicted as S_c in Figure A.3. Its upward slope reflects the assumption that the higher the price, the greater the quantity supplied, *ceteris paribus*.

When any variable that influences supply (other than the commodity's own price) changes, the supply schedule shifts. Suppose, for example, that the wage rate for coffee-bean pickers increases. This increase reduces the amount of coffee that firms will be willing to supply at any given price. The supply curve therefore shifts to the left. As depicted in

---

[3] There is no need, incidentally, for D_c' to be parallel to D_c. In general, this will not be the case.

FIGURE A.3   Hypothetical Supply Curve for Coffee

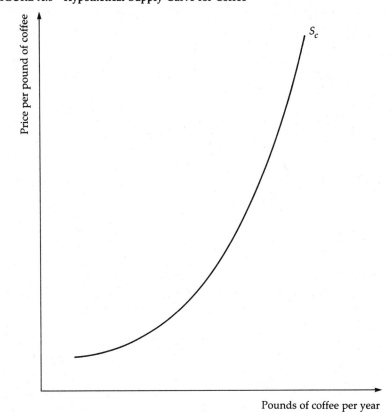

Figure A.4, the new supply curve is S'_c. More generally, when any variable other than the commodity's own price changes, the supply curve shifts. (A change in the commodity price induces a movement along the supply curve.)

Equilibrium

The demand and supply curves provide answers to a set of hypothetical questions: *If* the price of coffee is $2 per pound, how much will consumers be willing to purchase? *If* the price is $1.75 per pound, how much will firms be willing to supply? Neither schedule by itself tells us what will be the actual price and quantity. But taken together, the schedules determine price and quantity.

In Figure A.5 we superimpose demand schedule D_c from Figure A.1 on supply schedule S_c from Figure A.3. We want to find the price and

FIGURE A.4   Effect of an Increase in the Wages of Coffee Pickers upon the Supply of Coffee

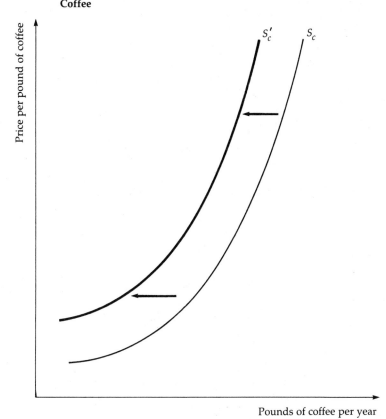

output at which there is an **equilibrium**—a situation which will tend to be maintained unless there is an underlying change in the system. Suppose the price is P_1 dollars per pound. At this price, the quantity demanded is Q_1^D and the quantity supplied is Q_1^S. Price P_1 cannot be maintained, because firms want to supply more coffee than consumers are willing to purchase. This excess supply tends to push the price down, as suggested by the arrows.

Now consider price P_2. At this price, the quantity of coffee demanded, Q_2^D, exceeds the quantity supplied, Q_2^S. Because there is excess demand for coffee, we expect the price to rise.

Similar reasoning suggests that any price at which the quantity supplied and quantity demanded are unequal cannot be an equilibrium. In Figure A.5, quantity demanded equals quantity supplied at price P_e. The associated output level is Q_e pounds per year. Unless something else in

FIGURE A.5   Equilibrium in the Coffee Market

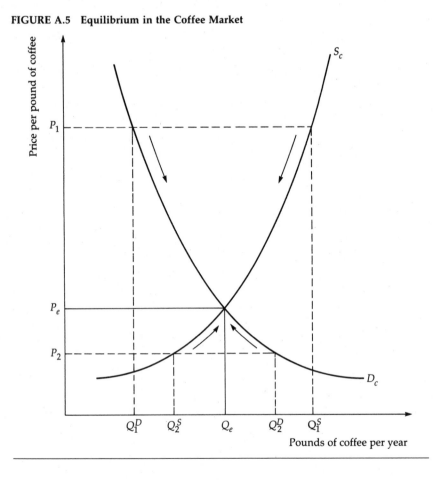

the system changes, this price and output combination will continue year after year. It is an equilibrium.

Suppose now that something else does change. For example, the weather turns bad so that a considerable portion of the coffee crop is ruined. In Figure A.6, D_c and S_c are reproduced from Figure A.5, and as before, the equilibrium price and output are P_e and Q_e, respectively. As a consequence of the weather change, the supply curve shifts to the left, say to S'_c. Given the new supply curve, P_e is no longer the equilibrium price. Rather, equilibrium is found at the intersection of D_c and S'_c, at price P'_e and output Q'_e. Note that, as one might expect, the crop disaster leads to a higher price and smaller output. (That is, $P'_e > P_e$ and $Q'_e < Q_e$.) More generally, a change in any variable that affects supply or demand creates a new equilibrium combination of price and quantity.

FIGURE A.6   Effect of Bad Weather on the Coffee Market

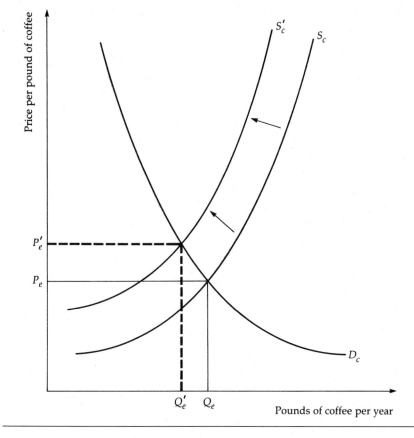

Supply and Demand for Inputs

Supply and demand can be used not only to investigate the markets for consumption goods, but also the markets for **inputs** into the production process. (Inputs are sometimes referred to as **factors of production.**) For example, we could label the horizontal axis in Figure A.5 "number of hours worked per year" and the vertical axis "wage rate per hour." Then the schedules would represent the supply and demand for labor, and the market would determine wages and employment. Similarly, supply and demand analysis can be applied to the markets for capital and for land.

Measuring the Shapes of Supply and Demand Curves

Clearly, the market price and output for a given item depend substantially on the shape of its demand and supply curves. Conventionally, the shape of the demand curve is measured by the **price elasticity of demand:** the absolute value of the percentage change in quantity demanded divided by the percentage change in price.[4] If a 10 percent increase in price leads to a 2 percent decrease in quantity demanded, then the price elasticity of demand is 0.2. An important special case is when the quantity demanded does not change at all with a price increase. Then the demand curve is vertical and elasticity is zero. At the other extreme, when the demand curve is horizontal, then even a small change in price leads to a huge change in quantity demanded. By convention, this is referred to as an infinitely elastic demand curve.

Similarly, the **price elasticity of supply** is defined as the percentage change in quantity supplied divided by the percentage change in price.

THEORY OF CHOICE: INDIFFERENCE CURVES AND BUDGET CONSTRAINTS

The fundamental problem of economics is that resources available to people are limited relative to people's wants. The theory of choice shows how people can make sensible decisions in the presence of such scarcity. In this section we develop a graphical representation of consumer tastes and show how these tastes can best be gratified in the presence of a limited budget.

Tastes

We assume that an individual derives satisfaction from the consumption of commodities.[5] In economics, the slightly archaic word **utility** is used as a synonym for satisfaction. Consider Oscar who consumes only two commodities, marshmallows and donuts. (Using mathematical methods, all the results for the two good case can be shown to apply to situations in which there are any number of commodities.) Assume further that for all feasible quantities of cookies and donuts, Oscar is never satiated—more consumption of either commodity always produces some increase in his utility.

In Figure A.7, the horizontal axis measures the number of donuts consumed each day, and the vertical axis shows daily marshmallow consumption. Thus, each point in the quadrant represents some bundle of marshmallows and donuts. For example, point *a* represents a bundle with seven marshmallows and five donuts.

Because Oscar's utility depends only upon his consumption of marshmallows and donuts, we can also associate with each point in the

---

[4] The elasticity need not be constant all along the demand curve.

[5] In this context, the notion of *commodities* should be interpreted very broadly. It includes not only items like food, cars, and stereos, but also less tangible things like leisure time, clean air, etc.

FIGURE A.7   Ranking Alternative Bundles

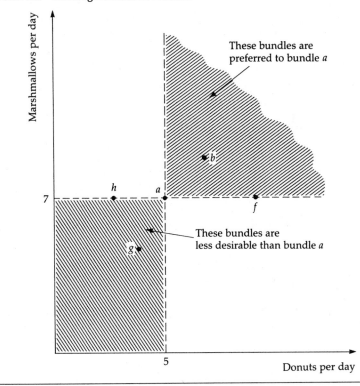

quadrant a certain level of utility. For example, if seven marshmallows and five donuts creates 100 "utils" of happiness, then point *a* is associated with 100 "utils."

Some commodity bundles create more utility than point *a*, and others less. Consider point *b* in Figure A.7, which has both more marshmallows and donuts than point *a*. Since satiation is ruled out, this means that *b* must yield higher utility than *a*. Bundle *f* has more donuts than *a* and no fewer marshmallows, and is also preferred to *a*. Indeed, any point to the northeast of *a* is preferred to *a*.

The same reasoning suggests that bundle *a* is preferred to bundle *g*, because the latter has fewer marshmallows and donuts than the former. Point *h* is also less desirable than *a*, because although it has the same number of marshmallows as *a*, it has fewer donuts. Point *a* is preferred to any point southwest of it.

We have identified some bundles that yield more utility than *a*, and some that yield less. Can we find some bundles that produce just the same amount of utility as point *a*? Presumably there are such bundles, but we need more information about the individual to find out which

FIGURE A.8   Derivation of an Indifference Curve

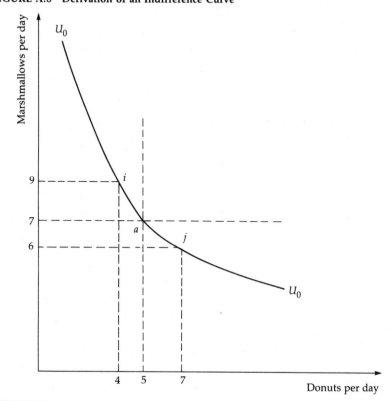

they are. Consider Figure A.8, where point *a* from Figure A.7 is reproduced. Imagine that we pose the following question to Oscar: "You are
now consuming seven marshmallows and five donuts. If I take away
one of your donuts, how many marshmallows do I need to give you to
make you just as satisfied as you were initially?" Suppose that after
thinking a while, Oscar (honestly) answers that he would require two
more marshmallows. Then by definition, the bundle consisting of four
donuts and nine marshmallows yields the same amount of utility as *a*.
This bundle is denoted *i* in Figure A.8.

We could find another bundle of equal utility by asking: "Starting
again at point *a*, suppose I take away one marshmallow. How many
more donuts must I give you to keep you as well off as you originally
were?" Assume that the answer is two donuts. Then the bundle with six
marshmallows and seven donuts, denoted *j* in Figure A.8, must also
yield the same amount of utility as bundle *a*.

We could go on like this indefinitely—start at point *a*, take away various
amounts of one commodity, find out the amount of the other commod-

ity required for compensation, and record the results on Figure A.8. The outcome is curve U_0U_0, which shows all points which yield the same amount of utility. U_0U_0 is referred to as an **indifference curve,** because it shows all consumption bundles between which the individual is indifferent.

By definition, the **slope** of a curve is the change in the value of the variable measured on the vertical axis divided by the change in the variable measured on the horizontal—the "rise over the run." The slope of an indifference curve has an important economic interpretation. It shows the rate at which the individual is willing to trade one good for

FIGURE A.9   **An Indifference Curve with a Diminishing Marginal Rate of Substitution**

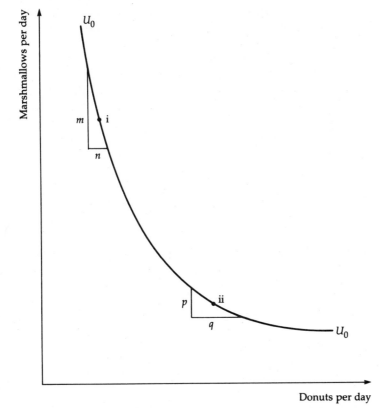

another. For example, in Figure A.9, around point i, the slope of the indifference curve is m/n. But by definition of an indifference curve, n is just the amount of donuts that Oscar is willing to substitute for sacrificing m marshmallows. For this reason, the absolute value of the slope of the indifference curve is often referred to as the **marginal rate of substitution** of donuts for marshmallows.[6] This is abbreviated MRS_{dm}.

Note that as drawn in Figure A.9, the marginal rate of substitution declines as we move down along the indifference curve. For example, around point *ii*, MRS_{dm} is given by p/q, which is clearly smaller than m/n. Introspection leads one to conclude that this makes sense. Around point *i*, Oscar has a lot of marshmallows relative to donuts, and is therefore willing to give up quite a few marshmallows in return for an additional donut—hence a high MRS_{dm}. On the other hand, around point *ii*, Oscar has a lot of donuts relative to marshmallows, so he is not willing to sacrifice a lot of marshmallows in return for yet another donut. The decline of MRS_{dm} as we move down along the indifference curve is called a **diminishing marginal rate of substitution.**

Recall that our construction of indifference curve $U_0 U_0$ was based upon bundle *a* as a starting point. But point *a* was chosen arbitrarily, and we could just as well have started at any other point in the quadrant. In Figure A.10, if we start with point *b* and proceed in the same way, we can generate indifference curve $U_1 U_1$. Or starting at point *k*, we can generate indifference curve $U_2 U_2$. Note that any point on $U_2 U_2$ represents a higher level of utility than any point on $U_1 U_1$, which in turn, is preferred to any point on $U_0 U_0$. If Oscar is interested in maximizing his utility, he will try to reach the highest indifference curve that he can.

The entire collection of indifference curves is referred to as the **indifference map.** Once we have the indifference map, we know everything there is to know about the individual's preferences.

Budget Constraint

Basic Setup. Suppose that marshmallows *(M)* cost 3 cents apiece, donuts *(D)* cost 6 cents, and Oscar's weekly income is 60 cents. What options does Oscar have? Whatever amounts he purchases must satisfy the equation

(A.1) $$3 \times M + 6 \times D = 60$$

In words, expenditure on marshmallows ($3 \times M$) plus expenditures on donuts ($6 \times D$) must equal income (60).[7] Thus, for example, if $M = 10$, then to satisfy Equation (A.1), D must equal 5 ($3 \times 10 + 5 \times 6 = 60$). Alternatively, if $M = 8$, then D must equal 6 ($3 \times 8 + 6 \times 6 = 60$).

It is useful to represent Equation (A.1) graphically. The usual way is to graph a number of points that satisfy the equation. This is straightfor-

---

[6] As noted below, *marginal* means *additional* or *incremental.* The indifference curve's slope shows the *marginal* rate of substitution because it indicates the rate at which the individual would be willing to substitute marshmallows for an *additional* donut.

[7] If Oscar is a utility maximizer, we can assume that he will not throw away any of this income. It is also assumed that 60 cents is net of any savings he desires to make.

FIGURE A.10   An Indifference Map

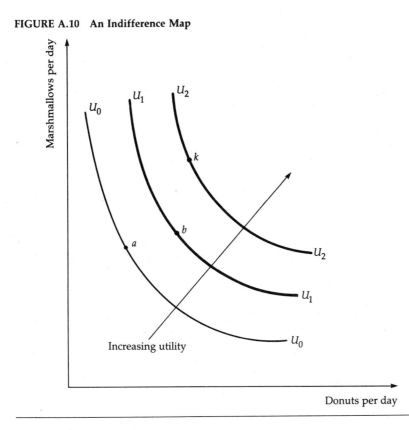

ward once we recall from basic algebra that (A.1) is just the equation of a straight line. Given two points on the line, the rest of the line is determined by connecting them. In Figure A.11, point r represents 10 marshmallows and 5 donuts, and point s represents 8 marshmallows and 6 donuts. Therefore, the line associated with Equation (A.1) is LN which passes through these points. By construction, *any* combination of cookies and donuts that lies along LN satisfies Equation (A.1). Line LN is known as the **budget constraint** or the **budget line.** Any point on or below LN (the shaded area) is feasible because it involves an expenditure less than or equal to income. Any point above LN is impossible because it involves an expenditure greater than income.

Two aspects of line LN are worth noting. First, the horizontal and vertical intercepts of the line have economic interpretations. By definition, the vertical intercept is the point associated with $D = 0$. At this point, Oscar spends all his 60 cents on marshmallows, buying 20 of them (60/3). Hence, distance OL is 20. Similarly, at point N, Oscar consumes zero marshmallows, but can afford a binge consisting of 10 do-

FIGURE A.11   A Budget Constraint

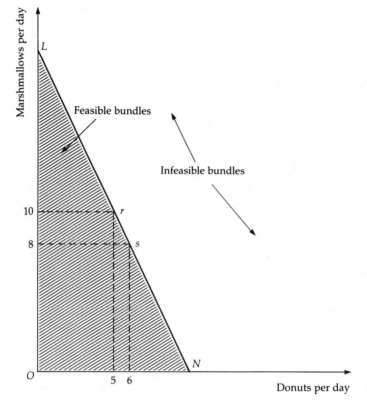

nuts (60/6). Distance *ON* is therefore 10. In short, the vertical and horizontal intercepts represent bundles in which only one of the commodities is consumed.

In addition, the slope has an economic interpretation. To calculate the slope, recall that the "rise" *(OL)* is 20 and the "run" *(ON)* is 10, so the slope (in absolute value) is 2. Note that 2 is the ratio of the price of donuts (6 cents) to the price of marshmallows (3 cents). This is no accident. The absolute value of the slope of the budget line indicates the rate at which the market permits an individual to substitute donuts for marshmallows. Because the price of donuts is twice the price of marshmallows, Oscar can trade two marshmallows for each donut.

Let us generalize this discussion. Suppose that the price per marshmallow is P_m, the price per donut is P_d, and income is I. Then in analogy to Equation (A.1), the budget constraint is

(A.2) $$P_m M + P_d D = I$$

If M is measured on the vertical axis and D on the horizontal, then the vertical intercept is I/P_m and the horizontal intercept is I/P_d. The slope of the budget constraint, in absolute value, is P_d/P_m. A common mistake is to assume that because M is measured on the vertical axis, the absolute value of the slope of the budget constraint is P_m/P_d. To see that this is wrong just divide the rise (I/P_m) by the run (I/P_d) : $(I/P_m) \div (I/P_d) = P_d/P_m$. Intuitively, P_d must be in the numerator because its ratio to P_m shows the rate at which the market permits one to trade M for D.

Changes in Prices and Income.   The budget line shows Oscar's consumption opportunities given his current income and the prevailing prices. What if any of these change? Return to the case where $P_m = 3$, $P_d = 6$ and $I = 60$. The associated budget line, $3M + 6D = 60$, is drawn as LN in Figure A.12. Now suppose that Oscar's income falls to 30. Substituting into Equation (A.2), the new budget line is described by $3M + 6D = 30$. To graph this equation, note that the vertical intercept is 10 and the horizontal intercept is 5. Denoting these two points in Figure

FIGURE A.12   Effect on the Budget Constraint of a Decrease in Income

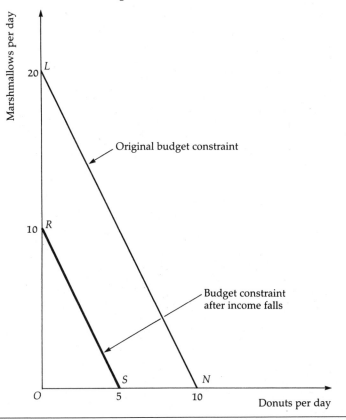

A.12 as *R* and *S*, respectively; and recalling that two points determine a line, we find that the new budget constraint is *RS*. The slope of *RS* in absolute value is 2, just like that of *LN*. This is because the relative price of donuts and marshmallows has not changed. When income changes but relative prices do not, a parallel shift in the budget line is induced. If income decreases, the constraint shifts in; if income increases, it shifts out.

Return again to the original constraint, 3M + 6D = 60, which is reproduced in Figure A.13 as *LN*. Suppose that the price of *D* increases

FIGURE A.13   Effect on the Budget Constraint of a Change in Relative Prices

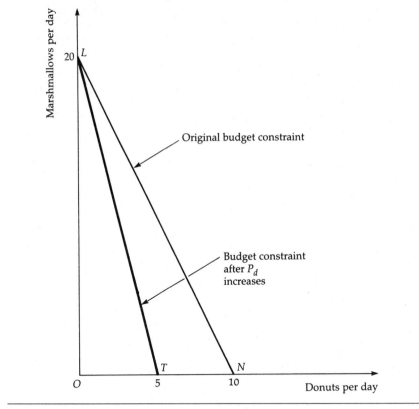

to 12, but everything else stays the same. Then by Equation (A.2), the relevant budget constraint is 3M + 12D = 60. To graph this new constraint, we begin by noting that it has a vertical intercept of 20, which is the same as that of *LN*. Because the price of *M* has stayed the same, if Oscar spends all his money only on *M*, then he can buy just as much as he did before. The horizontal intercept, however, is changed. It is now at five donuts (60/12), a point denoted T in Figure A.13. The new budget constraint is then LT. The slope of LT in absolute value is 4 (20/5). This value reflects the fact that the market now allows each individual to trade four marshmallows per donut.

More generally, when the price of one commodity changes and other things stay the same, the budget line pivots along the axis of the good whose price changes. If the price goes up, the line pivots in; if the price goes down, the line pivots out.

Equilibrium

The indifferent map shows what Oscar *wants* to do; the budget constraint shows what he *can* do. To find out what Oscar *actually* does, they must be put together.

In Figure A.14, we superimpose the indifference map from Figure A.10 upon budget line LN from Figure A.11. The problem is to find the

FIGURE A.14   Utility Maximization Subject to a Budget Constraint

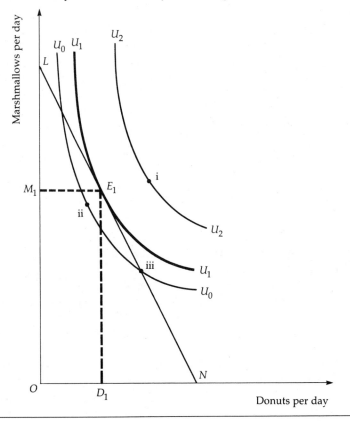

combination of M and D that maximizes Oscar's utility subject to the constraint that he cannot spend more than his income.

Consider first the bundle represented by point i on $U_2 U_2$. This point is ruled out, because it is above LN. Oscar might like to be on indifference curve $U_2 U_2$, but he simply cannot afford it.

Now consider point ii. That combination is certainly feasible, because it lies below the budget constraint. But it cannot be optimal, because Oscar is not spending his whole income. In effect, at bundle ii, he is just throwing away money that could have been spent on more marshmallows and/or donuts.

What about point iii? It is feasible, and Oscar is not throwing away any income. Yet he can still do better in the sense of putting himself on a higher indifference curve. Consider point E_1, where Oscar consumes D_1 donuts and M_1 marshmallows. Because it lies on LN, it is feasible. Moreover, it is more desirable than bundle iii, because E_1 lies on $U_1 U_1$, which is above $U_0 U_0$. Indeed, no point on LN touches an indifference curve that is higher than $U_1 U_1$. Therefore, the bundle consisting of M_1 and D_1 maximizes Oscar's utility subject to budget constraint LN. E_1 is an equilibrium because unless something else in the system changes, Oscar will continue to consume M_1 marshmallows and D_1 donuts day after day.

Note that at the equilibrium, indifference curve $U_1 U_1$ just "barely touches" the budget line. Intuitively, this is because Oscar is trying to achieve the very highest indifference curve he can while still keeping on LN. In more technical language, line LN is *tangent* to curve $U_1 U_1$ at point E_1. This means that at point E_1 the slope of $U_1 U_1$ is equal to the slope of LN.

This observation suggests an equation that can be used to characterize the point of utility maximization. Recall that by definition, the slope of the indifference curve (in absolute value) is the marginal rate of substitution of donuts for marshmallows, MRS_{dm}. The slope of the budget line (in absolute value) is P_d/P_m. But we just showed that at equilibrium, the two slopes are equal, or

(A.3)
$$MRS_{dm} = P_d/P_m$$

Equation (A.3) is a necessary condition for a utility maximization.[8] That is, if the bundle being consumed is not consistent with Equation (A.3), then Oscar could do better by reallocating his income between the two commodities. Intuitively, MRS_{dm} is the rate at which Oscar is willing to trade M for D. On the other hand, P_d/P_m is the rate at which the market allows Oscar to trade M for D. At equilibrium, these two rates must be equal.

Now let us suppose that the price of marshmallows falls by some amount. Figure A.15 reproduces the equilibrium point E_1 from Figure

---

[8] This statement is correct only if some of each commodity is consumed. If the consumption of some commodity is zero, then Equation (A.3) will, in general, not be satisfied.

FIGURE A.15   Effect on Equilibrium of a Change in Relative Prices

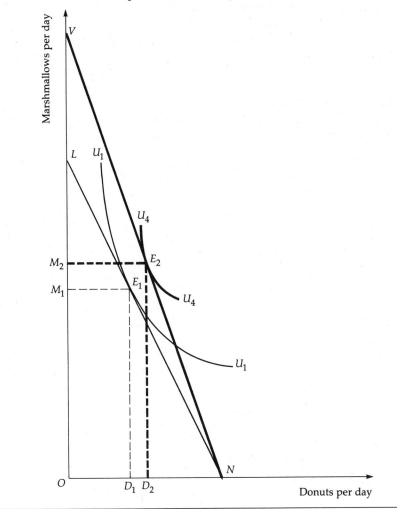

A.14. As we showed above, when a price changes *(ceteris paribus)* the budget line pivots along the axis of the good whose price has changed. Because P_m falls, the budget line LN pivots around N to a point that is higher on the vertical axis. The new budget line is VN. Given that Oscar now faces budget line VN, E_1 is no longer an equilibrium. The fall in P_m has created new opportunities for Oscar, and utility maximization requires that he take advantage of them. Specifically, subject to budget line VN, Oscar maximizes utility at point E_2, where he consumes M_2 marshmallows and D_2 donuts.

Note that at the new equilibrium, the amounts of both D and M have increased relative to the amounts consumed at the old equilibrium.

$(D_2 > D_1$ and $M_2 > M_1$.) In effect, the price decrease in marshmallows allows Oscar to purchase more marshmallows and still have money left over to purchase more donuts. While this is common, it need not always be the case. The change depends upon the tastes of the individual under consideration. Suppose that Bert faces exactly the same prices as Oscar, and also has the same income. Bert's indifference map and budget constraints are depicted in Figure A.16. For Bert, donut consumption is totally unchanged by the decrease in the price of marshmallows. On the other hand, Ernie's preferences, depicted in Figure A.17, are such that a fall in P_m leaves the amount of marshmallows consumed the same, and

FIGURE A.16   A Change in Relative Prices with No Effect on Donut Consumption

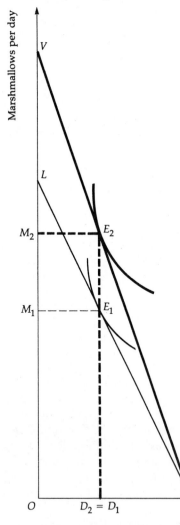

**FIGURE A.17   A Change in Relative Prices with No Effect on Marshmallow
Consumption**

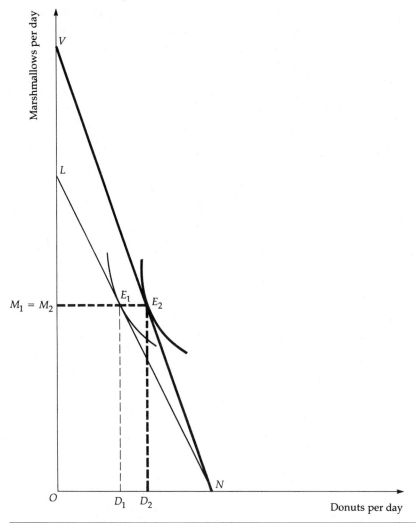

only the amount of donuts increases. Thus, unless we have information
about the individual's indifference map, we cannot predict just how he
or she will respond to a change in relative prices.

More generally, a change in prices and/or income changes the position of the budget constraint. The individual then *reoptimizes*—finds the
point that maximizes utility subject to the new budget constraint. This
will usually involve the selection of a new commodity bundle, but without information on the individual's tastes, one cannot know for sure

exactly what the new bundle will look like. We do know, however, that as long as the individual is a utility maximizer, the new bundle will satisfy the condition that the price ratio equal the marginal rate of substitution.

Derivation of Demand Curves

There is a simple connection between the theory of consumer choice and individual demand curves. Recall from Figure A.15, at the original price of marshmallows—call it P_m^1—Oscar consumed M_1 marshmallows. When the price fell to P_m^2, Oscar increased his marshmallow consumption to M_2. This pair of points may be plotted as in Figure A.18.

Repeating this experiment for various prices of marshmallows, we find the quantity of marshmallows demanded at each price, holding fixed money income, the price of donuts, and tastes. By definition, this

FIGURE A.18   Demand Curve for Marshmallows Derived from an Indifference Map

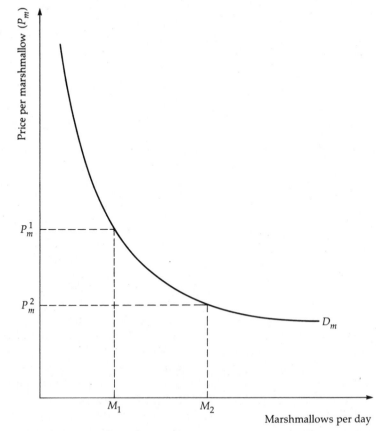

is the demand curve for marshmallows, shown as D_m in Figure A.18. Thus, we see how the demand curve is derived from the underlying indifference map.

Substitution and Income Effects

Figure A.19 depicts the situation of Grover, who initially faces budget constraint WN, and maximizes utility at point E_1, where he consumes

FIGURE A.19   Substitution and Income Effects of a Price Change

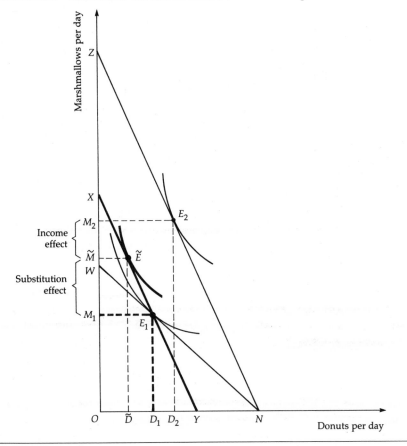

M_1 marshmallows. Suppose now that the price of marshmallows falls. Grover's budget constraint pivots from WN to ZN, and at the new equilibrium, E_2, he consumes M_2 marshmallows.

Just for hypothetical purposes, suppose that as the price of marshmallows falls, Grover's income is *simultaneously* adjusted so that at the new set of prices, he can *just* afford his original commodity bundle, E_1. If this hypothetical adjustment were made, what budget constraint would Grover face? Suppose we call this budget constraint XY. We know that XY must satisfy two conditions.

First, because the original bundle of E_1 is just affordable, XY must pass through point E_1.

Second, the slope (in absolute value) must be equal to the ratio of the price of donuts to the *new* price of marshmallows. This is because of the requirement that Grover be able to afford bundle E_1 at the *new* set of prices. Recall, however, that the slope of ZN is the ratio of the price of donuts to the new price of marshmallows. Hence, XY must have the same slope as ZN, that is, it must be parallel to ZN.

In Figure A.19, XY is drawn so that these two conditions are satisfied—the line is parallel to ZN and passes through point E_1. If Grover were confronted with constraint XY, he would maximize utility at a point like $\tilde{E}$, where his consumption of marshmallows is $\tilde{M}$.

Why should this hypothetical budget line be of any interest? Because drawing line XY helps us break down the effect of the change in the price of marshmallows into two components, the first from E_1 to $\tilde{E}$, and the second from $\tilde{E}$ to E_2.

1. The movement from E_1 to $\tilde{E}$ is a consequence purely of the change in the relative price of marshmallows to donuts. This movement shows that Grover substitutes marshmallows for donuts when marshmallows become cheaper, *even though* the original commodity bundle is available. Hence, the movement from E_1 to $\tilde{E}$ is called the **substitution effect.** Since the movement from E_1 to $\tilde{E}$ involves "compensating" income (in the sense of changing income so as to keep the original commodity bundle available), the movement from E_1 to $\tilde{E}$ is sometimes called the **income-compensated response** to a change in price.[9] In sum, the income-compensated response to a price change shows how the price change affects quantity demanded *when income is simultaneously altered so that the original bundle is just affordable.*

2. The movement from $\tilde{E}$ to E_2 is generated by the parallel shift of XY up to ZN. But recall from Figure A.12 that such parallel movements are associated with changes in income, holding relative prices constant. Hence, the movement from $\tilde{E}$ to E_2 is in effect due to a change in income, and is called the **income effect** of the price change.

Intuitively, when the price of marshmallows decreases two things happen. First, marshmallows become more attractive relative to donuts, inducing the substitution effect. Second, the decrease in price raises the individual's real income—his ability to afford commodities. When in-

---

[9] In this case, "income" is being kept the same in the sense that the same *commodity bundle* is available. It is also possible to define a substitution effect that keeps the same *utility* level available. For our purposes, there is no important difference between these.

come goes up, the quantity purchased generally changes, even without any change in relative prices.[10] This is the income effect. Any change in prices can be broken down into an income effect and a substitution effect.

We could repeat the exercise depicted in Figure A.19 for any change in the price of marshmallows. Suppose that for each price, we find the income-compensated quantity of marshmallows demanded, and make a plot with price on the vertical axis, and marshmallows on the horizontal. This plot is called the **income-compensated demand curve** for marshmallows. Note that the ordinary demand curve discussed at the beginning of this appendix shows how quantity demanded varies with price, holding I fixed, where I is income measured in terms of dollars. In contrast, the income-compensated demand curve shows how quantity demanded varies with price, holding the availability of the initial commodity bundle fixed.

MARGINAL ANALYSIS IN ECONOMICS

In economics, the word **marginal** usually means *additional* or *incremental*. Suppose, for example, that the annual total benefit per citizen of a 50-mile road is $42, and the annual total benefit of a 51-mile road is $43.50. Then the marginal benefit of the 51st mile is $1.50 ($43.50 − $42.00). Similarly, if the annual total cost per person of maintaining a 50-mile road is $38, and the total cost of a 51-mile road is $40, then the marginal cost of the 51st mile is $2.

The reason that economists focus so much attention on marginal quantities is that they usually convey the information required for rational decision making. Suppose that the government is trying to decide whether to construct the 51st mile. The key question is whether the *marginal* benefit is at least as great as the *marginal* cost. In our example, the marginal cost is $2 while the marginal benefit is only $1.50. Does it make sense to spend $2 to create $1.50 worth of benefits? The answer is no, and the extra mile should not be built. Note that basing the decision on *total* benefits and costs would have led to the wrong answer. The total cost per person of the 51-mile road ($40) is less than the total benefit ($43.50). Still, it is not sensible to build the 51st mile. An activity should be pursued only if its marginal benefit is at least as large as its marginal cost.[11]

Another example of marginal analysis: Farmer McGregor has two fields. The first is planted in wheat and the second in corn. McGregor

---

[10] If the good is normal, then the income effect of a price decrease will increase the quantity demanded, *and* vice versa if it is inferior. In Figure A.19, marshmallows are a normal good because M_2 exceeds M.

[11] If the marginal cost of an action just equals its marginal benefit, one is indifferent between taking the action and not taking it.

has seven tons of fertilizer to distribute between the two fields, and wants to allocate the fertilizer so that his total profits are as high as possible. The relationship between the amount of fertilizer and *total* profitability for each crop is depicted in Table A.1. Thus, for example, if

TABLE A.1   Total Profit

Tons of Fertilizer	Wheat	Corn
0	$ 0	$ 0
1	100	325
2	150	385
3	170	415
4	175	435
5	177	441
6	178	444

six tons of fertilizer were devoted to wheat, and one ton to corn, then total profits would be $503 (=$178 + $325).

To find the optimal allocation of fertilizer between the fields, it is useful to compute the marginal contribution to profits made by each ton of fertilizer. The first ton in the wheat field increases profits from $0 to $100, so the marginal contribution is $100. The second ton increases profits from $100 to $150, so its marginal contribution is $50. The complete set of computations for both crops is recorded in Table A.2.

TABLE A.2   Marginal Profit

Tons of Fertilizer	Wheat	Corn
1	$100	$325
2	50	60
3	20	30
4	5	20
5	2	6
6	1	3

Suppose that McGregor puts two tons of fertilizer on the wheat field and five tons on the corn field. Is this a profit maximizing allocation? To answer this question, we must determine whether any other allocation would lead to higher total profits. Suppose that one ton of fertilizer were removed from the corn field and devoted instead to wheat. As a consequence of removing the fertilizer from the corn field, profits from corn would go down by $6. But at the same time, profits from the wheat field would increase by $20 (the marginal profit associated with the third ton of fertilizer in the wheat field). Farmer McGregor would therefore be $14 richer on balance. Clearly, it is not sensible for McGregor to put two tons of fertilizer on the wheat field and five tons on the corn, because McGregor can do better (by $14) with three tons devoted to wheat and four to corn.

Is this latter allocation optimal? To answer, note that at this allocation, the marginal profit of fertilizer in each field is equal to $20. When the marginal profitability of fertilizer is the same in each field, there is *no way* that fertilizer can be reallocated between fields so as to increase total profit. In other words, total profits are maximized when the marginal profit in each field is the same. Readers who are skeptical of this result should try to find an allocation of the seven tons of fertilizer such that the total profit is higher than the $605 ($170 + $435) associated with the allocation at which the marginal profits are equal.

In general, if resources are being distributed across several activities, maximization of *total* returns requires that *marginal* returns in each activity be equal.[12]

PRODUCTION DECISIONS

Suppose that the only two commodities in the economy are marshmallows and donuts. All productive inputs are engaged either in marshmallow production or donut production. Provided that inputs are efficiently used, if more marshmallows are produced, then donut production must necessarily fall and vice versa. The **production possibilities curve** shows the maximum quantity of marshmallows that can be produced along with any given quantity of donuts. A typical production possibilities curve is depicted as CC in Figure A.20. Note that the curve does for the economy what the budget constraint does for the individual—it shows which bundles are feasible and which are not.

As shown in Figure A.20, one option available to the economy is to produce Ow marshmallows and Ox donuts. The economy can expand donut production from Ox to Oz, distance xz. To do this, of course, inputs have to be removed from the production of marshmallows and devoted to donuts. Marshmallow production must fall by distance wy if donut production is to increase by xz. The ratio of distance wy to distance xz is called the **marginal rate of transformation** of donuts for marshmallows (MRT_{dm}) because it shows the rate at which the economy can transform donuts into marshmallows. Just as MRS_{dm} measures the absolute value of the slope of an indifference curve, MRT_{dm} measures the absolute value of the slope of the production possibilities curve.

---

[12] More precisely, this result requires that the marginal returns be diminishing, as they are in Table A.2. In most applications, this is a reasonable assumption.

FIGURE A.20   A Production Possibilities Curve

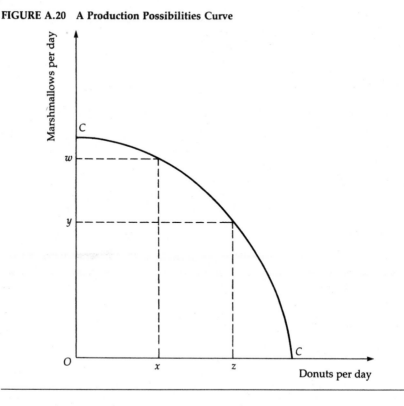

Suppose that the price of marshmallows is P_m, and the price of donuts is P_d. If firms aim to maximize profits, which point along CC will they select? To solve this problem, it is useful to begin by turning the question around: What combinations of donuts and marshmallows will yield (say) $100 in profit? Any combination of marshmallows and donuts that satisfies the equation[13]

(A.4) $P_m M + P_d D = 100$

will produce profits of $100. Equation (A.4) is represented graphically in Figure A.21, which measures donuts on the horizontal axis and marshmallows on the vertical. It is the straight line QR, whose slope (in absolute value) is P_d/P_m; its horizontal intercept is $100/P_d$; and its vertical intercept is $100/P_m$. Because line QR shows combinations of the two

---

[13] The reader may wonder how it is possible to write an expression for profits which ignores costs of production. Because all resources will be fully employed in production of either good, the only cost of producing more of one good is producing less of the other—the cost of other inputs is unchanged. Hence, only M and D need appear in the equation.

FIGURE A.21   An Iso-Profit Line

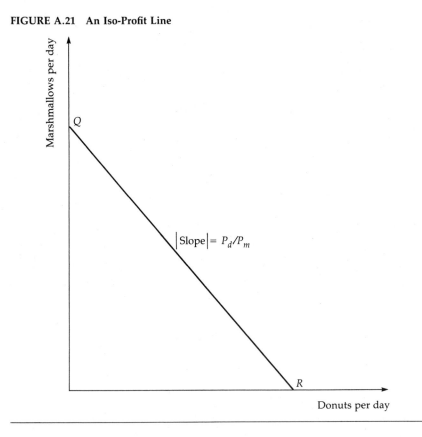

commodities that yield the same profit, it is referred to as an **iso-profit line.**

We can find the iso-profit line associated with any level of profits by substituting that level of profits on the right-hand side of Equation (A.4). For example, the iso-profit line associated with profits of $3,628 is $P_m M + P_d D = 3{,}628$. Note that:

1. Every iso-profit line has the same slope (in absolute value), P_d/P_m.
2. Iso-profit lines which represent greater profit levels have larger horizontal and vertical intercepts.

Observations (1) and (2) together imply that for any given price ratio, there exists a family of iso-profit lines. They are parallel to each other, and the iso-profit lines farther from the origin are associated with higher levels of profits. A set of iso-profit lines is drawn in Figure A.22.

We are now in a position to answer our original question: How do producers select the profit-maximizing combination on the production

FIGURE A.22   A Set of Iso-Profit Lines

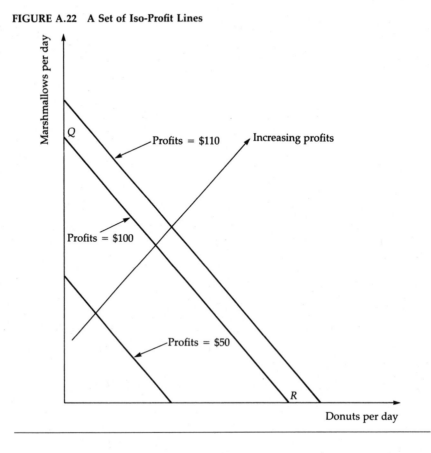

possibilities curve? We assume that producers would like to attain the highest iso-profit line they can. However, they are constrained by the fact that only certain output combinations are possible. Therefore, they select that combination which puts them on the highest iso-profit line *subject to the constraint* that this combination be on the production possibilities curve.

In Figure A.23 we reproduce the production possibilities curve from Figure A.20 and superimpose upon it a set of iso-profit lines. Profits are maximized at point E^*, where M^* marshmallows and D^* donuts are produced. Note that at E^*, the production possibilities curve and iso-profit line are tangent—they have the same slope. Recall that the slope of the production possibilities curve (in absolute value) is the marginal rate of transformation of donuts for marshmallows, MRT_{dm}. The slope of the iso-profit line (in absolute value) is P_d/P_m. Hence, at E^*,

(A.5) $$MRT_{dm} = P_d/P_m$$

FIGURE A.23   Selection of the Profit-Maximizing Combination of Outputs

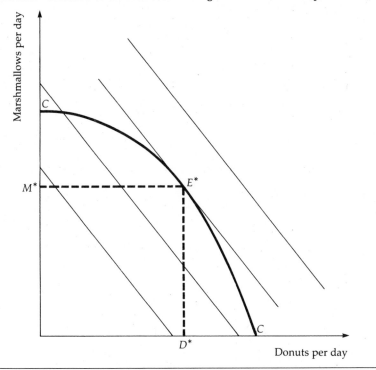

Note the similarity to condition $MRS_{dm} = P_d/P_m$ [Equation (A.3)], which characterizes the behavior of a utility-maximizing consumer. As long as consumers and producers face the same prices, then the marginal rate of transformation equals the marginal rate of substitution.

References

Aaron, Henry J. *Shelters and Subsidies*. Washington, D.C.: Brookings Institution, 1972.

Aaron, Henry J. *Who Pays the Property Tax? A New View*. Washington, D.C.: Brookings Institution, 1975.

Aaron, Henry J. "Inflation and the Income Tax: An Introduction." In *Inflation and the Income Tax*, ed. Henry J. Aaron. Washington, D.C.: Brookings Institution, 1976, pp. 1–31.

Aaron, Henry J. *Politics and the Professors—The Great Society in Perspective*. Washington, D.C.: Brookings Institution, 1978.

Aaron, Henry J. "Introduction and Summary." In *The Value-Added Tax—Lessons from Europe*, ed. Henry J. Aaron. Washington, D.C.: Brookings Institution, 1981, pp. 1–18.

Ackerman, Bruce A.; Susan Rose-Ackerman; James W. Sawyer, Jr.; and Dale W. Henderson. *The Uncertain Search for Environmental Quality*. New York: Free Press, 1974.

Andrews, William D. "A Consumption-Type or Cash Flow Personal Income Tax." *Harvard Law Review* 87 (April 1974), pp. 1113–88.

Andrews, William D. "The Achilles' Heel of the Comprehensive Income Tax." In *New Directions in Federal Tax Policy for the 1980s*, ed. Charles E. Walker and Mark A. Bloomfield. Cambridge, Mass.: Ballinger, 1983, pp. 278–84.

Armitage-Smith, George. *Principles and Methods of Taxation*. London: John Murray, 1907.

Arrow, Kenneth J. *Social Choice and Individual Values*. New York: John Wiley & Sons, 1951.

Arrow, Kenneth J. "The Economic Implications of Learning by Doing." *Review of Economic Studies* 29 (1962), pp. 155–73.

Arrow, Kenneth J. *The Limits of Organization*. New York: W. W. Norton, 1974.

Arrow, K. J., and R. C. Lind. "Uncertainty and the Evaluation of Public Investment Decisions." *American Economic Review* 60 (1970), pp. 364–78.

Atkinson, Anthony B. *The Economics of Inequality*. Oxford: Oxford University Press, 1975.

Atkinson, Anthony B., and Nicholas H. Stern. "Pigou, Taxation and Public Goods." *Review of Economic Studies* 41 (1974), pp. 119–28.

Atkinson, Anthony B., and Joseph E. Stiglitz. *Lectures on Public Economics*. New York: McGraw-Hill, 1980.

Auerbach, Alan J. *Stockholder Tax Rates and Firm Attributes*. National Bureau of Economic Research, Working Paper no. 817, 1982.

Auerbach, Alan J. "The Theory of Excess Burden and Optimal Taxation." Cambridge, Mass.: National Bureau of Economic Research, Working Paper no. 1025, 1982.

Auerbach, Alan J., and Harvey S. Rosen. *Will the Real Excess Burden Please Stand Up? (or, Seven Measures in Search of a Concept).* Cambridge, Mass.: National Bureau of Economic Research, Working Paper no. 495, 1980.

Auten, Gerald E., and Charles T. Clotfelter. "Permanent versus Transitory Tax Effects and the Realization of Capital Gains." *The Quarterly Journal of Economics,* November 1982, pp. 613–32.

Baily, Martin Neil. "Are the New Economic Models the Answer?" *The Brookings Review* 1, no. 1 (Fall 1982), pp. 11–14.

Ballard, Charles L.; John B. Shoven; and John Whalley. *The Welfare Costs of Distortions in the United States Tax System: A General Equilibrium Approach.* Cambridge, Mass.: National Bureau of Economic Research, Working Paper no. 1043, 1982.

Barlow, Robin; Harvey E. Brazer; and James N. Morgan. *Economic Behavior of the Affluent.* Washington, D.C.: Brookings Institution, 1966.

Barro, Robert J. "Are Government Bonds Net Wealth?" *Journal of Political Economy* 82 (1974), pp. 1095–117.

Barro, Robert J., and Chaipat Sahasakul. *Measuring the Average Marginal Tax Rate from the Individual Income Tax.* Cambridge, Mass.: National Bureau of Economic Research, Working Paper no. 1060, 1983.

Bator, F. M. "The Anatomy of Market Failure." *Quarterly Journal of Economics* 72 (August 1958), pp. 351–79.

Bator, F. M. "The Simple Analytics of Welfare Maximization." *American Economic Review* 47 (March 1957), pp. 22–59.

Baumol, William J. "Book Reviews—Economics and Clean Water." *The Yale Law Journal* 85, no. 3 (January 1976), pp. 441–46.

Baumol, William J. *Economic Theory and Operations Analysis.* 4th ed. Englewood Cliffs, N.J.: Prentice-Hall, 1977, Chapter 21.

Baumol, William J., and Hilda Baumol. "Book Review." *Journal of Political Economy* 89, no. 2 (April 1981), pp. 425–28.

Baumol, William J., and Alan S. Blinder. *Economics Principles and Policy.* 2d ed. New York: Harcourt Brace Jovanovich, 1982.

Baumol, William J., and Wallace E. Oates. *Economics, Environmental Policy, and the Quality of Life.* Englewood Cliffs, N.J.: Prentice-Hall, 1979.

Becker, Gary S. "Irrational Behavior and Economic Theory." *Journal of Political Economy* 70 (February 1962), pp. 1–13.

Becker, Gary S. "Crime and Punishment: An Economic Approach." *Journal of Political Economy* 76 (March–April 1968), pp. 169–217.

Becker, Gary S. "Altruism, Egoism, and Genetic Fitness: Economics and Sociobiology." *Journal of Economic Literature* 14, no. 3 (September 1976), pp. 817–26.

Becker, Gary S., and H. Gregg Lewis. "On the Interaction between the Quantity and Quality of Children." *Journal of Political Economy* 81 (March–April 1973), pp. S279–88.

Bewley, Truman F. "A Critique of Teibout's Theory of Local Public Expenditures." *Econometrica* 49 (1981), pp. 713–39.

Bhagwati, Jagdish N. "Introduction." *Journal of Public Economics* 18, no. 3 (August 1982), pp. 285–90.

Bhagwati, Jagdish N., and Koichi Hamada. "Tax Policy in the Presence of Emigration." *Journal of Public Economics* 18, no. 3 (August 1982), pp. 291–318.

Bishop, Robert L. "The Effects of Specific and Ad Valorem Taxes." *Quarterly Journal of Economics*, May 1968, pp. 198–218.

Bittker, Boris. "Federal Income Taxation and the Family." *Stanford Law Review* 27 (July 1975), 1392–1463.

Black, D. "On the Rationale of Group Decision Making." *Journal of Political Economy* 56 (February 1948), pp. 23–34.

Blank, Rebecca M. "Welfare, Wages and Migration." Mimeographed. Princeton, N.J.: Princeton University, 1983.

Blinder, Alan S. "The Level and Distribution of Economic Well-Being." In *The American Economy in Transition,* ed. Martin Feldstein. Chicago: University of Chicago Press, 1980.

Blinder, Alan S. "(Groucho) Marx Economics." *Boston Globe,* August 24, 1982, p. 51.

Blinder, Alan S.; Roger H. Gordon; and Donald E. Wise. "Reconsidering the Work Disincentive Effects of Social Security." *National Tax Journal* 33, no. 4 (December 1980), pp. 431–42.

Boffey, Phillip M. "The Debate over Dioxin." *New York Times,* June 25, 1983, p. 1.

Boskin, Michael J. "Efficiency Aspects of the Differential Tax Treatment of Market and Household Economic Activities." *Journal of Public Economics* 4 (1975), pp. 1–25.

Boskin, Michael J. "Taxation, Saving, and the Rate of Interest." *Journal of Political Economy* 86, no. 2 (April 1978), pp. S3–S28.

Boskin, Michael J.; Marcy Arvin; and Kenneth Cone. "Modelling Alternative Solutions to the Long-Run Social Security Funding Problem." Mimeographed. Stanford, California: Stanford University, January 1981.

Boskin, Michael J., and Eytan Sheshinski. "Optimal Income Redistribution when Individual Welfare Depends on Relative Income." *Quarterly Journal of Economics* 92 (1978), pp. 589–602.

Boskin, Michael J., and Eytan Sheshinski. *Optimal Tax Treatment of the Family: Married Couples.* Cambridge, Mass.: National Bureau of Economic Research, Working Paper no. 368, 1979.

Bowen, William G. *Economic Aspects of Education.* Princeton, N.J.: Industrial Relations Section, Princeton University, 1964.

Bowen, William G.; Richard Davis; and David Kopf. "The Public Debt: A Burden on Future Generations?" *American Economic Review* 50, no. 4 (September 1960), pp. 701–06.

Bradbury, Katherine L., and Anthony Downs, eds. *Do Housing Allowances Work?* Washington, D.C.: Brookings Institution, 1981.

Bradbury, Katharine L.; Anthony Downs; and Kenneth A. Small. *Urban Decline and the Future of American Cities.* Washington, D.C.: Brookings Institution, 1982.

Bradford, David F. "The Incidence and Allocation Effects of a Tax on Corporate Distributions." *Journal of Public Economics* 15, no. 1 (February 1981), pp. 1–22.

Bradford, David, and Wallace Oates. "Suburban Exploitation of Central Cities and Government Structure." In *Redistribution Through Public Choice*, ed. Harold Hochman and George Peterson. New York: Columbia University Press, 1974.

Break, George F. "Income Taxes and Incentives to Work." *American Economic Review* 47 (1957), pp. 529–49.

Break, George F. *Financing Government in a Federal System.* Washington, D.C.: Brookings Institution, 1980.

Break, George F., and Joseph A. Pechman. *Federal Tax Reform The Impossible Dream?* Washington, D.C.: Brookings Institution, 1975.

Brennan, Geoffrey, and James M. Buchanan. "Towards a Tax Constitution for Leviathan." *Journal of Public Economics* 8, no. 3 (December 1977), pp. 255–74.

Brittain, John A. *Inheritance and the Inequality of Material Wealth.* Washington, D.C.: Brookings Institution, 1978.

Broome, J. "Trying to Value a Life." *Journal of Public Economics*, February 1978, pp. 91–100.

Browning, Edgar K., and William R. Johnson. "The Trade-off between Equality and Efficiency." *Journal of Political Economy*, April 1984, pp. 175–203.

Buchanan, James M. "Social Choice, Democracy, and Free Markets." In *Fiscal Theory and Political Economy—Selected Essays*, ed. James M. Buchanan. Chapel Hill: University of North Carolina Press, 1960, pp. 75–89.

Buchanan, James M. "An Economic Theory of Clubs." *Economica* 32 (February 1965), pp. 1–14.

Buiter, W. H., and J. Tobin. "Debt Neutrality: A Brief Review of Doctrine and Evidence." In *Social Security vs. Private Savings*, ed. George M. von Furstenberg. Cambridge, Mass.: Balinger, 1979.

Carliner, Geoffrey. "Income Elasticity of Housing Demand." *Review of Economics and Statistics* 55 (1973), pp. 528–32.

Caves, Richard, and Ronald Jones. *World Trade and Payments.* Boston: Little, Brown, 1981.

Chirinko, Robert S., and Robert Eisner. "Tax Policy and Investment in Major U.S. Macroeconomic Econometric Models." *Journal of Public Economics* 20, no. 2 (March 1983), pp. 139–66.

"Chrysler's Stock Plea Angers Congressmen." *New York Times,* May 10, 1983, p. D6.

City of Clinton v. *Cedar Rapids and Missouri River RR. Co.,* 24 Iowa 475 (1868).

Classen, Kathleen P. "Unemployment Insurance and Job Search." In *Studies in the Economics of Search,* ed. Stephen A. Lippman and John J. McCall. Amsterdam: North-Holland, 1979, pp. 191–219.

Clendinen, Dudley. "Court Ban on Work at Home Brings Gloom to Knitters in Rural Vermont." *New York Times,* December 3, 1983, p. 8.

Clotfelter, Charles T. "Tax Evasion and Tax Rates: An Analysis of Individual Returns." *Review of Economics and Statistics* 65, no. 3 (August 1983), pp. 363–73.

Clotfelter, Charles. T. "Tax Cut Meets Bracket Creep: The Rise and Fall of Marginal Tax Rates, 1964–1984." *Public Finance Quarterly* 2, no. 2 (April 1984), pp. 131–52.

Clotfelter, Charles T., and C. Eugene Steuerle. "Charitable Contributions." In *How Taxes Affect Economic Behavior,* ed. Henry J. Aaron and Joseph A. Pechman. Washington, D.C.: Brookings Institution, 1981.

Clymery, Adam. "Poll Finds Trust in Government Edging Back Up." *New York Times,* July 15, 1983, p. 1.

Coase, Ronald H. "The Problem of Social Cost." *Journal of Law and Economics,* October 1960.

Coase, Ronald H. "The Lighthouse in Economics." *Journal of Law and Economics,* October 1974.

Cohen, Wilbur J. "Economic Well-Being and Income Distribution." In *The American Economy in Transition,* ed. Martin Feldstein. Chicago: University of Chicago Press, 1980.

Commissioner of Internal Revenue and the Chief Council for the Internal Revenue Service. *Annual Report 1981.* Washington, D.C.: U.S. Government Printing Office, 1982.

Congressional Budget Office. *Indexing the Individual Tax.* Washington, D.C.: U.S. Government Printing Office, 1980.

Congressional Budget Office. *Tax Expenditures: Current Issues and Five-Year Budget Projections for Fiscal Years 1983–1986.* Washington, D.C.: U.S. Government Printing Office, 1981.

Congressional Budget Office. *Federal Credit Activities: An Overview of the President's Credit Budget for Fiscal Year 1983.* Washington, D.C.: U.S. Government Printing Office, 1982a.

Congressional Budget Office. *Balancing the Federal Budget and Limiting Federal Spending: Constitutional and Statutory Approaches.* Washington, D.C.: U.S. Government Printing Office, 1982b.

Congressional Budget Office. *Financing Social Security: Issues and Options in the Long Run.* Washington, D.C.: U.S. Government Printing Office, 1982c.

Congressional Budget Office. *Tax Expenditures: Budget Control Options and Five-Year Budget Projections for the Fiscal Years 1983–1987.* Washington, D.C.: U.S. Government Printing Office, 1982d.

Congressional Budget Office. *The Federal Government in a Federal System: Current Intergovernmental Programs and Options for Change.* Washington, D.C.: U.S. Government Printing Office, 1983a.

Congressional Budget Office. *Tax Expenditures: Current Issues and Five-Year Budget Projections for Fiscal Years 1984–1988.* Washington, D.C.: U.S. Government Printing Office, 1983b.

Cooper, George. *A Voluntary Tax? New Perspectives on Sophisticated Estate Tax Avoidance.* Washington, D.C.: Brookings, Institution, 1979.

Corlett, W. J., and D. C. Hague. "Complementarity and the Excess Burden of Taxation." *Review of Economic Studies* 21 (1953), pp. 21–30.

"The Cuts in Federal Aid." *Newsweek,* June 29, 1981, pp. 66–67.

Danziger, Sheldon; Robert Haveman; and Robert Plotnick. "How Income Transfers Affect Work, Savings, and the Income Distribution." *Journal of Economic Literature* 19, no. 3 (September 1981), pp. 975–1028.

Danziger, Sheldon, and Robert Plotnick. "Demographic Change, Government Transfers and Income Distribution." *Monthly Labor Review* 100, no. 4 (April 1977), pp. 7–11.

Davidson, Mary. " 'New Federalism'—Old Discrimination." *New York Times,* October 8, 1982, p. A31.

Devarajan, S.; Fullerton, D.; and Musgrave, R. "Estimating the Distribution of Tax Burdens: A Comparison of Alternative Approaches."*Journal of Public Economics* 13 (1980), pp. 155–82.

Diamond, Peter A. "A Many-Person Ramsey Tax Rule." *Journal of Public Economics* 4 (1975), pp. 335–42.

Diamond, Peter A. "A Framework for Social Security Analysis." *Journal of Public Economics* 8, no. 3 (December 1977), pp. 275–98.

Diamond, Peter A., and Daniel L. McFadden. "Some Uses of the Expenditure Function in Public Finance." *Journal of Public Economics* 3 (1974), pp. 3–21.

Dorfman, Nancy S., assisted by Arthur Snow. "Who Will Pay for Pollution Control?—The Distribution By Income of the Burden of the National Environmental Protection Program, 1972–1980." *National Tax Journal* 28 (March 1975), pp. 101–15.

Downs, Anthony. *An Economic Theory of Democracy.* New York: Harper & Row, 1957.

Doyle, Michael W. "Stalemate in the North-South Debate: Strategies and the New International Economic Order." *World Politics* 35, no. 3 (April 1983), pp. 426–64.

Drinan, Robert F. "Education: To Cherish." *New York Times*, February 27, 1983, p. E17.

Due, John F., and Ann F. Friedlaender. *Government Finance Economics of the Private Sector.* 6th ed. Homewood, Ill.: Richard D. Irwin, 1977.

Eaton, Jonathan, and Harvey S. Rosen. "Taxation, Human Capital, and Uncertainty." *American Economic Review* 70, no. 4 (September 1980a), pp. 705–15.

Eaton, Jonathan, and Harvey S. Rosen. "Labor Supply, Uncertainty, and Efficient Taxation." *Journal of Public Economics* 14, no. 3 (December 1980b), pp. 365–74.

Economic Recovery Tax Act of 1981. Chicago: Commerce Clearing House, 1981.

The Economic Recovery Tax Act of 1981—A Summary and Analysis. New York: Price Waterhouse, 1981.

Economic Report of the President. Washington, D.C.: U.S. Government Printing Office, 1983.

Economic Report of the President. Washington, D.C.: U.S. Government Printing Office, 1984.

Edgeworth, F. Y. "The Pure Theory of Taxation." [1897] Reprinted in *Readings in the Economics of Taxation,* ed. Richard A. Musgrave and Carl S. Shoup. Homewood, Ill.: Richard D. Irwin, 1959, pp. 258–96.

Eisner, R., and Nadiri, M. I. "Investment Behavior and the Neo-Classical Theory." *Review of Economics and Statistics* 50, no. 3 (August 1968), pp. 369–82.

Executive Office of the President, Office of Management and Budget. *Special Analyses: Budget of the United States Government, Fiscal Year 1984.* Washington, D.C.: U.S. Government Printing Office, 1983, p. E-5.

Executive Office of the President, Office of Management and Budget. *Special Analyses: Budget of the United States Government, Fiscal Year 1985.* Washington, D.C.: U.S. Government Printing Office, 1984.

Facts and Figures on Government Finance—21st Biennial Edition. Washington, D.C.: Tax Foundation, 1981.

Facts and Figures on Government Finance—22nd Biennial Edition. Washington, D.C.: Tax Foundation, 1983.

Fainstain, Susan S. "American Policy for Housing and Community Development: A Comparative Examination," In *Housing Policy in the 1980s,* ed. Roger Montgomery and Dale Marshall. Lexington, Mass.: D.C. Heath, 1980, pp. 215–230.

Fair, Ray C. "The Optimal Distribution of Income." *Quarterly Journal of Economics* 85 (1971), pp. 551–79.

Fair, Ray C. "The Effects of Economic Events on Votes for President." *The Review of Economics and Statistics* 70 (May 1978), pp. 159–73.

Fair, Ray C. "The Effect of Economic Events on Votes for President: 1980 Results." *Review of Economics and Statistics* 44, no. 2 (May 1982), pp. 322–24.

Fama, Eugene F., and Merton H. Miller. *The Theory of Finance.* New York: Holt, Rinehart & Winston, 1972.

Feenberg, Daniel. *The Tax Treatment of Married Couples under the 1981 Tax Law.* Cambridge, Mass.: National Bureau of Economic Research, Working Paper no. 872, 1982.

Feldstein, Martin S. "The Effects of Taxation on Risk-Taking." *Journal of Political Economy* 77 (1969), pp. 755–64.

Feldstein, Martin S. "Corporate Taxation and Dividend Behavior." *Review of Economic Studies* 37 (1970), pp. 57–72.

Feldstein, Martin S. "Equity and Efficiency in Public Sector Pricing: The Optimal Two-Part Tariff." *Quarterly Journal of Economics* 86 (1972), pp. 175–87.

Feldstein, Martin S. "Tax Incentives, Corporate Saving and Capital Accumulation in the United States." *Journal of Public Economics,* 2 (1973), pp. 159–171.

Feldstein, Martin S. "Social Security, Induced Retirement, and Aggregate Capital Accumulation." *Journal of Political Economy* 82, no. 5 (September–October 1974a), pp. 905–26.

Feldstein, Martin S. "Unemployment Compensation: Adverse Incentives and Distributional Anomalies." *National Tax Journal* 27 (1974b), pp. 231–44.

Feldstein, Martin, S. "On the Theory of Tax Reform." *Journal of Public Economics* 6 (1976a), pp. 77–104.

Feldstein, Martin S. *Social Insurance.* Harvard Institute of Economic Research, Discussion Paper no. 477, Cambridge, Mass., 1976b.

Feldstein, Martin S. "Personal Taxation and Portfolio Composition: An Econometric Analysis." *Econometrica* 44 (1976c), pp. 631–50.

Feldstein, Martin S. "Does the United States Save Too Little?" *The American Economic Review Papers and Proceedings,* February 1977, pp. 116–21.

Feldstein, Martin S. "A Contribution to the Theory of Tax Expenditures: The Case of Charitable Giving." In *The Economics of Taxation,* ed. Henry J. Aaron and Michael J. Boskin. Washington, D.C.: Brookings Institution, 1980, pp. 99–122.

Feldstein, Martin S. "Social Security and Private Saving: Reply." *Journal of Political Economy* 90, no. 3 (June 1982a), pp. 630–42.

Feldstein, Martin S. "Inflation, Tax Rules, and Investment: Some Econometric Evidence." *Econometrica* 50, no. 4 (July 1982b), pp. 825–62.

Feldstein, Martin S. *Capital Taxation.* Cambridge, Mass.: National Bureau of Economic Research, Working Paper No. 877, 1982c.

Feldstein, Martin S., and Daniel Frisch. "Corporate Tax Integration: The Estimated Effects on Capital Accumulation and Tax Distribution of Two Integration Proposals." *National Tax Journal* 30 (March 1977), pp. 37–52.

Feldstein, Martin S., and Jerry Green. "Why Do Companies Pay Dividends?" *The American Economic Review* 73, no. 1 (March 1983), pp. 17–30.

Feldstein, Martin S., and David Hartman. *The Optimal Taxation of Foreign Source Investment Income.* Harvard Institute of Economic Research, Discussion Paper no. 563, Cambridge, Mass., 1977.

Feldstein, Martin S., and Joel Slemrod. "How Inflation Distorts the Taxation of Capital Gains." *Harvard Business Review.* September–October 1978, pp. 20–22.

Feldstein, Martin S., and Lawrence Summers. "Inflation and the Taxation of Capital Income in the Corporate Sector." *National Tax Journal* 32, no. 4 (December 1979), pp. 445–470.

Filimon, R.; T. Romer; and H. Rosenthal. "Asymmetric Information and Agenda Control: The Bases of Monopoly Power and Public Spending." *Journal of Public Economics* 17 (1982), pp. 51–70.

Finley, Murray. "Brown Lungs." *New York Times*, May 4, 1981, p. A23.

Friedman, Milton. *A Theory of the Consumption Function.* Princeton, N.J.: Princeton University Press, 1957.

Friedman, Milton. "Our New Hidden Taxes." *Newsweek*, April 14, 1980, p. 90.

Friedman, Milton. "Which Budget Deficit?" *Newsweek*, November 2, 1981, p. 88.

Frisch, Daniel J. *Issues in the Taxation of Foreign Source Income.* Cambridge, Mass.: National Bureau of Economic Research, Working Paper no. 798, 1981.

Fullerton, Don. "On the Possibility of an Inverse Relationship between Tax Rates and Government Revenues." *Journal of Public Economics* 19, no. 1 (October 1982), pp. 3–22.

Fullerton, Don; Yolanda K. Henderson; and John B. Shoven. *A Comparison of Methodologies in Empirical General Equilibrium Models of Taxation.* Cambridge, Mass.: National Bureau of Economic Research, Working Paper no. 911, 1982.

Fullerton, Don; John B. Shoven; and John Whalley. "Replacing the U.S. Income Tax with a Progressive Consumption Tax: A Sequenced General Equilibrium Approach." Cambridge, Mass.: National Bureau of Economic Research, Working Paper no. 892, 1982.

Funkhauser, Richard. "Ask about Acid Rain." *New York Times*, August 18, 1983, p. A27.

Galper, Harvey, and Eric Toder. "Measuring the Incidence of Taxation of Income From Capital." In *1982 Proceedings of the Seventy-Fifth Annual Conference on Taxation*, ed. Stanley J. Bowers. Cincinnati: October 1982.

"Gas Tax Rise Likely to Show Up at Pump." *New York Times*, April 1, 1983, p. D1.

George, Henry. *Progress and Poverty*, New York: Doubleday Publishing, 1914, Book VII.

Gillis, Malcolm, and Charles E. McLure. "Excess Profits Taxation: Post-mortem on the Mexican Experience." *National Tax Journal* 32, no. 4 (December 1979), pp. 501–11.

Goode, Richard. "The Economic Definition of Income." In *Comprehensive Income Taxation,* ed. Joseph A. Pechman. Washington, D.C.: Brookings Institution, 1977, pp. 1–37.

Goode, Richard. "The Superiority of the Income Tax." In *What Should Be Taxed: Income or Expenditure?* ed. Joseph A. Pechman. Washington, D.C.: Brookings Institution, 1980, pp. 49–74.

Goodwin, Michael. "City's Tax Incentive Panel Is Called Slipshod." *New York Times,* May 4, 1983, p. 1.

Graetz, Michael J. "Expenditure Tax Design." In *What Should Be Taxed: Income or Expenditure?* ed. Joseph A. Pechman. Washington, D.C.: Brookings Institution, 1980, pp. 161–298.

Gramlich, Edward M. "The New York City Fiscal Crisis: What Happened and What Is to Be Done?" *The American Economic Review, Papers and Proceedings* 66, no. 2 (May 1976), pp. 415–29.

Gramlich, Edward M. *Benefit-Cost Analysis of Government Programs.* Englewood Cliffs, N.J.: Prentice-Hall, 1981.

Gramlich, Edward M., and Patricia P. Koshel. *Educational Performance Contracting: An Evaluation of an Experiment.* Washington, D.C.: Brookings Institution, 1975.

Gramlich, Edward M., and Daniel L. Rubinfeld. "Microestimates of Public Spending Demand Functions and Test of the Tiebout and Median-Voter Hypotheses." *Journal of Political Economy* 90 (June 1982), pp. 536–60.

Gravelle, Jane G. "Effects of the 1981 Depreciation Revisions on the Taxation of Income From Business Capital." *National Tax Journal* 35, no. 1 (March 1982), pp. 1–20.

Greider, William. "The Education of David Stockman." *Atlantic Monthly,* December 1981, pp. 27–54.

Groves, T., and J. Ledyard. "Optimal Allocation of Public Goods: A Solution to the 'Free Rider' Problem." *Econometrica* 45 (1977), pp. 783–809.

Gujarati, D. *Basic Econometrics.* New York: McGraw-Hill, 1978.

Hagman, Donald C. "Proposition 13: A Prostitution of Conservative Principles." *Tax Review* 39, no. 9 (September 1978), pp. 39–42.

Hall, Robert E., and Alvin Rabushka. *Low Tax, Simple Tax, Flat Tax.* New York: McGraw-Hill, 1983.

Hamilton, Bruce. "Property Taxes and the Tiebout Hypothesis: Some Empirical Evidence." In *Fiscal Zoning and Land Use Controls, The Economic Issues,* ed. Edwin S. Mills and Wallace E. Oates. Lexington, Mass.: Lexington Books, 1975a, pp. 13–30.

Hamilton, Bruce. "Zoning and Property Taxation in a System of Local Governments." *Urban Studies* 12 (June 1975b), pp. 205–11.

Harberger, Arnold C. "Taxation, Resource Allocation, and Welfare." In *Taxation and Welfare,* ed. Arnold C. Harberger. Boston: Little, Brown, 1974a, pp. 25–62.

Harberger, Arnold C. "Efficiency Effects of Taxes on Income from Capital." in *Taxation and Welfare*, ed. Arnold C. Harberger. Boston: Little, Brown, 1974b, pp. 163–70.

Harberger, Arnold C. "The Incidence of the Corporation Income Tax." In *Taxation and Welfare*, ed. Arnold C. Harberger. Boston: Little, Brown, 1974c, pp. 135–62.

Harris, C. Lowell. "Property Taxation after the California Vote." *Tax Review* 39, no. 8 (August 1978), pp. 35–38.

Harrison, David, Jr., and Daniel L. Rubinfeld. "Hedonic Housing Prices and the Demand for Clean Air." *Journal of Environmental Economics and Management* 5 (March 1978), pp. 81–102.

Hartman, David G. *Tax Policy and Foreign Direct Investment in the United States.* Cambridge, Mass.: National Bureau of Economic Research, Working Paper no. 967, 1982.

Hausman, Jerry A. "Labor Supply." In *How Taxes Affect Economic Behavior*, ed. Henry J. Aaron and Joseph A. Pechman. Washington, D.C.: Brookings Institution, 1981, pp. 27–84.

Hausman, Jerry A. *Taxes and Labor Supply.* Cambridge, Mass.: National Bureau of Economic Research, Working Paper no. 1102, 1983.

Hemming, Richard. "Income Tax Progressivity and Labour Supply." *Journal of Public Economics* 14, no. 1 (August 1980), pp. 95–100.

Hendershott, Patric H., and James D. Shilling. "The Economics of Tenure Choice, 1955–79." In *Research in Real Estate*, ed. C. Sirmans. Greenwich, Conn.: Jai Press, 1982, pp. 105–33.

Henderson, James M., and Richard E. Quandt. *Microeconomic Theory: A Mathematical Approach.* 3d ed. New York: McGraw-Hill, 1980.

Hicks, J. R. "The Valuation of the Social Income." *Economica*, May 1940, pp. 105–24.

"A High Court Win for OSHA." *Newsweek*, June 29, 1981, p. 59.

Hitler, Adolf. *Mein Kampf* (translated by Ralph Manheim). Boston: Houghton Mifflin, 1971 (1925).

Hobbes, Thomas. *Leviathan.* New York: Meridian Books, 1963 (1651).

Hochman, H. M., and J. D. Rodgers. "Pareto Optimal Redistribution." *American Economic Review* 59 (1969), pp. 542–57.

"How Congress Slices the Pork." *Newsweek*, August 2, 1982, p. 18.

Howrey, E. Phillip, and Saul H. Hymans. "The Measurement and Determination of Loanable-Funds Saving." In *What Should Be Taxed: Income or Expenditure?* ed. Joseph A. Pechman. Washington, D.C.: Brookings Institution, 1980, pp. 1–31.

Ingram, Gregory K. "Discussion of 'Housing Behavior and the Experimental Housing Allowance Program: What Have We Learned?' " Mimeographed. Washington, D.C.: World Bank, 1981.

Inman, Robert P. "The Fiscal Performance of Local Governments: An Interpretative Review." In *Current Issues in Urban Economics,* ed. Peter Mieszkowski and Mahlon Straszheim. Baltimore: Johns Hopkins University Press, 1979, pp. 270–321.

Inman, Robert P. "The Economic Case for Limits to Government." *The American Economic Review, Papers and Proceedings* 72, no. 2 (May 1982), pp. 176–83.

Inman, Robert P., and Daniel L. Rubinfeld. "The Judicial Pursuit of Local Fiscal Equity." *Harvard Law Review* 92 (1979), pp. 1662–750.

Internal Revenue Service, *Statistics of Income Bulletin, Winter 1983–1984,* U.S. Government Printing Office, Washington, D.C., 1984.

Jantscher, Gerald R. "The Aims of Death Taxation," In *Death, Taxes and Family Property: Essays and American Assembly Report,* ed. Edward C. Halbach, Jr. New York: West Publishing Company, 1977, pp. 40–55.

Johansen, Leif. "The Theory of Public Goods: Misplaced Emphasis?" *Journal of Public Economics,* 7, no. 1 (February 1977), pp. 147–52.

Joines, Douglas H. "Estimates of Effective Marginal Tax Rates on Factor Incomes." *Journal of Business* 54, no. 2 (1981), pp. 191–226.

Joint Committee on Taxation. *Analysis of Proposals Relating to Broadening the Base and Lowering the Rates of Income Tax.* Washington, D.C.: U.S. Government Printing Office, 1982.

Jones, Reginald H. "Sunset-Legislation." *Tax Review,* December 1978, p. 53.

Jorgenson, Dale W. "Capital Theory and Investment Behavior." *American Economic Review* 53, no. 2 (May 1963), pp. 247–59.

Jorgenson, Dale W. "Econometric Studies of Investment Behavior: A Survey." *The Journal of Economic Literature* 9, no. 4 (December 1971), pp. 1111–47.

Kaldor, N. "Welfare Propositions of Economists and Interpersonal Comparisons of Utility." *Economic Journal,* September 1939, pp. 549–52.

Kenan, Amos. Smothering Israel. *New York Times,* October 26, 1982.

Keynes, John Maynard. *The General Theory of Employment, Interest, and Money.* New York, Harcourt Brace and World, 1965 (1936).

Kiefer, Nicholas N. "Federally Subsidized Occupational Training and the Employment and Earnings of Male Trainees." *Journal of Econometrics* 8 (1978), pp. 111–25.

King, Mervyn. "The Economics of Saving." Cambridge, Mass.: National Bureau of Economic Research, Working Paper no. 1247, 1983.

King, Mervyn A., and Don Fullerton, eds. *The Taxation of Income From Capital: A Comparative Study of the U.S., U.K., Sweden and West Germany.* Woodrow Wilson School, Princeton University, Discussion Paper no. 37, Princeton, N.J. 1982.

Klarman, Herbert E. "Syphilis Control Programs." In *Measuring Benefits of Government Investments,* ed. Robert Dorfman. Washington, D.C.: Brookings Institution, 1965, pp. 367–409.

Kristol, Irving. "Some Personal Reflections on Economic Well-Being and Income Distribution." In *The American Economy in Transition*, ed. Martin Feldstein. Chicago: University of Chicago Press, 1980, pp. 479–86.

Krutilla, John V., and Anthony C. Fisher. *The Economics of Natural Environments: Studies in the Valuation of Commodity and Amenity Resources*. Baltimore: The Johns Hopkins Press, 1975.

Ladd, Helen F. "An Economic Evaluation of State Limitations on Local Taxing and Spending Powers." *National Tax Journal* 3, no. 1 (March 1978), pp. 1–18.

Ladd, Helen F., and Fred C. Doolittle. "Which Level of Government Should Assist the Poor?" *National Tax Journal* 35, no. 3 (September 1982), pp. 323–36.

Laffer, Arthur B. "Statement Prepared for the Joint Economic Committee, May 20." Reprinted in *The Economics of the Tax Revolt: A Reader*, ed. Arthur B. Laffer and Jan P. Seymour. New York: Harcourt Brace Jovanovich, 1979, pp. 75–79.

Laidler, David. "Income Tax Incentives for Owner-Occupied Housing." In *The Taxation of Income From Capital*, ed. Arnold C. Harberger and Martin J. Baily. Washington, D.C.: Brookings Institution, 1969, pp. 50–76.

Lave, Lester B., and Gilbert S. Omenn. *Clearing the Air: Reforming the Clean Air Act*. Washington, D.C.: Brookings Institution, 1981.

Layard, Richard, ed. *Cost-Benefit Analysis*. New York: Penguin Books, 1977, pp. 1–70.

Leimer, Dean R., and Selig D. Lesnoy. "Social Security and Private Saving, New Time-Series Evidence." *Journal of Political Economy* 90, no. 3 (June 1982), pp. 606–29.

Lenin, Nikolai. "The Marxist Theory of the State and the Tasks of the Proletariat in the Revolution." In *Lenin on Politics and Revolution*, ed. James E. Connor. Indianapolis, Ind.: Bobbs-Merrill, 1968(1917), pp. 184–232.

Leonard, Herman B. "The Federal Civil Service Retirement System: An Analysis of Its Financial Condition and Current Reform Proposals." Cambridge, Mass.: National Bureau of Economic Research, Working Paper no. 1258, 1984.

Lerner, A. P. "The Burden of the National Debt." In *Income, Employment and Public Policy: Essays in Honor of Alvin H. Hansen*, ed. L. A. Metzler, et al. New York: W. W. Norton, 1948.

Lewin, Tamar. "New Alternatives to Litigation." *New York Times*, November 1, 1982.

Lindahl, E. "Just Taxation—A Positive Solution." In *Classics in the Theory of Public Finance*, ed. R. A. Musgrave and A. T. Peacock. New York: St. Martin's Press, 1958.

Lindbeck, Assar. *Tax Effects* versus *Budget Effects on Labor Supply*. Institute for International Economic Studies, Seminar Paper no. 148, Stockholm, 1980a.

Lindbeck, Assar. *Work Disincentives in the Welfare State*. Institute for International Economic Studies, Seminar Paper no. 164, Stockholm, 1980b.

Lipton, James. *An Exaltation of Larks,* New York: Penguin Books, 1977.

Lohr, Steve. "How Tax Evasion Has Grown." *New York Times,* March 15, 1981, Section 3, p. 1.

Lowi, Theodore, J. *The End of Liberalism.* New York: W. W. Norton, 1979.

Lubar, Robert. "Making Democracy Less Inflation-Prone." *Fortune,* September 22, 1980, pp. 78–86.

MacAvoy, Paul W. "The Nondecision Cotton Dust Decision." *New York Times,* July 5, 1981.

Marwell, Gerald, and Ruth E. Ames. "Economists Free Ride, Does Anyone Else? Experiments on the Provision of Public Goods, IV." *Journal of Public Economics* 15, no. 3 (June 1981), pp. 295–310.

Massie, Robert K. *Peter the Great—His Life and World.* New York: Random House, 1980.

McKean, R. N. "The Use of Shadow Prices." In *Cost-Benefit Analysis,* ed. Richard Layard. New York: Penguin Books, 1977, pp. 119–39.

McLure, Charles E., Jr. "The Theory of Tax Incidence with Imperfect Factor Mobility." *Finanzarchiv* 30 (1971), pp. 27–48.

McLure, Charles E., Jr. *Must Corporate Income Be Taxed Twice?* Washington, D.C.: Brookings Institution, 1979.

McLure, Charles E., Jr. "Tax Restructuring Act of 1979: Time for an American Value-Added Tax?" *Public Policy* 28, no. 3 (Summer 1980a), pp. 301–22.

McLure, Charles E., Jr. "Taxes, Saving, and Welfare: Theory and Evidence." *National Tax Journal* 33, no. 3 (September 1980b), pp. 311–20.

McLure, Charles E., Jr. "VAT versus the Payroll Tax." In *Social Security Financing,* ed. Felicity Skidmore, Cambridge, Mass.: MIT Press, 1981a, pp. 129–64.

McLure, Charles E., Jr. "The Elusive Incidence of Corporate Income Tax: The State Case." *Public Finance Quarterly* 9, no. 4 (October 1981b), pp. 395–413.

Meiselman, David I. "Breaking the Tax Barriers to Economic Growth." *Tax Review* 38, no. 8 (August 1977), pp. 29–32.

Meiselman, David I. "The Oil Excise Tax: Another Government Windfall." *Tax Review* (October 1979), pp. 33–37.

Melton, Carroll R. *Housing, Finance and Homeownership: Public Policy Initiatives in Selected Countries.* Chicago: International Union of Building Societies and Savings Associations, 1979.

Meltzer, Allan H., and Scott F. Richard. "A Rational Theory of the Size of Government." *Journal of Political Economy* 89, no. 5 (October 1981), pp. 914–27.

Mermelstein, David, ed. *Economics: Mainstream Readings and Radical Critiques.* New York: Random House, 1973.

Mieszkowski, Peter M. "Tax Incidence Theory: The Effects of Taxes on the Distribution of Income." *Journal of Economic Literature* 7 (1969), pp. 1103–24.

Mieszkowski, Peter M. "The Property Tax: An Excise Tax or a Profits Tax?" *Journal of Public Economics* 1 (1972), pp. 73–96.

Mincer, Jacob. *Schooling, Experience, and Earnings.* National Bureau of Economic Research. New York: Columbia University Press, 1974.

Mishan, E. J. "The Post-War Literature on Externalities: An Interpretative Essay." *Journal of Economic Literature* 9 (1971a), pp. 1–28.

Mishan, E. J. "Evaluation of Life and Limb: A Theoretical Approach." *Journal of Political Economy* 79, no. 4 (1971b), pp. 687–705.

Modigliani, F., and R. Brumberg. "Utility Analysis and the Consumption Function: An Interpretation of Cross-Section Data." In *Post-Keynesian Economics,* ed. K. K. Kurihara. London: Allen & Unwin, 1955.

Modigliani, F., and H. M. Miller. "The Cost of Capital, Corporation Finance, and the Theory of Investment." *American Economic Review* 48 (1958), pp. 261–97.

Monthly Tax Features 26, no. 9 (October 1982).

Mossin, Jan. "Taxation and Risk-Taking: An Expected Utility Approach." *Economica* 35 (1968), pp. 74–82.

Mueller, Dennis C. "Public Choice: A Survey." *The Journal of Economic Literature* 14, no. 2 (June 1976), pp. 395–433.

Munnell, Alicia H. *The Future of Social Security.* Washington, D.C.: Brookings Institution, 1977.

Munnell, Alicia H. "The Couple versus the Individual under the Federal Income Tax." In *The Economics of Taxation,* ed. Henry J. Aaron and Michael J. Boskin. Washington, D.C.: Brookings Institution, 1980, pp. 247–80.

Musgrave, Richard A. *The Theory of Public Finance.* New York: McGraw-Hill, 1959.

Musgrave, Richard A. "ET, OT and SBT." *Journal of Public Economics* 6, no. 1–2 (July–August 1976), pp. 3–16.

Musgrave, Richard A. "Theories of Fiscal Crises: An Essay in Fiscal Sociology." In *The Economics of Taxation,* ed. Henry J. Aaron and Michael J. Boskin. Washington, D.C.: Brookings Institution, 1980.

Musgrave, R. A.; K. E. Case; and H. Leonard. "Distribution of Fiscal Burdens and Benefits." *Public Finance Quarterly* 2 (1974), pp. 259–311.

Musgrave, Richard A., and Peggy B. Musgrave. *Public Finance in Theory and Practice.* 3d ed. New York: McGraw-Hill, 1980.

Musgrave, Richard A., and Tun Thin. "Income Tax Progression 1929–1948." *Journal of Political Economy* 56 (1948), pp. 498–514.

Nichols, Albert L., and Richard J. Zeckhauser. "Targeting Transfers through Restrictions on Recipients." *American Economic Review Papers and Proceedings* 72 (May 1982), pp. 372–77.

Niskanen, William A., Jr. *Bureaucracy and Representative Government.* Chicago: Aldine, 1971.

Nozick, Robert. *Anarchy, State and Utopia.* Oxford: Basil Blackwell, 1974.

Oakland, William H. "Proposition XIII—Genesis and Consequences." *National Tax Journal* 32, no. 2 (June 1979), pp. 387–409.

Oates, Wallace. "The Effects of Property Taxes and Local Spending on Property Values: An Empirical Study of Tax Capitalization and the Tiebout Hypothesis." *Journal of Political Economy* 77 (1969), pp. 957–71.

Oates, Wallace E. *Fiscal Federalism.* New York: Harcourt Brace, 1972.

Office of Management and Budget. *Special Analyses, Budget of the United States Government Fiscal Year 1984.* Washington, D.C.: U.S. Government Printing Office, 1983.

Ornstein, Norman J. "Chipping Away at the Old Blocks." *The Brookings Bulletin* 18, nos. 3 and 4 (1982), pp. 11–15.

Peacock, A. T., and J. Wiseman. *The Growth of Public Expenditure in the United Kingdom.* 2d ed. London: Allen & Unwin, 1967.

Pechman, Joseph A. *Federal Tax Policy.* Washington, D.C.: Brookings Institution, 1977a.

Pechman, Joseph A., ed. *Comprehensive Income Taxation.* Washington, D.C.: Brookings Institution, 1977b.

Pechman, Joseph A., ed. *What Should Be Taxed: Income or Expenditure?* Washington, D.C.: Brookings Institution, 1980.

Pechman, Joseph A. "Tax Policies for the 1980s." In *Economics in the Public Service,* ed. Joseph A. Pechman and N. J. Simler. New York: W. W. Norton, 1982, pp. 145–91.

Pechman, Joseph A., ed. *Setting National Priorities—the 1984 Budget.* Washington, D.C.: Brookings Institution, 1983.

Pechman, Joseph A., and Benjamin A. Okner. *Who Bears the Tax Burden?* Washington, D.C.: Brookings Institution, 1974.

Pechman, Joseph A., and P. Michael Timpane, eds. *Work Incentives and Income Guarantees: The New Jersey Negative Income Tax Experiment.* Washington, D.C.: Brookings Institution, 1975.

Pechman, Joseph A., et al. "The Nondefense Budget." In *Setting National Priorities—The 1982 Budget,* ed. Joseph A. Pechman. Washington, D.C.: Brookings Institution, 1981, pp. 45–132.

Pellechio, Anthony J. "Individual Gains and Losses from Social Security: Calculations in 1981 according to Social Security Law and an Agenda for Reform." Mimeographed. Rochester, N.Y.: University of Rochester, 1981.

Pellechio, Anthony J., and Gordon P. Goodfellow. "Individual Gains and Losses from Social Security Before and After the 1983 Social Security Amendments." Mimeographed. Washington, D.C.: Department of Health and Human Services, 1983.

Penner, Rudolph G. "The Nonsense Amendment." *New York Times.* March 28, 1982.

Perlez, Jane. "City and State Lobbyists Vie for Dwindling Federal Aid." *New York Times,* October 24, 1983, p. B1.

Phares, Donald. *Who Pays State and Local Taxes?* Cambridge, Mass.: Oelgeschlager, Gunn and Hain, 1980.

Pigou, A. C. *The Economics of Welfare.* New York: Macmillan, 1932.

Pommerehne, Werner. "Quantitative Aspects of Federalism: A Study of Six Countries." In *The Political Economy of Fiscal Federalism,* ed. Wallace Oates. Lexington, Mass.: D.C. Heath, 1977, pp. 275–355.

Projector, Dorothy S., and Mary P. Roen. *Family Demography and Transfer Payments During the 1970s.* Washington, D.C.: U.S. Department of Health and Human Services, Social Security Administration, 1982.

Ramsey, Frank P. "A Contribution to the Theory of Taxation." *Economic Journal* 37 (1927), pp. 47–61.

Rawls, John. *A Theory of Justice.* Cambridge, Mass.: Harvard University Press, 1971.

Rees, Albert. "An Overview of the Labor Supply Results." *The Journal of Human Resources* 9, no. 2 (Spring 1974), pp. 158–80.

Retirement and Survivor's Insurance, Regional SSA Program Circular 83-3, New York Region, January 31, 1983.

Robbins, William. "Costly Farm Price Supports Are under Sharper Scrutiny." *New York Times,* December 5, 1983, p. 1.

Roberts, Paul C. "The Keynesian Attack on Mr. Reagan's Plan." *The Wall Street Journal,* March 19, 1981, p. 26.

Rosen, Harvey S. "Housing Decisions and the U.S. Income Tax: An Econometric Analysis." *Journal of Public Economics* 11 (February 1979), pp. 1–23.

Rosen, Harvey S. "Is It Time to Abandon Joint Filing?" *National Tax Journal* 30 (December 1977), pp. 423–28.

Rosen, Harvey S., and Richard E. Quandt. "Estimation of a Disequilibrium Aggregate Labor Market." *The Review of Economics and Statistics* 40, no. 3 (August 1978), pp. 371–79.

Rosen, Kenneth T. "The Impact of Proposition 13 on House Prices in Northern California: A Test of the Interjurisdictional Capitalization Hypothesis." *Journal of Political Economy* 90, no. 1 (February 1982), pp. 191–200.

Royal Commission on Taxation. *Report of the Royal Commission on Taxation.* Vol. 3. *Taxation of Income,* Ottawa, Canada, 1966.

Rubinfeld, Daniel L. "The Economics of the Local Public Sector." Mimeographed. Ann Arbor: University of Michigan, 1983.

Ruhm, Thomas. "Improving the Investment Climate." *The Wall Street Journal,* June 29, 1981, p. 21.

Safire, William. "The Flat Tax." *New York Times,* April 30, 1982, p. A31.

Samuelson, Paul A. "The Pure Theory of Public Expenditure." *Review of Economics and Statistics* 36 (1954), pp. 387–89.

Samuelson, Paul A. "Diagrammatic Exposition of a Theory of Public Expenditure." *Review of Economics and Statistics* 37 (1955), pp. 350–56.

Samuelson, Paul A. *Economics.* 11th ed. New York: McGraw-Hill, 1980.

Sandler, Todd, and John T. Tschirhart. "The Economic Theory of Clubs: An Evaluative Survey." *Journal of Economic Literature* 18, no. 4 (December 1980), pp. 1481–521.

Sandmo, Agnar. "Optimal Taxation—An Introduction to the Literature." *Journal of Public Economics* 6 (1976), pp. 37–54.

Sandmo, Agnar. "Income Tax Evasion, Labour Supply, and the Equity-Efficiency Trade-off." *Journal of Public Economics* 16, no. 3 (December 1981), pp. 265–88.

Schoen, Elin. "Once Again, Hunger Troubles America." *New York Times Magazine*, January 2, 1983, p. 23.

Schorske, Carl E. *Fin-de-Siecle Vienna—Politics and Culture.* New York: Vintage Books, 1981.

Shabecoff, Philip. "Toward a Neutral Role for OSHA." *New York Times*, March 19, 1981, p. E9.

Shabecoff, Philip. "Mrs. Gorsuch as a Crusading Tiger? Critics Wonder Why?" *New York Times*, December 26, 1982.

Shoven, John B. "The Incidence and Efficiency Effects of Taxes on Income from Capital." *Journal of Political Economy* 84 (1976), pp. 1261–84.

Simon, Carl P., and Ann D. Witte. "The Underground Economy: Estimates of Size, Structure and Trends." In *Special Study on Economic Change.* Vol. 5. *Government Regulation: Achieving Social and Economic Balance.* Washington, D.C.: U.S. Government Printing Office, 1980, pp. 70–120.

Slemrod, Joel. "Do We Know How Progressive the Income Tax System Should Be?" *National Tax Journal* 36, no. 3 (September 1983), pp. 361–70.

Slemrod, Joel, and Nikki Sorum. "The Compliance Cost of the U.S. Individual Income Tax System." Mimeographed. Minneapolis: University of Minnesota, 1983.

Small, Kenneth A. *Geographically Differentiated Taxes and the Location of Firms.* Princeton, N.J.: Urban and Regional Research Center, Princeton University, 1981.

Smith, Adam. *The Wealth of Nations.* London: J. M. Dent and Sons, 1977 (1776).

Smith, Marvin M. "Unemployment Compensation." In *Setting National Priorities—The 1982 Budget*, ed. Joseph A. Pechman. Washington, D.C.: Brookings Institution, 1981.

Smith, Sharon P. *Equal Pay in the Public Sector: Fact or Fantasy.* Princeton, N.J.: Industrial Relations Section, Princeton University, 1977.

Smith, Vernon L. "Experiments with a Decentralized Mechanism for Public Goods Decisions." *American Economic Review* 70, no. 4 (September 1980), pp. 584–600.

Smith, Vernon L. "Microeconomic Systems as an Experimental Science." *American Economic Review* 72, no. 5 (December 1982), pp. 923–55.

Solon, Gary. *Work Incentive Effects of Taxing Unemployment Benefits.* Industrial Relations Section, Working Paper no. 149, Princeton University, Princeton, N.J., July, 1982.

Stark, Irwin. "Salary Disparities Continue." *New York Times,* July 1, 1983, p. A23.

"State Finds Evasion of Sales Taxes on Gas." *New York Times,* January 24, 1983, p. B1.

Stern, Nicholas H. "On the Specification of Models of Optimum Income Taxation." *Journal of Public Economics* 6, nos. 1, 2 (July–August 1976), pp. 123–62.

Steuerle, Eugene, and Michael Hartzmark. "Individual Income Taxation, 1974–79." *National Tax Journal* 34 (June 1981), pp. 145–66.

Stigler, George J. "Free-Riders and Collective Action." *Bell Journal of Economics* 5 (1974), pp. 359–65.

Stiglitz, Joseph E. "Taxation, Corporate Financial Policy, and the Cost of Capital." *Journal of Public Economics* 2 (1973), pp. 1–34.

Stiglitz, Joseph E. "Notes on Estate Taxes, Redistribution, and the Concept of Balanced Growth Path Incidence." *Journal of Political Economy* 86 (1978), pp. S137–50.

Stiglitz, Joseph E. *Modelling the Effects of Capital Gains Taxes on the Accrual and Realization of Capital Gains.* Final Report Prepared for the Department of the Treasury, Washington, D.C., 1981.

Stone, Lawrence. *The Family, Sex, and Marriage in England 1500–1800.* New York: Harper & Row, 1977.

Stuckart, Wilhelm, and Hans Globke. "Civil Rights and the Natural Inequality of Man." *Nazi Culture,* ed. George L. Morse. New York: Universal Library, 1968.

Sunley, Emil M., Jr. "Summary of the Conference Discussion." In *Comprehensive Income Taxation,* ed. Joseph A. Pechman. Washington, D.C.: Brookings Institution, 1977.

Tanzi, Vito. "Inflationary Expectations, Economic Activity, Taxes, and Interest Rates." *American Economic Review* 70 (March 1980), pp. 12–21.

Tax Policy Guide. Washington, D.C.: Citizens for Tax Justice, June 1982.

"Tax Reform Tra-La." *New York Times.* April 15, 1980.

Thaler, Richard, and Sherwin Rosen. "The Value of Saving a Life: Evidence From the Labor Market." In *Household Production and Consumption,* ed. Nestor E. Terleckyj. New York: Columbia University Press, 1976, pp. 265–98.

Thurow, Lester C. "The Income Distribution as a Pure Public Good." *Quarterly Journal of Economics,* May 1971, pp. 327–36.

Tiebout, Charles. "A Pure Theory of Local Expenditures." *Journal of Political Economy* 64 (1956), pp. 416–24.

Tobin, James. "Liquidity Preference as Attitude toward Risk." *Review of Economic Studies* 25 (February 1958), pp. 65–86.

Tobin, James. "On Limiting the Domain of Inequality." *Journal of Law and Economics* 13 (1970), pp. 263–77.

Tresch, Richard W. *Public Finance: A Normative Theory.* Plano, Texas: Business Publications, 1981.

Tucker, Robert C., ed. *The Marx-Engels Reader.* 2d ed. New York: W. W. Norton, 1978.

Tucker, William. *America in the Age of Environmentalism.* New York: Doubleday Publishing, 1982.

Tufte, Edward R. *Political Control of the Economy.* Princeton, N.J.: Princeton University Press, 1978.

Tullock, Gordon. "The Rhetoric and Reality of Redistribution." *Southern Economic Journal* 47, no. 4 (April 1978), pp. 895–907.

U.S. Bureau of the Census. *Current Population Reports,* series P-60, no. 136. Washington, D.C.: U.S. Government Printing Office, January 1983a.

U.S. Bureau of the Census. *Governmental Finance in 1981–82.* U.S. Government Printing Office, 1983b.

U.S. Bureau of the Census. *Current Population Reports,* series P-60, no. 140. Washington, D.C.: U.S. Government Printing Office, 1983c.

U.S. Bureau of the Census. *Historical Statistics of the United States, Colonial Times to 1970.* Washington, D.C.: U.S. Government Printing Office, 1975.

U.S. Bureau of the Census. *Statistical Abstract of the United States: 1982–83.* 103d ed. Washington, D.C.: U.S. Government Printing Office, 1982.

U.S. Congress. Senate. Subcommittee on Water Resources. *Corps of Engineers and Soil Conservation Service Projects.* 93rd Congress, 1973.

U.S. Department of Health, Education and Welfare, Office of the Assistant Secretary for Planning and Evaluation. *The Changing Economic Status of 5,000 American Families: Highlights from the Panel Study of Income Dynamics.* Washington, D.C.: U.S. Government Printing Office, 1974.

U.S. Department of Health and Human Services, Social Security Administration. *Social Security Bulletin, Annual Statistical Supplement 1982.* Washington, D.C.: U.S. Government Printing Office, 1982.

U.S. Department of the Treasury. *Blueprints for Basic Tax Reform.* Washington, D.C.: U.S. Government Printing Office, 1977.

U.S. Department of the Treasury, Internal Revenue Service. *Statistics of Income: Individual Tax Returns, 1981.* Washington, D.C.: U.S. Government Printing Office, 1983a.

U.S. Department of the Treasury, Internal Revenue Service. *Commissioner of Internal Revenue and Chief Counsel for the Internal Revenue Service: 1982 Annual Report.* Washington, D.C.: U.S. Government Printing Office, 1983b.

Wanniski, Jude. *The Way the World Works.* New York: Simon & Schuster, 1978.

"Watts Ouster Planned." *San Francisco Chronicle,* October 16, 1981.

Weicher, John C. "Urban Housing Policy." In *Current Issues in Economics,* ed. Peter Mieszkowski and Mahlon R. Straszheim. Baltimore: Johns Hopkins University Press, 1979, pp. 391–429.

Weicher, John C. *Housing—Federal Policies and Programs.* Washington, D.C.: American Enterprise Institute, 1980.

Weidenbaum, Murray L. "Reducing the Hidden Cost of Big Government." *Tax Review* 39, no. 7 (July 1978), pp. 31–34.

White, Lawrence J. "Effluent Charges as a Faster Means of Achieving Pollution Abatement." *Public Policy* 24, no. 1 (Winter 1976), pp. 111–25.

White, Michelle J. "Fiscal Zoning in Fragmented Metropolitan Areas." In *Fiscal Zoning and Land Use Controls,* ed. Edwin S. Mills and Wallace E. Oates. Lexington, Mass.: D.C. Heath, 1975, pp. 31–100.

Will, George. "Power to the President." *Newsweek,* October 12, 1981, p. 120.

Williams, Robert George. *Public Assistance and Work Effort.* Princeton, N.J.: Industrial Relations Section, Princeton University, 1975.

Willig, Robert. "Consumer's Surplus without Apology." *American Economic Review,* September 1976, pp. 589–97.

The Windfall Profits Tax: A Comparative Analysis of Two Bills. Congressional Budget Office, Staff Working Paper. Washington, D.C., 1979.

World Bank. *World Development Report, 1983.* New York: Oxford University Press, 1983.

Yitzhaki, Shlomo. "A Note on Optimal Taxation and Administrative Costs." *American Economic Review* 69, no. 3 (June 1979), pp. 475–80.

"Your Stake in the Fight over Social Security." *Consumer Reports,* September 1981, pp. 503–10.

Zodrow, George, ed. *Local Provision of Public Services: The Tiebout Model after Twenty-Five Years.* New York: Academic Press, 1983.

Author Index

Subject Index

Z

This book has been set Linotron 202 in 10 and 9 point Palatino, leaded 2 points. Part numbers are 36 point, and part titles 24 point Palatino Bold. Chapter numbers are 14 and 36 point Palatino; chapter titles are 18 point Palatino Bold. The size of the type page is 27 by 48 picas.